Organizational Behavior in Education

ninth edition

Organizational Behavior in Education

Adaptive Leadership and School Reform

Robert G. Owens

Distinguished Research Professor Emeritus
Hofstra University

Thomas C. Valesky

Florida Gulf Coast University

PEARSON

Boston   New York   San Francisco
Mexico City   Montreal   Toronto   London   Madrid   Munich   Paris
Hong Kong   Singapore   Tokyo   Cape Town   Sydney

Senior Editor: *Arnis E. Burvikovs*
Series Editorial Assistant: *Erin Reilly*
Marketing Manager: *Tara Kelly*
Editorial-Production Service: *Omegatype Typography, Inc.*
Composition Buyer: *Linda Cox*
Manufacturing Buyer: *Linda Morris*
Electronic Composition: *Omegatype Typography, Inc.*
Cover Administrator: *Linda Knowles*

For related titles and support materials, visit our online catalog at www.ablongman.com.

Between the time website information is gathered and then published, it is not unusual for some sites to have closed. Also, the transcription of URLs can result in typographical errors. The publisher would appreciate notification where these errors occur so that they may be corrected in subsequent editions.

Library of Congress Cataloging-in-Publication Data

Owens, Robert G.
   Organizational behavior in education : adaptive leadership and school reform / Robert G. Owens and Thomas C. Valesky. — 9th ed.
     p. cm.
   Includes bibliographical references and index.
   ISBN 0-205-48636-3
    1. School management and organization—United States. 2. Organizational behavior.
I. Valesky, Thomas C. II. Title.

LB2806.O9 2007
371.200973—dc22

                                             2006044801

Printed in the United States of America

10 9 8 7 6 5 4   RRD-VA   10 09 08 07

*This book is lovingly dedicated
to Barbara and Jill*

Contents

CHAPTER 3: Mainstreams of Organizational Thought   78

CHAPTER 6: Organizational Culture and Organizational Climate   181

CHAPTER 7: Organizational Change   224

CHAPTER 8: Adaptive Leadership   267

CHAPTER 11: Motivation   360

CHAPTER 12: School Reform   397

Preface

As we prepared this ninth edition, the first evaluation reports of the effectiveness of the No Child Left Behind Act (NCLB) were making their way into the news while demands by states for changes in the administration of the act were stiffening and making their way through the courts. The results of the evaluations of the performance of NCLB in meeting the goals set by the law were, at best, a decidedly mixed bag. They gave some glimmer of encouragement to those backers of the unprecedented federal intervention, who felt a need to find some encouragement, but very much left the eventual denouement as murky and doubtful as ever.

Meanwhile many other—remarkably different—school reform initiatives, largely privately funded, were going forward. The nongovernment efforts at school reform especially focused new attention on two problem areas.* One was the need for improving the instructional effectiveness of secondary schools. The other was the seeming intractability of the teaching–learning problems presented by students in big-city schools that are characteristically poor and culturally diverse. The remarkable difference between the federally sponsored effort and the privately sponsored efforts was easily seen in the divergence in the underlying approach to organizational behavior on which each effort was predicated. As we explain in discussing organizational change and school reform, the NCLB initiative has chosen to rely on punitive-coercive efforts to compel schools to improve in some unspecified way. The nongovernment approaches, on the other hand, seek to put into practice the best knowledge and understandings of organizational behavior drawn from a substantial body of research and scholarly work. Much in school reform has been accomplished, and very much remains to be done in the years ahead.

We would draw your attention to three special and important changes in this edition. One is the very welcome arrival of Thomas C. Valesky as coauthor beginning with this edition. He brings to this task not only a strong record of academic and administrative leadership in U.S. universities but also a wealth of experience as a practicing effective leader in American schools in Europe and South America as well as in the United States.

Another change is to improve and clarify coverage of the standards for school leaders of the Interstate School Leaders Licensure Consortium (ISLLC). This important contribution to the field of educational leadership should be known well by students. In the next few pages we not only describe and discuss the ISLLC standards but also show where in this book a broad range of the standards is covered. As an additional guide to readers, we have placed at the beginning of each chapter a summary of the ISLLC standards covered in that chapter.

---

*This was also a time when the term *problem* seemed to be disappearing from the conversation about schooling. It had become more semantically fashionable for writers and speakers to frame their observations in terms of issues, rather than to admit to perceiving problems.

Finally, we have expanded and strengthened the Reflective Exercises in each chapter to facilitate and encourage readers to engage in working with the concepts that are presented so as to internalize them and make them their own. We did this because the organizational world of the educational leader is demanding: fast-paced, confusing, often contentious. It is rarely a place where the leader has the luxury of time to lean back and ruminate about how best to deal with the insistent need to act. We strongly believe that it is insufficient for educational leaders to be well-informed about the science and scholarship that underlie best practice: they must have a well-formed understanding of how to use this knowledge. Therefore, throughout the book we emphasize the need for you to internalize these concepts, to work with them, to make a personal judgment and commitment regarding them. Through the Reflective Exercises we encourage you to begin developing a professional game plan, or theory of practice, that will guide you to effective action in the stress and confusion of everyday educational leadership.

This ninth edition also offers support to instructors in the form of the following supplements:

- **Test Bank,** developed by the authors and available online at an access-protected website
- **PowerPoint™ Presentation,** covers every chapter and is also available online at an access-protected website
- **Education Leadership Supersite,** a website that includes resources for students and faculty, available at www.ablongman.com/edleadership

Acknowledgments

We are grateful to the reviewers of the ninth edition for their comments and suggestions: Patricia Helene Earl, Marymount University; Lora Knutson, Governors State University; and Debra Touchton, Stetson University.

R.G.O.
T.C.V.

The ISLLC Standards for School Leaders

This book is a study of organizational behavior in schools and not a survey textbook of educational leadership. Therefore, it focuses on many, but not all, of the nearly two hundred knowledge, dispositions, and performance indicators of the six ISLLC standards. It's doubtful that any book can or should include content relative to all or even most of the indicators, or alternatively, that any textbook or program in educational leadership should be limited to only these indicators. As Joseph Murphy, who is one of the primary authors of the ISLLC standards, put it,

> . . . these indicators are examples of important knowledge, practices, and beliefs, not a full map. No effort was made to include everything or to deal with performances in the myriad of leadership contexts. Leadership is a complex and context-dependent activity. To attempt to envelope the concept with a definitive list of indicators is a fool's errand.[1]

The authors of the ISLLC standards assume that an entire program, not any single course, should engender all knowledge, dispositions, and performances of the ISLLC standards, but even then, programs should not be evaluated simply based on these indicators alone.

In a moment we will describe and discuss the ISLLC standards and the knowledge, dispositions, and performances that comprise a major focus of the chapters. In addition, at the beginning of each chapter, we provide learning objectives that both include and go beyond the ISLLC standards. Although we recognize that the ISLLC standards are not comprehensive of all aspects of school leadership and that there has been significant critical discourse in the profession about the standards, we also recognize that approximately forty states have adopted or adapted the ISLLC standards as the basis for state certification in educational leadership and as the basis for evaluating and approving university preparation programs. In view of their importance, therefore, we want to identify for you the ISLLC standards and their accompanying knowledge, dispositions, and performance indicators that are significant aspects of this book.

The ISLLC standards provide the basis for evaluating university programs by the National Council for Accreditation of Teacher Education (NCATE) and the National Policy Board for Educational Administration (NPBEA). A brief history of the development of the ISLLC standards might help the reader understand the importance of these standards. The NPBEA was formed in 1988 with membership from ten national associations including:

- American Association of Colleges for Teacher Education
- American Association of School Administrators
- Association of School Business Officials
- Association for Supervision and Curriculum Development

- Council of Chief State School Officers
- National Association of Elementary School Principals
- National Association of Secondary School Principals
- National Council of Professors of Educational Administration
- National School Boards Association
- University Council for Educational Administration

In 1994, the NPBEA formed the Interstate School Leaders Licensure Consortium (ISLLC) to develop standards for our profession. ISLLC was funded by a grant from the Pew Charitable Trusts, and the process of developing the standards was managed by the Council of Chief State School Officers (CCSSO) under the direction of Joseph Murphy and Neil Shipman. The NPBEA adopted the ISLLC standards in 1996. The NPBEA then formed a working group from among its membership to form the Educational Leadership Constituent Council (ELCC) that worked to develop a set of standards for evaluating programs in educational leadership to be used by NPBEA and NCATE. **The ELCC used the ISLLC standards as the primary basis for its program evaluation standards, which are entitled *Standards for Advanced Programs in Educational Leadership*. The first six standards mirror the ISLLC standards, and the seventh standard involves a required internship.**[2]

There has been considerable controversy surrounding the ISLLC standards, including the notions that the standards do not provide a supporting research base, that no weighting is given to the standards in terms of which standards (and the knowledge, dispositions, and performances) are more likely to lead to higher student achievement, and that the standards do not include or do not emphasize the importance of some critical areas, such as technology. The NPBEA acknowledged these criticisms and in the summer of 2005 formed a working group to begin work on a revision of the ISLLC standards. A ten-member steering committee was formed from nine of the member organizations (all except the National School Boards Association). The NPBEA agreed that the standards would be revised under important assumptions, including:

- The ISLLC and the ELCC standards revamping will be done at the same time.
- The ISLLC *Standards for School Leaders* need to be updated, not rewritten from scratch.
- The context in which both sets of standards are being revised has changed dramatically in the past decade.
- NPBEA will own the copyright to the revised two sets of standards.

The plan is to present the final revision of the standards to the NPBEA for approval in the spring of 2008. Despite the changes that will take place in the standards and subsequent program evaluation standards, most states have adopted some form of the initial ISLLC standards under which educational leadership programs are expected to continue to operate.[3]

The following tables are matrices of each ISLLC standard indicating the knowledge, dispositions, and performances that are contained in each chapter. Although some concepts are emphasized more than others, each of the concepts that is marked is covered to some degree in the chapter. By looking at each standard table, one can see which chapters in our book contain related content. It is clear that some standards are covered more thoroughly than others. For example, one can see from the table for Standard 4 that little related material is contained in this book, whereas from the tables for standards 3 and 5, one can see that this book contains a great deal of related content. By scanning across the rows for knowledge, dispositions, and performances, one can determine which chapter, if any, contains related material. We hope that this information is of value to students and professors alike, and we welcome any feedback that might guide us in making this information more useful in future editions.

ISLLC Standards by Chapter

STANDARD 1: A school administrator is an educational leader who promotes the success of all students by facilitating the development, articulation, implementation, and stewardship of a vision of learning that is shared and supported by the school community.

	1	2	3	4	5	6	7	8	9	10	11	12
Knowledge The administrator has knowledge and understanding of:												
Learning goals in a pluralistic society	●	●										
The principles of developing and implementing strategic plans							●					
Systems theory						●	●					
Information sources, data collection, and data analysis strategies						●	●		●			
Effective communication						●	●		●	●		
Effective consensus-building and negotiation skills						●	●	●	●	●		
Dispositions The administrator believes in, values, and is committed to:												
The educability of all		●				●						
A school vision of high standards of learning		●				●	●					
Continuous school improvement						●	●	●				
The inclusion of all members of the school community								●	●			
Ensuring that students have the knowledge, skills, and values needed to become successful adults		●							●			
A willingness to continuously examine one's own assumptions, beliefs, and practices	●	●				●		●		●		
Doing the work required for high levels of personal and organization performance						●	●					

	1	2	3	4	5	6	7	8	9	10	11	12
Performances The administrator facilitates processes and engages in activities ensuring that:												
The vision and mission of the school are effectively communicated to staff, parents, students, and community members						●		●				
The vision and mission are communicated through the use of symbols, ceremonies, stories, and similar activities						●						
The core beliefs of the school vision are modeled for all stakeholders						●						
The vision is developed with and among stakeholders						●	●	●				
The contributions of school community members to the realization of the vision are recognized and celebrated						●						
Progress toward the vision and mission is communicated to all stakeholders								●				
The school community is involved in school improvement efforts						●	●	●	●			
The vision shapes the educational programs, plans, and actions						●	●	●				
An implementation plan is developed in which objectives and strategies to achieve the vision and goals are clearly articulated						●						
Assessment data related to student learning are used to develop the school vision and goals						●	●					
Relevant demographic data pertaining to students and their families are used in developing the school mission and goals												
Barriers to achieving the vision are identified, clarified, and addressed						●	●					
Needed resources are sought and obtained to support the implementation of the school mission and goals						●						
Existing resources are used in support of the school vision and goals						●						
The vision, mission, and implementation plans are regularly monitored, evaluated, and revised						●	●		●			

Standard 2: A school administrator is an educational leader who promotes the success of all students by advocating, nurturing, and sustaining a school culture and instructional program conducive to student learning and staff professional growth.

	1	2	3	4	5	6	7	8	9	10	11	12
Knowledge The administrator has knowledge and understanding of:												
Student growth and development												
Applied learning theories												

	1	2	3	4	5	6	7	8	9	10	11	12
Applied motivational theories						●					●	
Curriculum design, implementation, evaluation, and refinement												
Principles of effective instruction												
Measurement, evaluation, and assessment strategies												
Diversity and its meaning for educational programs											●	
Adult learning and professional development models											●	
The change process for systems, organizations, and individuals						●	●					
The role of technology in promoting student learning and professional growth												
School cultures				●	●	●	●	●			●	

Dispositions
The administrator believes in, values, and is committed to:

	1	2	3	4	5	6	7	8	9	10	11	12
Student learning as the fundamental purpose of schooling		●			●	●						
The proposition that all students can learn		●										
The variety of ways in which students can learn												
Lifelong learning for self and others											●	
Professional development as an integral part of school improvement					●	●						
The benefits that diversity brings to the school community											●	
A safe and supportive learning environment						●						
Preparing students to be contributing members of society		●		●								

Performances
The administrator facilitates processes and engages in activities ensuring that:

	1	2	3	4	5	6	7	8	9	10	11	12
All individuals are treated with fairness, dignity, and respect					●	●		●			●	
Professional development promotes a focus on student learning consistent with the school vision and goals					●	●						
Students and staff feel valued and important					●	●		●			●	
The responsibilities and contributions of each individual are acknowledged				●	●	●					●	
Barriers to student learning are identified, clarified, and addressed				●	●	●						
Diversity is considered in developing learning experiences												
Lifelong learning is encouraged and modeled					●						●	
There is a culture of high expectations for self, student, and staff performance					●	●					●	

	1	2	3	4	5	6	7	8	9	10	11	12
Technologies are used in teaching and learning				●								
Student and staff accomplishments are recognized and celebrated				●	●	●					●	
Multiple opportunities to learn are available to all students		●										
The school is organized and aligned for success				●	●	●	●					
Curricular, cocurricular, and extracurricular programs are designed, implemented, evaluated, and refined							●					
Curriculum decisions are based on research, expertise of teachers, and the recommendations of learned societies				●			●					
The school culture and climate are assessed on a regular basis				●		●	●					
A variety of sources of information is used to make decisions				●		●						
Student learning is assessed using a variety of techniques		●										
Multiple sources of information regarding performance are used by staff and students		●										
A variety of supervisory and evaluation models is employed												
Pupil personnel programs are developed to meet the needs of students and their families												

Standard 3: A school administrator is an educational leader who promotes the success of all students by ensuring management of the organization, operations, and resources for a safe, efficient, and effective learning environment.

	1	2	3	4	5	6	7	8	9	10	11	12
Knowledge The administrator has knowledge and understanding of:												
Theories and models of organizations and the principles of organizational development			●	●	●	●	●	●	●	●	●	●
Operational procedures at the school and district levels			●	●	●	●						●
Principles and issues relating to school safety and security												
Human resources management and development			●	●	●	●			●	●	●	
Principles and issues relating to fiscal operations of school management												
Principles and issues relating to school facilities and use of space				●								
Legal issues impacting school operations												●
Current technologies that support management functions												

	1	2	3	4	5	6	7	8	9	10	11	12
Dispositions The administrator believes in, values, and is committed to:												
Making management decisions to enhance learning and teaching				●	●	●			●			
Taking risks to improve schools					●	●			●			●
Trusting people and their judgments				●	●	●		●	●	●	●	●
Accepting responsibility				●		●		●	●	●	●	
High-quality standards, expectations, and performances				●	●	●					●	●
Involving stakeholders in management processes					●	●			●	●	●	
A safe environment					●							
Performances The administrator facilitates processes and engages in activities ensuring that:												
Knowledge of learning, teaching, and student development is used to inform management decisions				●	●	●	●		●			
Operational procedures are designed and managed to maximize opportunities for successful learning			●	●	●	●						
Emerging trends are recognized, studied, and applied as appropriate				●	●		●		●			●
Operational plans and procedures to achieve the vision and goals of the school are in place				●		●			●			
Collective bargaining and other contractual agreements related to the school are effectively managed												
The school plant, equipment, and support systems operate safely, efficiently, and effectively						●						
Time is managed to maximize attainment of organizational goals												
Potential problems and opportunities are identified				●		●				●		
Problems are confronted and resolved in a timely manner									●	●		
Financial, human, and material resources are aligned to the goals of schools					●	●	●					
The school acts entrepreneurially to support continuous improvement										●		●
Organizational systems are regularly monitored and modified as needed			●	●	●	●	●			●		●
Stakeholders are involved in decisions affecting schools				●	●	●	●	●	●	●	●	●
Responsibility is shared to maximize ownership and accountability				●	●			●	●	●	●	
Effective problem-framing and problem-solving skills are used							●	●	●	●		
Effective conflict resolution skills are used										●		
Effective group-process and consensus-building skills are used				●	●	●	●	●	●	●		

	1	2	3	4	5	6	7	8	9	10	11	12
Effective communication skills are used				●		●		●		●		
There is effective use of technology to manage school operations				●								
Fiscal resources of the school are managed responsibly, efficiently, and effectively												
A safe, clean, and aesthetically pleasing school environment is created and maintained						●						
Human resource functions support the attainment of school goals			●			●	●	●			●	
Confidentiality and privacy of school records are maintained												

Standard 4: A school administrator is an educational leader who promotes the success of all students by collaborating with families and community members, responding to diverse community interests and needs, and mobilizing community resources.

	1	2	3	4	5	6	7	8	9	10	11	12
Knowledge The administrator has knowledge and understanding of:												
Emerging issues and trends that potentially impact the school community												
The conditions and dynamics of the diverse school community												
Community resources												
Community relations and marketing strategies and processes												
Successful models of school, family, business, community, government, and higher education partnerships												
Dispositions The administrator believes in, values, and is committed to:												
Schools operating as an integral part of the larger community												
Collaboration and communication with families												
Involvement of families and other stakeholders in school decision-making processes												
The proposition that diversity enriches the school												
Families as partners in the education of their children												
The proposition that families have the best interests of their children in mind												
Resources of the family and community needing to be brought to bear on the education of students												
An informed public												

	1	2	3	4	5	6	7	8	9	10	11	12

Performances
The administrator facilitates processes and engages in activities ensuring that:

	1	2	3	4	5	6	7	8	9	10	11	12
High visibility, active involvement, and communication with the larger community are priorities												
Relationships with community leaders are identified and nurtured												
Information about family and community concerns, expectations, and needs is used regularly												
There is outreach to different business, religious, political, and service agencies and organizations												
Credence is given to individuals and groups whose values and opinions may conflict				●			●	●	●	●	●	
The school and community serve one another as resources												
Available community resources are secured to help the school solve problems and achieve goals												
Partnerships are established with area businesses, institutions of higher education, and community groups to strengthen programs and support school goals												
Community youth family services are integrated with school programs												
Community stakeholders are treated equitably								●				
Diversity is recognized and valued												
Effective media relations are developed and maintained												
A comprehensive program of community relations is established												
Public resources and funds are used appropriately and wisely												
Community collaboration is modeled for staff												
Opportunities for staff to develop collaborative skills are provided												

Standard 5: A school administrator is an educational leader who promotes the success of all students by acting with integrity, fairness, and in an ethical manner.

	1	2	3	4	5	6	7	8	9	10	11	12

Knowledge
The administrator has knowledge and understanding of:

	1	2	3	4	5	6	7	8	9	10	11	12
The purpose of education and the role of leadership in modern society	●	●	●		●	●		●				
Various ethical frameworks and perspectives on ethics										●	●	
The values of the diverse school community												
Professional codes of ethics												

	1	2	3	4	5	6	7	8	9	10	11	12
The philosophy and history of education		●	●		●							●

Dispositions
The administrator believes in, values, and is committed to:

	1	2	3	4	5	6	7	8	9	10	11	12
The ideal of the common good	●	●										●
The principles of the Bill of Rights	●	●										
The right of every student to a free, quality education		●										●
Bringing ethical principles to the decision-making process					●			●	●	●	●	
Subordinating one's own interest to the good of the school community								●			●	
Accepting the consequences for upholding one's principles and actions								●	●	●		
Using the influence of one's office constructively and productively in the service of all students and their families								●		●		
Development of a caring school community						●		●				

Performances
The administrator:

	1	2	3	4	5	6	7	8	9	10	11	12
Examines personal and professional values	●				●	●		●		●	●	
Demonstrates a personal and professional code of ethics								●				
Demonstrates values, beliefs, and attitudes that inspire others to higher levels of performance					●			●				
Serves as a role model								●				
Accepts responsibility for school operations			●						●	●		
Considers the impact of one's administrative practices on others			●			●		●	●	●	●	
Uses the influence of the office to enhance the educational program rather than for personal gain								●	●			
Treats people fairly, equitably, and with dignity and respect			●		●	●		●	●	●	●	
Protects the rights and confidentiality of students and staff												
Demonstrates appreciation for and sensitivity to the diversity in the school community												
Recognizes and respects the legitimate authority of others			●					●				
Examines and considers the prevailing values of the diverse school community	●											
Expects that others in the school community will demonstrate integrity and exercise ethical behavior												
Opens the school to public scrutiny												

	1	2	3	4	5	6	7	8	9	10	11	12
Fulfills legal and contractual obligations												
Applies laws and procedures fairly, wisely, and considerately												

Standard 6: A school administrator is an educational leader who promotes the success of all students by understanding, responding to, and influencing the larger political, social, economic, legal, and cultural context.

	1	2	3	4	5	6	7	8	9	10	11	12
Knowledge The administrator has knowledge and understanding of:												
Principles of representative governance that undergird the system of American schools	●	●										●
The role of public education in developing and renewing a democratic society and an economically productive nation	●	●		●								●
The law as related to education and schooling												●
The political, social, cultural, and economic systems and processes that impact schools	●	●		●		●	●					●
Models and strategies of change and conflict resolution as applied to the larger political, social, cultural, and economic contexts of schooling							●					●
Global issues and forces affecting teaching and learning	●	●		●			●					●
The dynamics of policy development and advocacy under our democratic political system	●			●								●
The importance of diversity and equity in a democratic society												
Dispositions The administrator believes in, values, and is committed to:												
Education as a key to opportunity and social mobility	●	●		●								●
Recognizing a variety of ideas, values, and cultures	●	●				●						●
Importance of a continuing dialogue with other decision makers affecting education	●			●			●					●
Actively participating in the political and policy-making context in the service of education		●		●								
Using legal systems to protect student rights and improve student opportunities												
Performances The administrator facilitates processes and engages in activities ensuring that:												
The environment in which schools operate is influenced on behalf of students and their families	●			●		●						●
Communication occurs among the school community concerning trends, issues, and potential changes in the environment in which schools operate						●						●

	1	2	3	4	5	6	7	8	9	10	11	12
There is ongoing dialogue with representatives of diverse community groups												●
The school community works within the framework of policies, laws, and regulations enacted by local, state, and federal authorities	●											●
Public policy is shaped to provide quality education for students	●	●										●
Lines of communication are developed with decision makers outside the school community												●

Source: Council of Chief State Officers. (1996). *Interstate School Leaders Licensure Consortium (ISLLC) standards for school leaders.* Washington, DC: Author. The Interstate School Leaders Licensure Consortium (ISLLC) standards were developed by Council of Chief State School Officers (CCSSO) and member states. Copies may be downloaded from the Council's website at www.ccsso.org.

chapter 1

In Search of a Paradigm

LEARNING OBJECTIVES

After reading this chapter, you should be able to

- Specify and describe the concept of implicit basic assumptions about people, human nature, and the nature of relationships between people and their environments.
- Describe how basic assumptions are learned and developed.
- Describe how basic assumptions are said to be invisible and are rarely thought about or discussed.
- Compare and contrast the concept of basic assumptions about people with the beliefs and values that one holds about people.
- Identify the relationship between basic assumptions, beliefs, and values in organizational behavior.
- Compare and contrast modernism with postmodernism.
- Explain why it is important to examine and make manifest one's own basic assumptions, values, and beliefs about people.
- Describe the implications of structuralist thought for school leadership.
- Identify some important ways in which structuralism and poststructuralism differ.
- Compare and contrast psychoanalytic psychology, behaviorism, cognitive psychology, and social psychology.
- Compare and contrast sociological and anthropological approaches to schools as organizations.
- Analyze and discuss selected fundamental principles of organizational behavior that are embodied in the No Child Left Behind Act of 2001.

ISLLC Standards

STANDARD 1: A school administrator is an educational leader who promotes the success of all students by facilitating the development, articulation, implementation, and steward-ship of a vision of learning that is shared and supported by the school community.

Knowledge

The administrator has knowledge and understanding of:

- learning goals in a pluralistic society

Dispositions

The administrator believes in, values, and is committed to:

- a willingness to continuously examine one's own assumptions, beliefs, and practices

STANDARD 5: A school administrator is an educational leader who promotes the success of all students by acting with integrity, fairness, and in an ethical manner.

Knowledge

The administrator has knowledge and understanding of:

- the purpose of education and the role of leadership in modern society

Dispositions

The administrator believes in, values, and is committed to:

- the ideal of the common good
- the principles in the Bill of Rights

STANDARD 6: A school administrator is an educational leader who promotes the success of all students by understanding, responding to, and influencing the larger political, social, economic, legal, and cultural context.

Knowledge

The administrator has knowledge and understanding of:

- principles of representative governance that undergird the system of American schools
- the role of public education in developing and renewing a democratic society and an economically productive nation

- the political, social, cultural, and economic systems and processes that impact schools
- global issues and forces affecting teaching and learning
- the dynamics of policy development and advocacy under our democratic political system

Performances

The administrator facilitates processes and engages in activities ensuring:

- the importance of a continuing dialogue with other decision makers affecting education
- the school community works within the framework of policies, laws, and regulations enacted by local, state, and federal authorities
- public policy is shaped to provide quality education for students

A school is a world in which people live and work. Like any other social organization the world of the school has power, structure, logic, and values, which combine to exert strong influence on the ways in which individuals perceive the world, interpret it, and respond to it. In short, the behavior of people at work in an educational organization—individually as well as a group—is not merely a reflection of their idiosyncratic personalities but is influenced, if not defined, by the social norms and expectations of the culture that prevail in the organization. This interplay between individuals and the social environment of their world of work is powerful in giving rise to "organizational behavior," which means the behavior of people in the school organization. Those who would be educational leaders will find a clear grasp of the essentials of organizational behavior essential in deciding what to do as they engage in the practice of leadership. This simple statement sets forth the central assumptions underlying this book.

Because an understanding of organizational behavior cannot be handed to you in a neat package of rules, algorithms, and recipes, you have a very active role to play in reading this book and coming to an understanding of organizational behavior. By merely reading and remembering, much as countless students have read other textbooks before, you probably will learn a great deal that will be useful in your present work and will be even more useful as you increase your field of influence as a leader. But if you ponder what you read, question it, challenge it, and ask yourself—and discuss with other people—how it all fits into the practical realities of your work, your experience, and your personal view of the world, the book will be much more useful to you both now and in the future.

One reason for this is that you will encounter many people in your professional practice whose understanding of organizational behavior will be at a different stage of development from your own. Many people will be skeptical about some of the viewpoints that this book suggests. In this growing and developing field, it is important that you not merely understand and internalize your commitment to certain principles and practices of organizational behavior, but that you also understand why some may disagree with them and doubt their practical usefulness in the harsh realities of the embattled U.S. schools.

Moreover, as we have suggested, both our knowledge of organizational behavior and the culture in which the school exists will continue to evolve. In the face of such challenges, it is vital that you clarify what you think the fundamental principles of organizational behavior are and how they square with your personal values, beliefs, and vision of the role you want to play in your career.

Assumptions, Beliefs, Behaviors

Everyone in every culture accepts certain implicit basic assumptions about people, their human nature, the nature of human relationships, the nature of human activity, and the nature of the relationships between people and their environment. These assumptions are called basic assumptions because they give rise to our beliefs and values and, ultimately, the way we behave toward others.[1] The basic assumptions are learned in infancy and develop as we mature and are educated. They become so thoroughly internalized that they are taken for granted and are shared with and supported by others around us. The assumptions become an invisible part of the warp and woof of life, and they are rarely thought about enough to be considered or discussed.

These basic assumptions—invisible and so taken for granted as to be rarely thought about, much less talked about—give rise to values and beliefs that we are more readily aware of. Because we may discuss them from time to time, the values and beliefs are, therefore, more public than the basic assumptions from which they arise. For example, one of the marvels of the Declaration of Independence is that it publicly articulated the clear linkage between basic assumptions about the nature of humankind held by the Founding Fathers and the political beliefs that, in their view, ultimately arose from those assumptions.

Moreover, actions (that is, behaviors) flow from the values and beliefs that people embrace. In the case of the Founding Fathers the compelling logic of their assumptions about human nature, that all men are created equal, led them to the treasonable acts of declaring independence from and ultimately taking up arms against arguably the mightiest kingdom of the time. Few of us have the intellectual and moral integrity of the Founding Fathers, however, and sometimes a peculiar dissonance separates the beliefs and values that we publicly espouse and the organizational behavior that we engage in. In the case of the Founding Fathers, an example of this dissonance is easily seen in the discrepancy between the soaring pronouncement in the Declaration of Independence that all men are created equal and the fact that slavery was an accepted institution in the new republic. As we know, this contradiction was the fountainhead of seemingly endless political struggles and compromises that began at the Constitutional Convention in Philadelphia and have wracked the nation through generations until this very day, more than two centuries later.

Indeed, the contradiction nearly destroyed the nation in the bloody Civil War. Yet, some eighty-seven years after the writing of the Declaration of Independence, in his celebrated Gettysburg Address, Abraham Lincoln restated the proposition that all men are created equal and made clear to Americans that the purpose of the Civil War was finally to achieve that reality in practice. But while the basic assumption that all men are created equal endured and was thus powerfully reinforced, resistance also persisted, and the struggle to achieve equality in daily human behavior and political practice has endured as well. For many, the nadir of this saga was the Jim Crow period in the South that began in the 1870s and was finally broken in the great civil rights struggles that wracked the nation in the 1950s. This dissonance between underlying assumptions about the nature of humanity, on the one hand, and the things that we do—our behaviors—on the other hand, continues to exist in our own time.

Examples of such hypocrisy abound in education, as they do everywhere in our culture. Much is said about the need for children to get a good early start in schooling, with a rich and diverse program to lay a strong foundation for success in later years. However, we persist in spending minimally for preschool and early childhood education and spend increasingly more money at the middle and secondary school levels, despite the signs of seemingly intractable academic difficulty that are already well established early on.[2] Yet few would explicitly acknowledge that their basic assumption is that early childhood education is relatively unimportant and the "real work" of schooling begins after elementary school. Women's rights activists, people of color, the growing impoverished underclass, and oppressed racial and ethnic minorities in our culture discomfit many by pointing to similar discrepancies between espoused beliefs and values in the schooling enterprise, on the one hand, and actual schooling practices, on the other hand. If we want to make a difference in the organization we call school, it is first necessary to carefully make our basic assumptions manifest and consider how logical the connections are between those assumptions, our publicly espoused values and beliefs, and the organizational behavior in which we engage in professional practice.

As you undoubtedly know, this is a difficult, though necessary, thing to do. One reason that it is difficult is epistemological: What do we know about organizational behavior in education and how do we know it? Just as the social sciences and the humanities are now in a period of great philosophical and epistemological turmoil, so is the field of organizational behavior. Therefore, much as you need to know how we know what we know, there is no quick, simple answer: you must become at least somewhat aware of the academic turmoil that is going on and how this book is positioned in it.

Modernist and Structuralist Thought

Certainly, at least until the mid-twentieth century, the pervasive assumption in Western cultures was that the world we live in must be characterized by some underlying patterns of logic, system, and order. From that assumption arose the belief that these patterns could be discovered only by using systematic methods of study, generally called the scientific method, that were controlled and circumscribed by strict rules of procedure and evidence. It was thought that once the orderly, presumably recurring, patterns were made manifest and described, they would reveal the keys to controlling the course of events so as to improve the human condition. In many fields, organizational behavior included, this meant that credible ways of knowing must base their claims to knowledge only on behavior or other phenomena that could be observed directly, measured, and quantified, preferably under carefully controlled conditions. Claims to knowing based on other rules of procedure and evidence could be dismissed as intuitive, anecdotal, or otherwise unscientific and, therefore, not to be taken terribly seriously. Today, this rather dogmatic view of ways of knowing is often referred to as modernism.

A related assumption was that the world, being an orderly and logical place, could be described by classifying the relative parts, usually in some sort of hierarchical schema. Who can forget, for example, memorizing the classification systems that we were taught in biology for sorting out the various kinds of plants and animals and showing their logical relationships in the scheme of things?

Such classification systems are called taxonomies. Many readers of this book will recall what is generally called Bloom's *Taxonomy of Educational Objectives,*[3] which has had extraordinary impact on thinking and practice in both curriculum development and teaching methods. To create the taxonomy, according to which all educational objectives could be classified, Bloom and his colleagues created an admittedly arbitrary (though apparently logical) hierarchy of six major classes of objectives that started with knowledge and, in ascending order, went on to comprehension, application, analysis, synthesis, and evaluation. Thus, the schema sought to build a conceptual structure of educational objectives that ascended from the simple to the complex, the concrete to the abstract.[4] Teachers, curriculum developers, and textbook writers embraced this powerful idea as a new and better way to organize instruction into a more logical, orderly, and systematic pattern. Above all, the taxonomy was generally accepted as being "scientific": objective, neutral, value-free, dispassionate. The Bloom taxonomy is mentioned here as simply one of the more distinguished examples that illustrate the structuralist approach to understanding the interface between human behavior and the school as a context, one that has had enormous influence on the ways in which teachers organized and managed instruction in their classrooms. It has also had great impact on organizational behavior thought and administrative practice in education inasmuch as organizational theorists have, until recently, accepted the structuralist view of knowledge. Essentially, that is what past organizational theories—such as bureaucratic theory and social systems theory, to mention two of the best known—have been about. Cherryholmes's observation on structuralism is well worth noting:

> Structuralism as a pervasive and often unacknowledged way of thinking has influenced twentieth-century thinking in important ways. It promises order, organization, and certainty. Structuralism is consistent with teaching for objectives, standardized educational assessment, quantitative empirical research, systematic instruction, rationalized bureaucracies, and scientific management. As long as structural assumptions remain unacknowledged, they are immunized against criticism.[5]

Postmodernism and Poststructuralism

In the period of postmodernism and poststructuralism, a growing number of academic iconoclasts are engaged in processes of bringing the previously unexamined assumptions, from which our cultural and professional beliefs and values arise, into the open, making them explicit, questioning them, and seeking to forge a consensus around new assumptions on which to rebuild our thinking about truth, knowledge, and epistemology in organizational behavior. You will recognize that we are now entering an area of philosophical discourse of such complexity that it cannot be dealt with in great depth here. But it is such an important emerging issue in the study of organizational behavior today that it must be acknowledged and at least briefly described.

Poststructuralism was fueled by growing awareness that there is often an obvious disjunction between publicly espoused values and what we do in schools. We say, for example, that we believe in equity and equality, but many women, people of color, and poor people find inequality and inequity to be dominant characteristics of their lives in schools. But it is difficult for members of minority groups to raise questions about that issue because those who control the schools are usually able to suppress, sidetrack, redefine, or otherwise control the colloquy. The French intellectual Michel Foucault pointed out that the issue is an invisible web of power in the culture that controls our aspirations, how we think of ourselves, and what we do to deal with those issues in our lives.[6] Through that invisible web of power, those who control the culture decide what may be discussed, who is credible, and who is allowed to speak.

For example, college students who want to become teachers generally take the prescribed courses. Because they want to become teachers, and therefore want to be viewed as successful students, they manifest the beliefs and behaviors that will further those ends and that the faculty of the college espouses, rewards, and controls. Thus, the college weaves a web of visible and invisible power that influences students to espouse the "appropriate" values and beliefs and behave in "desirable" ways so that they will be seen as "good" potential teachers, meanwhile perhaps submerging and even extinguishing some of their own inner assumptions. Later, as professionals in the schools, they "adapt as a matter of everyday professional life to contractual organizational demands, to demands of professional discourse, to expectations of professional peers, and to informal as well as formal job expectations. Power helps shape subjective feelings and beliefs. . . . Often power is most effective and efficient when it operates as desire, because desire often makes the effects of power invisible."[7]

Power, more particularly the asymmetrical distribution of power in the culture, makes this part of the poststructuralist view of the world a political view. It is thus that polemic enters academic discourse that previous generations prized for its evenhandedness, "objectivity" (which postmodernists now doubt can exist), and dispassion. Thus, in academic discourse on organizational behavior and educational leadership today, one commonly hears such hot-button political terms as "oppression," "powerlessness," "political struggle," and "repression" being used with greater frequency as radical iconoclasts seek to develop a vocabulary intended to bring long-held, hidden basic assumptions into the open for reconsideration and thus to confront traditional thought. In this way, postmodernism contains an element of confrontation between radical members of minority groups and more conservative inheritors of power; the former seek to legitimize the preoccupation with the differences that create our particular identities (such as differences in race, ethnicity, sexual orientation, class, and gender), and the latter seek to emphasize universality and amalgamation in attempting to merge our personal identities with traditionally espoused group values.[8]

This is not some arcane philosophical discussion: it is, for example, the field on which the future direction of the school curriculum and teaching in U.S. schools is being forged. Defenders of traditional values and cultural norms such as William J. Bennett and Allan Bloom strongly advocate emphasis on traditional Western literature, music, art, languages, history, and culture in the classic tradition of Western civilization, which they think of as universal elements in good school curricula. Postmodernists—including women's rights activists, racial and ethnic minorities, new immigrants from non-European countries, and the poor—argue for a more diverse curriculum, one that is more inclusive of the literatures and histories of the majority of humankind. Thus, they argue for "Women's Studies, African American, Asian, African, Latin American, Hispanic, and Asian-American Studies."[9]

Poststructuralists also tend to think of ways of knowing—that is, research—less in the coolly detached terms of objective science and more in the sense of people's experience, feelings, intuition, and common sense. Poststructuralists often think of research in educational organizations as practitioners and academicians mutually engaged in a collaborative search for understanding rather than as aloof scientists studying their nameless "subjects" (or, worse, "S's") in the detached, impersonal way formerly associated with scientific investigations of organizational behavior in education. Evidence of this lies in the rapid increase of the use of various qualitative research methods, especially ethnography, which seek to examine life in schools primarily through the experiences, assumptions, beliefs, values, and feelings of the participants.

However, as will be described in the chapters ahead, no overarching, all-encompassing theory or metanarrative (see box) of organizational theory exists that would generally be agreed upon by everyone today. Except on the general conceptual level that was described earlier, there is no coherent body of thought that may accurately be described as *the* theory of organizational behavior. There is, though, an enormous body of literature that has been building at least since the mid-1920s, when organizational behavior was "discovered." That literature contains the thought, experience, and research of generations of scholars and practitioners as they struggled to understand human behavior in the workplace and its implications for effective management and leadership. As you might expect, while that vast literature reveals great diversity, it also reveals a steadily growing consensus about what we know.

That is why, as will be discussed more fully in the chapters ahead, most people today believe that it matters very much what kind of climate or culture prevails in a school. As teachers know well, many schools tend to evoke behavior that is conventional, conforming, submissive, and controlled—many would describe such schools as oppressive (students tend to say "jails")—by emphasizing powerful social norms and expectations that support and reward such behavior. Conversely, the norms of such schools discourage

Metanarrative

The word *metanarrative* literally means "big story" and is often used to mean the one story that is always right and that shapes and molds our perceptions of the world around us. Typically, metanarratives give rise to stories that powerfully legitimate mechanisms of social control. For example, a widely known and believed metanarrative is that told in the Christian Bible from Genesis 1 through the New Testament; it is generally spoken of as the story of the Bible.

A key characteristic of postmodernism was to question and challenge the metanarratives that have held sway in the Western world from the days of imperial Rome to the present time. For many people, one enduring metanarrative was the dogmatic belief in the superiority of Christianity to all other religions. According to this metanarrative, Christianity was the foundation of morality and civilization and, thus, provided the logic for converting all peoples to the Christian faith. This, in turn, was a dynamic source of energy that propelled the development of imperialism and colonialism. A dominant metanarrative of modernism, on the other hand, was the conviction that the logic and rationality of science provide the keys to understanding our world.

Other examples of important recent metanarratives are capitalism and communism or socialism, as well as the metanarratives of democracy and fascism. Indeed, the American Declaration of Independence coupled with Lincoln's Gettysburg Address comprises a classic statement of the democratic metanarrative. Following the destruction of the World Trade Center in New York in 2001, the clash between two major metanarratives that had previously existed almost unnoticed—that of Christian fundamentalism in America and Muslim fundamentalism—was suddenly and unexpectedly thrust to the forefront.

behavior that questions the established order and proposes changes that challenge the conventional ways of the past. In the United States today, many people—not only those from traditionally oppressed or ignored groups, such as women, people of color, ethnic and minority groups, and the burgeoning underclass—find such educational institutions incompatible with their own strongly held personal values such as empowerment, self-growth, personal fulfillment, and sense of self-worth. This book will help you to explore ways of understanding the extraordinarily powerful relationship between the school as an organization and the behavior of people who work in it, and what implications for praxis in educational leadership these understandings suggest.

Knowledge of organizational behavior is not only very powerful but also is arguably central to the most pressing issues in educational leadership today. This is a time of great intellectual turmoil in the field of education, a time of great epistemological skepticism in which all ideas rooted in the past are suspect. Indeed, some people seek to reject all theory and insist on a pragmatic approach to understanding organizational life in schools without seeming to understand that pragmatism is, in itself, a theory and an epistemological philosophy. Although this book takes a pragmatic approach to understanding behavior in education, it is based on understanding and accepting the fact that pragmatism is both an epistemological theory and a philosophy. Because of the epistemological skepticism that is rampant today and the antitheory bias that is sweeping through all the behavioral sciences, let us disclose at least the essence of the growing intellectual heritage that underlies this book.

The Nature of Scientific Progress

As dissatisfaction with public schooling has deepened over time, the search for simple direct solutions has not borne fruit in the sense of an emerging broad national consensus that points the way to effective school reform. Instead, efforts to improve the performance of schools have produced not widespread agreement as to how to bring about improvement but, rather, a frustratingly broad array of very different concepts, proposals, and programs, some of which are in conflict. By the time the No Child Left Behind Act of 2001 came before Congress for consideration, as we shall describe in a moment, many people wished to bring order out of seeming chaos and somehow clutched at the notion that what was needed was a more scientific, or evidence-based, approach to deciding what to do. They wanted, in other words, to see the emergence of a consensus on what should be done to make schools more effective. Apparently the hope was to legislate a simpler, more transparent understanding of what the problems and, therefore, the solutions were. The prevailing view at the time of the debate and adoption of the act by Congress was that an infusion of more rigorous scientific thought and methods would be instrumental in improving the performance of schools. However, this view embodies some critically important assumptions about the nature of science and scientific progress. *It requires those who would be educational leaders to think more carefully about those assumptions and about the nature of science and scientific progress.*

People used to think, and many who hold a modernist understanding of the world still do, that science brings about a steady cumulative acquisition of knowledge over the course of time. This view assumes that the nature of scientific inquiry is to use the discoveries of earlier investigations to explore further and thus extend our knowledge and understanding in an orderly and systematic way. This view envisions the growth and development of a science as a continuous, ever-expanding, increasingly certain understanding of the world.

This view of science and scientific methods was challenged in 1962 by Thomas S. Kuhn with the publication of a 180-page essay entitled *The Structure of Scientific Revolutions.*[10] Clearly "a profoundly influential landmark of twentieth-century intellectual history,"[11] it has been translated into sixteen languages and has sold well over a million copies—a remarkable number for such an intellectually rigorous book. Still in print today, Kuhn's work is studied not only by those in the so-called mature sciences (such as physics, chemistry, and astronomy), but by those in the less mature sciences (such as economics, history, education, and sociology) as well. As the demand for increased use of scientifically rigorous approaches to improving teaching and learning rises, it becomes important for educational leaders to understand the issues that Kuhn discussed.

Central to Kuhn's thesis was the recognition that science does not produce a steady, cumulative acquisition of knowledge. Rather, the history of science is characterized by a pattern consisting of tranquil periods during which "normal science" is practiced, punctuated occasionally by intellectually vigorous—or even, at times, intellectually violent—scientific revolutions. These scientific revolutions bring to the fore whole new conceptual understandings about the world we live in.

During periods of normal science, the basic task of scientists is to apply established theory to explain and understand the mysteries that abound in our universe, to grapple with the confounding intricacies, and to discern patterns in the apparent muddle of the world we live in. In the conduct of normal science there is wide general agreement within the profession as to what theory is acceptable and what methods are appropriate to use in conducting studies and investigations. This professional agreement is powerfully implemented by such means as peer review groups that control appointments to positions on university faculties, admission to professional associations and election of officers in them, and the distribution of research grant money, and that decide what gets published—especially in influential refereed journals—and what papers are read at prestigious conferences. Thus, during periods of normal science, the work of scientists consists largely of using currently accepted theory to frame explorations of questions that the theory has not yet explained. Usually, this work results in strengthening and extending the currently accepted theories, ideas, and practices.

Contrary to popular belief, Kuhn described scientists and scientific work during periods of normal science as being rather routine, what he called *puzzle solving*: fitting the remaining pieces of the puzzle in the right order so as to further demonstrate and support the currently accepted theory. Such scientists are neither breaking new ground to extend scientific knowledge nor being objective, independent thinkers in the popular stereotype of scientific work. They are generally conservative individuals who accept what they have been taught and seek to apply it to solving the problems that prevailing theory dictates.

Kuhn used the term *paradigm*[12] to describe this worldview shared by scientists, this intertwined set of theoretical and methodological beliefs and values that is accepted as being fundamental to a field of science. The scientific paradigm, then, sets forth a set of agreed-upon understandings—the rules of the game, if you will—subscribed to by those in the profession about accepted and approved ways in which problems are to be apprehended and explained. But a paradigm is more than merely a set of understandings and agreements arising from objective facts. A paradigm, even a scientific paradigm, is a system of beliefs that exists within a larger ideological context: it consists of interlocking scientific, social, and political views and commitments. Thus, it is not simply some esoteric scientific phenomenon isolated from the rest of the world; it is closely entwined with the realities of the social and political world. The social and political realities of the time and place are powerful players in shaping and molding a scientific paradigm.

A classic example of this, one that Kuhn used, is in the realm of astronomy, which had for centuries been dominated by the Ptolemaic paradigm that described the Earth as the center of the universe around which the sun and the planets revolve. This was of practical importance because astronomical observations were used to establish the calendar, and the calendar was vitally important in the life of the Roman Catholic Church. Yet, as time passed, astronomers encountered increasing difficulty—during a very long period of normal science—in resolving increasingly awkward discrepancies between their observations and the dictates of the well-accepted Ptolemaic paradigm. During the sixteenth century, as the need for calendar reform made it vital to resolve these discrepancies, a great furor was stirred by the increasing debate over the new, revolutionary paradigm arising from the work of Copernicus. He claimed that the evidence showed that Ptolemy had been wrong, that in fact the sun was at the center of the solar system; around it, the Earth and other planets revolved. Thus arose what was indeed a paradigmatic crisis that finally resulted in a scientific revolution that brought about the downfall of the time-honored Ptolemaic paradigm and gave rise to the then-new Copernican paradigm that still prevails today in astronomy.

Many other examples have been used to illustrate the concept of paradigms, scientific revolutions, and scientific progress. Though this thought is explored more fully in Chapter 2, four main points should be underscored here:

- Scientific progress is characterized by periods of normal science, during which the established paradigm is refined and strengthened, followed by the emergence of a new paradigm to replace the old.

- In a scientific revolution the new paradigm is very different from the old. It is not a modification of what went before, and it takes the science in a new direction. It renders the old paradigm incorrect and overthrows it.

- The emergence of a revolutionary paradigm is strongly resisted and denied by the established normal science. Thus, a scientific revolution is inevitably turbulent, volatile, and even intellectually violent. This is not a peaceful process, though, at its best, it may well be a civil process.

- Like a political revolution, a scientific revolution can succeed only when it wins the approval and acceptance not only of those in the scientific community but also of other relevant constituents.

The presence of a scientific paradigm is the most critical criterion that identifies a field as a mature science because it guides the research efforts of those who work in that scientific community. An immature science, on the other hand, lacks such an overarching paradigm to unify the efforts of the members of its community. In other words, the paradigm identifies and defines a field of science. Being an immature science, education has no overarching paradigm. This is a fundamental reason the effort to improve schools and teaching and learning is currently characterized by a cacophony of disparate theories, ideas, programs, and approaches—all of which are said by their adherents to yield results but none of which has unified the relevant constituencies in acceptance and endorsement. The last paradigm in American education was progressive education, presently gleefully maligned by many, which is discussed briefly later in this book.

Progressive education was not overthrown as incorrect by the breakthrough discovery of a new and different scientific paradigm; it was never demonstrated to be wrong or ineffectual through clinical trials or other scientific research. Rather, many of the basic pedagogical practices developed under progressive education continue to be widely in evidence in American classrooms today, even as efforts to demolish the movement persist and swell. The shift away from progressive education has been largely fueled not by any scientific breakthrough, but by a rising conservative social and political outlook that chooses to reject the essence of the ideas about human nature and human behavior on which progressive education was built. In this context, American educational leaders may correctly understand the bold changes in direction embodied in the No Child Left Behind Act as an attempt to legislate the establishment of a new paradigm in teaching and learning, rather than as a scientific revolution as Thomas Kuhn had described. In fact, the legislation called for scientific work to be done to justify the new paradigm after the fact instead of establishing a new paradigm based upon new ideas arising from a scientific revolution, which effectively turns Kuhn's analysis on its head.

But do not be misled: paradigm shifts and scientific revolutions occur from time to time in all sciences, no matter how mature they may be. This is the very nature of scientific progress. It is also why we continually witness previously well-established ideas and practices being challenged and overthrown either by the discovery of new scientific insights or by mounting evidence that the established ways are not producing the results that were predicted. In our modern scientific age, this has become the stuff of daily newspaper headlines. For some three decades, for example, menopausal women were routinely advised by their doctors to take hormones, which were thought to ease the problems normally associated with the onset of menopause. Among medical practitioners this was thought to be based on a well-developed body of solid scientific clinical evidence. Yet, early in the twenty-first century, this practice was thrown into great doubt and confusion as accumulating evidence clearly contradicted earlier beliefs and expectations held by medical practitioners and underscored the potential dangers of hormone therapy that had been largely downplayed. This was not necessarily because the earlier scientific studies had been badly done but simply because accumulating experience with the use of hormones had produced unanticipated, and often inexplicable, outcomes for many patients, and these constituted new evidence that had to be considered and could not be ignored.

A similar example, commonplace yet very important in the lives of many people, has to do with diet and weight control. The trend toward overweight and obesity in the American population has long been noted and its correlation with serious medical problems well understood. This was one of the early central findings of the famed Framingham Heart Study, which we shall describe shortly. Thus, increased scientific attention was focused on the role of diet in weight control.

This resulted, in the 1980s, in the introduction and strong promotion by the United States Department of Agriculture, with vigorous support from health-oriented associations, of the now-famed Food Guide Pyramid. The Food Guide Pyramid sought to interpret for consumers the best scientific thinking about diet as a practical guide to deciding how much of which kinds of foods should comprise one's daily diet. Essentially, it strongly advocated that a high-carbohydrate diet should be the basis of the American diet: that is, a diet that included a substantial portion of foods from refined carbohydrate-rich foods such as bread, grain, cereals, and pasta, with lesser amounts of fruits and vegetables, small amounts of protein-rich foods (such as fish and lean meat), and very little fat and oil. For over twenty years this was strongly advocated by the American government and prestigious health-oriented organizations, with strong support from the scientific community, as the diet that would, among other benefits, help individuals to keep their weight at healthy levels. Thus, the Food Guide Pyramid was established and widely promoted as the paradigm for healthy diet.

Several things happened over time, however, that brought this paradigm sharply into question by the end of the twentieth century. One was constantly mounting scientific evidence that the incidence of overweight and obesity, even among children, was markedly increasing. Indeed, by 2000, many were speaking of the overweight problem in America as an "epidemic" that was spreading so rapidly as to constitute a public health problem. Another was the widespread observation that many individuals who tried to reduce and control their weight with assiduous dieting using the accepted guidelines reported that it did not succeed. A third was the work of a practicing physician, Dr. Robert Atkins, who consistently reported that patients who undertook a diet that was dramatically different from the paradigm Food Guide Pyramid achieved weight loss and stability of their weight with a diet that included very few carbohydrates. He advocated a diet that included

- very low consumption of carbohydrate-rich cereals and grains and the foods made from them (such as bread, pasta, pizza, and sushi),
- emphasis on including many green vegetables in the daily diet (but not "starchy" ones such as potatoes, onions, or corn)
- meat (such as steak, lamb, pork, bacon, fish, and also eggs and cheese) as an important part of the diet, and
- very little consumption of foods rich in natural sugars such as orange juice and other fruit juices.

Predictably, as Kuhn had described, the established paradigm was strongly defended and the new approach was roundly attacked.

- Dieters who failed to lose weight, it was speculated, really were cheating and backsliding and needed to apply the Food Guide Pyramid more rigorously in their daily lives.
- Americans, in general, ate too much calorie-rich food, particularly fast food, and they did not exercise adequately.
- Children, it was claimed, simply indulged too much in rich, sweet, fatty foods and also did not exercise enough.
- As for the ideas of Dr. Atkins, he was largely marginalized by the defenders of the established paradigm as a quack who was persuading his gullible patients and readers to adopt a diet that, unproven by rigorously controlled independent clinical research, was clearly dangerous to their health.

As Kuhn had taught us, paradigm shifts are usually accompanied by conflict and contention; this was to be no exception.

As Kuhn has also taught us, however, the controversy would not be damped or suppressed and would not go away. Atkins's books became increasingly popular and increasing numbers of readers were persuaded to try his new, radically different approach to diet. At the same time, evidence from studies persistently reported that the overweight-obesity epidemic continued to flourish. In the early twenty-first century, it became progressively more apparent that the conflict between the concepts of the established paradigm (the Food Guide Pyramid) and the newer low-carbohydrate approach to diet actually hinged on a clash of assumptions (or theories) about some basic human physiology. By 2002 many researchers came to agree with Dr. Atkins that carbohydrates, especially refined ones like sugar and other vegetable-based sweeteners, white flour and rice, are quickly absorbed as energy by the body, while carbohydrates in excess of the body's immediate needs are stored as fat for future use. A secondary effect of this quick absorption is renewed hunger soon after a high-carbohydrate meal, for example, after a Chinese dinner of noodles, rice, wonton wrappers, egg-roll skins, syrupy ribs, and cornstarch thickeners. A low-carbohydrate diet, on the other hand, not only forces the body to seek energy by consuming its own stored fat but also suppresses appetite, since dietary fat and protein take longer to digest and enter the bloodstream than carbohydrates. Moreover, the body expends more energy burning fat than burning carbohydrates, yielding what Atkins calls a "metabolic advantage."[13]

As the turmoil mounted among those concerned about nutrition and health issues, it came as a surprise to many to learn that the long-established paradigm, the Food Guide Pyramid, had in fact never been systematically tested in controlled scientific studies. It was essentially an untested theoretical model. This criticism led the United States Department of Agriculture in 2000 to revise its pyramid and *Dietary Guidelines for Americans.* Unfortunately, although this version of the pyramid and the guidelines was better, it still fell short of utilizing the best research in the field of nutrition. The Harvard School of Public Health accused the government of being influenced by business interests, and it developed an alternative food pyramid to correct the problems inherent in the government's version.[14] This clash in the field of human nutrition represents a classic example of the beginning of a paradigm shift, and in the early 2000s, the resulting confusion and turmoil made it appear highly likely that a scientific revolution in human nutrition was underway.

Psychology

Modern psychology, the study of the mind, began in the late nineteenth century. Many people mark the date as 1879, the year in which William Wundt established the first psychological laboratory at the University of Leipzig, Germany, and, by coincidence, William James established a laboratory at Harvard. Since then the discipline of psychology has developed rapidly and, in the process, has produced a number of major approaches or scientific paradigms. Four of these paradigms are briefly described here because they are particularly germane to the study of organizational behavior in education.

Behaviorism

Behaviorists largely ignored the likelihood of possible connections between conceivable inner states of individuals—such as perceptions, feelings, and thoughts—and their behavior. Since these inner states, if they exist, cannot be observed or measured, behaviorists directed their attention to developing a science of human behavior in the classic modernist sense, focusing on overt manifestations of behavior that can be observed and measured, largely ignoring the possibility that inner drives (that cannot be observed) may be involved.

In behaviorism, observations of behavior should be reduced to quantifiable terms: How many times was the behavior observed? In what time frame? In what sequence? Because intrinsic (or inner) motivations cannot be observed, much less quantified or controlled, but depend on anecdotal evidence, behaviorists discounted them altogether. Thus, behaviorists focused on extrinsic motivation: rewards and punishments intended to reinforce desired behaviors and extinguish undesired behaviors. Food and release from pain were among the quantifiable, manipulable extrinsic rewards often used in the carefully controlled laboratory experiments that constituted the method of choice of behaviorists and became their hallmark.

Thus, human beings were not only reduced to being merely objects under study by behaviorists, but also they were actually replaced in the laboratory by rats, pigeons, and other animals, which were both cheaper and easier to control. "Animals, from a breeding house and often newly obtained fresh from American Railway Express platforms, were starved to three quarters or two thirds of their body weight to ensure adequate 'motivation.' When it is remembered that these rats were two to three months old, 'teenagers' in the human time scale, at the outset of the experimentation (to have waited longer would have increased laboratory costs), it is no wonder" that the psychology that emerged could be described as the psychology of desperate rats.[15]

Nonetheless, behaviorism had clearly emerged by 1933 as the definitional approach to understanding human behavior in academic departments of psychology in U.S. universities. B. F. Skinner is undoubtedly the practitioner best known to U.S. teachers and educators for his widely practiced proposals for applying behaviorism to schooling, especially the pedagogical methods for teaching children with maladaptive behavior. Behaviorism was very popular among those in business and industrial management for many years because it supported the idea that management had the moral and ethical right to control and dominate people. Employees were, in this view, more or less passive objects that should be controlled and manipulated by management using behaviorist techniques. This, it was reasoned, would be done in the best interests of the employees—whether or not they believed or understood that.

By the 1970s, behaviorism, and particularly its Skinnerian form, had mushroomed into a large-scale movement in U.S. schooling and remained so well into the 1980s. Behaviorism still remains influential in curriculum and instruction circles. It has been embraced, knowingly or otherwise, by many advocates of school reform. Such pedagogical notions as programmed instruction, diagnostic-prescriptive teaching, and behavior modification are behaviorist ideas familiar to many U.S. teachers. Much of the use of computers in the classroom is based on behaviorist notions of pedagogy. "The technology of behaviorism that Skinner [advocated] for the schools is to decide on goals, to find the reinforcers to produce those responses, to implement a program of reinforcers that will produce the desired behaviors, and finally to measure very carefully the effects of the reinforcers and to change them accordingly."[16] Thus behaviorism, especially B. F. Skinner's brand, was far from some idle academic theory that had little relevance to the real world of schools: in fact, it has been a powerful force in defining how U.S. teachers, administrators, reformers, and others think about students, teaching praxis, and the organization and leadership of schools. For example, Schmuck and Schmuck viewed with some alarm the impact of Skinnerian behaviorism on schooling in the United States. In 1974, they observed that, in the behaviorist view, "Evidence of learning consists of prescribed responses to stimuli presented in a program, on a standardized test, or by the teacher's question. In a good [behaviorist] program, the objectives are behaviorally defined, the information is presented in a logical and sequential manner"[17] and there are systematic methods for evaluating behaviors to be used as evidence of reaching the program's objectives. Systematic methods for evaluating the outcomes of instruction should be, in the behaviorist view, "objective" and tend to emphasize standardized testing. Skinner, moreover, made it very clear that since the processes of learning themselves are neither directly visible nor quantifiable, the pedagogical techniques of behaviorism "are not designed to 'develop the mind' or to further some vague 'understanding' . . . they are designed on the contrary to establish the very behaviors which are taken to be *evidence of learning*."[18]

That was in 1968, but it is not some hoary academic babble that has been rendered obsolete with the passage of time and the advancement of knowledge. Clearly, this view of teaching and learning is alive and well in our own time of school reform: many who advocate the standards movement and high-stakes testing in education reform today would be comfortable with it. As we shall explain more fully in Chapter 3, it is one of two recurring themes in debate and discussion of schooling that have clashed repeatedly for well over a century.

Psychoanalytic Psychology

A virtually 180-degree turn away from the behaviorist approach was the psychology of psychoanalysis. It was founded around the year 1900 by Sigmund Freud and a group of followers, notably Carl Jung in the early years. Whereas behaviorism was often spoken of as first-force psychology, psychoanalysis emerged as the second force.

Psychoanalysis was the key method of choice to explore the unconscious drives and internal instincts that were thought to motivate people and, thus, be the causes of behavior. In fact, it was Freud who introduced the revolutionary notion of *psychic energy*: a previously overlooked source of energy, different from physical energy, from which human thoughts, feelings, and actions arose. Both Freudian and Jungian psychoanalytic approaches tended, at that time, to focus on the need to diagnose and treat what was thought to be deviant or, at least, problematic behavior and tended to concentrate on such issues as social maladjustment and behavior disorders. The reader will no doubt recall such familiar concepts as the id, ego, and superego, which were of bedrock importance in teaching and studying human behavior as it was understood by psychoanalysts.

The preferred method of treatment of perceived behavioral disorders was, and still is, psychotherapy.

Psychoanalysts and psychotherapists of various types were important actors in some academic departments of psychology in U.S. universities in 1933, but they were far from dominant in the field because their research methods had little to do with such things as the design and execution of laboratory experiments, objective measurement, and mathematical analyses—all of which had become the hallmark of the scientific method and academic respectability among the status-conscious denizens of the upwardly mobile U.S. academy of the time. Nevertheless, the psychoanalytic/psychotherapeutic concepts of psychology were—as they still are—a widely known and influential force in the development of psychology.

Today, many U.S. teachers have studied the application of psychotherapeutic concepts to schooling through the work of such practical psychoanalysts as Bruno Bettelheim,[19] whose writing has been very popular among the general public as well, especially among parents and others interested in his chosen field of emotionally disturbed children.

Cognitive Psychology

Cognitive psychology is generally acknowledged as having begun in the 1960s as a major paradigm shift away from the then-dominant behaviorism. An important factor that triggered the paradigm shift was a devastating review by Noam Chomsky of some of B. F. Skinner's work on verbal behavior that made it clear that creative use of language cannot be explained by behavioristic theories.

Cognitive psychologists concentrate on the role of such phenomena as attention, motivation, perception, memory, learning, information processing, reasoning, problem solving, judgment, decision making, language processing, and sensation in generating human behavior. They often apply their theories and paradigms to such matters as

- *critical thinking,* for example, how we apply these cognitive phenomena to evaluating arguments and analyzing complex discussions, and

- *creative thinking,* for example, how we generate new insights, understandings, and alternatives that are divergent from the norm.

Those who trigger scientific or artistic revolutions by inventing new paradigms (such as Einstein, Mozart, and Monet) are typically skilled in thinking critically and creatively. This area of cognitive psychology opens up consideration of the contrasts between convergent thinking and divergent thinking. It is also closely related to the currently popular concept of left-brain and right-brain orientation in thinking.

Cognitive psychology, having been widely accepted as a principal component of the scientific paradigm of education, has had considerable impact on the practice of teaching and learning in school classrooms. Thus, of course, excellent instruction is seen as emphasizing such outcomes as the perception of relationships between and among the elements of a problem, in contrast with emphasis on rote memorization. Contemporary teachers who are thought to be excellent tend to strive to develop the motivations of students, as well as to incorporate a variety of ways of knowing and understanding in their teaching and, thus, the learning of their students. Therefore, considerable emphasis is given to the teaching of such things as study skills, social skills, problem solving, and organizational skills along with subject matter mastery. This perspective clashes remarkably with the views of many who are active in the political realm of school reform, as is evident in much of the No Child Left Behind Act.

Social Psychology

Social psychology is particularly useful in informing the educational leader about organizational behavior. Whereas behaviorism focused on the study of observations of manifest behavior and assumed nothing about possible inner factors that might influence it, and whereas psychoanalysis sought to study the inner forces of individuals as causes of behavior, social psychology interprets behavior as arising from an interaction between factors within each person and factors in the person's environment. This insight is largely credited to Kurt Lewin,* who is widely regarded as the founder of social psychology. It may be expressed as $B = f(p \cdot e)$, meaning that behavior is a function of the interaction between person and environment. This simple yet powerful concept was a major breakthrough of Lewin's, and it is called the *field theory* of human behavior. Social psychology encompasses a wide variety of fields of human behavior including leadership, socialization, motivation, social interaction, interpersonal relations, group processes, group dynamics, the formation and role of attitudes, public opinion, group behavior, and intercultural behavior. It is part of the core of organization studies and has been very influential in the development of sociological and anthropological concepts. Many social psychological concepts underlie modern approaches to classroom management and teaching-learning practices as well. An understanding of the basics of social psychology is indispensable to the educational leader.

When working in schools, as in any organization, an extraordinarily powerful aspect of the environment in shaping and molding behavior of participants is the culture and the climate provided by the organization. Although educational leaders have scant influence over the temperaments or personalities of the individuals whom they would lead, they have a wide range of possibilities for influencing the characteristics of the culture and the climate of the organization. Because the organization has no independent physical reality but exists only as a socially constructed reality, and because our construction of reality is dependent on our perception of what is real, it becomes clearer how the organization emerges as a primary factor in evoking behavior of people in it. This web of interactions between people and organization, and its implications for leadership, is not simple but it is powerful in influencing and shaping the behavior of people at work in educational organizations. It is the subject of the rest of this book.

*During his lifetime, Kurt Lewin pronounced his last name as Luh-veen.

Sociological and Psychological Points of View

The study of psychology took root in the United States in the years preceding World War I. The pioneers in the field, such as G. Stanley Hall (who was awarded the first U.S. doctorate in psychology in 1878) and William James, took intense interest in pedagogy and schooling and had enormous impact on educational thought. By the early 1920s, normal schools and, later, university schools of education had developed strong departments of educational psychology that reflected their views; these departments soon established themselves as dominant in shaping the curriculum of teacher education and, thus, the thinking of U.S. educators.

Today, psychology remains a predominant element in teacher education. Departments of educational psychology in schools of education commonly exert strong influences not only on the content of courses in teaching methods and curriculum but also on the content and methods of data collection and research. That is why courses in such topics as tests and measurements and statistics loom so large in the undergraduate and graduate studies of teachers: they represent critically important skill areas for the researcher in the laboratory of behavioral psychology and are commonly assumed to be somehow useful in teaching praxis. We know from the widespread belief that teachers often voice that such courses are viewed as having little application to teaching practice. The longtime dominance of educational psychology on educational thought in schools of education also helps to explain why present-day in-service education programs for teachers tend to focus so narrowly on technical aspects of pedagogy, usually with emphasis on instructional techniques in the classroom. It is common for teachers to view such programs as of dubious value to them in improving practice.

Sociology, on the other hand, developed in its early years with scant reference to schools other than as institutions that reflected such issues as social class, the effects of desegregation, and the role of schools in society. By the late 1970s, however, a small number of sociologists grew interested in the sociology of organizations, including educational organizations. They began to pick up on some of the ideas that had been explored by the sociologists who conducted studies in industrial settings, notably in units of the Western Electric Company, and to extend that field of inquiry. As the reform movement of the 1980s unfolded, educators became disenchanted with many of the proposals coming from psychologists—for example, proposals for more testing, increased emphasis on basic skills, and refinement of pedagogical techniques—and they began to listen more carefully to the thoughts of sociologists.

In thinking about schooling, psychologists and sociologists generally agree that the goals of schooling are

- academic achievement
- effective work habits
- civic values
- social behavior
- self-esteem
- self-reliance[20]

But they disagree on what must be emphasized to achieve these outcomes more effectively. Psychologists focus on how individual pupils learn, including particular learning styles, motivation, and relationships with both the teacher and classmates. "Sociologists," on the other hand, "look at the entire school and how its organization affects the individuals within it."[21] Thus, to achieve the goals of schooling, educational psychologists tend to focus on such things as

- the expectations that teachers have for the achievement of students
- the relationships between students and teachers
- the motivation of students
- time spent on teaching and learning
- the relationships between individual students and their peers

To achieve the same goals, organizational and educational sociologists tend to emphasize such things as

- how schools are led and managed
- how students are grouped
- the involvement of parents and community
- the ways in which students and teachers are assigned to work together
- the ways in which important decisions are made in the school as a whole

One should be careful about emphasizing the apparent dichotomy of these two different points of view. It is not a new idea in psychology that behavior is heavily influenced by the characteristics of the organizational environment, on which organizational sociologists tend to focus. Working independently, both Kurt Lewin and Henry A. Murray,[22] each a giant in the founding of modern psychology, accepted the premise as early as the 1930s that behavior is a function of the interaction between the person and the environment. This remains today a basic concept in understanding organizational behavior. In this book, that idea is expressed as $B = f(p \cdot e)$.[23]

This is a powerful understanding that has informed and inspired much of the study of organizational culture and organizational climate in schools. The study of organizational behavior is, in fact, the study of the internal needs and personality characteristics of the individual in dynamic tension with the environment created by the educational organization.

The recent tendency to emphasize restructuring of schools to achieve school reform emanates largely, but by no means exclusively, from contemporary thought of organizational sociologists, which generally has not been well represented in the curricula of schools of education. Many currently popular buzzwords in school reform reflect the renewed understanding that the interface of people with the organization is the nexus of school reform efforts. Thus, the vernacular of school reform in the 1990s resounded with calls for empowerment and power sharing, "reinventing" the school, school site management, restructuring the school, participative decision making, and humanizing the school. All of these suggest major changes in the organization of the schools to improve the growth-enhancing characteristics of their environments.

Although U.S. schools have tended throughout their history to ape the values and views of industry, commerce, and the military, it is becoming increasingly clear that schools are in fact distinct, if not unique, kinds of organizations that are different in important ways from industrial, commercial, governmental, or military organizations. Because schools are unique among organizations, they require ways of thinking, styles of leadership, and approaches to administrative practice that are especially suited to them.

The uniqueness of educational organizations resides in their educative mission, which demands that they be growth-enhancing organizations: fostering the learning and personal growth and development of participants, encouraging never-ending processes of maturing, enhancing self-confidence and self-esteem, satisfaction, taking initiative, and taking responsibility for one's actions. Educative organizations seek to increase the personal and interpersonal competencies of their participants, to constantly develop the skills of the group in collaborating, to make hidden assumptions explicit and to examine them for what they mean in terms of individual and group behavior, to enact cooperative group behavior that is caring and supportive of others, to manage conflict productively and without fear, and to share information and ideas fully and without fear. It is the business of schools, therefore, to develop a culture that places high value on, and supports and enhances, openness, high trust, caring and sharing, that always strives for consensus but supports and values those who think differently, and that prizes human growth and development above all. Educational leaders, then, strive for a vision of the school as one that seeks to be engaged in a never-ending process of change and development, a "race without a finish line," or *kaizen,* as the Japanese speak of constant growth achieved through small incremental steps, rather than one that seeks the big dramatic breakthrough, the mythical "silver bullet," that will, supposedly, finally make everything right.

The processes of becoming[24]—of people growing and developing as individuals and as groups, and of the organization doing so as well—combine to create the essence of enduring vitality in organizational life, while academic outcomes are transient, ephemeral evidence that the processes are working. The conundrum of power is a major characteristic of the environment of the educational organization: hierarchy prevails; we have never found a substitute for it in organizational life, but there is much that we can ethically and honestly do to share power and distribute it more equitably in efforts to minimize its deleterious effects on the behavior of people in the organization. In the process, we can make the school an ever more growth-enhancing environment.

The Relevance to School Leadership Today

One may well question how relevant the ideas that have been discussed thus far are to the practice of educational leadership in schools. Are these ideas merely the playthings of academics and philosophers or do they have real meaning to those who seek to make a difference as leaders in education?

The key to understanding how and why ideas such as modernism and postmodernism, or how sociological views of organizations differ from psychological views, are important to educational leaders lies, first, in understanding that the processes of developing educational leadership are highly dynamic, with constant, ongoing change and development. They have been changing and developing over the course of many years and will continue this dynamic process in the future. Knowing and accepting this as an enduring characteristic of the education enterprise is basic to preparing oneself to be an educational leader. Of the many wellsprings from which the dynamic processes of change and development in education are shaped and molded, two are of foremost importance:

- *The emergence of new knowledge about how people function in organizations.* Research and study are constantly modifying our understanding of the human experience in educational organizations. This is why it is necessary for the educational leader to stay abreast of emergent relevant studies of organizational behavior. Much of this book is devoted to exploring and interpreting knowledge about organizational behavior arising from recent scholarship and research.

- *The dynamic impact of changes in the larger society in which the schools exist.* In the affairs of humankind there is an unremitting ebb and flow of overarching changes that challenge all social institutions to adapt to new conditions, and schools are no exception. War and peace, economic prosperity and depression, the evolution of social values and beliefs, and sweeping technological-industrial changes are obvious among them. Some are more nuanced, such as the worldwide surging rise of conservatism—economic, political, religious—that emerged in the waning years of the twentieth century and swept across the globe as the twenty-first century unfolded. This may appear to have little to do with educational leadership but in fact, as we shall describe, it may have at least as much impact as all the discoveries or inventions of new knowledge by scholars.

The relentless, ceaseless interplay between the search for a better understanding of human nature and human behavior, on the one hand, and the evolutionary development of social and political beliefs and values in our culture, on the other hand, creates a dynamic environment in which the basic concepts of education and educational leadership are endlessly incomplete, always works in progress. This can be an uncomfortable environment for those who seek certainty and finality in the ideas that guide their professional work. But this is hardly unique to educational leadership: the need to be nimble, adaptable, and flexible is a central characteristic of all kinds of effective organizations and every profession today. It is at least as pressing in business, law, medicine, and just about every field of human enterprise in the world today as it is in education.

The educational leader—like leaders in all fields of human endeavor—inevitably faces a career in which new, resilient responses are constantly required to meet the challenges that will inescapably and unremittingly arise in the future. These challenges are likely to occur in cycles, as they have for over a century. Rest assured: the problems that seem overwhelming to us now will in time recede into the background as new, and apparently more demanding, challenges emerge in the future. In view of this unyielding progression, educational leaders need to develop not responses to the urgencies of the moment but rather a set of values, beliefs, and principles to guide them in developing effective strategies and actions in the ever-uncertain future. Taken together these values, beliefs, and principles mold and shape the educational leader's vision of what the school ought to be like, the direction in which it should be going, the end state that it should be striving for. And a core element in such a vision must be the ability to see the school as a nimble, adaptive organization that is able to detect emerging problems and to proactively develop effective solutions to them. It is generally agreed today that a school administrator who does not have such a vision that is clear and well developed will find it difficult, if not impossible, to be an effective educational leader.

This unremitting social-political process of change has been commented upon many times as being characteristic of the American approach to educational problems: new solutions to problems are invented, rise in popularity, and are enthusiastically tried for a few years. Then, when they fail to solve the problems, we grow impatient and cast them aside in favor of applying a new fad to a fresh set of different problems. The chronicle of schooling in the United States since the mid-twentieth century clearly supports the view that this pattern is an enduring characteristic of the American approach to educational problems. It seems certain to be repeated in the future. And the debate and contention that accompany each new proposed "quick fix" invariably involve clashes concerning assumptions about people, values, and beliefs about human nature and involve different ways of thinking—such as modernist and structuralist versus postmodern and poststructuralist, psychological versus sociological—as have been discussed in this chapter. The current iteration of this peculiarly American approach was launched with the passage by Congress and the signing by the president of the No Child Left Behind Act in 2002.

The No Child Left Behind Act of 2001

The power of the ideas that have been briefly discussed here to forge and give direction to practical matters in the tough world of educational leadership is clearly demonstrated in the federal omnibus bill on education that became the law of the land in January 2002. All the ideas that have been discussed here were contested in the debate and the rough-and-tumble of national politics for dominance in shaping and molding new rules and new dynamics in the roles to be played from that point on by Washington political moguls and by the states in educational policy and practice. Clearly, in the process one set of values and beliefs won the day in that legislative process, and competing values and beliefs did not prevail. And yet in the give-and-take of the democratic process, losers seek to become winners, and we would be naive to assume that the pendulum might not, in time, swing back to the former state of affairs. But that is not the situation at this moment; it is a possibility of the future. By any measure, the passage of the historic No Child Left Behind Act demonstrates that the ideas that have been discussed are not merely academic fluff but are at the heart of the need to make practical decisions about education.

When signed by President George W. Bush on January 8, 2002, the act reauthorized the Elementary and Secondary Education Act of 1965 in ways intended to be "the most far-reaching reform of the nation's public education system" since the creation of the Department of Education in 1979.[25] It can be seen as "perhaps the greatest achievement of the U.S. Department of Education in its then 29-year history [because] it signified a clear shift from the department's early role as data keeper and dispenser of student-aid funds to its emergent role as leading education policy maker and reformer."[26] Conversely, it has also been described as a historic, even breathtaking, intrusion by the federal government into the rights of states to control the education enterprise within their borders.

The No Child Left Behind Act promised to increase federal expenditures in education by 20 percent over the previous year, and it had three major goals:

- Closing the achievement gap for disadvantaged students.

- Improving the preparation of teachers and increasing their compensation so as to have every classroom in America staffed by a "highly qualified" teacher by the end of the 2005–2006 school year.

- Instituting closely monitored systems of accountability for students, teachers, and schools.

It was envisioned that these goals would be achieved by a number of federal mandates. A centerpiece of the effort to close the achievement gap was a provision in the act creating the Early Reading Initiative. It pledged $900 million per year over a six-year period to bolster reading instruction primarily in schools in poverty-stricken areas and an additional $75 million per year for preschool instruction in reading. The funding was not to be doled out automatically to the states, but had to be applied for by proposals from the then cash-starved states that described in detail the programs they would develop with the money from Washington so as to achieve the initiative's intention of raising the achievement of disadvantaged students in learning to read.

But the language of the act, some 1,184 pages long, bristles with 246 references to the word *research* and 116 references to the terms *scientific* and *scientifically* in describing the kinds of approaches to instruction that were desired by Congress in enacting the law. It was clear that what Congress wanted to accomplish was to support instruction based on evidence from scientific research, but this quickly gave rise to a controversy over what exactly "scientifically based" research or instruction means.

Some advocates for improving educational research seemed to insist that only controlled laboratory experimentation in the tradition of double-blind studies used in pharmaceutical research would be the gold standard for judging the scientific adequacy of the research on instructional methods. Pharmaceutical studies are called controlled laboratory experiments because they use two basic techniques:

- They normally employ a control group, whose members would unknowingly receive a placebo, and an experimental group, whose members, also unknowingly, receive the medication under study.

■ They include systematic efforts to control or minimize other variables that might be confusing. These could include such things as age of the subjects, sex, race, financial status, and so on.

The controlled laboratory experiment is, unquestionably, a powerful and highly reputable research method that is basic to the development of modern Western medicine. Many believe that this method of studying treatments and effects provides an almost mythical certitude regarding the effects of a drug treatment and offers a desirable model that should be emulated in educational research.

In fact, however, one of the confounding factors in such research is that in a surprising number of cases, individuals taking the placebo, perhaps a simple sugar pill, respond to it by getting better, while others in the control group do not get better. At the same time, there is sure to be variation in the observed effects of the experimental drugs on the individuals in the experimental group. Thus, even the best such studies can produce only statistical correlations to describe the outcomes; the best such studies are associational and cannot describe cause and effect with certitude. This is, quite simply, why one is well advised to proceed with caution whenever we are told that "research *proves*" anything. Actually, research in any field of human behavior can rarely be said to prove anything: some correlations can be very strong and yield high levels of confidence about predicted outcomes, and others may be weak and yield low levels of confidence. But the findings of even the strongest research designs most rigorously applied to research in human behavior, such as teaching and learning, are almost certain to be stated in terms of statistical associations: one may be assured that there is some level of probability that outcomes can be predicted, but that level nearly always falls short of certainty.

Consequently, prescribing a medication to an individual cannot guarantee predictable results but only a degree of likelihood that the predicted results may or may not be experienced. Moreover, lack of control over other variables not included in the study can confound the findings: for example, those in the sample populations of the study will vary in some degree in their lifestyles, in their outlook on the world, in social and cultural backgrounds, in physical fitness, and so on: a long list of possible uncontrolled—and even unknown—variables. Further, taking the medicine under study may produce a variety of side effects, often unpredicted, some of which may be so serious as to cast doubt on the wisdom of using the medicine at all. Thus, the outcome of such studies is something less than certitude: instead of a clean dividing line between success and failure, what such studies produce is some evidence that "some degree of health benefit is associated with some dosage of the experimental drug. Where there is a relationship between the experimental medicine and improved health, researchers note that there is an association—a statistical correlation—between the drug and the condition of the patient."[27] This is a rather simple, fundamental concept that the educational leader should keep in mind when confronted with discussions of educational research outcomes, and especially when confronted with strong advocacy for the use of methods of instruction in the school that are said to have been proven to work.

Research Methods in Education

Research in elementary and secondary education has, for over a century, been generally scorned in the academic community as being trivial, shallow, and largely lacking what is usually called scientific or academic rigor. Indeed, many academics contend that, because they perceive the field as lacking rigorous theoretical and scientific underpinnings, education cannot properly be called an academic discipline at all. This is a major reason why, among the contentious baronies that make up universities, schools of education have generally been held in low esteem on their own campuses. In fact, not a few elite universities have chosen to abolish their beleaguered schools of education in the belief that doing so would enhance the academic prestige of the university as a whole. It is also a major reason why educational research does not attract the financial support that is common in many other disciplines such as agriculture, medicine, physics, and business.

It cannot be denied that the quality of research in education has been and still is uneven. Further, research in education is hampered by the fact that it is not recognized as a bona fide scholarly discipline. By definition, a scholarly discipline includes a well-defined body of knowledge that arises from recognized theory and the use of research methods accepted as being appropriate to study the questions under investigation. This, of course, refers to what Thomas Kuhn called the scientific paradigm, which has already been discussed. History is a typical example: clearly, it has well-defined body of knowledge that we call history, and that body of knowledge is constantly under development and expansion by researchers who investigate interesting questions using systematic methods of study and recognized rules of evidence. Historians, for example, study history using theory unique to their discipline and well-recognized methods of historical research such as historiography. In a similar vein, cultural anthropologists study culture using anthropological theory unique to their discipline, as well as research methods and rules of evidence considered appropriate to the questions under investigation, such as ethnography and ethnology. Education, on the other hand, must draw its knowledge as well as its theory and research methods from a number of different, related disciplines. In addition to psychology, sociology, and anthropology these often include history, political science, and economics. Very often the educational researcher does not have the academic qualifications that would ordinarily be required of researchers to work in one of these related disciplines and thus lacks academic credibility to do a particular study. However, it should be noted that the quality of educational research has been rapidly improving since the middle of the twentieth century, as have the academic qualifications of those who are engaged in educational research. However, in academic circles it takes time, sometimes a lot of time, to painstakingly bring an emerging discipline to maturity and recognition. Psychology went through this process as it began to develop from biology, sociology required a long time to become accepted as an academic discipline, and so on.

Not surprisingly, lacking the strong support of their institutions as well as commitment from external sources of funding, few rigorous, large-scale, breakthrough studies exist in education comparable to, say, the legendary Framingham Heart Study that has been so powerful in shaping the modern practice of medicine and, indeed, the way most of us live today. This study began collecting data in 1948 from 5,209 men and women between the ages of thirty and sixty-two and continues today, having enrolled 5,124 of the adult children of the original participants and their spouses. Consider a few of the major findings of that research:

- Cigarette smoking was found to increase the risk of heart disease (1960).
- Cholesterol level and hypertension were found to increase the risk of heart disease (1961).
- The level of physical activity was found to be correlated with the risk of heart disease (1967).
- High blood pressure was found to increase the risk of stroke (1970).
- Menopause was found to be related to the risk of heart disease (1976).
- Sociopsychological factors were found to be related to the risk of heart disease (1978).
- High levels of high density lipid (HDL) cholesterol were found to reduce the risk of death (1988).

This extraordinary program of research has directly contributed to more than a thousand articles published in refereed medical journals and has transformed, in important ways, the curriculum in medical schools and the practice of medicine itself. This is indeed powerful research by any standard. But notice: there was no control group, no laboratory controls, none of the arcane mystery that is popularly thought to be inherent in good medical research. Conceptually, the design of the Framingham Heart Study was classically simple: data were systematically collected from a large, stratified random sample of individuals over the course of many years and examined for statistical relationships. Carrying out the research, however, has been complex, expensive, and difficult. This was a large-scale longitudinal study whose execution included two basic steps:

- gathering data from a selected population using repeated questionnaires, interviews, and tests over time, and
- seeing how, over time, selected factors (e.g., diet, exercise, genetic inheritance, smoking habits) correlated with the incidence of the onset of heart disease.

It is a truly elegant research design, simple and straightforward, and executed with remarkable precision and fidelity. Of course, being a large and long-lasting study, it has required careful and highly competent management. But the thing to be noted in the present discussion is that it is a classic correlational study. The Framingham Heart Study has great power to inform us, on the one hand, of certain associations between cardiovascular health and selected lifestyle practices and, on the other hand, to suggest new and important questions for researchers to explore more fully using equally rigorous, though perhaps different, research designs.

In education research there are few well-designed, large-scale studies similar to the Framingham study. One example that most educational researchers can agree upon that meets the gold standard for research is the longitudinal study done in Tennessee entitled Student-Teacher Achievement Ratio, popularly known as the STAR study. This was a legislated study that was conducted by the Tennessee State Department of Education and carried out by representatives from four state universities. From 1985 to 1989, 79 elementary schools stratified by inner-city, urban, suburban, and rural settings with approximately 7,500 students in 300 kindergarten through third grade classes were involved in this experiment. A U.S. Department of Education publication about class size stated the following regarding the research design of STAR:

> . . . the particular strengths of this initiative should be underscored. The within-school design was an effective way to control for differences among school settings including, but not limited to, the economic status of the student body, per-pupil expenditures, and the manner in which schools were administered. The value of this type of design cannot be underestimated. The random assignment was monitored carefully by state-level evaluators. A large and diverse population of students was longitudinally tracked over the 4 year period, and the data were collected, cleaned, and collated with a high degree of care.[28]

In the STAR study, students were randomly assigned to small classes ranging from 13 to 17 students, regular classes ranging from 22 to 26 students, and regular classes ranging from 22 to 26 with a full-time aide. Findings from standardized test measures of math and reading indicated that students in small classes benefited significantly among all types of schools when compared to regular classes or regular classes with aides. Regular classes with aides showed some increased achievement results when compared to regular classes, but these results were not significant. The most striking findings were that gains made in small classes in kindergarten and first grade were maintained over the four years of the study, that low SES (socioeconomic status) student gains outpaced high SES student gains, and that small class sizes reduced grade retention. Since significant differences can be found statistically with small gains, the researchers were also interested in knowing how large the gains actually were. To do this they calculated the effect size. Effect sizes were found to range from .15 to .34 for all students across the four years of the study. This means that students in small classes gained from 15 percent to 34 percent of one standard deviation compared to the larger classes. What this study found that was not significant is also important. There were no differences found in teacher in-service training, teacher grouping practices, and parent volunteer interaction with classes. In other words, small class size made the difference in achievement, not these other variables. Due to its research design, the STAR study is perhaps the best known, large-scale longitudinal study in education, and befitting this stature, STAR has been influential in many education policy decisions.[29]

In the context of the current brouhaha over the role of research in school improvement, and the many competing claims being made for research "evidence" that advocates proffer in support of the use of particular commercially produced instructional methods and materials, the educational leader should remember to examine the research designs and procedures on which the claims are based, as well as the statistical treatments given to the data reported, instead of taking the reported evidence at face value. The No Child Left Behind Act ushered in a new era for educational leaders, one in which school leadership was expected to be driven by data concerning educational outcomes to an unprecedented degree, an era in which one increasingly needed statistical evidence to support claims and beliefs about instructional practices, much as the Framingham Heart Study guides us today in dealing with choices about diet and exercise.

Indeed, these two emphases immediately raised a storm of questioning, debate, and argument because it was not clear what either of those provisions meant: did they mean that phonics drill was now to be the order of the day, to the exclusion of other methods of early reading instruction? And what did "scientifically based" instructional methods mean? To some, it appeared that quantitative laboratory research methods were being emphasized as a base for professional knowledge to the exclusion of knowledge obtained through other research methods. To some, it seemed evident that the emphasis on phonics in the provisions concerning reading instruction was an effort by a political majority to dictate the outcome of the long-running controversy over what constituted appropriate pedagogical strategies and techniques in the teaching of reading. Thus, it seemed manifest that the federal government was, for the first time in history, dictating how reading should be taught in the kindergartens and primary grades of schools throughout the land. Similarly, to others, it seemed equally manifest that the Washington bureaucracy had decided to back quantitative laboratory research exclusively in the study of teaching methods as the only acceptable form of research despite the fact that research in the social and behavioral sciences had generally, over the years, stressed the importance of qualitative field studies as well.

Clearly, the writing of the No Child Left Behind (NCLB) Act, and the debate and disputation that led to its final passage by Congress, had involved a battle in which modernist and postmodernist beliefs, values, and understandings had clashed and the modernist view of the world had won the political battle. This was hardly some unfathomable academic discussion by supposedly wooly-headed intellectuals that had little to do with the hard realities of leadership and day-to-day life in schools. It was a struggle between people with different understandings of human nature, human behavior, values, and beliefs about the human condition, and the struggle is not over.

These issues will be revisited many times in the twenty-first century as the application of the law unfolds and the effects are experienced, with all their ramifications. The contention over the No Child Left Behind Act was a struggle for the heart and soul of schooling in the United States, a struggle to wrest control of the direction in which schools had been going from those who had been in control and to force a change of course in a strikingly new, and hopefully more successful, direction.

States, education associations, and parent groups successfully flexed their own political muscles, and in 2005, the Bush administration eased up on some accountability measures. For example, some, though not all, special education children were permitted to take alternative state achievement tests if IEP teams decided that a student was making progress but his or her disability was preventing him or her from reaching grade level in the same time frame as other students. By the spring of 2005, twenty-one states sought some changes to NCLB resulting in lawsuits, state legislation, resolutions, and other actions such as requests for waivers from NCLB requirements. Connecticut became the first state to sue the federal government for not providing sufficient funding to support the mandates of NCLB, and the National Education Association (NEA) sued (in *Pontiac School District v. Spellings*) on behalf of nine school districts in Vermont, Texas, and Michigan asking for exemptions from all NCLB requirements that were not funded by the federal government. The NEA claimed that from the inception of NCLB in 2002 to early 2005, states had to pay a $28 billion shortfall between required costs of NCLB and federal funding.[30] They cited the law's own words in its reasoning: "Nothing in this Act shall be construed to authorize an officer or employee of the Federal Government to mandate, direct, or control a State, local education agency, or school's curriculum, program of instruction, or allocation of State or local resources, or mandate a State or any subdivision thereof to spend any funds or incur any costs not paid for under this Act."[31] In November 2005, the United States District Court for the Eastern District of Michigan granted the federal government's motion to dismiss *Pontiac v. Spellings*. The judge ruled that the federal government has the authority to require states to spend their own money to comply with the law. The NEA reportedly planned to appeal. Like the NEA, other education associations such as the American Association of School Administrators (AASA), the National Association of Secondary School Principals (NASSP), the National Association of Elementary School Principals (NAESP), the Council for Exceptional Children (CEC), and the National PTA became strong advocates for school districts in their lobbying efforts for changes to NCLB. It was an attempt to establish a new scientific paradigm in education by political action rather than by scientific revolution. It has everything to do with the day-to-day realities of being a leader in the schools. Anyone who would be an effective leader in the schools of America's future must have a clear understanding of the assumptions and beliefs that underlie the arguments of those on both sides of this confrontation.

Leadership as Coaching

Since the 1980s, much has been said in the literature on school reform and school leadership about the importance of educational leaders having a "vision" of what schools should ideally be like and how they can be changed from their present imperfect state to more nearly achieve the ideal that the leader and, presumably, the people in the school community, envision. This is, of course, offered as an antidote to the popular received wisdom that school administrators have traditionally been mindless bureaucrats who blindly follow the dictates of the frequently demonized "educational bureaucracy" that some critics claim is the organizational bane of public schooling.

The ISLLC Standards for School Leaders

One of the most influential calls for educational leaders to have such a vision is found in the set of six Standards for School Leaders proposed by the Interstate School Leaders Licensure Consortium (ISLLC) of the Council of Chief State School Officers as a basis for licensing school administrators in the United States.[32] These standards

Standard 1	*Standard 4*
A school administrator is an educational leader who promotes success of all students by facilitating the development, articulation, implementation, and stewardship of a vision of learning that is shared and supported by the school community.	A school administrator is an educational leader who promotes success of all students by collaborating with families and community members, responding to diverse community interests and needs, and mobilizing resources.
Standard 2	*Standard 5*
A school administrator is an educational leader who promotes the success of all students by advocating, nurturing, and sustaining a school culture and an instructional program conducive to student learning and staff professional growth.	A school administrator is an educational leader who promotes success of all students by acting with integrity, with fairness, and in an ethical manner.
Standard 3	*Standard 6*
A school administrator is an educational leader who promotes success of all students by ensuring management of the organization, operations, and resources for a safe, efficient, and effective learning environment.	A school administrator is an educational leader who promotes success of all students by understanding, responding to, and influencing the larger political, social, economic, legal, and cultural context.

FIGURE 1.1   Standards for School Leaders of the Interstate School Leaders Licensure Consortium (ISLLC). (From Interstate School Leaders Licensure Consortium, *Standards for School Leaders.* Washington, DC: Council of Chief State School Officers, 1996.)

were developed in a two-year collaborative effort by numerous individuals drawn from the ranks of state education agencies and representatives of professional associations. Published in 1996, they have had a nationwide impact on qualifications required for issuing licenses to educational administrators. So far more than forty states have adopted these standards. They comprise a scholarly yet practical approach to the problem of agreeing on what it is that school leaders should know and be able to do. Because they are compatible with the curriculum guidelines of the National Council for the Accreditation of Teacher Education (NCATE), they are also having an impact on the development of programs in institutions of higher education that prepare school leaders.*

The six ISLLC standards for school leaders are given in Figure 1.1. The first of these standards calls for the school administrators who would be leaders to have a "vision of learning" that shapes the educational programs they may advocate, as well as the ways in which they work with others in seeking to bring the vision to reality. This concept of a vision of learning is described by the Interstate Consortium, which developed the standards, as drawing upon a wide range of underlying concepts including systems theory, principles of strategic planning, consensus-building, high standards of learning,

*Please see the discussion about ISLLC standards and their connection to NCATE in the Preface of this book.

a belief in the educability of all, and numerous other forms of knowledge, beliefs, and attitudes. All of these are important subjects in this book and are discussed at length in the chapters ahead.

Few would argue with this premise. Clearly, educational leaders *should* have such a vision, and their professional behaviors *should* be shaped and guided by it. However, the real world in which educational leaders work is a very messy place that is normally steeped in uncertainty and confusion, ambiguities, conflict, and a chronic shortage of time and resources. How, as a practical matter, does the educational leader develop such a vision and implement it in the day-to-day work that administration and leadership require? The answer is that the educational leader must develop the skills and abilities of coaching.

Coaching as a Method of Teaching

Coaching is a time-honored and respected method of teaching, and it is one that school leaders must master. Mortimer Adler has pointed out that there are three principal methods of teaching well, and each one is distinctive.[33]

- *One teaching method is didactic instruction.* This method of teaching relies on clearly presenting information to students, often through lectures by teachers and such activities as having students read books, watch films, and do practice exercises. These instructional techniques are commonly supplemented by such techniques as discussions, demonstrations, the use of examples, and field trips—all intended to link new concepts to previously learned concepts so as to build and strengthen learning. Most readers of this book are skilled in didactic instruction, but as they assume the role of educational leaders, they will find that it is a way of working with teachers that is generally not productive. Many in-service programs intended to improve the instructional skills of teachers founder because they emphasize didactic teaching methods, which are not always well received by adult learners.

- *Another teaching method is Socratic.* This method is often useful when the students have already learned a great deal of information but the goal is to get them to connect relevant ideas, to think critically, to analyze, to hypothesize about and explore the pros and cons of ideas, to assess the quality of countervailing claims, and to internalize new learnings so that they will be applied in daily life. In using the Socratic method, the teacher often poses a conceptual conundrum and encourages the students to explore and discuss the issues that the conundrum raises. This teaching method has limited, but sometimes useful, applications for the school leader in working with teachers.

- *A third teaching method is coaching.* Coaching assumes that the learners have a solid basic understanding of what they are doing, which has been previously imparted by both didactic and Socratic teaching. The coach "stands back to observe performance and then offers guidance, identifies weaknesses, points up principles, offers guiding and often inspiring imagery, and decides what kind of practice to emphasize."[34] As former teachers, school leaders learn that coaching is a familiar basic teaching method that they find very useful in working with teachers.

To many readers, the coaching metaphor immediately conjures the imagery of sports. It is quite true that in football, basketball, gymnastics—indeed, in almost any sport—"the coach applauds strengths, identifies weaknesses, points up principles, offers guiding and often inspiring imagery, and decides what kind of practice to emphasize."[35] However, coaching is also a basic approach to leadership and teaching that is widely used in many situations where one is dealing with advanced students or professional colleagues. High schools that are successful in teaching advanced students, such as those who are preparing to enter challenging competitions in fields as diverse as science, music, dance, and mathematics, usually find coaching to be the method of choice. University professors normally use coaching techniques in working with advanced graduate students, and it is commonly the method of choice in working with students at the doctoral level. Coaching is often sought by many accomplished professionals with proven track records—among them presidents, opera stars, world-class athletes, and international luminaries of the theater—many of whom routinely seek the help of coaches even as they are recognized as masters of their professions. In contemporary business management, which emphasizes leadership no less than educational administration, coaching is also widely accepted as an effective way to motivate and enhance the competencies of others—that is, to lead.

Conclusion

This chapter has described and discussed some of the different paradigms, metanarratives, and perspectives, or worldviews, in thinking about and trying to understand issues of behavior in educational organizations. The fact that various people use different worldviews in trying to understand human behavior in organizations inevitably means that educational leaders will be confronted with conflict and controversy as a normal part of their work. It also makes clear that there is no one paradigm to unify and give direction to those who are concerned about schools, teaching, and learning.

Precisely because there is no overarching paradigm, it becomes especially important for educational leaders to think through the issues and develop a clear understanding of their own position on the different, often conflicting, points of view. For this reason, it is vital for the educational leader to develop a clear vision of the school, and of teaching and learning, and how that vision can be implemented in practice in the schools. In this book, the plan to implement and achieve the educational vision that the leader holds is called a game plan.

All of the issues discussed in Chapter 1 underlie the exploration of major topics of leadership and organizational behavior in education that are developed further in the chapters ahead.

Reflective Activities

A contribution from athletic coaching to American English is the concept of a "game plan," and it is very useful in dealing with the problem of turning an educational vision into effective leader behavior that brings about improvement in the learning of all the students in the school. By developing a game plan and supervising its implementation in the midst of the uncertainties, confusion, and stress of the game, the coach transforms the vision of the game into a coherent plan of action that is intended not only to achieve results but to motivate and enhance the abilities of the players as well. This is precisely what effective educational leaders do, too. While it is unarguable that a clear, articulate, well-grounded vision of learning in the school is absolutely necessary for effective instructional leadership, it is also clear that it is not sufficient. To be effective, to get results, the vision must be developed into a workable implementation plan. Moreover, let us repeat, the game plan must not only get results in terms of improved student learning but, at the same time, it must motivate and enhance the competencies of the teachers. It is the responsibility of the school leader, the coach, to develop and supervise the implementation of that plan.

This is a theme that you will encounter in each chapter as we encourage you to think more deeply about your educational vision and the game plan you need to make it happen. In the next chapter this theme is further discussed and its relationship to the concept of *theory of practice,* the well-accepted academic term for this concept, is explained. In succeeding chapters you will find opportunities and, we hope, challenges for you to examine your own beliefs and values about leading people and coaching them to improve the instructional outcomes of the students in the school.

It is generally accepted today that school leaders are administrators whose professional practice is dedicated to promoting the success of all students, regardless of their race, family background, gender, or any other social, financial, or personal characteristics. As a basis for developing such a practice, it is essential for leaders to create, articulate, and implement a vision of learning in the school that they seek to make a reality. This vision of learning gives direction and shape to the leader's day-to-day activities and priorities. By sharing the vision with others—teachers, students, and parents—the leader engages them to unite in the effort to make it happen. Quite simply, the vision of learning in the school—having been thought through and embraced as the organizing core for exercising leadership—becomes the way in which the central issues of learning, teaching, and school improvement are constantly held highly visible in the foreground as the administrator confronts the never-ending necessity to make choices in a world where resources, such as time and money, are never enough and expectations are always beyond our full grasp.

In this book, that vision for learning is called a game plan because it is not just wishful thinking or an idle dream: the vision becomes a plan that will guide you in choosing effective strategies and ways of implementing them in the real world of schools. The metaphor of the game plan is taken from sports, of course. The vision becomes a plan that organizes the work of the leader and establishes priorities for action. In other words, where do you want to go and how do you intend to get there? When communicated to others in such a way that they embrace it as their own, the vision organizes their work and establishes the priorities of everyone on the school's team. No serious coach would take an athlete into an arena or send a team into a game without a strategy and a plan for implementing it, and no serious school leader should try to lead a faculty and staff in making the school more effective without a game plan either.

You will find more about the concept of a game plan in Chapter 2.

However, to get started, focus now on the notion of a vision for the school that you would like to lead. The vision is the end state, the intentions of where you want to go with the school. Perhaps nothing is as important than that educational leaders lift their eyes from the mundane world of the present and envision the future possibilities—not a dream—of what a school really should and could be. The vision that you have of the school you would like to lead will express not merely the direction in which the school should be moving but what, in the end, such a school would be like. Free yourself now from the fetters of past practice, custom, or the way in which things are done in your school district. Think afresh: How do you envision what a school should be like? What *really* should be going on in such a school? How would you describe an effective school to others? What values and beliefs about learning in schools do you think are very important to address? What vision do you have for a really effective school?

Select one or two of the concepts that were introduced in Chapter 1 and describe, in a paragraph or two, how they would be involved in implementing your vision for learning. Dream a little. Write freely. This is not the end; this is the beginning.

Suggested Reading

Aronowitz, Stanley, and Henry A. Giroux, *Postmodern Education: Politics, Culture, and Social Criticism.* Minneapolis: University of Minnesota Press, 1991.

> A polemical discussion of the politics of class, race, and gender in the present postmodernist period of U.S. education. The writing is dense and often obscure but presents knowledgeable, passionate, and important information for those who have not kept abreast of this emerging field.

Cherryholmes, Cleo H., *Power and Criticism: Poststructural Investigations in Education.* New York: Teachers College Press, 1988.

> An excellent tour of poststructuralist thought in education that provides an always challenging, often exciting, discussion of newer ways of thinking about schools and how they are being studied.

Educational Researcher, Volume 31, Number 8, November 2002.

> The theme of this issue of *Educational Researcher* is "scientific research in education." It contains six articles by nine distinguished authors, which discuss aspects of the report *Scientific Inquiry in Education,* which is strongly recommended on the next page. This was triggered by the emphasis in the No Child Left Behind Act on the importance of using scientific research methods in designing programs for improving instruction. The articles contained in this issue of *Educational Researcher,* together with the original report, *Scientific Inquiry in Education,* will provide the educational leader with an invaluable guide to the issues and problems that comprise the current controversy about educational research. These readings are strongly recommended to anyone who hopes to be an educational leader.

Foster, William, *Paradigms and Promises: New Approaches to Educational Administration.* Buffalo, NY: Prometheus Books, 1986.

> A book on theory in administration that explains critical theory and strongly advocates it as a basis for the study of educational administration. "Administrators of educational settings are critical humanists. They are humanists because they appreciate the usual and unusual events of our lives and engage in an effort to develop, challenge, and liberate human souls. They are critical because they are educators and are therefore not satisfied with the status quo; rather, they hope to change individuals for the better and to improve social conditions. A scientific model of administration, to the degree that this depends on a positivist model of science, comes under attack here because we feel that it inadequately considers the many social, cultural, and educational issues in our society" (pp. 17–18).

Interstate School Leaders Licensure Consortium, Standards for School Leaders. Washington, DC: Council of Chief State School Officers, 1996.

> The Interstate School Leaders Licensure Consortium sought to develop common standards that would under-

lie the licensing of school leaders, and inasmuch as many states have adopted them as their own standards, it has been highly successful. The Standards are, of course, a wish list, but they represent the collaborative effort of many knowledgeable people and have accordingly had great impact. Individuals who are now preparing to become school leaders should study this document closely.

Kuhn, Thomas S., *The Structure of Scientific Revolutions.* Chicago: The University of Chicago Press, 1962.

This important small book is "must" reading for educational leaders today. It not only helps us to understand how scientific progress is shaped and developed, but also explains some of the difficulties that immature sciences—such as education—have in increasing their scientific credibility. Given the recent attempts to legislate a paradigm for teaching in the United States, instead of encouraging a scientific paradigm, the issues discussed by Kuhn take on new importance for educational leaders.

Shavelson, Richard J., and Lisa Towne (eds.), National Research Council Committee on Scientific Principles for Education Research. *Scientific Inquiry in Education.* Washington, DC: National Research Council, National Academy Press, 2002.

One of the most powerful and controversial provisions of the No Child Left Behind Act requires those who receive federal funds under the act to use evidence-based strategies in their school reform efforts. This requirement put education research at center stage as questions arose about what the term "evidence-based strategies" meant. In an effort to clarify this issue, the National Research Council convened a committee that produced this report. Essentially, the report defines and discusses what scientific inquiry in education is and what standards are appropriate to use in judging its quality. The main thrust of the report is to encourage the development of a scientific culture in the education profession. This is a landmark document that will undoubtedly have a profound long-term impact on the much-delayed development of research in education. Some practitioners may think that such dull stuff is best left to those in the ivory tower, but that would be very wrong: of all the provisions in the No Child Left Behind Act, this is the one that gives greatest promise, over time, of finally moving education into the ranks of a full-fledged profession.

chapter 2

Toward a Theory
of Practice

LEARNING OBJECTIVES

After reading this chapter, you should be able to

- Define theory.

- Identify three ways in which theory is useful in the study and practice
of organizational behavior.

- Define and describe the two principal sets of opposing views—one on
education, the other on organization—that invariably cause conflict
for educational leaders.

- Specify and describe the major issues that persist today in the ongoing
Great Educational Debate.

- Describe and discuss *A Nation at Risk* and its historic impact on
schooling in the United States today.

- Compare and contrast the educational views of E. D. Hirsch, Jr., on
the one hand, and those of Howard Gardner on the other hand.

- Define theory of action and describe how it is relevant to educational
leadership.

- Define and describe theory of practice.

- Describe the major educational issues and strategies for change that
were addressed at the three national summit meetings on education.

- Describe the educational-political strategy for school reform that
emerged from the national summit meetings on education.

- Define and describe Multiple Intelligences Theory (MIT).

- Define and describe the key differences between traditional IQ theory
and MIT.

- Describe the major differences between traditional IQ theory and the
theory of learnable intelligence.

ISLLC Standards

STANDARD 1: A school administrator is an educational leader who promotes the success of all students by facilitating the development, articulation, implementation, and stewardship of a vision of learning that is shared and supported by the school community.

Knowledge

The administrator has knowledge and understanding of:

- learning goals in a pluralistic society

Dispositions

The administrator believes in, values, and is committed to:

- the educability of all
- a school vision of high standards of learning
- ensuring that students have the knowledge, skills, and values needed to become successful adults
- a willingness to continuously examine one's own assumptions, beliefs, and practices

STANDARD 2: A school administrator is an educational leader who promotes the success of all students by advocating, nurturing, and sustaining a school culture and instructional program conducive to student learning and staff professional growth.

Dispositions

The administrator believes in, values, and is committed to:

- student learning as the fundamental purpose of schooling
- the proposition that all students can learn
- preparing students to be contributing members of society

Performances

The administrator facilitates processes and engages in activities ensuring that:

- multiple opportunities to learn are available to all students
- student learning is assessed using a variety of techniques
- multiple sources of information regarding performance are used by staff and students

STANDARD 5: A school administrator is an educational leader who promotes the success of all students by acting with integrity, fairness, and in an ethical manner.

Knowledge

The administrator has knowledge and understanding of:

- the purpose of education and the role of leadership in modern society
- the philosophy and history of education

Dispositions

The administrator believes in, values, and is committed to:

- the ideal of the common good
- the principles in the Bill of Rights
- the right of every student to a free, quality education

Performances

The administrator:

- examines personal and professional values
- examines and considers the prevailing values of the diverse school community

STANDARD 6: A school administrator is an educational leader who promotes the success of all students by understanding, responding to, and influencing the larger political, social, economic, legal, and cultural context.

Knowledge

The administrator has knowledge and understanding of:

- principles of representative governance that undergird the system of American schools
- the role of public education in developing and renewing a democratic society and an economically productive nation
- the political, social, cultural, and economic systems and processes that impact schools
- global issues and forces affecting teaching and learning

Dispositions

The administrator believes in, values, and is committed to:

- education as a key to opportunity and social mobility
- recognizing a variety of ideas, values, and cultures
- actively participating in the political and policy-making context in the service of education

Performances

The administrator facilitates processes and engages in activities ensuring that:

- public policy is shaped to provide quality education for students

This is a book for students of education who aspire to become educational leaders. As you contemplate moving into the ranks of educational leadership, you may be certain of at least one thing from the outset: the world in which you will work as an educational leader is, and will continue to be, embedded in controversy, conflict, and contention. Perhaps some people in our culture may go through life as detached observers; leaders may not. Leaders engage in the business of not merely observing the human condition, but also—however modestly—making a difference in the outcomes of the issues of their day. Moreover, educational leaders do not merely survive in their competitive, conflicted, fast-paced world of work. To paraphrase William Faulkner, they prevail: they succeed in the work and find it challenging, zestful, and rewarding.

Therefore, if you choose the path of leadership for your professional future, even if you do not now aspire to a high position in the scheme of things, to be successful you must prepare yourself to prevail in that new role. There is a great deal of scholarly evidence to support the commonplace observation that effective leaders are characteristically confident and self-assured even in the face of uncertainty. This need to deal confidently with ambiguity is a core factor in making the transition from teaching or counseling to school administration. Such a move is more than a step to extend or enrich one's career. It is a career change: a move from one career to another. Normally, one literally leaves teaching to take up administration. At the moment of appointment to a position as administrator one no longer holds the title of teacher but has a different title: assistant principal, principal, or whatever the case may be. Also at that moment—at least at the level of school principal and often at lower ranks in the organization—you not only leave the classroom but also leave the teachers' union bargaining unit and are classified as management. There is no gainsaying that training and experience in teaching are important to success in educational administration; they clearly are. It is also indisputable that a career in leadership requires knowledge, skills, and attitudes that are not necessarily required for effective teaching.

Preparation for leadership in education includes becoming increasingly familiar with and comfortable working in an environment characterized by uncertainty, paradox, and—not infrequently—confusion. Upon appointment to administrative position, leaders acquire power and cachet—no matter how minor or trivial their new role may seem—and are, therefore, inevitably pulled and hauled from many different directions by those who want to enlist that power and cachet in support of their causes. Preparation for prevailing in this environment is, in part, cognitive: learning basic principles of organization and the behavior of people who work in them, which this book is about. But acquiring the essential organizational knowledge is, in itself, inadequate. Preparation for leadership also requires an individual to internalize this knowledge. Only by internalizing organizational knowledge can one use it as a guide to developing the kinds of leader behavior that will be authentic, consistent, and effective even under conditions that may seem to be contentious or bordering on the chaotic. That part of the preparation process is in your hands. Only you can develop a theory of practice that will guide *your* practice of educational leadership.

Later in this book we will discuss more fully the idea that conflict is a normal part of organizational life. Differences of opinion, dispute, debate, and discussion are not to be avoided, nor should we seek to eliminate them entirely. Properly managed, conflict in an organization—as well as in one's individual life—can and should be welcomed as a source of dynamism that strengthens and energizes both the individual and the organization and offers opportunities for leaders to lead. It is very difficult to be an effective leader in an organization in which the participants are satisfied with things as they are, "rocking the boat" by raising questions or proposing new ideas is frowned upon, and no one feels a need to change the way things are done. As we shall discuss more fully later in a chapter devoted to organizational culture, organizations in which participants seem to be smug and complacent may be unwittingly revealing symptoms of deep organizational malaise. In fact, one of the important things that leaders do is to raise the awareness of people that change is needed and convince them that it can be accomplished.

Dealing with divergent opinions and disputation is a given to anyone who would exercise leadership in any organization because, as we shall explain more fully in a later chapter, leadership is—by definition—exercised in an environment that demands that choices be made from among competing points of view. After all, if everyone in the organization agreed from the beginning on what should be done, there would be little need for leadership.

Two Principal Sources of Conflict

Leaders in education are likely to encounter conflict that arises from various sources, many of which may be idiosyncratic to their local community, or their particular school system, or the region in which they are located. However, there are two overarching sources of conflict that all educational leaders are certain to encounter, regardless of where or at what level they work.

- One source lies in the different ways in which different people can and do understand what educational organizations are and how they are best led and managed.
- The second source lies in the pervasive disagreement among people in our society about the nature of education itself and what the goals of schooling should be.

The educational leader encounters conflict, or the appearance of it, as an ordinary part of practice. In a dynamic and open society such as ours in which education is clearly in the public realm, the level and intensity of conflict are closely related to the extent to which there is broad agreement in society as to the purposes and methods of schooling. We like to think, fantasize perhaps, that in some time in the past there was little controversy over schools and schooling: that there was broad agreement about what schools should be accomplishing and how. Whatever the truth may be, that time (if it ever existed) is in the past and is not relevant to the situation we face today. All school districts and all states today abound with groups and coalitions of single-issue critics: ethnic groups, gays, conservatives, women, tax cutters, liberals, the poor—one could go on and on.

The "Great Debate": Traditional versus Progressive Education

One single, overarching, long-standing struggle has dominated educational thought in the United States for well over a century, beginning in the 1870s, with each side declaring victory from time to time. While, overall, progressive ideas have steadily gained increased popularity and have occasionally been in ascendancy, at the beginning of the second millennium it is clear that traditional conservative concepts of schooling have seized the momentum of the school reform movement. Thus, many teachers and parents, believing in the tenets of progressive education, are dismayed to find their views at odds with the prevailing educational philosophy of the day.

Traditional concepts of schooling emphasize the primacy of subject matter, the importance of passing an inherited body of knowledge on to the young, drill, memorization of facts, the authority of the teacher, and formal instructional methods. Although those holding such traditional views have consistently presented tough-minded challenges to progressive educational thought, the signature ideas and practices of progressivism had already irrevocably transformed the practice of teaching in the United States by the 1940s and had become generally recognized as the standard of good educational practice.[1] Such "progressive" ideas and classroom instructional practices as the primacy of practical experience in learning (learning by doing), individual instruction, informality in the classroom, group discussion, team learning, and laboratory instruction had become defining characteristics of good teaching and good schools and were important standards by which regional accrediting agencies and state evaluators judged the quality of schools. The belief that art, music, poetry, dance, athletics, and other cultural pursuits are important contributors to the history of the human race tends to be a central value in such schools. It remains so today, even as the clash between traditional and progressive approaches to schooling in the United States continues unabated. These ideas, beliefs, and practices are, and will remain, important standards for judging the quality of teaching and schooling even as the disputation continues on in the twenty-first century.

The Beginnings of the Great Educational Debate

The conflict and disputation over public schooling that you have personally witnessed and experienced during your career is nothing new; it has been going on since the 1870s. Much of the present-day conflict over schooling in the United States is a continuation and extension of the clash of two very different and very opposing points of view about schooling that erupted in the late 1800s and that have been battling for dominance in the United States literally for generations. "At its simplest level, one could say it is a debate between education broadly and narrowly conceived, between the primacy of the child and the primacy of subject matter, between spontaneous and formal approaches to schooling, and between education designed to transform the nation's cultural heritage and one designed to preserve it."[2] The clash has often been referred to as the "progressive" versus the "traditional." It has waxed and waned "with bitter intensity throughout the 20th century. And it is no less heated or closer to resolution today than it was in the beginning."[3]

During the era in which progressive education developed and flourished, spanning the years from 1873 through the depths of the Great Depression in the 1930s, immigration seemed to be flooding the United States and large-scale industrialization was rapidly transforming it from an agricultural society into an urban-industrial society. It was a time that was, in some remarkable ways, much like our own time. It was the era that saw the emergence of new super-rich corporate giants such as financier John Pierpont Morgan, steel magnate Andrew Carnegie, oilman John D. Rockefeller, automaker Henry Ford, and railroad tycoon Jay Gould. It was a time, also, of new technology that was, then as now, the province of young entrepreneurs. For example, Thomas Edison was twenty-eight when he sold a license to use the wax-process stencil that he had invented to nineteen-year-old Albert Blake Dick, who created the mimeograph machine with it and became rich and famous. John D. Rockefeller founded his first oil venture in Titusville, Pennsylvania, when he was twenty. Charles A. Lindbergh flew the Atlantic when he was twenty-five. Chauncy "Chance" Vought founded Chance Vought Aircraft to manufacture the airplanes that he was designing when he was twenty-seven and then went on to be instrumental in creating United Aircraft.

It was a time of transformation in the nation, fueled not only by the financiers, entrepreneurs, and technical wonks who were building the great new industries, transportation systems, and communications systems that would alter life in the United States forever but also by the great masses of immigrants from abroad and migrants from the farms to cities. It was they who would provide the muscle and energy in the factories and on the construction sites and for most of them it would be a new life, very often one of squalor. Unlike their forebears they would now be city dwellers, tenants in rented housing, employees dependent on their weekly pay envelopes, living away from the traditional support systems of their families and communities.

In this era of massive industrialization and urbanization, many became very concerned about the welfare of the large number of workers and their families who were, in a single generation, being relocated and socialized into a new way of life, a new culture that was just in the process of being invented. Corporate abuse of workers abounded, government agencies were often corrupt, social support for those in need was skimpy, and health care was often nonexistent. It was the time of the muckrakers who documented the plight of the urban poor and who exposed corruption in education and city government and the often deplorable working conditions that powerless workers had to endure. Lincoln Steffens, editor of *McClure's* magazine, may have invented investigative reporting by exposing corruption in city government. Ida Tarbell published a book that revealed a good deal that was seamy in the history of the Standard Oil Company. Jacob Riis, using flash photography for the first time to create incredibly powerful pictures of the human condition in inner cities, revealed to middle- and upper-class Americans how the other half lived. Nobel laureate Jane Addams, founder of Hull House, was a feisty and powerful activist for better working conditions, improved city services, and expanded social and health services. Pulitzer Prize winner Upton Sinclair wrote a series of books documenting widespread abysmal working conditions—*The Jungle,* perhaps his most notable work, focused on the Chicago stockyards—and then went on to write exposés of other kinds of organizations.

A political movement soon emerged that "sought to curb the excesses of modern capitalism by regulating industry and commerce, emphasizing concern for human over corporate welfare, and placing the scientific expertise of the university at the service of the government. . . . It was in this heady, fractious period that reformers turned to the schools."[4] In 1873 Francis Wayland Parker—the superintendent of the Quincy, Massachusetts, public schools—became prominent by establishing perhaps the first schools using what were to become known as progressive methods: they used group instructional activities and informal instruction methods, stressed science and the real world in which the children lived, and eschewed harsh disciplinary methods. Parker was a true educational pioneer who took up academic life only after he had demonstrated the practicality of his ideas convincingly in the real world of public schools in less than idyllic communities.

> At a time when public schools were dominated by recitation, memorization, and drill, Parker advocated placing the child at the center of education and building schools around their students' motivation and interests. Under the Quincy System, as it came to be called, textbooks gave way to magazines, newspapers, and materials developed by teachers. Students learned geography by exploring the local countryside. And they studied an integrated curriculum that stressed learning by doing and expression through the arts.[5]

These ideas appealed to many people and they took root and flourished: progressive education was on the upswing and it spread rapidly. The most pressing problems were in the cities, and many cities across the nation were in the vanguard of the Progressive movement: the public schools of Gary (Indiana), Denver, Houston, and St. Louis were prominent among them. While each community developed its own unique approach to implementing the new ideas, they tended to be "associated with more active learning, cooperative planning by teachers and students, a greater recognition of individual differences, attempts to relate learning to 'real life,' and efforts to broaden the school's mission to address health, vocational, social, and community issues."[6]

In the early years of the twentieth century, this new approach to public schooling involved such legendary figures as John Dewey, a world-class philosopher and educator; psychologist Edward L. Thorndike, internationally acclaimed for his original work on the nature of intelligence; G. Stanley Hall, an eminent psychologist and president of Clark University, who did pioneering work in the study of adolescence; and educator William Heard Kilpatrick of Teachers College, Columbia University, who was Dewey's most noted acolyte.

The Backlash of the 1950s

Powerful though the progressive education movement had been in rescuing American schooling from the formalistic rote-recitation constrictions of traditional teaching and moving it toward a more enlightened recognition of the central role of students as growing, developing individuals, some of its adherents went too far. Some advocated rejecting traditional concepts of subject matter altogether and advocated schools that prepared students for—among other things—worthy home membership, the use of leisure time, and entry-level vocational preparation.[7] In 1944 the National Education Association spearheaded a concept of "Education for All American Youth" that envisioned high schools that would track some students into college-preparation courses and would send 60 percent of the students into lower-level courses that would presumably prepare them for entry-level employment. In 1945 the "life adjustment movement" appeared. Backed by the United States Office of Education, it advocated simplified courses for the 60 percent of high school students who were not expected to go to college, courses that emphasized such things as the ability to read a newspaper, fill out a job-application form, or balance a checkbook. "The result was a proliferation of nonacademic and often pedestrian high school courses,"[8] and this led directly to a powerful backlash from a broad spectrum of people who had become increasingly uneasy about the "modern" changes in American schooling.

One of the first critics to be heard from was Arthur E. Bestor, who had earned a reputation as a historian of the nineteenth-century New Harmony communal colony on the banks of the Wabash River in southern Indiana. His smash hit book in 1953 was *Educational Wastelands: The Retreat from Learning in Our Public Schools.* It was a devastating, shocking, and hugely profitable critique in the era of the Brave New World, when many hoped and dreamed that, in contrast to their own lifetimes—which had been dominated by the Great Depression followed by the enormity of World War II—the old contests for international dominance would not be inherited by their children. In the Cold War years there was not much to cheer them, however.

Vice Admiral Hyman G. Rickover, the iconoclastic and strangely magnetic individual in charge of developing the U.S. atomic-powered attack submarine to confront the much-feared and mysterious Russian opponent in the dark and dangerous depths of the oceans of the world, foresaw the collapse of the American way of life being deliberately and carelessly engineered in the schools of the nation in competition with the schools of the Soviet Union.[9] A 1959 book buttressed with a foreword by the venerated Edward R. Murrow and a preface by Charles Van Doren, then still admired in his role as a youthful and popular intellectual on a television game show, was a runaway best-seller and raised primordial fears that, in the life-and-death contest with the fearsome Soviet Union, the future of the nation was being decided—most unfavorably—in the high school classrooms. Meanwhile, former school board member Albert Lynd had published a sensational exposé titled *Quackery in the Public Schools.*[10] In a similar vein, another former school board member, Mortimer Smith, had found publishing gold in *The Diminished Mind: A Study of Planned Mediocrity in Our Public Schools.*[11] Amidst these sensational and highly popular exposés, the esteemed chancellor of the University of Chicago weighed in with the more sober but nonetheless devastating *Education for Freedom,* which, predictably, decried the public schools' straying from the heritage of the Great Books, which Robert Maynard Hutchins thought contained the essence of human civilization. Altogether these critics lambasted the schools for denigrating academic learning, lacking serious goals, and undermining the traditions of liberal education.

All of this became mere background, however. It was merely the warmup for the main event, which came when the Soviet Union launched a 184-pound satellite on October 4, 1957, to orbit the earth every ninety minutes and followed it up the next month with *Sputnik II,* which had a live dog aboard as passenger. In the paroxysm of deep foreboding and fear that swept across the United States, schooling was quickly identified as a major culprit for the national embarrassment and became a primary target for immediate and massive change. Suddenly school had to be made more demanding; the future of the nation required a tougher curriculum and greater effort from children in school. The schools of the Soviet Union were extolled as models because they emphasized demanding academic training, made heavy use of authoritarian traditional teaching methods, made heavy use of examinations, and eschewed such frills as sports, driver training, and other extracurricular activities. The National Defense Education Act was swept through the

Congress, providing substantial funding for strengthening instruction in mathematics, sciences, and foreign languages. Notions of progressive education were widely shouldered aside as U.S. schools and teachers were pressed to retool to prepare their students for the grim and dangerous future of global competition that many thought surely lay ahead.

The Neoprogressives Emerge in the 1960s

The cyclical nature of the pulling and hauling that is the signature of the ongoing struggle between traditional, conservative views of schooling and more liberal, progressive views was powerfully manifest in the 1960s. Against a backdrop of the protracted tragedy of the Vietnam War, spectacular and disheartening assassinations of political and racial leaders, noisy rebelliousness among youth, and urban uprisings against institutional injustice, progressive views surged to the fore of education. During this time a new group of critics cried out against the social inequities and the dull, mindless course work they saw as the lot of those hapless children trapped in the public schools of inner cities. This group of largely youthful critics once again sounded progressive themes and practices as urgently necessary to deal with the realities, often harsh, that they saw firsthand in urban schools. John Holt, in simple yet withering prose, described vividly how the schools that children were required to attend doomed them to failure in coping with the realities of the world they lived in. Jonathan Kozol, in *Death at an Early Age,* wrote a searing indictment from the front lines, from the classrooms of the Boston public schools, that vividly described "the destruction of the hearts and minds of the Negro children in the Public School System."[12] In *36 Children* Herbert Kohl described his experiences in his first year of teaching.[13] He told, for example, of his efforts to find ways (often subversive ways, in the eyes of the system) to breathe life and freshness into classroom routines and encourage children to explore, invent, create, and find excitement in their learning.

The Contemporary Debate on Schooling

The former president of Yale University and commissioner of baseball, A. Bartlett Giamatti, has described truth as being perhaps a dynamic compound of opposites, savage contraries for a moment conjoined. If this is so, then the polemic disputation one finds so readily in current literature on the state of U.S. education may represent the process of interfusing a new amalgam that may eventually be generally accepted as the basis for understanding the state of affairs in schooling. As the twentieth century drew to a close, however, the student of educational leadership found a literature characterized more by *Sturm und Drang* than by coolly reasoned analyses in search of truth.

In retrospect the confrontive, heated style of discussion of issues and problems in education is thought by many to have been touched off by an opening salvo in 1983, when the White House released an incendiary document highly critical of American education.[14] The document was called *A Nation at Risk,*[15] and its release by the Reagan White House amidst a well-orchestrated nationwide publicity blitz was an astonishing event in U.S. history, let alone U.S. schooling. The report had been prepared by a prestigious committee under the direction of the secretary of education. The president, Ronald Reagan, took the extraordinary step of endorsing it in a speech, which was in itself a historic intervention in education by any president—especially one who had campaigned on the promise to eliminate the United States Office of Education, which had sponsored the report. Subsequently, as president, George Bush also endorsed the report.

The title of the work was an alarming tocsin at a time when the Cold War was still tense and fraught with danger, the Berlin Wall was intact, and we still had nuclear-capable bombers aloft flying in relays twenty-four hours a day ready to retaliate in the event of nuclear attack. It immediately catapulted issues in U.S. education into the realm of the highest possible concern: literally, the security of the nation itself. It was, to put it mildly, a new, if not novel, thesis: that what went on in U.S. classrooms posed a threat to the security of the nation.

A Nation at Risk made many allegations of numerous "failures" of U.S. schools and went on to charge that the educational achievement of U.S. students was dismal in comparison with that of students in other lands. Further, it described U.S. schools as being not very well organized and run and depicted educators in them as being a dispirited and not very able lot. Upon its release, scholars eagerly examined the report and quickly noticed that the "evidence" on which the claims of failures and shortcomings were based was not in the document, nor were the claims cited well so that one could examine the basis for the charges. The document was, therefore, difficult to discuss meaningfully, let alone challenge, while it became the basis for any number of startling sound bites and breathless discussions in both print and electronic media.

Clearly, the school reform movement that was thus kicked off has been the greatest and most sustained concerted national effort to change the central core of assumptions and structures of the public schools in the history of the Republic. Since its inception "the country has been searching for some magical way to reform and restructure public schools. We have tried—and are still trying—all sorts of alchemical nostrums [that we hope] will turn educationally leaden schools into schools of educational gold."[16] Over the years the discourses on school reform have been well leavened with bold calls for sweeping changes such as restructuring education, reinventing schools, and recreating the nation's educational goals. During the same years, instead of finding a new amalgam of truth, some cojoining of contraries that Giamatti hoped for, the discourses have grown increasingly polarized, tendentious, and partisan. As Clark Kerr, President Emeritus of the University of California, observed, "Seldom in the course of policymaking in the U.S. have so many firm convictions held by so many been based on so little convincing proof."[17] We will cite only three examples from this large and fast-growing body of literature. The very titles of the first two of these books make manifest how far we have drifted from reasoned discourse in the public discussion of these issues.

Thomas Sowell, a Senior Fellow at the Hoover Institution, chose to title his book *Inside American Education: The Decline, the Deception, the Dogmas.*[18] Its title, redolent of William L. Shirer's history-making exposé of the Nazi regime, is a tendentious polemic that, in 368 pages of relentless attack, finds virtually nothing of value in U.S. schools. Moreover, to deliver his message, Sowell chose to heavily lard it with hot button words—referring to U.S. public schools as "a vast tax-supported empire," speaking of "deceptions and dogmas" in the schools that are "technically sophisticated brainwashing," and decrying much of what the schools do as "anti-American . . . totalitarian . . . sinister curriculum developments" while "cowardly and irresponsible management [is] more concerned about institutional image and ranking than with fiscal integrity or commitment to educate our youth."[19]

In summing up, Sowell asserts that the schools must be reorganized and that this first requires that "We need to face the harsh reality of the kind of people we are dealing with, the kind of bitter fight we can expect from them if we try to disturb their turf and perks—and the bleak future of our children if we don't."[20] What kind of people are these educators in the schools, and what have they done? Sowell's answer begins thus:

> They have taken our money, betrayed our trust, failed our children, and then lied about the failures with inflated grades and pretty words. They have used our children as guinea pigs for experiments, targets for propaganda, and warm bodies to be moved here and there to mix and match for racial balance, pad enrollments. . . . They have proclaimed their special concern for minority students, while placing those students into those colleges where they are the most likely to fail.[21]

David C. Berliner and Bruce J. Biddle present a remarkably different view in their 1995 book, *The Manufactured Crisis: Myths, Fraud, and the Attack on America's Public Schools.*[22] Using somewhat more restrained language than Sowell, their blunt analysis starts with the proposition that the current crisis in education is based on a series of specific myths that—though they have become widely believed—are simply and demonstrably not true. Moreover, this did not happen by accident, nor was it the product of dynamic social forces: this, the authors contend, was planned and orchestrated "by identifiable persons to sell America the false idea that their public schools were failing and that because of this failure the nation was in peril."[23] Thus, *A Nation at Risk* and its aftermath is seen by them as a campaign of disinformation by the Reagan administration to put the con into play and that this was later supported by the Bush presidency. Many of the myths, half-truths, and outright lies that make up the Manufactured Crisis—the massive and orchestrated con game—are described in this book, each of them being countered with carefully marshaled evidence and reason that destroys the myth. A few of the myths are as follows:

1. Student achievement in U.S. primary schools has recently declined.
2. The performance of U.S. college students has also fallen recently.
3. The United States spends a lot more money on its schools than other nations do.
4. Investing in the schools has not brought success. Indeed, money is unrelated to school performance.

Berliner and Riddle, both highly reputable scholars with acknowledged strong research credentials, leave little doubt that efforts to perpetuate these myths in attacking the public schools clearly arise from deliberate distortion for the purpose of furthering certain sociopolitical intentions. They do their best to help the reader to understand why they think so by encouraging examination of the data on which the mythical claims are based. To their great credit, the last 135 pages of *The Manufactured Crisis* are devoted to a quiet and level-headed discussion of "real problems in American education," which many readers will find useful.

Berliner and Riddle are not alone in their skepticism. There is growing dismay in the ranks of education scholars at the widespread propagation of distortions and misinformation about the condition of public education that have become daily grist for the U.S. press and U.S. politicians as well. For example, Gerald Bracey has published a series of reports in the journal *Phi Delta Kappan* that has diligently examined and documented the sources of some of the most egregious and damaging myths and untruths that are routinely passed off as facts about schools and the achievement of students in them.[24]

In a 1998 book entitled *The Way We Were?*,[25] Richard Rothstein pointed out that the popular indictment of the public schools—including the alarming *A Nation at Risk* report in 1983—rests not on clear and documented evidence but on generalizations that "everyone seems to know," beginning with the conviction that "our schools are in desperate need of reform." Thus, everyone seems to know that "The quality of public education seems to have declined, and schools are not up to the task of readying young people for the challenges"[26] that lie ahead. Everyone seems to know, Rothstein continues, that a watered-down curriculum ensures that all students, regardless of whether or not they have mastered necessary skills, can graduate. "Social promotion" without a requirement to master grade-appropriate skills is said to now be commonplace, so even elite colleges must run remedial courses for freshmen in basic math and literacy. Instead of teaching basic skills, everyone seems to know that schools concentrate on "self-esteem" and "values clarification" while discarding traditional values along with traditional skills, so that students no longer absorb the moral values that schools once inculcated. And, so, the litany of things that "everyone seems to know" about the apparent decline of the public schools goes on and on.

Moreover, Rothstein continues, "Most Americans agree with these indictments. . . . Most adults remember that when they were students, public schools were safer, more academically serious, and focused both on basic learning and on more advanced thinking skills. They believe schools now do worse, even though a modern economy demands that they do better."[27] *"But," Rothstein's research reveals, "this story, whatever partial truths it contains, is more a culturally embedded fable that has remained unchanged for a century rather than a factual account."*[28]

Rothstein began his study by asking this question: If schools are worse today than they used to be, then when, exactly, was the golden—or at least silver—age of education? Was the golden age in the 1960s and 1970s? he wondered. Apparently not, because that was the time that best-selling author Vance Packard's thundering accusation was that we were becoming a nation of illiterates, asserting that there was "indisputable evidence that millions of presumably educated Americans can neither read nor write at satisfactory levels."[29] That was also the period during which best-seller Jacques Barzun was bemoaning declining literacy as partly due to "the loss of proper pedagogy in the lower schools."[30] And it was in 1961 that the Council for Basic Education issued its startling report, *Tomorrow's Illiterates,* charging that a third of ninth graders could read at only the second- or third-grade level because phonics had been abandoned in the schools.[31] And it was in 1967 that Jeanne

Chall published a widely read textbook on reading instruction, entitled *Learning to Read,* that alleged that most problems in reading instruction were traceable to the abandonment of phonics in that decade.[32] Clearly, the decades of the 1960s and 1970s were not the golden age of education. Perhaps it was in the 1950s? Rothstein looked there.

The 1950s were dominated by the Cold War, the centerpiece of which was the intense competition between the Soviet Union and the United States, and that was serious business indeed. It was the time of McCarthyism, blacklisting of suspect intellectuals—such as writers, directors, and actors—and the fear that Communism had insidiously infiltrated all aspects of American life and culture, including education, to undermine American institutions and sap values from within. Indeed, the nadir of the Cold War was in 1957, when the Soviet Union launched *Sputnik I* and *Sputnik II* and our national humiliation at believing that we had lost the space race was largely ascribed to the abysmal failure of public schools, which were described as having become weak, flabby, and ineffectual.

So, in search of the golden age of American schooling, Rothstein looked back to the 1940s, then the 1930s, back to World War I, the early 1900s, and even to the nineteenth century, and never did discover a golden age. What he did find, however, was an endless recycling of complaints much the same as those we hear in our own day. In 1902, for example, the editors of the *New York Sun* asserted that when they went to school, children "had to do a little work . . . spelling, writing and arithmetic were not electives, and you had to learn." But now, in 1902, schooling seemed to them to be a vaudeville show in which the child must be kept amused and learns what he pleases.[33] Thus, Rothstein concludes (paraphrasing a well-worn Will Rogers adage), "The schools ain't what they used to be and probably never were," despite the unending din of criticism with which we are all familiar today. It seems clear that "what everyone seems to know" is, as Rothstein has described, a culturally embedded fable.

This, of course, supports the obvious weakness in the time-honored assault on public schooling: if the criticisms are—and long have been—correct, why have the gloomy outcomes forecast by the doomsayers not come to pass? More than twenty years after the *A Nation at Risk* report, for example, how does it happen that the economy of the United States has managed to weather periods of bearish stock market prices, recession, and other inevitable variations to continue to stand in the second millennium as the envy of the world? Is it the fault of schooling in Japan and Germany that the economies of those global competitors have wallowed in the doldrums for years, apparently unable to respond to persistent initiatives to spark them into new growth? How do we explain that the United States has achieved continually escalating levels of productivity, unmatched in competing industrial nations, that have yet to peak? Why has the technological growth of the nation not faltered in competition with other nations, given the allegedly poor education of the generations of young people coming out of school to take up the task of developing new technologies in such fields as space exploration, computer technologies, biomedical sciences, and quantum physics, to mention only a few areas in which the United States stands peerless? One could go on, but the point is clear. There is a disconnect between the dismal predictions that have been made for generations about educational achievement in the United States and the actual achievement in virtually every field of human endeavor—including the economy, the arts, letters, sciences, and other areas of human achievement.

Indeed, the disconnect is so obvious that some thoughtful observers have described disinformation as being an important part of contemporary attacks on schooling.

This observation is not offered here in any sense as an excuse for complacency, let alone self-satisfaction, on the part of educational leaders. This is a fast-paced world, one that is dominated by ceaseless global change. Our educational organizations must be nimble and adaptable, and so we must always strive to do better, achieve more. While much has been accomplished in American education, we may not rest on our laurels; much work lies ahead. We must never slacken our efforts to develop ever better schools, more equal educational opportunity, and greater social justice in schooling. On the other hand, there is no cause for despair by educational leaders: while there is much that can be fairly criticized, much room for improvement, there is also a great deal of evidence that we have done well and are continuing to do well. The evidence is not only in the great achievements in the social, political, economic, and cultural life of our society but also in the remarkable resilience demonstrated by the schools themselves in adapting to social changes of nearly incredible scope. These include rapidly changing demographics in the schools arising from ongoing massive immigration and migration, evolving social-political policies of inclusion and education of children with special needs, and the continuing push for greater equality in dealing with such issues as gender, race, and ethnicity. While the agenda is incomplete—a work in progress, if you will—educational leaders can and should face the challenges of the future with justifiable confidence, optimism, and enthusiasm. If it is true that every challenge presents an opportunity, this time of challenge is also a moment of great opportunity for educational leaders. That opportunity may lie in a tectonic shift—or, more precisely, a scientific paradigm shift—that is now underway in American education.

A Paradigm Shift in Education

We appear to be in the midst of a true scientific revolution in education, a major paradigm shift that makes it likely that the traditional concept of equality of educational opportunity is being fundamentally transformed. The paradigm shift pivots on understanding the nature of human intelligence on which the learning theory that we use to organize schools and programs of instruction in them rests. That paradigm—the consensus among scientists as to what intelligence is—has direct and significant implications for educational leadership because it is the basic foundation upon which all else in education stands. The paradigm concerning the nature of human intelligence is the only foundation on which educational leaders may build the "visions" for educational excellence that are now so much demanded of them. The paradigm drives how we organize schools, what we teach in them, how we teach, how we group students for instruction, and everything else for which educational leaders are responsible. Thus, the scientific paradigm of human intelligence drives and shapes the educational vision of schools that school leaders hold. This is, therefore, the key to developing a game plan for educational leadership.

A Passion for Equality

The American people are remarkably passionate idealists in many ways. A central American ideal is that of equality, especially equality of opportunity. This ideal is embodied in the noble sentiments that Thomas Jefferson wrote in the introduction to the Declaration of Independence: "We hold these truths to be self-evident, that all men are created equal, that they are endowed by their Creator with certain unalienable Rights, that among these are Life, Liberty, and the pursuit of Happiness." Since those words were penned in one of the most revered American documents, virtually enshrined as American Scripture,[34] the concept of equality has been embraced, observed, and embellished by successive generations that have struggled ceaselessly to achieve the ideal as reality in daily life rather than merely regarding it as a lofty and distant goal. As a result, today, Americans seek literal equality. Differences in outcome—whether in voting rights, access to housing, job opportunities, fairness in lending, access to schooling, or whatever—are taken as legally sufficient evidence of unequal opportunity. Thus has evolved a remarkably egalitarian, if still flawed, society that is engaged in the apparently unending process of perfecting itself, and it is distinctively American.

The current brouhaha over the quality and effectiveness of American schooling takes on a different perspective from the past when viewed through the prism that this egalitarian ideal provides. Though often obscured in the hardball vehemence of public controversy over school reform, controversy that involves many agendas that are tangential to education, perhaps the central educational issue is that of equal educational opportunity. This is no longer understood to be merely equal opportunity to be present in the schoolhouse, which desegregation was largely about. Equal educational opportunity today implies that, once in the schoolhouse, each individual will have equal access to effective teaching that will achieve desired educational outcomes. To a remarkable extent, this issue revolves around one's understanding of the nature of intelligence.

The Traditional Paradigm of Intelligence

In 1994 a group of fifty-two internationally known scholars, who viewed themselves as working in the mainstream of science, described what Kuhn might call the existing or traditional paradigm of science on intelligence in this way:

1. Intelligence is a very general mental capability that, among other things, involves the ability to reason, plan, solve problems, think abstractly, comprehend complex ideas, learn quickly and learn from experience. It is not merely book learning, a narrow academic skill, or test-taking smarts. Rather, it reflects a broader and deeper capability for comprehending our surroundings—"catching on," "making sense" of things, or "figuring out" what to do.

2. Intelligence, so defined, can be measured, and intelligence tests measure it well. They are among the most accurate [that is, reliable and valid] of all psychological tests and assessments. They do not measure creativity, character, personality, or other important differences among individuals, nor are they intended to.

3. While there are different kinds of intelligence tests, they all measure the same intelligence. Some use words or numbers and require specific cultural knowledge (such as vocabulary). Others do not, and instead use shapes or designs and require knowledge of only simple universal concepts (many/few, open/closed, up/down).[35]

This paradigm of intelligence that has prevailed in the cognitive sciences for a century has two characteristics that are particularly important in this discussion:

- Intelligence is a unitary whole: a single, though complex, phenomenon.
- Like one's body build or skin color, IQ is a fixed and unchangeable personal characteristic.

But what is the source of intelligence? Is it a fixed inherited characteristic? That is, is it genetically determined? Or is intelligence amenable to development from environmental sources such as nutrition, social support, and opportunities to learn? This, of course, raises the nature-nurture controversy that educators know so well.

The existing traditional paradigm of intelligence began to unfold and develop just about a century ago—in 1904—when Alfred Binet was asked by the French minister of education to develop a way to identify those children in school who needed special help. Binet promptly set about devising a way to measure intelligence so that one could express the results in numerical terms, much as one weighs and measures the physical characteristics of the bodies of children. By comparing the intelligence test score of an individual child with the distribution of all of the scores of many children taking the same test, one could discern whether or not the score of an individual was above or below the average of scores of many other children of that age. This gave rise to the concept of *mental age*: if, for example, ten-year-old François's test score equaled that of most twelve-year-olds he would be considered bright—that is, two years ahead of his peers—having a mental age of twelve. If, however, his ten-year-old classmate Hélène scored at the level of most eight-year-olds, she would be considered less intelligent, having a mental age of eight. Within a few years, a German psychologist came up with the idea of dividing the mental age by the chronological age of the child and multiplying the resulting quotient by 100 to yield the "intelligence quotient," or IQ. Thus, François would be said to have an IQ of 120, while Hélène's IQ would be 80.

If one obtained the IQs of a large sample of individuals, their frequency distribution would predictably fall into a bell-shaped pattern that is familiar to most readers of this book. This is predictable because the distribution of data from any measure of individuals, such as height, shoe size, or weight, would also normally fall into this bell-shaped pattern, which is why it is called the *normal curve of distribution* or the *normal curve.* Not surprisingly, it is also popularly called the *bell curve* (because it somewhat resembles a cross section of a bell such as the Liberty Bell). In a normal distribution the bell curve shows, as would be expected from such measures of individuals, a small number of very low scores, a small number of very high scores, and a strong tendency for most of the scores to cluster toward the middle of the distribution. The dispersion of the data, from low scores to high, is shown along the horizontal axis; it can be spread out or compressed, depending

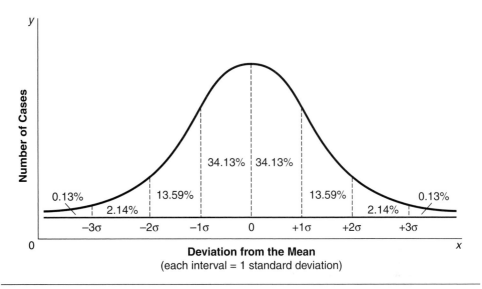

FIGURE 2.1 When displayed in graph form, the distribution of IQ scores from a large population typically takes the form of a bell-shaped curve.

on the shape and appearance desired for display purposes. The unit of the spread is called a *standard deviation* and ordinarily a standard deviation of 15 is used to array scores from intelligence tests; a smaller standard deviation will produce a narrow, sharply arched curve, while a larger standard deviation will produce a lower, more elongated curve. In any case the data—that is, the distribution of the scores from the intelligence test—remain the same; only the graphic depiction changes. A typical ideal bell curve that might display the distribution of IQ scores is shown in Figure 2.1.

The distribution of scores shown in Figure 2.1 shows that about 68 percent of those who took the test are within 1 standard deviation of the mean score. Many people, thinking of this group as within the "average" range, would say that the scores of about 16 percent of those who took the test are below the average range and those of another 16 percent are above it. One could readily use such a distribution to identify the "best and the brightest," on the one hand, and the "losers," on the other hand, and, as we all know, this has often been done in making decisions not only in schools but also in hiring practices and other highly important matters.

The Bell Curve

In 1994 a book entitled *The Bell Curve*[36] examined the effects of the application of this paradigm over the course of time to such things as deciding who would be selected to attend the best schools and elite universities and who would be proffered the choicest jobs in the most prestigious firms. The study showed that the inevitable effect of this ongoing practice in a modern technological-industrial society would be the emergence of a social class system, a meritocracy based on perceived cognitive ability.

The rise of this select, elite meritocratic social class was described as, in turn, inevitably fostering the creation and perpetuation of other ever more entrenched (lower-ranking) social classes. Moreover, the authors described how these social classes being inevitably established by the ever-increasing demand for high-level cognitive skills in the modern world of complex and technological work were becoming heritable in terms of race and ethnicity. Other twentieth-century observers had previously commented on the profound social changes afoot in advanced industrial nations, but they had focused on such characteristics as poverty, social class, and education as the basic causal dynamics driving these great social changes. These ideas had given rise to many schooling programs intended to mitigate the impact of these causes and bridge the widening chasm between educational attainment of children from poor families and those from affluent families.

The new view described in *The Bell Curve* was, however, perhaps the first major study to point to cognitive ability, or intelligence, as the key factor in these tectonic changes in the social structure. It had long been known that cognitive ability is a major factor in determining whether or not individuals will achieve greater or lesser social status than their parents. That knowledge had, in fact, been the springboard for the development of many school enrichment programs aimed at mitigating the effects of poverty such as Title I and preschool education. However, when the authors of *The Bell Curve,* Richard Herrnstein and Charles Murray, presented evidence that

1. described intelligence as being largely an inherited characteristic that does not readily respond to educational and enrichment interventions, that
2. seemed to demonstrate that cognitive ability is unequally distributed among the races as well, and that
3. there is a strong tendency for those with similar abilities to marry one another

they were clearly describing the inevitable emergence of a permanent new social class structure in American society, one based on a meritocratic class system. Perhaps more alarming is their observation that in this meritocracy those with similar abilities tend to intermarry. This would mean that "there will be less regression to the mean in the cognitive ability of children of the intellectually talented and, therefore less intergenerational reassortment. Under these circumstances a meritocracy begins to look like an aristocracy, a perception that is strongly reinforced when the intellectual elite segregate themselves from the rest of society by living in separate neighborhoods, sending their children to private schools."[37] This scenario was described as having begun to unfold in the second half of the twentieth century, when the percentage of high school graduates in the top IQ quartile who went directly to college—perhaps the most effective mechanism for sorting people by cognitive ability—zoomed from about 55 percent in 1950 to about 72 percent in 1980 and was destined to continue increasing.

Some cognitive psychologists greeted *The Bell Curve* with approbation and seemed to view it as skillfully illuminating the existing paradigm of intelligence and changes in social structure that were accompanying the increasing demand for highly competent intellectual workers as the high-tech global economy continued to expand. Overwhelmingly, however, the book was savaged by the popular press and academics as being an incendiary assault on the highest ideals and most cherished beliefs in the American egalitarian tradition. Not only was the book itself excoriated, but the authors were personally accused of being racists, fascists, frauds, and worse, much worse. Few could remember when a serious academic treatise had been received with such an overwhelming storm of opprobrium. Clearly, Herrnstein and Murray had seized the third rail; they had broken the last taboo: in a society whose central value is equality, no matter how imperfect the reality may be at the moment, there is little tolerance for those who question that core goal in American life. Herrnstein and Murray may have skillfully drawn from the scientific paradigm that they had inherited to back up their analysis but, if so, that scientific paradigm—while it still represented the mainstream of thought of many cognitive psychologists—was deemed unacceptable by many, intolerable; in their view, a new approach had to be found.

A New Paradigm of Intelligence or the Lake Wobegon Syndrome?

The traditional paradigm of intelligence has long had a powerful impact on educational leadership at all levels of schooling and continues to be the scientific paradigm in cognitive psychology. School leaders have generally accepted this paradigm and the learning theory that it implies and therefore have recognized the need for some means for sorting students according to ability as a basis for organizing curriculum and instruction. Recognizing that there is a spread of abilities in the student population, schools have commonly been organized using variations of the concept of ability grouping for instruction to conform to this perceived reality. For example, a time-honored standard of excellence in elementary school teaching is the skill that teachers demonstrate in using ability grouping to organize instruction within their classrooms. At the secondary level, it is common practice to offer courses at different levels of difficulty, when practical, and to sort students into them using scheduling techniques. College instructors have, not infrequently, tried to assign marks to students competitively according to the normal curve of distribution, so-called marking on the curve, even though the small numbers of students in such classes frequently make this statistically indefensible.

But in an era where schools are expected to "leave no child behind," there is an increasing conviction that all children—in America, at any rate—start out in life with equal intellectual abilities. There has been, as we have pointed out, a notably persistent gap between the learning outcomes of poor children and those of children from affluent families, and the gap has continued to exist despite efforts to close it. Because there are many minority people in the ranks of the poor, the educational achievement gap takes on racial overtones. In the emerging view, it is the task of the school to teach each child so that equality is not merely the opportunity for all individuals to be present in school and to receive instruction but that the actual learning of all children is more nearly equal than historically has been the case. This is more than an important shift; it is a tectonic shift:

from accepting equality of opportunity to learn as the standard of excellence in schooling to demanding equality of educational achievement, or outcomes, as the standard.

But, one may protest, how can this be? We accept as a scientific verity that there is a normal distribution of intellectual abilities in the population. More than a century of scholarly work devoted to developing and refining intelligence tests around the world has demonstrated this time and again, and this distribution is predictably depicted by the curve of normal distribution. How, then, is it reasonable to expect that the intervention of schooling can yield achievement outcomes that are significantly different from the curve of normal distribution? Yet it seems clear that this is exactly the expectation with which many people approach the issue of school reform.

To skeptics this sounds much like Lake Wobegon, the mythical Minnesota bastion of small-town values and rural innocence that humorist Garrison Keillor, on his weekly radio show *A Prairie Home Companion,* unfailingly describes as being a place where all the women are strong, all the men are good-looking, and all the children above average. It's an idea so preposterous that it is an exemplar of humor, and it has drawn an appreciative chuckle from his large radio audience for years. To many educators it so aptly describes the emerging new demands on schools—which seem similarly preposterous—that the term *Lake Wobegon syndrome* has become standard in the professional jargon of educators.

The point is, of course, that it seems to many teachers and other educators as though when schools are properly run, all the pupils and students should score above average on their examinations. But the issue takes on a markedly different perspective if we consider the possibility that the current well-established paradigm theory of intelligence is fundamentally wrong. If this is the case, and if we become convinced that American public schools and their pedagogical practices are organized on the basis of a flawed understanding of the nature of intelligence and, therefore, a flawed learning theory, it may not be surprising that the educational achievement gap between the poor and the affluent has persisted for so long despite continued diligent efforts to close it. Moreover, if a new and more correct understanding of the nature of intelligence exists, educational leaders need to learn what it is and perhaps reconsider the learning theory that they use, in the light of the new paradigm, to decide how schools should be reorganized and how pedagogical practices in them should be revised so as to be more effective. It seems clear that we may be at this moment present at the beginning of a scientific revolution that, if it succeeds in supplanting the existing paradigm, could pave the way to the emergence of a new paradigm and great opportunities for educational leadership.

Multiple Intelligences Theory

First, let's review briefly a few of the core theories on which the existing paradigm of intelligence is constructed:

- Intelligence is a single, unitary mental factor that is often referred to as the "g factor" (meaning general intelligence). This is what intelligence tests are designed to measure.

- Intelligence processes are neural processes, and the quality of these processes is dependent upon the nervous system that is present in the individual at birth.
- The nervous system is inborn, dependent on inherited chromosomes, and the level of its functioning is little changed by such external events in life as schooling or poverty. Intelligence is, therefore, relatively stable over time.

This was summarized in a classic statement by Henry H. Goddard—the scholar whose opus magnum was the translation of Binet's work into English. Goddard observed that "our thesis is that the chief determinant of human conduct is a unitary mental process which we call intelligence: that this process is conditioned by a nervous mechanism which is inborn: that the degree of efficiency to be attained by that nervous mechanism and the consequent grade of intellectual or mental level for each individual is determined by the kind of chromosomes that come together with the union of the germ cells: that it is but little affected by any later influences except such serious accidents as may destroy part of the mechanism."[38] Goddard's work in 1920 was followed by generations of research studies into the working of the brain and the mind, which produced a much better understanding of intelligence and learning theory and, at the same time, a steady erosion in the confidence that Goddard's beliefs are correct. Jean Piaget and, later, Jerome Bruner, for example, fundamentally challenged the notion that external influences—such as schooling—had little effect on cognitive functioning.

Many readers of this book know something of the work of the Swiss scholar Jean Piaget, who regarded learning as part of child development. He described learning as a progressive growth process during which—over time and with proper stimulation and guidance—the individual builds on the simpler processes that were learned in earlier years by integrating higher-order logical processes and, thus, the growth in logical thought matures and develops. Piaget's work had great influence on the education and work of schoolteachers, especially American schoolteachers, in the 1970s and 1980s. Jerome Bruner, working in the constructivist theoretical framework, was much influenced by Piaget's thinking and also had great influence on teachers and their methods in the later decades of the twentieth century. Bruner's view was that learning is an active process in which students construct new understandings upon a base of their existing knowledge. The active process involves the learner in selecting and transforming information, constructing hypotheses, and—in short—developing logical cognitive processes and ways of discovering and learning new ideas and new information. But this, in Bruner's view, required carefully structured, skillful, Socratic-type teaching in order for it to happen.

Piaget and Bruner had clearly challenged the notion that intellectual functioning was fixed and unchangeable. They believed that, by aiding and abetting the inborn tendency of individuals to develop cognitively, teachers and schools could facilitate the growth and maturity of their students' cognitive skills. They also challenged the conviction of the behaviorists, which represented the clearly dominant approach to psychology at that time, that (1) one could not deal with the internal functioning of learners because it was unseen and not manipulable and that (2) the manipulation of rewards and punishments was key to designing successful teaching–learning strategies. But they had not directly challenged the belief that intelligence is a fixed, inborn, unitary characteristic of each individual. That would be done by a later generation of scholars whose work began to appear near the end of the twentieth century.

For example, Daniel Goleman argued that the important competencies in life included self-awareness, self-discipline, persistence, and empathy, and that these are more important for success in life than IQ. Moreover, he contended, in a worldwide best-selling book in 1995, that these competencies can be taught to children. This cluster of competencies he called "emotional intelligence," and he went on to explain in a 1998 book that these competencies are more important for outstanding performance and leadership than either intellect or technical skill.

Gardner's Multiple Intelligences Theory (MIT)

In his landmark work on the nature of human intelligence or, more correctly, human intelligences, Howard Gardner has drawn attention to the shift during the twentieth century of psychologists away from focusing on the external objects of the physical world in explaining human behavior to focusing on the preoccupation with the mind, and especially cognitive thought, that depends so heavily on symbols such as language, mathematics, the visual arts, body language, and other human symbols.[39] Gardner's great contribution in explaining human thought and behavior has been to give us a new way to think about intelligence: not as a single characteristic, or even as a group of characteristics that can be summed up with the single measure of IQ. Gardner explained that there are several kinds of intelligence that are independent of one another, yet each of them enables one to engage in intellectual activity in different ways. Many have found it persuasive that Gardner, who formerly taught neurology in a medical school, has identified specific areas in the brain that are involved in each of the different kinds of intelligence.

Gardner has observed:

> In the heyday of the psychometric and behavioristic eras, it was generally believed that intelligence was a single entity and that it was inherited; and that human beings—initially a blank slate—could be trained to learn anything, provided that it was presented in an appropriate way. Nowadays an increasing number of researchers believe precisely the opposite; that there exists a multitude of intelligences, quite independent of each other; that each intelligence has its own strengths and constraints; that the mind is far from unencumbered at birth; and that it is unexpectedly difficult to teach things that go against early "naive" theories or that challenge the natural lines of force within an intelligence and its matching domains.[40]

Howard Gardner has described seven dimensions of intelligence:*

- *Linguistic intelligence.* The ability to understand words and how they are combined to produce useful language. This is important for writers, poets, and journalists.

*In 2000, Gardner proposed the possibility that there are several other dimensions of intelligence. However, they were not as clearly stated and described as the original seven dimensions that were proposed in 1984 and that are the basis of this discussion.

- *Logical-mathematical intelligence.* The ability to see patterns, order, and relationships in seemingly unrelated events in the world around us and to engage in logical chains of reasoning. One thinks of scientists, mathematicians, engineers, and architects.

Before we present the remainder of the list of intelligences, we should point out that Gardner believes that a major problem in schools as they are organized and operated today is that they tend to restrict much of their curriculum and teaching to the linguistic and the logical-mathematical dimensions of intelligence. Learning in these areas is especially esteemed, is considered by many to be of a higher order, and is usually emphasized in assessing the outcomes of schooling. There are, however, five other intelligences that are widely recognized in our culture and that, Gardner argues, are valid ways of learning and thinking:

- *Musical intelligence.* The ability to discern pitch, melody, tone, rhythm, and other qualities of musical symbolism and integrate them into intellectual activity such as reasoning. Musicians, composers, singers, and rap artists come to mind.
- *Spatial intelligence.* The ability to accurately perceive and think in terms of the visual qualities of the world and its dimensions, and to manipulate and transform them in creative ways. This is important for architects, artists, sculptors, photographers/cinematographers, and navigators.
- *Bodily-kinesthetic intelligence.* The ability to control one's bodily motions, the capacity to handle objects skillfully,[41] and the skill to combine these into a language with which one may express oneself "with wit, style, and an esthetic flair,"[42] as Norman Mailer said with boxers in mind. Gardner's example of mimes, particularly Marcel Marceau, makes vivid the concept of bodily-kinesthetic intelligence, but one thinks also of dancers, figure skaters, and many athletes.
- *Intrapersonal intelligence.* The ability to access and understand the inner self: feelings, reactions, aspirations. This refers to the self-aware individual who understands and is comfortable with his or her personal emotions and is able to differentiate between various feelings and use them in thinking about the world. One thinks of novelists and playwrights such as Alice Walker, Eugene O'Neill, Marcel Proust, and James Baldwin, all of whom used autobiographical themes to explore the world. Cinema *auteurs* ranging from Marcel Pagnol to Woody Allen also readily come to mind, as do gurus whose wisdom transcends their own provincialism.
- *Interpersonal intelligence.* "The ability to notice and make distinctions among other individuals and, in particular, among their moods, temperaments, motivations, and intentions."[43] This ability "permits a skilled adult to read the intentions and desires—even when these have been hidden—of many other individuals and, potentially, to act upon this knowledge—for example, by influencing a group of disparate individuals to behave along desired lines."[44] Outstanding examples include Martin Luther King, Jr., Eleanor Roosevelt, Lyndon B. Johnson, and Mohandas Gandhi. Individuals who possess high levels of interpersonal intelligence might find it useful

in exercising educational leadership, but it appears to be a form of intelligence rarely sought by university programs of preparation in educational administration.

Gardner's description of intelligences illuminates some important ways in which people bring different inner resources to the behavioral equation in organizations—not only students, but adults such as teachers and administrators as well. It is important to remember that these different kinds of intelligence are present in each of us, but that the mix in each of us is so idiosyncratic that in any group one will find some range of individual differences. This suggests that an approach to developing an educational game plan that fails to take these differences into account is flawed at the outset.

It is, moreover, important to remember that these intelligences are human characteristics, not options or preferences that individuals choose. As Gardner has shown, though one's intelligences develop over time as one matures physiologically, their development also depends to a great extent on learning from the environment. Thus, one does not learn to read, write, and calculate simply because one has matured (and is, therefore, presumably "ready" to learn), but also because, for example, along the way one has seen others read, write, and calculate.[45] This underscores the importance of interaction between the person and the culture in the individual's environment in shaping human behavior.

Gardner's MIT has had a profound impact on the learning theory that underlies the practice of American teachers and school leaders and is currently being used in many schools across the country as a basis for organizing curriculum and instruction. Many of these schools participate in an organization called Project SUMIT (Schools that Use Multiple Intelligences Theory) under the sponsorship of Harvard University's Project Zero, which is conducting systematic studies of these schools and the effects of MIT in them. Project SUMIT also publishes case studies, descriptions of teaching methods and practices, and other information that is useful to those who want to learn more about the application of MIT to the improvement of school outcomes.

Perkins's Learnable Intelligence Theory

Clearly, Gardner has raised credible objections to the paradigmatic theory that intelligence is a single unitary human characteristic and has convinced many that there are, in fact, at least seven kinds of intelligence. These provide the educator with the keys to a learning theory for organizing the school, creating the curriculum, and selecting pedagogical methods that will facilitate learning and achievement in a much broader spectrum of students than had previously been thought possible. Gardner's colleague in Project Zero at the Harvard University Graduate School of Education, David Perkins, has taken aim at the second fundamental concept of traditional IQ: the theory that intellectual capability is inherited and fixed. Perkins says:

> [T]he old IQ lives! Many people firmly believe in intelligence as a fixed, genetically determined characteristic of themselves and others. Historically, many people have thought that some racial groups differ in their fundamental intellectual capacities. It is unpopular to express such a view today, but certainly the attitude persists. More broadly, a view of intelligence as fixed pervades our reasoning about human performance. . . . We attribute failure

to fundamental lack of ability. Likewise, when people succeed conspicuously, we laud their talent and envy their genes. Curiously, this pattern of thinking figures much more in United States culture than, for instance, in Japan [where] parents lay much more emphasis on the role of effort in success: The way to deal with a difficult problem or a puzzling concept is to persevere systematically until you have mastered it.[46]

But Perkins agrees with Gardner in emphasizing that intelligence is not a single characteristic. He is not so sure that there are seven dimensions, however. He believes that there are in fact three dimensions of intelligence:

- "The first is *neural intelligence,* the contribution of neural efficiency to intelligent behavior,"[47] much as the theorists and psychometricians in the traditional paradigm have claimed.

- "The second is *experiential intelligence,* the contribution of a storehouse of personal experience in diverse situations to intelligent behavior."[48]

- "The third is *reflective intelligence,* the contribution of knowledge, understanding and attitudes about how to use our minds"[49] in intelligent ways.

The latter two kinds of intelligence, Perkins argues, are not recognized by those who support traditional IQ theory—who claim that intelligence cannot be learned—yet they are the keys to learnable intelligence. You can, Perkins argues, know your way around "in much the same sense that you can know your way around your neighborhood, the game of baseball, or the stock market. To acquire such knowledge, people can 'learn their way around' important kinds of thinking, gaining concepts, beliefs, feelings, and patterns of action that allow them to handle problem solving, decision making, explanation, and other intellectually demanding activities better."[50] This analysis brings to mind the age-old dichotomy between the ability of one who has "street smarts" to thrive and succeed in an environment that one with "book smarts" cannot hope to cope with. The point is that to be "smart" is to be intelligent, and Perkins emphasizes that this is not limited to either facility in understanding words and how they are combined or facility in understanding logical-mathematical patterns of order in the world around us, though these are the two aspects of intelligence and learning that have long been emphasized in schools. And to make the point, Perkins draws upon a report from the Rand Corporation entitled *Global Preparedness and Human Resources*:

> The report examined what people from the corporate and academic sectors felt what was needed to meet the escalating challenges of the times. Their answer: General cognitive skills were rated more highly than knowledge in an academic [subject], social skills, [or] personal traits. Good thinking counts most. . . .[51]

Similarly, a study of the international role of schooling found that success in today's global market of competitiveness and economic productivity depends on workers who are skillful thinkers and learners, yet in U.S. schools they found that

> [f]ewer than four in ten young adults can summarize in writing the main argument from a lengthy news column—one in four whites, one in four blacks, and two in ten Hispanics.

> Only twenty-five out of 100 young adults can use a bus schedule to select the appropriate bus for a given departure or arrival—three in 100 blacks and seven in 100 Hispanics. Only 10 percent of the total group can select the least costly product from a list of grocery items on the basis of unit-pricing information—twelve in 100 whites, one in 100 blacks, and four in 100 Hispanics. . . . These findings make it clear that only a tiny fraction of our workers can function effectively in an environment requiring strong communications skills and the application of sophisticated understanding to complex real-world problems.[52]

Of course, observations such as these are commonplace to readers of this book as we contemplate the educational outcomes that are essential today and increasingly so in the years ahead. Many seize upon observations such as these to mount insistent demands for more "back to basics," more readin', writin', and 'rithmetic, tougher academic standards, more drill and practice, and more demanding examinations. Perkins takes a very different tack, and it has proven to be very popular: that schools should be increasingly engaged in teaching more thinking skills, because real learning is a consequence of thinking. We should, he argues, be developing "smart schools" that teach better thinking and, therefore, better learning to every child.[53]

Smart Schools

Perkins asserts that "we need schools that put to work, day in and day out, what we know about how to educate well. We can call such schools 'smart schools'—schools wide awake to the opportunities of better teaching and learning."[54] In Perkins's view smart schools exhibit three characteristics:

1. *They are informed.* "Administrators, teachers, and indeed students in the smart school know a lot about human thinking and learning and how it works best. And they know a lot about school structure and collaboration and how that works best."[55]

2. *They are energetic.* "The smart school requires spirit as much as information. In the smart school, measures are taken to cultivate positive energy in the structure of the school, the style of administration, and the treatment of teachers and students."[56]

3. *They are thoughtful.* "Smart schools are thoughtful places, in the double sense of caring and mindful. First of all, people are sensitive to one another's needs and treat each other thoughtfully. Second, both the teaching/learning process and school decision-making processes are thinking centered . . . putting thinking at the center of all that happens is crucial."[57]

These are important ideas for an educational leader who is engaged in the process of creating a vision for teaching and learning in the school, which we have called a "game plan." we have added emphasis to the important linkage that Perkins makes between the values and behavior of the educational leader, on the one hand, and the quality of educational life in the school, on the other hand.

Perkins goes on to say that these characteristics of smart schools—being informed, energetic, and thoughtful—are not revolutionary and, indeed, they are not. Perkins readily admits that they go back at least as far as John Dewey and were central to the progressive education movement that provided the dominant theory of learning until the mid-1940s, when the pendulum of popularity began to swing away from the progressive movement and toward life adjustment education. The three characteristics of smart schools are largely common sense, Perkins points out, yet *they are not common practice in schools.* And that observation is a consistent theme in this book because it is a central theme for understanding organizational behavior in schools.

Emotional Intelligence

A moment ago we briefly described the emerging understanding that emotional intelligence is today seen as being an important form of intelligence, one of the multiple intelligences that individuals possess. A common cliché in our culture is that of the individuals who were recognized as "brains" in traditional school course work, people who seemed to do well effortlessly in examinations and could ". . . send an IQ test sky-high, but who don't quite make good in either their personal or working lives. They rub others the wrong way; success just doesn't seem to pan out."[58] Of course, on the flip side of the cliché are the individuals who—though not outstanding in either course work or examinations at school or in IQ tests—do well at other things such as socializing easily with others, or immersing themselves in creative work such as music or new technologies, or being respected members of a team. Such individuals may go on in life and to the surprise of many become respected members of the community, successful in their personal lives and in their business or professional lives as well.

This, you will recognize, is the old "book smarts" versus "common sense" dichotomy, which has attracted the attention of cognitive scientists since the early twentieth century. In 1920, for example, in the heyday of developing IQ tests, Edward Thorndike pondered the importance of what he called "social intelligence," which he recognized as being quite different from "general intelligence." Twenty years later, in 1940, David Wechsler, one of the founding fathers of IQ testing, urged that measures of emotional and social intelligence should be included along with intellective aspects of general intelligence to get a more complete assessment of general intelligence. In 1948, shortly after the end of World War II, R. W. Leeper explored the idea that "emotional thought" was intertwined in the development of "logical thought." But through all these years the boom in IQ testing continued, largely unsullied by these ideas. So, although this understanding of the emotional side of intelligence is hardly new, it has only recently entered the mainstream of the conversation.

When Howard Gardner began writing about multiple intelligences in 1983, as we have described, he drew on previous scholarship, of course, but he also spelled out afresh the meanings and the power of *intrapersonal intelligence* and *interpersonal intelligence*. Gardner had been talking about emotional intelligence and social intelligence, though he did not use those terms, and how the two are mutually interconnected. Gardner demonstrated how these intelligences—while markedly different from more traditionally respected *linguistic intelligence* and *logical-mathematical intelligence*—are crucially important for the achievements in life of many people. In 1990 Peter Salovey, of the University of New Hampshire, and John D. Mayer, of Yale University, coined the term *emotional intelligence*[*] and described it as being " . . . the ability to perceive emotions, to access and generate emotions so as to assist thought, to understand emotions and emotional meanings, and to reflectively regulate emotions in ways that promote emotional and intellectual growth."[59]

In a 1995 book called *Emotional Intelligence,* Daniel Goleman suddenly transformed the subject from being an obscure academic field of interest for a handful of cognitive scientists to one that is today of wide interest and was on the best-seller lists for a long time. Goleman vividly delineates the relevant research of modern neuroscience as it describes our "two minds"—the rational and the emotional—that are rooted deep in the brain and how, often undetected by us, they interact to shape the way that we perceive and react to the world around us. He convincingly explains that emotional abilities are not fixed and inherent but that individuals can learn to harness both their rational and emotional minds so that they effectively work together. Moreover, Goleman explains that if one does not learn to harness the two minds together, the emotional can cripple the rational. This, of course, readily helps to explain why it is commonplace to see bright, even learned, individuals who stumble as leaders. Goleman goes on to advocate that schools need to learn a new approach to curriculum that includes developing emotional intelligence as well as rational intelligence and, thus, make possible an entirely new concept of the meaning of excellence in educational achievement.

Later in this book, when we are dealing more directly with leadership, we shall return to this theme to consider the power of emotional intelligence in approaching the challenges of leadership.

The Debate Continues

More than a century after it began, the debate continues, with no sign of achieving closure soon. An educational leader must be well grounded in this debate and know with clarity where she or he stands on the issues and what implications that has for professional practice. The traditional camp continues to believe that schools should stress the acquisition of subject matter, memorization of facts, and examination by standardized tests. The progressive camp believes that it is crucial for students to learn to think critically, to do so using the methods of the scholarly disciplines (such as science, math, history, music, and art), and to use their analytical skills in dealing with problems in real life. One camp believes that children should learn a body of received knowledge and that doing so is, in itself, the goal of "being educated." In a widely popular book, E. D. Hirsch, Jr., for example, compiled a list of 4,552 facts that he believes every child should know if he or she is to be considered culturally literate.[60] He thinks that children should be taught so as to be able to answer questions like these:

- Who wrote *Macbeth*?
- What is a limerick?

---

*Some scholars, such as Reuven Bar-On, choose to use the term *social-emotional* intelligence.

- What does *nouveau riche* mean?
- What is a non sequitur?
- What is a carnivore?
- What does *regression* mean?
- Who was Spiro Agnew?

Hirsch advocates using such a compendium of knowledge as the basis for creating a core curriculum in schools. Many agree with him. Indeed, this approach has had great appeal, and it has been the central idea for organizing a number of charter schools.

Others have sought to extend Hirsch's work with their own additional lists of facts to be learned. These generally attempt to add more current knowledge drawn from more contemporary culture. Among these is *Test Your Countercultural Knowledge,* in which the authors, Kathy A. Zahler and Diane Zahler, suggest questions such as these:

- Who was Cesar Chavez?
- What is the *I Ching* used for?
- How did Janis Joplin die?
- What does *macrobiotic* mean?
- Which countries were in SEATO?
- Who was Timothy Leary?[61]

Interesting questions, and the issue being raised is this: Are we sure that the information needed to answer Hirsch's questions is inherently more important than the information needed to answer the Zahlers' questions? Is the word *carnivore* really more important than *macrobiotic*? "Is it inherently more important to know about Spiro Agnew's life than it is to know about Cesar Chavez's?"[62]

Howard Gardner might respond by saying, "Probably not." Gardner is the author of *The Disciplined Mind: What All Students Should Understand.* Notice the differences between the titles of Gardner's book and Hirsch's. While Hirsch focuses on what students need to know, meaning facts, Gardner speaks of the disciplined mind and the need for students to *understand.* There is a big difference between these points of view and, in terms of how you try to develop curriculum, organize a school, and instruct children, it makes all the difference in the world which view is central to your theory of practice. This difference is at the core of the continuing disputation between conservative traditional views of schooling and progressive views.

Gardner contends that our greatest cultural heritage is not a storehouse of facts and information but, rather, the academic disciplines, ways of engaging in disciplined thinking, such as the mathematics, sciences, music, art, history, and literature that we have inherited. It is these disciplines, with their methods for seeking information, analyzing it, and communicating what is learned—these human-created methods and structures for approaching long-standing problems—that constitute education in his view, not the memorization of an assortment of facts. Thus, educated people use disciplined methods of thinking: "Historians evaluate documents and testimony to reconstruct plausible accounts of past events. Scientists generate hypotheses about how the world works, collect data relevant to those hypotheses, analyze the data objectively, and then revise or endorse the original hypotheses or theories."[63] The arts are also disciplines: How do you create musical harmony? Paint a portrait? Write a sonnet?

He adds: "The disciplines are arguably the most important human inventions of the last two millenniums."[64] Teaching students critical thinking and analytical skills of the disciplines should therefore be the centerpiece of a school program, Gardner contends, so that they can use their learning in the lifelong pursuit of further learning and problem solving.

Hirsch coyly seeks to finesse the obvious link between this long-standing educational debate and politics in the United States. "During the last two decades," he writes, "when Democrats have controlled a school board, the district has tended to favor the whole-language method of teaching reading, to encourage the use of calculators for 'math understanding' (instead of memorizing the multiplication table) and to disparage multiple-choice tests, all positions connected with progressive education but not logically with the platform of the Democratic Party."

"By contrast," Hirsch continues, "when a majority of school-board members have been Republican, the district has tended to favor the explicit teaching of phonics, the memorization of the multiplication table and the use of standardized tests, positions properly associated with educational conservatism but not necessarily with political conservatism."[65]

The National "Summit Meetings" on Educational Standards

But the connection with politics is undeniably plain for all to see. Indeed, since President Reagan chose to intervene in the school debate, which was a political first in the history of the nation, it has become a staple in presidential politics and in state-level politics as well.

Following the appearance of *A Nation at Risk* in 1983, a series of three "educational summit meetings" was held to stimulate and encourage the school improvement movement that the report had triggered. The first of the three was convened on September 27–29, 1989, by President George Bush and the National Governors' Association at the University of Virginia. It was attended by 49 governors and their staffs, and they focused on ways to set new performance goals for the schools of the nation.

The second summit meeting was held on March 26–27, 1996, at the IBM Executive Conference Center, located on the border of New York and New Jersey just outside of New York City. This time the group in attendance was more diverse: President Clinton was there, as were 40 governors and corporate executives, and in addition there were 40 individuals who were described as "education experts." That meeting concluded with a commitment by those present to work on creating mandated educational standards in every state. At the time, only 14 states had adopted standards setting forth what students should know and be able to do. That meeting ended with an enthusiastic and much-heralded call to make the achievement of U.S. children in math and sciences first in the world by the year 2000. This was the much-ballyhooed Year 2000 Initiative.

In 1999 the third of these national conferences was held, again at the Executive Conference Center of IBM. It was hosted by Louis V. Gerstner, chairman of IBM, who had emerged as a driving force behind the national movement for higher educational standards. It brought together President Clinton, 28 governors, 21 state school superintendents, 34 corporate executives, and some 40 education leaders and officials including state officials, school board members, and superintendents. Also included were the president of the National Education Association and his counterpart from the American Federation of Teachers, though, as in previous summit meetings, rank-and-file teachers and school principals were excluded. The purpose of this meeting was to consider their progress and plan the next steps.

In one sense, progress had been close to startling: in 1999, 49 states had or would very soon have some form of statewide standards in place. The lone holdout was Iowa. At this summit meeting some states, notably North Carolina and Texas, were pleased to report rising achievement in test scores. In the case of North Carolina, the governor ascribed that state's improved test scores to a program that provided teachers with incentive raises of as much as $1,500 when the test performance of the students in their schools rose and threatened dismissal if it did not. On the other hand, the ambitious goals of the Year 2000 Initiative, to make the achievement of U.S. students in math and science preeminent in the world by the year 2000, was and would be very far from being reached.

Some serious concerns were expressed about the summit meetings' central goal: accountability through the strict application of clear standards on test performance. For example:

- Some expressed concern at the possibility that in some high-stakes testing, such as exit tests for high school, the apparent public high standards were being undermined by lenient test scoring so as to reduce the number of failures.
- Indeed, part of the backdrop for the conference included the recent news that more than half of all fourth graders in New York State—even in some of the elite school districts—had failed a statewide English test. Worse, it had been revealed that the tests of some 8,600 pupils in New York City had been erroneously scored as "failed" by the publisher that had provided and scored the tests.
- New York had also that year mandated that all students take and pass the traditionally stringent Regents Examinations to advance in high school, and experienced observers were surprised to see such a high percentage of students pass. It was soon revealed that the examinations had been scored in a more lenient fashion than in past years.
- Moreover, conferees lamented that, even though many states had adopted performance standards for schools, no state had a majority of students in either fourth grade or eighth grade who were judged to be "proficient readers."
- It was clear that the 1999–2000 school year would see a significant rise in students being failed and held back in grade as the new achievement standards were put in place across the country and that this trend would be exacerbated in the years ahead.

There was no clear plan for dealing with that problem, and the conferees mulled it over without reaching any clear decision on how to deal with it.

But the conferees moved forward, determined to somehow confront and deal with what Gerstner called the "pain" that students and teachers were encountering as the new programs and testing for higher standards were being administered—that is, the pain of failing the qualifying examinations and the pain of being held back in grade. They were eager to take up new issues in the years ahead. These included improving teacher quality, promoting choice in schools, and strengthening accountability for achieving the standards that were being set. Thus, the quest for improving the effectiveness of schools moved on amidst debate, disagreement, conflict, and—as Gerstner conceded—not a little pain.

However, if Giamatti was right, from this struggle a new amalgam of truth must eventually emerge that will guide us into the future of educational development. This textbook is not a place to deal extensively with this struggle except to note that it exists, has been going on for many years, and makes up an important context in which educational leaders must work. You can neither understand organizational behavior in education nor hope to work usefully as an educational leader without having some clear and definite understanding of the issues in this struggle and, more than that, without having a personal commitment on where you stand and how that commitment will guide your actions as an educational professional. You must decide where you stand on these tough issues, and why, and how your conviction will shape your leader behavior. You cannot equivocate on issues such as these and hope to prevail in educational leadership in the United States. Thus, it is critical that you get involved in developing a clear theory of practice to guide you in making your own decisions about professional practice.

Theory of Action

A *theory of action* is a theory that gives rise to some judgment, given the nature of truth that the theory describes, as to how theoretical knowledge can be applied in dealing with practical problems. For example, in the nineteenth century, as the theory that germs can cause infection and disease gradually became credible to surgeons and physicians, it ceased to be merely an academic theory and became a theory of action. Doctors, especially surgeons, slowly began to recognize the value of antiseptic methods in surgery, and they sought to use them in their medical practice. A great breakthrough came in the work of Joseph Lister, who, in 1865, discovered that carbolic acid was an effective antiseptic material that killed dangerous microorganisms. Soon, standard antiseptic methods in the surgery included liberal use of carbolic acid: instruments and even patients were scrubbed and sprayed with carbolic acid in efforts, which seem draconian by the standards of today's practice, to kill the germs that were thought to cause infection. In time, however—still using the germ theory of disease—doctors gradually changed the ways in which they applied it in practice. Aseptic methods became the more accepted way of applying the theory: the concept was one of keeping the surgical environment clean and sterile, free of germs, in the first place. Surgeons took to washing their hands, wore surgical gowns and masks, and found better ways to sterilize things than with liberal scrubs of carbolic acid. As early as 1874, Robert Wood Johnson had developed the first ready-to-use sterile dressings, directly applying Lister's knowledge of germ theory to medical practice. By 1885, his company, the Johnson & Johnson Company, was manufacturing sterile self-adhesive dressings—the forerunner of the now-ubiquitous Band-Aid. Today, of course, the same germ theory guides the actions of doctors but their actions in practice are different. Those who believe in the theory and practice of modern Western medicine take such things as disposable rubber gloves, autoclaving, the use of disposable instruments, maintaining sterile environments in the surgical unit, and the use of antibiotics as the actions that one ordinarily expects of doctors as they practice medicine.

To illustrate the basic interaction between theory of action and theory of practice we have chosen to use simple examples from the realm of modern Western medicine. It is important to note, however, that in medicine—just as in the realms of education, organization, and leadership—there are a number of theories of practice that compete in the marketplace of ideas to inform the practitioner. Modern Western medicine is far from being the only source for medical theory in action. There are today many alternative approaches to medical practice, each supported by theories unique to a specific approach. Many patients, for example, prefer to be attended by doctors of osteopathy rather than doctors of medicine. Holistic medicine and homeopathic medicine are surging in popularity in the West and around the world, as is an array of alternative medical practices that often have roots in ancient non-Western cultures. Acupuncture has a wide following and is slowly finding its way into the practice of some Western medical practitioners. Relaxation therapy, once thought to be exclusive to the ashrams of Indian yogis, has been embraced by many in the West including an increasing number of highly respected practitioners of modern Western medicine. Worldwide, various forms of faith-healing (which draw their theories in action from many different concepts of religious faith and practice), homeopathy, and folk medicine continue to be the accepted basis for medical practice for large numbers of people. Those who practice medicine must decide which of these many competing theories—which explanations for events observed in nature—they will accept and act on to guide their actions in practice.

It can be reasonably argued that U.S. school administrators and supervisors are among the most skeptical professionals in the world when it comes to theory. As a group they tend to reject what is often characterized as the "ivory tower" thinking of academic theorists, which many practicing school administrators see as fuzzy and reflecting little understanding of the hard realities that confront the practitioner on the job. To many, the word *theory* itself conjures images of impractical or esoteric thought or perhaps idle daydreaming. It often suggests the notion of some unattainable ideal state or speculation or even guesswork. In contrast, practicing educational administrators tend to view themselves as confronting a demanding and fast-moving environment in which action is required in order to solve problems and temporizing is not tolerated. Perhaps when the word *theory* is heard, many conjure an image of the intrepid TV defense attorney announcing that he has "a theory about this case," when all he means is that he has a hunch—shrewd or otherwise. Since theory means none of these things, let us begin by demystifying the word *theory*.

Theory is the term that is used for systematically organized knowledge thought to explain observed phenomena. The alternative to using theoretical knowledge is to scurry through the maze of professional leadership practice mindlessly hoping to take the right actions but guessing all the way. In that sense, there is perhaps nothing more practical than good theory, for it provides the foundation for taking appropriate action in a busy, complex world where few problems are truly simple, where time is chronically short, and where any decision usually leads only to the need for further decisions. Such is the nature of administrative work in which educational leaders are normally involved.

While it is true that some academic theorizing can be enormously complex, with arcane subtleties beyond the ken of nonexperts, this is not necessarily true of all theory, nor is it a necessary characteristic of elegant, powerful theory. Consider, for example, the story of Isaac Newton observing an apple falling from a tree in an orchard in 1666 and then—brilliant mathematician that he was—calculating what eventually were recognized as the laws of gravity. Gravity: what a simple, exquisite, powerful—and, one must add, theoretical—concept. Understanding how to calculate the relationships between the mass and speed of two bodies may be beyond many of us, but the central concept has become basic to our understanding the world we live in.

But many things that we commonly observe in daily life are not so simple. For generations, for example, it was widely believed that the center of the universe was the Earth. Evidence to support that idea had been developed in the second century by Claudius Ptolemy, a Greco-Egyptian astronomer, and had been elaborated into a geocentric theory of the universe that was not seriously challenged for well over thirteen centuries. That theory held, of course, that the Earth stood still while the sun and the other planets orbited around it. To many who lived during those years, evidence that supported Ptolemaic theory included the common observation that, when dropped, things tend to fall downward—toward what was thought to be the center of the universe. Moreover, when an Earthling looked up, she could readily observe that the sun was moving about the Earth, causing day and night as it arced across the sky. Using this geocentric explanation of easy-to-observe everyday events, our forbears spoke confidently of the obvious: people were sure that they could easily see the sun rise in the morning and travel around the Earth during the day and then set in the evening. Plainly, the evidence then available strongly supported the theory that the Earth was the center of the solar system.

However, in the early 1500s the Polish astronomer Nicholas Copernicus recorded and published careful systematic observations of celestial events that eventually convinced some cognoscenti that, in fact, it is the sun that is at the center of the solar system and that the Earth rotates and is in orbit around the sun. This was confirmed in 1632 when Galileo published his *Dialogue Concerning the Two Chief World Systems,* which was based on the observations that Galileo made directly with the aid of his telescope. Even though Galileo was imprisoned and forced to renounce his findings in 1633, the genie was out of the bottle: the Copernican, or heliocentric, view of the solar system has not been seriously challenged since. Indeed, Galileo's work became a turning point in the development of Western science.

Today, because of this theorizing and testing of theory, when you look up at the heavens you may speak of the "sunrise" and the "sunset," but we use those terms merely as figures of speech. Most of us are quite certain that the Earth rotates on its axis and is in orbit around the sun. This helps us to understand better what is going on, to explain it and to comprehend predictions of future events. While it is helpful to us individually at that level, modern heliocentric theory is much more powerful than that. For example, it provides scientists and engineers with ways of understanding and explaining the solar system that are so solid that it has been and continues to be basic to the designing and carrying out of our huge programs for exploring the solar system and of space beyond. Clearly, this theory is not some idle speculation; it is part of the theoretical bedrock on which our achievements in space have been built since the 1950s, and on which our plans for future space exploration have been constructed. Clearly no idle dream, no plaything of fuzzy-thinking academics, this theory—like every good theory—is part of the practical stuff of living effectively in the real world. To paraphrase Kurt Lewin, the founder of social psychology: nothing is more practical than good theory.[66]

Just as we have theories of the causes of disease and theories about the solar system, life in our scientific-technological era relies on a rich base of theoretical understandings. Theories of aerodynamics describe and explain the forces that make it possible for heavier-than-air machines—airplanes—to fly. Because they understand the theory, reasonably able middle school children can explain why it is that steel ships float. Not surprisingly, we also have theories about organizations and the people who work in them. Just as there are theoretical reasons that underlie the beliefs that we should wash our hands frequently, exercise regularly, and maintain a nutritionally sound diet, there are theoretical underpinnings to our understanding of schools as organizations and how to make them ever more effective.

For example, suppose that you accidentally cut your finger. What would you do? Very likely you would wash the cut, then apply some antiseptic, and cover it with a sterile bandage. To most readers this would be an ordinary, unremarkable response to having a cut finger. But it is an ordinary, unremarkable response only to someone who knows about, and accepts, the germ theory of disease and the prophylactic practices that have been developed from that theory. To such people, the germ theory of disease is a theory of action. That is, it is a systematic explanation of phenomena that guides us to take actions that seem to be sensible, logical, and reasonable because they are compatible with the explanation of reality that the theory provides.

Theory is useful because it provides a basis for thinking systematically about complex problems, such as understanding the nature of educational organizations. Theory enables us to do four useful things: (1) *describe* what is going on, (2) *explain* it, (3) *predict* future events under given circumstances, and—essential to the professional practitioner—(4) think about ways to exercise *control* over events. This lays the groundwork for the professional practice of school leadership. When we accept, internalize, and act on a theory of action, that theory becomes an important element in our theory of practice.

Theory of Practice

A *theory of practice* is a composite of theories of action that underlies, and gives direction to, one's professional practice. A theory of practice is one's personal view of causal relationships: it arises from the processes of gathering, organizing, and integrating facts and experiences that one has encountered. It is the theory of practice that coheres, unifies, consolidates, makes consistent, and makes sense of hundreds of daily decisions and actions that the leader takes and that guide the leader inexorably to a seemingly unerring sense of what is the right thing to do. Because the typical reader of this book is demonstrably already a successful teacher and has almost certainly been entrusted with other leadership roles, the focus of the book is on further developing the intellectual underpinnings of leadership in schools. The focus is on combining one's various theories of action into a coherent theory of practice. The foundation for a theory of practice in educational leadership rests on three intellectual pillars:

- *A systematic understanding of the behavior of adults at work in the school.* Thus, the book will focus on understanding such aspects of human behavior as motivation, decision making, and conflict. This realm of behavior theory seeks to explain the different ways in which we may attempt to understand the behavior of people, whether or not they are functioning in the context of organizational life. There are many, often competing, theories of human behavior that can be used to guide our understanding.

- *An understanding of the organizational context in which people work.* This realm of organizational theory seeks to explain the different ways in which we may approach the problem of organizing and coordinating the cooperative efforts of many people in order to achieve things that cannot be done individually. The central concern in the study of organizational behavior is the dynamic interaction between the organization and the people who populate it.

- *Leader behavior.* This aspect of organizational theory examines how leaders interact with people in the organization in ways that cause them to be understood and accepted as leaders—not only by followers but by other participants in the organization as well.

But do not be misled: while it is important for potential school leaders to have a solid grasp of the knowledge that underlies leadership, knowledge alone is not sufficient. Each of us who would lead must develop and articulate a coherent theory of practice based on our idiosyncratic understanding of that knowledge and how it may be used in action. It is your theory of practice that informs your method of school leadership, that guides you in deciding what to do and what not to do when choices are difficult and urgent, and that renders your behavior as a leader understandable, believable, and therefore trustworthy to others.

Throughout this book you will be challenged to reflect on ideas that you have read and to use them in thinking through the ways in which you hope to engage in the practice of being a school leader. By engaging in this reflective thinking, it is hoped that you can move beyond merely *knowing about* some of these ideas to a higher level of thinking in which you consider how you can *use these ideas* in your professional practice. How, for example, can you incorporate them into ways of thinking about problems and issues that confront you? How can you use them in developing the plans you make, the actions you take, and the ideas that you propose as a school leader? The concept of developing theories of action and combining them to form a theory of practice lends itself very well to the study of organizational behavior in education.

The Game Plan: A Coaching Metaphor

Another way of thinking about theories of action and combining them into a theory of practice is to apply the metaphor of the coach of a sports team. This is the preferred metaphor in many popular books intended for an audience of managers in business and industrial organizations. Coaches are unquestionably leaders and, arguably, theoreticians. Every successful coach is, above all, a student of the game, just as you are being urged to become a student of educational organization. We expect that the coach is able to analyze and think through the game as a basis for planning and developing strategies and tactics that will win in the future. As spectators of sports contests, we know that every team—in football, basketball, hockey, or any other sport—must operate from a "game plan" that is understood and shared by all who are involved.

The coach must also weave the dynamics of the human behavior of the team players with the strategic notions that underlie the plan. That is called "team building." Those who are being coached must not merely know of the game plan, in addition, each individual in the group must be personally committed to it and have confidence that the plan is solid and will work. This involves the use of playbooks, classroom sessions, tutoring, practice sessions, one-on-one encounters, and all of the teaching techniques that teachers and coaches know so well. More important, it involves developing the dynamics of human relationships on the team that build trust, collaboration, and high morale. The coach does not hope or assume that the team members will somehow understand that there is a plan that governs how the game is played; an important part of coaching is to make sure that everyone understands the game plan and what role each has in executing it. Ultimately the coach uses the game plan in the heat and confusion of the action as a guide for making decisions as the situation develops and conditions change. One would hardly expect a coach to go into a game without a game plan.

Unpredictable developments and rapid, unforeseen changes constantly confront coaches, just as they confront all organizational leaders. An essential characteristic of the game plan is, therefore, that it be a guide to action—a plan that can be readily modified and adapted to new emerging conditions, not something that is fixed and rigid. This adaptability is, in fact, a crucial element in the game plan, just as it is in a theory of practice. It is what makes it possible for the team to respond nimbly and deftly to emerging circumstances that were unforeseen, rather than to continue hammering away at a game plan that is not working. In the context of this discussion, it is appropriate to think of your theory of practice as a game plan.

Conclusion

The central purpose of this book is to help you in the career-long process of developing, testing, and refining a theory of practice, or a game plan, in school leadership. While the focus is on understanding the interface between organization and human behavior as a basis for making a difference in schools, one must be very aware of one key factor that frames all actions in educative organizations—that is, the long-running fundamental disagreement between those who hold a traditional-conservative view of what education should be and how schools should be organized and run, on the one hand, and those who hold progressive-liberal views, on the other hand. The reader is challenged to think through a clear and committed position on these contentious issues as an important step in developing a game plan, or theory of practice, for educational leadership.

Reflective Activities

1. Apply the three characteristics of Perkins's "smart schools" by describing several organizational structures, or common routines, that once established might lead to the type of school Perkins identifies as "smart."

2. The three national "summit meetings" on educational standards resulted in a set of national goals for education, the establishment of educational standards in all states, and the push for tough accountability measures using high-stakes testing. Later, NCLB made these tests a reality. We indicate in this chapter that serious students of educational leadership should be knowledgeable about these issues and take a stand that guides their actions as education professionals. Where do you stand on these issues at this point in time? Write a paragraph or two describing your beliefs. Use one or more references from the research literature that support your stand.

3. Identify and describe a specific *theory* that guides your actions in your answer to the preceding exercise.

4. *Working on the Game Plan.* A game plan normally takes into consideration two principal factors: first, the strategies and tactics that are most likely to gain your objectives based on your analysis of the game and, second, the dynamic relationship between these strategies and tactics with the people on your team. Reflecting on the contemporary debate on education and school reform, which is an important part of the context of educational leadership today, write a paragraph in which you do three things:

   a. Describe at least one key idea from Chapter 2 that will guide your behavior as an educational leader.

   b. Explain the rationale for your choice. Why is it a key idea? What are the behavior implications of the idea for educational leadership?

   c. Show how your behavior based on this idea should improve the performance of those whom you lead.

Suggested Reading

Berliner, David C., and Bruce J. Biddle, *The Manufactured Crisis: Myths, Fraud, and the Attack on America's Public Schools.* Reading, MA: Addison-Wesley, 1995.

Two highly reputable scholars provide a careful, well-documented analysis of the principal myths and distortions from which many attacks on U.S. public schooling have been launched. The authors recognize, however, that there are serious problems and shortcomings in U.S. public schools. Chapters 6 and 7 provide ninety-two pages of thoughtful discussion of real problems in U.S. education and proposed ways of dealing with them.

Gardner, Howard, *The Disciplined Mind: What All Students Should Understand.* New York: Simon and Schuster, 1999.

This is a rarity in the literature on schooling: a thoughtful, superbly informed, and well-disciplined analysis of the problems that lie at the heart of the education profession. In it, Gardner, clearly a first-rate scholar, articulately stakes out a position that defines present-day progressive-liberal views on education and clarifies the issues that differentiate that view from the traditional-conservative approach so ably espoused by Hirsch. Educational leaders who do not know Gardner are inherently at a great disadvantage in the current incarnation of the great debate on schooling.

Hirsch, E. D. Jr., *The Schools We Need: And Why We Don't Have Them.* New York: Doubleday, 1996.

Hirsch, the author who was made famous by *Cultural Literacy,* offers a literate, scholarly, and often compelling argument that became the textbook for forcing schools to reform by advocating hard work, knowledge acquisition, and rigorous testing. He evades the obvious observation that educational ills in the United States arise in large part from a society disrupted by clashing ethnic groups and disintegrating families by arguing that *because of these problems* a "demanding curriculum" (meaning memorizing a lot of facts) is the best way to go. This is an important book and should be known well by educational leaders throughout the United States.

Kohn, Alfie, *The Schools Our Children Deserve: Moving beyond Traditional Classrooms and "Tougher Standards."* Boston: Houghton Mifflin, 1999.

This important book is a cautionary discourse on the future of U.S. schooling and "must" reading for anyone who would be an educational leader. Former teacher Kohn joins Berliner and Biddle in questioning whether today's schools are really floundering or whether some romanticized notions about "the good old days," which he calls "aggressive nostalgia," are coloring our perceptions. Drawing on a wealth of research, Kohn argues that the demand for tougher standards reflects a lack of understanding of how children actually learn and why.

Rothstein, Richard, *The Way We Were? The Myths and Realities of America's Student Achievement.* Washington, DC: The Brookings Institution, 1998.

While this book carefully dispels the fantasy that there was at one time a golden age in which schooling in America was far better and more effective than it is today, it has much more to offer than a trip down memory lane. Rothstein's informative discussions of the ins and outs of such tests as the much-talked-about School Achievement Tests and the Iowa Tests of Basic Skills, how they came to be what they are, and how they are affected by such things as the socioeconomic status of students and dropout rates in schools alone make this must reading for anyone preparing for leadership in American schooling.

Sowell, Thomas, *Inside American Education: The Decline, the Deception, the Dogmas.* New York: The Free Press, 1993.

This slashing, take-no-prisoners attack on public education in the United States is from a Senior Fellow of the Hoover Institution who represents the ultraconservative perspective well. A must read for those who work in the schools and have not studied the thinking and tactics of right-wing critics.

Tucker, Marc S., Judy B. Codding, and Richard Rothstein, *Standards for Our Schools: How to Set Them, Measure Them, and Reach Them.* New York: John Wiley & Sons, 2002.

This book is about what the future of schooling must be in America in an era of increasingly global technology. It compares the outlook and attitudes of European and Asian students with those of American students and emphasizes the need for Americans to think of their future in terms of professional or occupational aspirations and how these relate to their schooling opportunities. The authors argue strongly that standards-based education, based on professional and professional occupational standards, can transform schools by providing students with focus and motivation that they do not now have.

chapter 3

Mainstreams of Organizational Thought

LEARNING OBJECTIVES

After reading this chapter, you should be able to

- Define and describe organizational behavior as a field of scientific study.
- Define and describe organizational behavior as a field of practice.
- Describe the shift in organizational theory that occurred in the twentieth century from human–machine systems to human social systems.
- Define leadership and administration.
- Identify the two major organizational theories or strategies for organizing and leading.
- Describe and discuss the principles of scientific management.
- Define and describe bureaucracy.
- Define and describe classical organizational theory.
- Compare and contrast Taylorism, or scientific management, with classical organizational theory.
- Describe the role that the work of Mary Parker Follett played in the shift toward human relations theory in organization.
- Describe the Western Electric Studies (the Hawthorne Studies) and some of their major findings.
- Explain the paradox of organizational structure.
- Identify and describe the four key organizational characteristics of schools and school districts.

ISLLC Standards

STANDARD 3: A school administrator is an educational leader who promotes the success of all students by ensuring management of the organization, operations, and resources for a safe, efficient, and effective learning environment.

Knowledge

The administrator has knowledge and understanding of:

- theories and models of organizations and the principles of organizational development
- operational procedures at the school and district levels
- human resources management and development

Performances

The administrator facilitates processes and engages in activities ensuring that:

- operational procedures are designed and managed to maximize opportunities for successful learning
- organizational systems are regularly monitored and modified as needed
- human resource functions support the attainment of school goals

STANDARD 5: A school administrator is an educational leader who promotes the success of all students by acting with integrity, fairness, and in an ethical manner.

Knowledge

The administrator has knowledge and understanding of:

- the purpose of education and the role of leadership in modern society
- the philosophy and history of education

Performances

The administrator:

- accepts responsibility for school operations
- considers the impact of one's administrative practices on others
- treats people fairly, equitably, and with dignity and respect
- recognizes and respects the legitimate authority of others

Over the course of the past century we have learned that there are, essentially, two ways of thinking about educational organizations. One is the traditional way: to think of organizations as hierarchical systems in which power and intelligence are concentrated at the top; hence, initiative and good ideas originate there and are passed down through command and control as programs and procedures that people in the lower levels put into practice. The other, newer way—discovered in chrysalid fashion over the course of the twentieth century—is to think of organizations as cooperative, collegial, even collaborative systems in which good ideas exist everywhere in the organization and can be made manifest and put into action only when those in the hierarchy of command and control act in ways that release the capabilities and motivations of subordinates. There is a lot more to it than that, of course, and Chapter 3 gives you some background on the history of the development of these ideas in education. Without that background, one cannot intelligently engage in the current debate on school reform because the debate—though often openly political rather than educational—nearly always arises from the different concepts that the debaters have about such issues as how to make an organization more effective and what leadership is.

Like most readers of this book, you are probably an experienced and highly skilled professional teacher who is preparing to qualify for a position of leadership where you work: perhaps as a chairperson, an assistant principal, or a principal. If so, you are undoubtedly not only a busy person but inclined to be tough-minded and practical, not especially interested in academic discourse that is not directly related to your needs. Therefore, you may ask yourself, why should I be studying organizational behavior in education? What is important to me in this chapter? Let me deal with this in the form of three questions.

Organizational Behavior

Because educational leaders work with and through other people to achieve organizational goals, understanding the behavior of people at work is fundamental to the success of their efforts. All human behavior is mediated and modulated by the context in which it occurs. The context can be overarching and distant, such as the impact of the historical culture of our social and ethnic traditions, for example, or it can be highly proximate. Normally our behavior can and does appropriately shift—usually very swiftly as we move from one context to another—depending, for example, upon whether we are at home for a quiet time with our family, engaged in a job interview, participating in a religious service, or attending a casual gathering of a few friends.

Organizational behavior is defined as the study of human behavior in the context of an organization. The context could be any kind of organization, of course: military organizations often do such studies; so do churches and other voluntary organizations. But usually the term *organizational behavior* is applied to the study of the behavior of people at work, and that is the case in this book. Organizational behavior (OB) is both a field of scientific inquiry and a field of applied practice.

As a field of scientific inquiry, organizational behavior seeks to illuminate the behavior of individuals and groups of people in the social and cultural context of organizations. Like education, organizational behavior is a cross-disciplinary field: no single academic discipline claims it as its exclusive realm. Students of organizational behavior from a number of recognized disciplines can, and do, legitimately conduct inquiry in this field. Collectively, these disciplines are known as the "social sciences."

The social sciences are the disciplines from which organizational behavior derives (1) its intellectual base of knowledge and theory and (2) the research methods that give credence to claims of scientific legitimacy. Thus, scholars in organizational behavior tend to have academic grounding in one or more of the five principal social science disciplines: cultural anthropology, sociology, social psychology, political science, and economics. Although they all seek to shed light on understanding the behavior of people in organizational environments, people from each of these disciplines tend to frame problems and choose research methods in ways that fit into the particular traditions of the discipline with which they are associated. Not surprisingly, political scientists often focus on the ways in which people in organizations tend to form coalitions and use power. Cultural anthropologists tend to look at the values and belief systems of people in the organization and how these are revealed through the artifacts that are used, the customs of the place, the history of the organization, and the myths and stories that are told. Social psychologists are inclined to study the behaviors of people as they are influenced by the social milieu in the organization. Yet the boundaries separating these disciplines are not as impermeable as one may think. When designing, executing, and interpreting inquiry into issues of organizational behavior in real-world organizations, a great deal of overlapping of ideas and methods associated with these various disciplines occurs.

Indeed, collaborative interdisciplinary inquiry has been a hallmark of organizational behavior inquiry since the field first began to emerge in the 1930s. One of the celebrated collaborations in the history of organizational behavior inquiry was that of Kurt Lewin, who is generally credited with founding the discipline of social psychology, and cultural anthropologist Margaret Mead in the 1940s. He, a renowned experimentalist in social psychology, and she, equally renowned as a field researcher in cultural anthropology, demonstrated and modeled interdisciplinary collegiality in studying human social behavior. Among their pioneering discoveries was the process of group decision making that has since become a central concept in organizational behavior.

Organizational behavior is also a field of applied science—that is, it is a field of professional practice that seeks to apply knowledge from the social sciences to solve practical problems in improving the performance of organizations. For example, organizational behavior is a standard subject for study at both the undergraduate and graduate levels of schools of business administration in U.S. universities. The intent is, of course, to improve the leadership and management, and thus the performance, of business organizations in today's global, fast-changing, competitive environment. Similarly, it is studied in military colleges and graduate institutions for similar implications for application in that field. This book examines some of the knowledge and theory that social scientists have been building for over half a century with a view to their possible application to improving leadership and administration in education.

With these observations in mind, we can define organizational behavior as a field of social-scientific study and application to administrative practice that seeks to understand and use knowledge of human behavior in social and cultural settings for the improvement of organizational performance. Thus, organizational behavior is an arena in which social scientists and school administrators can seek to collaborate, however imperfectly, to bridge the gulf between arcane academic inquiry and the everyday challenges of improving the performance of schools.

Organization and Behavior

The two concepts *organization* and *behavior* gradually began to be linked as the second half of the twentieth century unfolded. In the beginning, ideas about organization tended to come from people with engineering backgrounds. Military tradition has, for centuries, provided much of the logic that underlies organizational concepts that continue to be taken for granted even today. These organizational concepts tended to strongly emphasize the linear, logical, hierarchical, authoritarian, and disciplinary structure that one would expect of the military tradition. Generally, these concepts were adopted uncritically by the large-scale industrial and business organizations that developed so rapidly in the late nineteenth and early twentieth centuries. The people who took the lead in designing and managing these organizations were usually engineers whose interest in human factors was largely focused on fitting people into the machine system so as to create more efficient and manageable human–machine systems.

As the twentieth century unfolded, social scientists came to realize that the ubiquity of organizational life mandated that they seriously consider the nature of organizations as human environments. Beginning as early as the 1930s, serious scientific studies of the human side of organization began to be undertaken in earnest. This was a period that ushered in the Great Depression and an era of unprecedented labor–management strife in industry, and the topic had become too significant to ignore. By the end of the 1940s the engineers had largely been displaced as organizational theorists. From that time on, the major thinkers in the field of organization would come almost exclusively from the ranks of the social and behavioral scientists.

Why Study Organizational Behavior?

The short answer is because organizational behavior provides the indispensable foundation of knowledge that is absolutely essential if one hopes to achieve success in educational leadership. After all, leadership, and administration as well, means working with and through other people to achieve organizational goals. Although those who are appointed as school principals are usually selected from the ranks of teachers who are thought to be especially effective, after their appointments they engage very little in the technical aspects of teaching that earned them their reputations. Indeed, the shift from classroom teaching to a school leadership position, such as the principalship, is really a career change. So different are the skills needed to do the work, and the outcomes by which one's success is judged, that one literally leaves teaching and enters a new and very different occupation. Often, newly appointed school leaders find that knowledge of traditional subjects in the curriculum of educational administration—such as school law, curriculum theory, or educational finance—does little to ensure success in leadership.

After appointment as principal, one's work consists primarily of working with and through other adults: one confers with people, individually and in small groups; one plans and runs meetings, sometimes small and sometimes large; one has innumerable encounters with people, some planned but many impromptu and necessarily hurried. It is often assumed that intelligent adults, such as successful teachers, are smart enough to work with and through other people effectively. Yet if you are a school teacher, you may have already witnessed school principals at work who are simply not as capable as they should be in motivating teachers and parents, leading them, and developing the dynamic teamwork in the school and its community that is demanded in this era of school reform. A major cause of such failure is often the fact that the principal simply does not have a strategic plan, sometimes called a "theory of practice," as to how to deal with the all-critical human dimension of the school enterprise.

Many newly appointed principals have good intentions about improving the performance of the school by improving morale, enriching the quality of life in the school, and building teamwork. Many wish to introduce new technical changes as well: adding new curricula, perhaps, or reorganizing the structure of the school. But very often they are ill prepared by either their experience in the classroom or traditional course work in graduate school to think through and plan their approach to school leadership, and have given little thought to the relationship between their day-to-day and hour-by-hour behavior on the job and the outcomes that they so earnestly desire as leaders. Study of organizational behavior in education can help you, first, by focusing your attention on these issues and, second, by encouraging you to make some personal decisions as to how you would plan to practice being a leader on the job. Aside from a general knowledge of pedagogy and schooling, perhaps the single most useful professional tool that the teacher can bring to the role of educational leader is skill in planning for both long-range and short-range activities on the job. One of the outstanding characteristics of successful teachers is their skill in planning their work, both in the formal sense of written plans as well as in the sense of coherent mental maps of what work to do and how to do it. Astonishingly, this is the very skill that many people seem to abandon first when appointed to the principalship and, instead, go in to work every day more or less waiting to see what crises will unfold. Every principal quickly finds that there are always many, many crises and emergencies sure to arise that seem to fill every hour of the day, compete urgently for attention, and keep one "putting out fires" from early in the morning until the evening hours. Such a demanding job, with its never-ending time pressures, requires a principal who not only understands organizational behavior and its importance to school leadership, but who has also internalized a personal commitment to constantly keep leadership and human concerns high on the list of priorities.

Why Study the History of Organizational Behavior?

This chapter presents a history of the development of modern organizational thought from its beginnings in 1887 to the present time. Prior to that time, little serious consideration had been given to organizational thought, other than the concept of hierarchical command that arose in the mists of time past and was perpetuated in monarchic dynasties and their military and ecclesiastical establishments. It is the patrimony of many of their intellectual heirs in present-day business, government, and military organizations. But, as we shall see, since 1887 a great deal of thought and study has been given to the search for alternative ideas for organizing and leading that are better suited to modern realities. The central theme of that search, which developed throughout the twentieth century, has been growing awareness and understanding of human behavior and its importance in determining the effectiveness of the organization. But new knowledge has not replaced the old. Traditional concepts of organization continue to compete with newer knowledge and, indeed, are still dominant in the marketplace of ideas. But, in Western cultures at least, there has been a growing trend in which the importance of the human dimension of the organization is increasingly understood and recognized.

In the twenty-first century, we know that we can deliberately choose between two competing strategies of leading and organizing: a traditional top-down hierarchy or a more collegial participative approach. Today both strategies are being used in education, as well as in business, government, and the military, and each has its sometimes fierce advocates. As a school leader you may be certain of one thing, at least: you will be constantly pulled by advocates of traditional authoritarian leadership and hauled by those who see the fundamental importance of the human dimension of the school. You may be certain that, as an educational leader, you will regularly be called on to make personal decisions as to which path to follow. Only by knowing the contributions of those who came before us, those who pioneered in building the knowledge that we have for thinking about organizations and leadership, can you prepare yourself to make the strategic and tactical decisions that will undergird your leadership with steadfast purpose, consistency, and effectiveness.

Why Study Theory?

This chapter describes a number of theories about organization that were developed mostly in the second half of the twentieth century. But, the practical-minded reader may ask, why study theory? Why not just tell us what works and leave the theorizing to someone else? The answer to this question lies in the fact that there is often confusion about what theory is. Chapter 2 presented an introductory general discussion of theory that included definitions and emphasized the usefulness of theory in dealing with everyday issues in our lives. Chapter 4 extends that discussion by focusing particularly on organizational theory, which is, of course, a central theme in this book. But for the moment it should be understood that one cannot even think about different ways of organizing human beings in collective effort without using theory. Simply to speak of such common organizational notions as leadership or top-down hierarchical authority is to engage in theoretical discussion. Trying to discuss educational organization without some reference to theory is a lot like trying to discuss the prevention of sickness and disease without reference to such basic sanitary practices as washing, bathing, and constructing sealed wells for drinking water, ideas that rest on the germ theory of disease. It is insufficient for us to know that one should wash one's hands regularly, bathe from time to time, and have a source of safe drinking water. It is when we know *why* these are good, healthful practices that we become personally, deeply committed to them as being very important to achieving an important goal in life. Thus, no matter how busy we are, we do not fail to keep these practices high on our list of daily priorities: although they are theoretically important to us, they are equally important in a practical sense.

It is theory that provides the rationale for what one does. Practice simply cannot be isolated from theory. Paul Mort said it well: "There is nothing impractical about good theory. . . . Action divorced from theory is the random scurrying of a rat in a new maze. Good theory is the power to find the way to the goal with a minimum of lost motion and electric shock."[1]

Public Administration as a Beginning

In one sense, administration is one of the most ancient of all human endeavors. There is little question, for example, that the Egyptians organized and administered vast, complex enterprises that required sophisticated planning, complex organization, skilled leadership, and detailed coordination at least 2,000 years before the birth of Christ. To put it in perspective, the task of constructing the pyramids took 100,000 men twenty years to complete.

Similarly, the Chinese are known to have had highly systematic, large-scale administrative systems at about the same time as the pyramids were built, which used many of the management concepts still in use today. Moses, implementing the plan given to him by his father-in-law, by which the people of Israel would be ruled, is cited in modern management textbooks as establishing the pyramidal design of organization still so much in vogue today. The administrative system of the Catholic Church, a far-flung organization at one time numbering nearly a half million cardinals, archbishops, bishops, and parish priests, is still studied for its remarkably centralized administrative system and is compared with the vastly more complex administrative system of modern-day global corporations. And, of course, great military leaders from Alexander the Great to Caesar, to Napoleon, to Douglas MacArthur have long been studied for what they can teach us about planning, organizing, leading, and motivating.

Today, of course, the teaching of administration and leadership is commonplace in universities at both the graduate and undergraduate levels. Most major universities now boast of schools of business administration, usually well attended and heavily bankrolled. Schools of government and public administration are appearing increasingly as their prestige and endowments increase. Schools of hotel administration and hospitality administration, including the culinary arts, are far from unknown. These invariably include departments that support research and course offerings in organizational behavior.

Less specialized institutions of higher learning—such as undergraduate colleges—today almost universally offer courses in organization, administration, and leadership. Virtually all schools of education offer programs of instruction in this area, though nearly always at the graduate level.

The proud civil services of nineteenth-century Great Britain, France, and a few other European nations, which served so effectively in building great worldwide empires, were accepted for a long time as models of public administration. They embodied the belief that policy decisions in government properly belong in the political realm but that those policies should be implemented by civil servants whose jobs are not dependent on the winds of politics and who are free to develop good administrative procedures. This belief is based on the conviction that a disinterested administrative organization staffed by professional, impartial experts is more effective than one that is entwined in the politics of making policy. Today, this concept—as an ideal, at least—underlies the administrative secretariats of a number of international organizations such as the United Nations, the North Atlantic Treaty Organization, and the European Union.

In the United States, however, the concept of "civil service" has generally been less focused on the British and European ideals of professionalism and expertness and more concerned with being an alternative to the spoils system and political corruption in public employment. This happened despite the efforts of Princeton's young assistant professor, Woodrow Wilson, who crystallized early thinking about the professionalization of administration with the publication of his now-famous essay, "The Study of Administration," in 1887. He felt that the improvement of administrative techniques depended on scholarly study and learning in the specialized field of administration itself.

"The object of administrative study," he wrote in an often-quoted statement, "is to rescue executive methods from the confusion and costliness of empirical study and set them upon foundations laid deep in stable principle."[2] Thirty-one years old when he published this article, Wilson was far ahead of his time in arguing earnestly for the inclusion of the study of administration as a subject fit for serious treatment by universities. Forty years were to pass before the first textbook on the principles of public administration for which he called was published (1927). The search for principles was essential to the development of an administrative science, as differentiated from administrative folklore or custom.

Impact of the Industrial Revolution

At about the close of the nineteenth century—the time of Woodrow Wilson's scholarly contributions—businesspeople in Western Europe and the United States were stepping up their efforts to increase profits from industry. Then, as now, it was generally believed in that burgeoning era of industry that greater profitability required lowering the unit cost of producing goods. One way to do this, of course, was to step up mass production through the use of such innovations as the assembly line. The leadership of pioneering industrial giants such as Henry Ford is widely recognized in connection with such technological breakthroughs. In this era of industrial expansion, the key people were the engineers and technically oriented scientists—as they are in our own day of technological revolution. These were the people who could build the machines and then combine them into assembly line units. This was the era of the engineering consultant and the drive for efficiency.

Frederick W. Taylor and Scientific Management

Frederick W. Taylor is a name well known to many students of administration. He had been an engineer at the Midvale and Bethlehem steel companies at the close of the 1800s and, in the early 1900s, became one of the top engineering consultants in U.S. industry. We know that Taylor read Wilson's essay and was influenced by it. From about 1900 to 1915, as he worked to solve practical production problems in factories all over the United States, Taylor developed what later became known as his four "principles of scientific management":

1. Eliminate the guesswork of rule-of-thumb approaches to deciding how each worker is to do a job by adopting scientific measurements to break the job down into a series of small, related tasks.

2. Use more scientific, systematic methods for selecting workers and training them for specific jobs.

3. Establish a clear division of responsibility between management and workers, with management doing the goal setting, planning, and supervising and workers executing the required tasks.

4. Establish the discipline whereby management sets the objectives and the workers cooperate in achieving them.

Notice, especially, the last two of Taylor's principles: they formally differentiate between the roles and responsibilities of managers, on the one hand, and those of workers, on the other hand. They mandate a top-down hierarchical relationship between managers and workers. This traditional concept of labor–management relationships was hardly original with Taylor, but its formalization as a basic principle of organization and management has proven to be extremely powerful in shaping the assumptions and beliefs of managers and, thus, their thinking about such concepts as collaboration and teamwork, which were to emerge in the years ahead. These two of Taylor's principles still provide the justification for many school administrators and school board members to resist—openly or covertly—such ideas as collegial, collaborative approaches to goal setting, planning, and problem solving and other "bottom-up" approaches to school reform in favor of more traditional authoritarian approaches. Indeed, over the course of the next seventy-five years—certainly until the present time—these two of Taylor's principles of scientific management would be the arena in which new and very different ideas about management behavior would evolve.

Frederick Taylor's principles of scientific management became enormously popular, not only in industry but also in the management of all kinds of organizations, including the family. A best-seller of the 1950s, *Cheaper by the Dozen*, vividly recounts how "efficiency" invaded every corner of the family life of Frank B. Gilbreth, one of Taylor's closest colleagues and an expert on time-and-motion study. Taylor's principles of scientific management were aimed primarily at lowering the unit cost of factory production, although he and his followers claimed that these principles could be applied universally;[3]

they became almost an obsession in the press and throughout our society.[4] In practice, Taylor's ideas led to time-and-motion studies, rigid discipline on the job, concentration on the tasks to be performed with minimal interpersonal contacts between workers, and strict application of incentive pay systems.[5]

The Beginning of Modern Organizational Theory

At the same time that Taylor's ideas and their application were having enormous impact on life in the United States, a French industrialist was working out some powerful ideas of his own. Henri Fayol had a background quite different from Taylor's, which helps to account for some of the differences in perception of the two men. Whereas Taylor was essentially a technician whose first concern was the middle-management level of industry, Fayol had the background of a top-management executive. It would be useful to mention briefly some of the ideas Fayol advanced to give us a better perspective on what he contributed to the growth of thought in administration:

1. Unlike Taylor, who tended to view workers as extensions of factory machinery, Fayol focused his attention on the manager rather than on the worker.
2. He clearly separated the processes of administration from other operations in the organization, such as production.
3. He emphasized the common elements of the process of administration in different organizations.

Fayol believed that a trained administrative group was essential to improving the operations of organizations, which were becoming increasingly complex. As early as 1916, Fayol wrote that administrative ability "can and should be acquired in the same way as technical ability, first at school, later in the workshop."[6] He added that we find good and bad administrative methods existing side by side "with a persistence only to be explained by lack of theory."[7]

In his most notable work, *General and Industrial Management,*[8] Fayol established himself as the first modern organizational theorist. It was Fayol who defined administration in terms of five functions: (1) planning, (2) organizing, (3) commanding, (4) coordinating, and (5) controlling. It should be noted that, in the sense in which he used these terms, "commanding" and "controlling" mean what are now called "leading" and "evaluating results." More than sixty years after its initial publication, many still find this insightful approach to administration practical and useful.

Fayol went further by identifying a list of fourteen "principles," among which were (1) unity of command, (2) authority, (3) initiative, and (4) morale. Avoiding a rigid and dogmatic application of his ideas to the administration of organizations, Fayol emphasized that flexibility and a sense of proportion were essential to managers who adapted principles and definitions to particular situations—quite a different interpretation from that of Taylor, who held firmly to the uniform, emphatic application of principles.

Emergence of Bureaucratic Organizational Theory

By the time of Fayol and Taylor, it was clear that the Western world was becoming an "organizational society." As giant industrial organizations grew in the early 1900s, so did government and other organizational aspects of life. The relatively simple social and political structures of the preindustrial era seemed inadequate in an urban industrial society. Life was not always completely happy in this new social setting, and a great deal of friction—social, political, and economic—resulted. The increasing sense of conflict between people and organizations became a major factor in the struggle of learning to live successfully in this new kind of world, this industrial world in which the individual was, at every turn, a part of some organization. The years before World War I were punctuated by frequent outbursts of this conflict, such as labor unrest, revolution, and the rise of Communism. In this setting, a German sociologist, Max Weber, produced some of the most useful, durable, and brilliant work on an administrative system; it seemed promising at that time and has since proved indispensable: *bureaucracy.*

At a period when people and organizations were dominated by the whims of authoritarian industrialists and entrenched political systems, Weber saw hope in bureaucracy. Essentially, the hope was that well-run bureaucracies would become fairer, more impartial, and more predictable—in general, more rational—than organizations subject to the caprices of powerful individuals. Weber felt that well-run bureaucracies would be efficient, in fact, would be the most efficient form of organization yet invented. Such a viewpoint may not reflect modern experiences with bureaucracies, but Weber was convinced that a *well-run* bureaucracy would be very efficient for a number of reasons, one of which was that bureaucrats are highly trained technical specialists, each skilled in a specific, limited portion of an administrative task.

According to Weber, the bureaucratic apparatus would be very impersonal, minimizing irrational personal and emotional factors and leaving bureaucratic personnel free to work with a minimum of friction or confusion. This, he concluded, would result in expert, impartial, and unbiased service to the organization's clients. In the ideal bureaucracy Weber envisioned certain characteristics that are, in a sense, principles of administration:

1. A division of labor based on functional specialization.
2. A well-defined hierarchy of authority.
3. A system of rules covering the rights and duties of employees.
4. A system of procedures for dealing with work situations.
5. Impersonality of interpersonal relations.
6. Selection and promotion based only on technical competence.[9]

Part of Weber's genius lay in his sensitivity to the dangers of bureaucracy, while at the same time he recognized the merits of bureaucracy in *ideal* circumstances. He emphasized very strongly the dangers of bureaucracy, even so far as to warn that massive, uncontrollable bureaucracy could very well be the greatest threat to both Communism and free-enterprise capitalism.[10] It is helpful, in trying to understand the flow of ideas that guided the development of administration, to be aware that although he produced his work at about the same time that Taylor and Fayol did (that is, from about 1910 to 1920), Weber was almost unknown in the English-speaking world until translations of his work began to appear in the 1940s. This helps to explain why his systematic work on bureaucracy did not receive widespread attention in educational administration until after World War II.

We have thus far considered the ideas of three people who represent many others and a prodigious amount of effort in their time. Each pointed to the need for the principles and the theories that, by 1900, were generally regarded as essential if the administration of our growing organizations was to become more rational and more effective. The American, Taylor, emphasized the principles that viewed administration as management—the coordination of many small tasks so as to accomplish the overall job as efficiently as possible. Efficiency was interpreted to mean the lowest net-dollar cost to produce the finished article. Taylor assumed that labor was a commodity to be bought and sold, as one buys oil or electricity, and that by using "scientific management," the manager could reduce to a minimum the amount of labor that must be purchased.

The Frenchman, Fayol, emphasized broader preparation of administrators so that they would perform their unique functions in the organization more effectively. He felt that the tasks that administrators perform are, presumably, different from those that engineers perform but equally important.

Germany's Max Weber held that bureaucracy is a theory of organization especially suited to the needs of large and complex enterprises that perform services for large numbers of clients. For Weber, the bureaucratic concept was an attempt to minimize the frustrations and irrationality of large organizations in which the relationships between management and workers were based on traditions of class privilege.

The Rise of Classical Organizational Theory

These three individuals—Taylor, Fayol, and Weber—were giants in the pre–World War I years and led the way in the early efforts to master the problems of managing modern organizations. There is no precise and universally agreed-upon beginning or end of this era; however, the period from 1910 to 1935 generally can be thought of as the era of scientific management. Scientific management had a profound and long-lasting impact on the ways in which schools were organized and administered. Raymond E. Callahan, in *Education and the Cult of Efficiency,* vividly described how school superintendents in the United States quickly adopted the values and practices of business and industrial managers of that time.[11] Emphasis was on efficiency (that is, low per-unit cost), rigid application of detailed, uniform work procedures (often calling for minute-by-minute standard operating procedures for teachers to use each day throughout a school system), and detailed accounting procedures. Though some educational administrators harbored doubts about all of this, there was a rush among school superintendents to get aboard the bandwagon of the day by adopting the jargon and practices of those with high status in the society—business executives. Typifying this, Ellwood Cubberley—long one of the leading scholars in U.S. education—took the clear position in 1916 in a landmark textbook that schools were "factories in which the raw materials are to be shaped and fashioned into products to meet the various demands of life."[12]

This view was widely held over the period roughly from before World War I until very close to the outbreak of World War II. Because the concept of scientific management called for the scientific study of jobs to be performed, professors of educational administration undertook to describe and analyze what school superintendents did on the job. Fred Ayer, at the University of Texas, for example, surveyed superintendents to find out what kind of work they did in 1926–1927. Nearly all reported "attending board meetings, making reports, and supervising teachers, 80 percent . . . reported that they went to the post office daily; and each week half of them operated the mimeograph machine, . . . 93 percent inspected toilets, and 93 percent inspected the janitor's work."[13] To prepare individuals to become school superintendents, therefore, programs of study often featured courses in budgeting, heating and ventilating, methods for performing janitorial services and sanitation tasks, writing publicity releases, and record keeping. Professors of educational administration, in turn, commonly conducted studies to determine, for example, the cheapest methods of maintaining floors—such as the most efficient techniques for mopping or sweeping, oiling and/or waxing—so that they could provide prospective school superintendents with the skills necessary to train janitorial workers.

As the study of the problems of organization, management, and administration became established more and more firmly in the universities—just as Wilson and Fayol had predicted—the principles of scientific management received increased attention and also challenge from scholars and practitioners. In particular, as the hierarchical-authoritarian notions of organizational life formalized by Taylor and his followers gained ascendancy, mounting conflict arose from the clash between the demands of the organization for submissiveness and discipline on the part of workers and the need of individuals to experience a reasonable sense of reward and satisfaction from their work. This was publicly manifested in the 1920s and 1930s by increasing labor unrest. Nevertheless, management specialists continued to focus on developing and refining top-down hierarchical ideas about the management of organizations.

Luther Gulick and Lyndall Urwick stand out among the many scholars who attempted to synthesize what is now known as the "classical" formulation of principles, which would be useful in developing good, functional organizations. Central to the work of these two men was the idea that elements of the organization could be grouped and related according to function, geographic location, or similar criteria. They emphasized the drawing up of formal charts of organizations that showed the precise ways in which various offices and divisions were related. Gulick and Urwick published a widely acclaimed book in 1937[14] and were still highly influential after World War II.[15] Many school administrators are familiar with some of the organizational concepts that were popularized by such classical writers.

Scientific Management versus Classical Organizational Theory

Frederick Taylor was an engineer who spent many years designing and perfecting the machines and machine systems of mass-production factories that were mushrooming in his day. He got into management through his concern about the unique ability of human beings to interfere with the reliability, orderly predictability, and linear logic of his beloved machine systems. Scientific management, therefore, focused on ways to make individuals at work more reliable, more predictable, and less prone to such human failings as fatigue. Its focus, we would say today, was on the human–machine interface.

Scientific management taught that it was important to hire the right people, train them well to work with the machine, and keep the job requirements within the physical limits of the individual. Furthermore, Taylor urged consideration of worker motivation and that meant, to him, only money. The motivation to work, as he saw it, was a simple economic transaction between the individual worker and the employer. Pay should be closely pegged to the difficulty of the job and productivity achieved.

Much of what Taylor taught now seems both commonsensical and old-fashioned, almost banal. In the first quarter of the twentieth century it was not so; these were new and powerful ideas at that time. In fact, they were widely seen as a serious threat to the American worker because they demanded the surrender of individuality and the human spirit in return for dollars.

It is testimony to Taylor's greatness that we still accept many of his ideas and have moved beyond those that have not stood the test of time. Many people are surprised to learn that Taylor was a true pioneer in connecting motivation to performance on the job. Few today think that money is the only motivator, but before Frederick Taylor few had thought of motivation as being important at all.

Classical organizational theory, in contrast to Taylorism, came to view the total organization, rather than the individual worker, as the focus of attention. Classical organizational theorists tend to view motivation as being more important than Taylor did and also as being a more nuanced concept: money is not the only motivator for people at work. Classical theorists understand that an organization is much more than the interface of human and machine; it is a complex web of social relationships and interdependencies, and motivation often involves more than money. It includes ideals, values, beliefs, and the need for personal satisfactions. Also, classical theorists—such as Max Weber and Elton Mayo, among many others—were concerned with such organizational issues as division of labor, organizational hierarchy and power, and defined lines of authority. One can learn a great deal about classical ideas about organizational theory, leadership, and motivation from viewing films such as *Twelve O'Clock High* and *The Godfather.*

Organizational Concepts of Classical Theory

Classical organizational theorists have sought to identify and describe some set of fixed "principles" (in the sense of "rules") that would establish the basis for management. The best known of these dealt with organizational structure. For example, central to the classical view of organization is the concept of hierarchy, which, in the jargon of classical theorists, is the *scalar principle.* (In practice it is usually referred to as "line and staff.") The contention is that authority and responsibility should flow in as direct and unbroken a path as possible from the top policy level down through the organization to the lowest member. This general principle is rather widely accepted by organizational theorists today, being most often attacked because of the rigid insistence with which many classical thinkers tend to apply the concept in practice, limiting lateral relationships between parts of the organization. It is, thus, no accident that organizational charts of U.S. school districts today frequently show vertical lines of authority and responsibility with little or no interconnection between operating divisions of the organization. Thus, the organizational chart of a typical school district will show the elementary schools reporting up the line through the director of elementary education to the superintendent, with no interconnections to the middle schools or the secondary schools. In fact, in such a district there ordinarily is no functional connection between the three levels or divisions of the district.

Another central classical principle of organization is *unity of command*: essentially, that no one in an organization should receive orders from more than one superordinate. Fayol, a strict interpreter of this point, was sharply critical of Taylor because the latter favored something called "functional foremanship," which permitted a worker to receive orders from as many as eight bosses (each being a specialist). As organizations and work became more complex over time, this principle has been greatly weakened by the need to modify it so often to meet changing conditions. The organizational charts of school districts frequently reflect this principle, although in actual operation it is routinely ignored.

For example, a teacher of music in the elementary schools may be assigned to several schools and spend time as an itinerant going from one school to another to offer classes and organize groups in music. Although the organizational chart of the school district may show the music teacher as reporting to the director of music, and although the teacher may be formally evaluated by the director, when working in a given school this teacher actually comes under the direction of the principal. In these situations, teachers receive instructions from at least two superordinates and are held responsible by both of them—although the principal and the director may neither coordinate their interests and intentions nor be in agreement on them.

The *exception principle* holds that when the need for a decision recurs frequently, the decision should be established as a routine that can be delegated to subordinates (in the form of rules, standard operating procedures, or administrative manuals). This frees those in higher positions from routine detail to deal with the exceptions to the rules. This principle, too, has received wide acceptance: it underlies the delegation of authority and the concept that all decisions should be made at the lowest possible level in the organization. This has proved to be the most generally applicable principle of classical theory.

Span of control is the most widely discussed of the major ideas from classical organizational theory. The essence of the concept is to prescribe (and thereby limit) the number of people reporting to a supervisor or administrator. Much of the thinking about this principle arose from military organizations, which—under highly stressful, unstable, emergency conditions—need a dependable system of control and coordination. The problems in applying the concept to other kinds of organizations have led to more controversy than understanding. Whereas many theorists suggest having a small number of people reporting to an administrator (usually between three and six), many firms deliberately put executives in charge of larger numbers of people so as to force them to delegate more decision making to their subordinates.

The Ideas of Mary Parker Follett

The work of Mary Parker Follett was unique in the development of management thought. Her ideas were rooted in the classical traditions of organizational theory but matured in such a way that she, in effect, spanned the gap between scientific management and the early industrial psychologists. Follett's first organizational study, done for her master's thesis at Radcliffe, was a major analysis of the speakership of the House of Representatives of the United States Congress, a significant administrative and leadership position that had received little systematic study until that time. It was published as a book that was a standard in the field for years.

Then, for many years, Follett managed an innovative volunteer program in Boston that offered a large-scale program of educational and recreational opportunities in public school facilities during the afternoon and evening hours. The program was designed specifically to meet the needs of the large number of homeless boys, street kids, who lived in Boston and other major U.S. cities at the turn of the century and who badly needed safe places where they could study in the evening, receive supportive guidance, and engage in wholesome recreational activities. Much of the financial support for this volunteer social program came from business executives, and through working with them, Follett came to learn a great deal about U.S. corporate leaders and what they thought about organizations and workers. She increasingly became concerned that corporations, through their management practices, were doing much to create the problems that her programs were attempting to ameliorate. The stock market crash of 1929, followed by the Great Depression, was a galvanizing event for her and for many others that starkly illuminated the realization that large business corporations had become social institutions whose concentration of power called into question the U.S. tradition of unrestrained corporate action.

Her ideas were instrumental in modifying the trend toward rigidly structuralist views in classical management theory, provided a rationale that was helpful in ushering in the human relations movement, and pioneered conceptualizing about what today is called contingency theory.

Follett, first, viewed management as a social process and, second, saw it inextricably enmeshed in the particular situation. She did not see authority as flowing from the top of the organization's hierarchy to be parceled out among those in lower ranks. It was better practice, in her view, that orders should not be given by one person; rather, all should seek to take orders from the situation itself. She saw that the administrator has three choices of ways to handle conflict: (1) by the exercise of power, (2) by compromise, or (3) by "integration" (that is, bringing the conflict into the open and seeking a mutually acceptable, win-win resolution).

In 1932, Follett sought to summarize her views by developing four principles of sound administration. The first two were *coordination by direct contact of the responsible people concerned* and *coordination in the early stages.* These clashed with the typical classical preoccupation with hierarchical communication and control: Follett advocated placing control in the hands of those in the lower levels of the organization, which requires opening up communication horizontally across the organization as well as down the hierarchy. The third principle was *coordination as the reciprocal relating of all the factors in the situation* (which laid the basis for the "law of the situation"). This emphasized the importance of linking departments in ways that enabled them to self-adjust to the organization's needs at lower levels of the organization. Finally, *coordination as a continuing process* recognized that management is an ever-changing, dynamic process in response to emerging situations—a sharp contrast to traditional, static, classical views that sought to codify universal principles of action.

Classical and Neoclassical Administrative Concepts

Though classical concepts of organization and administration—that is, the concepts associated with bureaucracy and scientific management—were developed early in the twentieth century and stood for a time unchallenged by competing concepts, it would be an error to view the classical approach as something that once flourished and is now gone from the scene. Nothing could be further from actuality.

Bureaucracies flourish among us today, of course: government bureaucracies, such as the Internal Revenue Service and state departments of motor vehicles, are among the obvious examples encountered every day. Even in the case of nonbureaucratic organizations, however, many scholars as well as administrators essentially believe that the classical views are the best basis for administrative practice.

Many contemporary advocates of accountability programs, competency-based programs, and management by objectives operate from classical organizational concepts. These newer manifestations of the older classical concepts are often referred to as *neoclassical* or, in some cases, *neoscientific.*

Numerous federal interventions in public schooling—such as the Elementary and Secondary Education Act (ESEA), P.L. 93-380, the Emergency School Assistance Act (ESAA), P.L. 92-318, and the Comprehensive Employment and Training Act (CETA), P.L. 93-203—are organized and administered in conformity with classical concepts of bureaucracy. Planning, Programming, and Budgeting Systems (PPBS) and Zero-Based Budgeting Systems (ZBBS) are designed to implement the basic ideas of classic bureaucratic organizational strategies (as are most so-called rational planning and management systems). They are examples that are widely called neoclassical today.

The Human Relations Movement

In time, as the principles of scientific management were applied to industry with greater care, a need to be more precise about the effect of human factors on production efficiency was felt. The Western Electric Company was one of the more enlightened industrial employers of the time and, in routine fashion, cooperated with the National Research Council in a relatively simple experiment designed to determine the optimum level of illumination in a shop for maximum production efficiency. Western Electric's Hawthorne plant near Chicago was selected for the experiment. Before the research was over, an impressive team of researchers was involved; of its members, Elton Mayo is probably the best known to educators.

The original experiment was very well designed and executed, and it revealed that there was no direct, simple relationship between the illumination level and the production output of the workers. Because one of Taylor's principles suggested strongly that there would be such a relationship, this study raised more questions than it answered.

The Western Electric Studies

The original experiment in what became known as the Western Electric Studies (often called the Hawthorne Studies) was really quite simple. The question to be studied could be put this way: In a room where women sit at benches assembling devices from parts, what is the optimum level of illumination that is required for the workers to be most productive in their jobs? An experiment was designed and conducted to find out.

In 1927 the investigators divided the workers into two groups. One group was the *control group:* throughout the experiment their work went on as it had before, with no changes being made. For the other group, the *experimental group,* there would be some experimental interventions. In this case, the interventions consisted of nothing more than installing electric light bulbs of different sizes. They started with the rather low-wattage lamps that the workers were accustomed to and that were ordinarily used in such work-shop situations and took note of the productivity of the workers. Then they installed bulbs with higher output of illumination and recorded the productivity of the workers. Productivity rose.

Since productivity went up, and since the only change that was known to have occurred was the amount of illumination, it seemed evident that there was some causal relationship between the level of illumination and the productivity of workers. It appeared that the level of illumination might be a *cause* of variations in productivity. A reasonable hypothesis might be that productivity increases as the level of illumination increases. Or would there be some limit, some level of illumination beyond which productivity would no longer increase? Is it possible that there is an optimum level of illumination that, if exceeded, would result in declining productivity? Because the researchers had started these studies with the intention of finding the optimum illumination required for optimum output, these kinds of questions hinted at interesting hypotheses that could only be confirmed or rejected through further experimental study. The experimenters again increased the light output of the bulbs in order to see what would happen. Productivity rose.

Taylor's principles of scientific management had clearly suggested that there would be an optimum amount of illumination to trigger optimum output by the workers. But the Western Electric Studies could not find any optimal amount of illumination that was associated with maximum productivity. When the wattage of the bulbs in the work areas was increased, the productivity of the workers increased. But when the wattage of the bulbs was held steady, productivity continued to rise. The confused experimenters undertook studies in which the amount of illumination was actually *reduced,* and productivity did not decline. Meanwhile, the people in the control group continued working at the same rate of productivity that they had experienced before the studies. The experiments did not confirm any of the hypotheses that were being tested. Something was afoot here, and those who were in control of the studies did not know what it was. Quietly, one of the breakthrough moments of modern organizational behavior had arisen.

After pondering the surprising results from the initial series of studies, the investigators drew up a list of six questions that clearly revealed a broadening of their concept of the working environment and its impact on human behavior. The questions also revealed deepening awareness of possible connections between productivity and the attitudes and beliefs of workers as well as their physical selves. The questions that sparked the continuation of the Hawthorne Studies were these:

1. Do employees actually become tired?
2. Are pauses for rest desirable?
3. Is a shorter working day desirable?
4. What is the attitude of employees toward their work and toward the company?
5. What is the effect of changing the type of working equipment?
6. Why does production decrease in the afternoon?

These were rather simple, straightforward questions, but it is obvious that the answers to a number of them would be psychological, rather than physical, in nature. These questions triggered one of the most far-reaching series of experiments in the history of administration, which became known as the Western Electric Studies and which led to discoveries that are not yet fully understood. However unexpected it may have been, one major finding of these studies was the realization that human variability is an important determinant of productivity. Thus, in the 1920s the basis for the human relations movement was established.[16]

New concepts were now available to the administrator to use in practice. Among them were (1) morale, (2) group dynamics, (3) democratic supervision, (4) personnel relations, and (5) behavioral concepts of motivation. The human relations movement emphasized human and interpersonal factors in administering the affairs of organizations. Supervisors, in particular, drew heavily on human relations concepts, stressing such notions as "democratic" procedures, "involvement," motivational techniques, and the sociometry of leadership.

Sociometry

The human relations movement attracted social and behavioral scientists, particularly group dynamicists who had already been studying the phenomena of human behavior of individuals interacting with one another in dyads and in groups. Numerous studies carried out in group and organizational settings laid the groundwork for better understanding of the nature of human groups and how they function. Illustrative of the better early work of group dynamicists is that of Jacob Moreno, who developed and refined the techniques of sociometric analysis. Moreno sensed that within groups there are informal subgroups— identifiable clusters of people that form essentially on the basis of how much they like or dislike one another.[17] Moreno developed techniques of gathering information from

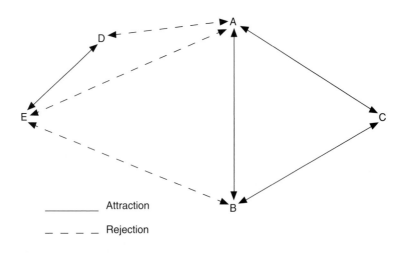

FIGURE 3.1   Simple sociogram of five-person group.

members of organizations as to the attraction they had for one another; the data were often gathered by interview, but other techniques (such as simple questionnaires) also were used. From such information, *sociograms* were developed that portrayed the dynamics of the *informal social structure* of human groups. A typical sociogram of a group of five people might look like Figure 3.1, for example. By asking the members of the group simple questions (such as with whom they would be most willing to work), it is possible to ascertain a great deal about the informal social structure of the group.

Behavior Patterns in Groups

Another fruitful line of investigation emanating from the human relations approach was the work of Robert Bales. He developed a systematic technique for analyzing the patterns of interaction between the members of a group. Essentially, Bales's interaction analysis technique consisted of recording key facts about the discussions that occurred between individuals: how many took place between specific individuals, who initiated them, which of these were between two individuals and which were addressed to the group as a whole, and so on.[18] Bales's work not only provided a workable technique that others could use to study the interaction patterns of groups, but also permitted him to draw some generalizations about groups that have proved to be useful.

For example, Bales was the first to document that successful groups tend to include people who play two key roles: it is necessary for someone (or, perhaps, several individuals in a group) to keep the group focused on *accomplishing its task;* at the same time, it is necessary for every successful group to have someone to see that the group pays attention to *maintaining productive human relations* within the group. These two dimensions of group behavior—task orientation and maintenance orientation—have proved to be of lasting value in understanding the dynamics of group functioning.

Leadership as a Group Function

Leadership has long been a subject of great interest to those concerned with organizations, and social scientists were not long in realizing that—unlike the classical view—leadership is not something that "great people" or individuals with formal legal authority provide for their subordinates; rather, it is a process involving dynamic interaction with subordinates. Benjamin Wolman, for example, found that members of groups tend to elect to leadership positions individuals who are perceived to have the ability (or "power") to satisfy the needs of the group and who are, at the same time, perceived as ready to accept the responsibility.[19] Bales noted that groups tend to confer leadership on individuals not so much on the basis of how well they are liked as on the basis of the ideas that the individuals contribute to the groups and the help that they give the groups in carrying out the ideas.[20] Helen Jennings found that dominant, aggressive people are not likely to be perceived by group members as leaders but, in fact, are likely to be rejected and isolated by the group.[21]

These few examples may serve in this discussion to illustrate some of the kinds of sociological, psychological, and social psychological investigations that were undertaken in large numbers during the human relations era. This was a time when, in fact, social psychology began to mature as a scientific and academic discipline. Kurt Lewin contributed richly to studies of organizational behavior during this period, especially in the area of group decision making.[22] More importantly, Lewin early developed crucial insights and theoretic views that were of great help to those who came after him. His work and that of his students, for example, inspired the laboratory method of personal growth training (that is, T-groups or sensitivity training), which, in turn, laid the basis for the contemporary practice of organization development, discussed in Chapter 7.

Muzafer Sherif, whose studies of street gangs as human social systems became landmarks of insight and research methodology, went on to produce one of the early textbooks in social psychology.[23] George Homans (*The Human Group,* 1950), Felix Roethlisberger (*Management and Morale,* 1950), William Foote Whyte ("Human Relations in the Restaurant Industry," 1948), Fritz Redl ("Group Emotion and Leadership," 1942), Philip Selznick ("The Leader as the Agent of the Led," 1951), and Alvin W. Gouldner (*Studies in Leadership,* 1950) are only a few of the more famous contributors to the outpouring of theory and research during this period that was to establish an irreversible trend in thought and understanding about behavior in human organizations.

In U.S. education, the human relations movement had relatively little impact on school district administrators (for example, superintendents of schools), as compared with a substantial impact on supervisory levels (for example, supervisors, elementary school principals). Superintendents, in general, continued to emphasize such classical concepts as hierarchical control, authority, and formal organization, whereas supervisors emphasized to a much greater extent such human relations concepts as morale, group cohesiveness, collaboration, and the dynamics of informal organization. A review of the proceedings and publications of representative organizations, such as the American Association of School Administrators (AASA) and the Association for Supervision and Curriculum Development (ASCD) readily reveals that, for the most part, those who saw their roles as educational administrators tended to emphasize attention to budgets, politics, control, and the asymmetrical exercise of power from the top down, whereas those who were primarily concerned with instruction and curriculum placed much more emphasis on participation and communication and deemphasized status–power relationships. This difference in emphasis persisted at least into the 1980s, though administrators moved somewhat to embrace human relations ideas.

The Paradox of Organizational Structure

So much has been said and written about organizational structure that many people have come to think of organizations as real, material things: tangible, concrete, ponderable, almost like buildings, with their foundations deep in the earth and their structures soaring aloft so as to define how we must behave in order to live with them, to come to terms with them.

But organizations are not real: they merely exist as concepts in our minds and in the minds of other people. As much as anything, organizations are social conventions. Palpable though they may seem, they cannot be touched or grasped; you cannot seize an organization in your hand or weigh it, kick it, or measure it. Organizations are human inventions and only concepts at that. If you learn nothing else about organizations, this is one basic bedrock idea that you must learn. Organizations are what we think they are and what others think they are, nothing more.

The Organizational Theory Movement

Classical and bureaucratic approaches to organizations tend not only to emphasize organizational structure and the highly rational logic of hierarchical control over people, but also to reify these concepts: treating the organization as tangible, concrete, virtually touchable and even living. In the early literature on organization this was called the *formal* organization. Today, it is generally known as *structuralism.* Structuralists tend to think that a properly structured organization will improve organizational performance. When we combine small school districts into larger ones, or adopt school-based management, or modify the interface between elementary schools and high schools by creating middle schools, structuralist thought is guiding our administrative practice.

But the organization, with all its formal structure and the rules and regulations to interpret and reinforce that structure, is populated by human beings with their very human and personal beliefs, attitudes, assumptions, hopes, and fears, and such inner states of these people, collectively, go a long way to make the organization what it actually is. Thus, psychological thinking enters the study of organization and administration. Those who emphasize this concept of organization are convinced that changes in the relations between human beings in the organization have enormous power to affect the performance of the organization. This is variously called the *informal* organization or, as it was indelibly labeled in 1960, the *human side* of the organization. Often today it is referred to simply as *people approaches* to organization. When we seek to involve people more fully in making decisions that affect them, attend to their motivational needs more adequately, or increase collegiality and collaboration through teamwork, we are using people approaches to organizational problems.

In the five-year period between 1937 and 1942, however, three significant books appeared that laid the groundwork for what was to develop during the post–World War II era into a new major influence on thought and practice in administration. The first of these landmark books was Chester Barnard's *The Functions of the Executive,* which appeared in 1938. Barnard, a vice president of the New Jersey Bell Telephone Company, selected and integrated concepts from the many schools of thought that had appeared since the publication of Wilson's essay, and he introduced a number of new insights of his own. Barnard was in close communication with the scientists who conducted the Western Electric Studies. One of his most important contributions, and one that is germane to this discussion, was to illuminate the crucial importance of better understanding the relationship between the formal organization and the informal organization. In this pioneer work Barnard made it clear (1) that it was illusory to focus exclusively on the formal, official, structural facets of administering organizations and (2) that the effective executive must attend to the interaction between the needs and aspirations of the workers, on the one hand, and the needs and purposes of the organization, on the other hand.

The next year, 1939, the second of these three significant books appeared: *Management and the Worker,* by Felix J. Roethlisberger and William J. Dickson. These two scholars presented a new view of the dynamic mutual interaction between the formal organization and the informal organization. Based on evidence gathered from the Western Electric Company research, the authors described and documented, for example, the surprising sophistication of the informal organization and its power to exercise control over not only the behavior of workers but also (without their realizing it) over the behavior of supervisors and managers who thought that they were exercising the control. Their emphasis on "individual needs, informal groups, and social relationships was quickly endorsed by other social scientists and led to a 'philosophy of management' concerned primarily with human relationships in formal organizations."[24]

Finally, the third of this triumvirate of early books was Herbert A. Simon's *Administrative Behavior,* which was published in 1947. Even the title, with its emphasis on behavior, foreshadowed a fresh approach to understanding administrative practice. Simon—a professor with a strong background in political science, psychology, and business administration—sought to illuminate the importance of human behavior in such critical administrative processes as making decisions. This book, more than any other, established a fresh new concept of administration and set the pace for social and behavioral scientists who sensed in the post–World War II era that there was great promise in this new approach.

Although the adherents of classical and human relations approaches did not vanish in the years that followed, the most vigorous administrative research was in the areas of extending and developing the newer behavioral concepts. Scientists from a number of disciplines, or traditions, were to publish a steady stream of research and theory during the ensuing years. A list of a few of the better-known books published in the 1950s and 1960s, roughly classified by the academic tradition of their authors, presents a rather clear overview of the way the field developed:

Psychology and Social Psychology

ALVIN W. GOULDNER, ED., *Studies in Leadership* (1950)

CHRIS ARGYRIS, *Personality and Organization* (1958)

BERNARD M. BASS, *Leadership, Psychology, and Organizational Behavior* (1960)

MUZAFIR SHERIF, ED., *Intergroup Relations and Leadership* (1962)

RENSIS LIKERT, *The Human Organization: Its Management and Value* (1967)

Sociology

AMITAI ETZIONI, *A Comparative Analysis of Complex Organizations* (1961)

PETER M. BLAU AND W. RICHARD SCOTT, *Formal Organizations* (1962)

CHARLES PERROW, *Organizational Analysis: A Sociological View* (1970)

Anthropology

WILLIAM FOOTE WHYTE, *Men at Work* (1961)

ELIOT DISMORE CHAPPLE AND LEONARD R. SAYLES, *The Measure of Management* (1961)

HARRY F. WOLCOTT, *The Man in the Principal's Office* (1973)

Political Science

VICTOR A. THOMPSON, *Modern Organization* (1961)

ROBERT V. PRESTHUS, *The Organizational Society* (1962)

MARILYN GITTEL, *Participants and Participation: A Study of School Policy in New York City* (1967)

Management

DOUGLAS MCGREGOR, *The Human Side of Enterprise* (1960)

RENSIS LIKERT, *New Patterns of Management* (1961)

ALFRED J. MARROW, DAVID G. BOWERS, AND STANLEY E. SEASHORE, *Management by Participation* (1967)

Human Relations and Organizational Behavior

The term *human relations* is a broad one that refers to the interactions between people in all kinds of situations in which they seek, through mutual action, to achieve some purpose. Thus, it can properly be applied to two people seeking to develop a happy and productive life together, a social club, a business firm, a school, or, indeed, an entire government or even a whole society. The social structure that regulates the human interactions that are the subject of human relations may be formal, clear, and readily apparent (for example, a government, a firm), or it may be informal, even diffuse, and, therefore, difficult to describe accurately (for example, the power structure of a group of prison inmates, the social system of a school faculty, or a neighborhood).

Organizational behavior is a narrower, more precise term that falls under the broader, more general meaning of human relations. Organizational behavior is a discipline that seeks to describe, understand, and predict human behavior in the environment of formal organizations. A distinctive contribution and characteristic of organizational behavior as a discipline is the explicit recognition that (1) organizations create con-textual settings, or environments, that have great influence on the behavior of people in them and that (2) to some extent the internal environment of an organization is in-fluenced by the larger context in which the organization itself exists (for example, the social, political, economic, and technological systems that support the organiza-tion). Moreover, the internal environment or context of the organization (which is so influential in eliciting and shaping human behavior) is not merely physical and tangi-ble but also includes the social and psychological characteristics of the living human system.

Because management/administrative science has effective performance of goal-seeking formal organizations as its central focus, organizational behavior is closely linked with that science also. Management and administration necessarily must bear responsibil-ity for establishing internal arrangements of the organization so as to achieve maximum effectiveness. In the early years of human relations it was common for managers and administrators to speak of the human relations of employees or human relations of the firm as though the organization and the wellsprings of its employees' behavior were separate though related. Contemporary administrative science, on the other hand, views goal-directed organizational behavior as essential to results-oriented, cooperative endeav-ors that cannot be teased out from the management policies and administrative practices of the system.

Educational administration was affected very little by the evolution of administration as a field of study until the middle of the twentieth century, largely because the teaching of educational administration was sequestered from the mainstreams of scholarly thought and research. Schools of education in even the most prestigious universities tended to have almost no contact with the business schools and the behavioral science departments on their own campuses. Traditionally, educational administration had been taught by former school superintendents whose knowledge of their subject came largely from years of hard-earned experience in the "front lines." Courses in educational administration tended to focus on practical, "how-to-do-it" problems, drawing on the past experience of practicing adminis-trators. Emphasis was typically given to sharing the techniques of these administrators for solving problems—techniques that had been tried in school districts such as the ones with which the students were familiar.

Research in educational administration during the first half of the twentieth cen-tury consisted principally of status studies of current problems or the gathering of opin-ion. With rare exceptions, little research in educational administration dealt with the testing of theoretical propositions, and virtually none of it involved the insights and research methods that had been developed by behavioral scientists. As Van Miller has observed:

> A lot of the study of administration has been a matter of looking backward or sideways at what was done or what is being done. It is striking to contemplate how much administrative experience has been exchanged and how little it has been studied scientifically. The current excitement arises from the fact that within recent years educational administration has be-come a field of study and of development as well as a vocation.[25]

By the mid-1950s a new concept of organization was gaining wide acceptance among students of educational administration. This new concept recognized the dynamic interrelationships between (1) the structural characteristics of the organization and (2) the personal characteristics of the individual. It sought to understand the behavior of people at work in terms of the dynamic interrelationships between the organizational structure and the people who populated it.

Using this insight, students of organization began to conceptualize organizations—such as school systems and schools—as *social systems*. Although it is true that nearly any human group[26] constitutes a human social system (including such diverse groups as street gangs, hobby clubs, and church congregations), the concept that began to emerge in this post–World War II era was that *organizations* constitute a *particular kind* of social system: essentially, they are characterized by a clear and relatively strong *formal* structure. For example, unlike such informal human social systems as the office bowling team or the secretaries who eat lunch together, school systems and schools (and, indeed, all formal organizations) may be characterized as follows:[27]

1. They are specifically goal oriented.
2. The work to be done so as to achieve goals is divided into subtasks and assigned as official duties to established positions in the organization.
3. These positions are arranged hierarchically in the formal organization, and authority relationships are clearly established.
4. General and impersonal organizational rules govern, to a large extent, what people do in their official capacity and also, to a large extent, shape and delimit the interpersonal interactions of people in the organization.

Beginning in the mid-1950s, increasing attention was devoted to efforts to better understand the relationships among (1) these characteristics of organizational structure, (2) the personality (and consequent "needs") of individuals in the organization, and (3) behavior on the job. For example, numerous studies of leader behavior conducted in the 1950s and 1960s revealed remarkable agreement on the point that leadership can be best understood in terms of two specific kinds of behavior: (1) behavior that gives structure to the work of the group (for example, how the work is to be done, when, by whom, and so forth) and (2) behavior that is perceived by subordinates as showing consideration for the subordinates as human beings. These empirically derived insights were widely applied to business, industry, the military, and many other kinds of organizations, as well as to school systems and schools.[28]

The generalization that seemed to arise from empirical tests of this view was that one leadership style promised to be more effective than any other: namely, a style characterized by behavior that emphasized *both* initiating structure *and* consideration for people. In this way, of course, both the demands of the organization and the needs of individuals in dealing with the organization would be met. One study typical of this period, using the popular social systems model, found that school principals who displayed a style that emphasized concern for people tended to view teachers as professionals to a greater extent than did principals who stressed the role of initiating structure in the work group.[29]

In the years from roughly 1955 to 1970, there was a great outpouring of theorizing and research in educational administration which explored the basic concepts of social system (either explicitly or implicitly) as applied to public school systems and schools. Neal Gross, using sociological methods of inquiry, sought to illuminate the reasons school board members and school superintendents in New England made the decisions that they did.[30] Daniel Griffiths initiated landmark work on decision making in educational administration which added considerably to our understanding of the importance of the decision-making behavior of administrators.[31] One of many studies based on Griffiths's work, for example, suggests that if the administrator confines himself or herself to establishing clear processes and procedures for making decisions (rather than actually making the final decisions), the administrator's behavior will be more acceptable to subordinates.

A team of researchers, who were especially interested in understanding the processes of curriculum change in schools, conducted a study to explore the question "To what extent do administrators and teachers in a given school system tend to agree or disagree in their perceptions of decision-making roles and responsibilities?" Among the many findings arising from this complex and comprehensive study, one of the most outstanding—according to Griffiths—was that consideration for subordinates is more valuable behavior for the superintendent to exhibit than behavior intended to initiate structure in the group.

University graduate programs of study for educational administrators soon reflected the influence of social and behavioral science views of organizational behavior. In many cases, courses featuring some of the newer behavioral views—such as leadership, motivation, decision making, organizational climate, conflict management, and organizational change—took their place alongside courses on budgeting, financing, law, and school plant, site, and facilities. It soon became standard practice for writers of textbooks on the school principalship, general administration, and personnel administration to attempt to establish the relevance of organizational behavior research and concepts to the specific areas that the book addressed. Many professors, in their research and consulting activities, used these new ideas in their analysis of practical problems in actual schools, as well as in the design of in-service training activities.

Conclusion

Much of the current debate about school reform and educational leadership—whether in academic literature, in the popular press, or in discussions between practitioners—manifests different, frequently incompatible, ideas about the nature of schools as organizations and the behavior of people who work in them. This debate has its roots in the larger debate about whether organizations are best understood as hierarchical, bureaucratic systems or as collegial, collaborative systems. That debate emerged in the first half of the twentieth century with the publication of the Western Electric Studies and has been continually stimulated by the growth and spread of research in group dynamics and human resources development. Though the human resources view has over time steadily grown in influence in the realms of business and the military as well as in education, many individuals in executive and leadership positions still cling to classical notions of hierarchical power relationships. It is important for the student of education to be aware of this, and it is especially important to examine the issues and make a clear personal commitment on where to stand on those issues as a guide to professional practice in educational leadership.

The struggle to develop understanding of human resources approaches to organizational behavior has led to the development of a number of theoretical views that can be helpful in clarifying issues confronting the educational leader. Chapter 4 examines a number of these newer views.

Reflective Activities

1. Examine the concepts from this chapter related to scientific management, bureaucratic organizational theory, and classical organizational theory. Which concepts, if any, do you believe are viable for today's schools? Describe why you believe these can still be effective.

2. Organizations have elements of scientific management, bureaucratic organizational theory, classical organizational theory, and/or human relations concepts that predominate. Using the concepts presented in this chapter, describe the management model of the organization (for example, school) where you are employed. In your opinion, is the existing model of management in your school or work environment the most effective for the organization? If so, indicate why. What specific outcomes do you believe are attributable to this model of management? If it is not a desirable organizational model, what would you suggest as an alternative?

3. Complete a sociogram of the teachers and administrators in your grade level, department, and/or school, whichever is most helpful to you in analyzing informal relationship structures. Analyze the results in terms of how many informal groups exist and the size of these groups. Are they influential? Are they loners? Are they connected to the formal decision-making structure of the school?

4. *Working on Your Game Plan.* Chaper 3 described two different approaches to understanding organizations and behavior. One is from the classical perspective (organizations are characteristically hierarchical and bureaucratic) and the other is from the human relations perspective (organizations are characteristically collegial and collaborative). In our present era of school reform, both of these perspectives are alive and well and competing for your attention and your allegiance as a leader. As you plan to exercise leadership in schools, write a paragraph for your game plan expressing your thoughts and present commitment on two issues:

- What ideas from these two perspectives on organization and human behavior do you find most useful in analyzing the problems of being a leader in schools? How would you translate those ideas into things that you do—or how you would do them—as a leader on the job?

- What connection do you perceive between the ideas that you discussed and present-day human problems in the schools (such as motivation, student achievement, or morale)?

Suggested Reading

Callahan, Raymond E., *Education and the Cult of Efficiency.* Chicago: University of Chicago Press, 1962.

    Recounts the events of an early period in the twentieth century when U.S. business and industrial leaders sought to improve public schooling by forcing school boards across the country to adopt their organizational values and goals. If you think that what goes around comes around, you will find a powerful message for today in this fascinating account.

Etzioni, Amitai, *Modern Organizations.* Englewood Cliffs, NJ: Prentice-Hall, 1964.

    A remarkably lucid, easy-to-read explanation of the fundamentals of modern organizational thought. Truly a classic in the literature of organization and behavior.

Morgan, Gareth, *Images of Organization.* Beverly Hills, CA: Sage Publications, 1986.

    This well-written book describes seven different ways of thinking about organizations, using such metaphors as organizations as machines, as political systems, as cultures, and so on. The author goes on to describe the advantages and disadvantages of using each metaphor.

Organizational Theory in the Modern Period

LEARNING OBJECTIVES

After reading this chapter, you should be able to

- Identify five organizational mechanisms often used to establish and maintain control and coordination in bureaucratic organizations.
- Describe and explain, with examples, how much of the current school reform movement uses bureaucratic ideas and practices.
- Explain how human resources development concepts of organization differ from bureaucratic concepts.
- Identify and describe Theory X and Theory Y.
- Explain the concept of an organization as an open social system.
- Describe how role theory is related to social systems theory.
- Explain and discuss the concept $B = f(R \bullet P)$.
- Explain the role of the following factors in evoking the behavior of people in an organization: task, structure, people, and technology.
- Explain the key differences between viewing an organization in traditional classical terms and viewing it as an organic system.
- Describe some key ways in which chaos theory differs markedly from traditional systems theory.

ISLLC Standards

STANDARD 2: A school administrator is an educational leader who promotes the success of all students by advocating, nurturing, and sustaining a school culture and instructional program conducive to student learning and staff professional growth.

Knowledge

The administrator has knowledge and understanding of:

- school cultures

Dispositions

The administrator believes in, values, and is committed to:

- preparing students to be contributing members of society

Performances

The administrator facilitates processes and engages in activities ensuring that:

- the responsibilities and contributions of each individual are acknowledged
- barriers to student learning are identified, clarified, and addressed
- technologies are used in teaching and learning
- student and staff accomplishments are recognized and celebrated
- the school is organized and aligned for success
- curriculum decisions are based on research, expertise of teachers, and the recommendations of learned societies
- the school culture and climate are assessed on a regular basis
- a variety of sources of information is used to make decisions

STANDARD 3: A school administrator is an educational leader who promotes the success of all students by ensuring management of the organization, operations, and resources for a safe, efficient, and effective learning environment.

Knowledge

The administrator has knowledge and understanding of:

- theories and models of organizations and the principles of organizational development
- operational procedures at the school and district levels
- human resources management and development
- principles and issues relating to fiscal operations of school management

Dispositions

The administrator believes in, values, and is committed to:

- making management decisions to enhance learning and teaching
- trusting people and their judgments
- accepting responsibility
- high-quality standards, expectations, and performances

Performances

The administrator facilitates processes and engages in activities ensuring that:

- knowledge of learning, teaching, and student development is used to inform management decisions
- operational procedures are designed and managed to maximize opportunities for successful learning
- emerging trends are recognized, studied, and applied as appropriate
- operational plans and procedures to achieve the vision and goals of the school are in place
- potential problems and opportunities are identified
- organizational systems are regularly monitored and modified as needed
- stakeholders are involved in decisions affecting schools
- responsibility is shared to maximize ownership and accountability
- effective group-process and consensus-building skills are used
- effective communication skills are used
- there is effective use of technology to manage school operations
- a caring school community is developed

STANDARD 6: A school administrator is an educational leader who promotes the success of all students by understanding, responding to, and influencing the larger political, social, economic, legal, and cultural context.

Knowledge

The administrator has knowledge and understanding of:

- the role of public education in developing and renewing a democratic society and an economically productive nation
- the political, social, cultural, and economic systems and processes that impact schools
- global issues and forces affecting teaching and learning
- the dynamics of policy development and advocacy under our democratic political system

Dispositions

The administrator believes in, values, and is committed to:

- education as a key to opportunity and social mobility
- the importance of a continuing dialogue with other decision makers affecting education
- actively participating in the political and policy-making context in the service of education

Performances

The administrator facilitates processes and engages in activities ensuring that:

- the environment in which schools operate is influenced on behalf of students and their families

From its beginnings in the mid-1920s until roughly the mid-1970s, the search for understanding of organizational behavior was dominated and controlled by scholars who believed in traditional methods of laboratory science, which were drawn from logical positivism. This is now referred to as the modern period. Throughout subsequent decades, therefore, the scholars who dominated the study of organizational behavior demanded the use of a single way of thinking about organizations and the behavior of people in them. They demanded the use of theory and scientific techniques for testing theory—techniques that they thought were objective, detached from the people being studied, and relied on mathematical proof as the highest goal of investigation. However, it eventually became obvious that this severely delimited approach of the logical-positivist tradition borrowed from the physical sciences was relatively barren for the school practitioner, yielding little that could be applied with confidence to the praxis of educational leadership. Indeed, some leading scholars had endeavored to point out that the fundamental fatal flaw in this narrowly "scientific" approach lay in the rigid demand by influential academicians that only hypothetico-deductive ways of thinking be used in attempting to understand organizational life. Nevertheless, a number of ways of thinking about organizations—that is, a number of useful organizational theories—were developed during the modern period that have proved over time to be useful to school leaders in thinking about and implementing leadership strategies. These theories also can be helpful to you in thinking about organizations and the behavior of people in them. This overview starts with a brief grounding in what theory is, then proceeds to compare and contrast bureaucratic theory and human resources theory. Finally you are presented with several systems models of organization, in which various scholars have sought to describe their understanding of the interrelationships between the notion of organizational structure and the people who populate the organization.

Describing systems models of organizational life is a great deal like the chalk-talk diagrams that a TV commentator uses during a football game. They can lay out and describe the concepts that underlie the game, but they must be understood in the context of the uncertainty and unpredictability that are always present in human endeavor. Models are useful for giving you a mental road map of how organizations work, something that you can use in the practical business of sorting out organizational problems and planning to solve them. They are helpful in clarifying important issues involving organizational behavior. But they are not *literal* depictions of an organizational mechanism, as they are sometimes mistakenly taken to be. For example, some people have rhapsodized about systems theories of organizations using the metaphor of old-fashioned clockworks, in which pendulums swing with unerring predictability, gears whir, springs unwind, balance wheels, cogs, escapement, and other parts all move synchronously in near-perfect predictable relationships to produce the desired result, namely, to tell the correct time. Organizations, after all, especially educational organizations, are human endeavors, and—to the despair of those seeking simplicity, precision, system, order, and certainty in human affairs—cannot be reduced to mechanistic systems. We are dealing with *human social systems.*

Organizational Theory

Discussion of different perspectives that may be used in thinking about organizations—such as bureaucratic and nonbureaucratic—is really discussion of organizational theory. Many practicing educational administrators are skeptical of theory, often thinking of it as some ideal state or idle notion (commonly associated with the pejorative "ivory tower"), whereas they must deal with the tough practicalities of daily life. The position being taken here is that, far from being removed from daily life, theory is crucial in shaping our everyday perception and understanding of commonplace events.

Theory Defined and Described

Theory is systematically organized knowledge thought to explain observed phenomena. Just as we have theories about the causes of disease, the forces that make it possible for airplanes to fly, and the nature of the solar system, we also have theories about organizations and how they work. Just as there are theoretical reasons that underlie the fact that we know that we should wash our hands frequently, exercise regularly, and maintain a nutritionally sound diet, there should be theoretical underpinnings to our understanding of schools as organizations and how to make them ever more effective.

Theory is useful insofar as it provides a basis for thinking systematically about complex problems, such as understanding the nature of educational organizations. It is useful because it enables us to *describe* what is going on, *explain* it, *predict* future events under given circumstances, and—essential to the professional practitioner—think about ways to exercise *control* over events.

Two Major Perspectives on Educational Organizations

Since the dawn of organizational studies in the twentieth century, people have generally elected to conceptualize organizations in one of two ways. One, the classical, traditional view, is often called "bureaucratic," though in the rhetoric of educational reform in recent years many choose to speak of it as the "factory model" of organization. Whatever name is used, bureaucratic organization is epitomized by the image of the eighteenth-century army of Frederick the Great with its characteristically mechanical regimentation, top-down authority, and "going by the book." To this day, bureaucratic organization remains by far the most common ideal of organization worldwide. Indeed, to many people, this is the defining concept of what an organization is.

As time passed, two things happened that have created seemingly irreversible challenges to bureaucratic concepts of organization and have given rise to newer ways of thinking about organization:

1. *The constant growth and accelerating tempo of change in the world.* The seemingly geometric acceleration in the development of technology and changes in politics,

economics, and society have generally left rigid bureaucracies floundering and unresponsive.

2. *The worldwide rise in expectations for increased democracy, personal freedom, individual respect and dignity, and opportunities for self-fulfillment.* Whereas prior to World War II teachers perforce submitted to the authority of the bureaucratic organization and unhesitatingly accepted its dictates with little thought of marching to their own personal drummer, that era in educational organizations is long gone, and seemingly gone forever.

Organizations, particularly educational organizations, are so ubiquitous—so commonplace—that we frequently deal with them with scant examination of the assumptions about them that we often take virtually for granted. A major concern of contemporary organizational views is to clarify and differentiate between the assumptions that underlie the two major competing views of what organizations are all about: classical (or bureaucratic) views, on the one hand, and the newer perspectives, often called "human resources development," on the other hand. Consider, for example, two contrasting approaches to the problem of coordinating and controlling the behavior of people to achieve the goals of the organization.

Bureaucratic Views

The bureaucratic approach tends to emphasize the following five mechanisms in dealing with issues of controlling and coordinating the behavior of people in the organization:

1. *Maintain firm hierarchical control of authority and close supervision of those in the lower ranks.* The role of the administrator as inspector and evaluator is stressed in this concept.

2. *Establish and maintain adequate vertical communication.* This helps to ensure that good information will be transmitted up the hierarchy to the decision makers and orders will be clearly and quickly transmitted down the line for implementation. Because the decision makers must have accurate information concerning the operating level in order to make high-quality decisions, the processing and communicating of information up the line is particularly important but often not especially effective. The use of computers to facilitate this communication is highly attractive to adherents of this concept.

3. *Develop clear written rules and procedures to set standards and guide actions.* These include curriculum guides, policy handbooks, instructions, standard forms, duty rosters, rules and regulations, and standard operating procedures.

4. *Promulgate clear plans and schedules for participants to follow.* These include teachers' lesson plans, bell schedules, pull-out schedules, meeting schedules, budgets, lunch schedules, special teacher schedules, bus schedules, and many others.

5. *Add supervisory and administrative positions to the hierarchy of the organization as necessary to meet problems that arise from changing conditions confronted by*

the organization. For example, as school districts and schools grew in size, such positions as assistant principal, chairperson, director, and coordinator appeared. As programs became more complex, positions for specialists appeared; director of special education, coordinator of substance abuse programs, school psychologist, and school social worker are a few examples.

The widespread acceptance of these as the preferred mechanisms for exercising control and coordination in schools is illustrated by the reform movement that burst on the scene in the early 1980s. The effectiveness of schools arose as a major theme in the public agenda on education in the 1980s to join the linked duo that had been inherited from the 1970s—equality and access. Although there had been a steadily growing body of research literature on effective schools and what they were like, a virtually unrelated "reform movement" suddenly erupted in 1983 that—in the popular press and electronic media, at least—seized the center stage and strongly influenced numerous efforts to improve the functioning of schools. This is of interest to us here because it illustrates the very strong conviction of many educational leaders that bureaucratic theory is highly useful in thinking about schools and how to improve them.

During the biennium of 1982–1983, led by *A Nation at Risk,* issued by the National Commission on Excellence in Education, no fewer than ten major reports were published on the state of public education in the United States. Each of these cataloged various deficiencies perceived by the reporters and proffered an array of corrective measures to deal with them. If nothing else, they stand as testimony to the widespread concern about the effectiveness of public schooling at the time, and they were the source of considerable popular discussion of the shortcomings of public schooling in the press and electronic media. Indeed, for the first time in the history of the Republic—thanks in large part to the interest stimulated by these reports (and approximately twenty others that were to appear by mid-1985)—the president of the United States chose to elevate the discussion of the condition of U.S. public schools to the level of presidential discourse and politics. The Educational Commission of the States counted no fewer than 175 state-level active task forces on education that were issuing recommendations in 1983. By 1985, a total of some thirty reports and calls for reform had appeared in print. This extraordinary outpouring of concern for the effectiveness of public schools in the United States resulted in a dazzling array of observations and recommendations for improvement and an unprecedented, broad-scale discussion of what became known as the movement for public school "reform." One veteran observer called it "the best opportunity for school renewal we will get in this century." Considering that a mere sixteen years then remained in the century, that seemed like a hardly overoptimistic assessment.

The profusion of recommendations emanating from this body of work was predominantly based on traditional assumptions about the nature of schools held by at least some of those who conducted the studies and certainly many who read them. Of course, there were many variations and differences among the recommendations of the reports, some being partially in conflict with one another. Essentially, however, the gist of the major recommendations ran as follows.

Somehow, goals of the schools (then described by John Goodlad as being mired in a conceptual swamp) should be simplified, clarified, and limited; all students should be required to complete some sort of core curriculum (bereft of "soft, nonessential courses" as the Education Commission of the States put it); mastery of the English language should be emphasized, but greater stress should also be given to math, the sciences, and computer technology; teachers should be paid more, trained better, and provided with better working conditions; schools should be more effectively linked to outside leadership groups—principally partnerships with business and more effective relationships with the state and federal governments; the school day and school year should be extended and reorganized with a keen eye to time on task, and more homework should be assigned to students; the status of teaching and teachers should be enhanced by such means as improving compensation, creating career ladders so as to reward superior teachers for superior teaching performance, and professionalizing the working environment of teachers; and stronger educational leadership should be developed, chiefly at the level of the school principalship.

In sum, the recommendations emanating from these reports on the state of education in the United States have been described as barren in terms of large-scale influence, containing few fresh ideas and few promising initiatives, and offering essentially warmed-over ideas of modest conceptual strength.[1] In response to the stimulus of the various reports, every state and numerous local school districts sought quickly to implement some of the recommendations. Predictably, the manner of implementation has weighed heavily on the side of traditional bureaucratic mandates intended to compel schools to effect change.

For example, many states issued new rules, regulations, and mandates to "toughen up" the curriculum in local schools. Frequently, these were aimed at such things as reducing the number of elective courses and increasing the number of required courses, as well as dictating the assignment of homework by teachers. The impact of such efforts at reform in improving the instructional effectiveness of schools remains problematic.

This is well illustrated by the effort to extend both the school year and the school day. At the time of its appearance in 1983, one of the popular recommendations of *A Nation at Risk* was that "school districts and state legislatures should consider the seven-hour school day and the 200 or 220 day school year" as a means of providing more time for instruction. This would appear to be a relatively simple change to effect, requiring only a clear mandate from the state. Though several states did mandate additional days to be added to the minimum pupil–teacher contact days, the net effect nationwide was simply to move some states closer to the already existing national average of 180 days of instruction per year. Arkansas, for example, decided to move from its 175-day school year to a 180-day year by 1989. Colorado went from 172 school days per year to 176 in 1984. Several other states extended the work year *for teachers* while holding the number of instructional days *for students.* Thus, Florida, Tennessee, and North Carolina each requires 180 days of student–teacher contact time while permitting the employment of teachers for additional days to cover emergency closings, in-service training programs, and other administrative purposes. The net effect has been scant change nationally. In 1985 the school year ranged from a high of 184 days in Washington, D.C., to a low of

173 days in North Dakota, with 29 states clustered at the national average of 180 school days. Viewing the resistance to a longer school calendar from employers in agriculture and the travel industry as well as from the general public, the Education Commission of the States concluded in 1985 that the 200- or 220-day school year was "not realistic" and that "there may be a bigger payoff in wringing more honest instruction time out of the regular day, and this may be the only acceptable solution as far as parents and the public are concerned."[2] In other words, it does not appear likely that schools will move much beyond the "time on task" concept that had been widely implemented in schools long before the appearance of the report.

Virtually all of the "reform" proposals have assumed a top-down strategy similar to this; that is, decisions are made in the legislature or another place high in the hierarchy, such as the state education department, and handed down to be implemented by teachers in their classrooms. For example, the California Business Roundtable—composed of large business corporations in the state—managed to get the legislature to enact (and the governor to sign) a new major education law for California that was funded for $2.7 billion over a two-year period—money that the schools desperately needed in the wake of the stringent cutbacks that had been imposed as a result of Proposition 13. The new law—150 pages long—prescribed in detail things that were to be done in the classrooms (for example, what textbooks to use, how many minutes of instruction would be given in a particular subject) and specified how the state education bureaucracy would audit and verify compliance with all these complex provisions. Similarly, the New York State Board of Regents developed an Action Plan accompanied by the "Part 100 Regulations" that enabled the Regents to reach into virtually every public school classroom in the state to direct, implement, and verify compliance with a comprehensive set of highly detailed directives for changes in school practice. These specify not only policy directions (such as the goals or intent desired) but also, by directives, such things as requiring certain remedial instruction to be carried on in rooms separate from regular classrooms, specifying the types of instruction to be used, and indicating the periods of time. In the 1980s, every state developed and implemented similar plans—more or less comprehensive, perhaps, but virtually all using bureaucratic assumptions as the basis for change strategy.

Clearly, there is a strong tendency for contemporary educational reformers to have in mind a set of assumptions about the nature of schools on which the logic of their efforts pivots. Those assumptions are the same as those underlying the old-fashioned factory, in which management decided what was to be done, directed the workers to do it, then supervised them closely to be sure that the directives were followed in full. Denis Doyle and Terry Hartle observed:

> It simply doesn't work that way. The impulse to reform the schools from the top down is understandable: it is consistent with the history of management science. The explicit model for such reform was the factory; Frederick Taylor's scientific management revolution did for the schools the same thing that it did for business and industry—created an environment whose principal characteristics were pyramidal organization. . . . The teacher was the worker on the assembly line of education; the student, the product; the superintendent, the chief executive officer; the school trustees, the board of directors; and the taxpayer, the shareholder.[3]

Top-Down School Reform Persists

Though Doyle and Hartle may be right—and many agree that they are—top-down educational reform strategy continues to dominate the political scene, as the No Child Left Behind Act of 2001 clearly demonstrates. The outcome of the entire enterprise unquestionably rests on the unshakable conviction of those in political power in Washington and the state capitals that

1. they have the best ideas about how to bring about improvement in school outcomes in the classrooms of the 15,000 school districts throughout the land,
2. they have sufficient knowledge about the circumstances in those classrooms to make the judgments necessary to draw up action plans and legal mandates to implement them, and
3. top-down organizational strategy is incontestably the most promising option available to bring about the desired changes that are sought in the schools.

The No Child Left Behind Act was—in the history of the Republic until that time—the boldest venture on the part of the federal government to redirect the schooling of children throughout the land. It will take time to see how well founded the confidently held beliefs of politicians in Washington and in the state capitals actually were.

Human Resources Development Views

Doyle and Hartle go on to present a different set of assumptions about the organizational characteristics of schools and the behavior of teachers in their classrooms—a view that places the teacher foremost in creating instructional change and, therefore, questions the wisdom of any change strategy that seeks to force change upon the teacher arbitrarily and without his or her participation in the processes of deciding what should be done. As we have seen, this is far from a new view of organization. But recent failures of bureaucratic methods to rectify severe organizational difficulties—especially in the corporate world—coupled with the emergence of such newer organizational perspectives as loose coupling and the power of organizational cultures to influence behavior has brought human resources development concepts to the fore as a major new way to think about organizational problems.

Whereas bureaucratic theory stresses the primacy of the organization's officially prescribed rules, and their enforcement, as a means of influencing individual participants to perform dependably in predictable ways, human resources development emphasizes using the conscious thinking of individual persons about what they are doing as a means of involving their commitment, their abilities, and their energies in achieving the goals of the organization. The central mechanism through which the organization exercises coordination and control is the socialization of participants to the values and goals of the organization, rather than through written rules and close supervision. Through this intense socialization the participant identifies personally with the values and purposes of the organization and is motivated to see the organization's goals and needs as being closely congruent with his or her own. Thus, the culture of the organization epitomizes not only what the organization stands for but also the aspirations of the individual participants themselves.

The culture of an organization makes clear what the organization stands for—its values, its beliefs, its true (as distinguished from its publicly stated) goals—and provides tangible ways by which individuals in the organization may personally identify with that culture. The culture of an organization is communicated through symbols: typically stories, myths, legends, and rituals that establish, nourish, and keep alive the enduring values and beliefs that give meaning to the organization and make clear how individuals become and continue to be part of the saga of the organization as it develops through time.

In this view, close inspection and supervision are far from the only means of ensuring the predictable performance of participants. Personal identification with the values of the organization's culture can provide powerful motivation for dependable performance even under conditions of great uncertainty and stress. Consider, for example, what it is that causes an individual to join an organization, stay in it, and work toward that organization's goals. A response to this fundamental question is facilitated by Douglas McGregor's Theory X and Theory Y.[4]

Theory X and Theory Y

Theory X rests on four assumptions that the administrator may hold:

1. The average person inherently dislikes work and will avoid it whenever possible.
2. Because people dislike work, they must be supervised closely, directed, coerced, or threatened with punishment in order for them to put forth adequate effort toward the achievement of organizational objectives.
3. The average worker will shirk responsibility and seek formal direction from those in charge.
4. Most workers value job security above other job-related factors and have little ambition.

Administrators who—tacitly or explicitly—accept the assumptions underlying this explanation of humankind will, of course, use them as a guide to action in dealing with employees in the organization. Theory Y, however, embraces some very different assumptions about the nature of people at work:

1. If it is satisfying to them, employees will view work as natural and as acceptable as play.
2. People at work will exercise initiative, self-direction, and self-control on the job if they are committed to the objectives of the organization.
3. The average person, under proper conditions, learns not only to accept responsibility on the job but also to seek it.

4. The average employee values creativity—that is, the ability to make good decisions—and seeks opportunities to be creative at work.

Administrators who—tacitly or explicitly—favor this explanation of the nature of human beings at work could reasonably be expected to deal with subordinates in ways that are quite different from those who hold Theory X views.

These theories are not presented here as something for the reader to accept or reject; they are merely proffered as a simple illustration of how organizational views are actually used by practitioners of educational administration in their work—a guide to rational decisions and actions "on the firing line."

Theory X and Theory Y are obviously two different, contrasting explanations of real-world conditions. They are clearly based on differing assumptions about people. Those of us with administrative, management, or leadership responsibilities tend to believe that one of these theoretic statements is more accurately representative of the nature of human beings than the other. Those of us whose behavior is congruent with our beliefs and perceptions will act in ways that are harmonious with the theoretic statement that we think is true. Those who tend to hold a Theory X view of people, for example, will tend to believe that motivation is basically a matter of the carrot and the stick; they will tend to accept readily the necessity for close, detailed supervision of subordinates, and they will tend to accept the inevitability of the need to exercise down-the-line hierarchical control in the organization. Collaborative, participative decision making will tend to be viewed as perhaps a nice ideal in the abstract but not very practical in the real world.

As Chris Argyris put it, Theory X views give rise to Behavior Pattern *A* on the part of leaders.[5] This pattern of behavior may take one of two principal forms:

1. Behavior Pattern *A, hard,* is characterized by no-nonsense, strongly directive leadership, tight controls, and close supervision.
2. Behavior Pattern *A, soft,* involves a good deal of persuading, "buying" compliance from subordinates, benevolent paternalism, or so-called good (that is, manipulative) human relations.

In either case, Behavior Pattern *A,* whether acted out in its hard or its soft form, has the clear intention of manipulating, controlling, and managing in the classical sense. It is based on Theory X assumptions about the nature of human beings at work.

Argyris went on to explain that Theory Y assumptions about people give rise to Behavior Pattern *B.* This is characterized by commitment to mutually shared objectives, high levels of trust, respect, satisfaction from work, and authentic, open relationships. Pattern *B* leadership may well be demanding, explicit, and thoroughly realistic, but it is essentially collaborative. It is a pattern of leader behavior that is intended to be more effective and productive than Pattern *A,* because it is thought to reflect a more accurate understanding of what people at work are really like.

In this discussion of the relationship between theory and understanding organizational behavior in schools, it should be emphasized—as Argyris cautioned—that Behavior Pattern *A, soft,* is often superficially mistaken for Behavior Pattern *B.* This ambiguity has caused considerable confusion among those trying to apply these theoretic ideas to schools:

> Behavior associated with Theory Y assumptions . . . is basically developmental. Here supervisors focus on building identification of and commitment to worthwhile objectives in the work context and upon building mutual trust and respect in the interpersonal context. Success in the work and the interpersonal contexts are assumed interdependent, with important satisfactions for individuals being achieved within the context of accomplishing important work.[6]

The important differences in the assumptions that underlie Behavior Pattern *A, soft,* and Behavior Pattern *B* are compared and contrasted in Figure 4.1.

But the Behavior Pattern *A, soft,* approach often used by supervisors to manipulate teachers into compliance with what is basically highly directive management—in the guise of "good human relations"—has done much in U.S. education to discredit the plausibility of Theory Y as applicable to the real world of schools and school systems. "By treating teachers in a kindly way," Sergiovanni observes, "it is assumed that they will become sufficiently satisfied and sufficiently passive so that supervisors and administrators can run the school with little resistance."[7]

The utility of theorizing in this way is illustrated by the work of Rensis Likert. In more than thirty years of research in schools as well as in industrial organizations, Likert has identified a range of management styles, called Systems 1, 2, 3, and 4. Further, his studies support the hypothesis that the crucial variable that differentiates more effective from less effective organizations is human behavior in the organization:

> The main causal factors [of organizational effectiveness or ineffectiveness] are the organizational climate and the leadership behavior which significantly affect how subordinates deal with each other individually and in work groups in order to produce the end results. These variables can be used to define consistent patterns of management. . . . The range of management styles begins with System 1 which is a punitive authoritarian model and extends to System 4, a participative or group interaction model. In between is System 2, a paternalistic authoritarian style that emphasizes [person-to-person] supervision in a competitive (or isolative) environment, and System 3, which is a [person-to-person] consultative pattern of operation.[8]

Essentially, these four categories of management systems are descriptions of conditions that may be found in schools and school systems. By the 1970s, Likert and others were conducting a number of studies in school settings to ascertain whether these same factors of organizational behavior are applicable to the unique characteristics of effective school systems. Those studies support the view that "the more effective schools are those with a participative environment more toward System 4, while the less effective are much more authoritarian, toward a System 1 pattern of operation."[9]

Figure 4.2 shows that there is a remarkable compatibility between Douglas McGregor's work and that of Likert. Both were basically concerned, not with being nice to people or making work pleasant, but with understanding how to make work organizations more

ASSUMPTIONS UNDERLYING BEHAVIOR PATTERN A, *SOFT* (Theory X, *soft*)	ASSUMPTIONS UNDERLYING BEHAVIOR PATTERN B (Theory Y)

With Regard to People

1. People in our culture, teachers among them, share a common set of needs—to belong, to be liked, to be respected.	1. In addition to sharing common needs for belonging and respect, most people in our culture, teachers among them, desire to contribute effectively and creatively to the accomplishment of worthwhile objectives.
2. Although teachers desire individual recognition, they, more importantly, want to feel useful to the school.	2. The majority of teachers are capable of exercising far more initiative, responsibility, and creativity than their present job or work circumstances require or allow.
3. They tend to cooperate willingly and to comply with school, department, and unit goals if these important needs are fulfilled.	3. These capabilities represent untapped resources that are currently being wasted.

With Regard to Participation

1. The administrator's basic task is to make each teacher believe that he or she is a useful and an important part of the team.	1. The administrator's basic task is to create an environment in which teachers can contribute their full range of talents to the accomplishment of school goals. The administrator works to uncover the creative resources of the teachers.
2. The administrator is willing to explain his or her decisions and to discuss teachers' objections to his or her plans. On routine matters, teachers are encouraged in planning and in decision making.	2. The administrator allows and encourages teachers to participate in important as well as routine decisions. In fact, the more important a decision is to the school, the greater are the administrator's efforts to tap faculty resources.
3. Within narrow limits, the faculty unit or individual teachers who comprise the faculty unit should be allowed to exercise self-direction and self-control.	3. Administrators work continually to expand the areas over which teachers exercise self-direction and self-control as they develop and demonstrate greater insight and ability.

With Regard to Expectations

1. Sharing information with teachers and involving them in school decision making will help satisfy their basic needs for belonging and for individual recognition.	1. The overall quality of decision making and performance will improve as administrators and teachers make use of the full range of experience, insight, and creative ability that exists in their schools.
2. Satisfying these needs will improve teacher morale and will reduce resistance to formal authority.	2. Teachers will exercise responsible self-direction and self-control in the accomplishment of worthwhile objectives that they understand and have helped establish.

FIGURE 4.1   Comparison of assumptions underlying Argyris's Behavior Pattern A, *soft*, and Behavior Pattern B. Adapted from Thomas J. Sergiovanni, "Beyond Human Relations," in *Professional Supervision for Professional Teachers*, ed. Thomas J. Sergiovanni (Alexandria, VA: Association for Supervision and Curriculum Development, 1975), pp. 12–13. Copyright © 1975 ASCD. Reprinted by permission. All rights reserved.

121

THEORY X	*System 1*	*Management is seen as having no trust in subordinates.*
		a. Decision imposed—made at the top.
		b. Subordinates motivated by fear, threats, punishment.
		c. Control centered on top management.
		d. Little superior–subordinate interaction.
		e. People informally opposed to goal by management.
	System 2	*Management has condescending confidence and trust in subordinates.*
		a. Subordinate seldom involved in decision making.
		b. Rewards and punishment used to motivate.
		c. Interaction used with condescension.
		d. Fear and caution displayed by subordinates.
		e. Control centered on top management but some delegation.
	System 3	*Management seen as having substantial but not complete trust in subordinates.*
		a. Subordinates make specific decisions at lower levels.
		b. Communication flows up and down the hierarchy.
		c. Rewards, occasional punishment, and some involvement are used to motivate.
		d. Moderate interaction and fair trust exist.
		e. Control is delegated downward.
THEORY Y	*System 4*	*Management is seen as having complete trust and confidence in subordinates.*
		a. Decision making is widely dispersed.
		b. Communication flows up and down and laterally.
		c. Motivation is by participation and rewards.
		d. Extensive, friendly, superior–subordinate interaction exists.
		e. High degree of confidence and trust exists.
		f. Widespread responsibility for the control process exists.

FIGURE 4.2   Likert's Management Systems Theory related to McGregor's Theory X and Theory Y.

effective, which is as pressing a need in business and industry as it is in education. This general point of view is widely and strongly supported by a vast amount of organizational research. Robert R. Blake's and Jane Srygley Mouton's organizational research,[10] Gordon Lippitt's studies of organizational renewal,[11] and Paul Berman's and Milbrey McLaughlin's extensive studies of change in U.S. schools[12] are only a few of the many studies that support the general theoretic position that pioneers such as McGregor and Likert held.

Traditional classical organizational views would indicate the opposite practices: tighten up, exercise stronger discipline and tougher management, and demand more work from subordinates. In the parlance of neoclassical theory, the focus is on teacher accountability, specified performance objectives, and cost–benefit analysis. Yet much of the best research in organizational behavior strongly suggests that this latter approach would be, at best, self-defeating.

A word of caution is in order here. Bureaucratic and human resources perspectives have been compared and contrasted as ideal cases for the purpose of clarifying and delineating the very real, basic differences between them. In the real world of educational administration, of course, one rarely encounters ideal cases, which is not to suggest that organizations cannot properly be classified as being bureaucratic or nonbureaucratic. Indeed, they can be and often are. However, nor does it mean that to be described as nonbureaucratic an organization must be totally devoid of policies, regulations, standard operating procedures, or hierarchical organization, or that to be described as bureaucratic an organization must be totally devoid of sensitivity to or respect for people. This is particularly true of schools, which are bureaucratic in some ways and nonbureaucratic in some very important ways. What it does suggest is that organizations may be properly described as *relatively* bureaucratic or nonbureaucratic. It also suggests that schools are undoubtedly far more organizationally complex than was traditionally understood prior to the mid-1980s.

Organizational Structure and People

A major theme, perhaps the dominant one, in organizational theory for at least a half-century has been the interaction between organizational structure and people. It can be argued, for example, that the structure of an organization is the prime determinant of the behavior of people in the organization. Charles Perrow pointed out that

> one of the persistent complaints in the field of penology, or juvenile correctional institutions, or mental hospitals, or any of the "people-changing" institutions is the need for better workers. Their problems, we hear, stem from the lack of high-quality personnel. More specifically, the types of individuals they can recruit as guards, or cottage parents, or orderlies typically have too little education, hold over-simplified views about people, tend to be punitive, and believe that order and discipline can solve all problems.[13]

He went on to describe a study in which applicants for positions in a juvenile correction institution were, when tested, found to be quite enlightened and permissive, whereas after they had worked in the institution for a while they became less permissive and took a punitive, unenlightened view regarding the causes of delinquency and the care and handling of delinquents. Perrow offered this as an illustration of the power of organizations to shape the views and attitudes—and, thus, behavior—of participants.

On the other hand, much of the literature of organizational theory is devoted to the view that the people in the organization tend to shape the structure of the organization. Much attention is given to the impact of the behavior of people—in the processes of making decisions, leading, and dealing with conflict—on the structure, values, and customs of organizations. Increasingly, attention has been devoted to the possibilities of improving organizations not by changing their structures as a way of inducing more effective organizational behavior, but by training participants in more effective group processes as a way of bringing about desirable changes in organizational structure.

General Systems Theory

Attempts to describe, explain, and predict organizational behavior generally depend—as does all modern scientific thought—on systems theory. A biologist, Ludwig von Bertalanffy, is generally credited with having first outlined, in 1950, the notion of what is now known as general systems theory.[14] The nature of his work and its significance to the science of biology are suggested by the following statement:

> An organism is an integrated system of interdependent structures and functions. An organism is constituted of cells and a cell consists of molecules which must work in harmony. Each molecule must know what the others are doing. Each one must be capable of receiving messages and must be sufficiently disciplined to obey. You are familiar with the laws that control regulation. You know how our ideas have developed and how the most harmonious and sound of them have been fused into a conceptual whole which is the very foundation of biology and confers on it its unity.[15]

This statement captures the basic ideas of a way of considering and analyzing complex situations that have come to be preeminent in both the physical and the social sciences.

If we substitute *organization* for organism, *group* for cell, and *person* for molecule in the above statement about biology, it has relevance for thinking about organizations:

> An *organization* is an integrated system of interdependent structures and functions. An *organization* is constituted of *groups* and a *group* consists of *persons* who must work in harmony. Each *person* must know what the others are doing. Each one must be capable of receiving messages and must be sufficiently disciplined to obey. . . .[16]

Basic Concepts of System

The systems approach to understanding and describing phenomena is well established in both the physical sciences and the social sciences. Social scientists tend to draw their illustrations and analogues from the biological sciences.

A young child, for example, might think of a nearby pond as a wonderful playground, away from the ever-watchful eyes of grown-ups. A fisherman might see it as a great place in which to fill his creel. A farmer might think of it as a good source of water for irrigating his crops. A biologist, however, would tend to view the pond as a system of living things, all of which are interdependent in many ways and all of which are dependent in some ways on the larger environment in which the pond exists (for example, the air and sunlight). In terms of understanding the pond and being able to describe it, it is obvious that we are dealing with different levels of insight. However, in terms of being able to predict more accurately the consequences of things that might be done to the pond—such as pumping a large volume of water from it or removing large numbers of its fish—the biologist clearly has the advantage.

It is this advantage in dealing with cause and effect that has made systems theory so attractive to those concerned with organizational behavior. There is a strong tendency in our culture to ascribe single causes to events; in fact, the causes of even relatively simple organizational events are often very complex. We may be unwilling to accept this fact and, as a way of rejecting it, choose to apply simplistic cause-and-effect logic to our problems.

This was illustrated by congressional interest in reducing automobile accidents in this country, which started out by concentrating on the automobile as a primary cause of accidents. From this flowed a logical line of thought: if we require automobile manufacturers to improve the design of their cars and install certain mechanical safety features, the result would be a reduction in the appalling carnage on our highways.

In fact, however, more careful study seemed to show that automobile accidents are caused by an enormously complex, interrelated set of variables. Automobile design is clearly one, but others include road conditions and such relatively intangible factors as social mores and the psychological state of the driver. As we dig behind each of these conditions (for example, Why was the road built that way? Why was the driver drunk? Why didn't the driver yield the right of way?), we find that each is part of a complex set of interrelated factors of its own. Clearly, significant reduction in automobile accidents must eventually require analysis of the interrelated factors of these complex subsystems of causative factors.

Peter Senge and the Fifth Discipline

New ways of thinking are required in a world that is dominated by change, ambiguity, and the need for nimble, sure-footed organizational performance. Under those conditions, schools must become quick learners. In some very popular publications over the years, Peter Senge has sought to clarify how systems thinking is essential in helping an educational organization to become a learning organization. Senge calls systems thinking the "Fifth Discipline," since he sees it as essential to integrate with four other disciplines: personal mastery, mental models, team learning, and shared vision. "Within every school district, community, or classroom," Senge says, "there might be dozens of different systems worthy of notice: the governance process of the district, the impact of particular policies, the labor–management relationship, curriculum development, the approaches to disciplining students, and the prevailing modes of staff behavior. Every child's life is a system. Every educational practice is a system."* In this complex environment, Senge believes, people who have experience with systems thinking can act with more leverage than a short-attention-span culture generally permits.

*Peter Senge and others, *Schools That Learn: A Fifth Discipline Fieldbook for Educators, Parents, and Everyone Who Cares About Education* (New York: Doubleday/Currency, 2000), p. 78.

Systems theory, then, puts us on guard against the strong tendency to ascribe phenomena to a single causative factor. Similarly, if our car is not running well, we often take what is, in effect, a systems approach to the problem: we get a tune-up from someone who understands the functions and interrelatedness of the subsystems (for example, the ignition system, the fuel system, the exhaust system) that comprise the engine.

These two concepts—the concept of subsystems and the concept of multiple causation—are central to systems theory.

Social Systems Theory

Systems can be divided into two main classes: "open" systems, which interact with their environments, and "closed" systems, which do not interact with their environments. Social systems theory generally deals with open systems, because it is virtually impossible to envisage a social system, such as a school, that is not interactive with its environment. When observers describe certain schools or school systems as closed systems, they generally mean that those organizations tend to try to limit the influence of the community and tend to proceed as though unrelated to the larger real world in which they exist. Thus, in the late 1960s and into the 1970s, it was popular to describe unresponsive school systems that resisted constructive change as closed systems. Though the calumny has a certain ring of scientific credibility, it is in fact technically impossible. The input–output relationship of the school to its larger environment is an endless cyclical interaction between the school and its larger environment.

Figure 4.3 shows schooling as a process involving (1) *inputs* from the larger societal environment (for example, knowledge that exists in that society, values that are held, goals that are desired, and money), (2) the *process* that occurs within the social system we call a school (involving subsystems of organizational structure, people, technology, and work tasks), and—resulting from that process—(3) *outputs* to society (in the form of changed individuals). In this sense it is impossible for a school to be, in fact, a closed system. Indeed, in recent years professional educators have become increasingly aware of the extent and importance of the interaction between the school and its environment—which is, conceptually, the basis for much of what goes on under the rubrics of accountability and community relations.

A Contextual Approach

The input–output concept is often called a "linear model"; it is, in effect, a theory that attempts to explain how things can be described in the real world. It is a seductive concept—seemingly logical, rational, and orderly. It lends itself well to concepts of efficiency, such as cost effectiveness; one can relate the value of inputs to the value of outputs and arrive at relative cost efficiency. It was for a long time a popular concept in analyzing the apparent relative effectiveness of competing programs and technologies. It is now generally recognized that this theoretical model contributed little to our understanding of the ways in which educative organizations function. For example, it presupposes that when students

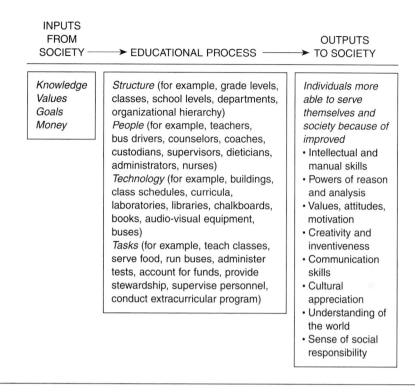

INPUTS
FROM
SOCIETY ⟶ EDUCATIONAL PROCESS ⟶ OUTPUTS
TO SOCIETY

| *Knowledge* *Values* *Goals* *Money* | *Structure* (for example, grade levels, classes, school levels, departments, organizational hierarchy) *People* (for example, teachers, bus drivers, counselors, coaches, custodians, supervisors, dieticians, administrators, nurses) *Technology* (for example, buildings, class schedules, curricula, laboratories, libraries, chalkboards, books, audio-visual equipment, buses) *Tasks* (for example, teach classes, serve food, run buses, administer tests, account for funds, provide stewardship, supervise personnel, conduct extracurricular program) | *Individuals more able to serve themselves and society because of improved* • Intellectual and manual skills • Powers of reason and analysis • Values, attitudes, motivation • Creativity and inventiveness • Communication skills • Cultural appreciation • Understanding of the world • Sense of social responsibility |

FIGURE 4.3   Schooling as an input–process–output system.

and teachers go to school each day, their dominant concerns are to achieve the formal, official goals of the school. Even a casual observer soon learns, however, that actually these people bring to school with them a host of their own beliefs, goals, hopes, and concerns that are more significant and more powerful to them. Clearly, the many subtle ways in which teachers, administrators, and students accommodate to the rules, regulations, and discipline of the school have more to do with the need to survive in a frustrating, crowded environment than with commitment to the achievement of some remote and often ambiguous educational goals.

A more useful approach to understanding educative organizations and the behavior of people in them is to focus our attention on what actually goes on in them. Thus, our attention is centered on examining the inner workings of that system we call an organization. This requires us to see the organization as a whole system that creates the setting, the context, in which the whole pattern of human behavior that characterizes the organization occurs. With this approach we seek to study organizations as systems that create and maintain environments in which complex sets of human interactions (both group and individual) occur with some regularity and predictability. In this view, our understanding of educative organizations requires us to examine the relationships between human behavior and the context (environment, ecology) that are characteristic of the organization. Thus, as we shall discuss in detail in Chapter 6, the organizational culture (climate, ecology, ethos) of the system we call an organization becomes critical to our understanding.

The realm of organizational behavior tends to focus primarily on the school district or on the school as a system. Some scientists, in studying organizational behavior, have unwittingly encouraged the illusion that a school can, in fact, be a closed social system. Andrew Halpin and Don Croft, for example, in their highly influential study of the organizational climate of schools "concentrated on internal organizational characteristics as though they function independently from external influences"[17] and, further, used the terms "open" and "closed" to describe the profiles of schools that represented selected characteristics of what they chose to call "organizational climate."[18] This was, to some extent, a convenience for the researchers: it is, indeed, difficult to study and discuss the behavior of people in a system without assuming (implicitly or otherwise) that the organization is separate from its environment. Many studies of organizational behavior in schools have, in fact, focused on the internal functioning of schools—that is, have treated the schools as closed systems—as though they function independently of influences from their larger outside environments.[19]

In the physical realm, a burning candle has become a classic illustration of an open system: it affects its environment and is affected by it, yet it is self-regulating and retains its own identity. If a door is opened, the candle may flicker in the draft, but it will adjust to it and return to normal at the first opportunity—provided, of course, that the environmental change (the draft) was not so overwhelming as to destroy the system (that is, to extinguish the flame).

It is not so simple to describe *social* systems on even this superficial level. Daniel Griffiths spoke of the organization (the system) as existing in an environment (the suprasystem) and having within it a subsystem (the administrative apparatus of the organization). His diagram is presented in Figure 4.4. The boundaries of the various systems and subsystems are suggested in the figure by the tangential circles; however, we must bear in mind that these boundaries are permeable, permitting interaction between the systems and their environments. One application of this viewpoint can be illustrated by labeling

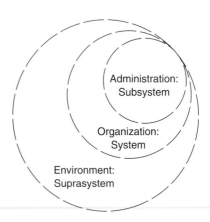

FIGURE 4.4

An organization viewed as an open social system. From Daniel E. Griffiths, "Administrative Theory and Change in Organizations," in *Innovation in Education,* ed. Matthew B. Miles (New York: Teachers College Press, 1964), p. 430. © 1964 by Teachers College, Columbia University. Reproduced by permission of the publisher.

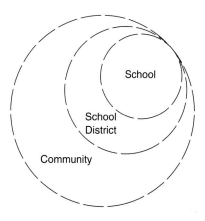

FIGURE 4.5
A social systems view of the school.

the figure, as in Figure 4.5. It then becomes obvious that factors that interfere with the interactive and adaptive relationships among the components of the interrelated parts of the system could pose a threat to the functioning of the whole. One form of interference would be a loss of permeability of one or more of the boundaries, thus tending to make the system closed and less sensitive to environmental change.

Where does the individual fit into all of this? This becomes clearer if we modify the original model, as in Figure 4.6. Here, again, relabeling the diagram can specify—a little more clearly at least—one way in which the view would apply to people working in schools. The individual is functioning in the organization not only as an individual but also as one who occupies a certain *role* within the social system in the organization. In the hypothetical case illustrated in Figure 4.7, the person occupies the role of teacher in the chemistry department of John F. Kennedy Senior High School, a situation possessing a

FIGURE 4.6
Levels of interaction of the individual and the organization. From Richard C. Lonsdale, "Maintaining the Organization in Dynamic Equilibrium," in *Behavioral Science and Educational Administration*, ed. Daniel E. Griffiths. The Sixty-Third Yearbook of the National Society for the Study of Education, Part II (Chicago: National Society for the Study of Education, 1964), p. 143. Reprinted by permission.

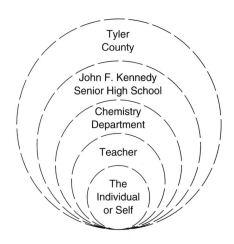

FIGURE 4.7
A social systems view of the individual in a
hypothetical school organization.

number of useful implications for anyone interested in analyzing, predicting, and perhaps controlling organizational behavior.

When we consider the individual person carrying out a unique role in an organization, we become concerned with the complex web of human involvement and its attendant behavior in organizational life. As the individual, with all the needs, drives, and talents that human beings have, assumes an official role, he or she shapes that role to some extent and is also shaped by it. The dynamic interaction of people with varying psychological makeups in the organizational setting is the domain of role theory.

Role Theory

In attempting to analyze face-to-face interpersonal behavior of people in organizations, Erving Goffman, in *The Presentation of Self in Everyday Life,*[20] drew a useful analogy between real-life situations and the unfolding of a play on the stage. People in organizations have definite roles to perform, and many interactive factors help to determine precisely what kind of "performance" each role will receive. Each "actor" must interpret his or her role, and this interpretation depends to some extent on what the individual brings to the role. But behavior in a role as part of an organization—no less than for an actor on the stage—is influenced to some extent by dynamic interplay with other people: other actors and the audience. Role performances are also shaped by the expectations of the director and others attempting to control the situation. Presumably, each actor attempts, to some degree, to behave in conformity with these expectations—and the expectations of colleagues and other referent groups as well. Goffman described the actors in an organization as being on stage when they are formally carrying out their roles, but he points out that backstage there is a different behavioral standard. Those of us connected with schools, for example, know that a certain kind of behavior is exhibited by teachers in the presence of students and their parents, which differs from their behavior in the relative privacy of the teachers' lounge.

Role theory has been used extensively by observers and researchers in many kinds of organizations to better understand and predict organizational behavior. A vocabulary of generally understood terms is fairly well established in the literature. Some of the more commonly used terms are described as follows.

Role.   Role[21] is a psychological concept dealing with behavior enactment arising from interaction with other human beings. The various offices or positions in an organization carry with them certain expectations of behavior held both by onlookers and by the person occupying the role. These expectations generally define the role, with some additional expectation that the individual will exhibit some idiosyncratic personality in role behavior.

Role description.   This refers to the actual behavior of an individual performing a role or, more accurately, one's perception of that behavior.

Role prescription.   This is the relatively abstract idea of what the general norm in the culture is for the role. What kind of role behavior is expected of a teacher in this country, for example?

Role expectation.   This refers to the expectation that one person has of the role behavior of another. Teachers, for example, expect certain behaviors from a principal, and the principal has expectations of behaviors for teachers. Thus, as teacher and principal interact in their roles in the school, they have complementary role expectations.

Role perception.   This term is used to describe the perception that one has of the role expectation that another person holds for him or her. In dealing with the PTA president, for example, the principal knows that the president has some role expectation of the principal. The principal's estimate of that expectation is role perception.

Manifest and latent roles.   Naturally, a person plays more than one role in life; indeed, an individual may well play more than one in an organization. In the case of multiple roles, the term *manifest role* refers to the obvious role that one is performing, but one also occupies *latent roles*. For example, in the classroom, a teacher's manifest role is that of "teacher"; but the teacher may also be the building chairperson for the teachers' union, and that role—while he or she is teaching—is a latent role. A history teacher may also be an activist in a consumers' rights organization and thus holds a latent, as well as a manifest, role.

Role conflict.   This is commonly thought to be a source of less than satisfactory performance in organizations. There are many sources of role conflict, all of which inhibit optimum performance by the role incumbent. An obvious role conflict is a situation in which two persons are unable to establish a satisfactory complementary or reciprocal role relationship, which can result from a wide variety of causes and—not infrequently—may involve a complex set of conflict behaviors. Confusion over role expectation and role perception is commonly observed.

Moreover, role conflict frequently exists within a single individual. The role expectation may clash with the individual personality needs of the role incumbent. A case in point is that of a school principal who was employed by a school district largely because of his innovative skill and strong leadership qualities; when a taxpayers' revolt in the school district suddenly caused a sharp reversal of school board policy, the superintendent was dismissed, and the school board put strong emphasis on economy of operation and conformity to mediocre educational standards. The school principal was plunged into a role conflict situation in which he could not perform to his or anyone else's satisfaction and ended up seeking another job with a more manageable amount of conflict.

A common source of tension from role conflict is the expectation that the incumbent, perhaps an administrator, will be empathetic and understanding in dealing with his or her subordinates and will still enforce the rules of the organization and strongly support the school board in dealing with teachers as members of a collective bargaining unit. Many administrators feel this sort of conflict when they zealously attempt to build trust, confidence, and high morale in the teaching staff and then are required to conduct a formal evaluation or to participate in a grievance procedure that seems to be in conflict with those goals.

Role ambiguity. This arises when the role prescription contains contradictory elements or is vague. Role ambiguity is rather commonly observed in the attempt to preserve the distinction between administration and supervision: the first is generally seen as a "line" authority, whereas the other is thought to be a "staff" responsibility. Yet supervisors are often perceived as being in hierarchical authority over teachers; not infrequently, supervisors feel that they are being maneuvered, against the spirit of their role, into the exercise of authority over teachers, which threatens their more appropriate collegial relationship with them.

Role conflicts such as those described produce tensions and uncertainties that are commonly associated with inconsistent organizational behavior. In turn, this inconsistent behavior, being unpredictable and unanticipated, often evokes further tension and interpersonal conflict between holders of complementary roles. Frequently, those who must perform their roles under the conditions of ambiguity and tension outlined here develop dysfunctional ways of coping with the situation.

Thus, although we may find such socially acceptable avoidance behavior as joking about the conflict or ambiguity, in organizations in which this kind of avoidance is not acceptable rather elaborate and mutually understood avoidance patterns may exist. These can include a studied avoidance of any discussion of the problem or substituting any kind of "small talk" instead. A common avoidance technique is found in ritualistic behavior that permits parties to get through their role performances with a minimum of actual conflict. Vagueness, pomposity, complex structure, clichés, and obscure vocabulary in communication are popular avoidance techniques.[22]

Role set. The notion of *role set* is helpful in clarifying some of the concepts of role theory as they are found to be operational in organizations. If we were to observe a work group, we would, of course, find it possible to sort out the participants into subgroups in a variety of ways. One way would be in terms of role. In the case of the role set that will be used here as an illustration, the pivotal role player may be thought of as an administrator.[23] Naturally, he or she has superordinates in the hierarchy of the organization, people to whom he or she reports (see Figure 4.8). These are key people in the individual's referent group, and they convey their role expectations in many ways. But the administrator not only has superordinates; he or she also has subordinates, or people who report to him or her. As shown in Figure 4.9,

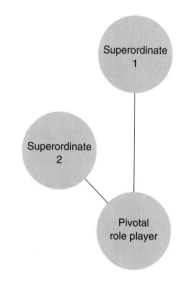

FIGURE 4.8
Relationship of role player to superordinates in the
work group. Adapted from Warren G. Bennis, *Changing
Organizations* (New York: McGraw-Hill Book Company,
1966), p. 193. Reprinted by permission.

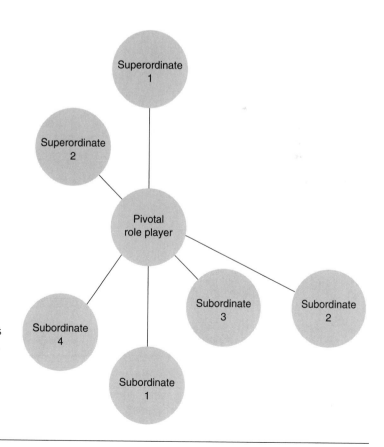

FIGURE 4.9 Relationship
of a pivotal role player to
superordinates and subordinates
in the work group. Adapted from
Warren G. Bennis, *Changing
Organizations* (New York:
McGraw-Hill Book Company,
1966), p. 193. Reprinted by
permission.

subordinates also are significant persons in the administrator's group, and they, too, communicate role expectations to the administrator. Thus, the role player's position becomes pivotal, and it is obvious that the role expectations being communicated are likely to be somewhat in conflict.

The role set is incomplete, however, until a third group of referents is added: the role player's colleagues. With their addition to the role set, as in Figure 4.10, we see the administrator in a pivotal position in relationship to subordinates and superordinates. When we realize that, in this example, twelve persons—two super-ordinates, four subordinates, and six colleagues—are acting as *role senders* (that is, they are communicating role expectations to the administrator), it is evident that the interpersonal dynamics of the role set are complex.

Undoubtedly some role conflict will be present in such a situation, as well as some role ambiguity. Robert Kahn and his colleagues have used this operational concept of role theory to describe and measure role conflict and role ambiguity and

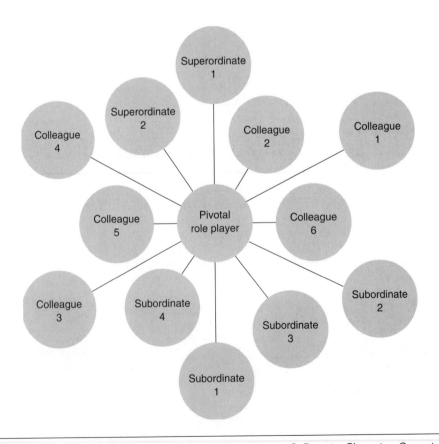

FIGURE 4.10 Illustration of role set. Adapted from Warren G. Bennis, *Changing Organiza-tions* (New York: McGraw-Hill Book Company, 1966), p. 193. Reprinted by permission.

to correlate their presence with attitudes that members of the set have toward their work situation and to the behavioral functioning of these people in the work group.[24] Thus, role set is an important concept considering the ecology of the social setting in which the individual makes his or her contribution to the organization. It is a useful way of conceptualizing the connection between the person and the organization.

To possess knowledge of role theory and some of its concepts is, in itself, of little use. However, the construct can be useful in analyzing some of the interpersonal behavior that we encounter in the work groups of organizations. For example, leaders are concerned with facilitating the acceptance, development, and allocation of roles that are necessary for the group to function well.

Functional Roles in the Group

Kenneth Benne and Paul Sheats have pointed out that a group must fill three types of roles:[25]

1. *Group task roles.* These roles help the group to select the problems to be worked on, to define these problems, and to seek solutions to these problems.
2. *Group building and maintenance roles.* These roles facilitate the development of the group and its maintenance over time.
3. *Individual roles.* These roles enable group members to satisfy their own idiosyncratic needs as individuals.

Although we must be wary of too much labeling, let us consider Benne and Sheats's further description of possible specific roles that are available to group members in meeting two critical needs of a group:

> *Group task roles:* These are roles that help the group to achieve its tasks. They include the roles of (a) initiating action and contributing ideas, (b) seeking information, (c) seeking opinions from the group, (d) giving information, (e) giving one's opinion, (f) coordinating the work of group members, (g) helping to keep the group focused on goals, (h) the evaluator-critic, (i) the energizer who prods the group to action, (j) the procedural technician who attends to routine "house-keeping" tasks of the group, and (k) the recorder.[26]

Benne and Sheats stressed that each of these roles must be played by someone in the group; the leader must either assume these essential roles or see that they are allocated to other members of the group. Part of the leader's responsibility is to provide for the creation of an environment in the group in which these roles can be developed and carried out. Other specific roles are suggested under the second major category:

> *Group building and maintenance:* These roles help the group develop a climate and processes that enable the members to work harmoniously and with a minimum of lost time, such as (a) encouraging members to keep at the task, (b) harmonizing differences between ideas and between individuals, (c) facilitating communication (for example, by helping silent

individuals to speak up and encouraging equal use of "air time"), (d) setting high standards of performance for the group, (e) providing the group with feedback as to its own processes and actions.[27]

These roles are obviously quite different in nature and function from the group task roles. Of course, it is possible that an individual group member will take on more than one role or that two or more members will share a given role.

Role Related to Social Systems Theory

The foregoing discussion enables us to return to social systems with somewhat more insight. The basic notion is that the organization may be understood as a "social system." Jacob Getzels and Egon Guba described this view as follows:

> We conceive of the social system as involving two major classes of phenomena, which are at once conceptually independent and phenomenally interactive. There are, first, the *institutions* with certain *roles* and *expectations* that will fulfill the goals of the system. Second, inhabiting the system are the *individuals* with certain *personalities* and *need-dispositions,* whose interactions comprise what we generally call "social behavior." . . .
>
> . . . [T]o understand the behavior of specific role incumbents in an institution, we must know both the role expectations and the need-dispositions. Indeed, needs and expectations may both be thought of as motives for behavior, the one deriving from personal propensities, the other from institutional requirements. What we call social behavior may be conceived as ultimately deriving from the interaction between the two sets of motives.
>
> The general model we have been describing may be represented pictorially as indicated [in Figure 4.11]. The nomothetic [organizational] axis is shown at the top of the diagram and consists of the institution, role, and role expectations, each term being the analytic unit for the term next preceding it. . . . Similarly, the idiographic [individual] axis, shown at the lower portion of the diagram, consists of individual, personality, and need-dispositions, each term again serving as the analytic unit for the term next preceding it. A given act is conceived as

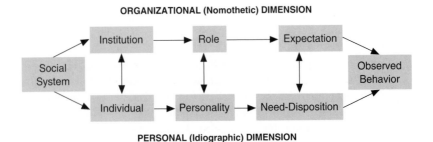

FIGURE 4.11   Model of the organization as a social system (the so-called Getzels-Guba model). Adapted from Jacob W. Getzels and Egon G. Guba, "Social Behavior and the Administrative Process," *The School Review,* 65 (Winter 1957), 423–441.

deriving simultaneously from both the nomothetic and the idiographic dimensions. That is to say, social behavior results as the individual attempts to cope with the environment composed of patterns of expectations for his behavior in ways consistent with his own independent pattern of needs.[28]

Viewed in this way, each behavioral act is seen as stemming simultaneously from the nomothetic and the idiographic dimensions. But how do these dimensions interact? What proportion of each dimension is present in organizational behavior? That depends, of course, on the individual and on the institutional role and is best expressed as a function of the interplay between the two dimensions. Getzels gave us this general equation to express it:

$$B = f(R \bullet P),$$

where B = observed behavior,
R = institutional role, and
P = personality of the role incumbent.[29]

Thus, the school, as an organization, creates certain offices and positions that are occupied by individuals. The offices and positions represent the nomothetic dimension of the organization, and role expectations held by the organization for incumbents are specified in a number of ways. These may range from elaborate written job descriptions to the more subtle (and usually more powerful) group norms established by custom and tradition. By this means, the organization not only establishes some formal, minimal level of job performance that would be acceptable but also communicates rather elaborate specifications of behavior in roles that may well extend to the kinds of clothes worn on the job, the manner of speech used, and so on.

Idiographic—Nomothetic

In the study of human social behavior, as in the organization sciences, two modes of analysis are generally used. One mode seeks to discover scientific principles or laws that are generally true, applicable in all situations, and are endlessly repeatable. It is called the *nomothetic* approach (from the ancient Greek *nomos,* or "law," and *thetos,* "prescribed"). Another approach, sometimes thought to be antithetical, is called "idiographic" (from the Greek *idios,* personal or private, and *graphos,* to display or write). The idiographic mode focuses on the human beings who populate the organization and their uniqueness from one organization to another and from time to time even in the same roles. Nomothetic analyses focus on the formal structure of the organization (typically described in organization charts, operations manuals, and other rules and "laws") that is generally thought to be replicable from organization to organization and from time to time. More commonly, we speak of the *structure* of the organization (nomothetic) and the *human* side of the organization (idiographic). These terms and concepts are widely used in the study of history, psychology, geography, and other human sciences.

FIGURE 4.12

The interplay of role and personality in organizational behavior. Behavior is a function of organizational role and personality, or B = *f* (R · P). Adapted from Jacob W. Getzels, "Administration as a Social Process," in *Administrative Theory in Education*, ed. Andrew W. Halpin (Chicago: Midwest Administration Center, University of Chicago, 1958), p. 158. Reprinted by permission.

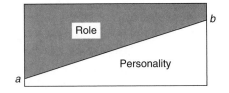

But the individuals who are incumbent in the offices and positions have their own personality structures and needs, which represent the idiographic dimensions of the organization. To some extent, even in highly formal organizations, the role incumbents mold and shape the offices in some ways in order to better fulfill some of their own expectations of their role.

The mechanism by which the needs of the institution and the needs of the individual are modified so as to come together is the work group. There is a dynamic interrelationship in the work group, then, not only of an interpersonal nature but also between institutional requirements and the idiosyncratic needs of individual participants. The shaping of the institutional role, the development of a climate within the social system, and the personalities of the participants all interact dynamically with one another. Organizational behavior can be viewed as the product of this interaction.

How much organizational behavior can be ascribed to role expectation and role prescription, and how much is traceable to the personality needs of the role incumbent? In other words, if B = *f*(R • P), what values can be assigned to R and P, respectively? A useful way of picturing the problem is shown in Figure 4.12. We can see that, for some people, a role can have far greater influence in prescribing behavior than for others.

For example, there has been considerable study of individuals who exhibit an authoritarian personality syndrome and of their impact on others.[30] Such an individual possesses a combination of personality characteristics that are stable, describable, and go far in shaping his or her view of the world. Typically the authoritarian individual tends to think in terms of relatively simple dichotomies: things are seen in black-or-white terms (with few shades of gray), concrete ideas are typical (with little patience for abstract thinking or ambiguity), and he or she identifies strongly with the "in" group (and particularly with authority figures). Authoritarian individuals, being insecure in ambiguous circumstances, place little trust in others and seek to control as much of the environment as possible (including the people around them). Such a person tends to seek a role in which he or she is seen as strong and in which control can be exercised. Behavior in that role tends to be relatively consistent: dogmatic, seeking absolute solutions to complex problems, and exercising power for personal gratification.

Mary Crow and Merl Bonney describe the impact of such people when they take on the leadership roles of a school district:

Picture a moderate-sized urban school system in Middle America. The clean-cut, conservatively dressed superintendent has made it clear who is on his side and who isn't. Among his supporters are the building principals, men who are much more like the superintendent: wanting to be tough disciplinarians, yet subservient to the boss. Of these principals, teachers will tell you that more competent candidates were often passed over for principalships in favor of these supporters who would be no threat to the superintendent's job. . . . At the first faculty meeting of the year, the superintendent comes across forcefully. He stresses how important it is that his teachers be honest, upstanding citizens, maintain good discipline in their classes, and work hard if they wish to be successful in his system. . . . Students are afraid of teachers; teachers are afraid of principals; principals are afraid of the superintendent; and the superintendent is afraid of the board.[31]

Though this is admittedly a stereotype of one kind of personality frequently found in leadership roles in U.S. school districts, everyone shapes his or her own role to *some* extent; hence, as shown in Figure 4.12, point *a* would not ordinarily be at zero; on the other hand, in any organization everyone plays some sort of institutional role, and, therefore, point *b* is somewhat below the 100 percent mark. The line *ab,* however, suggests the possible range of variation of the function of role and personality that organizations normally encounter.

Different kinds of roles in different kinds of organizations do suggest that some role players will be closer to point *a* (that is, will permit very little infusion of personality into the role). Conversely, we know that some kinds of roles demand greater personality involvement, as illustrated in Figure 4.13. One generally supposes that the role of an army private is very largely prescribed and clearly limits the extent to which the private can meet his or her individual personality needs. Closer to the other extreme would be an artist who exhibits highly creative behavior, with a minimum of organizational constraint, and who expresses personal idiosyncratic needs to a great degree.

Equilibrium

People participate in organizations in order to satisfy certain needs. Presumably, the organization has needs of its own, which are fulfilled by the participants who function in its various roles. This is illustrated by the Getzels-Guba social systems model, with its stress on the interplay between the nomothetic (organizational) needs and the idiographic (personal) needs of the "actors" who fill the various roles. There is obviously a *quid pro quo* relationship between the role player and the organization, the maintenance of which

FIGURE 4.13

Personality and role factors in organizational behavior of an army private and an artist (proportions are approximate). Adapted from Jacob W. Getzels, "Administration as a Social Process," in *Administrative Theory in Education*, ed. Andrew W. Halpin (Chicago: Midwest Administration Center, University of Chicago, 1958), p. 158. Reprinted by permission.

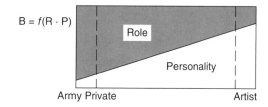

$B = f(R \cdot P)$

Role

Personality

Army Private   Artist

can be thought of as a state of *equilibrium* between the needs of the organization and those of the individual. As long as this state of equilibrium exists, the relationship presumably will be satisfactory, enduring, and relatively productive.

On a very rudimentary level, the notion of equilibrium between the needs of the organization and its participants is illustrated by the well-known case of Schmidt at Bethlehem Steel. Schmidt, as he was called in Frederick W. Taylor's description,[32] was a pig-iron handler who picked up, carried, and loaded pig iron—12.5 tons in a ten-hour day for $1.15 per day. Obviously, the company needed men to do the pig-iron handling, and this need was satisfied by the men whose role was that of handler. Presumably, as long as the needs and satisfactions exchange was in a state of balance or equilibrium, the organization functioned adequately. In his account Taylor described how he applied his "scientific principles" to the task of rigorously training Schmidt to increase Schmidt's daily workload to 47.5 tons. The needs–inducements balance was maintained by boosting the pay by 60 percent, to $1.85 per day. Schmidt and the company apparently found the needs–inducements arrangements mutually satisfactory, because Schmidt was described as staying on the job for "some years."

Chester Barnard discussed equilibrium as "the balancing of burdens by satisfactions which results in continuance"[33] of participation of both the individual and the organization in a mutual relationship. In his lexicon, the term "effectiveness" was the "accomplishment of the recognized objectives of cooperative action."[34] "Efficiency" referred to the ability of the organization to sustain the continued participation of individuals by offering adequate satisfactions to them.

Barnard described the organization as inducing cooperation by distributing its "*productive* results" to individuals. "These productive results," he wrote, "are either material or social, or both. As to some individuals, material is required for satisfaction; as to others, social benefits are required. As to most individuals, both material and social benefits are required in different proportions."[35] Barnard pointed out—and this is familiar to us all—that the definition of what constitutes "adequate satisfactions" to individuals in the organization varies, depending in great measure on the makeup and circumstances of the individual involved. Some people certainly find great satisfaction in material reward, especially money, and in order to get it will accept an organizational role that may be insecure, unpleasant, or strenuous. Regardless of the many possible negative aspects of such a role, as long as there is enough material reward, such people may well find the inducement satisfying. Others, for whatever reasons, might find a higher income not worth the price that must be paid.

In the recent history of educational administration, this can be seen in connection with the role of the superintendent of schools and, to a lesser degree, with that of the high school principal. Although the salaries being offered to superintendents are reaching very high levels, many qualified people are not attracted to this role, and many incumbents have shifted to university teaching or to other fields altogether. Long working hours, arduous demands, and enormous pressures are some of the drawbacks of the superintendency; in many cases there is little reward in terms of achievement or self-fulfillment. In order to attract and hold capable people as superintendents, school districts must proffer a combination of material and psychological rewards that incumbents will find attractive.

Similarly, not many years ago, an important problem in the United States was attracting good teachers to rural areas and keeping them there in spite of the low pay, inadequate school facilities, and limited cultural opportunities, which made teaching in such areas relatively unrewarding to many. Today, of course, the situation is reversed; other careers and schools in nonurban areas offer considerable reward to many teachers, whereas the bleak, hostile, frustrating environment of the teacher in the poor urban school is barely adequate—both in terms of money and a sense of fulfillment—for many capable teachers.

In discussing organizational equilibrium from the systems theory point of view, we must remember that there is not only a needs–inducements relationship between the individual participant and the organization; the organization itself is part of a larger system. Further, if the system is open—as in the case of schools and school systems—the organization will interact actively with the external systems that comprise its environment. An expanded version of the Getzels-Guba social system model, shown in Figure 4.14, depicts this interaction of the school with its larger environment. Presumably, changes in the environment will stimulate a reaction by the organization, either *static* or *dynamic*. If the reaction is static, the system responds so as to keep relationships in

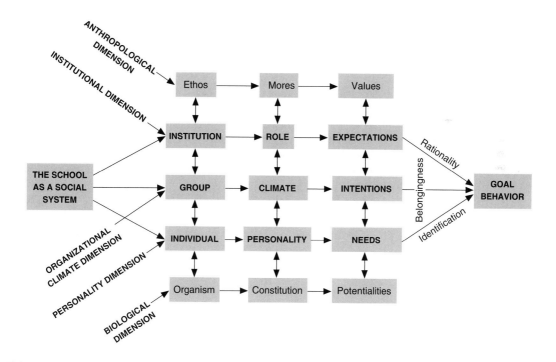

FIGURE 4.14 Dimensions of the school as a social system. Adapted from Jacob W. Getzels and Herbert A. Thelen, "The Classroom Group as a Unique Social System," in *The Dynamics of Instructional Groups: Sociopsychological Aspects of Teaching and Learning*, ed. Nelson B. Henry. N.S.S.E. Yearbook LIX, Part II (Chicago: National Society for the Study of Education, 1960), p. 80. Reprinted by permission.

their original state, that is, the *status quo* is maintained. Dynamic equilibrium, however, is characterized by a rearrangement of the internal subsystems of the organization or by a change in its goals in order to adjust to changing circumstances in its external environment. Dynamic equilibrium, in other words, helps to keep the system in a steady state by being adaptable.

Homeostasis

This biological term has been applied to organizations and refers to the tendency of an open system to regulate itself so as to stay constantly in balance. The biological organism tends to retain its own characteristics, to maintain itself and to preserve its identity, but, at the same time, it has compensatory mechanisms that enable it to adapt to and survive environmental changes within certain limits. Homeostatic processes in human beings include the body's tendency to maintain a constant temperature and to maintain blood pressure by repairing a break in the circulatory system through coagulation. Homeostatic mechanisms in school systems and schools, such as well-developed communication systems and decision-making processes, enable them to adapt to and deal effectively with changes in their environment.

Feedback

Feedback is described by John Pfiffner and Frank Sherwood:

> In its simplest form, feedback is the kind of communication an actor receives from a live audience. If the crowd is enthusiastic, the performer reacts with similar enthusiasm. There is in a way a closed circuit between performer and audience with continuing interchange of information. . . . Essential to feedback is the notion that the flow of information is actually having a reciprocating effect on behavior. This is why the term loop is frequently associated with feedback. This circular pattern involves a flow of information to the point of action, a flow back to the point of decision with information on the action, and then a return to the point of action with new information and perhaps instructions. A primary element in this process is the sensory organ, the instrument through which information is obtained.[36]

Systems that do not have sensitive antennae picking up accurate feedback information or—perhaps worse—that do not provide for the accurate transmission of feedback information to decision makers, find it difficult to react appropriately to environmental changes. Such systems tend to be in a static, rather than in a dynamic, equilibrium with their environments. They tend to lack the self-correcting, homeostatic processes essential to maintaining themselves in environments characterized by change.

We have, then, in the social systems view, an organization that is, by definition, an open system. This means, in part, not only that the organization has internal subsystems but also that it is part of a suprasystem. Moreover, the organization is in an interactive relationship with this suprasystem: it exchanges inputs and outputs with it. To some extent, the organization affects its environment (the suprasystem) and is also affected by changes that occur in the suprasystem.

It can resist and deny changes in the suprasystem or environment by ignoring or fighting them or by attempting to insulate itself from them (that is, by becoming more closed). It can attempt to accommodate to environmental change by homeostatic adaptation (that is, by adopting a policy of "business as usual"). Or, finally, the organization can adapt to environmental changes by developing a new balance, a new equilibrium. In a world such as ours, dominated by rapid and extensive change, it would appear that the organization with poor feedback mechanisms or weak homeostatic characteristics would show declining performance and increasing evidence of disorganization.

It is important to remember that essential to systems theory is the concept that *systems are composed of subsystems that are highly interactive and mutually interdependent.* It would seem clear from the Getzels-Guba model of the school as an open social system, which has already been described, that at least two subsystems can be identified and their interaction at least suggested: (1) the organizational or institutional system and (2) the human system. However, useful as this model was in early attempts to understand the dynamics of organizational behavior, it is incomplete. By the mid-1980s it was clear that organizations possess more than these two subsystems and that analysis of organizational behavior requires us to use more complex concepts. One of the more currently useful approaches is to conceptualize organizations—for example, the school system and the school—as *sociotechnical systems.*

Sociotechnical Systems Theory

By definition, an organization exists for the purpose of achieving something: reaching some goal or set of goals. It seeks to do this by accomplishing certain tasks.[37] Rationally, of course, the organization is structured, equipped, and staffed appropriately to accomplish its mission. The main goal of a school district, for example, requires it to operate schools, a transportation system, and food services. The district must employ people, provide legally mandated services, and perhaps engage in collective bargaining. There are numerous tasks that the school district must organize internally in order to achieve its goals.

In order to achieve an assigned task—which may include a large number of subtasks and operationally necessary tasks—we build an organization: that is, we give it *structure.* It is the structure that gives an organization order, system, and many of its distinctive characteristics. The structure establishes a pattern of authority and collegiality, thus defining roles: there are top-management executives and middle-management supervisors, bosses and workers, each of whom attempts to know the extent of his or her own legitimate authority as well as that of others. Structure dictates, in large measure, the patterns of communication networks that are basic to information flow and, therefore, to decision making. Structure also determines the system of work flow that is, presumably, focused on achieving the organization's tasks.

The organization must have *technological resources* or, in other words, the "tools of its trade." "Technology," used in this sense, does not only include such typical hardware items as computers, milling machines, textbooks and chalk, and electron microscopes.

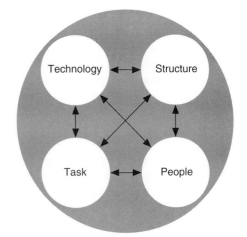

FIGURE 4.15

Interacting subsystems in a complex organization. Adapted from Harold J. Leavitt, "Applied Organizational Change in Industry: Structural, Technological and Humanistic Approaches," in *Handbook of Organizations*, ed. James G. March. © 1965 by Rand McNally & Company, Chicago, Figure 1, p. 1145.

Technology may also include program inventions: systematic procedures, the sequencing of activities, or other procedural inventions designed to solve problems that stand in the way of organizational task achievement. Thus, the teacher's daily lesson plan, the high school class schedule, and the district's curriculum guides are illustrative of technology in educational organizations.

Finally, of course, the organization must have *people.* Their contribution to the task achievement of the organization is ultimately visible in their acts—that is, their organizational behavior. It is this behavior that selects, directs, communicates, and decides.

These four internal organization factors—*task, structure, technology,* and *people*[38] (Figure 4.15)—are variables that differ from time to time and from one organization to the next. Within a given organization these four factors are highly interactive, each tending to shape and mold the others. As in any system, the interdependence of the variable factors means that a significant change in one will result in some adaptation on the part of the other factors. Important in determining the nature and interrelationship of these internal organizational arrangements in a school district or school is the response of the organization to changes occurring in the larger system in which it exists.

Suppose, for example, that an academically oriented high school admits limited numbers of talented students by competitive examination for the express purpose of preparing them for college. If the board of education rules that the school be converted into a comprehensive high school to meet the needs of the total youth population (which, of course, would be a change in the organization's goal), it is apparent that a number of internal adjustments would be necessary for the school to achieve its new goal reasonably well. Many of these changes would be compensatory in nature. For example, to accommodate those students interested in a business career, it would be necessary to teach courses in business (task). To do this, business education equipment would have to be installed (technology), business education teachers would have to be employed (people), and a department of business education might be created (structure). However, some of the changes flowing from the board's directive might be retaliatory rather than compensatory. For example, if some people in the school sought to resist these changes, their former cooperative and productive behavior would be replaced by alienation and conflict. This, in turn, could disrupt the normal communications patterns in the school, thereby producing a structural change.

A technological change, such as the introduction of a comprehensive, computer-related instructional system in a high school, could bring about important side effects: it could change the goals of the school by making it possible to achieve new things and, simultaneously, by rendering certain traditional tasks obsolete. A change in people would include the employment of new personnel with technical skills, affecting the work activities of others in the school by making some activities unnecessary and requiring certain new activities to be introduced. Finally, the introduction of new departments and changes in those involved in the decision-making processes would be structural changes flowing out of the technical change originally initiated.

Thus, in coordinating the internal processes of the school district or school, it is necessary to attend to the dynamic interaction of the four subsystems: people, structure, technology, and task. However, if it is proposed to introduce a significant change through primarily one of the target variables, it is clear that the other variables soon will be affected. Change efforts that are basically technological in nature result in some compensatory or retaliatory behavior on the part of people and in some structural adjustments within the organization. Those who seek to bring about significant structural rearrangements in the school, such as differentiated staffing plans, must reckon with the people involved and the way they will react to the change.

Although it is easy to speak of different administrative strategies and to categorize various tactics and procedures as "belonging" to one strategy or another, we must recognize the symbiotic interrelationship that exists among the internal organizational subsystems with which we are concerned: task, technological, structural, and behavioral.

The schematic diagram in Figure 4.16 illustrates the key internal and external relationships of a school system or school. The figure provides only a few illustrative examples of the many things that are normally included in the task, technology, and structure subsystems. In conceptualizing the human subsystem, the reader is cautioned to note that it is insufficient to name or label the occupational roles of participants (such as teachers, nurses, and custodians). In terms of the dynamics of internal organizational functioning, the values, beliefs, and knowledge possessed by individuals in the human system are fully as important as the facts that the individuals are present and that the organization has formalized ways of dealing with them (such as rules, grievance procedures, and personnel policies). It should be obvious that the human subsystem is the only one that has nonrational (that is, affective, not irrational) capability.

Contingency Theory

Theorizing, thinking, research, and experience with organizations have been accompanied by an observable tendency for individuals (whether theorists or practitioners) to adopt

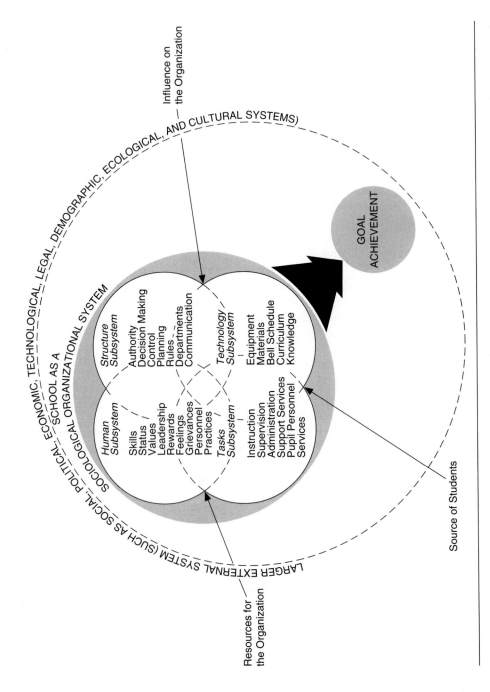

FIGURE 4.16 Four primary organizational subsystems characterize the internal arrangements of school systems and schools. Adapted from Robert G. Owens and Carl R. Steinhoff, *Administering Change in Schools* (Englewood Cliffs, NJ: Prentice-Hall, 1976), p. 143.

advocacy positions. Those who favor classical approaches to organization, for example, have consistently supported the notion that a hierarchy of authority based upon rank in the organization is essential to the very concept of organization. Human relations adherents may differ on many points but are almost unanimous in espousing supportive, collaborative, people-centered leadership and highly participative management styles as superior to other approaches. Behavioral adherents have, with a fair degree of consistency, sought to find the best, most productive way to integrate the key elements of the classical and human relations approaches. The result, for many years, was the development of competing advocacy positions, which showed very mixed results when attempts were made to apply any one of the positions to organizations: none of the three approaches is demonstrably superior in *all* situations.

Traditional (classical or neoclassical) approaches to the administration of school systems and schools have tended not only to use a hierarchical model of organization (drawn from the tradition of the military and large corporations) but also to emphasize the importance of rational, logical, and potentially powerful control systems, whereby decisions are made at the top of the hierarchy and implemented at the bottom. As a conceptually ideal state, at least, the whole is characterized by hierarchically maintained order, system, and discipline. Remember, as in the discussion of Douglas McGregor's Theory X presented earlier in the chapter, classical concepts may be used in either hard (coercive) or soft (manipulative) form.

Rational Planning Models

These models, such as Planning, Programming, and Budgeting Systems (PPBS), Program Evaluation and Review Technique (PERT), Management by Objectives (MBO), and Zero-Based Budgeting (ZBB), are adapted from massive, military-industrial enterprises that were created for such purposes as building and maintaining huge fleets of enormous, technologically complex systems of weapons (such as intercontinental ballistics missiles, atomic-powered submarines, and giant aircraft) and, lest we forget, carrying out vast space exploration programs.

The approach, characterized by use of modern rational systems concepts and technology (as differentiated from *social* systems concepts), is traditional, classical in viewpoint, and *mechanical* in operation. Organizations are said to be mechanical when the primary basis for managing the system features the following:

1. Highly differentiated and specialized tasks with precise specification of rights, responsibilities, and methods.
2. Coordination and control through hierarchical supervision.
3. Communication with the external environment controlled by the top offices of the hierarchy.
4. Strong, downward-oriented line of command.
5. One-to-one leadership style emphasizing authority–obedience relationships.
6. Decision-making authority reserved for top levels of the hierarchy.

The concepts of *mechanical* and *organic* systems are widely discussed in the literature of organizational theory.[39] These concepts help us to discuss and analyze specific organizational situations without resorting to such potentially pejorative dichotomies as the bureaucratic-humanistic or democratic-authoritarian ones, which, in our culture, are obviously value laden. Organic organizational systems are recognizable by the fact that they emphasize a different approach to managing the system:

1. Continuous reassessment of tasks and responsibilities through interaction of those involved, with functional change being easy to arrange at the working level.
2. Coordination and control through interaction of those involved, requiring considerable shared responsibility and interdependence.
3. Communication with external environment relatively extensive and open at all levels of the organization.
4. Emphasis on mutual confidence, consultation, and information sharing—up and down, laterally, and diagonally across the organization—as the basis of organizational authority.
5. Team leadership style, featuring high levels of trust and group problem solving.
6. Wide sharing of responsibility for decision making at all levels in the organization.

These two views of organization in public education have long represented what John Goodlad described as two irreconcilable modes of thought that have struggled for dominance.

> They have been with us for a long time. William James characterized them as "the hard and the tough" and the "soft and the tender." . . . So far as the rhetoric of schooling is concerned, these two themes rise and fall like tides, one usually flooding as the other ebbs. Each during its high [tide] deposits its share of debris on the beach and occasionally changes the shoreline a little. But the vast interior of schooling is disturbed scarcely at all.
>
> During the 1960s, both modes of thought struggled for attention. But the avant garde was represented by the soft and tender. Teachers were exhorted to open up their classrooms; open-space schools were the work of an enlightened school district. But all of this [was] replaced [in the late 1970s] with the rhetoric of "back to the basics." . . . The cry is picked up in the daily press, on radio and television, and at P.T.A. meetings. There is a flurry of activity—more of it outside the schools than within. Hundreds of conventions carry the theme; legislative bills are enacted—for accountability by objectives, competency-based teacher education and, of course, proficiency tests for high school students. This activity builds up for two or three years, is intense for from three to five years, but then . . . falls from its own weight. . . . What bothers me most is that educators contribute so significantly to these excesses. Indeed, they pick them up and, for a brief while, make dubious reputations out of them. Usually, too, they are just a little late so that they are swinging exuberantly to one drumbeat at about the time an alternate drumbeat is coming on strong.[40]

The ebb and flow of the tides of rhetoric and viewpoint—alternately bringing a mechanical-bureaucratic-hierarchical emphasis to the fore, then a soft human relations–

humanistic sweep followed, perhaps, by a more manipulative, soft mechanical emphasis—historically has been painfully evident in the administration of U.S. public schooling. Many school superintendents, principals, and others, having witnessed this reality, have decided to eschew any theoretical or analytical approach but have elected what is generally described by practitioners as an eclectic or pragmatic approach: to go out into the real world of school districts and to do whatever seems to work. After all, the argument goes, "theory doesn't make any difference." This is not only a gross misreading of what organizational studies have to teach us, but it also offers no hope whatever of setting educational administration on a solid foundation of knowledge from which systematic administrative practice may be developed.

A contingency approach to organization takes a different view: although there is no one best way to organize and manage people in all circumstances, there are certain designs of organizational structure and describable management methods that can be identified as being most effective under specific situational contingencies. The key to understanding and dealing effectively with organizational behavior, from a contingency point of view, lies in being able to *analyze* the critical variables in a given situation. Effective administrator behavior (that is, behavior likely to increase achievement of the organization in attaining its goals, to improve the culture for working and learning, and to deal as productively as possible with conflict) is not seen as characterized by a universal fixed style (for example, nomothetic or idiographic) but reveals a repertoire of behavioral styles tailored to the contingencies of the situation. In sum, three basic propositions underlie the contingency approach to organizational behavior in schools:

1. There is no one best universal way to organize and administer school districts or schools.

2. Not all ways of organizing and administering are equally effective in a given situation: effectiveness is contingent upon appropriateness of the design or style to the situation.

3. The selection of organizational design and administrative style should be based on careful analysis of significant contingencies in the situation.

Open System Related to Contingency Theory

As we have described, contingency theory represents "a middle ground between (a) the view that there are universal principles of organization and management and (b) the view that each organization is unique and that each situation must be analyzed separately."[41] Contingency approaches represent a rather sensible theoretical development that seems to have value in dealing with the theory–practice gap.[42] The basic contribution of contingency thinking lies not in providing ready-made, pat answers to complex problems or easy recipes for "how to do it"; it lies, rather, in providing us with new ways of analyzing the interrelationships within and among the interacting parts of the organizational system.[43] One critical set of relationships arises from the interaction of the organization (which, remember, is an open system) with its environment.

One of the early influential attempts along this line was the work of Paul Lawrence and Jay Lorsch,[44] who viewed organizations as open systems that are capable of differentiating their internal subsystems in response to a variety of environmental contingencies. Organizations that deal successfully with uncertain environments (that is, environments that are apt to call for relatively sudden change in the organization) tend to differentiate internally more than less successful organizations do; yet they are able to maintain high levels of integration between the various subunits. Such organizations are characterized by joint decision making, clear interdepartmental linkages, and well-developed means of dealing with conflict between units of the organization. Organizations that function in environments characterized by change and instability must, to be effective, organize differently to meet the need for planning, decision making, and conflict management than do those organizations that deal with relatively stable environments.

As environmental conditions change, the organization needs to adapt by responding with an appropriate structure and administrative system. Stable technologies and stable environmental conditions call for mechanistic organizations, characterized by rigidity and by explicitly defined tasks, methods, and job descriptions. In contrast, organizations facing unstable or changing technologies and environments require relatively flexible structures, with emphasis on lateral rather than vertical communications, expert power (rather than hierarchical power) as the predominant base of influence, loosely defined responsibilities, and emphasis on exchanges of information rather than on giving direction.[45]

Response to Technological Change

Critics who fault U.S. schools for failing to make full use of modern technology often have hardware technologies in mind (such as computers, television and videotape, and other machines) and have a limited grasp of the extensive software technology that is widely used in U.S. education. The term *technology* properly includes such "software" as procedures for sequencing instruction; scheduling the interface of time, people, and material resources; specialized programs and curriculum guides; and techniques for generating and managing information. Thus, the term—when applied to school organizations—must include such diverse forms as curriculum guides, the high school schedule, biology laboratories and band rooms, the testing program, and methods for classifying, grouping, and promoting students. The array of technology utilized in schooling has considerable power to affect behavior in the entire sociotechnical system, as was suggested earlier.

But, again, technology is usually developed outside of the school system or school; its impact is a result of the interaction of the open sociotechnical system with its environment. New technological developments of every description tend to alter the contingencies that affect the internal arrangements of the school. They are, in effect, one aspect of the large environment in which school systems or schools as organizations exist.

Interaction with the External Environment

The school system or school, as a sociotechnical system, is in constant dynamic interaction with the larger external environment in which it exists. As used here, *environment* refers to the suprasystem in which the school district or school exists: the social, political, and economic systems of our culture. Thus, demographic shifts resulting in changing enrollments and increasing percentages of older people in the population, changing attitudes toward individual freedom, emphasis on women's right to equality, shifting patterns of social mobility, dissatisfaction with the performance of schools, massive changes in legal-judicial philosophy, increased taxpayer resistance, organization of teachers into labor unions, and even mounting distrust of authority and institutions in our society in general are among the many environmental contingencies to which public school organizations have had to adapt in recent years.

Internal arrangements of the organization are largely contingent upon circumstances in that environment. Changes in the environment cause the organizational system to respond with changes in its internal arrangements. Those internal arrangements are best understood as containing four dynamically interactive subsystems: *tasks* to be performed, *structure* of the organization, *technology* utilized to perform the tasks, and the *human* social system.

One way that the social, political, and cultural environment of the school district or school has an impact is in setting goals to be achieved. Although educators play a part in establishing the goals of schooling, the process is ultimately in the political realm: state legislatures representing the body politic, for example, are normally instrumental in formalizing important aspects of the goals of schooling. Legislation of minimum competency standards for graduation and/or promotion can have a powerful impact on what schools seek to achieve. Federal initiatives have had a widespread, direct effect on school goals—not only for youngsters with special educational needs but for virtually all other students as well.

Other political processes, such as approving budgets and levying taxes or electing school board members, also serve as means for influencing the goals of schools. Frequently, a display of potential political power is sufficient to effect reassessment and revision of organizational goals. Not infrequently, of course, judicial intervention is a means of implementing goal changes in schooling. This is readily observable in situations in which federal district courts not only have ordered the desegregation of school districts but also have specified the means by which this is to be achieved (for example, intradistrict transportation and interdistrict transportation). Courts also have not infrequently required changes in curricula, testing procedures, and methods of selecting and assigning staff. All of these represent some of the ways that the environment of the school organization affects the internal functioning of the organization; the organization will either adapt smoothly and easily, or it may resist.

Thus, a groundswell of popular support for "back to basics" might appear in a local school district that motivates the board of education and the administrative staff to initiate a goal-setting and educational planning project with community involvement. As a result, the schools would likely revise their curricula, shift their teaching style, perhaps reorganize their grade structure, and adopt new textbooks—that is, make internal rearrangements in response to changes in the organization's environment.

Not infrequently, however, schools will resist external changes and maintain the status quo, almost regardless of the degree or power of the new environmental contingencies. Our history with regard to desegregation, equal rights, and nondiscriminatory practices—even in the face of concentrated, massive, statutory, judicial, and political action—makes it clear that there are many occasions when schools attempt to close off the organizational system in order to deflect the impact of changes in the larger environment, rather than seek ways of making appropriate internal rearrangements so as to adapt to them. From a contingency point of view, this tends to put the school or school system out of touch with the real-world contingencies in which these organizations exist. In terms of organizational behavior, a negative result in such a case is likely to be leadership and administrative styles that—in the long run—are not the most effective and may even be counterproductive.

Contingency Theory and Organizational Behavior in Schools

Operationally, using the contingency approach in the practice of school administration does not necessarily have to be terribly exotic or to require highly sophisticated methods. It does, however, require the administrator to use some analysis of relevant contingencies in the situation at hand as a basis for selecting a way of dealing with them. Since administration is working with and through individuals and groups to achieve organizational goals, a fundamental issue to consider is "What will likely yield the most productive behavior (in terms of achieving organizational goals) from my subordinates in this situation?" An important assumption underlying this question is, of course, that different administrative styles are likely to evoke predictably different responses from people.

For example, an issue that often confronts the administrator concerns leadership style. Is a good leader one who sets goals, directs subordinates as to what to do, and checks closely to see that they do things as directed? Or is a good leader one who involves subordinates in setting goals, collaborates with them in deciding what to do and how to do it, and provides coordination of the group in evaluating progress and results? In the parlance of public school administrators, which is better: "directive" leadership or "democratic" leadership?

A contingency approach to this issue starts with clarifying what is meant by "good." Because the administrator's intent is to maximize the achievement of organizational goals, "good" is probably best redefined as "effective." The question then becomes: Which leadership style is most effective—that is, which will likely contribute most to the goal performance of the school system or school?

As we shall discuss more fully in Chapter 8, contemporary understanding of the dynamics of leader behavior makes it clear that there is apparently no one most effective style: effectiveness of leadership style clearly depends on its appropriateness in terms of the critical contingencies in a given situation. The power of the leader, the quality of relationships with subordinates, the clarity of the structure of the task to be done, the degree of cooperation required to implement decisions, and the levels of skill and motivation of subordinates are a few of the many contingencies that can be assessed by the administrator and related to predictable outcomes of various specific alternative ways to lead. In the contingency view, the effective leader is able to match leadership style to the contingencies of the situation in order to achieve the behavior on the part of subordinates that will contribute most to achieving the goals of the school district or school.

Similarly, a contingency orientation is helpful in dealing with issues of motivation, decision making, organizational change, organizational culture, and conflict management. The remaining chapters of this book explore these aspects of organizational behavior in schools.

Conclusion

Open systems theory is the basis for contemporary analysis of organizational behavior. Social systems theory, such as the Getzels-Guba model, has provided a useful way of conceptualizing organizational behavior as a function of the interaction between the demands of organizational requirements and the needs-dispositions of individuals in the organization. Although the Getzels-Guba model often has been used to stress this internal dynamic relationship of the organization, the expanded version of the model clearly illustrates the dynamic relationship between the organizational system itself and its external larger environment, the suprasystem.

Role theory not only helps us to understand the idiographic–nomothetic relationship in greater detail but also illuminates many of the broader interpersonal relationships that exist in schools and school systems. Although role theory lacks the power to explain the organization in its entirety, it is useful as a framework for examining relationships between person and organization, as well as interpersonal behavior.

Sociotechnical concepts help us to understand the dynamic interrelationship among the structure, tasks, technology, and human aspects of educational organizations as a force in evoking and molding the behavior of people. In the typical high school, for example, people's daily lives are deeply affected by the schedule, which governs all and often defines the possible. Architects design buildings that evoke psychological responses and shape behavior. The choice to equip a classroom with movable desks or screwed-down desks has an impact on behavior. A curriculum that mandates individually prescribed instruction also mandates behavior. The need to transport students to and from school on buses has an impressive impact on the school as an organization and on the behavior of people in it.

But the fact that educational organizations are *open* systems has additional behavioral consequences. A school, for example, is subject to two major external forces that define the very nature of its internal arrangements. One of these forces is the fact that the school *is* a school: it is probably more like other schools from coast to coast than different from them. Professional standards and expectations expressed through teacher training institutions, accrediting associations, the entrance requirements of colleges, the wares of the educational-industrial complex, and the speakers at annual conventions—all of these are but a representative few of the many professional influences that reach in from the outside and define what a school *is* in behavioral terms.

The *second* cluster of these forces represents the broader social-cultural influences that reach in from the outside and establish norms for behavior in the school. These include such diverse sources as community standards, tradition, judicial decisions, statutory law, and—not least, by any means—the broad generalizations embodied in such concepts as "Western culture." More specifically, perhaps, is the impact of the "youth subculture" that has become so influential in Western nations. Because the school is an open system, this facet of the school's environment has a powerful impact on its internal functioning. The fact that children watch television, are exposed to a drug culture, and are developing new concepts of sex, marriage, and the family does shape the nature of life in schools. All of these, together, combine to create an *organizational* culture that is powerful in determining how people perceive things, value them, and react to them.

Thus, the concept of the educative organization as an open sociotechnical system enables one to see the internal arrangements of a particular organization as at once unique and part of an interaction with its larger suprasystem. This is the view of schools that people like Goodlad have when they speak of the "culture" of the school, and it is discussed again in Chapter 6, on organizational culture.

In contemporary organizational theory, this concept is coupled with contingency theory: the view that there is no one universal "best" way of dealing with organizational issues. Contingency approaches to organizational behavior require developing a systematic understanding of the dynamics of organizational behavior in order to be able to diagnose or analyze the specific situation that exists.

Organizational theory provides a systematic body of knowledge on which we base assumptions about the nature of organizations and the behavior of people in them. Far from being the impractical plaything of scholars, theory is used constantly by administrators—albeit often in an intuitive and unexamined way—as a basis for the professional work they do every day.

Bureaucratic theory has long been, by an overwhelming margin, the most widely used perspective in developing assumptions about educational organizations. Human resources theory has, however, been steadily developing and gaining greater acceptance as research following the tradition of the Western Electric Studies has been pushed forward and as bureaucratic responses to the problems of schools have failed to work as well as had been expected. Since the 1960s, human resources development theory has been considerably strengthened by the emergence of such newer perspectives as concepts of loose coupling.

It is recognized today that, as a broad generalization, schools characteristically tend to use human resources approaches in the management of the instructional behavior of teachers and to use bureaucratic approaches in the management of other, more routine aspects of the enterprise. Each of these two theoretic approaches gives rise to different assumptions about the nature of people and, therefore, of effective ways of managing them—Theory X and Theory Y.

Reflective Activities

1. Analyze how the five mechanisms of the bureaucratic approach to controlling and coordinating behavior of individuals in an organization are used in your work environment. To what extent are these used? Do they support the achievement of organizational goals? What recommendations do you have for their continued use, modification, or termination?

2. Using role theory and the Getzels-Guba model as described in this chapter, analyze your organization as a social system. Alternatively, use the expanded model of Getzels and Thelen of a school as a social system. Briefly define the group roles, individual roles, and organizational expectations that seem to define or direct the goal behaviors of your organization. Can you identify any changes in roles or expectations that might help improve organizational effectiveness?

3. *Working on Your Game Plan.* Chapter 4 revisited and extended the theme of two divergent views of organization—bureaucratic views and human resources development views. The question be-

comes, which of these views do you use in analyzing educational organizations as a basis for your leadership game plan?

Review the initial ideas that you wrote for your game plan after reading Chapters 2 and 3 and revise them and incorporate them into a new statement that adds the following two concepts from Chapter 4:

a. Theory X and Theory Y

b. Sociotechnical systems theory (Figure 4.16)

Add and incorporate two distinct points to the plan document that you are developing, using such systems frameworks as those proposed by Chris Argyris or Rensis Likert. Point 1 is to articulate your own personal position on Theory X and Theory Y as an educational leader and some initial ideas as to what this would mean about your behavior as a leader on the job. Given that and using Figure 4.16 as a guide, Point 2 is to think through the best strategy for entering the organizational system so as to exercise leadership in it.

Suggested Reading

Firestone, William A., and Bruce L. Wilson, "Using Bureaucratic and Cultural Linkages to Improve Instruction: The Principal's Contribution." *Educational Administration Quarterly,* 21 (Spring 1985), 7–30.

Discusses the two kinds of "linkages" available for principals to use in influencing the instructional behavior of teachers: bureaucratic and cultural. An excellent source of references to the literature for those who wish to probe this topic more fully.

Flood, Robert Louis, *Rethinking the Fifth Discipline: Learning Within the Unknowable.* New York: Routledge, 1999.

An excellent introduction to systems thinking, which underlies all modern approaches to scientific thought. This is a readily accessible discussion that uses nontechnical language. Flood compares systems thinking to other kinds of thinking—such as scientific reductionism and spiritualism/theism—and shows the historical connection to its emergence during the Enlightenment. Recommended to the educational leader who seeks to better understand the emerging emphasis on scientific methods in educational research.

Meyer, John W., and Brian Rowan, "The Structure of Educational Organizations." In John W. Meyer and W. Richard Scott, eds., *Organizational Environments: Ritual and Rationality.* Beverly Hills, CA: Sage Publications, 1983.

A provocative analysis of schools from a sociological perspective that challenges the conventional tradition of bureaucratic logic and order. The entire book, of which this chapter is part, will be of great interest to the serious student.

Meyer, Marshall W., *Theory of Organizational Structure.* Indianapolis: Bobbs-Merrill Educational Publishing, 1977.

In this seventy-eight-page book, sociologist Meyer first discusses the various functions of organizational theory. He then goes on to describe a theory of organizational structure that departs from traditional bureaucratic concepts. Much in this book is directly related to the emerging new perspectives on the structure of educational organizations.

Weick, Karl E., "Educational Organizations as Loosely Coupled Systems." *Educational Administration Quarterly,* 21 (1976), 1–19.

While Weick did not invent the concept of loosely coupled systems, in this article he did lay the foundation for a major shift in the theory of schools as organizations. This is a classic that should be read in the original.

c h a p t e r 5

The Human Dimension of Organization

LEARNING OBJECTIVES

After reading this chapter, you should be able to

- Define administration.
- Describe the image of schools as organizations often held by individuals who advocate technical solutions to problems of education.
- Describe the assumptions about rationality, order, and system that underlie traditional concepts of schools as organizations.
- Describe and discuss the concepts of anthropomorphizing and reifying organizations.
- Describe the differences between the ways that school principals describe schools and the ways that academicians describe them.
- Describe human capital and explain how it relates to school administration.
- Discuss the relationship between administrative practice and the concept of human resources as assets.
- Describe the concept of growth-enhancing environments and discuss how it relates to teacher tenure.
- Define and describe organizational culture.
- Describe how organizational culture is related to academic performance in schools.
- List and describe the six characteristics of effective schools that you think are most important.
- Identify and describe the four principal contemporary approaches to school reform.
- Explain why understanding the human and social dimensions of organization is central to understanding organization itself.

ISLLC Standards

STANDARD 2: A school administrator is an educational leader who promotes the success of all students by advocating, nurturing, and sustaining a school culture and instructional program conducive to student learning and staff professional growth.

Knowledge

The administrator has knowledge and understanding of:

- school cultures

Dispositions

The administrator believes in, values, and is committed to:

- student learning as the fundamental purpose of schooling
- professional development as an integral part of school improvement

Performances

The administrator facilitates processes and engages in activities ensuring that:

- all individuals are treated with fairness, dignity, and respect
- professional development promotes a focus on student learning consistent with the school vision and goals
- students and staff feel valued and important
- the responsibilities and contributions of each individual are acknowledged
- barriers to student learning are identified, clarified, and addressed
- lifelong learning is encouraged and modeled
- there is a culture of high expectations for self, student, and staff performance
- student and staff accomplishments are recognized and celebrated
- the school is organized and aligned for success

STANDARD 3: A school administrator is an educational leader who promotes the success of all students by ensuring management of the organization, operations, and resources for a safe, efficient, and effective learning environment.

Knowledge

The administrator has knowledge and understanding of:

- theories and models of organizations and the principles of organizational development
- operational procedures at the school and district levels
- human resources management and development

Dispositions

The administrator believes in, values, and is committed to:

- making management decisions to enhance learning and teaching
- taking risks to improve schools
- trusting people and their judgments
- high-quality standards, expectations, and performances
- involving stakeholders in management processes

Performances

The administrator facilitates processes and engages in activities ensuring that:

- knowledge of learning, teaching, and student development is used to inform management decisions
- operational procedures are designed and managed to maximize opportunities for successful learning
- emerging trends are recognized, studied, and applied as appropriate
- financial, human, and material resources are aligned to the goals of schools
- organizational systems are regularly monitored and modified as needed
- stakeholders are involved in decisions affecting schools
- responsibility is shared to maximize ownership and accountability
- effective group-process and consensus-building skills are used
- human resource functions support the attainment of school goals

STANDARD 5: A school administrator is an educational leader who promotes the success of all students by acting with integrity, fairness, and in an ethical manner.

Knowledge

The administrator has knowledge and understanding of:

- the purpose of education and the role of leadership in modern society
- the philosophy and history of education

Dispositions

The administrator believes in, values, and is committed to:

- bringing ethical principles to the decision-making process

Performances

The administrator:

- examines personal and professional values
- demonstrates values, beliefs, and attitudes that inspire others to higher levels of performance
- treats people fairly, equitably, and with dignity and respect

T he previous chapter introduced some systematic ways of thinking about organizations and the people who work in them, which is the field of systems theory of organization. Many of these ways of thinking, or theories, such as the Getzels-Guba model, have proven almost indispensable to students in educational administration. However, in this chapter we shall see that these ways of thinking have some distinct limitations. Perhaps the most serious one is that, although they depict relationships between the organizational structure and the people who populate the organization in graphic ways, they tend to subscribe to a theory of action that emphasizes bureaucratic control over the human realities in organizations.

This chapter describes some aspects of the very important shift in organizational paradigm from traditional modernism, with its emphasis on perfecting and refining bureaucratic management strategies and techniques, to an approach that emphasizes the potential for improving organizational performance from within, from the bottom up, by fostering the growth and development of the people who inhabit the organization. The overarching concept of this paradigm is that of building human capital: that organizations become more effective as the people in them grow and develop personally and professionally over time so that they become increasingly effective not only in their individual work but as participants in a work group that also is becoming increasingly adept and effective in cooperative endeavor.

Reconceptualizing the Nature of Organizations

This book addresses the problem of understanding the behavior of people at work in educational organizations. This is the central problem confronting educational administrators because administration is defined as "working with and through other people, individually and in groups, to achieve organizational goals." In terms of administrative practice, then, we need to address an essential question: Which are the best and most effective ways of working with and through other people?

This is no arcane academic question. How you answer it goes to the heart of how you go about the work of school administration, whether as a department chairperson, a school principal, a superintendent of schools, or any position in between. Nor is it a simple question. Teachers know, from working with children and their parents, that people are complex, idiosyncratic, and full of contradictions, and that their behavior often seems baffling and difficult to grasp.

Moreover, we understand now much better than we did twenty years ago that schools, like all organizations, are complex and confusing places that are—at their best—filled with contradiction, ambivalence, ambiguity, and uncertainty. These understandings help us realize that many of the most important problems confronting school administrators are neither clear-cut nor amenable to technical solutions.

This is not a problem peculiar to school administration nor is it limited to schools as organizations. It is a problem that is generally shared by all professions and all organizations. Consider how Donald Schön describes what he calls a "crisis of confidence in professional knowledge":

In the varied topography of professional practice, there is a high, hard ground overlooking a swamp. On the high ground, manageable problems lend themselves to solutions through the application of research-based theory and technique. In the swampy lowland, messy, confusing problems defy technical solution. The irony of this situation is that the problems of the high ground tend to be relatively unimportant to individuals or society at large, however great their technical interest may be, while in the swamp lie the problems of greatest human concern. The practitioner must choose. Shall he remain on the high ground where he can solve relatively unimportant problems according to prevailing standards of rigor, or shall he descend to the swamp of important problems . . . ?[1]

For many years now, educational administrators have been urged to concentrate on technical solutions to the problems of education. The educational standards movement that we described in Chapter 2 is just such a technical approach, which relies on the technology of norm-referenced objective tests to produce the results desired. Essentially, those who back the standards movement believe that establishing new detailed curriculum standards at the state level that are directly linked to required statewide high-stakes objective achievement tests that must be taken by children at the local level will force local administrators and teachers to revamp practices in their schools in order to achieve the demanded results. Adherents of this strategy usually refer to this as "setting educational standards."

Other popular technical approaches include not only the use of electronic technology, such as computers and the Internet, but also structural technology, such as the creation of magnet schools, charter schools, and other forms of school choice, as well as instructional technology, such as the invention of new pedagogical techniques in the classroom.

The perspective of schools and school reform that has been adopted by many people who advocate these various technologies has been tightly bound to the image of schools as production organizations in which teaching is viewed as routinized labor which, if properly systematized and subjected to bureaucratic controls, will lead logically to the desired outcomes. Adherents of these views of schools have tended to believe that teachers can learn only through formal training that normally consists of lectures, directed workshops, and formal conferences, all of which are controlled and directed by external experts who know what the problems are and what the teachers need to deal effectively with them. Thus, we have witnessed the rise of a virtual obsession to develop training programs to meet every conceivable problem confronting the schools as well as a proliferation of "expert" consultants ready to fly in to dispense their wisdom and quickly depart with their high fees safely in their pockets.

But important educational problems, those that are in the swampland that Donald Schön described, are typically messy: ill defined, ill understood, and complicated. Messy problems tend to be understood, or framed, in terms of the things about them that we are apt to notice. What you may notice, though, comes mainly from your own background, values, and perspectives. As Schön observed:

A nutritionist, for example, may convert a vague worry about malnourishment among children in developing countries into the problem of selecting an optimal diet. But agronomists may frame the problem in terms of food production; epidemiologists may frame it in terms of diseases that increase the demand for nutrients or prevent their absorption; demographers tend to see it in terms of a rate of population growth that has outstripped agricultural activity; engineers, in terms of inadequate food storage and distribution; economists, in terms of insufficient purchasing power or the inequitable distribution of land or wealth.[2]

Similarly, as administrators seek to deal with the problems of education, their approach depends primarily on how they conceptualize their options, how they frame the problems. As in the case of malnutrition of children, there are many ways of framing a response. But people are limited in their ability to make sense of problems, to frame them, by the number and variety of frames that they are familiar with and that they can draw on to give them insight and perspective on the messy, ill-defined problems that every professional encounters in the swampy lowlands.

As we have described, for much of the last century one single perspective dominated thinking about educational organizations: the structural perspective. This is the familiar notion of hierarchical control, bureaucratic offices, the familiar organization chart, and rules and regulations such as "standard operating procedures."

After 1975, organizational thought took a major turn away from such formal theorizing, which emphasized the machinelike characteristics that many scholars believed underlay the ways in which they worked, toward a markedly increased emphasis on the human dimensions of organization. This shift was caused by a combination of several forces that came together simultaneously. One of these forces was intellectual: the development of a new analysis of the fundamental concept of what an organization actually is.

A New Paradigm of Organizational Theory

As we have described, the period from the early 1950s to the mid-1970s produced an outpouring of theory and research in educational administration, so much so that in retrospect the period—the modern period—is often called the era of the Theory Movement in educational administration. However, by the 1970s concern was being increasingly expressed that the theories and the research that had been spawned did not fully describe schools as they were experienced by people in them. Research, and indeed the academic establishment in leading universities at that time, was dominated by those who accepted logical-positivist assumptions about schools as organizations and about ways of understanding them. In other words, they assumed that there was some rational, logical, systematic order underlying the organizational realities of schools that must be discovered. Further, they thought that the means of discovery must be the approach to inquiry that emphasizes measurement, sampling, quasi-experimental methods, and quantification. Moreover, it was believed that these assumptions and these methods of discovery were the only way to improve the training of educational practitioners. Wayne Hoy and Cecil Miskel claimed, for example, that "The road to generalized knowledge can lie only in tough-minded scientific research, not in introspection and subjective experience."[3]

However, by 1974, T. Barr Greenfield articulated serious concerns about then-existing organizational theory that had been developing among both practitioners and a growing number of scholars. The crux of the concerns was that academicians, in their search to understand educational organizations and the behavior of people in them—to make sense of the "swamp" that Donald Schön spoke of—had become transfixed with the wish to be objective, to emphasize mathematical descriptions, and, worst of all, they had come to think of organizations as tangible, concrete entities that exist independently and that are governed by systematic laws and principles. "In common parlance," Greenfield said, "we speak of organizations as if they were real."[4] But they are not real, he went on to explain: "they are invented social realities"[5] that exist only in the minds of people, rather than as tangible, independent realities. Thus, the argument runs, we anthropomorphize when we speak of organizations as imposing themselves on people or of organizational systems "behaving" in certain ways. The essence of organization is human beings who populate the organization; it is they who choose, act, and behave, even if in their own minds they reify the organization as they do so.

Nevertheless, we are continually confronted by evidence that academic assumptions often contrast remarkably with the experiences of individuals engaged in the work of school administration. This pervasive discrepancy between the academic view of the world and that of the practitioner may well explain the lack of enthusiasm that practitioners chronically express for the preparation that they have received at the university.[6] For example, striking differences exist between academic literature on the principalship and principals' written reflections on their own practices:[7]

- Principals describe concrete everyday experiences, whereas academics emphasize theory and abstract relationships.

- Principals communicate through metaphors, examples, and stories, whereas academics use models and the language of science.

- Principals are aware of limits on rationality, whereas academics stress rationality and defining problems in formal terms.

- Principals describe schools in human and emotional terms wherein school personnel agonize over and celebrate their daily ups and downs, whereas academics describe them in terms of detached abstraction.

- Principals see schools as ambiguous and even chaotic places, whereas academics describe an image of rationality and orderliness.

Rise of Qualitative Research Methods

As early as 1964, James Bryant Conant—Nobel laureate, former president of Harvard University, and chairman of the National Defense Research Committee during World War II—had reported that when he undertook studies of U.S. schools in the 1950s it became necessary for him to eschew the hypothetico-deductive way of thinking that he had used for so many years in chemistry; instead, he had to learn to use inductive reasoning because the nature of educational problems was so different from that of scientific problems. In a readable little book called *Two Modes of Thought: My Encounters with Science and*

Education, he discussed the differences between kinds of thinking appropriate to the sciences and education. In it he observed, "What goes on in schools, colleges and universities may be classified as applied social science, or a practical art in which the social sciences were now impinging."[8]

In 1963, Carl Rogers discussed "three ways of knowing" about human behavior and the contexts in which it occurs:

1. Subjective knowing, which "is fundamental to everyday living."

2. Objective knowing, which Rogers thought was not really objective but actually more of a consensus between and among trusted colleagues who were thought to be qualified to make judgments about the "truth" of observed events.

3. Interpersonal, or phenomenological, knowing, in which one can know about the frame of mind of an individual by checking hypotheses with the individual or, alternatively, by validating hypotheses by checking independently with several other observers. Rogers gave a simple example in describing the situation in which you may feel that a colleague is sad or depressed. How can you confirm that hypothesis? One way would be to simply ask the person in an empathetic way. Another would be to wait and see if others comment to you on their own independent observations and feelings about the colleague's state of mind. Rogers believed that in a mature behavioral science all three ways of knowing would be acknowledged and used in combination, rather than using one way and ignoring the others.[9]

Twenty-five years later, in 1988, Arthur Blumberg enriched this line of thinking about educational organizations when he suggested that it is useful to think of school administration as a craft rather than as a science, and so to think about knowledge and understanding as craft workers do. A craft, he contended, is unlike science in important ways. A craft (he used pottery as one example) is learned in day-to-day practice with tools and materials in which the practitioner develops "a nose for things," an intimate feel for the nature of the materials being worked with, a sense of what constitutes acceptable results, an almost intuitive sense of process, an understanding of what to do and when to do it, and a feel for the need for action. Blumberg argued convincingly that by shifting from the concept of science to the concept of craft, one discovers new and useful ways of knowing about organizational behavior in education.[10] However, like many people who advocate the use of pragmatic approaches such as this in our search for understanding of behavior in schools, Blumberg failed to recognize that the use of the craft metaphor is but another theoretical approach to understanding, as had been the work of Rogers, Conant, and so many others who sought to break out of the straitjacket of logical positivism.

By the 1980s, many students of education, who were well aware of these discrepancies, began to eschew traditional formal theorizing and the limitations of traditional quasi-experimental research methods and to find better ways of studying human behavior in schools. They began to go into the schools, instead of sending questionnaires and compiling statistics, to see what was going on and to talk to individuals at schools in order to understand how they were experiencing their lives. The results of such inquiries produced lively, rich narrative descriptions of life in present-day schools that illuminated the confusions, inconsistencies, ambiguities, and general messiness so characteristic of schools' organizational life.

Indeed, studies using these research methods, called *qualitative* or *ethnographic methods,* became the intellectual backbone of the educational reform movement of the 1980s. Gone were the spare statistical studies, so often elegant in style but yielding "no significant difference"; they were replaced by lively, richly documented accounts of human beings at work that yielded insight and understanding of what was happening to people and how they were responding to their experiences.

This was a major shift in ways of thinking about and studying organizational behavior, and it arose directly from abandoning the old certainties of logical positivism in favor of significant new directions in understanding organizational behavior in schools. To get some flavor of the newer thinking, we now present a brief explanation of some of the ideas about organization that began to emerge as traditional organizational theory collapsed.

Educational Organizations as Loosely Coupled Systems

Commonly, we are apt to think of and describe a school system or a school in classical structural terms: for example, as a hierarchically linked pyramid of units subject to strong central control and command (as bureaucracies and military organizations are usually described). Students of organization have recognized for quite some time, however, that school systems and schools are in fact characterized by structural looseness: schools in a district have considerable autonomy and latitude, and teachers in their classrooms are under only very general control and direction of the principal. As Charles Bidwell has pointed out,[11] this is a functionally necessary arrangement, given the nature of the school's task, clients, and technology. Karl Weick captured this reality with vivid imagery, which he credited to James G. March:

> Imagine that you're either the referee, coach, player or spectator in an unconventional soccer match: the field for the game is round; there are several goals scattered haphazardly around the circular field; people can enter or leave the game whenever they want to; they can throw balls in whenever they want; they can say "that's my goal" whenever they want to, as many times as they want to, and for as many goals as they want to; the entire game takes place on a sloped field; and the game is played as if it makes sense. And if you now substitute in that example principals for referees, teachers for coaches, students for players, parents for spectators, and schooling for soccer, you have an equally unconventional depiction of school organizations. The beauty of this depiction is that it captures a different set of realities within educational organizations than are caught when these same organizations are viewed through the tenets of bureaucratic theory.[12]

We can contrast this image of reality with the conventional explanation of how schools go about doing things: namely, by planning, goal setting, and applying such rational processes as cost-benefit analyses, division of labor, job descriptions, authority vested in official office, and consistent evaluation and reward systems. The only problem with this latter conventional view is that it is rare to find schools that actually work that way; more often than not, people in educational organizations find that rational concepts such as these simply do not explain the way the system functions.

Because so much of educational organization defies explanation by existing rational concepts, the suggestion is that we give serious thought to newer, more unconventional ideas that may lead us to more accurate understanding, such as the notion of "loose coupling." In general, the term *loose coupling* means that although subsystems of the organization (and the activities that they carry out) are related to one another, each preserves its own identity and individuality. In a high school, for example, the guidance office is usually shown on an organization chart as reporting to the principal's office; yet the linkage is usually loose, with relatively infrequent interaction and typically a slow response of one to the other; the linkage is, in short, relatively weak and unimportant. The coupling—the very glue that holds the organization together—may be described as, at best, "loose."

Educational Organizations as Dual Systems

The concept of loose coupling as a distinctive characteristic of schools and other educational organizations has been powerful in explaining aspects of their organization that were previously ill understood. It does not, however, explain them fully: an observer can easily find much in schools that smacks of bureaucratic or classical organization as well as much that is loosely coupled.

By the mid-1980s there was general agreement among students of organizations that educational organizations are loosely coupled in some significant ways and are highly bureaucratic in other ways, and that this is important in understanding them and the behavior of people in them. For example, in reporting the results of a study of 188 elementary schools in thirty-four school districts in the San Francisco area, John Meyer and Brian Rowan showed that

> the inspection of instructional activity is delegated to the local school and takes place infrequently. For example, only one of the thirty-four superintendents interviewed reported that the district office evaluates teachers directly. Nor does it appear that principals and peers have the opportunity to inspect and discuss teachers' work: Of the principals surveyed, 85 percent reported that they and their teachers do not work together on a daily basis. Further, there is little evidence of interaction among teachers: A majority of the principals report that there are no day-to-day working relations among teachers within the same grade level, and 83 percent report no daily work relations among teachers of different grades. Teachers reaffirm this view of segmented teaching. Two-thirds report that their teaching is observed by other teachers infrequently (once a month or less), and half report a similar infrequency of observation by their principals.[13]

Considerable other research evidence corroborates the observation that supervision by school administrators is rather infrequent.[14]

Of course, control may be exerted by means other than direct inspection (which public school people usually call "supervision"). For example, evaluating student learning, maintaining close and detailed specification of the curriculum, and ensuring that students have mastered the work of a previous grade before being promoted to the next are among the many ways that schools may exercise strong control over teaching. These views are, of course, at the core of the No Child Left Behind Act.

Thus, the central core activity of the school—instruction—is viewed as being loosely coupled to the extent that it is not directly controlled by administrators. Although administrators bear general responsibility for the instructional programs of schools, their authority to control the instructional behavior of teachers is rather limited and, since the advent of collective bargaining, appears to be declining. For example, Meyer and Rowan reported that only 12 percent of the principals they studied indicated that they have real decision power over the methods that teachers use, and a mere 4 percent said that they are extremely influential in determining the instructional methods used by teachers.[15]

Administrators, however, do have access to bureaucratic means by which to structure the work of teachers and, thereby, have indirect means of influencing the instructional behavior in the school. *The control of time* is one means: time schedules, the frequency with which students are pulled out for special classes and other activities, the frequency of interruptions of classroom instruction, and the burden of paperwork required of teachers all mold the teaching behavior of teachers and all are influenced by the administrator as a key actor. *The assignment of students to classes* (how many and what kind) is also considerably influenced by administrators and constrains the teachers' work behavior. *Grouping* is another way in which administrators can influence instruction—for example, students may be grouped heterogeneously or homogeneously; teachers may work alone in self-contained classrooms, on teaching teams, or in departments. Principals also influence instructional behavior of teachers through their *control of resources:* teaching space, the availability of equipment, access to the copying machine, and even the availability of such mundane basic supplies as paper and pencils. Yet, although these bureaucratic means are powerful in some ways in influencing the instructional behavior of teachers, they are relatively indirect. Further, as teachers have come to realize the power of these mechanisms, they have increasingly sought to gain some share in controlling them through collective bargaining. Thus, principals are increasingly constrained in their ability to dictate teaching schedules and class sizes, and even in their ability to impose paperwork on teachers.

Whereas the core technical activity of the school is, thus, loosely coupled (as contrasted with what one would expect from a classic bureaucratic organization), noninstructional activities are often tightly coupled. The issuing of paychecks in timely fashion, the deployment of buses, the management of money, and pupil accounting (attendance, for example) are among the numerous noninstructional activities that are closely controlled by administrators and therefore may be described as tightly coupled. In contrast to the nebulous authority that administrators reported over the instructional activities of teachers in their research, Meyer and Rowan reported that 82 percent of the principals surveyed claim to make decisions about scheduling, 75 percent about the assignment of pupils to classes, and 88 percent (either alone or in consultation with other school administrators in the district) about hiring new personnel. These activities may be said to be tightly coupled inasmuch as they are carefully controlled by direct administrative oversight.

One may conclude that looseness in controlling the instructional behavior of teachers is somehow wrong and insist—in the tradition of classic bureaucratic thought—that it be tightened up. Indeed, many contemporary observers take such a view, and this explains many political initiatives undertaken in recent years by governors, legislatures, and a few state departments of education to "toughen up" standards and educational requirements by imposing new requirements and limitations on schools. These often include adding required instruction to the curriculum, increased testing of both students and teachers, and more detailed specification of teaching methods. However, the issue being raised here is not whether schools ought to be loosely coupled or tightly coupled. Our interest is in better understanding the organizational characteristics of educational organizations *as they exist* (rather than as someone may wish they were) so that we may better understand the leadership of people in them.

Indeed, recent studies strongly suggest that there are powerful mechanisms through which the organization exerts considerable control over the instructional activities of teachers that have heretofore been largely unseen and unrecognized. These mechanisms are in contrast with the hierarchical line of authority embodied in classical bureaucratic thought. Whereas we traditionally think of organizations exercising control exclusively through such formal mechanisms as supervision down the line of authority, a useful newer perspective is that, in educational organizations at least, powerful control is exercised through the use of far more subtle and indirect means: the development of organizational culture. Understanding this can be a powerful insight in understanding schools and universities and how to lead them effectively.

Building Human Capital

Capital is ordinarily thought of in terms of tangible assets such as cash, raw materials, real estate, machinery and equipment, and intellectual property such as ideas, inventions, and creations. But economists have, for a long time, understood the concept of *human* capital: that is, that the knowledge that people have, their skills, attitudes, and social skills, are also assets to any human enterprise. The human resources available to an organization are, therefore, a form of human capital. In fact, it turns out that they are potentially highly valuable assets that can increase in value over time—which, by definition, assets should do—or decrease in value, depending largely on how they are managed.

Applied to societies, nations, or regions, this concept helps to explain why some societies, though rich in tangible assets such as minerals or water power, may be less productive than others. Those societies and nations in which people have high levels of education and well-developed work skills, are favorably disposed toward the discipline of the workplace, and have a social tradition that places high value on hard work and productivity tend to become wealthier than those that do not.[16] This concept was demonstrated spectacularly in Western Europe shortly after World War II with the Marshall Plan.

Most of Europe lay in ruins after World War II: many factories were gone, equipment ruined or worn out, currency systems in shambles, distribution and transportation systems nearly wrecked, and not a few cities and towns reduced to rubble. As a result, unemployment was rampant, poverty was commonplace, and despair was everywhere. George C. Marshall and Harry S. Truman persuaded a reluctant Congress to fund a large-scale plan, the Marshall

Plan, to rebuild the currency and banking systems, the cities, the factories, the transportation and communications systems, and, generally, to get people back to work and productive once again. A key to the plan was that the human capital needed to bring recovery about was already in place in Western European nations: Western Europeans were a well-educated populace, possessing high levels of work skills and managerial skills; they were not only able but also wanting to work; and they had a long tradition of pride in high-quality work and achievement. Because these human resources were in place, the infusing of a substantial amount of start-up money enabled Western Europe to quickly rebuild, and citizens rapidly achieved levels of productivity higher than those that had existed prior to the war.

The concept of building human capital underlies much of the historic effort to improve the lot of societies through the spread of education and the development of social infrastructures, as well as the physical and economic infrastructures of third-world nations through international aid. Today, many developing nations that are emerging as prosperous societies with rising standards of living, especially countries in the Pacific Rim area such as Japan, South Korea, Taiwan, Hong Kong, Thailand, Singapore, and China, manifest the power of the concept of human capital. Not a few business leaders in the United States view the need to reform U.S. schooling through the lens of human capital, often referring to the reform of education as an investment in human capital. The concept is apt for application to thinking about organizations as well and lies at the heart of the notion of human resources management.

Administrators are customarily held accountable for the financial and physical assets of the school district, such as buildings, equipment, and money. The processes of preparing and approving the annual budget, then the administration of the budget over the course of the fiscal year, and finally a formal accounting of stewardship are familiar and important activities in every school district. Permitting tax-levy funds to be used unwisely or allowing assets to deteriorate through misuse or neglect are, justifiably, considered to be evidence of mismanagement. Only in the 1970s, however, did accountants as well as organizational theorists begin to realize the extent to which mismanagement of an organization's human resources can be detrimental to the organization's effectiveness.

One form of mismanagement is, obviously, to spend too much on human resources; this has led to downsizing, outsourcing, contracting for services, using temporary and part-time employees, and other efforts to reduce payroll costs. Another way of mismanaging human resources, perhaps more important because it is less obvious and often unseen immediately, is failing to place adequate value on the skills, abilities, motivations, and commitment of the people in the organization.

In a typical U.S. school district, over 80 percent of the annual operating budget is allocated to personnel services and related costs. Obviously the human resources of the school enterprise require a substantial outlay of tax-levy funds. Not only are the administrators responsible for maintaining the quality and effectiveness of these resources, but they also must manage them—as one would manage any assets—so that their value to the school district increases over time. People, therefore, should be managed so that their skills, motivations, attitudes, and knowledge develop, improve, and increase over time rather than level off at a steady pace or, worse yet, decline. This way of managing, so as to develop and increase the value of the organization's human resources, is the process of building human capital.

Human Resources as Assets

In building human capital, it is insufficient to assume that if employees do not actually quit, the state of the organization's human resources is acceptable. Research has shown, for example, that the processes of building and administering the budget are often handled in ways that create considerable pressure on individuals and groups, which leads to strife, apathy, tension, strain, aggression, and a pervasive feeling of failure. These responses tend, of course, to give rise to counterproductive behaviors that are directly related, not to the fact that budget decisions had to be made, but to the leadership processes that leaders and administrators choose to employ in dealing with the budget.[17]

As Rensis Likert observed, "if bickering, distrust, and irreconcilable conflict become greater, the human enterprise is worth less; if the capacity to use differences constructively and engage in cooperative teamwork improves, the human organization is a more valuable asset."[18] Many problems stem from a negative climate in the organization—such as low morale, inadequate effort, lack of cooperation, complaints, and employee turnover.[19] Thus there is impressive evidence that the internal characteristics of the organization that tend to evoke destructive organizational behavior arise largely from the choices that administrators make in deciding how to carry out their work. Indeed, it is often largely the behavior of administrators that needlessly causes the dysfunctional feelings and behaviors commonly observed in struggling or failing organizations.

A continuing difficulty in dealing with this issue has been to find ways to make administrators aware of the dense relationship between their behaviors, policies, and practices and their impact on the human side of the enterprise. In dealing with tangible assets, such as money or real estate, it is often possible for accountants to demonstrate with numbers the bottom-line results of choices that managers make affecting the value of tangible assets entrusted to their care. One can show that deferring maintenance on buildings is an expensive practice, that purchasing wisely can save money, or that turning down thermostats reduces fuel costs. It is much more difficult to make such cause-and-effect linkages between administrative practices and their impact on the value of human resources. A local taxpayer association may cheer on a heavy-handed administrator who ruthlessly cuts teaching positions to slash the budget, but what is the cost if student achievement nosedives and dropout rates soar? Antiunion residents may be elated to see the superintendent of schools get tough at contract bargaining time, but what is the cost if resentment undermines the motivation of teachers and teamwork between administrators and classroom teachers falters? The American Accounting Association has supported a great deal of work to develop ways of dealing with such human resources issues in industrial and commercial organizations. This is called "human resources accounting." The central continuing problem with human resources accounting lies in the difficulty of measuring and quantifying the impact of management behavior on human attitudes, motivation, and work behavior. However, this work has given rise to a set of concepts that are helpful in understanding organizational behavior.

Human resources are valuable. In fact, in the case of educational organizations, they are often the most valuable resources available to create and maintain a high-performing organization. If thought of and treated as assets, the people in the organization—the human resources from which human capital is formed—are expected to have greater value in the future than at the present time. This is the essential nature of assets. Therefore, one can properly think of the costs of recruiting and hiring new people, training and supporting them, encouraging their professional growth and development, and managing them sensitively and skillfully as investment in people and—one would hope—their eventual higher productivity as return on that investment.

Instead of increasing in value over time, however, it is commonplace to assume that the human resources in schools decline in value over the years. For example, many observers of schooling complain that school faculties contain a lot of "deadwood," particularly older teachers, who are often described as "burned out." This is often thought to be a consequence of tenure, which allegedly causes teachers to become not only complacent but uncaring. As a proposed remedy, legislation is frequently called for that would make it easier to fire teachers for little substantial cause. If this is true, it is not only costly but—worse—hinders the school's effective performance. But if it is true, one must ask, what is the cause? Is it that teachers tend to be a basically selfish and uncaring lot who, once they have some job security, shed any sense of professional responsibility? Is it that teaching is somehow a young person's game and at some point teachers should be dismissed because of age? Perhaps, but there is little that we know about organizational behavior that supports either of these propositions. Rather, research in organizational behavior suggests that it is more likely that in a supportive organizational environment, one that facilitates continuous personal growth and professional fulfillment, teachers turn out to be increasingly effective over the course of time. This fortuitous state of affairs is ordinarily found to exist in schools that are described as highly effective. Creating such a growth-enhancing organizational environment is the responsibility of those in charge of the schools, namely, school administrators. It is the process through which one builds human capital in schools.

Organizational Culture as a Bearer of Authority

Like all workplaces, an educational organization—each school and each university—is characterized by a distinctive organizational culture. In this sense "organizational culture" refers to the *norms* that inform people about what is acceptable and what is not, the dominant *values* that the organization cherishes above others, the *basic assumptions and beliefs* that are shared by members of the organization, the *rules* of the game that must be observed if one is to get along and be accepted as a member, and the *philosophy* that guides the organization in dealing with its employees and its clients. These elements of organizational culture are developed over a period of time by the people in the organization working together. They evolve during the history of the organization and are shared and subscribed to by those who are a part of that history.

The culture of the educational organization shapes and molds assumptions and perceptions that are basic to understanding what it means to be a teacher. The culture informs the teachers as to what it means to teach, what teaching methods are available and approved for use, what the pupils or students are like—what is possible, and what is not. The culture also plays a large role in defining for teachers their commitment to the task: it evokes the energy of the teachers to perform the task, loyalty and commitment to the organization and what it stands for, emotional bonds of attachment to the organization and its ideals. These give rise to teachers' willingness not only to follow the rules and norms governing their behavior in the organization but, more than that, to accept the ideals of the organization as their own personal values and, therefore, to work energetically to achieve the espoused goals of the organization.[20]

Do certain kinds of organizational cultures promote greater effectiveness in educational organizations? The consensus is a resounding "yes," as we describe more fully in Chapter 6. It is widely accepted today that the single most critical factor in improving the performance of an organization is to change its culture. For example, Terrence E. Deal and his associates have contended that it is strong organizational culture that distinguishes high-performing companies from less successful companies in competitive markets.[21] In a highly popular and best-selling book, Thomas J. Peters and Robert H. Waterman, Jr., argued that successful U.S. corporations are characterized by the presence of specific, describable cultures that clearly differentiate them from others that seek to compete with them.[22] Similarly, Rosabeth Moss Kanter has argued persuasively that companies that have what she calls an "open culture" are more innovative and more successful than those that do not.[23] Edgar Schein has described the relationship between organizational culture and the ability of administrators to exercise leadership.[24] A growing body of literature concerning the role of organizational culture in educational organizations (discussed in later chapters of this book) strongly suggests that organizational culture is as powerful in creating effective educational organizations as it is in creating profit-making corporations.

Five Basic Assumptions of Effective Schools

For well over two decades, researchers have studied the characteristics of effective schools, seeking to find out what they tend to be like in contrast with less effective schools. The result is an accumulated body of research that suggests that effective schools, or high-achieving schools, tend to be organized and operated on the basis of five basic assumptions:[25]

1. Whatever else a school can and should do, its central purpose is to teach: success is measured by students' progress in knowledge, skills, and attitudes.

2. The school is responsible for providing the overall environment in which teaching and learning occur.

3. Schools must be treated holistically: partial efforts to make improvements that deal with the needs of only some of the students and break up the unity of the instructional program are likely to fail.

4. The most crucial characteristics of a school are the attitudes and behaviors of the teachers and other staff, not material things such as the size of its library or the age of the physical plant.[26]

5. Perhaps most important, the school accepts responsibility for the success or failure of the academic performance of the students. Students are firmly regarded as

capable of learning regardless of their ethnicity, sex, home or cultural background, or family income. "Pupils from poor families do not need a different curriculum, nor does their poverty excuse failure to learn basic skills," Stewart Purkey and Marshall Smith have asserted, adding, "Differences among schools do have an impact on student achievement, and those differences are controllable by the school staff."[27]

Thus, the effective schools concept turns 180 degrees from traditional educational thought that tends to blame the victim, namely, the student, for low academic achievement. Though one of the outstanding characteristics of effective schools is that they take responsibility for meeting the educational needs of students to a greater degree than their less successful counterparts, this is still a concept that many educational practitioners find difficult to accept. Especially in those schools seemingly overwhelmed, as many inner-city and not a few suburban schools are, by poor children, children from diverse cultural backgrounds, and children from nontraditional families, it is not easy to focus the responsibility for the motivation and achievement of students on the school rather than on the students or forces outside the school. Nevertheless, this is the essential lesson from the effective schools research.

The question remains: What is it, specifically, that the schools do in order to fulfill this responsibility? Listen to Purkey and Smith, who developed a penetrating analysis of the effective schools research literature in the mid-1980s:

> The most persuasive research suggests that student academic performance is strongly affected by school culture. This culture is composed of values, norms, and roles existing within institutionally distinct structures of governance, communication, educational practices and policies and so on. Successful schools are found to have cultures that produce a climate or "ethos" conducive to teaching and learning . . . efforts to change schools have been most productive and most enduring when directed toward influencing the entire school culture via a strategy involving collaborative planning, shared decision making, and collegial work in an atmosphere friendly to experimentation and evaluation.[28]

Thus, the effective schools research suggests "increased involvement of teachers and other staff members in decision making, expanded opportunities for collaborative planning, and flexible change strategies that can reflect the unique 'personality' of each school. The goal is to change the school culture; the means requires staff members to assume responsibility for school improvement, which in turn is predicated on their having the authority and support necessary"[29] to create instructional programs that meet the educational needs of their students.

A survey of the research literature has identified a cluster of thirteen organizational and operational characteristics that effective schools tend to exhibit.[30] They fall into two groups. The first group contains nine characteristics that can be implemented quickly at minimal cost by administrative action:

1. School-site management and democratic decision making, in which individual schools are encouraged to take greater responsibility for, and are given greater latitude in, educational problem solving.

2. Support from the district for increasing the capacity of schools to identify and solve significant educational problems; this includes reducing the inspection and management roles of central office people while increasing support and encouragement of school-level leadership and collaborative problem solving.

3. Strong leadership, which may be provided by administrators but also may be provided by integrated teams of administrators, teachers, and perhaps others.

4. Staff stability to facilitate the development of a strong cohesive school culture.

5. A planned, coordinated curriculum that treats the students' educational needs holistically and increases time spent on academic learning.

6. Schoolwide staff development that links the school's organizational and instructional needs with the needs that teachers themselves perceive should be addressed.

7. Parental involvement particularly in support of homework, attendance, and discipline.

8. Schoolwide recognition of academic success, both in terms of improving academic performance and achieving standards of excellence.

9. An emphasis on the time required for teaching and learning; for example, reducing interruptions and disruptions, stressing the primacy of focused efforts to learn, and restructuring teaching activities.

These are not the only characteristics of effective schools and certainly they are not the most crucial. However, they are relatively easy and inexpensive to implement quickly, and they set the stage for the development of a second group of four characteristics that have great power to renew and increase the school's capacity to continue to solve problems and increase effectiveness over time:

10. Collaborative planning and collegial relationships that promote feelings of unity, encourage sharing of knowledge and ideas, and foster consensus among those in the school.

11. Sense of community, in which alienation—of both teachers and students—is reduced and a sense of mutual sharing is strengthened.

12. Shared clear goals and high achievable expectations, which arise from collaboration, collegiality, and a sense of community and which serve to unify those in the organization through their common purposes.

13. Order and discipline that bespeak the seriousness and purposefulness of the school as a community of people—students, teachers and staff, and other adults—that is focused by mutual agreement on shared goals, collaboration, and consensus.

Clearly, the critical school characteristics listed in the second group are more complex than those in the first group, more difficult to achieve and sustain over time, yet they combine to produce great power to establish the improvement of educational effectiveness as a central focus of life within the school. The power, of course, lies in developing within the school a culture—norms, values, and beliefs—that unites those in the school in their unending quest of seeking increased educational effectiveness. Many if not most school-improvement plans can be faulted precisely for seeking to "install" the relatively simpler first-order characteristics and falling short of seriously engaging in the culture-rebuilding suggested by the more complex second-order characteristics cited here.

Turmoil in School Reform

By the beginning of the twenty-first century, school reform was a widespread and highly energized disarray of competing theories and calls for action. Three main approaches were competing with each other for allegiance and support from the many constituencies concerned with the problem. The Congress of the United States sought to mandate a denouement by choosing one of the three main competing approaches to school reform and enacting it into law in January 2002 with the passage and signing of the No Child Left Behind Act. Many believed that this would end the competition and apparent disarray by forcing the emergence of a single approved approach over the competing approaches. Perhaps, but more than a century of educational history in the United States suggests that a more likely outcome will be more pluralistic, with each of the three approaches making some contribution. In the meantime, there is, and will be, considerable confusion and contention as a solution to the problem is forged—perhaps creating a new amalgam of consensus—in our democratic culture. Educational leaders like you are an important constituency of schooling, and which approach to school reform a leader accepts has the potential of making a great deal of difference in the direction that the school reform movement will ultimately take.

Although, as we described in Chapter 2, a case can be made that descriptions of the plight of the public schools are overstated, if not just wrong, many people believe that we are past that argument and that it is irrelevant to most of us. The need for school reform is widely accepted within the education profession as well as in the general public. A few, particularly those who advocate abandoning the public schools altogether, many of whom are identified with conservative economic and political leanings, continue to hammer away at the credibility of public enterprises in hopes of destroying their foundations. Although it is not clear that they will not ultimately prevail, a more likely scenario seems to be that public schooling still enjoys public support and will not be destroyed in the end. But it seems equally clear that schooling in the United States will continue the processes of change and development that have been ongoing since the late nineteenth century.

Three Approaches to School Reform

As we have said, those who are engaged in school reform generally fall into one of three groups:

1. One group advocates the use of some form of market competition as a basis for school reform. This group includes those who believe that education should be improved by abandoning the concept of government-operated schools altogether and turning to private enterprise to do the job in a competitive open market. The theory is not merely that private-sector managers are inherently more capable of running schools better and at lower cost than public-sector managers, but that the discipline inherent in the competition of the marketplace will produce more flexible, more nimble, more responsive—in a word, better—schools. This group of reformers includes those who believe that parents should have options in choosing the schools that their children attend. Many who favor this approach think that introducing competition—that is, by making the choice of schools competitive in a diverse marketplace of many kinds of educational opportunities—would in itself have a tonic effect on the quality of all schools. This is often called "school choice" when the schools available are limited to the various public schools in a district or a state. However, some advocate that parents should be issued vouchers drawn on the public treasury that may be redeemed at any school—public, private, or church related. This is called a "voucher plan."

2. Another group is composed of those who believe that it is necessary for each state to (1) mandate a fixed body of knowledge that is thought to be basic and that each student must be required to learn, (2) determine the achievement level of each student in this task by administering statewide standardized examinations, and (3) require a prescribed passing grade on examinations before a student is promoted from one grade to the next or is allowed to graduate from high school. This is usually called the "educational standards movement" of school reform. These concepts, of course, are core elements of the No Child Left Behind Act.

3. A third group seeking to raise academic standards and school achievement is composed of those who believe that schools should be improved from within so that the schools and their teachers have the skills, resources, conditions, and habits that make the schools more responsive, more challenging, and simply better places for children to learn. This includes emphasis on strong leadership, a collaborative climate, and the continuous development of theory of practice. It is a strategy of developing the capacity of the organization to support people—teachers, principals, superintendents, parents—in improving their own professional practice. Creating charter schools, to free them from bureaucratic officialism, is seen by some as a necessary prerequisite for this approach.

These three strategies for school reform are discussed in greater detail in Chapter 12.

Conclusion

The essay "The Study of Administration," which Princeton's Assistant Professor Woodrow Wilson published in *Political Science Quarterly* in the summer of 1887, marked the beginning of serious study of administration. During the century that was to follow, students of organization struggled to do what had never before been done: to increase through systematic inquiry our understanding of organizations and the behavior of people who work in them. Two very clear long-term trends developed that, together, set the stage for where we are now and where we are going.

The Effort to Create an Administrative Science

The search for deep and stable principles believed to be the foundations of administrative thought and practice led first to the quest for a science of administration. The effort was fueled by the conviction that some fundamental rational logic, system, and order must underlie organization. These were to be discovered through objective, value-free scientific research using measurement and expressing descriptions in mathematical terms.

Once these factors were discovered, it was thought, systematic principles for engaging in the practice of administration could be scientifically derived from them. By the middle of the twentieth century, though, many observers were having doubts, not merely about the assumptions of system and rationality in organizations that guided the processes of scientific discovery but also that the assumed order and logical system even existed at all. These doubts arose from two main observations. First, practicing administrators saw little relationship between the reality of organizational life as they experienced it and the theories of organizational life that academicians espoused. Second, scant convincing evidence was generated to support the "scientific" assumptions as being more valid than other insightful, thoughtful views.

Formal challenges to this logical-positivist paradigm began to be published in 1974, the so-called theory movement collapsed, and today students of educational administration, at least, have coalesced around a new paradigm that is in the process of being developed at this time. The new paradigm rejects anthropomorphism, which can lead us to reify organizations and think of them as existing in some sort of freestanding way independent of human beings, when organizations actually are social inventions that exist only in the minds of people. We now think not so much of analyzing organizations in mathematical terms but of making sense of them in human terms. We accept that organizations do not act or think; people do.

Thus, at the dawn of the second century of organizational study, few seriously believe that the time is ripe to develop a science of administration if, indeed, such a science ever will be developed. This does not mean, however, that we have failed either to discover some basic principles of organizational behavior or to develop increased understanding of organizational life. Far from it. The patient theorizing and research carried out over the course of a century has produced a rich legacy of knowledge that administrators can use in practice. But it is not marked by the logical precision and mathematical certitude that the pioneer scholars had expected it to have.

Centrality of the Human Dimension of Organization

Perhaps the most powerful learning to have arisen during the first century of organizational studies concerns what is now obvious: that the key to understanding organization lies in understanding the human and social dimensions. Early scholars emphasized organizational structure, chiefly as a hierarchy of power, and the discipline of inducing those of the lower ranks to submit to the power and authority, perceived as legitimate, of those in the higher ranks of the hierarchy. Toward the middle of the twentieth century, triggered by the Western Electric research, students of organization began to grasp what Douglas

McGregor was later to describe as "the human side of enterprise." This was the realization that human motivation, aspiration, beliefs, and values have wondrous power in determining the effectiveness of efforts to lead and develop organizations.

At first, still obeisant to the then widely held conviction of the legitimacy of hierarchical authority, this was interpreted as "human relations," meaning taking steps to ameliorate and reduce the resistance of workers to their powerlessness. Human relations, as it was interpreted by administrators, typically became ameliorative inducements for people to submit to organizational authority. The inducements ranged from health insurance plans to simple civility in daily encounters; from providing pleasant working environments to legitimizing the feelings of employees about their work. But throughout the human relations era, administrators clung to the notion that while they might act civilly, even kindly, to subordinates, power in the organization is hierarchical and, by right, ought to be exercised asymmetrically from top down.

But the "battle of the century," both in organizational studies and in the larger world, has been the struggle between centralized authority and individual freedom, between entrenched power elites and ordinary people. Organizations of all kinds, often once revered, are now suspect, viewed with hostility, and often described as oppressive. The ability to establish and maintain organizational discipline through traditional top-down hierarchical exercise of power has been rapidly eroding in all kinds of organizations from nation-states to school districts. The larger canvas, the backdrop, is of course revealed in the collapse of traditional political hegemonies that began to unfold in the late 1980s in Eastern Europe, the former Soviet Union, and South Africa as people around the world demanded greater power and freedom from centralized organizational constraints, greater control over their own lives and destinies.

In the world of U.S. education this theme is insistently echoed, if in muted tones, in oft-repeated themes that call for efforts to improve the performance of schools by restructuring them so as to increase the power of teachers to make critical educational decisions, facilitate collaborative decision making, and create collegial growth-enhancing school cultures. This is, of course, a marked departure from traditional thinking and is based on the conviction that overemphasis on bureaucratic structures, top-down exercise of power, and centralized control have demonstrably failed to produce the organizational results that advocates of traditional organizational theory had claimed it would.

Where We Are and Where We Are Going

At the present time, traditional bureaucratic approaches to organization and the newer approaches that emphasize the human dimensions of organization exist side by side and often compete for the attention and loyalty of educational administrators. Bureaucracy is far from dead in educational organizations, and many people are confident that imposing change from the top down is the most effective way to reform them. On the other hand, nonbureaucratic approaches to organizing and administering have been rapidly gaining support in recent years. These two approaches will continue to compete in the marketplace of ideas for years to come, with the concept of building human capital continuing to gain ground because it so well meets contemporary conditions.

Reflective Activities

1. In this chapter we point out the discrepancies between the academic view of the world and that of the practitioner. As an aspiring leader, what is your opinion of these discrepancies? How will your opinion affect the way in which you lead an organization?

2. Locate a primarily quantitative research article and a primarily qualitative research article about organizational behavior. Compare and contrast the different research design and data collection methods. Describe the findings in these articles. How are the research methods in each type of article useful in understanding organizations? In your view, which type of research paradigm is best?

3. Reflect on the results from the Meyer and Rowan study. Analyze how the leadership in your organization uses bureaucratic means to influence the instructional behavior of teachers. Are these ideas effective? Suggest others ideas that might be effective in influencing instruction.

4. Using the research on effective school characteristics, identify those elements in your school that are currently used and those that are not. Are those characteristics used in your school effective? If so, why? Is not, what do you suggest to improve their effectiveness?

5. *Working on Your Game Plan.* Consider the following advertisement, which appeared word for word (except for changes in the names) in a national newspaper in December 1999. Assume that you are interested in applying for the principalship that is advertised. After reviewing the work that you have done thus far on your game plan, and after reviewing Chapter 6, prepare a draft of the letter of interest that the ad requests.

   Because you are limited to a one-page letter (including the heading block, inside address, and signature block), it is evident that

---

COLUMBIA-PROSPECT

July 1, 2008 Vacancy

PRINCIPAL

Alexander Hamilton High School

Join and lead an outstanding High School with a talented faculty, a supportive community, motivated and wonderful students.

If you . . .
- Have a vision of educational excellence
- Are collaborative
- Are bright, articulate, and reflective
- Believe that all students can meet or surpass State standards
- Have a wonderful sense of humor
- Enjoy being involved in an exciting educational environment where students and faculty are treated with respect and appreciation
- Wish to lead and learn with a dynamic and talented faculty

Alexander Hamilton High School could be your dream come true!

Please send a one-page letter that describes you and your interest in this position by January 3, 2008 to:

> **Columbia-Prospect Search
> c/o Regional Services
> P.O. Box 834
> Moorestown, PA 33908**

---

*No phone calls, please.
Written replies only. AA/EOE*

---

you cannot address every point raised in the ad. In preparing your draft, you must choose, at most, a few points that you consider important and with which you can present yourself to advantage.

It would be interesting, and probably a learning opportunity, to discuss with others how they handled this problem and why they chose to say what they did.

Suggested Reading

Meyer, Marshall W., and Associates, *Environments and Organizations.* San Francisco: Jossey-Bass, 1978.

Structuralism, in the classical bureaucratic tradition, has long dominated thinking about organizations in sociology. This important book marks a sharp departure from that tradition and introduces the newer organizational theorizing that is emerging in that discipline. Excellent chapter on "The Structure of Educational Organizations." Highly recommended.

Mink, Oscar G., Barbara P. Mink, and Keith Q. Owens, *Developing High Performance People: The Art of Coaching.* Reading, MA: Addison-Wesley Longman, 2000.

The authors describe coaching as the art of encouraging others to experience their own power, and they try to show how leaders can use coaching to create high-performance environments, as present-day school reform efforts demand. Starting from understanding how people learn and grow on the job, they deal with issues involved in helping workers to deal with barriers to their performance, participate with others in self-managed teams, and work toward improving the performance of the organization.

Mintzberg, Henry, *The Structuring of Organizations.* Englewood Cliffs, NJ: Prentice-Hall, 1979.

A well-organized, comprehensive, and lucid discussion of contemporary problems of designing and building organizations. Describes the characteristics of five specific kinds of organizations and their implications for administration.

Parker, Glenn M., *Cross-Functional Teams: Working with Allies, Enemies, and Other Strangers.* San Francisco: Jossey-Bass, 1994.

Though primarily concerned with corporate management, this book about managing and leading collaborative teams does include among its examples some noteworthy team efforts in public school education in the United States. It is a how-to manual that gives advice and practical guidance on such issues as overcoming communication barriers, building bridges between groups, and working together to produce fluid and productive collaboration.

Peters, Thomas J., and Robert H. Waterman, Jr., *In Search of Excellence: Lessons from America's Best-Run Companies.* New York: Harper & Row, 1982.

Long on the best-seller lists, this is a must for those who want to find out how modern organizational theory is being used in the competitive corporate world. Though it focuses on business and industry, it contains a great deal of food for thought for educators.

chapter 6

Organizational Culture and Organizational Climate

LEARNING OBJECTIVES

After reading this chapter, you should be able to

- Describe the concept that school leaders can enhance the motivation of people by bringing about changes in the psychosocial environment of the organization.

- Specify and describe the physical and material factors that give rise to the organizational ecology of schools.

- Specify and describe the human social system factors that give rise to the organizational milieu of schools.

- Specify and describe the organizational structure factors that give rise to the organization of schools.

- Specify and describe the psychosocial characteristics that give rise to the organizational culture of schools.

- Describe the relationship between and among the four internal organizational dimensions: ecology, milieu, organization, and culture.

- Describe the roles and functions of artifacts, values, and basic assumptions in creating and maintaining the culture of a school.

- Describe and discuss the roles of social norms and basic assumptions in creating and maintaining the culture of a school.

- Define organizational climate.

- Describe the relationship between organizational climate and the four psychosocial dimensions of the school.

- Define the term *interaction–influence system* and state the ways in which it can affect the organizational effectiveness of the school.

- Explain why organizational culture cannot be studied directly but must be inferred from observing organizational behavior in schools.

ISLLC Standards

STANDARD 1: A school administrator is an educational leader who promotes the success of all students by facilitating the development, articulation, implementation, and stewardship of a vision of learning that is shared and supported by the school community.

Knowledge

The administrator has knowledge and understanding of:

- information sources, data collection, and data analysis strategies
- effective communication
- effective consensus-building and negotiation skills

Dispositions

The administrator believes in, values, and is committed to:

- the educability of all
- a school vision of high standards of learning
- continuous school improvement
- a willingness to continuously examine one's own assumptions, beliefs, and practices
- doing the work required for high levels of personal and organization performance

Performances

The administrator facilitates processes and engages in activities ensuring that:

- the vision and mission of the school are effectively communicated to staff, parents, students, and community members
- the vision and mission are communicated through the use of symbols, ceremonies, stories, and similar activities
- the core beliefs of the school vision are modeled for all stakeholders
- the vision is developed with and among stakeholders
- the contributions of school community members to the realization of the vision are recognized and celebrated
- the school community is involved in school improvement efforts
- the vision shapes the educational programs, plans, and actions
- an implementation plan is developed in which objectives and strategies to achieve the vision and goals are clearly articulated
- assessment data related to student learning are used to develop the school vision and goals
- barriers to achieving the vision are identified, clarified, and addressed
- needed resources are sought and obtained to support the implementation of the school mission and goals
- existing resources are used in support of the school vision and goals
- the vision, mission, and implementation plans are regularly monitored, evaluated, and revised

STANDARD 2: A school administrator is an educational leader who promotes the success of all students by advocating, nurturing, and sustaining a school culture and instructional program conducive to student learning and staff professional growth.

Knowledge

The administrator has knowledge and understanding of:

- school cultures

Dispositions

The administrator believes in, values, and is committed to:

- student learning as the fundamental purpose of schooling
- professional development as an integral part of school improvement
- a safe and supportive learning environment

Performances

The administrator facilitates processes and engages in activities ensuring that:

- all individuals are treated with fairness, dignity, and respect
- professional development promotes a focus on student learning consistent with the school vision and goals
- students and staff feel valued and important
- the responsibilities and contributions of each individual are acknowledged
- barriers to student learning are identified, clarified, and addressed
- there is a culture of high expectations for self, student, and staff performance
- student and staff accomplishments are recognized and celebrated
- the school is organized and aligned for success
- the school culture and climate are assessed on a regular basis
- a variety of sources of information is used to make decisions

STANDARD 3: A school administrator is an educational leader who promotes the success of all students by ensuring management of the organization, operations, and resources for a safe, efficient, and effective learning environment.

Knowledge

The administrator has knowledge and understanding of:

- theories and models of organizations and the principles of organizational development
- operational procedures at the school and district levels
- principles and issues relating to school safety and security
- human resources management and development

Dispositions

The administrator believes in, values, and is committed to:

- making management decisions to enhance learning and teaching
- taking risks to improve schools
- trusting people and their judgments
- accepting responsibility
- high-quality standards, expectations, and performances

- involving stakeholders in management processes
- a safe environment

Performances

The administrator facilitates processes and engages in activities ensuring that:

- knowledge of learning, teaching, and student development is used to inform management decisions
- operational procedures are designed and managed to maximize opportunities for successful learning
- operational plans and procedures to achieve the vision and goals of the school are in place
- the school plant, equipment, and support systems operate safely, efficiently, and effectively
- potential problems and opportunities are identified
- financial, human, and material resources are aligned to the goals of schools
- organizational systems are regularly monitored and modified as needed
- stakeholders are involved in decisions affecting schools
- effective group-process and consensus-building skills are used
- effective communication skills are used
- a safe, clean, and aesthetically pleasing school environment is created and maintained
- human resource functions support the attainment of school goals

STANDARD 5: A school administrator is an educational leader who promotes the success of all students by acting with integrity, fairness, and in an ethical manner.

Knowledge

The administrator has knowledge and understanding of:

- the purpose of education and the role of leadership in modern society

Dispositions

The administrator believes in, values, and is committed to:

- development of a caring school community

Performances

The administrator:

- examines personal and professional values
- considers the impact of one's administrative practices on others
- treats people fairly, equitably, and with dignity and respect

STANDARD 6: A school administrator is an educational leader who promotes the success of all students by understanding, responding to, and influencing the larger political, social, economic, legal, and cultural context.

Knowledge

The administrator has knowledge and understanding of:

■ the political, social, cultural, and economic systems and processes that impact schools

Dispositions

The administrator believes in, values, and is committed to:

■ recognizing a variety of ideas, values, and cultures

Performances

The administrator facilitates processes and engages in activities ensuring that:

■ the environment in which schools operate is influenced on behalf of students and their families
■ communication occurs among the school community concerning trends, issues, and potential changes in the environment in which schools operate

B ecause the behavior of people in organizational life arises from the interaction between their motivational needs and characteristics (temperaments, intelligences, beliefs, perceptions) and characteristics of the environment, or because $B = f(p \cdot e)$, it follows that the organizational environment is a key to influencing organizational behavior. Moreover, although educational leaders have little ability to alter the inner drives and motivational forces of individuals in the organization, they have considerable latitude to alter the organizational environment.

But remember, the organization, and therefore its environment, is a socially constructed reality: it is not tangible. Of course, the building is tangible enough, as are the furniture, equipment, files, and other artifacts that make up the physical entity that we often call "school." But these are not the organization. The organization exists largely in the eye and the mind of the beholder: it is, in reality, pretty much what people think it is.

Coordinating and influencing the behavior of people so as to achieve the goals of the organization is perhaps the central concern of administrators and leaders. Previous chapters in this book have pointed out that there are two different, contrasting ways of thinking about and acting on this problem. That is, there are two different theoretic approaches to it: one is the traditional bureaucratic approach; the other uses the concept of building human capital through human resources development. These two theoretic approaches were compared and contrasted in some detail in Chapter 5.

If educational administrators have little ability to directly alter or influence the inner state of organizational participants—in other words, their motivation—they have considerable ability to do so through indirect means. By fostering the creation of organizational environments that enhance the personal growth of organization members— environments that are supportive of creativity, team building, and participation in solving problems—school leaders can tap into the powerful energy of inner motivational forces that traditional organizational environments routinely repress and discourage. What is being discussed here is, of course, largely the social-psychological environment of the organization rather than only the physical environment. It is the realm of organizational climate and organizational culture.

Human Resources Development

The inner state of organizational participants is an important key to understanding their behavior. Thus, although immediate antecedent conditions may well evoke behavioral responses, so do the perceptions, values, beliefs, and motivations of the participants. In other words, participants commonly respond to organizational events very much in terms of learnings that have developed through their experience over time and not merely to events immediately preceding their behavior. Therefore, the educational leader is much concerned with the forces and processes through which organizational participants are socialized into the organization: how they develop perceptions, values, and beliefs concerning the organization and what influence these inner states have on behavior. In contemporary organizational behavior literature, this is the realm of organizational climate and organizational culture.

Neither organizational climate nor organizational culture is a new concept. They have a long tradition in the literature of organization studies, going back at least as far as the Western Electric research of the 1930s, which noted—as described earlier—that some management styles elicited feelings of affiliation, competence, and achievement from workers, leading to more productive work than had been done previously, as well as eliciting greater satisfaction from workers than under different styles of management. Beginning in the 1940s, Kurt Lewin and his colleagues and students conducted numerous studies to explore the proposition that organizations could be made more effective by using planned interventions designed to shift the social norms of managers and workers alike. Perhaps the most notable of these early efforts occurred in the Weldon Manufacturing Company, which made men's pajamas, after its merger with the Harwood Manufacturing Corporation.[1]

Many different names have been used over the years to allude to the subtle, elusive, intangible, largely unconscious forces that comprise the symbolic side of organizations and shape human thought and behavior in them.[2] In the late 1930s, Chester Barnard described culture as a social fiction created by people to give meaning to work and life.[3] In the 1940s, Philip Selznick used the term *institution* to describe what it is that creates solidarity, meaning, commitment, and productivity in organizations,[4] Marshall Meyer and his associates used the term somewhat similarly in the 1970s.[5] In the 1960s, the term *organizational climate* became very popular with students of organization, in no small measure due to the research on elementary schools by Andrew Halpin and Don Croft.[6] In his studies of universities in the 1970s, Bernard Clark used the term *organizational saga*.[7] Michael Rutter and his colleagues noted the importance of "ethos" in determining the effectiveness of the high schools that they studied.[8] These studies are illustrative of a substantial body of research literature that seeks to describe and explain the learned pattern of thinking, reflected and reinforced in behavior, that is so seldom seen yet is so powerful in shaping people's behavior. This pattern of thinking and the behavior associated with it provide stability, foster certainty, solidify order and predictability, and create meaning in the organization.[9]

Defining and Describing Organizational Culture and Climate

An observer who moves from school to school ineluctably develops an intuitive sense that each school is distinctive, unique in some almost indefinable yet powerful way. This sense, seemingly palpable when we are in a school, more than describes that school: it *is* that school. As we have stated, many different terms have been used to identify that sense of the unique characteristics that organizations have. People sometimes use such terms as *atmosphere, personality, tone,* or *ethos* when speaking of this unique characteristic of a school. But the term *organizational climate* has come into rather general use as a metaphor for this distinctive characteristic of organizations. But just what is organizational climate? And how is it created?

Climate is generally defined as the characteristics of the total environment in a school building.[10] But we need to understand what those characteristics are, and to lay the groundwork for that we turn to the work of Tagiuri.

Renato Tagiuri described the total environment in an organization, that is, the organizational climate, as composed of four dimensions:

1. *Ecology* refers to physical and material factors in the organization: for example, the size, age, design, facilities, and condition of the building or buildings. It also refers to the technology used by people in the organization: desks and chairs, chalkboards, elevators, everything used to carry out organizational activities. See Figure 6.1.

Ecology
Physical and Material Factors

Building and Facilities
Age of building
Size of building
Design of building
Equipment and furniture
Condition of building
Facilities

Technology
Scheduling/sequencing inventions
(e.g., bell schedule, scope and sequence of curriculum)
Information/communication inventions
Books
Computers
Video
Film
Chalkboard
Pedagogical inventions
Student grouping
Instructional techniques
Testing

FIGURE 6.1   Some illustrative examples of the characteristics that give rise to the ecology of a school.

Milieu of the School
Human Social System Factors

Skills	*Morale*
Motivation	*Size of the group*
Job satisfaction/rewards	*Race, ethnicity, and gender issues*
Status	*Socioeconomic level of students*
Feelings	*Education levels attained by teachers*
Values	*Leadership*

FIGURE 6.2   Some illustrative examples of the characteristics that give rise to the milieu of a school.

2. *Milieu* is the social dimension in the organization. This includes virtually everything relating to the people in the organization—for example, how many there are and what they are like. This would include race and ethnicity, salary level of teachers, socioeconomic level of students, education levels attained by the teachers, the morale and motivation of adults and students who inhabit the school, level of job satisfaction, and a host of other characteristics of the people in the organization. See Figure 6.2.

3. *Social system* (organization) refers to the organizational and administrative structure of the organization. It includes how the school is organized, the ways in which decisions are made and who is involved in making them, the communication patterns among people (who talks to whom about what), what work groups there are, and so on. See Figure 6.3.

4. *Culture* refers to the values, belief systems, norms, and ways of thinking that are characteristic of the people in the organization. It is "the way we do things around here." This aspect of the organization's total environment is described more fully a little later in this chapter. See Figure 6.4.

As Figure 6.5 on page 190 shows, these four dimensions or subsystems are dynamically interrelated. In creating Figure 6.5, we have substituted the term *organization* for Tagiuri's original term *social system* because it seems to be more descriptive of what that dimension actually encompasses. Much of the organization dimension of climate arises from factors that administrators control directly or strongly influence. It is important, we think, that administrators understand the close connections between the choices they make about the way they organize and the climate manifested in the organization. To some, *social system* conveys a sense of a somewhat uncontrollable natural order of things whereas

Organization of the School
Organizational Structure Factors

Organization of:

Instruction

Supervision

Administration

Support services

Pupil personnel services

Decision-making practices

Communication patterns

Control mechanisms

Patterns of hierarchy/collegiality

Planning practices

Formal structure

(e.g., departments, emphasis on rules)

FIGURE 6.3   Some illustrative examples of the characteristics that give rise to the organization of a school.

organization makes the influence of the administrator's responsibility for establishing that order a little clearer.

However, contemporary thought does not view each of the four dimensions as being equally potent in producing the character and quality of the climate in a given organization. Recent research has concentrated attention on the primacy of the culture of the organization in defining the character and quality of the climate of an organization.

Culture of the School
Psychosocial Characteristics

Assumptions

Values

Norms

Ways of thinking

Belief systems

History

Heroes/heroines

Myths

Rituals

Artifacts

Art

Visible and audible behavior patterns

FIGURE 6.4   Some illustrative examples of the characteristics that give rise to the organizational culture of a school.

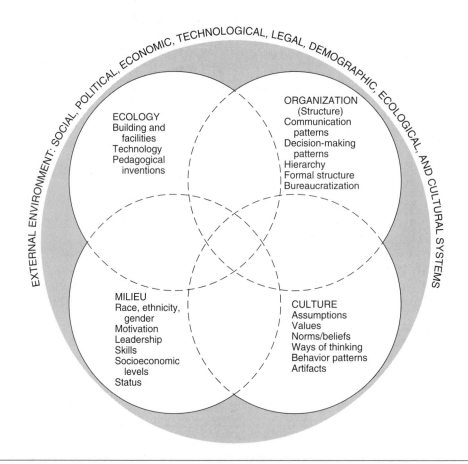

FIGURE 6.5   The four internal dimensions or subsystems of the organization—ecology, milieu, organization, and culture—are dynamically interactive within the organization, whereas the organization itself is dynamically interactive with its external environment.

Research on Organizational Culture

Research on organizational culture, which had stood for some time in the wings of organization studies, shifted to center stage in 1981–1982. It was a dramatic shift and was due to the publication of two books. The first of these, William Ouchi's *Theory Z*, appeared in 1981 and became the first book by a researcher of organizational behavior to enjoy a lengthy stay on the nonfiction best-seller lists.[11] Published at a moment when U.S. corporate managers were groping for some solution to their difficulties in meeting Japanese competition, Ouchi—a Japanese American—compared and contrasted the management styles used in the two nations. He found that Japanese management practices tended to be quite different from those applied in the United States and that some of them (not all, due to societal differences) could profitably be adopted by U.S. corporations.

Taking his cue from McGregor's Theory X–Theory Y, he named his approach Theory Z to suggest a new alternative. Theory Z accepts the main assumptions of human resources development (HRD):

> Of all its values, commitment of a Z culture to its people—its workers—is the most important. . . . Theory Z assumes that any worker's life is a whole, not a Jekyll-Hyde personality, half machine from nine to five and half human in the hours preceding and following. Theory Z suggests that humanized working conditions not only increase productivity and profits to the company but also the self-esteem for employees. . . . Up to now American managers have assumed that technology makes for increased productivity. What Theory Z calls for instead is a redirection of attention to *human* relations in the corporate world.[12]

In 1982, another research report appeared on the best-seller lists. Called *In Search of Excellence*, it described eight management characteristics that sixty-two successful U.S. corporations had in common.[13] Cutting across the eight characteristics was a consistent theme: the power of values and culture in these corporations, rather than procedures and control systems, provides the glue that holds them together, stimulates commitment to a common mission, and galvanizes the creativity and energy of their participants. These values are not usually transmitted formally or in writing. Instead, they permeate the organization in the form of stories, myths, legends, and metaphors—and these companies have people who attend to this awareness of organizational culture: "The excellent companies are unashamed collectors and tellers of stories, of legends and myths in support of their basic beliefs. Frito-Lay tells service stories. Johnson & Johnson tells quality stories. 3M tells innovation stories."[14]

Why did organizational culture stay in the wings in the United States so long? And why is it today a central concern in U.S. management? One answer to the first question is that the human underpinning of organization has long been considered to be soft. Technology is hard. Money is hard. Organizational structure, rules and regulations, policy decisions—these are hard, in the lexicon of many administrators and managers. The things that one can measure, quantify, and control are hard. In this view, the human side of organization is soft. Values, beliefs, culture, behavioral norms have, therefore, widely been believed to be less powerful in getting things done.

But it helps to clarify what culture is: a system of shared values and beliefs that interact with an organization's people, organizational structures, and control systems to produce behavioral norms. In practical terms, *shared values* means "what is important"; *beliefs* means "what we think is true"; and *behavioral norms* means "how we do things around here." With the obvious success of companies using these ideas, and with the ideas themselves clarified, the concept of organizational culture suddenly became of practical importance to managers and administrators. As Peters and Waterman put it, "Now, culture is the 'softest' stuff around. Who trusts its leading analysts—anthropologists and sociologists—after all? Businessmen surely don't. Yet culture is the hardest stuff around, as well."[15]

It became clear to U.S. businesspeople that an organizational culture that stifles innovation and hard work may be the biggest stumbling block to adapting to uncertain times. The lesson was not lost on educational administrators: confronted by shrinking finances, faltering public support, divided constituencies with conflicting interests, and rampant charges of organizational ineffectiveness, they became riveted by the implications of organizational culture for educational organizations.

Organizational Culture and Organizational Climate Compared and Contrasted

The terms *culture* and *climate* are both abstractions that deal with the fact that the behavior of persons in organizations is not elicited by interaction with proximate events alone but is also influenced by interaction with intangible forces in the organization's environment. As we shall explain more fully, *culture* refers to the behavioral norms, assumptions, and beliefs of an organization, whereas *climate* refers to perceptions of persons in the organization that reflect those norms, assumptions, and beliefs.

Organizational Culture

Though many definitions of organizational culture are found in the literature, the high degree of agreement between and among them makes it relatively easy to understand what culture is and how it relates to and differs from organizational climate. *Organizational culture* is the body of solutions to external and internal problems that has worked consistently for a group and that is, therefore, taught to new members as the correct way to perceive, think about, and feel in relation to those problems.[16]

Culture develops over a period of time and, in the process of developing, acquires significantly deeper meaning. Thus, "such solutions eventually come to be assumptions about the nature of reality, truth, time, space, human nature, human activity, and human relationships—then they come to be taken for granted and, finally, drop out of awareness."[17] Therefore, "culture can be defined as the shared philosophies, ideologies, values, assumptions, beliefs, expectations, attitudes, and norms that knit a community together."[18] In this case, the community is an organization—a school, for example—and all of these interrelated qualities reveal agreement, implicit or explicit, among teachers, administrators, and other participants on how to approach decisions and problems: "the way things are done around here."[19]

"At the heart of most . . . definitions of culture is the concept of a learned pattern of unconscious (or semiconscious) thought, reflected and reinforced by behavior, that silently and powerfully shapes the experience of a people."[20] This pattern of thought, which is organizational culture, "provides stability, fosters certainty, solidifies order and predictability, and creates meaning."[21] It also gives rise to simpler, though highly compatible, common-sense definitions, such as "[Organizational culture] is the rules of the game; the unseen meaning between the lines in the rulebook that insures unity"[22] or "Culture consists of the conclusions a group of people draws from its experience. An organization's culture consists largely of what people believe about what works and what does not."[23]

Although anthropologists and sociologists understand that culture—whether of a larger society or of an organization—can be inferred by observing the behavior of people, it is not really a study of that behavior. Through the observation of behavior one can develop an understanding of the systems of knowledge, beliefs, customs, and habits of people—whether it be in a larger society or an organization. In studying organizational culture, therefore, one looks at the artifacts and technology that people use, and one listens to what they say and observes what they do in an effort to discover the patterns of thoughts, beliefs, and values that they use in making sense of the everyday events that they experience. Thus, organizational culture is the study of the wellsprings from which the values and characteristics of an organization arise.

Two Major Themes in a Definition of Organizational Culture

Two themes consistently pervade the literature describing and defining organizational culture: one theme is *norms* and the other theme is *assumptions.* Norms and assumptions are widely regarded as key components of organizational culture.

Norms

An important way in which organizational culture influences behavior is through the norms or standards that the social system institutionalizes and enforces. These are encountered by the individual as group norms, which are ideas "that can be put into the form of a statement specifying what members . . . should do."[24] They are, in other words, "rules of behavior which have been accepted as legitimate by members of a group."[25] They are, of course, unwritten rules, that nonetheless express the shared beliefs of most group members about what behavior is appropriate in order to be a member in good standing.[26]

Assumptions

Underneath these behavioral norms lie the assumptions that comprise the bedrock on which norms and all other aspects of culture are built. These assumptions deal with what the people in the organization accept as true in the world and what is false, what is sensible and what is absurd, what is possible and what is impossible. We agree with Edgar Schein: these are not values, which can be debated and discussed. Assumptions are tacit, unconsciously taken for granted, rarely considered or talked about, and accepted as true and nonnegotiable.[27] The cultural norms in the organization—informal, unwritten, but highly explicit and powerful in influencing behavior—arise directly from the underlying assumptions.

Specifying What Organizational Culture Is

Edgar Schein described organizational culture as being composed of three different but closely linked concepts. Thus, organizational culture may be described as follows:

1. It is a body of solutions to external and internal problems that has worked consistently for a group and that is, therefore, taught to new members as the correct way to perceive, think about, and feel in relation to those problems.
2. These eventually come to be assumptions about the nature of reality, truth, time, space, human nature, human activity, and human relationships.

3. Over time, these assumptions come to be taken for granted and finally drop out of awareness. Indeed, the power of culture lies in the fact that it operates as a set of unconscious, unexamined assumptions that is taken for granted.[28]

Thus, culture develops over a period of time and, in the process of developing, acquires significantly deep meaning. Therefore, culture can be defined as the shared philosophies, ideologies, values, assumptions, beliefs, expectations, attitudes, and norms that knit a community together.[29] The school is viewed as having all of these interrelated qualities that reveal agreement, implicit or explicit, among teachers, administrators, and other participants on how to approach decisions and problems: "the way things are done around here."[30] As with most definitions of organizational culture, this pivots on the concept of a learned pattern of unconscious thought, reflected and reinforced by behavior, that silently and powerfully shapes the experience of a people.[31]

In Schein's model (Figure 6.6), the most obvious manifestations of organizational culture are visible and audible: these are artifacts such as tools, buildings, art, and technology, as well as patterns of human behavior, including speech. Because these are visible, they have been frequently studied usually using naturalistic field methods such as

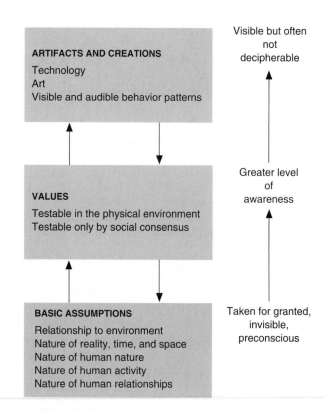

FIGURE 6.6
Schein's model of levels of culture. Edgar H. Schein, *Organizational Culture and Leadership* (San Francisco: Jossey-Bass, 1985), p. 14 (Figure 1). Reprinted by permission.

observation, interviews, and document analysis. Though these manifestations are readily visible, they are merely symbolic of the culture itself, which is not visible and which is not even in the awareness of the people we observe. Therefore, to make sense of the artifacts and the behaviors that we observe, we must decipher their meaning, and this is difficult to do.

Below this publicly visible level of the manifestations of culture lie the values of the organization, sometimes encoded in written language such as in a mission statement, a statement of philosophy, or a credo. Documents such as these move us closer to understanding the basic assumptions of the organization but they, too, merely reflect the basic assumptions that are the essence of the culture.

Finally, at the third and lowest level, we find the essence of the culture: those assumptions that are taken for granted, invisible, and outside of consciousness. These have to do with the relationships of individuals to the environment; the nature of reality, time, and space; the nature of human nature; the nature of human activity; and the nature of human relationships. These assumptions, of which the organization's members are unaware, form patterns but they remain implicit, unconscious, and taken for granted unless they are called to the surface by some process of inquiry.

How Organizational Culture Is Created

The organizational culture of the school arises over time and is shaped and defined by intersecting and overlapping symbolic elements, as shown in Figure 6.7.

The traditions of the school and its rituals, developing as time passes, are told, retold, and embellished to newcomers and old-timers alike in the stories and myths that convey the history of this particular school. These embody the values and beliefs of the people in the school and exert great power in establishing and maintaining the behavior norms that characterize the place—often more powerfully than rules and regulations can. The heroes and heroines of the school are very important in conveying organizational culture because they embody and are important in enacting these symbolic elements.

An important aspect of organizational culture, as it is for culture in general, is that it endures through the generations. Each school is different because its history is unique, and that history is constantly in development as the school moves toward its future. Anyone hoping to alter the culture of a school must seek to alter the course of the school's history, and the leverage points for that are in the symbolic elements that define and shape the organizational culture of the school.

Symbolism and Culture

Though organizational culture is usually studied through inferences derived from the observation of organizational behavior, the focus is not limited to the impact of the environment on the behavior of individual persons. It extends to understanding what the elements of such environments are, how they develop, and how these elements relate to one another so as to form (in effect) the lexicon, grammar, and syntax of organization. Thus, for example,

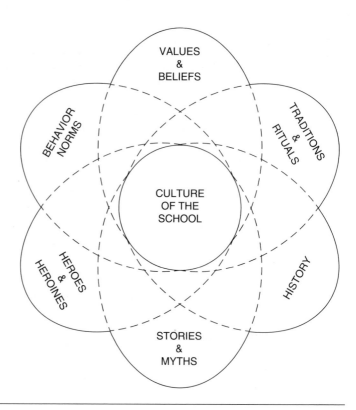

FIGURE 6.7
Overlapping symbolic elements describe the culture of a school.

the study of symbolism is central to the study of organizational culture: the rituals, myths, traditions, rites, and language through which human meanings and values are transmitted from one generation of the organization to another.

A school climate may be characterized by certain perceptions held by participants as to the nature of the organization ("What things are really like here"), but how are those perceptions developed, communicated, and transmitted? A school may be viewed by members as holding certain values, extolling particular virtues, standing for describable standards and practices that have a deep effect on the behaviors of the members. But how are these made explicit and communicated to the members? What are the mechanisms used by the organization to influence and control behavior in predictable, desired ways? In schools, as well as in societies, the answer is through institutionalized rituals and symbols. Understanding these is essential to understanding culture.

In many societies, for example, marriage rites constitute powerful symbols that evoke a great deal of behavior considered right and proper, if not inevitable. This might include deciding where the married couple live, how the members of the family take on new roles (such as mother-in-law), and division of labor between the sexes. Thus, the institution of marriage, symbolized by ceremonies and rituals handed down through the generations, communicates values to people that the society holds to be important. Much more than that, the communication results in behaviors that may seem ordinary and even mundane to the participants but that are powerful in developing their perceptions as to what is right or wrong or even possible.

Similarly, to join the faculty of a typical U.S. high school brings with it many obligations and expectations. Some of these are inexorably demanded by the daily schedule of classes (the bell schedule), which signals powerfully to participants who should be where—and doing what—virtually every minute of the day. To many educators the schedule is such an inherent part of the culture of the school as to be taken for granted, accepted without question, an overriding symbol of what defines the school itself. That is a powerful cultural feature of the high school, and it has great impact on what participants do, see as possible, and value as important in the life of the school. The bell schedule is one of many powerful cultural symbols that help to create the organizational climate found in a high school in the United States.

Organizational Climate

Organizational climate is the study of *perceptions* that individuals have of various aspects of the environment in the organization. For example, in their pioneer study of organizational climate in schools, Andrew Halpin and Don Croft examined "the attributes of leadership and group behavior" found to exist in elementary schools.[32] To do this, they asked teachers to describe their perceptions of certain human interactions in a sample of elementary schools that seemed to result from such causes as the principal's behavior in his or her official role in the hierarchy, the personality characteristics of individual teachers, the social needs of individual teachers as members of a work group, and such group characteristics of the teachers in the school as morale. A major outcome of the Halpin and Croft research was the demonstration that, by using the set of perceptions that the Halpin-Croft questionnaire probed, the organizational climate of elementary schools may be systematically assessed.

The notion of satisfaction is usually closely associated with the concept of organizational climate. That is, to what extent are the perceptions that participants have of the environment of the organization satisfying to them? This association of satisfaction with the perceptions of participants is implicit in some techniques for studying climate, whereas many studies have inquired directly into possible discrepancies between the participants' perceptions of the existing state of affairs in contrast to whatever desired state the respondents think ought to prevail.

Studies of organizational climate depend heavily on eliciting the perceptions of participants. This has led to the use of questionnaires in which respondents are asked directly about their perceptions. Although interviews could also be an effective means of gathering such information, this has not been done very often, whereas the development of questionnaires has proliferated.

Earlier studies of organizational climate in schools tended to gather data from adults, almost always teachers, with occasional inquiries of principals. In more recent years, the trend in school climate studies has been in the direction of examining the perceptions of pupils and students rather than of adults in the school.

The Affective Aspects of Culture and Climate

The culture of an organization exerts powerful influence on the development of climate. Inasmuch as the culture of the organization, even though it is intangible, influences the way participants perceive events and make sense of those events, it is clear that culture has influence on the attitudes and feelings of participants. Rosabeth Moss Kanter captured much of the impact of organizational culture and climate in reporting her studies comparing highly successful and less successful U.S. corporations.

She speaks of high-performing companies as having a culture of pride and a climate of success. By a "culture of pride" she means that "there is emotional and value commitment between person and organization; people feel that they 'belong' to a meaningful entity and can realize cherished values by their contributions."[33] With this feeling of pride in belonging to a worthwhile organization with a record of achievement, of being a member rather than merely an employee, the confidence of the individual is bolstered: confidence that the organization will be supportive of creative new practices and will continue to perform well, and confidence also that the individual will be effective and successful in his or her own realm of work in the organization.

Kanter's research led her to believe that the culture of pride is widely found in organizations that are integrative, which means organizations that emphasize the wholeness of the enterprise, that actively consider the wider implications of things that they do, and that thrive on diversity and stimulate challenges to traditional practices. These organizations tend to a large extent to be successful because their cultures foster a climate of success.

In contrast, Kanter described less successful organizations as being segmented. In segmented organizations members find it difficult even to discover what is going on beyond their own little sphere of operations, much less to deal with problems that affect the whole organization. People are kept isolated, stratified, away from the larger decisions in the organization, focused on the narrow piece of action in which they are directly involved. In these organizations, people find it difficult to take pride in the organization because they really know little about it and what it is doing. Thus, such organizations are characterized by climates of something other than success.

Multiple Cultures

Although a given organization will have an overall organizational culture, many organizations also have additional workplace cultures. In other words, in describing organizational culture we must be aware that subunits of the organization have cultures of their own which possess distinctive attributes. As an example, consider the school district that has central administrative offices, a senior high school, a junior high school, and several elementary schools.

Whereas the school board and top-level administrators in such a district may understand that the district as an organization has a shared set of understandings, assumptions, and beliefs reflected in and reinforced by the behaviors of people—in short, an organizational culture—they should also understand that each school will be characterized by its own culture. The culture of a given school is likely to reflect certain of the principal characteristics of the school district's organizational culture and yet is different in some ways. Moreover, the cultures of the various schools are likely to differ. Further, it is more than likely that the central office will exhibit an organizational culture of its own that is distinctive from that of any of the schools.

To carry the illustration further, consider the organizational culture of the senior high school in that district. The school itself will have an organizational culture, as I have described, and it will also have workplace cultures within it. For example, the counselors in the guidance and counselling department of the school may interpret their role—and that of the department—as being supportive and helping in their relationship to students, encouraging students to grow and mature in the ability to make informed decisions regarding their lives and to increasingly take charge of their lives. In their work, such counselors tend to value developing high trust relationships with students in order to engender openness in dealing with problems. Across the hall, however, one might find the unit responsible for managing attendance and discipline. Quite possibly the faculty in this unit could adopt—for whatever reasons—a shared understanding that toughness counts along with fairness, that it is the responsibility of the school to be sure that students toe the mark and to mete out punishment when they fail to do so, and to leave no mistake as to who is in charge. One could go on, demonstrating that other departments in the school are likely to exhibit cultures of their own—in some ways distinctive and in other ways mirroring the culture of the school as a whole.

The fact that multiple cultures are likely to be found in school districts and schools is not surprising inasmuch as the subunits of the organization do many of the same culture-building things that the larger organization itself does. It is the subunits—such as schools and departments—that regularly bring together people who share some constellation of interests, purposes, and values; they are the settings in which people seek social affiliation in face-to-face groups; they facilitate the sharing and cooperative effort required to get the work done. These functions of the subunits provide the impetus for developing multiple cultures in the organization, rather than a single organizational culture from top to bottom.

Indeed, it appears likely that Theory X administrators tend to think of organizational culture as being conceptualized at top levels in the organization and managed in such a way as to be implemented down the line of authority. This approach to the development of organizational culture, which is in harmony with classical concepts of organization, is problematic inasmuch as it is difficult to change the assumptions of people and compel their sharing of assumptions with others by issuing directives. On the other hand, Theory Y administrators are likely to more readily accept the concept of multiple cultures existing within the organization. The development of multiple cultures within the organization is facilitated by the use of participative methods associated with human resources development.

No concept in the realm of organizational behavior relies more heavily on social systems concepts than does organizational culture. Clearly, however, the culture of an organization is readily seen as important to eliciting and shaping the behavior of participants, which gives rise to the notion of *person–environment interaction*.

How Organizational Climate Is Created

Figure 6.8 shows that the organizational climate of a school is produced by the dynamic interaction of four variables: ecology, milieu, organization, and culture. People who work in the school, as well as the students there, experience this interaction. Their perceptions of the organization are inevitably molded by that experience. They thus come to understand what the place stands for, what is valued and what is not, what is true even if unvoiced and what is true or untrue of what *is* voiced. But, as we have said, although all of these subsystems have an impact on the formation of organizational climate, it is generally thought that they do not all have equal impact, though there is scant evidence to support that widely held belief. However, these are the levers for change available to the school leader who seeks

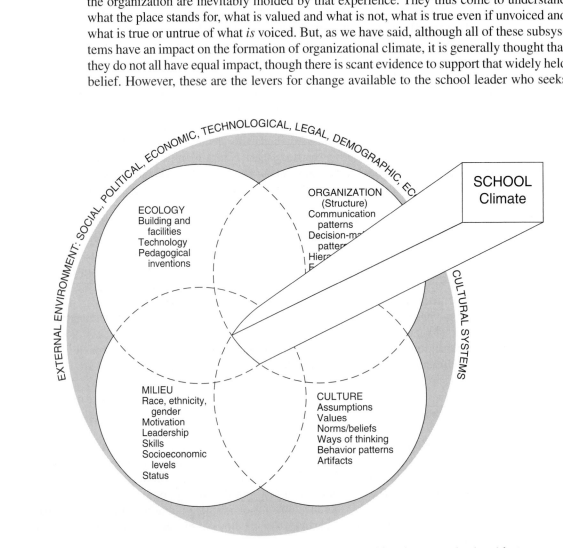

Organizational climate arises from overlapping and interaction of four key organizational factors.

FIGURE 6.8   The organizational climate of the school is the product of the interaction of the four internal dimensions, or subsystems: ecology, milieu, organization, and culture.

to shift the organizational climate of a school. Given the dynamic ways in which these subsystems interact, changes in one of them will result in changes in the others.

For many years, scholars as well as practitioners have tended to concentrate their efforts to change organizations on such things as restructuring the organization, retraining the employees or hiring new people, building new buildings or using new technology. The expectation usually is that changing one of these will in time result in commensurate changes in other of the organization's subsystems and thus involve the entire organization. However, by the beginning of the twenty-first century, organization theorists as well as practicing leaders were overwhelmingly in agreement that organizational culture is powerful in determining the course of change in an organization. Not a few believe that it is often the most powerful determinant.

Group Norms

An important way in which organizational culture influences behavior is through the norms or standards that the social system institutionalizes and enforces. These are encountered by the individual as group norms, which are "an idea that can be put in the form of a statement specifying what members . . . should do."[34] They are, in other words, "rules of behavior which have been accepted as legitimate by members of a group."[35] Groups typically exert pressures on an individual to conform to group norms that are more pervasive than the individual is likely to comprehend. These pressures are often felt as an obligation to behave in certain ways; this is often manifested in positive forms, such as support from the group for opinions and behavior that the group approves and wishes to reinforce.

Especially if the individual highly values the esteem and acceptance of members of the group and, more especially, if the group is highly cohesive, the pressure to conform to group standards and expectations can even influence one's perceptions of reality. One tends to see things in terms of the expectations of the group. Thus, the interaction of the individual with groups reaches far deeper than merely observable behavior: it strongly influences the development of perceptions, values, and attitudes.

Person–Environment Interaction

Any discussion of organizational culture has its roots in the work of Kurt Lewin, who demonstrated that understanding human behavior requires us to consider the whole situation in which behavior occurs.[36] The term *whole situation* is defined as meaning both the person and the environment. Essentially, then, behavior is a function of the interaction of person and environment. Thus, as we know, B = f(p • e). Consequently, in conceptualizing organizational culture, it is necessary to think of the person and the organizational environment as complementary parts of one situation. They are inseparable.

The group is an important part of the environment that the individual encounters as a member of an organization. "The postulate that behavior is a function of the interaction of organism and environment is widely accepted," it has been pointed out, but "the concept of environment has been a difficult one for psychologists to deal with empirically."[37]

This is, in part, because formal models of the organization (such as organizational charts) provide tidy, rational diagrams, but people often do not behave in the ways that the model depicts.[38] On the other hand, the behavior of individuals in organizational settings does not arise *only* from the personal characteristics of the individuals but is also influenced by the total situation in which they find themselves.[39]

The perspective of organizational culture helps us to understand that the environment with which people interact is constituted of more than the immediate circumstances in which they find themselves. A crucial aspect of understanding the culture of an organization is to understand the organization's history and its traditions because individuals in an organization are socialized to accept them. Thus, unseen but present in every human encounter with the organization is the understanding and acceptance by participants of values and expectations that are inherent in the tradition of the organization. Organizations normally expend considerable effort, both formally and informally, to transmit and reinforce these values and expectations through socialization processes.

In many a U.S. high school, to return to an earlier example, it is difficult for teachers and administrators alike to conceptualize organizing their work in any other way than by using a bell schedule built upon Carnegie Units of Instruction. Indeed, the tradition of using "units" as the building blocks of the U.S. high school's daily class schedule is so time honored and so taken for granted that few teachers today even know what a Carnegie Unit of Instruction is, even though it is one of the most dominant influences on their professional practice.

Carnegie Units were invented in 1905 by the Carnegie Foundation for the Advancement of Teaching as a way of standardizing high school instruction so that colleges would have an easier time comparing the transcripts of applicants. It was, and is, a measure of time: 120 hours of classroom instruction. Thus, one unit of a subject requires the student to be present in the classroom for 120 hours. The implications for scheduling are apparent: for example, if one decides to build a schedule around class periods that are forty-eight minutes long, so as to allow passing time between classes, then a one-unit class should meet 150 times during the year. This lays the basis for the traditional bell schedule that not only wields such power over the behavior of teachers and students, but also shapes their perceptions of what school is and ought to be, defines what is possible and not possible, and dictates what is right and what is wrong.

This is a strong tradition in secondary education in the United States, often associated with quality and sound professional practice, that has continually been reinforced by the teachers' own experience as students in high schools, by their university training, and by their experience as professionals. It is an illustration of the forces that are always present in organizational culture as part of the unseen, intangible environment that shapes and molds the behavior of participants. The Carnegie Unit illustrates the stubborn persistence that cultural artifacts typically display, surviving to influence thinking and behavior in the organization long after they have outlived their intended purpose. For many years, educators have doubted that time spent in class is the most useful indicator that we have to gauge what kind and quality of learning a student was achieving. Yet, reinforced in law and regulation, a venerable hallmark that many people associate with the "quality" of school's instructional program, the Carnegie Unit remained unchallenged for eighty-eight years as one of the key national quality standards in secondary schooling. In 1993 the Pennsylvania State Board of Education, the first state to do so, voted to abolish the use of the Carnegie Unit by the end of the century and to establish a set of required academic goals for students to achieve instead. The move, however—even though applauded by the Carnegie Foundation itself as desirable—has met fiercely entrenched opposition. Today, of course, many U.S. high schools are endeavoring to create new schedules—often called "block schedules"—that are intended to tailor instructional time to the pedagogical requirements of various subjects and also to facilitate changing the ways in which teachers and students work together in class.[40] As used today, block scheduling generally provides more class time for discussion, group work, individual critiques, and other pedagogical techniques in addition to presentations by the teacher.

The term *tradition* used in this sense does not necessarily mean repeating old solutions to newly emerging problems. Some organizations try to create what might be called new cultural traditions in an effort to break the habits of the past and emphasize the value of originality and creativity in finding fresh solutions to problems encountered in the life of the organization. Contemporary examples are readily found in the relatively young entrepreneurial computer firms in the Silicon Valley and other locations that place high value on bold thinking and inventiveness. Apple Computer is frequently cited as an illustration of an organization that was built on this concept.

Concept of Behavior Settings

Roger Barker theorized that environments have great influence in evoking and shaping the patterns of behavior of the people in them.[41] Indeed, according to his view of what is now known as "ecological psychology," the influence of environment is so great that it tends to overcome many individual differences among people who populate organizations. The result is that, in specific organizations, people tend to exhibit patterns of behavior that are so regular and distinct that we tend to view their behavior as "belonging to" those particular organizations. Barker posited, therefore, that organizational behavior is best understood in terms of *behavior settings,* referring to the whole complex physical and psychological environment with which people are in constant interaction.

In a remarkable pioneer study of the relationship between the size of high schools and the behavior of students in them, Roger Barker and Paul Gump discovered, for example, that the extent to which students participate in extraclass and extracurricular activities is directly related to the size of the school.[42] In similar research, Leonard Baird showed that the achievement of students, as well as the degree of their participation in extraclass activities, is related not only to the size of the school but also to the type of community in which the school is located (for example, small city, suburb, or large city).[43] In another study, Baird found that success at college was related not so much to the size of the high school from which students came as it was to the size of the college itself.[44]

The round of "school reform" and "school improvement" of the 1970s was notable for its emphasis on bigness: led by the studies of James B. Conant under the auspices of the Ford Foundation, the United States undertook to build bigger schools and create bigger school districts. Bigger was thought to be better because the financial economies of scale that were envisioned would permit schools to be more diverse, richer in resources, and supportive of greater opportunities for students. By the mid-1990s, however, there was increasing awareness that high schools with 2,000 to 5,000 students or more were being seen "as Dickensian workhouses breeding violence, dropouts, academic failure and alienation," whereas "schools limited to about 400 usually [had] fewer behavioral problems, better attendance and graduation rates, and sometimes higher grades and test scores."[45] To create more growth-enhancing behavior settings in their schools, cities across the country—including New York, Philadelphia, Denver, Chicago, and San Francisco—are busily trying various ideas ranging from simply creating smaller schools in separate buildings to trying schools-within-a-school plans. Some are experimenting with the "charter school" idea in which schools that undertake to reinvent themselves are encouraged and supported by being excused from some of the legal and bureaucratic constraints that burden the public school enterprise.

Barker's work has had considerable influence on Seymour Sarason, whose book, *The Culture of the School and the Problem of Change,* speaks so lucidly and persuasively of the necessity of finding ways of altering the patterns of activities, group norms, and the temporal qualities that are characteristic of U.S. public schools before we can hope to change the impact that they have on the people in them.[46] This milieu, which Sarason called the "culture of the school," is not necessarily planned or deliberately created; it tends, instead, to be a phenomenon that is generated from (1) the activities of people in the school (for example, lecturing, listening, moving about according to schedule), (2) the physical objects in the environment (for example, walls, furniture, chalkboard, playground), and (3) the temporal regularities observed (for example, the length of classes, the pattern of the daily schedule, the pattern of the school calendar).

The influence of this interaction among activities, physical environment, and temporal regularities is seen as not only pervasive and relatively stable, but also as having great power to mold the behavior of the people in the organization. Sarason has extended this insight to attempts to plan and create settings in new organizations that presumably would elicit the kinds of behaviors thought to be functional and productive in terms of the organization's mission.[47]

The Interaction–Influence System

A central concept in organizational behavior is that of the interaction–influence system of an organization. We should keep in mind that the basic function of organizational structure is to establish patterns of human interaction to get the tasks accomplished (who deals with whom, in what ways, and about what). Thus, departments, teams, schools, and divisions are typical formal structures, whereas friendship groups, people who work in close proximity to one another, and coffee-klatch groups are typical informal structures. The interactions between and among people thus put into contact with each other in conducting the day-to-day business of the organization establish the norms that are powerful in shaping organizational behavior.

The interaction–influence system of the organization deals simultaneously with structure and the processes of interaction. The two are mutually interdependent in such a dynamic way that they cannot be considered independently. In this sense, the interaction–

influence patterns in shaping the organizational behavior of work groups are roughly the counterparts of person and environment in eliciting and shaping the behavior of individuals.

The interaction processes in the interaction–influence system include communication, motivation, leadership, goal setting, decision making, coordination, control, and evaluation. The ways in which these interactions are effected in the organization (their characteristics and quality) exercise an important influence on eliciting and shaping human behavior. Efforts to describe the organizational culture of educative organizations are, therefore, efforts to describe the characteristics of the organization's interaction–influence system.

Describing and Assessing Organizational Culture in Schools

The study of organizational culture presents nettlesome problems to the traditional researcher primarily because important elements of culture are subtle, unseen, and so familiar to persons inside the organization as to be considered self-evident and, in effect, invisible. Collecting, sorting, and summarizing data such as the significant historical events in the organization and their implications for present-day behavior, the impact of organizational heroes on contemporary thinking, and the influence of traditions and organizational myths is a task that does not lend itself to the tidiness of a printed questionnaire and statistical analysis of the responses to it. As the work of Ouchi, Peters and Waterman, Kanter, and Deal and Kennedy demonstrated, it is necessary to get inside the organization: to talk at length with people; to find out what they think is important to talk about; to hear the language they use; and to discover the symbols that reveal their assumptions, their beliefs, and the values to which they subscribe. For that reason, students of organizational culture tend to use qualitative research methods rather than traditional questionnaire-type studies. This has raised vigorous debate in many schools of education as to the epistemological value of qualitative research methods as contrasted with the more traditional statistical studies (of the experimental or quasi-experimental type) that have long been the stock-in-trade of educational researchers.

Relationship between Organizational Culture and Organizational Effectiveness

Do various organizational cultures produce different outcomes, in terms of effectiveness, in the organization achieving its goals? The issue is far from simple: measuring organizational effectiveness is, in itself, a complex undertaking, and the traditional need felt by many people in management to control and direct subordinates in the *command* sense of the term tends to tinge with emotion discussion of the issue.

To a large extent, accepted conventions of research and rules of evidence, discussed previously, form the heart of this controversy. It has long been accepted in the logic of science that cause-and-effect relationships are best established by such rationalistic research designs as the controlled experiment. Experimental research, of course, requires one to control the relevant variables under study.

A substantial body of carefully controlled experimental research conducted in laboratory settings strongly undergirds the psychological concepts on which students of organizations draw in conceptualizing organizational behavior.[48] However, studies of actual organizations in the real world often must be conducted under conditions where such control is not possible. There is an analogous situation here with the extensive research literature on the possibility that "cigarette smoking causes cancer in humans," which is not a body of controlled experimental research that proves that cigarette smoking is the single causative factor. Research evidence suggesting (however strongly) a causal link between cigarette smoking and the incidence of cancer in humans is generally derived from such nonexperimental research as survey studies (many of which are longitudinal in design) or controlled research conducted on animals. Generally, there is such a strong association between the incidence of smoking and the incidence of cancer that many people accept that a cause-and-effect relationship exists. In terms of scientific rules of evidence, however, this is not proof and one can argue that, until evidence from fully controlled experiments is produced, the cause-and-effect relationship cannot be accepted as conclusive.

So it is with the link between organizational culture and organizational effectiveness: no significant body of experimental research in which the variables are fully controlled exists; therefore, discussion of the issue must be in the realm of association of significant variables. There is little question that many students of organizational behavior have ducked this issue by contenting themselves with refining techniques for defining and describing the variables of organizational culture or, in some cases, cautiously suggesting a possible relationship.

Cause and Effect

Rensis Likert sought to link organizational performance to the internal characteristics of the organization. His analysis is that the performance of an organization is determined by a three-link chain of causes and effects.

The first link in the chain is composed of the *causal variables,* which are under the control of the administration. Thus, administration (management) can choose the design of the organization's structure (mechanistic or organic, bureaucratic or flexible). Similarly, administration can choose the leadership style (for example, authoritarian or participative); it can choose a philosophy of operation (for example, teamwork or directive, problem solving or rule following). The choices that administration makes in selecting the options available are critical to and powerful in determining the nature of the management system in the organization (namely, Systems 1, 2, 3, or 4). These are seen as causing the interaction–influence system of the organization—in other words, its culture—to have the characteristics that it does have.

Intervening variables flow directly from (are caused largely by) these causal variables (that is, the choices that administration makes). Thus, the nature of motivation, communication, and other critical aspects of organizational functioning is determined.

End-result variables, the measures of an organization's success, depend heavily, of course, on the nature and quality of the internal functioning of the organization.

This analysis fits nicely with recent reports of qualitative research in U.S. public schools—such as Theodore Sizer's *Horace's Compromise,*[49] Ernest Boyer's *High School,*[50] and John Goodlad's *A Place Called School*[51]—and their counterparts from the corporate world—such as *In Search of Excellence, Theory Z, Corporate Cultures,* and *The Change Masters.* For, as Rosabeth Moss Kanter pointed out in the last work and as we discussed earlier, innovative companies are marked by a culture of pride and a climate of success in which the organizational norms support success-oriented effort—and that depends on the values which the leaders enact in the daily life of the organization.

The Problem of Measuring School Effectiveness

Any effort to relate organizational culture (however described and measured) to the effectiveness of educative organizations confronts the difficulties of assessing the effectiveness dimension. This problem requires that we identify indicators of organizational effectiveness for schools and ways of measuring them. Needless to say, this problem has been receiving markedly increased attention over the years.

In research parlance, we are dealing with sets of variables. Organizational climate and other internal characteristics of the school (for example, style of leadership, communication processes, motivational forces) are examples of *independent* variables. Other independent variables are characteristics of the situation in which the school, as an organization, is embedded. This, of course, would include such characteristics of the community as its wealth, its social-cultural traditions, political power structure, and demography. Very often it seems clear that these two independent variables are highly interactive, but little has been done to explore this possibility. For example, we have scant firm evidence of what impact the situational variables with which a school contends have on shaping the characteristics of the interaction–influence system of the school. We must remember that the school is an open system, interactive with and responsive to its external environment. Though organizational culture focuses on the internal arrangements of schools, those always reflect, to some degree, the larger environment of the school's situation.

Dependent variables are indicators of organizational effectiveness. These can be grouped roughly as objective indicators and subjective indicators. Measures of achievement (such as test scores) and measures of some behaviors (for example, dropouts, absences) often can be quantified objectively. Very often we use subjective measures of school effectiveness, too. These could include performance ratings by various of the school's publics, as well as surveys of attitudes toward the school's performance.

One recent, sophisticated attempt to "get at" the complexities of this problem was a study by Wilbur Brookover and his associates of a random sample of 2,226 Michigan elementary schools. The dependent variable, by which effectiveness was measured, was the mean achievement scores of fourth-grade pupils in the standardized Michigan Assessment Program.

The key independent variable was a measure of school climate that was developed from the following definition:

> The school climate encompasses a composite of variables as defined and perceived by members of this group. These factors may be broadly conceived as the norms of the social system and expectations held for various members as perceived by the members of the group and communicated to members of the group.[52]

The investigators noted that a good deal of the previous research of this kind had used the socioeconomic status (SES) of the children or the racial composition of the school as a proxy for organizational climate. Among such studies that are well known to educators are the famous "Coleman report"[53] and the work of Christopher Jencks on inequality of schooling.[54] In this case, however, the researchers chose to devise an instrument to measure climate directly in the schools under study. The climate variable was essentially a measure of the norms and expectations in the school. Appropriately enough, the researchers called this the Student Sense of Academic Futility. Thus, the principal independent variables in the study were (1) mean school-level SES, (2) racial composition of the school (that is, percentage of students who were white), and (3) climate of the school.

In commenting on their findings, the investigators said, "The first and foremost conclusion derived from this research is that some aspects of school social environment clearly make a difference in the academic achievement of schools."[55] Although large differences existed between the achievement levels in various schools, the socioeconomic and racial composition of the student bodies in those schools accounted for only a small percentage of the variance. The crucial variable, strongly associated with objective measures of student achievement, was the social climate of the school (measured, in this case, by the student's sense of academic futility).

The researchers concluded that this concept of climate, at least, is clearly related to school achievement:

> If we apply these findings to the school desegregation issue, it seems safe to conclude that neither racial nor socioeconomic desegregation of schools automatically produces higher school achievement. If the unfavorable social-psychological climate which typically characterizes segregated black and lower SES schools continues to prevail for the poor or minority students in the desegregated schools, desegregation is not likely to materially affect achievement of the students. If the social-psychological climate relevant to the poor and minority [students] is improved in conjunction with desegregation, higher achievement is likely to result.[56]

Strong research support for a close relationship between the culture of the school and outcomes also comes from a study of twelve inner-city London schools,[57] which posed the following research questions:

1. Do a child's experiences at school have any effect?
2. Does it matter which school a child attends?
3. If so, which are the features of the school that matter?

The first question was prompted, of course, by a number of U.S. studies that raise serious questions as to what effect attendance at school actually has (for example, Coleman's and

Jencks's work). The second and third questions deal specifically with the cause-and-effect problem under discussion here.

To measure school outcomes the researchers used the following dependent variables: (1) pupil behavior, (2) pupil attendance, and (3) regularly scheduled public school examinations. The study showed, first, that there was a marked difference in the behavior, attendance, and achievement of the students in various secondary schools. Second, these differences between schools were not accounted for by the socioeconomic or ethnic differences of their students: clearly, students were likely to behave better and achieve more in some schools than in others. Third, these differences in student behavior and performance

> were *not* due to such physical factors as the size of the school, the age of the buildings or the space available; nor were they due to broad differences in administrative status or organization [for example, structure]. It was entirely possible for schools to obtain good outcomes in spite of initially rather unpromising and unprepossessing school premises, and within the context of somewhat differing administrative arrangements . . . the differences between schools in outcome *were systematically related to their characteristics as social institutions.*[58]

Key among these latter characteristics (that is, the independent variables) were (1) the behavior of teachers at work, (2) the emphasis placed on academic performance, (3) the provision for students to be rewarded for succeeding, and (4) the extent to which students were able to take responsibility. All these factors, the researchers pointed out, were open to modification by the staff rather than fixed by external constraints. In short, this research strongly suggests that organizational culture (which they call "ethos") is a critical factor in student behavior and achievement. Moreover, much as Likert did, they pointed out that organizational culture is in the control of the people who manage the organization.

Joyce Epstein reported studies in schools which describe the perceptions of students' satisfaction with school in general, their commitment to school work, and their attitudes toward teachers.[59] Taken together, these are thought by Epstein to describe the quality of school life as the students perceive it. Further, this perception is described as, of course, being related to the behaviors of the students as participants in the organization. To conduct such studies, Epstein developed and validated a twenty-seven-item questionnaire designed to be used across school levels (that is, elementary, middle, and high school).

Rudolf Moos reported large-scale research in the United States, in both secondary school and college settings, that supports the mounting evidence in the literature that the learning and development of students are significantly influenced by characteristics of organizational culture.[60] After studying some 10,000 secondary school students in more than 500 classrooms, he was able to identify characteristics of classroom organizational culture that facilitate academic achievement, on the one hand, and those that induce stress, alienate students, and thereby inhibit learning, on the other hand. He measured the variances from classroom to classroom in such contextual influences as (1) stress on competition, (2) emphasis on rules, (3) supportive behavior by the teacher, and (4) extent of innovative activities. They were the independent variables. Moos then correlated these measures with measures of dependent variables, such as (1) student rate of absence, (2) grades earned, (3) student satisfaction with learning, and (4) student satisfaction with the teacher.

In college settings Moos studied 225 living groups (for example, coed and single-sex residence halls, fraternities and sororities), involving about 10,000 students. Using questionnaires, he measured distinctive characteristics of these various groups such as (1) emphasis on intellectuality, (2) social activities, and (3) group unity. He then sought to assess the effects of these variables on such dependent variables as (1) students' concepts of themselves, (2) personal interests and values, (3) aspirations, and (4) achievement.

Essentially, Moos found that students' learning and development are strongly influenced by the nature and qualities of the person–environment interaction in such educational settings as secondary school classrooms and college residence arrangements. An interesting aspect of his research is his attempt to demonstrate how organizational culture and human behavior are influenced not only by the interaction–influence system of the group but also by other factors in the environment such as room design, schedule of activities, and layout of the building. In his view, our knowledge of the causes and effects of organizational culture enables us to create and manage specified learning environments by controlling critical variables (such as competition, intellectuality, and formal structure). This, in turn, improves our ability to place students in the settings best suited to their needs—settings in which they will feel most comfortable and be most successful. This, he contends, is highly practical knowledge that can be used to develop administrative policies and pedagogical practices that are effective in dealing with student apathy, alienation, absenteeism, and dropouts.

Describing and Assessing Organizational Climate in Schools

To describe and assess the climate of a school requires (1) the development of a clear concept of what the key factors are in the interaction–influence system that determines climate, (2) the creation of some method of collecting data that describes these factors (usually a paper-and-pencil questionnaire), and (3) a procedure by which the data may be analyzed and, ultimately, displayed in a way that informs us.

Literally scores of ways of describing and assessing organizational climates of various kinds of organizations have been proffered in the literature. Most of these can be dismissed because they are largely intuitive in nature, giving little attention to a clear, systematic concept of the nature of climate itself on which to develop data-gathering and data-analysis procedures. This leaves at least a dozen well-developed scientific approaches that have been used in many kinds of organizational settings, ranging from the crews of space capsules to universities, from prisoner-of-war camps to the employees of large offices. Because our focus here is on education, only climate-assessment techniques that deal specifically with educational organizations are discussed. Criteria for selecting the three climate-assessment techniques included in the discussion were as follows:

1. The contribution that the theoretic construct on which the technique is based can make to our understanding of the organizational climate itself.

2. The relative frequency with which the technique actually has been used in studies of education.

3. The scientific quality of the technique.

Organizational Climate Description Questionnaire (OCDQ)

With the publication in 1962 of a research report titled *The Organizational Climate of Schools,*[61] Andrew W. Halpin and Don B. Croft introduced the notion of organizational climate to educators. Because, by definition, organizational climate is experienced by people in the organization, they assumed that the *perceptions* of these people are a valid source of data. Though one may argue that perceptions themselves are not objective reflections of reality (but may be influenced by subjective factors), the point is that whatever people in the organization *perceive* as their experience is the reality to be described. The purpose of an assessment of organizational climate is to obtain an objective description of those perceptions. Therefore, Halpin and Croft sought to elicit from teachers the critical factors that they generally agreed were central to describing the climate of a school. It should be remembered that at the time of the Halpin and Croft research the concept of organizational cultures was unknown. It is now understood that climate is the study of the perceptions of participants of factors in the organizational environment that are likely to reflect the culture of the organization.

Eventually they identified two clusters of factors. One cluster consisted of four factors that describe the teachers' perceptions of the teachers as a human group:

Intimacy: the degree of social cohesiveness among teachers in the school.

Disengagement: the degree to which teachers are involved and committed to achieving the goals of the school.

Espirit: the apparent morale of the group.

Hindrance: the extent to which teachers see rules, paperwork, and "administrivia" as impeding their work.

The other cluster of climate factors was the collective perception of teachers concerning the principal:

Thrust: the dynamic behavior with which the principal sets a hardworking example.

Consideration: the extent to which the principal is seen as treating teachers with dignity and human concern.

Aloofness: the extent to which the principal is described as maintaining social distance (for example, cold and distant or warm and friendly).

Production emphasis: the extent to which the principal tries to get teachers to work harder (for example, supervising closely, being directive, demanding results).

Halpin and Croft's central finding (based on initial data obtained in seventy-one suburban elementary schools) was that descriptions of the teachers as a human social group tend to be associated with the teachers' perceptions of the principal in relatively consistent patterns. For example, some schools—said to have a *closed climate*—appear thus in the perceptions of teachers: teachers tend not to be highly engaged in their work, they do not work well together, and their achievement as a group is minimal. The principal in such a school is seen by the teachers as ineffective in leading them, as creating a great deal of hindrance to their work, and as not inclined to be concerned about their personal welfare. Teachers get little satisfaction from their work, morale is low, and there is likely to be a high turnover of teachers. The principal is seen as aloof and impersonal, and tends to urge teachers to work harder. Such a principal tends to emphasize rules, is often arbitrary, and generally "goes by the book"—keeping good records and getting reports out punctiliously. Such a principal is viewed by teachers as working with little personal drive, as being not terribly inventive or creative in reducing the obstacles and annoyances that teachers encounter, and as often philosophically ascribing problems in the school to outside forces over which he or she has no control.

Using the OCDQ, Halpin and Croft identified a range of types of climates that ran from the "closed" (as just described) to the *open climate* school, which is, of course, quite different. The teachers of a school with an open climate tend to see the principal's behavior as an easy, authentic integration of the official role and his or her own personality. Such a principal works energetically, shows concern and even compassion for teachers, and yet is well able to lead, control, and direct them; he or she is not especially aloof or distant, seems to know how to follow rules and regulations with minimum hindrance to teachers, and does not feel the need to monitor teachers and supervise them closely, yet is in full control. Under such leadership, teachers obtain considerable satisfaction from their work and are suffi-ciently motivated to overcome most difficulties and frustrations. The teachers are proud to be part of the school, do not feel burdened by busywork, regulations, and administrivia, and have enough incentive to solve their own problems and keep the organization moving.

Comments on the OCDQ

The OCDQ concept of organizational climate produced some useful ways of viewing and describing aspects of the interaction–influence systems of schools (especially elementary schools with their simpler organizational structure). Its factor structure was, however, de-veloped from a strictly deductive process (rather than from an empirical study of schools), and, indeed, little has been done since the instrument was originally developed to validate it or modify it as a result of experience. Its usefulness for measurement purposes is now somewhat limited, and more recent approaches—which have been under constant processes of testing and revision—are being used increasingly.

Organizational Climate Index (OCI)

George C. Stern developed a different approach to the description and measurement of organizational climate. The basic rationale that underlies Stern's understanding of climate emanates directly from the Lewinian view that individuals and groups in organizations must be understood in the context of their interaction with the environment B = f(p • e). In this view, behavior is related to *both* person and environment. Efforts to assess the climate of a given organization must, therefore, measure *both* characteristics of individuals and characteristics of the environment.

Stern, a psychologist, saw an analogy between human personality and the personality of the institution, and he drew on the much earlier work of Henry A. Murray, who had developed the concept of *need-press* as it shaped human personality.[62] Murray postulated that personality is the product of dynamic interplay between need, both internal and external, and press, which is roughly equivalent to the environmental pressures that lead to adaptive behavior.[63] Two questionnaire instruments were devised to determine the need-press factors Stern felt influenced the development of climate in institutions of higher education: the Activities Index (AI), which assessed the need structure of individuals, and the College Characteristics Index (CCI), which probed the organizational press as experienced by persons in the organization.[64]

Over the years, these two questionnaires have been used on a number of campuses, where they have helped researchers assess organizational climate in higher education settings. Differences among various institutions of higher learning—denominational colleges, state universities, liberal arts colleges, and teachers colleges, among others—are observable for measurable factors such as staff and facilities, achievement standards, aspirations of students, extent of student freedom and responsibility, academic climate, and social life on the campus. The level of intellectual press seems to be particularly valuable in explaining important differences among collegiate institutions.

George Stern and Carl Steinhoff developed an adaptation of the CCI, applicable to schools and other organizations, called the Organizational Climate Index (OCI), which was first used in 1965 in a study of the public schools in Syracuse, New York.[65] The OCI presents teachers with statements that could apply to their schools; the teachers then are asked to mark these statements true or false as applicable to their schools. Analysis of the data from studies of a number of schools has led to the formulation of the six OCI Factors:

Factor 1: Intellectual Climate. Schools with high scores on this factor have environments that are perceived as being conducive to scholarly interests in the humanities, arts, and sciences. The staff and the physical plant are seen to be facilitative of these interests, and the general work atmosphere is characterized by intellectual activities and pursuits.

Factor 2: Achievement Standards. Environments with high scores on this factor are perceived to stress high standards of personal achievement. Tasks are successfully completed, and high levels of motivation and energy are maintained. Recognition is given for work of good quality and quantity, and the staff is expected to achieve at the highest levels.

Factor 3: Personal Dignity (Supportiveness). Organizational climates scoring high on this factor respect the integrity of the individual and provide a supportive environment that would closely approximate the needs of more dependent teachers. The working environment conveys a sense of fair play and openness.

Factor 4: Organizational Effectiveness. Schools with high scores on this factor have work environments that encourage and facilitate the effective performance of tasks. Work programs are planned and well organized, and people work together effectively to meet organizational objectives.

Factor 5: Orderliness. High scores on this factor are indicative of a press for organizational structure and procedural orderliness. Neatness counts, and teachers are pressured to conform to a defined norm of personal appearance and institutional image. There are set procedures and teachers are expected to follow them.

Factor 6: Impulse Control. High scores on this factor imply a great deal of constraint and organizational restrictiveness in the work environment. Teachers have little opportunity for personal expression or for any form of impulsive behavior.

Schools with high scores on the development press dimension are characterized by organizational environments that emphasize intellectual and interpersonal activities. In general, these environments are intellectually stimulating, maintain high standards for achievement, and are supportive of personal expression. Such schools characteristically tend to motivate people, are concerned about their personal needs, and accept (indeed, encourage) a wide range of behavior styles among participants.

A school's score on the control press (task effectiveness) dimension is computed by adding together the scores for Factors 4 and 5. Schools high in control press are characterized by internal environments that emphasize orderliness and structure. Rules and going through channels are important in such schools, and concepts of what constitutes appropriate behavior tend to be clear-cut, narrow, and emphasized. In short, schools with such environments tend to be task oriented rather than people oriented.

In sum, the two key dimensions that describe the organizational climate of a school, using the Stern-Steinhoff OCI, are development press and control press which combine to describe its organizational climate. As the OCI has been applied to a number of schools, normative data have been developed that are useful for interpreting the score of an individual school. Obviously, schools with high development press (that is, meeting the intellectual-cognitive needs of teachers and also their social-emotional needs) are associated with a good deal of freedom to exercise initiative and to fulfill their motivational needs. Schools that emphasize control (for example, rules, close supervision, directive leadership), on the other hand, provide an environment that offers less opportunity for teachers to grow and develop as mature professional people.

Comments on the OCI

Though the Stern need-press theory of the psychological environments in educative organizations has not enjoyed the popularity among those concerned with public schools that the OCDQ has, it has been used in a number of studies. A deterrent to early popularity was the length and complexity of the questionnaires (the full OCI once had 300 items). Another deterrent was the relative complexity of the data analysis and interpretation procedures. A short form of the OCI that is simple to use has been available since 1975, however. This can be scored by hand, and school norms for elementary, junior high, senior high, rural, suburban, and urban, which also are simple to use, have been published.

Among the many strengths of the need-press approach are that (1) it is based on a strong (if not simple) concept of organizational climate that has held up well and (2) it has a long history of meticulous research that has yielded assessment instruments that have been carefully scrutinized for validity and reliability. Consequently, the OCI is a powerful assessment tool that yields relatively rich and fine-grained data suited to the analysis of climates of individual schools. It is, at the same time, capable of producing the kinds of normative data needed to study groups of schools (for example, the schools in a given district or the schools involved in an experimental project).

In addition, the OCI appears to be applicable to a wide variety of educative organizations—elementary, secondary, and college,[66] urban or suburban. Various forms of the questionnaire instruments also make it possible to obtain data from pupils and students, as well as from adults such as teachers.

Four Management Systems

Having studied organizational climates extensively, Rensis Likert identified four management systems. Each is describable in terms of organizational climate and leadership behavior, as measured in terms of the organization's characteristics. System 1 is called *exploitive-authoritative* (or punitive-authoritarian) and, as is shown in Figure 6.9, is based on classical management concepts, a Theory X view of motivation, and a directive leadership style. System 2 is *benevolent-authoritative* (or paternalistic-authoritarian). It emphasizes a one-to-one relationship between subordinate and leader in an environment in which the subordinate is relatively isolated from others in work-related matters. System 3, called *consultative,* employs more of a participative leadership style in which the leader tends to consult with people *individually* in the process of making decisions. System 4, the *participative* (or group interactive) model of an organizational system, uses Theory Y concepts of human functioning and emphasizes team interaction in all of the critical organizational processes.

As Likert observed:

> The interaction–influence networks of our schools all too often are proving to be incapable of dealing constructively even with the internal school problems and conflicts, not to mention the conflicts impinging from the outside. Moreover, the present decision-making structure of the schools requires patterns of interaction that often aggravate conflict rather than resolving it constructively.
>
> Faculty meetings, for example, almost always employ parliamentary procedures that force a System 2 win-lose confrontation. The systematic, orderly problem solving that small groups can use does not and cannot occur in large meetings. . . . [I]t is distressing to observe the extraordinary capacity of *Robert's Rules of Order* to turn the interaction of sincere, intelligent persons into bitter, emotional, win-lose confrontation.[67]

SYSTEM 1: EXPLOITIVE AUTHORITATIVE

Motivational Forces

Taps fear, need for money and status. Ignores other motives, which cancel out those tapped. Attitudes are hostile, subservient upward, contemptuous downward. Mistrust prevalent. Little feeling of responsibility except at high levels. Dissatisfaction with job, peers, supervisor, and organization.

Communication Pattern

Little upward communication. Little lateral communication. Some downward communication, viewed with suspicion by subordinates. Much distortion and deception.

Interaction–Influence Process

No cooperative teamwork, little mutual influence. Only moderate downward influence, usually overestimated.

Decision-Making Process

Decision made at top, based on partial and inaccurate information. Contributes little motivational value. Made on person-to-person basis, discouraging teamwork.

Goal-Setting Process

Orders issued. Overt acceptance. Covert resistance.

Control Process

Control at top only. Control data often distorted and falsified. Informal organizations exists, which works counter to the formal, reducing real control.

SYSTEM 2: BENEVOLENT AUTHORITATIVE

Motivational Forces

Taps need for money, ego motives such as desire for status and for power, sometimes fear. Untapped motives often cancel out those tapped, sometimes reinforce them. Attitudes are sometimes hostile, sometimes favorable toward organization, subservient upward, condescending downward, competitively hostile toward peers. Managers usually feel responsible for attaining goals, but rank and file do not. Dissatisfaction to moderate satisfaction with job, peers, supervisor, and organization.

Communication Pattern

Little upward communication. Little lateral communication. Great deal of downward communication, viewed with mixed feelings by subordinates. Some distortion and filtering.

Interaction–Influence Process

Very little cooperative teamwork, little upward influence except by informal means. Moderate downward influence.

Decision-Making Process

Policy decided at top, some implementation decisions made at lower levels, based on moderately accurate and adequate information. Contributes little motivational value. Made largely on person-to-person basis, discouraging teamwork.

Goal-Setting Process

Orders issued, perhaps with some chance to comment. Overt acceptance, but often covert resistance.

Control Process

Control largely at top. Control data often incomplete and inaccurate. Informal organization usually exists, working counter to the formal, partially reducing real control.

FIGURE 6.9 Likert's four management systems. From David G. Bowers, *Systems of Organization: Management of the Human Resource* (Ann Arbor: University of Michigan Press, 1976), pp. 104–105. Reprinted by permission.

Motivational Forces	Communication Pattern
Taps need for money, ego motives, and other major motives within the individual. Motivational forces usually reinforce each other. Attitudes usually favorable. Most persons feel responsible. Moderately high satisfaction with job, peers, supervisor, and organization.	Upward and downward communication is usually good. Lateral communication is fair to good. Slight tendency to filter or distort.

Interaction–Influence Process	Decision-Making Process
Moderate amount of cooperation teamwork. Moderate upward influence. Moderate to substantial downward influence.	Broad policy decided at top, more specific decisions made at lower levels, based on reasonably accurate and adequate information. Some contribution to motivation. Some group-based decision making.

Goal-Setting Process	Control Process
Goals are set or orders issued after discussion with subordinates. Usually acceptance both overtly and covertly, but some occasional covert resistance.	Control primarily at top, but some delegation to lower levels. Informal organization may exist and partially resist formal organization, partially reducing real control.

SYSTEM 4: PARTICIPATIVE GROUP

Motivational Forces	Communication Pattern
Taps all major motives except fear, including motivational forces coming from group processes. Motivational forces reinforce one another. Attitudes quite favorable. Trust prevalent. Persons at all levels feel quite responsible. Relatively high satisfaction throughout.	Information flows freely and accurately in all directions. Practically no forces to distort or filter.

Interaction–Influence Process	Decision-Making Process
A great deal of cooperative teamwork. Substantial real influence upward, downward, and laterally.	Decision making done throughout the organization, linked by overlapping groups and based on full and accurate information. Make largely on group basis encouraging teamwork.

Goal-Setting Process	Control Process
Goals established by group participation, except in emergencies. Full goal acceptance, both overtly and covertly.	Widespread real and felt responsibility for control function, informal and formal organizations are identical, with no reduction in real control.

FIGURE 6.9 Continued

He went on to point out that in meetings of 50 to 100 faculty members there is little like-lihood of creative problem solving, as factions of members joust through parliamentary maneuvering, and, in the end, few emerge with anything like genuine commitment to the actions that are finally taken.

In discussing Likert's approach to this problem, David Bowers pointed out that a place to begin is to understand what an organization is and what it is not. Bowers observed:

> An organization is not simply a physical plant or its equipment. It is not an army of positions, nor a collection of persons who fill these positions. It is not a sequence of work tasks or techni-cal operations. It is all of these things, to be sure, but it is fundamentally something more. The basic building block of the organization is the face-to-face group, consisting of the supervisor and those subordinates immediately responsible to him [sic]. *The organization consists most basically of a structure of groups, linked together by overlapping memberships* into a pyramid through which the work flows.[68]

Thus, the organization is conceptualized as a roughly pyramidal structure whose basic unit is the face-to-face work group: people who regularly interact (communicate, influence, motivate) at work, together with their supervisor. Examples are department chairpersons and teachers in the departments, head librarians plus librarians and library aides, grade chairpersons and homeroom teachers, and so on. Such groups are (1) small enough to permit the development of effective group process that facilitates individual participation and (2) close enough to the task to be performed to make effective, creative decisions. To keep such groups coordinated requires effective communication between and among them: the primary work groups must be effectively linked together. Especially, Likert pointed out, it is essential that groups be linked *upward* in the organization so that the groups lower in the organizational pyramid have the capability of interacting with and influencing higher levels of the organization.

> The capacity to exert influence upward is essential if a supervisor (or manager) is to per-form his supervisory functions successfully. To be effective in leading his own work group, a superior must be able to influence his own boss, that is he needs to be skilled both as a supervisor and as a subordinate.[69]

Essentially, then, every supervisor or every administrator is a member of two face-to-face work groups: the group for which he or she is responsible and the group to which he or she is responsible. The total organization is composed of a planned system of such work groups that overlap and that are linked together by individuals who have roles in both of the overlapping groups. These individuals serve as "linking pins" between the groups—a role that requires them to facilitate communication, decision making, and other influence processes between levels of the organization and, also, across the organization.

Such a structure is not totally new in U.S. schooling, of course. The traditional high school principal's cabinet, for instance, generally includes chairpersons who link the departments to the cabinet. In turn, the principal is usually a member of a districtwide group (often also called a "cabinet") comprising other principals, central office people, and the superintendent. The superintendent, in turn, links the superintendent's cabinet to the school board (see Figure 6.10). However, Likert has suggested that, first, such an

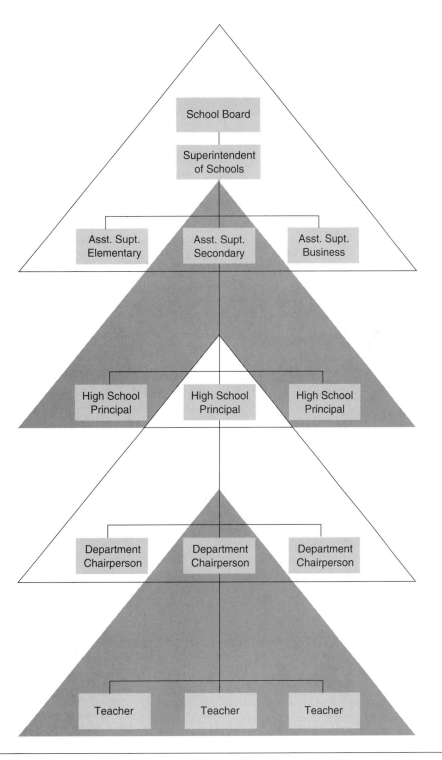

FIGURE 6.10 The linking-pin concept as applied to the decision-making structure of a medium-sized school district.

organizational system can be extended and elaborated to include all facets of the school district organization (including elementary schools).[70] Second—and more important—Likert has described how such an arrangement can facilitate the development of a more functional interaction-influence system: one that is not characterized by the traditional, directive, downward-oriented concepts of line-and-staff organization but instead is characterized by free communication and influence, up, down, and across the organization, featuring a teamwork approach to problems at all levels.

In sum, "the effectiveness of the interaction–influence system of an organization and the capacity of this system to deal with difficult problems depend on the effectiveness of the work groups of which the structure consists and on the extent to which multiple linkage is provided."[71] Considering, therefore, the dynamic interdependence between structure (for example, linked, overlapping groups) and the influence system (for example, directive or collaborative) brings us to the issue of participation in making decisions. One seeking to develop a collaborative interaction–influence system must attend to developing a leadership or administrative style that will develop the skills and motivation of subordinates that support such an approach. In other words, one would seek to move from System 1 to System 4. This conforms to the major approaches to motivation that are discussed in Chapter 5.

Conclusion

The concept of organizational culture has emerged as central in the analysis of organizational behavior and organizational effectiveness. Organizational culture is the body of solutions to problems that has worked consistently for a group and that is therefore taught to new members as the correct way to perceive, think about, and feel in relation to those problems. Over time, organizational culture takes on meaning so deep that it defines the assumptions, values, beliefs, norms, and even the perceptions of participants in the organization. Though culture tends to drop from the conscious thoughts of participants over time, it continues to powerfully create meaning for them in their work and becomes "the rules of the game."

Studies of schools have strongly supported the belief that organizational culture is a fundamental factor in determining the quality of educational organizations. Culture cannot be studied directly but is inferred from observed behavior such as language, use of artifacts, rituals, and symbolism commonly encountered in the workplace.

Organizational climate, which is the study of the perceptions of participants of certain intangible aspects of the environment, reflects the culture. Studies of organizational climate ordinarily use questionnaires to elicit perceptions from participants. The trend in the study of organizational climate in schools has been away from the study of the perceptions of adults toward the study of those of pupils and students.

As the study of organizational culture moved to a central position in organizational behavior in education, it was accompanied by increasing use of such qualitative research methods as participant observation and open-ended unstructured interviews to replace traditional statistical research methods. The use of qualitative research methods makes it possible to produce richly detailed "thick" descriptions of the organizational culture of schools, which are necessary in order to explain what is happening in them. Although the use of such methods is relatively recent in the study of organizational behavior in comparison with traditional statistical methods, they are derived from a long and respected research tradition in anthropology and sociology as well as educational administration. Qualitative research methods, such as ethnography, are based on very clear concepts of the nature of inquiry that are quite different from conventional rationalistic concepts and observe rules of procedure and rigor that are equally clear and different from those of conventional quantitative methods.

Much of the research on organizational culture, in both corporate and educational organizations, is related to the effectiveness of the organizations. Many studies describe relationships between performance of the company (in such terms as market share, sales, and profitability) and the organizational culture within the company. Comparable support exists for a similar thesis in education. In large measure, clearly establishing such causal connections in schooling is hampered by the extraordinary complexity of the organization and the confusion and ambiguity among and between various constituencies of schooling concerning the criteria for determining what high performance is in a school.

A substantial and growing body of empirical evidence, derived from rigorous research in schools and other educative organizations, indicates that the effectiveness of these organizations, in terms of student learning and development, is significantly influenced by the quality and characteristics of the organizational culture. Not surprisingly, the research clearly suggests that schools that emphasize supportiveness, open communication, collaboration, and intellectuality, and that reward achievement and success, outperform (in terms of achievement, attendance, dropout rate, frustration, and alienation) those that emphasize competition, constraint and restrictiveness, and rules and standard operating procedures, and that reward conformity. Further, by delineating the critical factors involved, the concepts arising from this body of research make it possible and practical to plan and manage organizational culture purposefully. It would be difficult to overemphasize the implications arising from this research for administrative practice in an era marked by declining confidence in schools and school systems and by increasing demands for accountability for performance.

Reflective Activities

1. Using the figures and the discussion in this chapter on school climate, analyze how your school's interaction–influence system establishes the organizational behavior that affects the climate. In other words, how do people go about their everyday business of interactions that is connected to and influenced by the elements that comprise school climate?

2. How would you characterize the system in your school using Likert's four management sys-

tems? That is, which system is most like your school? Give one or two specific examples that support your choice.

3. *Working on Your Game Plan.* This chapter described the overlapping symbolic elements that shape and define the organizational culture of a school. Among them are the myths and stories that people tell about the school, the heroes and heroines who are often recalled, the history of the school, the traditions of the school,

and the rituals that are ordinary events in the school. Consider a school that you know well and choose three of the following symbolic elements:

1. Heroes/heroines
2. Stories
3. Myths
4. Rituals
5. Traditions
6. History
7. Values
8. Beliefs

In a paragraph on each of the three elements you have chosen, describe how they are ordinarily manifested in that school. After writing your three descriptive paragraphs, compare notes with others who have done this exercise by reading what you and they have written and discussing the different observations that have been made about the organizational culture of schools.

Suggested Reading

Branden, Nathaniel, *Self-Esteem at Work: How Confident People Make Powerful Companies.* San Francisco: Jossey-Bass, 1998.

One would be hard pressed to name a personal characteristic that is more essential to being effective as a leader than a healthy sense of self-esteem. Your self-esteem has profound effects on your thinking processes, emotions, desires, values, goals, and ways of interpreting events. Self-respect and self-confidence are important aspects of self-esteem, and they are closely tied to your ability to learn, make appropriate decisions, and respond effectively to change. Indeed, Branden believes that self-esteem is the single most illuminating key to your behavior. This book helps readers to understand the concept of self-esteem and offers useful advice on how to develop it. This is important for anyone who would be an educational leader, who would take responsibility for schools in today's era of great change and seek to develop their culture so as to make them better.

Combs, Arthur W., and Donald L. Avila, *Helping Relationships: Basic Concepts for the Helping Professions,* 3rd ed. Boston: Allyn and Bacon, 1985.

Usually, educational leaders think of themselves as administrators: officers, more or less, in the hierarchical line of authority in the organization. However, if you accept the idea that a powerful way of strengthening schools is to develop their organizational cultures so that they will encourage and support creativity, change, and psycho-social growth, you are taking on the role of a helping professional. Changes in organizational culture cannot be brought about by command; they must be developed from within—from within people individually and from within the social group collectively. Combs and Avila offer valuable understanding about the role of facilitating as a helper and give solid advice that you will rarely find in courses on educational administration.

Deal, Terrence E., and Kent D. Peterson, *The Principal's Role in Shaping School Culture.* Washington, DC: U.S. Department of Education, Office of Educational Research and Improvement, 1990.

Although some academics still debate whether one can or should deliberately change the culture of schools, the pragmatic practitioner, in view of the mounting evidence of the importance of culture in evoking organizational behavior, tends to conclude that the issue is not whether one can or should, but how to do it. This little publication addresses the process in simple terms and provides the reader with a ten-point program on "how to build an effective culture."

Fullan, Michael, and Andy Hargreaves, *What's Worth Fighting for in Your School?* New York: Teachers College Press, 1996.

This book encourages principals and teachers to think more deeply about school reform, especially about school cultures that have long encouraged teachers to work individually in near isolation in the classroom. The authors make a strong, yet quiet, case for developing school cultures that facilitate greater collaboration, with teachers working together for improving the work of the school, and explore how principals can support and abet the process.

Levine, Sarah L., *Promoting Adult Growth in Schools: The Promise of Professional Development.* Boston: Allyn and Bacon, 1989.

This book starts with an examination of the professional lives of school teachers and finds what many have found before: that teaching is isolating, inhibiting of personal growth and development, and for these reasons is unsatisfying and rewarding. Moreover, this is inevitably reflected in the effectiveness of the schools. Levine goes on, however, to discuss what can be done by school principals and others to change this situation so as to develop schools as growth-enhancing environments for the adults who work in them. Contains a great deal of useful, practical advice.

Lieberman, Ann, ed., *Building a Professional Culture in Schools.* New York: Teachers College Press, 1988.

Note that the title of this book uses the term "professional culture" rather than "organizational culture." This is not by chance: it reflects the belief that schools should be developing a very definite kind of culture. It is an interesting book of readings in which a number of currently popular writers, including activists, researchers, academics, and unionists, advocate various aspects of developing schools which are more collegial and in which teachers provide greater leadership than in the past.

Lutz, Frank W., and Laurence Iannaccone, *Understanding Educational Organizations: A Field Study Approach.* Columbus, OH: Charles E. Merrill, 1969.

Two pioneers in the long history of qualitative research in educational administration—known particularly for their study of the exercise of power in schools—describe their theory, their research methods, and procedures to use in the field. A sound introduction for the reader inexperienced in using field methods in the study of school culture.

Nixon, Bruce C., *Making a Difference: Strategies and Real-Time Models to Transform Your Organization.* New York: AMACOM, 1997.

Nixon calls for a fundamental shift away from hierarchical organization to a more collaborative, empowering way of organizing and working in order to meet the current need for creative, nimble responses to rapid change. Though intended for corporate leaders, this book offers excellent descriptions of how organization development methods can be built into the daily work of running the organization (hence, the term *real time*). Provides many practical insights as to how culture can be changed and the organization "turned around."

Ott, J. Steven, *The Organizational Culture Perspective.* Pacific Grove, CA: Brooks/Cole, 1989.

A comprehensive textbook that provides a readable survey of contemporary organizational culture theory and research. Although it deals primarily with corporate culture, and includes numerous examples from business and industry, educators will find it a useful source for illuminating concepts of organizational culture that are readily applicable to educational settings.

Rubin, Hank, *Collaboration Skills for Educators and Nonprofit Leaders.* Chicago: Lyceum Books, 1998.

In working for organizational renewal from the inside out—that is, working with organizational culture and climate—much is said about the need for increased collaboration, team building, and reaching out to engage people in the community. But where do leaders learn the specific skills and techniques for doing this kind of facilitative work? Rubin points out that there is no degree program in collaborative leadership. The answer, at the moment, is to learn these methods on the job. And this book can help. It is a practical and insightful guidebook by someone who knows and understands schools and nonprofit organizations.

Sarason, Seymour B., *The Culture of the School and the Problem of Change.* Boston: Allyn and Bacon, 1971.

Based on his own extensive experiences in schools, this classic small volume presents a sensitive, insightful description of schools, how they are really organized, and what this means for developing effective ways of facilitating change in them. An easy-to-read book that endures as an exceptional example of the use of the concept of culture as an organizer for the analysis of the school as an organization.

Schein, Edgar H., *The Corporate Culture Survival Guide.* San Francisco: Jossey-Bass, 1999.

The *opus magnum* of the master of organizational culture, who has been working the territory for over forty years. Sadly, it is single-mindedly focused on corporate organizations, with nary a thought about schools. However, if you want to understand the nature of organizational culture from the pen of the master, you will find this a highly rewarding book. School people will gain much by reading this book and then pondering how its corporate illustrations can be applied to school organizations. It is a worthwhile exercise. Very highly recommended to those who want to advance from the dilettante stage of understanding.

Tieger, Paul D., Barbara Barron-Tieger, and Marly A. Swick, *The Art of Speedreading People: How to Size People Up and Speak Their Language.* New York: Little, Brown, 1999.

There is little question that the ability to understand others and to address them in their "native" language is a great asset to a leader. This book approaches that problem from the psychological concept of personality typing: Are you an extrovert or an introvert? Sensor or intuitive? Thinking or feeling? Judging or perceiving? The authors help you to understand yourself a little better using these dimensions and then show you how to apply this skill to understanding and interpreting others with whom you communicate. It is a powerful tool for those leaders who choose to work with and through other people in collaborative, collegial, mutually respectful ways.

chapter 7

Organizational Change

LEARNING OBJECTIVES

After reading this chapter, you should be able to

- Identify and describe the concept of natural diffusion of change in education.

- Compare and contrast natural diffusion with planned, managed diffusion in educational change.

- Describe the concept of empirical-rational strategies of planned change.

- Identify and describe the agricultural model of the empirical-rational change strategy.

- Describe and give examples of the power-coercive strategy of change in U.S. schooling.

- Describe the concept of organizational self-renewal.

- Identify the three essential core activities that an organization *must* perform in order to survive.

- Describe the interrelationship between the concepts of the learning organization and organization development (organization self-renewal).

- Identify and discuss the concepts of force-field analysis.

- Describe the three-step change process in the life cycle of an organization.

ISLLC Standards

STANDARD 1: A school administrator is an educational leader who promotes the success of all students by facilitating the development, articulation, implementation, and stewardship of a vision of learning that is shared and supported by the school community.

Knowledge

The administrator has knowledge and understanding of:

- the principles of developing and implementing strategic plans
- systems theory
- information sources, data collection, and data analysis strategies
- effective communication
- effective consensus-building and negotiation skills

Dispositions

The administrator believes in, values, and is committed to:

- a school vision of high standards of learning
- continuous school improvement

Performances

The administrator facilitates processes and engages in activities ensuring that:

- the vision is developed with and among stakeholders
- the school community is involved in school improvement efforts
- the vision shapes the educational programs, plans, and actions
- assessment data related to student learning are used to develop the school vision and goals
- barriers to achieving the vision are identified, clarified, and addressed
- the vision, mission, and implementation plans are regularly monitored, evaluated, and revised

STANDARD 2: A school administrator is an educational leader who promotes the success of all students by advocating, nurturing, and sustaining a school culture and instructional program conducive to student learning and staff professional growth.

Knowledge

The administrator has knowledge and understanding of:

- the change process for systems, organizations, and individuals
- school cultures

Performances

The administrator facilitates processes and engages in activities ensuring that:

- the school is organized and aligned for success

- curricular, cocurricular, and extracurricular programs are designed, implemented, evaluated, and refined
- curriculum decisions are based on research, expertise of teachers, and the recommendations of learned societies
- the school culture and climate are assessed on a regular basis

STANDARD 3: A school administrator is an educational leader who promotes the success of all students by ensuring management of the organization, operations, and resources for a safe, efficient, and effective learning environment.

Knowledge

The administrator has knowledge and understanding of:

- theories and models of organizations and the principles of organizational development

Performances

The administrator facilitates processes and engages in activities ensuring that:

- knowledge of learning, teaching, and student development is used to inform management decisions
- emerging trends are recognized, studied, and applied as appropriate
- financial, human, and material resources are aligned to the goals of schools
- organizational systems are regularly monitored and modified as needed
- stakeholders are involved in decisions affecting schools
- effective problem-framing and problem-solving skills are used
- effective group-process and consensus-building skills are used
- human resource functions support the attainment of school goals

STANDARD 6: A school administrator is an educational leader who promotes the success of all students by understanding, responding to, and influencing the larger political, social, economic, legal, and cultural context.

Knowledge

The administrator has knowledge and understanding of:

- the political, social, cultural, and economic systems and processes that impact schools
- models and strategies of change and conflict resolution as applied to the larger political, social, cultural, and economic contexts of schooling
- global issues and forces affecting teaching and learning

Dispositions

The administrator believes in, values, and is committed to:
- importance of a continuing dialogue with other decision makers affecting education

All that we know about schools as organizations and the behavior of people in them is brought into play when we confront the need to plan and manage change, or reform, in them. In fact, the fundamental issue in planning and managing change in a school is the need to bring about the important changes in the organizational culture of the school. As we shall describe, by recognizing the need to bring about the changes in key aspects of the organizational culture of the school, the leader finds powerful leverage points for triggering planned and managed organizational change.

Critics of American schooling have a propensity to depict schools as static bureaucracies, stodgy, lumbering about, and unable to adapt to emerging demands for high performance. Although there is some justification for this view, of course, schools are also the product of a long history of change. Transmitted from generation to generation as part of the cultural heritage of the school, this history has been powerful in developing some of the basic assumptions about change that are now well enmeshed in the warp and woof of the culture of schools. And, as we described earlier, the pattern of these basic cultural assumptions in the organization—which are normally unchallenged and rarely discussed—has great power to form the beliefs and values of people who work at the school and are, therefore, central in thinking about ways to change things. We are talking about a central element of the bedrock foundation of the culture of the school that shapes and molds the abilities of people in the school to conceptualize bold, fresh, creative ways that significantly break with the past and hold out the promise of transforming the school into a high-performance organization. As a point of departure, we turn now to a very brief review of some of the major themes that have shaped the tradition of change in the recent history of schooling.

Because the Constitution makes no mention of education, each state, at its founding, assumed responsibility for providing public school education in its state constitution. As the nation developed and expanded westward in the nineteenth century, public school education was developed almost entirely as a matter of concern of the various states while the federal government generally remained uninvolved. Each state created local school districts designating local school boards or committees in them to administer and control the state's constitutionally mandated responsibilities for schooling. This was a remarkably suitable arrangement for a time when the nation was largely agrarian, communities were small, distances between them were great, and the transportation and communication technology of the time were important limiting constraints. Local school districts levied and collected taxes (either directly or indirectly) on property (such as land, buildings, and livestock) in their districts to fund their operations and functioned under the relatively limited and largely benign supervision that the states had chosen as their role. However, powerful winds of social and economic change were freshening by the mid-nineteenth century and would ultimately sweep up the schools: the westward expansion of the nation; the development of science, technology, and industry; a swelling tide of immigration; and a trend toward urbanization. These and other major social-political changes of the time sparked new interest in redefining education's role in the scheme of things. In retrospect we can see that, as early as 1857, a tectonic shift began to rumble through the field of public schooling in the United States, and ever since it has been picking up speed and power for change that continue even now.

In 1857 Congressman Justin Smith Morrill of Vermont introduced a bill into the House of Representatives that would create endowments called land grants that, with matching funds from the state, could be used to establish and maintain a college in each state to teach not only classical studies but agriculture, the sciences, and technologies as well. The uniqueness of the land-grant colleges lay in two key concepts underlying them: one concept was to combine the study of traditional academic subjects with the study of more "practical" subjects such as the sciences and technologies that were emerging at the time, and the other concept was that these colleges would be owned and operated as public enterprises of the state at taxpayer expense. This bold innovative move was not well received by then-existing institutions of higher education in the United States, which were largely private preserves dedicated to meeting the needs of students from affluent families who were seeking education in the European tradition to enhance their positions of social privilege. By contrast, the newer land-grant institutions would meet the needs of working-class people who wanted to combine more practical technical studies with studies in the traditional liberal arts. At the outset the Morrill Act, as it became known, did not have an easy time of it politically: the first time that the bill was passed by both houses of Congress it was vetoed by conservative President James Buchanan in 1861. It would not be until a second try in 1862, when the southern members of the Congress were absent for the Civil War, that it was passed again by Congress and signed into law by President Abraham Lincoln. This was a landmark intervention by the federal government that not only led directly to the transformation of higher education in the United States but also heralded a new expansion of federal involvement in education that would eventually lead to the inclusion of elementary and secondary education as we see today. After passage of the first Morrill Act, the states had acquired a powerful partner in education that was not going to go away.

Behind this event, however, an overarching theme hovers almost unseen in the background, a theme that has been at the core of educational debate in the United States since at least the early eighteenth century and that continues today. The immediate questions that we might ask are these: Why did Justin Morrill, the Congress, and Abraham Lincoln all agree in thinking that it was necessary for the government to establish the land-grant colleges? What important public interest was to be served by them? The answers to these questions are too complex for a full discussion here but one central issue is clear: a persistent concern about the purposes of education. For example, who benefits from education? Is education a private good that benefits only those who have the money and leisure to afford it? Or is it a public good that benefits not only those who receive it but also the body politic as a whole? And, if the latter, what kind of education does the public interest require?

These were the kinds of questions that Benjamin Franklin had raised, and for which he proffered answers, as far back as 1749 when he proposed the establishment of an academy in Philadelphia in 1749. Franklin's brainchild, the academy, was a bold, new idea: he thought that the academy should focus on teaching the English language, including speaking, spelling, composition, and grammar; and such subjects as arithmetic, mathematics, astronomy, and accounting; history, including English translations of classical Greek and Roman texts; handwriting; the decorative arts; and more. He thought that classrooms in the academy should be equipped with maps and globes, mathematical instruments, apparatus for science and physics experiments, and collections of pictures of machines, celestial mechanics, specimens, architecture, art, and so on. Such an approach to schooling was radically different from the traditional classical schooling at that time, such as had been the hallmark of the prestigious Boston Latin School founded in 1635. That school along with others that followed it emphasized study of the classics and humanities in their original ancient Greek and Latin texts and considered the English language as inferior and unworthy of study. For over a century such schools in the United States had produced a stream of students who could fluently read and translate the ancient texts and who could discuss their contents in their original languages. Boston Latin School, and others like it, had been established expressly to offer this kind of classical curriculum in order to prepare boys to study for the ministry and the learned professions, and many at the time thought that it did so very well.

A hundred years later, however, things were different and schools were pressed to meet the challenge of new needs. Franklin's new idea for schooling, the academy, was announced at the height of the Age of Enlightenment and it embodied all the new ideas of that great middle-class movement. Franklin was then one of the world's leading Enlightenment scholars and he saw a need for schools to educate boys who would be prepared to take their places in the practical affairs of business, industry, and commerce that were then burgeoning not only in prosperous Philadelphia but also throughout the Western world. The new need, he saw, was not for more church ministers but for people who had the skills to work in the counting houses; to design, build, and navigate the ships; to develop industrial processes and techniques; to fill the emerging needs of government service; and to go on to advanced studies in the arts and sciences. Others saw this need as well and the academy movement in American schooling flourished and spread as people throughout the growing nation embraced its educational concepts.

The history of these themes and these questions illustrates the process of growth and development in education and schooling that have unfolded unceasingly since that time throughout the centuries right up until our own time. Educational goals continue to change and develop as social, cultural, and economic realities continue to develop. It is no different in our time and will continue to be so into the future.

We are speaking here of change in the organization that has certain basic characteristics:

- It is change that is *planned and directed* toward the achievement of specific new, higher organizational outcomes. This is in sharp contrast with the unplanned organizational drift that traditionally passes for change in many organizations and that normally occurs over time in any organization. Planned and directed change, on the other hand, seeks to transform an ordinary organization, or even a low-performing one, into a high-performing organization.

- It is change that *involves the whole organization*—an entire school or school district—rather than merely pieces of the organization.

■ It is change that *increases the capacity of the organization* to more effectively confront the continuing need for change now and in the future, leaving the organization stronger, healthier, more resilient, and more adaptable than it was before. This makes planned and directed organizational change very different from the ever-present temptation for a quick fix.

■ It is change that is *sustainable over time* and, thus, has a permanence that differentiates it from the constant ebb and flow of fads and fashions that has historically been so characteristic of schools.

In the United States, the terms *school reform, comprehensive school reform,* and *whole school reform* are used interchangeably and embody the four concepts just described. A core defining concept shared by all of these terms is that the reform is intended to change, or re-form, the entire school organization or the entire school system in important ways. This concept arises from systems thinking, which recognizes the dynamic interactive nature of the interrelated parts of the whole organization: we cannot significantly change one part of the school without having impact on other parts of the interdependent whole. Small-scale changes that have little or no effect on the rest of the organization are viewed as being little more than tinkering.

School reform, which involves increasing the capacity of the entire organization to be highly effective in achieving high-performance goals, stands in direct contrast with the long historical tradition in American schooling of repeated small-scale piecemeal changes that generally resulted in little significant improvement of the overall learning outcomes of all students. Whereas schools have demonstrated remarkable ability to remain essentially stable and seemingly unchanged despite a history of numerous small-scale changes over the years, school reform efforts seek to lift the organizational performance of schools as a whole. In the larger field of organizational studies, which includes business and industrial organizations as well as nonprofit organizations, such change is generally called simply organizational change. Both terms—*school reform* and *organizational change*—are believed by many to have a moral implication, such as the need to correct existing errors or abolishing malpractice, involved in transforming the organization.

With the advent of the No Child Left Behind Act, with its promises of Draconian punishment of schools that fail to demonstrate adequate annual yearly progress in pupil achievement, it is safe to say that schools in the United States have never before been so focused on the need for planned, controlled, and directed organizational change. This, of course, underscores the need for understanding the processes of organizational change in order for leaders to create effective strategies by which to plan, direct, and control them in order to achieve the outcomes desired. Clearly, this new era calls for leaders to approach organizational change in ways that are very different from the past.

This chapter begins with a brief overview of how schools in the United States have dealt with the issues of change in the past, which was characteristically passive and unplanned. It is important to have an understanding of this historical perspective because it is an indelible part of the culture and tradition of schools and still pervades much of the thinking by educators about organizational change processes. We then move on to consider the three very different and distinct ways, or strategies, for thinking about and planning organizational change that are well established in theory and practice, not only in schools but in business organizations as well. These three newer strategic approaches to change provide the leader with ways of thinking through the complexities and uncertainties that are inherent in the real-world environments of schools.

Educational organizations are expected not only to be vehicles for social change; they are expected also to preserve and transmit traditional values to younger members of society at the same time as they are expected to prepare them to deal with an ever-changing world. Thus, schools and other educational organizations must confront not merely change but also the integration of stability *and* change. And many observers, impatient to bring about change in schools, have pointed out again and again that the more things change in schools, the more they remain the same. Yet, as Matthew Miles has reminded us:

> Many aspects of schools as organizations, and the value orientations of their inhabitants, are founded on history and constitute . . . genotypical properties. These are important to the schools; they help maintain continuity and balance in the face of the school's ambiguous mission and its vulnerability to external pressures from parents and others. Therefore, it is likely that, while rapid shifts in specific school practices are relatively more possible, changes touching on the central core of assumptions and structures will be far more difficult to achieve.[1]

This is a useful concept for leaders to use in thinking through problems of bringing about organizational change in schools. It is drawn from biology, which describes how the genetic constitution of the individual produces persistent identifying characteristics, while interaction of the genotype with the environment results in distinctive visible adaptive properties. The notion is that schools as organizations are characterized by a genotypical core of traditions, values, and beliefs that identify them as schools and that differentiate them from other kinds of organizations. It is almost, as the description suggests, as though schools have a genetic predisposition to maintain their identity and core characteristics over time. Yet schools do interact with and are shaped by their ever-changing environments, resulting in the emergence of visible phenotypical properties. This helps explain why exasperated would-be school reformers often feel that the more things change, the more they stay the same.

School Reform and Change

Clearly, the school reform movement that was kicked off with publication of *A Nation at Risk* in 1983[2] has been the greatest and most sustained, concerted national effort to change the central core of assumptions and structures of the public schools in the history of the Republic. Since its inception, "the country has been searching for some magical way to reform and restructure public schools. We have tried—and are still trying—all sorts of alchemical nostrums we hope will turn our educationally leaden schools into schools of educational gold."[3] Over the years the discourses on school reform have been well leavened with bold calls for sweeping changes such as restructuring education, reinventing schools, and recreating our educational goals. Yet so little had changed in U.S. schooling by 1990 that Seymour Sarason pondered the seeming intractability of the schools in the face of years of reform effort and predicted the failure of educational reform[4] unless the strategies and tactics of change were themselves changed.

The essence of Sarason's analysis was that schools seemed to be intractable only because the strategies and tactics selected to carry out reform efforts had largely been ineffective in significantly altering the central core of assumptions and structures—that is to say, the organizational culture—of schools. He explained that the nucleus of that core of organizational behavior is power, particularly the power of assumptions about power: especially whether power is assumed to be authority conferred or denied by one's position in the hierarchy or is assumed to arise from mutual collaboration among people of all levels and at every position in the organization. Thus, according to Sarason, if we want to bring about significant change in the schools, we must come to terms with the power of culture to shape the assumptions and beliefs of people in the school, the power that motivates, the power used in attempts to lead, the power to participate in making important decisions, the power that gives rise to organizational behavior in schools.

What is there about the strategies and tactics of the reform movement that have generally failed to make much progress in achieving reform? Sarason, one of the most astute observers of schools and change, thinks the problem is that school reform generally avoids dealing with power relationships in the school, which he sees as central to bringing about educational change.

Power Relationships and School Restructuring

School reform literally means to give new form to the school,[5] that is, to change the school in fundamental ways. This concept is popularly called "restructuring." But the question is, how can schools be restructured? The key lies in changing power relationships in the school. How do we bring about such change? Since the public schools are ultimately controlled by the body politic acting through representative political agencies—such as school boards, state legislatures, or the U.S. Congress—political strategies to bring about change in schools can be very powerful. Ordinarily, political change strategies try to change power relationships in the schools by mandate. This is plainly exemplified by the No Child Left Behind Act, which mandated a broad array of goals, tests, and changes in the schools along with prescribed rewards and punishments to enforce the mandates that Congress and the Bush administration believed would bring about fundamental change in the functioning of the 106,000 K–12 schools in the United States and, consequently, would improve their instructional effectiveness. Clearly, then, those who wield legal hierarchical power can attempt to force change upon schools by altering the power relationships in them by fiat.

On the other hand, schools—like other organizations—can be changed from within. Sarason, for example, spoke approvingly about ways of altering power relationships by involving everyone in the organization in the process of change. Sarason pointed out that such a strategy makes two major contributions to our thinking about bringing about organizational change in educational organizations:

- It conceptualizes the organization as a whole, not this part or that part.

- It is essentially and explicitly an educational rationale in that it seeks to promote the personal and vocational development of everyone. "I use the word *educational*," Sarason explained, "because it aims to expand people's knowledge of and commitment to their individual . . . growth."[6]

In short, Sarason pointed out that two distinctly different strategies are possible for changing educational organizations, and few students of organization would disagree:

- a strategy for changing the educational organization from the outside in and from the top down or

- a strategy seeking to bring about change from the inside out and from the bottom up.

If we seek to change the inner core of assumptions and structures of the school, rather than merely the formal official aspects of the organization, the question becomes: which of the two approaches is more effective?

Aims of Educational Reform

For example, what kinds of changes does educational reform seek to bring about in the schools? What inner assumptions do we seek to change? From his analysis of the rhetoric, Sarason listed five aims that most agree would constitute major changes in the inner core of assumptions that are so difficult to bring about:

- To reduce the wide gulf between the educational accomplishments of children of different social classes and racial backgrounds.

- To get students to experience schooling as a process to which they are attracted, not a compulsory one they see as confining and boring.

- To enable students to acquire knowledge and skills that are not merely rote learning or memorized abstractions, but rather are acquired in ways that interrelate the learning and give personal purpose, now and in the future, to each student.

- To engender interest in and curiosity about human accomplishments, past and present. To get students to want to know how the present contains the past—that is, to want to know this as a way of enlarging their own identities: personal, social, and as citizens.

- To acquaint students with the domain of career options and how schooling relates to these options in the fast-changing world of work.[7]

If these encompass at least a substantial part of the aims of educational reform, why is it that there is so little agreement in the U.S. school reform movement as to the strategies and tactics for achieving them? Why is it that, as we described in Chapter 5, there are three major approaches to school reform currently competing with each other? Once again, the answer lies in the different ways in which people conceptualize the problem. It depends, to no small extent, on one's theory of action. We deal with the school reform movements themselves in more detail in Chapter 12 of this book. But in preparation for that, let us now identify and briefly discuss the array of major strategies and tactics of organizational change that are available to organizations generally—schools, corporations, military, or any other kind of organization.

The Tradition of Change in American Education

Historically, change in education in the United States was viewed largely as a process of "natural diffusion." That is, new ideas and practices arose in some fashion and spread in some unplanned way from school to school and from district to district. The result was that schools generally changed very slowly: in the late 1950s Paul Mort observed that it then took about fifty years for a newly invented educational practice to be generally diffused and accepted in schools throughout the country and that the average school lagged some twenty-five years behind the best practice of the time.[8]

Natural Diffusion Processes

Mort observed a pattern to this unplanned process of diffusion:

> Educational change proceeds very slowly. After an invention which is destined to spread throughout the school appears, fifteen years typically elapse before it is found in three percent of the school systems. . . . After practices reach the three percent point of diffusion, their rate of spread accelerates. An additional 20 years usually suffices for an almost complete diffusion in an area the size of an average state. There are indications that the rate of spread throughout the nation is not much slower.[9]

This is well illustrated by the introduction and spread of kindergartens. In 1873—nearly twenty years after the introduction of private kindergartens to the United States from Germany—the city of St. Louis established the first public school kindergartens. By the mid-1950s, kindergarten education had been firmly established in the profession as a desirable educational practice, and, indeed, such federally funded projects as Head Start provided strong stimuli for spurring its development. However, as late as the 1967–1968 school year (ninety-four years after the introduction of kindergartens in St. Louis), only 46 percent of the nation's school districts provided kindergarten education for their children.[10]

For many years, Mort was considered the leading student of educational change in this country. The main thesis of his work was that adequacy of financial support is the key factor in determining how much lag a school system exhibits in adopting innovative practices. Vigorously active in his many years as a teacher and researcher at Teachers College, Columbia University, Mort left a storehouse of knowledge and a large number of devoted students who have heavily influenced the thinking of school administrators with regard to the factors that enhance change and innovation in schools. Largely because of this influence, per pupil expenditure has long been considered the most reliable predictor of a school's chances of adopting educational innovations.

The systematic underpinnings of the cost–quality relationship in education are generally felt to have been established in 1936 by Paul Mort and Francis Cornell's study of Pennsylvania schools.[11] Numerous studies dealing with the relationship between expenditure and measures of school output have followed, which generally support the not too surprising notion that high expenditure is generally associated with various indicators of superior school output. A troublesome fact was noted rather early in this research, however: it is possible for school districts to have high per pupil costs and still have inferior schools.[12] Considerable research has been undertaken since 1938 to explain this fact, much of it exploring the nature of the cost–quality relationship itself. Mort tended to think of this relationship as linear: more money would tend to assure higher educational quality, and there was no point of diminishing returns. Since 1965, however, increasing attention has been paid to the possibility that cost–quality relationships in education are actually curvilinear and have an optimum point beyond which additional expenditure fails to yield increased school output.[13]

Sociological Views of Diffusion

Although it would be absurd to say that penurious circumstances would enhance the schools' efforts to reduce the lag in change, more recent research tends to emphasize the influences of social structure on the amount and rate of change. For example, Richard O. Carlson studied the rate and pattern of the adoption of "new math" in a West Virginia county.[14] Carlson reported that the position that a superintendent of schools held in the social structure of the school superintendents of the county made it possible to make reasonable predictions about the amount and rate of innovation in that superintendent's school district. When the superintendent was looked on as a leader by his or her peers, as influential among other superintendents, and as being in communication with many of them, his or her district tended to adopt innovations early and thoroughly. Contrary to the bulk of existing research on cost–quality relationships, Carlson did not find a parallel between innovation and the financial support level of the school district. If nothing else, such studies—and Carlson's study represents only one of many sociological studies of organizational change and innovation—indicate that money spent is only one factor in the adaptability of schools, to use Mort's term. Within limits that are not yet clear, it is probably not even the major factor.

Planned, Managed Diffusion

The strategy by which money is spent may have a greater impact on change in schools than conventional indices such as per pupil expenditure may indicate. One of the more spectacular and better-known attempts to alter significantly the pattern of change in the public schools in the post-*Sputnik* era was undertaken by the Physical Science Study Committee (PSSC) in 1956 under the leadership of Professor J. R. Zacharias of the

Massachusetts Institute of Technology.[15] Briefly, the PSSC group wanted to improve the teaching of physical science in U.S. high schools. Retraining thousands of teachers, developing new curricula for all sizes of school districts, and persuading the local school boards to buy the needed materials and equipment might have taken half a century to accomplish using traditional methods. Instead, within ten years after the project was inaugurated, high schools were considered to be behind the times if they did not offer a PSSC course.

This incredibly swift mass adoption was achieved by a strategy that involved three phases: (1) inventing the new curriculum, (2) diffusing knowledge of the new curriculum widely and rapidly among high school science teachers, and (3) getting the new curriculum adopted in local schools. This strategy involved the use of a number of new ideas. In addition to bypassing local school districts wherever possible, the PSSC group invested its money in novel and powerful ways. First, by spending $4.5 million in two and one-half years to hire a full-time professional team, a portable, self-contained curriculum package was developed and tested in practice. This package included filmed lessons, textbooks, teachers' guides, tests, and laboratory guides and apparatus—a completely unified, integrated unit that could be moved *in toto* into almost any high school. Second, physics teachers were introduced to the new techniques by attending institutes, for which they received financial grants and stipends. Some forty institutes were made available each year throughout the country for this purpose. Third, by providing funds to be matched by the federal government (largely through the National Defense Education Act), the PSSC group persuaded local school boards to buy the package for their schools.

Three Strategies of Planned Change

Contemporary approaches to change are dominated by efforts to develop strategies and tactics that may enable us to plan, manage, and control change. In this book, the taxonomy suggested by Robert Chin is used as the basis for discussion.[16] As we shall explain, Chin posited that three major "strategic orientations" are useful in planning and managing change:

1. Empirical-rational strategies.
2. Power-coercive strategies.
3. Normative-reeducative strategies.

Empirical-Rational Strategies of Change

The traditional processes of unplanned dissemination of new ideas to schools have given way to strategies of planned, managed dissemination intended to spread new ideas and practices swiftly. Much research and study have been devoted to these strategies, which focus primarily on more closely linking the findings of research to the practices of education. This link requires improving communication between researchers and practitioners (users, consumers of research) so that the traditional, scornful distance between them will be replaced by a more productive, cooperative (if not collaborative) relationship.

This approach sees the scientific production of new knowledge and its use in daily activities as the key to planned change in education. It is referred to broadly as "knowledge production and utilization" (KPU). Numerous models for implementing the strategy have been proposed and tried; all of these attempt to develop an orderly process, with a clear sequence of related steps leading from the origination of new knowledge to its ultimate application in practice. The aim is to bridge the gap between theory and practice. To do this requires not only that the functions or activities of the process be described but also that someone (or some agency) be designated to carry them out.

Research, Development, and Diffusion (R, D, and D)

Various models for implementing KPU concepts of change appear under different appellations, depending on the number of steps that are seen as important. An R and D model, for example, suggests that someone ought to be conducting research and that someone ought to be developing some useful products from that research. As in all KPU models, "research" is meant here to be the invention or discovery of new knowledge, regardless of its applicability to immediate problems. In R and D work, the quality and validity of the research are of paramount importance. The model recognizes, however, that the research scientist is not always the person best equipped to translate research findings into useful products.

The *development* phase of R and D includes such things as solving design problems, considering feasibility in real-world conditions, and cost. Development essentially means translating research into products that are practical for use; these can range from school buildings to pupil seating, from textbooks to comprehensive packaged curricula, or from instructional techniques to new types of football helmets. In free enterprise societies this stage has been largely the province of profit-seeking firms that have the necessary financial resources and entrepreneurial skills.

The *diffusion* phase of R, D, and D is seen as a third and distinctive phase; it is, more or less, the marketing activities of R, D, and D. The aim is to make the new products readily available in an attractive, easy-to-use form at a reasonable cost to the adopter.

Of course, the ultimate goal is to get the new ideas into use. Some, therefore, treat *adoption* as a separate aspect of the process and may even call it "research, development, dissemination, and adoption" (R, D, D, A) to emphasize this point. As David Clark and Egon Guba have made clear,[17] the processes of adoption are not simple. They described a three-stage process: (1) *a trial,* during which the new product is tested in some limited way, (2) *installation,* a process of refinement and adaptation to local conditions if the trial appears promising, and finally—if all goes well—(3) *institutionalization,* which means that the innovation becomes an integral part of the system. A test of institutionalization is whether or not the invention continues in use if external support and encouragement are withdrawn (see Figure 7.1).

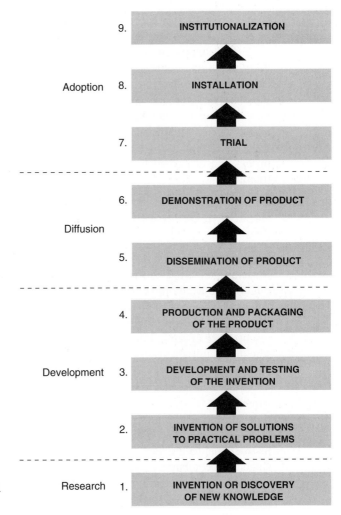

FIGURE 7.1
Concept of the research, development, diffusion, and adoption (R, D, D, A) model of change.

The "Agricultural Model"

It would be difficult to overemphasize the impact that the U.S. experience with planned, controlled change in agriculture has had on the thinking of those who advocate KPU strategies for education. Rural sociologists early discovered the processes and links that facilitated the rapid spread of new and better farming practices through the social system. The development of a network of land grant universities, agricultural experimentation stations, and the ubiquitous county agent are a few of the readily visible key parts of the extensive system that helps farmers to use new, yet proved, knowledge in the practical business of boosting production and lowering costs. When agriculture is compared to the public schools in terms of the speed with which new knowledge and techniques are put into widespread use, it is quickly apparent that agriculture has adopted innovations with far less lag than schools have. Thus, much of the model building and formalistic process development usually found in KPU approaches to change in education is based on efforts to replicate the "agricultural model" in terms appropriate to education.

Beginning in the late 1950s, federal activity was considerably increased in this direction. For example, the National Defense Education Act (NDEA) of 1958 triggered the production of the spate of innovative curriculum packages that appeared in the 1960s.[18] Title IV of the Elementary and Secondary Education Act (ESEA) of 1965 provided for the creation of twenty regional educational laboratories and ten Educational Research and Development Centers throughout the country. The Educational Resources Information Center (ERIC) also appeared, with federal support, in the 1960s. This nationwide network of twenty information clearinghouses seeks to facilitate the rapid communication of research and development activities in forms that will be useful to those in education. The National Institute of Education (NIE) was organized in 1972 expressly for the purpose of fostering research, experimentation, and dissemination of knowledge that could be applied to the improvement of public schooling. The creation of a cabinet-level Department of Education in the executive branch of the federal government in 1979 was strongly supported by many who believed that such an agency was needed to exercise greater order, system, and control in educational KPU. Thus, in a span of a quarter-century, the nation moved vigorously to systematize and stimulate planned KPU in education through federal leadership, in place of the traditional, relatively unplanned, scattered, local, and small-scale efforts of the past.

Assumptions and Implications of KPU Approaches to Change

KPU approaches to change are based on two critical assumptions: (1) that the new knowledge (product, technique) will be perceived by potential adopters as desirable and (2) that adopters—being rational and reasonable—will do what is desirable because it is in their own interest. In other words, "the belief is that good ideas will be used to improve education."[19] It typifies what Robert Chin has described as an *empirical-rational strategy of change*: that is, the new knowledge or practice is empirically demonstrated to be good, and, therefore, one rationally expects it to be adopted.[20] It is a strategy that fits neatly into the traditions and values of Western scientific-technological culture.

To facilitate adoption, new ideas have to reach the adopters in practical form. Thus, the local physician uses a new "wonder drug" with patients in the office when it is available in convenient containers and when the directions permit easy application with familiar implements. Increasingly, schools are being offered relatively complete instructional "delivery systems" that seek to provide comprehensive packages for instruction that, in turn, are based on demonstrably effective concepts and are complete enough to meet a significant need of the school. These are often referred to as "innovations," and much attention is given to the difficulties of "installing" innovations in schools.

The term *innovation* has been severely debased through misuse in the literature on organizational change and stability. Some people simply use it more or less as a synonym for "change." For example, H. G. Barnett posited that "innovation is any thought, behavior or thing that is new because it is qualitatively different from existing forms."[21] But such a broad generalization fails to convey the essence of innovation as it is used in organizational change. In fact, it fails to differentiate innovation from "organizational drift": the inevitable, unplanned, incremental changes that pervade all organizations that exist in a culture whose dominant characteristic is change. Innovation has acquired a pejorative sense in educational circles owing to the frequency with which innovations have been introduced, tried, used, and abandoned.

In this book, the term *innovation* is used in referring to planned, novel, deliberate, specific change that is intended to help the organization (1) achieve existing goals more effectively or (2) achieve new goals. The concept of specificity is crucial: "innovations in education . . . ordinarily have a defined, particular, specified character."[22] Thus, one usually speaks of *an* innovation as something that can be specified in terms of (1) concepts, (2) a set of operating procedures, and (3) a relevant technology to which we attach a name (for example, magnet schools, alternative education, the DISTAR reading program, individually prescribed instruction, and minimal competency testing). Thus, not all organizational change can be described as innovation; indeed, as we shall describe shortly, much desirable organizational change is not necessarily innovative in the sense that the term is used here.

The point to be emphasized, however, is that such empirical-rational strategies of change as KPU and R, D, and D tend to focus on innovation. The concept is that good ideas are developed outside the school and are ultimately *installed* in the school. Thus, there is much concern about problems of disseminating the innovation and of installing the innovation in adopting schools. At the installation level, those who favor the innovation see it as empirically proven and view adoption as rational; conversely, they tend to view barriers to installation at the school level as nonrational (if not irrational). It is at this point that the empirical rationalist becomes concerned not with *educational* change in a broad sense, but with *organizational* change to facilitate the adoption process.

Other Empirical-Rational Strategies

To simplify this discussion, we have focused on one empirical-rational strategy, namely, linking basic research to practice by building diffusion networks and stimulating applied research. This typically involves creating research and development centers, linking state education departments to regional educational laboratories, and developing consortia of universities and school districts. Other empirical-rational strategies for change include the following.

Personnel Selection and Replacement

This strategy includes "clearing out the deadwood" (through dismissal, early retirement, reorganization, transfers), as well as changing the criteria for the certification and employment of new people. Though many proponents of school reform advocate use of this strategy, many administrators confronted with a chronic shortage of teachers consider it of problematic value.

Utopian Thinking

Futurists seek to develop scientific techniques for improving forecasting of the future. Their efforts are, of course, based on the highly rational premise that skill in predicting the future can be helpful in making decisions at the present time. Their empirical-rational attempts to project what *might* exist in the future, what the alternatives *may* be, and what *ought* to be can lead to planned efforts to direct the course of events toward some desired goal, rather than to accept whatever may occur.

Power-Coercive Strategies of Change

A power-coercive approach to change differs significantly from an empirical-rational one in its willingness to use (or threaten to use) *sanctions* in order to obtain compliance from adopters. Sanctions are usually political, financial, or moral. In the power-coercive point of view, rationality, reason, and human relations all are secondary to the ability to effect changes directly through the exercise of power.

One way of exercising political power is to gain control over the political institutions that pass legislation, issue executive orders, and hand down court decisions. This is commonly accompanied by financial sanctions to heighten their coercive effect. The popularity of this strategy in the United States is visible in the welter of legislation, judicial decisions, and governmental regulations—each with sanctions for noncompliance—that draw so much time and attention from educational policymakers and administrators. The No Child Left Behind Act is an exemplar of power-coercive change.

Robert Chin and Kenneth Benne described the restructuring of power elites as another power-coercive strategy to bring about change.[23] It is well recognized that our society has a power structure in which relatively limited groups have extraordinary power to effect change, either to make things happen or to keep them from happening. Instead of accepting the existing power structure as fixed and inevitable, it is possible to change the power structure. If this is done—either by shifting power to new hands or by spreading power more equitably among more people—it is possible to achieve new goals.

This has, of course, been well illustrated by the efforts of minority groups and women to gain representation in the key decision-making groups concerning schools, such as school boards, administrative positions, and boards that control finances. It is illustrated, too, by teachers—long maintained in a powerless and dependent state—who have unionized in an effort to shift their power relationships with administrators and school boards so as to bring about change. A third illustration is the coalition of groups concerned about the education of the handicapped, which has resulted in a series of laws and judicial decisions that have sharply rearranged the power structure in some key areas of educational decision making.

Normative-Reeducative or Organizational Self-Renewal Strategies

Both empirical-rational and power-coercive strategies of change share two assumptions: (1) that good ideas are best developed outside of the organization and (2) that the organization is the target of external forces for change. Implicit in these strategies is the notion that organizations, when left to their own devices, generally emphasize stability over change and generally are resistant to change; they therefore must be *made* to change. There is little question that both of these strategic orientations are effective under certain conditions. But there also is little question that educational organizations have demonstrated remarkable resilience in dealing with these external forces for change by maintaining considerable stability over time and often frustrating even vigorous empirical-rational and power-coercive efforts.

Notice the significant differences between No Child Left Behind (NCLB) as a strategy of organizational change in schools and that of the Zacharias-PSSC undertaking that we described earlier. PSSC is an example of the empirical-rational approach of planned, managed change. It sought to improve instructional outcomes by creating and disseminating a carefully planned, coordinated package of curriculum, teacher training, and teaching materials for use in classrooms throughout the nation. It provided schools, and the teachers in them, with practical concepts, skills, and techniques for improving instruction. Teachers involved in a PSSC program generally felt professionally and personally rewarded by the experience of participating. The change strategy of NCLB, on the other hand, was starkly different: to directly exert the invincible political and financial power of the federal government to coerce schools to achieve, in some unstated fashion, ever-higher scores on mandated standardized tests of student achievement. Schools, and teachers in them, were left scrambling to find acceptable ways of responding to the coercion. Teachers involved tended to feel threatened and diminished by the experience. These two federal programs of intervention in education clearly demonstrate the theoretic and practical differences between empirical-rational and power-coercive strategies of organizational change in schools. They also clearly demonstrate that the decision to select one strategy over the other is a matter of deliberate choice between competing alternative theories, or understandings, of organization and behavior.

The Rand Study of Federal Programs Supporting Educational Change

The nature and extent of this frustration are illustrated by research conducted by the Rand Corporation for the United States Office of Education between 1973 and 1977. The concerns that led to this research were well expressed in 1975, in a publication of the National Institute of Education, which reflected the then-prevailing mood of the Congress:

> Over the past decade and a half, the federal government has spent over a billion dollars on research and development on the country's educational problems, and billions more on categorical aid to schools and districts. Yet, the problems remain intractable, and the repeated

research finding that innovations produce "no significant differences" has engendered such frustration that some have begun to despair of the schools' potential for improvement. A disturbingly familiar national behavior pattern is beginning to manifest itself in education. We are a "can-do," "quick-fix" society. The answer to a problem is a program. If the program fails, we try another one, and if a whole series of programs fails, we tire of that problem and go on to fresher ones.[24]

That was the situation in 1975 and, after the first nationwide appraisal of the effectiveness of NCLB by the federal government's venerable National Assessment of Educational Progress (NAEP), it appeared to hold true in 2005. The NAEP study, which compared test results in math and reading since 1990 and also compared the nationwide results from NCLB tests given in 2003 and 2005, revealed that NCLB had produced what could be most enthusiastically described as mixed results. One of the primary goals of NCLB was to reduce the achievement gap between white and minority students but, in 2005, NAEP found at best only modest, if any, gains in that area. Although the appraisal found that math scores in fourth and eighth grades were up in 2005 as compared with 1990, the rate of improvement had been slowed after implementation of NCLB as compared to the rate of improvement that had occurred in the early 1990s, prior to NCLB. Indeed, one cause for concern from the NAEP study in 2005 was that the data showed that greater educational progress in learning outcomes had been made in the years prior to NCLB than in the years after its implementation.

In an effort to understand this situation, Rand undertook a study of federally funded programs that had been designed to introduce and spread innovative practices in public schools. "These change agent programs," it was noted, "normally offer temporary federal funding to school districts as 'seed money.' If an innovation is successful, it is assumed that the district will incorporate and spread part or all of the project using other sources of funds."[25] (Recall the discussion earlier in this chapter concerning the adoption and institutionalization of innovations, and see again Figure 7.1.)

The study consisted of a series of related investigations of 293 projects in eighteen states sponsored under the following federal programs:

1. Elementary and Secondary Education Act (ESEA), Title III—Innovative Projects.
2. ESEA, Title VII—Bilingual Projects.
3. Vocational Education Act, 1968 amendments, Part D—Exemplary Programs.
4. Right to Read Program.

The research focused on two main issues: (1) the kinds of strategies and conditions that tend to promote change in the school and the kinds that do not and (2) the factors that promote or deter the institutionalization of innovation (which has been tried and adopted) after the federal "seed money" runs out.[26]

Although there is no pretense of summarizing this large and complex research here, the salient finding is clear: the differences among school districts in the extent to which they successfully adopted and implemented innovations are explained not so much by either (1) the nature of the innovation itself or (2) the amount of federal funding but, rather, by the *characteristics of the organization and the management of the local school districts and schools themselves.* For example:

> In cases of successful implementation, the districts were generally characterized by . . . a "problem-solving" orientation. That is, they had identified and frequently had already begun to attack the problem before federal money became available. By contrast, failures in implementation were associated with an "opportunistic" orientation. These districts simply supplemented their budgets with money that happened to be available.[27]

School districts that were successful in implementing innovative programs also tended to exhibit other characteristics:

- They tended to reject rigidly packaged innovations that did not permit adaptation to local conditions.
- They were strongly involved in developing their own local materials rather than simply adopting materials that had been developed elsewhere.
- They engaged in continuous planning and replanning rather than in one-shot planning at the beginning of a project.
- They engaged in ongoing training of people as needs arose in the projects and as defined by the participants (rather than in one-shot training at the outset or in having training needs identified by outside "experts").
- Consistent technical assistance was available locally for projects, rather than one- or two-day visits from outside "experts."
- Innovative projects received strong support from key administrators at both the district and the school level (for example, the superintendent of schools and the principal).

In sum, this research gives strong support to the view, long held by applied behavioral scientists, that organizational characteristics of the target school systems and schools at which empirical-rational and power-coercive strategies of change are aimed are crucial to determining the effectiveness of those schools *and* their capacity to change.

In the words of the NIE report, increasing of productivity is not primarily

> a problem which can be solved by installing new accountability systems, teaching administrators improved purchasing techniques, or utilizing superior technology, but is a problem of improving the organizational culture (problem-solving and decisionmaking structures, incentives to change, skills in managing collaborative planning and implementation, mutual support and communication, opportunities for relevant training, etc.) in which people work.[28]

This development at the local school district and school level is viewed as a necessary precondition to effective utilization of knowledge, no matter how it is produced, packaged, and disseminated:

No matter how good the channels which transmit knowledge and products to practitioners, it appears that such products will spread slowly and see little effective use until schools and districts develop the capacity to engage in an active search for solutions to their own problems, to adapt solutions to the particulars of their own situation, and equally important, to adapt themselves as organizations to the requirements of the selected solutions.[29]

A Normative-Reeducative Strategy

These views express the essence of the third major strategy orientation to change identified by Chin: the normative-reeducative strategy. This orientation, widely known as "organizational self-renewal," is based on an understanding of organizations and people in them that is quite different from the orientation usually held by the empirical-rational or power-coercive views, which are essentially classical or bureaucratic and tend to see the organization as a creation apart from people. Organization theory, in this view, "deals with human *response* to organization rather than with human activity in *creating* organizations."[30]

Normative-reeducative strategies of change, on the other hand, posit that the norms of the organization's interaction–influence system (attitudes, beliefs, and values—in other words, culture) can be deliberately shifted to more productive norms by collaborative action of the people who populate the organization. Andrew Halpin would describe this as shifting from a closed climate to a more open climate. In George Stern's terminology it would be enhancing the development press of the organizational climate. Rensis Likert would speak of moving away from System 1 management style toward System 4 (see Chapter 6).

Organizational Health

To be effective, an organization must perform three essential core activities *over time:*

1. Achieve its goals.
2. Maintain itself internally.
3. Adapt to its environment.[31]

These are the defining characteristics of healthy organizations.

Thus, the organization must be effective and stable, yet capable of changing appropriately. Organizations differ in their ability to accomplish these things; in other words, they exhibit different degrees of *organizational health.* A healthy organization "not only survives in its environment, but continues to cope adequately over the long haul, and continuously develops and extends its surviving and coping activities. Short-run operations on any particular day may be effective or ineffective, but continued survival, adequate coping, and growth are taking place."[32]

The unhealthy organization, on the other hand, is steadily ineffective. It may cope with its environment effectively on a short-term basis with a "crash program," a concentrated drive to meet a particularly threatening situation, or other "administration-by-crisis" techniques, but in the long run the unhealthy organization becomes less and less able to cope with its environment. Rather than gaining in its ability to cope with a situation, it declines in this capacity over time and tends to become dysfunctional.

No single output measure or time slice of organizational performance can provide a reliable, accurate measure of organizational health: a central concern is the organization's continuing ability to cope with change and to adapt to the future. This ability is best viewed in the perspective of time. There are, however, some relatively specific indicators of organizational health:

1. *Goal focus.* This is the extent to which people in the organization understand and accept the achievable and appropriate goals of the organization.

2. *Communication adequacy.* This is vertical and horizontal internal communication and external communication with the environment, and the ease and facility of communication (as against the amount of "noise" and "distortion" that can inhibit and confuse communication).

3. *Optimal power equalization.* An important element of this dimension is the issue of collaboration versus coercion.

4. *Human resources utilization.* This is the effective use of personnel so that they feel they are growing and developing in their jobs.

5. *Cohesiveness.* This is the extent to which participants like the organization and want to remain in it in order to influence the collaborative style.

6. *Morale.* This is exhibited as feelings of well-being and satisfaction.

7. *Innovativeness.* This is the tendency to devise new procedures and goals, to grow, to develop, and to become more differentiated over time.

8. *Autonomy.* Rather than being merely a "tool of the environment" that responds passively to outside stimuli, the autonomous organization tends to determine its own behavior in harmony with external demands.

9. *Adaptation.* Healthy organizations should be able to change, correct, and adapt faster than the environment.

10. *Problem-solving adequacy.* This includes mechanisms for sensing and perceiving problems, as well as those for solving problems permanently and with minimum strain.[33]

Organizational Self-Renewal

It is a commonplace observation, of course, that organizations have a tendency to atrophy over time, becoming obsessed with maintaining themselves, increasing their bureaucratic rigidity, and seeking to shore up traditional practices. In a world characterized by rapid change, such organizations tend to be viewed as *un*healthy, emphasizing maintenance of the organization at the expense of the need for constant adaptability so as to keep pace with the change in the demands and expectations of its external environment.

The concept of organization self-renewal was first comprehensively described by Rensis Likert.[34] He described managing the interaction–influence system of the organization in ways that would stimulate creativity, promote growth of people in the organization, and facilitate solution of the organization's problems. Gordon Lippitt later elaborated a well-developed approach to the processes of renewal based on the view that every organization has a life cycle (birth–youth–maturity) with different renewal needs at each stage of its existence.[35] Matthew Miles and Dale Lake described an application of the concept to school systems in the Cooperative Project for Educational Development.[36]

Organization self-renewal postulates that effective change cannot be imposed on a school; rather, it seeks to develop an internal capacity for continuous problem solving. The processes of renewal include the increased capacity to (1) sense and identify emerging problems, (2) establish goals, objectives, and priorities, (3) generate valid alternative solutions, and (4) implement the selected alternative. An outcome of renewal processes is to shift the culture of the school from emphasis on traditional routines and bureaucratic officialism toward a culture that actively supports the view that much of the knowledge needed to plan and carry out change in schools is possessed by people in the schools themselves.[37] Furthermore, it recognizes that "the optimal unit for educational change is the single school with its pupils, teachers, principal—those who live there every day—as primary participants."[38]

The self-renewing school possesses three essential characteristics: *first,* its culture supports adaptability and responsiveness to change. Such a culture is supportive of open communication, especially from the bottom up, and places a high priority on problem solving. *Second,* it has a set of clear-cut, explicit, and well-known procedures through which participants can engage in the orderly processes of systematic, collaborative problem solving. *Third,* the school is not a parochial institution relying solely on internal energy, ideas, and resources for solving problems. Rather, it is a school that knows when and how to reach out to seek appropriate ideas and resources for use in solving its problems.[39]

The Learning Organization

Some organizations, notably low-performing ones, are characterized by a remarkable inability to sense that they have problems—to detect a disconnect with their external environment—and, thus, have little ability to anticipate and adapt to changes in their external environment. In the case of schools this is commonly observed when the demographics of the community change rapidly, which is common in the United States, as well as when technological changes shift rapidly, which is endemic worldwide. In fast-changing environments, such as those we confront today, school organizations must—as a matter of survival—develop increased ability to sense, even predict, the problems posed by their environments and invent solutions to them. Thus develops the concept of the "learning organization": an organization, whether it be corporate or educational, that learns to adapt to unfolding changes in the environment. This process of increasing the capacity of the organization, qua organization, to learn, to adapt, is often called "organization development" (OD).

OD is an approach to increasing the self-renewal capability of school districts and schools. OD has been defined in many ways because it is difficult to capture the full essence of such a complex approach to improving organizational performance. However, after a comprehensive study of OD in U.S. and Canadian schools, this definition was proposed:

> Organization development in school districts is a coherent, systematically-planned, sustained effort at system self-study and improvement, focusing explicitly on change in formal and informal procedures, processes, norms or structures, using behavioral science concepts. The goals of OD include *both* the quality of life of individuals as well as improving organizational functioning and performance.[40]

In practice, OD involves a cluster of at least ten concepts that characterize the process:

1. The goal of OD.
2. System renewal.
3. A systems approach.
4. Focus on people.
5. An educational strategy.
6. Learning through experience.
7. Dealing with real problems.
8. A planned strategy.
9. Change agent.
10. Involvement of top-level administration.

Each of these ten OD concepts is briefly described here.[41]

1. The Goal of OD

The primary goal of OD is to improve the functioning of the organization itself. Improving the productivity and effectiveness of the organization is seen as largely dependent on developing the organization's capability to make better-quality decisions about its affairs—decisions affecting its structure, its tasks, its use of technology, its use of human resources, and its goals. The primary approach to this is to develop a work-oriented culture in the organization that will maximize the involvement of the organization's people in more effective decision making regarding matters of importance to them and to the goals of the organization.

Although OD may very well lead to the adoption of a new program or curriculum, to a restructuring of the organization, or to a commitment to new goals, these are not considered to be first steps to improved effectiveness of schools and school systems. Nor does OD assume—as some have speculated—that significant organizational change will result from programs limited to improving the personal and interpersonal skills of individuals or groups, whether through counseling, sensitivity training, conventional education, or any other means. This is not likely to be enough to alter significantly established norms that shape the work-related behavior of the organization: rules, expectations, traditions, and habits.

2. System Renewal

Organization development rejects the notion that atrophy is inevitable in organizations. Stated positively, the view is that an organization can develop self-renewing characteristics, enabling it to increase its capability, to adapt to change, and to improve its record of goal achievement.

This concept of system self-renewal sees the organization not as being helplessly buffeted about by exigencies and changes thrust on it, but as growing in its ability to initiate change, as having an increasing impact on its environment, and as developing an increasing capability to adapt to new conditions and solve new problems over time. Perhaps more important is its ability to develop a growing sense of purpose and direction over time. The view is of an energized system marked by increasing vitality and imaginative creativity.

The self-renewal concept is at the center of the difference between organization development and organization improvement. The goal is not merely to overcome an immediate problem and arrive at a new "frozen" state of organizational functioning. The concept is one of building into the organizational system the conditions, the skills, the processes, and the culture that foster continual development of the organization over a sustained period of time. Although OD may be triggered by a specific event—such as creating a new school or facing up to community criticism—the event itself merely provides an entry point for action.

If OD techniques are used to develop responses to the event and then are dropped, rather than continued and extended, then the project is not OD at all but another piecemeal change effort so characteristic of public schools. The concept of management by crisis is so firmly embedded in U.S. educational administration that developing planned, systematic, and sustained approaches has quite possibly become the central problem of administering change in schools.

3. A Systems Approach

Organization development is based on the concept of the organization as a complex sociotechnical system. Such a view of the organization, of course, emphasizes the wholeness of the organizational system and the dynamic interrelatedness of its component subsystems: human, structural, technological, and task.

The school, for example, is a sociotechnical system. It comprises subsystems, of course—departments, grade levels, informal groups, teams, and work groups—that are in a constant state of dynamic interrelationship. The school is also a subsystem of larger systems: the school district, for example, and the community in which it functions.

We have explained that such a view has fundamental implications for those concerned with administering organizational change; these are translated into certain basic assumptions:

1. To effect change that has long-term staying power, one must change the whole system and not merely certain of its parts or subsystems.

2. Moreover, because of the dynamic interrelatedness and interdependence of the component subsystems, any significant change in one subsystem will produce compensatory or retaliatory changes in other subsystems, as we described in Chapter 4.

3. Events very rarely occur in isolation or from single causes. Systems concepts of the organization emphasize the importance of dealing with events as manifestations of interrelated forces, issues, problems, causes, phenomena, and needs. The world of the organization is recognized as the complex system that it is, and ascribing single causation to phenomena or treating events as isolated incidents can mask our full understanding of them.

4. The organizational system is defined not by walls or membranes, but by existing patterns of human behavior. These patterns are not static but are in constant dynamic equilibrium—as the concept of force-field analysis illustrates. Therefore, the crucial information that the administrator requires comes from analyzing the specific field of forces at a particular time, rather than from analyzing generalized historical data from the past or from other organizations. Force-field analysis is described later in this chapter.

4. Focus on People

The main concern for OD is the human social system of the organization rather than task, technology, or structure dimensions. Specifically, the focus is on the organizational culture that characterizes the climate of beliefs influencing behavior—such as the ways in which superordinates and subordinates deal with one another, the ways in which work groups relate to each other, and the extent to which people in the organization are involved in identifying organizational problems and seeking solutions to them. Attitudes, values, feelings, and openness of communication are typical concerns for OD. It matters what people think, how open their communication is, how they deal with conflict, and to what extent they feel involved in their jobs, because these kinds of human concerns help determine how much work gets done and how well. People who have learned to keep their thoughts to themselves, to be discreet in proffering a new idea or in voicing doubt or criticism, contribute little to the organization's ability to diagnose its problems and find solutions. The culture of many schools encourages this kind of behavior—leaving decisions to the upper echelons and frowning upon lower-level participants who "cause trouble" by raising questions.

Commonly, the school's culture carefully structures organizational behavior so as to minimize open, free, and vigorous participation in central decisions—witness the typical faculty meeting with its crowded agenda of minutiae or the superintendent's *pro forma* appearances before the staff, which are filled with routine platitudes. Organizations with such characteristics tend to be relatively inflexible, slow to change, and defensive in a fast-changing environment.

In the OD view, one of the great resources available to an organization trying to improve its effectiveness is its own people. By encouraging people to become involved, concerned participants, rather than making them feel powerless and manipulated by unseen and inscrutable forces, the organization can draw ever-increasing strength, vitality, and creativity from its people.

5. An Educational Strategy

Organization development seeks to stimulate organization self-renewal by changing the behavior of people in the organization in significant ways through education. In this sense, however, education has little relationship to conventional, in-service education concepts that usually (1) are chiefly concerned with the acquisition of cognitive knowledge and (2) take place in a typical classroom setting that emphasizes the learner as a dependent recipient of knowledge.

The educational strategy and processes of OD focus primarily on the elements important to shaping the organizational climate and culture of the organization: the complex web of dynamic organizational variables that so deeply influences the way people feel about their role in the organization, the attitudes and expectations they develop toward their coworkers, and the quality of the relationships between individuals and groups within the organization. Conventionally, these kinds of problems—involving conflict, communication barriers, suspicion and fear, and questions of organizational effectiveness—have been skirted carefully in organizations: they are too "touchy," too sensitive to treat adequately. OD seeks ways not only to face such problems, which are central to the organization's functioning, but also to increase the participants' ability to solve them in productive ways. Because it changes the norms of the organization through a strategy of study and learning, the process is a normative-reeducative strategy.

6. Learning through Experience

The concept of learning by doing applied to organizational life is the basis for learning in OD. Educative techniques strongly stress the building of knowledge and skill in organizational behavior through a two-step, experience-based process in which a work-related group of people (1) shares a common experience and then (2) examines that experience to see what it can learn from it.

This can be done in relatively controlled conditions of laboratory training, such as in a T-group. It also can be a study of real-life experiences that group members actually have shared in the organization. But the basis for learning is the group's actual experience, not hypothetical situations. The group members are encouraged to question and to raise issues concerning group functioning, drawing insights and learning directly from this experience.

One purpose of this insistence on examining experience in this way is to develop within the participants a long-lasting set of techniques and understandings that will enable them to learn and profit repeatedly from their own experiences over a sustained period of time. If this can be developed as a significant part of the group life of an organization, it can be a strong element of the desired self-renewal process.

7. Dealing with Real Problems

Organization development is carried out in an organization in order to deal with pressing problems. In some cases these problems may be serious enough to threaten the very survival of the organization, although they usually are not so dramatic. The educational processes do not involve learning about someone else's problem or discussing general cases but are directed to the specific organization under consideration—with its special conditions that make it unique.

What kinds of problems might call for OD in a school? An attempt to catalog such a wide range of possibilities would not be helpful, but it might be useful to mention a few typical situations:

1. Conditions of rapid change—such as the need to respond to powerful school-reform initiatives from the state that, if the responses are not adequate, might threaten the existence of the school itself.
2. A leadership crisis, such as when a new superintendent finds that there is little response to his or her initiatives.
3. Poor organizational effectiveness (however it is measured) that must be resolved in ways other than defensiveness or seeking excuses.
4. A high level of conflict, whether evidenced by excessive bickering and infighting or by the apathy characteristic of withdrawal from too painful a situation.

Often, of course, these kinds of problems are interrelated; opening up one for examination and solution may well lead to other problems that were not considered to be of great concern at the outset. This heuristic characteristic of OD concepts and processes has great power to penetrate to the central problems of the organization. Therefore, the major criterion in identifying the problem to be worked on in the initial stages is that it be of genuine concern to the organization's participants—something they feel is important to them, rather than something about which only someone else is concerned.

Organization development efforts should be viewed in the long-term sense suggested by the self-renewal concept, enabling the process to start with seemingly superficial problems and eventually reach the core. Thus, OD is not a one-shot approach to the alleviation of some limited, narrowly defined crisis, after which it will be abandoned. Indeed, as OD techniques become more popular and respectable in the eyes of administrators and managers, there is rising concern that the demand for such a "Band-Aid" approach (identifying OD with management by crisis rather than with the development of self-renewal) could discredit more ethical OD approaches.

8. A Planned Strategy

Another characteristic of OD—again in harmony with its overall systems approach—is that the effort must be planned systematically. The technology of OD embraces a wide range of possible activities and techniques. But they, in themselves, do not constitute OD. Indeed, a defining characteristic of OD is that it is a form of planned change: a strategy in which goals have been identified and a design for achieving them has been laid out. The plan must be specific: identifying target populations, establishing a timetable, and committing resources necessary to its fulfillment. The plan also must be specifically tailored to the particular circumstances of the organization.

Emphasizing the importance of a plan for OD should not imply rigidity. Indeed, if the effort is initially successful, it is probable that the increasing involvement of participants will require modifying and shaping the plan over time. It is important to provide for this in the planning stages, lest the effort turn into just another in-service program. Conversely, however, haphazard introduction of bits and pieces of OD technology, without clear, purposive planning and the commitment to carry it through, can do more harm than good.

It has been noted, for example, that the decision to undertake OD in an organization can, in itself, produce some organizational improvement: it is often a signal to members involved that the culture is changing and that new ideas and new ways of doing things are becoming more of a possibility and reality. Obviously, a badly mounted OD program or the sudden termination of one that has been started following raised hopes (because, perhaps, of the administrator's timidity or the lack of sufficient resources for the program) can result in an understandable backlash of feeling.

An OD program is a complex and sophisticated undertaking; it involves a wide range of possible interventions that deal with potentially sensitive matters. A highly qualified OD specialist often can facilitate the planning and carrying out of such a program by helping the administrator develop a practical OD design tailored to the specific realities of his or her organization. Designing an OD project offers both the administrator and the behavioral scientist the rare opportunity to collaborate in a common cause.

9. Change Agent

OD is characterized by the participation of a change agent who has a vital and specific role to play, at least in the initial stages of the change effort. Indeed, OD—in the various forms currently known to us—is impossible without a competent change agent. This person may have various official titles in different organizations; regardless, the term *consultant* is almost always used among OD practitioners to refer to the specialist who helps an organization design and carry out an OD program.

The consultant is so vital to the success or failure of OD that a substantial part of the literature is devoted to descriptions of his or her role, function, and specialized competencies, the nature of his or her relationships to client organizations, and so forth.

Finding an appropriate consultant and establishing an effective working relationship with him or her may well be the administrator's most crucial role in establishing OD in his or her school. Indeed, the need for consultant help has been the source of some of the thorniest problems in implementing OD. There can be much confusion, under the best of circumstances, about the consultant: what his or her role is, from whom he or she takes orders, what impact his or her presence has on the usual relationships between administrators and teachers—these are some of the problem areas that commonly appear in OD work. They are the subject of considerable study and discussion among OD consultants themselves as they attempt to shape their own roles in appropriate ways.

In general terms, consultants may be either from outside the organization (external consultants) or from within the organization (internal consultants). In their early history, OD efforts depended exclusively on external consultants. Of course, the relationship of the external consultant to the organization is temporary and requires that extra money be found to cover the consulting fees. One reaction to this has been efforts to train individuals appropriately so that they may function as internal consultants;[42] typically, once such a position has been budgeted, it tends to become a long-term, institutionalized arrangement. It appears likely that the role of internal change agents, or consultants, will become increasingly visible and formalized in school districts in the years ahead. However, the need for external consultants to deal with particularly complex and difficult problems of change will probably not be completely eliminated.

Some limited progress has been made in developing procedures for carrying out certain crucial aspects of OD activities without the direct assistance of behavioral science consultants.[43] At this stage of the development of OD, however, the consultant is a key individual. Policy and administration problems in dealing with OD consultants are discussed later in this book.

10. Involvement of Top-Level Administration

Inevitably, one must conclude from the social systems orientation of OD that one cannot change part of the system in constructive ways without affecting other parts of the system. For example, management cannot presume to change the organization without being part of the process. Organizational change is not a matter of "us" (the administration) changing "them" (the teachers and other subordinates) or even of changing "it" (the organization as some sort of entity detached from "us"). Administration must be an active partner involved in the development process to assure that all subsystems of the organizational system stay appropriately linked together in a dynamic, interactive way. This is one of the identifying characteristics of the increasingly effective organization.

In operational terms, OD recognizes that organizations are hierarchical and will continue to be so. When subordinates see that the administration is doing something to the organization in the name of improving its effectiveness—something in which administrators are not involved except as observers—the subordinates are very likely to be wary and less than fully committed. On the other hand, if the administration is already interested in the undertaking, committed to it, and involved in visible ways, subordinates are much more inclined to view the effort as valid and will be more highly motivated to involve themselves. In any organization, subordinates tend to develop highly sensitive antennae that pick up reliable indications of what is really important at higher levels through all the static and noise that may surround the issuance of official statements.

This was illustrated in the case of a large suburban school district. Located in a highly industrialized community, the district was undergoing the stresses and strains related to the social and ethnic problems that have become so commonplace in recent years. The new superintendent—who was young, bright, articulate, energetic, and with an enviable record in other districts—moved early to bring the principals and other key administrators together and organize them as a team. With a new and greater opportunity to play a crucial role in establishing policy and dealing with districtwide problems, this group was soon involved in important districtwide issues that had significant implications for each school. Unfortunately, the team quickly ran into difficulties: wrangling broke out, decisions arrived at in meetings were undercut by private deals made outside of the team (often involving school board members), and some members created an alliance to control voting on issues before the team on the basis of the self-interest of their departments or schools. A number of principals—who had enjoyed considerable autonomy under the previous superintendent to "wheel and deal" with school board members in behalf of their individual schools—felt that the whole team idea was simply a scheme to undermine them. The superintendent discussed these problems with the group and won easy agreement that a consultant should be brought in to help them find solutions.

During an exploratory meeting, the consultant was able to establish a basis for working with the group. In addition to agreeing on some goals and some modes of operating, the group agreed to certain ground rules. One, suggested by the consultant and quickly supported unanimously, was that all members of the group must attend each scheduled training session if possible. This was a highly capable and sophisticated group, and after a few meetings with the consultant there was a general feeling that real progress was being made and that the training effort should be continued. At the session following that decision, the superintendent announced that, because of the eruption of an unforeseen crisis, he would have to rush off soon after the group convened.

At the next session, he strongly endorsed the training effort and expressed keen interest in it but had to hurry off to another emergency. At the subsequent session, three principals—after a decent interval—withdrew and hurried off to attend to "emergencies" at their schools. Needless to say, the superintendent's team members realized that, as soon as the original crisis had eased, the training program no longer was a high-priority matter at the top, and they responded accordingly.

A Sociotechnical View

Those who are inexperienced in participative approaches to management often think of them as being "soft," "permissive," and incompatible with the structure, discipline, and power that characterize organizations. In fact, however, what is needed is a new, more effective, approach to management: an approach that stresses more functional administrative structures and seeks more effective organizational behavior. Although the new structures may well be more flexible and adaptable than those of the past, they will not be fuzzy or ill defined; nor will the more effective work-related behaviors be lacking in clear, exact description and definition.

When the administrator confronts the need for more involvement of staff in decision making or seeks to move the organization in a more "organic" or self-renewing direction, does it mean that system, orderly procedures, and control must be abandoned? The answer is, of course, negative. In fact, quite the opposite is true: the need is to provide organizational structures that will enhance and facilitate the development of more adaptive decision-making styles to replace the rigid hierarchical structures characteristic of the mechanistic organization.

The shift in organizational system development, then, is not away from the clarity, order, and control associated with traditional views of organizational structure toward an ill-defined, disorderly, laissez-faire administration. What is sought, administratively, is a new and more functional basis for *task* analysis, *structural* arrangements, selection and use of *technology,* and selection and professional development of individual *people* and groups of people on the staff.

The rationality of this view—which is a sociotechnical orientation—becomes increasingly apparent when we acknowledge that technological change and innovation are likely to play an increasingly important role in organizational change in schools in the future. The function of the administrator, then, is to develop organizational structures that, while providing clearly for such imperatives as coordination of effort toward goal attainment, ensure the development of more adaptive ways of integrating people, technology, task, and structure in a dynamic, problem-solving fashion.

Force-Field Analysis

How can one analyze an organizational learning situation so as to better understand how to deal with it? Force-field analysis has proven to be a useful analytic approach for both the researcher and the administrator.[44]

Basically, this approach sees a social or organizational *status quo* as a state of equilibrium resulting from the balance between two opposing sets of forces. There are forces for change, sometimes called *driving forces,* and these are opposed by forces for remaining unchanged, sometimes called *restraining forces.* When these force fields are in balance, as in Figure 7.2, we have equilibrium—no change. Obviously, when one or another of these forces is removed or weakened, the equilibrium is upset and change occurs, as shown in Figure 7.3. On a very simple level, such an imbalance can be brought about by the introduction of a new work technique or the acquisition of new skills by participants. But an organization is essentially a stable entity generally characterized by equilibrium; an imbalance of equilibrium will bring about readjustments that will again

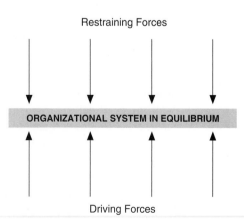

FIGURE 7.2
Force field in equilibrium.

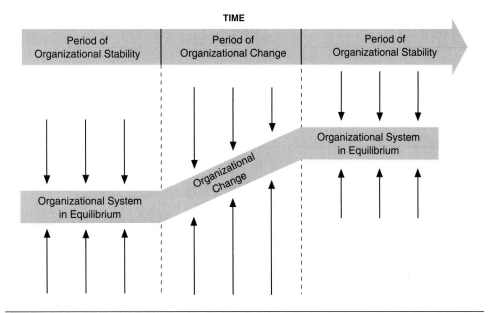

FIGURE 7.3 Imbalance of force field causes organizational change until a new equilibrium is reached.

lead to a new organizational equilibrium. This simple concept can become very complex when applied to a large-scale organization. But it also can be a practical aid to the administrator who seeks to understand his or her organization better so as to facilitate either change or stability in the organization. The analytic process of identifying restraining forces and driving forces ranges from a very simple approach at the rudimentary level to rather sophisticated techniques.

Force-field analysis eventually led its creator, Kurt Lewin, to a fundamental three-step change strategy that has come into increasingly popular use. It is predicated on the notion that in order to effect organizational change, it is first necessary to break the equilibrium of the force field: that is, the organization must be *unfrozen.* Once that is done, it is possible to introduce *change*—to move the organization to a new level. But no one knows better than educational administrators how fragile change can be and how easily the organization can slip back into its old ways. Therefore, the third step in the three-step change process is *refreezing.* This is an institutionalizing process that serves to protect and ensure the long-range retention of the change. Of course, refreezing smacks of a new *status quo;* in Lewin's view, the desired amount of flexibility could be built in by establishing "an organizational set up which is equivalent to a stable circular causal process."[45] Unfreezing can be a highly traumatic experience to a very rigid and resisting organization, But it can also be built in as a normal part of its life cycle, as suggested in Figure 7.4, in order to achieve greater organizational flexibility over time.

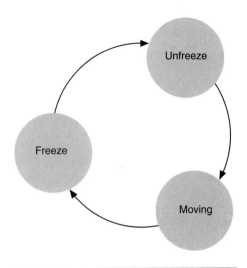

FIGURE 7.4

A three-step change process as an ongoing
life cycle of an organization.

The value of a force-field analysis is diagnostic: it permits the preparation of plans for specific action designed to achieve the changes sought. The success of such a plan will depend in large measure on the clarity with which the likely consequences of proposed action are perceived. Of the four major organizational subsystems—task, technological, structure, and human—only the human subsystem has the capacity to react differentially to differing conditions.

Great art and literature teem with depictions of heroic achievements of people moved by such feelings as love, faith, courage, and duty. Much of the literature on organizations is concerned with apathy, anger, frustration, and apprehensions of people and their great power to inhibit the organization's goal achievement. Although administrators must be deeply concerned with the work to be performed in the school, the structure of the organization, and the technology that is used, none of these has the capability of resisting plans for action. It is only the human subsystem that has that capability.

But it is not productive for the administrator to view opposition to change in any form—whether as outright resistance, apathy, skepticism, or whatever—as obdurate behavior. If "increasing the driving forces" is interpreted by the administrator as meaning the stepped-up use of authority and power to get people behind the change effort, it is highly predictable that the result will be strong reactions against the change. Pressure generates counterpressure, and in the school setting, where the administrator's coercive power is sharply limited, it is not likely that the equilibrium of the force field can be broken by such an approach. At the very least, it is predictable that, as the pressure is relaxed—as it must be eventually—there will be a tendency for the organization to retreat to its old ways under the pressure of the restraining forces.

In school situations it is likely to be more effective to help bring the restraining forces into the open as legitimate in the process of change. By creating a culture in which feelings can be expressed instead of secretly harbored, by opening communication and valuing the right to question and challenge, and by helping those who would oppose the forces of change to examine and deal with the concerns that cause their resistance, it is likely that (1) unforeseen probable consequences of proposed actions will be brought into the planning process and, perhaps more important, (2) the level of resistance will be diminished.

As the opposition helps to shape and mold decisions, its views are also shaped, molded, and modified in the process. *To obtain this kind of participation requires the existence of a developmental, or growth-enhancing, organizational culture that characteristically*

1. is intellectually, politically, and aesthetically stimulating.
2. emphasizes individual and group achievement.
3. places high value on the personal dignity of individuals.
4. accepts divergent feelings and views in a nonjudgmental way.
5. is oriented to problem solving rather than to winning or losing in intraorganizational skirmishes.

The establishment of orderly problem-solving processes that provide maximum participation for those who will be affected by the change is necessary to develop the collaborative approach suggested here. Although the point of view is important, it must be accompanied by effective specific procedures for making it work, creating the climate needed and ensuring that the way in which decisions are reached is understood and workable. Development of a new organizational culture and building the group skills needed for open, collaborative decision making require definite training and practice. These things are not achieved through cognitive understanding and determination alone: they require the development of new insights, new values and commitments, and new group process skills that are best taught and learned in problem-solving situations.

It must be remembered that the creation of a new organizational culture—a new environment for working and solving problems—requires participants to develop new and more effective responses to events, to act differently than they have done in the past. As every educator is keenly aware, such changes in human functioning do not often occur as a result of learning *about* the new, more effective ways of doing things. Opportunities must be provided wherein the new behaviors may be developed in practice: in short, *learning by doing* is required. The goal is to develop new and more productive norms of work-oriented behavior through reeducation.

Change is likely to be stabilized and maintained in the organization over time, when the new, more effective level of performance can be maintained without coercion and without continuous expenditures of administrative energy and vigilance to keep it going. Indeed, this is one practical criterion by which the administrator may judge whether or not change has been accomplished.

An appropriate plan for organizational change must be cognizant of these realities. It must also recognize that the goal of changing an organization in significant ways presents a challenge in terms of difficulty and in terms of the time span required. There are no quick and easy solutions, though there will probably never be a shortage of those who claim to possess such solutions. Hersey and Blanchard's admonition on this point is highly appropriate:

Changes in knowledge are the easiest to make, followed by changes in attitudes. Attitude structures differ from knowledge structures in that they are emotionally charged in a positive or a negative way. Changes in behavior are significantly more difficult and time consuming than either of the two previous levels. But the implementation of group or organizational performance change is perhaps the most difficult and time consuming.[46]

Research on the Effectiveness of OD

In reporting a major study of OD in schools, Fullan, Miles, and Taylor pointed out that a problem of assessing OD efforts to develop the self-renewal, problem-solving capacity of school systems and schools lies in the fact that many so-called OD projects are partial, incomplete, short-term activities lacking the planning, scope, and sustained effort required for success.[47] In many cases, for example, a few days of "human relations training" for teachers, or the use of an outside consultant for a few sessions, is incorrectly labeled an "OD project." Often the effort is limited to attempts to reduce conflict or otherwise to ameliorate unpleasant aspects of organizational culture, with little or no intention of significantly affecting organizational structure or processes of decision making. For reasons such as these, surveys of OD activities in education tend to show spotty success; yet those school districts that are successful with OD generally tend to institutionalize it and maintain it over time. Not a few school districts now have OD school renewal projects that have been functioning for several years.

Philip Runkel and Richard Schmuck, at the Center for Educational Policy and Management (CEPM) at the University of Oregon, have conducted the most comprehensive research and development work in this field. In assessing whether or not OD has been successful in a district or school, they caution against accepting superficial claims about *any* effort at change:

> Our experience in looking for outcomes has taught us that they are not simple. . . . Editors of scientific journals and providers of funds should demand detailed documentation when a researcher claims that one or more schools have "installed" or "adopted" some particular new way of doing things. The depth and variety in the ways that a new structure such as team teaching can be installed or adopted in a school are stupefying, and so are the ways a principal can cover up with verbiage the fact that the innovation really has not taken hold in his school at all. Statements that go no farther than, "In a school that had adopted a team teaching the previous year, . . ." or "We shall install team teaching in X schools next year . . . ," should never be accepted without skepticism.[48]

Their findings regarding OD in schools include these:

- Success is more likely when the school faculty senses a readiness to change and welcomes the OD project.
- Entering into OD may be the most critical phase of the project and requires a skilled and experienced OD consultant to avoid hidden pitfalls.
- Open, active support from administrators is critical to success.

- OD is more likely to be helpful in a school in which the staff is in substantial agreement on goals.

- An OD project can be thought of as consisting of four main phases: (1) entry, (2) diagnosis of organizational problems, (3) institutionalization, and (4) maintenance.

After witnessing the "continuing, frustrating failure of promising innovations to alter school practice in desired ways,"[49] John Goodlad undertook to lead a five-year research and development project addressing the problems of personal and institutional renewal in education. Goodlad started by pointing out that the conventional model for studying educational change is to manipulate certain instructional interventions (such as class size or teaching method) and to look for changes in pupil outcomes. As shown in Figure 7.5, such a research design treats pupil outcomes as the dependent variable and instruction (for example, methods and materials) as the independent variable. However, Goodlad's long-term observation of the difficulty of installing and sustaining instructional reforms led him to realize that "the explanatory thesis for this difficulty . . . is that the regularities of the school sustain certain practices, through expectations, approval, and reward. Teachers, as individuals, usually are not able to run successfully against these regularities or to create the schoolwide structures and processes necessary to sustain new practices."[50] This suggested the need to focus on the entire culture of the school; further, "We see everything constituting the culture of the school—its operational curriculum, written and unwritten rules, verbal and nonverbal communication, physical properties, pedagogical regularities, principal's leadership behavior and so on."[51] This led to research design in which the school's culture is the independent variable, and *both* (1) the behavior of the teacher and (2) pupil outcomes are seen as dependent on that culture, whereas *at the same time,* pupil outcomes are seen as dependent on teacher behavior (see Figure 7.6).

In practical terms Goodlad judged that although the relationships, as shown in Figure 7.7, probably correctly represent important elements of reality for schools, the design is much too complex for the practical study of schools in the real world. He, therefore, settled on a study of the causes of the culture of the school, as shown in Figure 7.6.

The central proposition of Goodlad's research was "that entire schools can and should be regarded as malleable and capable of changing, and that, as schools change in their cultural characteristics, so do the people in them."[52] Furthermore, a basic assumption was that in order to succeed, a client school must exhibit an internal sense of need, a

FIGURE 7.5

Conventional model for effecting and studying ends–means relationships when the focus is on instruction and pupil outcomes. From John I. Goodlad, *The Dynamics of Educational Change* (New York: McGraw-Hill Book Company, 1975), p. 113. Reprinted by permission.

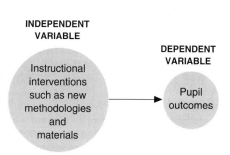

FIGURE 7.6

A paradigm for studying ends–means–effects relationships and for improving schooling and learning. From John I. Goodlad, *The Dynamics of Educational Change* (New York: McGraw-Hill Book Company, 1975), p. 117. Reprinted by permission.

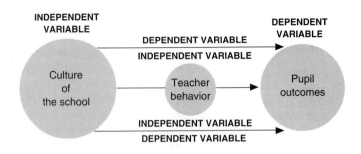

desire to change. The principal experimental intervention was to train faculty members of schools to engage in a four-step process called DDAE (dialogue, decision making, action, and evaluation), which is essentially an OD intervention aimed at developing self-renewal in the schools. A significant additional feature of Goodlad's work was to join the participating schools in this five-year project into a "league" so that they could provide one another with a sense of mutual support and nurturance during the experimental period.

As Goodlad reported:

In the high DDAE schools there were more cooperative teaching arrangements, more friendship networks among teachers, and more task-oriented communication among teachers. Teachers had more influence in decision-making, especially in areas affecting schools as total units. The quality of principal leadership was higher and principal influence depended more on competence. The principals in high DDAE schools were more apt to see teacher influence on schools as a desirable condition. These schools ranked higher on indices of school climate. By contrast, there were more self-contained classrooms in low DDAE schools. Teacher influence was more narrowly limited to areas affecting only a few people rather than the school as a whole and the principal was more apt to see teacher influence on schoolwide

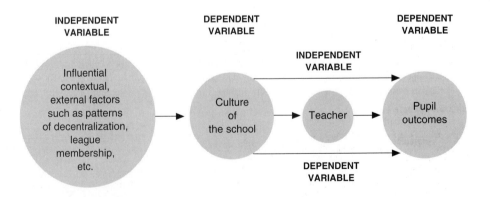

FIGURE 7.7   A paradigm for improving and studying educational practice with changes in the entire culture of a school the focus of attention. From John I. Goodlad, *The Dynamics of Educational Change* (New York: McGraw-Hill Book Company, 1975), p. 114. Reprinted by permission.

decisions as undesirable. The principal's influence was more likely to depend upon status and power to reward.[53]

The characteristics of high DDAE seemed to be associated in a school with significant potential for ongoing growth and self-renewal. But a visitor to such a school would have difficulty in isolating *an* innovation in that school because

> most of those being widely advocated were there: considerable use of audiovisual aids, especially by two or three children at a time and on their own; some of the new curricular materials; modified, flexible classroom space; multiage or non-graded groups and classes; use of parent volunteers in the instructional program; team planning, teaching, and evaluation.[54]

This kind of observation is characteristic of the self-renewing school: it is a growing and developing organization, not because of some agreement with an outside agency to employ a given innovation but, rather, because it is continuously engaged in systematic problem solving and is able to select appropriate technology from all that is available.

Conclusion

There are three basic strategies from which one may choose in planning and managing organizational change in schools:

1. *Empirical-rational strategies* are based on the concept that change can be fostered by systematically inventing or discovering better ideas and making them readily available in useful form to schools. Adherents of this strategy are often confounded by the difficulties usually encountered in the processes of installing new practices in the target schools. Typical difficulties are (1) ignoring the new ideas, (2) resisting or rejecting the new ideas, or (3) modifying the ideas or practices in such ways that, when put into practice, they have been significantly changed.

2. *Power-coercive strategies* are based on the use (or potential use) of sanctions to compel the organization to change. The No Child Left Behind Act of 2001 is a compendium of power-coercive strategies complete with required timetables for action, requirements for reporting compliance, and various sanctions and rewards intended to coerce the schools to comply with the demands for prescribed changes.

3. *Normative-reeducative strategies* are based on the notion of bringing about change in schools by improving their problem-solving capabilities as organizations. This is generally known as *organizational self-renewal.* This requires shifting the normative values of the school's culture (interaction-influence system) from those usually associated with hierarchical (bureaucratic, mechanistic, classical) organization to more creative, problem-solving norms. Techniques and processes for bringing about organizational self-renewal focus on developing increased skills among the staff members of individual schools in studying and diagnosing their own organizational problems systematically and in working out solutions to them. The term

organization development (OD) is widely applied to these techniques for increasing the self-renewal capacity of schools.

The critical importance of helping schools to develop their own capacity for self-renewal was not widely understood (outside of the field of organizational behavior) until the failure of extensive applications of both empirical-rational and power-coercive strategies to achieve desired levels of success had produced widespread frustration and concern. By the 1980s, it was clear to thoughtful people concerned with education that the long-neglected area of developing self-renewal in schools would have to be addressed seriously if change in U.S. schooling was to move forward. By thus improving the organizational health of schools, it appears possible to make schools more proactive than defensive and to reach out responsively to adopt new ideas and implement changing goals of society.

Though schools are organizations and, therefore, share many of the traits of other kinds of organizations, it must be remembered that we know relatively little about their specific organizational characteristics. Although research on the organizational characteristics of schools is increasing, until very recently our assumptions about them have been derived largely from studies in other kinds of organizations (for example, business firms, military organizations, government agencies). But schools do possess special properties (not all necessarily unique) that may well affect the ways in which they should deal with issues of stability and change.

A common observation is, for example, that they are largely populated by a nonvoluntary clientele. Six other special properties undoubtedly must be considered in planning change:[55]

1. *Their goals are diffuse,* usually stated in general, even abstract terms, with effectiveness measurement being difficult and uncertain.

2. *Their technical capability* is low, with a weak specific scientific base underlying educational practice.

3. *They are loosely coupled systems,* which gives rise to coordination problems: activities are not always clearly connected to goals, and control (for example, accountability) is difficult to establish. (Recall the discussion in Chapter 5 that pointed out that this organizational feature of schools is not necessarily entirely negative: it also can be a source of flexibility and adaptability.)

4. *Boundary management is difficult* inasmuch as "the skin of the organization seems overly thin, over-permeable to dissatisfied stakeholders."[56]

5. *Schools are "domesticated" organizations,* noncompetitive, surviving in a relatively protected environment, and with little incentive for significant change.

6. *Schools are part of a constrained, decentralized system:* 15,000 school districts in the United States with well over 100,000 buildings, each nominally autonomous, yet with many national constraints (for example, standards for test achievement, national textbook market, accreditation and certification requirements, statutes and case law).

In this organizational context, a legacy of study and practical experience that stretches back to the Western Electric Studies underscores the pragmatic necessity of developing and improving people-oriented change strategies in schools.

Reflective Activities

1. Reflect on a major change that has occurred in a school or organization with which you are familiar. Using Kurt Lewin's concept of force-field analysis, identify the driving forces and the restraining forces that were in play prior to and during the change process that helped unfreeze and drive the organization toward change.

2. In your preceding example, determine which of Robert Chin's strategic orientations (empirical-rational, power-coercive, or normative-reeducative) was used to plan and manage the change process. Using the content in this chapter, provide specific examples of how the change process followed the particular orientation you identify. Was the process successful in bringing about change that resulted in a positive organizational climate? Why or why not?

3. Find a research article that investigates organizational characteristics and their effects on schools. Write a short summary that identifies the purpose of the study, the independent and dependent variables, the research methods used, and the findings of the study. Share this information with fellow students. As a class, list those organizational characteristics that have a positive impact on the dependent variables studied.

4. *Working on Your Game Plan.* Consider this advertisement for an elementary school principal. Prepare a draft of a letter that responds to the interests of the school district and reflects your ideas about a theory of practice, or game plan.

"Each Child Is an Individual of Great Worth and Is Entitled to Develop to His or Her Fullest Potential"

Sunny Isles Elementary School District
(K-6   ADA 21,350)
South Florida's Gulf Coast

Sunny Isles, a culturally and ethnically diverse school district, is seeking outstanding candidates with the following attributes:

Student Advocate • High Integrity • Vision • Energetic • Empathetic • Compassionate • Accountable • Collaborative • Change Agent • Instructional Leader • Effective Communicator

ELEMENTARY PRINCIPAL

Salary: $84,000 to $87,500
Plus excellent fringe benefits
(207 days)

IMMEDIATE OPENINGS
Open Until Filled

Those interested in being considered for this position should submit a letter of interest that describes how their experience, background, aspirations, and goals can serve as a positive influence in the lives of children.

Please Contact
Ronald H. Kirby
Assistant Superintendent, Human Resources
(741) 327-2100 • FAX (741) 327-9601

Please visit our website at:
http://www.siesd.k12.fl.us
(To see the Job Postings' Web page, scroll down to the "Human Resources" banner and click on Employment Opportunities.)

EQUAL OPPORTUNITY EMPLOYER
Culturally Diverse and Bilingual Candidates
Are Encouraged to Apply

Suggested Reading

Argyris, Chris, *Knowledge for Action: A Guide to Overcoming Barriers to Organizational Change.* San Francisco: Jossey-Bass, 1993.

One of the most respected students of organizational change offers practical guidance for improving the abilities of organizational members to solve the human problems of working together. Invaluable for the educational leader who wants to improve collegial behavior and implement empowerment on the job.

Darling-Hammond, Linda, *A Blueprint for Creating Schools That Work.* San Francisco: Jossey-Bass, 1997.

A distinguished scholar and observer of U.S. schooling, Darling-Hammond thinks that what is wrong with schools today is excessive bureaucratization and administrative red tape that in the end leaves teachers little time for teaching. She rails against the "factory model" of the school that processes students instead of teaching them. This, she believes, accounts for the relatively poor showing of U.S. students against their contemporaries in other parts of the world. She advocates recreating schools so that good teachers flourish, and change from the inside out is encouraged. Her data include numerous interviews with people on the firing line, and her emphasis is on learner-centered schools.

Evans, Robert, *The Human Side of School Change: Reform, Resistance, and the Real-Life Problems of Innovation.* San Francisco: Jossey-Bass, 1996.

The book presents an insightful observation of leadership that makes a difference. For example, Evans describes the life cycle of a leadership theory: (1) it begins outside of education, developed by political scientists from studies of gifted historical figures or by management experts from studies of gifted business leaders (no one would ever think of basing a leadership model on studies of gifted school administrators!); (2) it gains favor in corporate America and comes to be a hot concept in management writing; (3) as it nears its apex of influence, someone decides to apply it to education, even if it has little apparent relevance to school; (4) it grows hot in educational circles as it begins to cool in the corporate world; (5) it is often misapplied in education; and (6) well after it has lost its cachet among business leaders, it lingers on in schools until its popularity finally dies away there too. There is much more, and this book is well worth reading by educational leaders-to-be.

Hirsch, E. D., Jr., *The Schools We Need: And Why We Don't Have Them.* New York: Doubleday, 1996.

Kirkus Reviews calls this "A brick hurled at the windows of the K–12 establishment for serving up content-lite curricula that leave U.S. elementary and secondary schools among the worst in the developed world." Hirsch zeros in on what he calls the artifact, supposedly child-centered, ideology propagated by Columbia University's Teachers College as the basis for all our problems. He goes on, of course, to flesh out the indictment and point the way—the only way—out of the current dilemma: Hirsch's way.

Kohn, Alfie, *The Schools Our Children Deserve: Moving beyond Traditional Classrooms and "Tougher Standards."* Boston: Houghton Mifflin, 1999.

Amazon.com puts it this way: "Teacher-turned-writer Alfie Kohn takes on traditional-education giants like E. D. Hirsch, along with practically every state government raising the bar and toughening standards, in this attack on the back-to-basics movement. An established critic of America's fixation on grades and scores, Kohn has written a detailed, methodical treatise that accuses politicians and educators of replacing John Dewey, the father of public education, with test-tutoring king Stanley Kaplan." This is a must-read for prospective educational leaders.

Levesque, Karen, Kristi Rossi, Denise Bradby, and Peter Teitelbaum, *At Your Fingertips: Using Everyday Data to Improve Schools.* Berkeley, CA: MPR Associates: National Center for Research in Vocational Education, 1998.

This is a practical step-by-step guide to selecting, analyzing, and reporting critical information in an easy-to-understand and compelling manner so as to marshal valid, reliable, and trustworthy data to communicate more effectively with parents and other audiences in school reform efforts. The book encourages and supports home-grown, locally designed school improvement initiatives. It shows how data that are ordinarily collected can and ought to be put to good use to focus our attention on otherwise intractable problems.

Maeroff, Gene I., *The Empowerment of Teachers: Overcoming the Crisis of Confidence.* New York: Teachers College Press, 1988.

Written by a professional writer who is a Senior Fellow at the Carnegie Foundation and was a consultant for the Rockefeller Foundation, and under a grant from the Rockefeller Foundation, this book strongly argues the case for teacher empowerment, which is an idea supported by both foundations. It includes an incisive analysis of the professional circumstances of public school teachers today and shows how, by restructuring schools to provide greater autonomy to teachers, they may be significantly changed. Maeroff believes, of course, that these changes will result in marked improvement in the performance of schools.

Senge, Peter, *The Fifth Discipline: The Art and Practice of the Learning Organization.* New York: Doubleday & Company, 1990.

Senge observes that the industrial age assembly-line model for education has shaped our schools more than we can imagine—producing generations of "knowers," not lifelong learners, people beautifully prepared for a world that no longer exists. He describes the Yale School Development Program as a genuine pioneer in creating the learner-centered education that will be vital for our future. One may have reservations as to what Yale has contributed to all this but Senge, drawing on fields from science to spirituality, shows why it matters to have a learning organization. This has been an enormously popular book and deserves the attention of all education leaders.

c h a p t e r **8**

Adaptive Leadership

LEARNING OBJECTIVES

After reading this chapter, you should be able to

- Define leadership.
- Describe the difference between leadership and command.
- Define and discuss power as a reciprocal relationship between leaders and followers.
- Explain why the decline of coercive power among school principals has increased the need for leadership.
- Describe and discuss the two-factor theory of leadership.
- Describe the concept of leadership as a relationship with followers.
- Explain how a Theory X leader and a Theory Y leader tend to behave differently.
- Define and describe the concept of transforming leadership.
- Compare and contrast transformational leadership and transactional leadership.
- Describe the role played by one's vision of the future in exercising leadership.
- Explain why it is important for school leaders to empower others to participate in creating a vision of the mission of the school.
- Critically examine the assertion that principals should be leaders and not managers.
- Describe and explain the two major trends in understanding leadership that developed over the course of the twentieth century.
- Describe and explain the link between leadership and organizational culture.

ISLLC Standards

STANDARD 1: A school administrator is an educational leader who promotes the success of all students by facilitating the development, articulation, implementation, and stewardship of a vision of learning that is shared and supported by the school community.

Knowledge

The administrator has knowledge and understanding of:

- effective consensus-building and negotiation skills

Dispositions

The administrator believes in, values, and is committed to:

- continuous school improvement
- the inclusion of all members of the school community
- a willingness to continuously examine one's own assumptions, beliefs, and practices
- doing the work required for high levels of personal and organization performance

Performances

The administrator facilitates processes and engages in activities ensuring that:

- the vision and mission of the school are effectively communicated to staff, parents, students, and community members
- the vision is developed with and among stakeholders
- progress toward the vision and mission is communicated to all stakeholders
- the school community is involved in school improvement efforts
- the vision shapes the educational programs, plans, and actions

STANDARD 2: A school administrator is an educational leader who promotes the success of all students by advocating, nurturing, and sustaining a school culture and instructional program conducive to student learning and staff professional growth.

Knowledge

- school cultures

Performances

The administrator facilitates processes and engages in activities ensuring that:

- all individuals are treated with fairness, dignity, and respect
- students and staff feel valued and important

STANDARD 3: A school administrator is an educational leader who promotes the success of all students by ensuring management of the organization, operations, and resources for a safe, efficient, and effective learning environment.

Knowledge

The administrator has knowledge and understanding of:

- theories and models of organizations and the principles of organizational development

Dispositions

The administrator believes in, values, and is committed to:

- trusting people and their judgments
- accepting responsibility

Performances

The administrator facilitates processes and engages in activities ensuring that:

- stakeholders are involved in decisions affecting schools
- responsibility is shared to maximize ownership and accountability
- effective problem-framing and problem-solving skills are used
- effective group-process and consensus-building skills are used
- effective communication skills are used

STANDARD 4: A school administrator is an educational leader who promotes the success of all students by collaborating with families and community members, responding to diverse community interests and needs, and mobilizing community resources.

Performances

The administrator facilitates processes and engages in activities ensuring that:

- credence is given to individuals and groups whose values and opinions may conflict
- community stakeholders are treated equitably

Like two sides of the same coin, leadership and decision making are inseparable. Leadership cannot be a solo performance: by definition, as we shall see, the only way that leaders can exercise leadership is by working with and through other people, the followers. Thus, leadership is always an ensemble performance. The subject of this chapter, leadership theory, focuses on conceptualizing the range of ways from which one may choose in deciding how to engage with others in exercising leadership. Contemporary leadership theory is not neutral in making this behavioral choice: it contends that some ways of working with followers are predictably more effective than others.

On the other side of the coin, decision-making theory focuses on the array of ways from which one may choose to implement the leadership theory that has been selected. Decision-making theory is the subject of the next chapter; thus, these two chapters are closely interrelated.

Adaptive Leadership

At one time schools may have existed in a world that moved at a relatively leisurely pace that seemed stable and enduring. One thinks of the fictional Charles Chipping, the steadfast master of the Brookfield School in *Goodbye, Mr. Chips,** who devoted a lifetime of work—fifty-eight years—shepherding generations of boys through the school and inculcating them with the values and traditions that the school had nourished in upper-crust Britons since the founding of the school in 1492. In such an environment, tradition is a valid and powerful organizational characteristic that leaders may do well to support and reinforce. In such a world, an effective educational leader may appropriately stay with well-worn verities and unchanging practices that have been validated over the course of time.

Schools do not exist in that kind of world today, of course. In today's fast-paced world dominated by change, the school, and particularly the school leader, must be constantly sensitive to emerging changes in the external environment that call for nimble, deft, rapid responses by the organization. One of the key concepts of organizational theory is the role of change and stability in the environment of the organization in selecting a strategy for leadership.

Certainly, as the pressure to improve the performance of schools has gained momentum and ever-widening support, the need for effective leadership in school administration has been increasingly emphasized. But there are many different and often conflicting ways of thinking about and understanding the nature of leadership. One popular concept or theory of leadership is the time-honored top-down style. This is, of course, based on the belief that the best ideas are, or ought to be, found at the higher levels of the organization and are passed down to be implemented by those at the lower levels. This traditional understanding of leadership comes to us from the military traditions of ancient Rome, and it is currently exemplified in the No Child Left Behind Act.

Those who supported the enactment of this approach to school reform into federal law in 2001 confidently believed that they knew what had to be done in the schools and classrooms in order to improve the learning of students. Their beliefs are clearly spelled out in the law itself, which includes the required use of phonics in teaching reading, the

---

*A short novel by James Hilton that appeared in *The Atlantic Monthly* in April 1934. It reflected Hilton's own experiences as Senior Master of Classics at a similar school in Cambridge. In the 1939 film version of the story Robert Donat won the Academy Award for Best Actor in competition with Clark Gable (*Gone With the Wind*), James Stewart (*Mr. Smith Goes to Washington*), and Laurence Olivier (*Wuthering Heights*).

regular use of standardized tests to monitor learning, the punishing sanctions to be levied against schools that fail to demonstrate improvement in student learning, and the insistence on using instructional methods that are supported by evidence of their effectiveness derived from "scientific research." Those who advocate this exercise of top-down power from Washington, unparalleled in the history of schooling in the United States, tend to describe it as an exercise in educational or political leadership.

Contemporary scholarly thought about leadership, however, is dominated by the recognition that change, complexity, and uncertainty are dominant characteristics of the environment to which organizations today must nimbly adapt. A growing body of literature addresses the need to find new and better ways to lead under these unstable and unpredictable conditions that confront organizations, conditions that are increasingly being described as chaotic.[1] Essentially, the leader in these circumstances is confronted with the need to deal with two very different kinds of problems:

- *Some problems are technical.* They are relatively clear-cut, if not simple, and can be solved by applying technical expertise; the outcome can be predicted with some confidence. Such problems normally can be solved by technically competent individuals, and that fact might well favor the use of top-down methods of leadership.
- *Other problems are adaptive.* These problems, by definition, are so complex and involve so many ill-understood factors that the outcomes of any course of action are unpredictable.[2] Common examples of adaptive problems include the reduction of crime, the reduction of poverty, and the implementation of educational reform. Solving these kinds of problems requires leadership methods that make the knowledge of many people at various levels in the organization accessible and facilitate the involvement and cooperation of these people in leadership processes. Leadership in dealing with adaptive problems, therefore, as we shall explain more fully in this chapter, requires collaboration between many individuals over time in an iterative process, much as was described in Chapter 7 (see Figure 7.4).

Problems confronting schools today, particularly problems of school reform, are clearly adaptive problems and require adaptive leadership concepts and techniques that are discussed in this chapter. But first we need to review some fundamentals of leadership. For example, leadership of any kind is basically about the exercise of power, and this is where we begin.

Power and Leadership

There is a vast literature on leadership containing hundreds of definitions of leadership. However, there is general agreement on two things:

1. Leadership is a group function: it occurs only when two or more people interact.
2. Leaders intentionally seek to influence the behavior of other people.

Thus, any concept of leadership deals with exercising influence on others through social interaction. To understand leadership, we must examine the nature and quality of the social interactions involved. The heart of the matter is power: What kind of power is involved, and how is it exercised?

In an era when single-issue groups—such as racial, ethnic, and gender groups—that are part of the social mosaic in the United States view educational organizations as oppressive and those in the organizational hierarchy as minions of an oppressive system, many cringe from even acknowledging power as an aspect of leadership in other than pejorative terms. Indeed, the subtext of discussions of power in educational organizations is that power is, by definition, a form of oppression of those in the lower levels of the organization. For example, the authors of one set of case studies of leadership in schools attempted simply to avoid the use of the word "leadership" because they perceived it as tainted with their strongly negative view of hierarchy as pernicious oppression. Thereupon they tried to substitute the term *distributive leadership* because in their view it "emphasizes process over power."[3]

However, one must understand that those who lead are necessarily powerful people because power is the basic energy for initiating and sustaining action that translates intention into reality when people try to work collaboratively.[4] One cannot lead and be powerless. But the exercise of power is not necessarily oppression, indeed cannot be oppressive, in the exercise of leadership as it is being discussed here. Let us explain.

There are different kinds of power through which one may attempt to influence others, and they come from different sources. Understanding leadership requires one to understand the difference between the power of those who lead and the power of those who command. The two are frequently confused with one another. The difference between leadership and command lies in the sources from which power is derived.

Leadership Different from Command

Those who occupy official positions in the hierarchy of an organization exercise vested authority, which is the legitimate right to command. Vested authority rests on legal power that is customarily granted to official positions in the hierarchy such as dean, superintendent, or principal. Because the legal power of office is granted by those higher in the hierarchy, subordinates, in theory at least, have no control over it and must yield to it. In practice, of course, such absolute power is rarely found in U.S. educational organizations. When it is exercised, it is often viewed as oppression. Teachers' unions, for example, were created expressly to mediate and limit the arbitrary exercise of power of school boards and school district administrators over teachers; there is no doubt that they have generally been highly effective.

The power of leaders, on the other hand, is voluntarily granted by followers who accept the leader's influence and direction by shared agreement, no matter how informally the agreement is arrived at. Leaders do not wield legal power vested in an official office; rather, they exercise power that followers have willingly entrusted to them. Why do followers entrust power to leaders? Often, and perhaps at the highest level, because the followers are drawn to the ideas of the leader, because they share the values and beliefs of the leader, and because they are convinced that the leader can represent the followers well in the inevitable conflict with others for control of resources to achieve what the leader and the followers are bound in mutual commitment to achieve.

The key to understanding the difference between the power of officeholders and the power of leaders lies in who controls the power. Followers can, and often do, withdraw the support that they have voluntarily entrusted to the leader. They can also voluntarily increase their grant of support, which increases the power of the leader. The Rev. Dr. Martin Luther King, Jr., for example, is generally acknowledged as one of the great and powerful leaders of the twentieth century, yet he had little legal authority to make his followers do anything. Nevertheless, Dr. King had extraordinary power to influence the behavior of followers and, ultimately, the course of the nation.

What Dr. King did have was ideas, a set of values and beliefs, and a clear vision of a better, more just, more morally perfect future that embodied all of these ideas and values. It was the intense wish of his followers to share in achieving these that motivated them to empower him with their strong, active support. Thus, Dr. King was a very powerful man who could mobilize vast numbers of people for a common purpose and set in motion momentous events, yet he was no oppressor. He had learned much about leadership from studying Mohandas Gandhi, who was, of course, a master of the art. Gandhi's lifework stands as a monument to the effectiveness of leadership, since he emerged victorious in 1947 from head-to-head confrontation with the determined oppression of seemingly invincible forces of entrenched colonialism.

Position power, such as that of a superintendent of schools or a school principal, provides the incumbent in an office in the hierarchy with legal authority for at least the potential for forcible domination and coercion. This is not leadership. It is superordination. We must distinguish between superordination and leadership:

> The source of superordination is *vested authority* [while] the source of leadership is *entrusted authority*. Authority is vested in a superordinate when power resides in the institution, and obedience is owed the superordinate by the subordinate in virtue of the role each occupies, roles the subordinate cannot alter.

> Authority is entrusted to a leader when power resides in the followers themselves, and cooperation is *granted* the leader by the follower . . . a judgment . . . the follower can alter. The superordinate may legitimately *compel* subordination; the leader can legitimately only *elicit* followership. The relationship between subordinate and superordinate is *compulsory,* between follower and leader *voluntary.*[5]

Power Defined

Power is commonly considered to be the capacity to influence others,[6] and different kinds of power can be used to exercise that influence. The classic, generally accepted description identifies five kinds, or sources, of power:[7]

- *Reward power.* Controlling rewards that will induce others to comply with the power wielder's wishes.

- *Coercive power.* Having control of potentially punishing resources that will induce others to avoid them.

- *Expert power.* Having knowledge that others want for themselves so much that they will be induced to comply with the power wielder so as to acquire the knowledge or benefit from it.

- *Legitimate power.* Having authority conferred by holding a position in an organization that is recognized by others as having a legitimate right to obedience.

- *Referent power.* Personal charisma of the power holder, or ideas and beliefs so admired by others that they are induced by the opportunity to be not only associated with the power holder but, as far as possible, to become more like him or her.

Thus, the exercise of power is a reciprocal relationship between the power holder and others. One has power not only when he or she controls resources that can reward or punish people, for example, money and access to more power for the followers themselves (such as participation in making decisions),[8] but also when he or she has ideas about the future of the organization that people find exciting and want to support.

The strength of the leader's power depends on the range of the sources of power drawn on. Leaders who draw on one source of power are inherently weaker than those who draw on multiple sources of power. Especially since the advent of teachers' unions and the broadening judicial interpretations of the constitutional rights of teachers, many school principals perceive that their power to lead has been undercut because the official power inherent in the office to coerce teachers into compliance has waned markedly, as has the power to control their compensation. Actually, the degradation of the coercive power of principals has *increased* the need for leadership. Strong school leaders still have access to significant sources of power:

- Although the power of principals to control the appointment, assignment, compensation, tenure, and promotion of teachers has been sharply curbed, those represent only one aspect of reward power, and, as we shall discuss, they have little to do with the power to lead. Many teachers find helping behavior from principals to be highly rewarding if it is nonjudgmental, supportive, collaborative, and caring in the tradition of self-development.[9] When they find such behavior by the principal rewarding enough, their support for the principal increases and the principal's power to lead increases as a result.

- Teachers continue to recognize the authority of official positions in the organization because they value the organization. They largely defer to the legitimate power of those occupying official positions in the hierarchy of the organization.

- Teachers generally resent and reject principals who pose as pedagogical experts by demanding that lesson plans be submitted for prior approval and principals who conduct critiques of observed teaching in the paternalistic, judgmental manner that they may think appropriate for technical experts. However, teachers view favorably support from principals for fresh ideas. Teachers tend to recognize and see as powerful those principals who are expert in using collaborative, collegial methods of working together to identify and solve mutual problems. Such methods are personally reward-ing to teachers at the higher levels of Maslow's concept of motivation and facilitate continuing personal self-growth.

- Principals who have fresh, exciting ideas—who have a vision of the future—that others embrace and want to share are building referent power. Teachers tend to admire principals who express their vision coherently and vividly, who inspire en-thusiasm, who involve others in dialogue intended to mold and develop the ideas, and who cause them to see a connection between the vision and their own desire to achieve something meaningful, to be part of a new and better future that is unfold-ing. This is an important source of power for principals who would be leaders.

Leadership Defined

Although they do exercise various kinds of power, *leaders engage with followers* in seeking to achieve not only the goals of the leader but also significant goals of the fol-lowers. Thus, "Leadership over human beings . . . is exercised when persons with certain purposes mobilize, in competition or in conflict with others, institutional, political, psy-chological and other resources so as to arouse and satisfy the motives of followers." That is as good a definition of leadership as we have at this time.[10]

These two kinds of power—position power and the authority voluntarily granted to leaders by followers—are not necessarily mutually exclusive. A university dean may have considerable legal clout in decisions regarding reappointment and tenure, yet at the same time have power that comes from strong support of a leader by the faculty. The litmus test is who controls the grant of power: a dean who loses the support of the faculty will also have lost considerable power to influence followers and get things done even though his or her official position power remains undiminished. Presidents of the United States combine the official power of office with the power from supporters who willingly accord them great power. For example, the collapse of Richard Nixon's presidency after Water-gate had little to do with the official legal power of the office of the president; without the support of followers, his position in office was untenable.

Two-Factor Leadership Theory Abandoned

Most of the formalistic theorizing that dominated the study of leadership only a few years ago has been largely abandoned. Instead, the seminal insights of Burns, which we have been discussing, gave rise to a new understanding of leadership and have gained ascen-dancy. The approach prior to Burns's work, which was studied by most present-day edu-cational administrators, generally defined the behavior of leaders in two dimensions:

- One dimension was the emphasis that the leader gives to getting the job done. This was often called *initiating structure* because it often involves structuring the work: delineating the relationship between the leader and the members of the work group, specifying the tasks to be performed, and endeavoring to establish well-defined patterns of organization, channels of communication, and methods of procedure, scheduling, and designating responsibilities. It was also often called *production emphasis* or *task emphasis,* for obvious reasons.

- The other dimension was the emphasis that the leader gives to developing friendship, mutual trust, respect, and warmth in relationships between the leader and followers.[11] These behaviors were usually labeled *consideration* or *concern for people.*

Bernard Bass spoke of leaders as tending to be either "follower focused" (i.e., emphasizing concern for people) or "task focused" (i.e., emphasizing rules and procedures for getting the task done):

> A task-focused leader initiates structure, provides the information, determines what is to be done, issues the rules, promises rewards for compliance, and threatens punishments for disobedience. The follower-focused leader solicits advice, opinions, and information from followers and checks decisions or shares decision making with followers. The . . . task-focused leader uses his or her power to obtain compliance with what the leader has decided. The follower-focused leader uses his or her power to set the constraints within which followers are encouraged to join in deciding what is to be done.[12]

This two-dimensional theory held that leadership consists of a mix of these two kinds of behavior and that effectiveness as a leader depends on choosing the right blend in various kinds of situations. The general tendency is for individuals to favor one of these behavioral orientations while placing less emphasis on the other. It would be virtually impossible, in U.S. schools at least, for a leader to totally lack either one of the two behavioral dimensions of leadership. Students of leadership who wish to denigrate this concept of leader behavior, which has fallen into disrepute in academic circles, often achieve their purposes by reporting that they do not find leaders who are *always* task oriented or *always* people oriented.

In the two-dimensional approach to understanding leadership, great emphasis was given to leadership style. For example, one commonly hears complaints that educational leaders in the past emphasized the task, or managerial, dimension of leader behavior—which is often called the "autocratic leadership style"—and few emphasized the consideration dimension—which defines the democratic style of leadership. Thus, individual styles of various leaders were described as tending to be autocratic or democratic, task oriented or people oriented, directive or collegial, and one could adopt a leadership style thought to be appropriate to the leader's personality, on the one hand, or the situation in which the leader works, on the other hand. All of this emanated from efforts to reduce the study of leadership to a science, and therein lay its weakness. In education today, recognition is rapidly growing that leadership cannot be reduced to formulas and prescriptions but must be attuned to the human variables and confusions that normally abound in busy, complex, and contradictory—that is, messy—human organizations.

It is helpful to bear two things in mind:

- Understanding of leadership is now undergoing great upheaval in all fields of human endeavor, not just in schools, and we have much to learn from enlightened leaders of business, industry, and the military, as well as from enlightened educational leaders.

- The direction of change in this upheaval is away from the old concepts of leadership as the downward exercise of power and authority and toward developing respect and concern for the followers and the ability to see them as crucial sources of knowledge, creativity, and energy for improving the organization—sources heretofore largely untapped by administrators whose focus tended to be on hierarchical control.

Leadership as a Relationship with Followers

Whenever we try to lead people we become part of their environment and, therefore, part of their "equation" for organizational behavior, $B = f(p \cdot e)$. Leaders are, therefore, not merely concerned with the leadership style and techniques that they intend to use but also with the quality and kinds of relationships that they have with followers. Leadership is not something that one does to people, nor is it a manner of behaving toward people: it is working with and through other people to achieve organizational goals.

What distinguishes leaders from other authority figures is the unique relationship between leaders and followers. Leaders relate to followers in ways that

- Motivate them to unite with others in sharing a vision of where the organization should be going and how to get it there.

- Arouse their personal commitment to the effort to bring the vision of a better future into being.

- Organize the working environment so that the envisioned goals become central values in the organization.

- Facilitate the work that followers need to do to transform the vision into reality.

How do leaders do these things? That depends, first, on what they think leadership is, and that is defined in terms of the character and quality of the relationship between leader and follower. This arises from the bedrock assumptions that the would-be leader holds about people and the world in which they work, the world from which all our cultural beliefs and values arise.

Using Douglas McGregor's concepts, one who accepts Theory X assumptions about followers tends to think about leadership pretty much as the stereotype of the traditional boss overseeing a gang in the field or on the shop floor: issuing orders, checking up, and prodding to keep things moving. One who accepts Theory Y assumptions about people at work tends to think about leadership more in terms of collaborating with others to reach organizational goals and achieve the organization's mission, sharing enthusiasm for the work to be done, providing help in solving problems, and supporting and encouraging. In the United States today, people working in education who subscribe to Theory X assumptions commonly mask them behind the kind of Theory X soft behavior that was discussed in Chapter 4, so as not to appear insensitive and undemocratic. Theory X soft behavior by the leader poses some serious moral and ethical problems, which we will discuss later in this chapter.

The key to understanding leadership, then, lies in understanding your own concept of the human nature of followers and how leaders relate to them. For example, Niccolo Machiavelli's assumptions about human nature were set forth in his advice to a young man of the ruling class in the fifteenth century. Machiavelli's treatise, *The Prince,* once was required reading for students in educational administration and is still widely admired today. It taught that the exercise of leadership by those who inherit positions of power as a privilege of membership in a dominant elite social class required the ruthless exercise of position power, the use of guile and deception when expedient to achieve the leader's personal agenda, and indifference to the concerns of others.

This Machiavellian view of leadership is still very prevalent, though, of course, it usually is expressed obliquely in cautious terms and is usually disguised in Theory X soft behavior so as to appear reasonably adapted to the democratic demands of our time. The central idea is that leadership consists largely of commanding and controlling other people. Consider, for example, this observation intended for a mass audience of readers from the management ranks of corporations:

> A leader is a leader only insofar as he [sic] has followers. If we want our subordinates to do something and they do not do it, then, plainly, they have not followed our lead. Likewise, if we want our charges to accomplish something, quite apart from how they go about it, and they do not accomplish it, then, again they have not followed our lead. Now these are the only two ways that we can be leaders: we can want certain *actions* and we can want certain *results. The degree in which we get what we want is the measure of our leadership.*
>
> A follower is a follower only insofar as he [sic] does what a leader wants in order to please the leader . . . we are all social creatures, and so we want to please the boss. . . . Work is done for the boss. We grow for our parents, learn for our teacher, win for our coach. Even the most independent of us presents his [sic] work as a gift for the boss.[13]

This statement says a great deal about the writers' assumptions about the human nature of followers and how leaders relate to them. On the other hand, consider this statement of assumptions about leadership from a modern military perspective:

> When you lead in battle you are leading people, human beings. I have seen competent leaders who stood in front of a platoon and all they saw was a platoon. But great leaders stand in front of a platoon and see it as 44 individuals, each of whom has hopes, each of whom has aspirations, each of whom wants to live, each of whom wants to do good.[14]

This expresses a very different view of human nature than was embodied in Max Weber's now classic work on bureaucracy. Weber's work first appeared in the early years of the twentieth century and became known in the United States only after World War II, when translations from the German were published in English.

Your Understanding of Human Nature Is Critical

At the turn of the twentieth century, the emergence of giant industrial corporations was transforming society in Europe. Max Weber saw that the old aristocracies could not provide the new kinds of leadership required in the expanding government, business, and industrial organizations of the day. To replace the absolute power inherited by privileged social classes, which was enjoyed by members of the German Junkers of Weber's day and *The Prince* of Machiavelli's day, and to reject the exercise of traditional autocratic rule in modern industrial, commercial, and government organizations that were then emerging around the world, Weber supported the rise of a disciplined and orderly organization composed of offices arranged hierarchically, with legally assigned power and authority descending from the top to the bottom. Weber approvingly gave this kind of organization a name: "bureaucracy."[15]

In contrast to autocratic rule, the "law" of the bureaucratic organization lies in its written rules and regulations, official standard operating procedures, written memos, chain of command, and acceptance of the concepts of hierarchical superordination and subordination. It is a vision of organization that is rational, logical, impersonal, formal, predictable, and systematic, and it reflects beliefs about the nature and needs of the human beings who populate the organization: bureaucratic theory generally holds that people tend pretty much to be motivated by the lower levels of Maslow's hierarchy of needs, with emphasis on pay and benefits, job security, and advancement in rank.

Weber's work has had enormous influence in establishing and maintaining bureaucracy as the most pervasive and credible organizational concept in the world. Yet few who are taught the virtues of bureaucratic organization in their universities understand or even know that it was the same Max Weber, sociologist and theologian, who also wrote powerfully on the Protestant Work Ethic as a defining characteristic of human nature. Weber was convinced, and convinced many other people at the time, that Protestantism was undergirded by certain fundamental moral and ethical imperatives that were played out in the world of work, the so-called Protestant Work Ethic, in ways that were superior to those of non-Protestant cultures. Thus, in reality, Weber viewed bureaucracy as embodying and codifying in the world of work certain views of human nature that he believed were inherent in Protestant theology. The two were, in his mind, closely linked.

Let us return the theme of this discussion of leadership to the concept of organizational behavior that $B = f(p \cdot e)$. In exercising leadership, the leader has an array of options from which to choose in influencing the nature and quality of the organizational environment with which members interact in the course of their daily work. How one chooses depends on one's understanding of what kinds of behaviors are desirable and sought, on the one hand, and how they are likely to be elicited in the organization's environment, on the other hand. If, for example, you think that Machiavelli understood the realities of modern educational organizations, then his advice on leadership will be appealing and appear practical. If, on the other hand, you think that schools are best understood as bureaucracies, then you will do your best to create a bureaucratic environment for people to work in.

However, if you think of people in Theory Y terms, then you will try to create the organizational environment likely to elicit and support the high motivation and high levels of effort that they will find satisfying in their work. Such an environment is growth enhancing and engages the members of the organization in personal growth and development as well as in organizational growth and development—that is, a healthy state of increasing ability to identify and solve its own problems in an ever-changing world. An important part of such an organizational environment is leadership. It is precisely because bureaucratic organizations lack this internal dynamic for organization development in the context of constant change in the world, as do autocratic organizations, that they are such poor exemplars for the study of leadership.

Bureaucratic View of Leadership

Commonly, the traditional bureaucratic officeholder tends to emulate the Lone Ranger when attempting leadership:

> The Lone Ranger, an imposing masked figure, rides up on a white horse to overcome great odds in solving the problems of the day. The model of the vanquishing leader—a bit mysterious, generous, but aloof—is a very common theme. Think of the setting: helpless, disorganized townsfolk are being threatened by some bad guys. The Lone Ranger, helped just by his trusty and loyal sidekick, arrives in the nick of time, with the right blend of courage and cunning, faces down the bad guys by being just a little quicker, smarter, and tougher, leaves a silver bullet as a symbol of his having solved the problem, and at the end, rides stoically off into the sunset. The grateful townspeople wonder who that masked man is—and wish he could stay—but are left to go about their mundane tasks no wiser or better prepared to deal with the next big problem. When again faced with a major crisis, they'll just have to hope for a return of the thundering hoofbeats and another last-minute rescue by the daring hero.[16]

Thus, the townsfolk or, in our case, the faculty of the school or department, learn nothing from their experience that leaves them better prepared to continue the process of solving problems in the future, nor have they been motivated by the Lone Ranger to improve their problem-solving skills: the problem has been solved for the moment, but the school has not increased its ability to solve problems as a result of the experience. For all the good work that he achieved, one must fault the Lone Ranger's performance as a leader because he did not leave the townsfolk functioning at a higher level than when he encountered them.

In contrast, contemporary thinking about leadership contends that leaders, unlike mere power wielders and bureaucratic managers, work with followers in ways that change both leaders and followers so that over time they perform at increasingly higher levels of functioning than they achieved initially. This view of leadership is called "transforming" leadership.[17]

Transforming Leadership

The idea of transforming leadership was conceptualized by James MacGregor Burns[18] and has directly influenced the thinking of scholars ever since. Burns's insights were later developed and elaborated by Bernard Bass.[19] They have subsequently been used as the basis of research, such as that of, for example, Warren Bennis,[20] Rosabeth Moss Kanter,[21] and Judy B. Rosener,[22] each of whom studied corporate leaders. More recently, the ideas of transforming leadership were used by Thomas Sergiovanni to organize a critique of school reform.[23]

Transforming Leadership Compared and Contrasted with Transactional Leadership

The heart of Burns's analysis was to compare and contrast traditional "transactional" leadership with the newer idea of transforming leadership. Having explained that leadership is different from simply wielding power over people, Burns went on to explain that there are two basic types of leadership. In the most commonly used type of leadership, the relationship between leader and followers is based on quid pro quo transactions between them. Transactional educational leaders can and do offer jobs, security, tenure, favorable ratings, and more in exchange for the support, cooperation, and compliance of followers.

In contrast "the transformational leader looks for potential motives in followers, seeks to satisfy higher needs, and engages the full person of the follower. The result of transforming leadership is a relationship of mutual stimulation and elevation that converts followers into leaders and may convert leaders into moral agents."[24] This evokes a third, and higher level, of leadership—the concept of "moral leadership" that began to receive so much attention in education in the 1990s.

Moral Leadership

The concept of moral leadership comprises three related ideas:

- First, the relationship between the leader and the led is not one merely of power but is a genuine sharing of mutual needs, aspirations, and values. The genuineness of this sharing is tested by whether or not the participation of followers is a matter of choice that is controlled by the followers.

- Second, the followers have latitude in responding to the initiatives of leaders: they have the ability to make informed choices as to who they will follow and why. As we shall explain more fully, the concept of transforming leadership means that followers voluntarily involve themselves in the leadership process. Among other things, followers voluntarily grant power and authority to leaders and are free to withdraw that grant. Therefore, in the highest level of transforming leadership, which is moral leadership, the followers must have access to alternative leaders from whom to choose, and they must have knowledge of alternative plans and programs that they can embrace.

- Third, leaders take responsibility for delivering on the commitments and representations made to followers in negotiating the compact between leader and followers. "Thus, moral leadership is not mere preaching, or the uttering of pieties, or the insistence on social conformity. Moral leadership emerges from, and always returns to, the fundamental wants and needs, aspirations, and values of followers."[25] In this sense, moral leadership is very different from the thin veneer of participation that administrators frequently use to give their relationships with followers some patina of genuine involvement while control remains firmly in the administrators' hands.

A Progression

A progression is clearly inherent in the concept of transforming leadership:

- At the lowest level of functioning is the exercise of power to exact the compliance of followers, which is not leadership at all.
- At the entry level of leadership is transactional leadership, wherein the leader and followers bargain with each other to establish a "contract" for working together.
- At a higher level of functioning is transforming leadership, in which the leaders and followers mutually engage in common cause, joined by their shared aspirations and values.
- At the highest level is moral leadership, which demands motivating emotional stimuli, such as a shared mission, a sense of mutual purpose, and a covenant of shared values interwoven with the daily life and practices of ordinary people so as to inspire new and higher levels of commitment and involvement.

A Process of Growth and Development

The levels in this progression in transforming leadership increasingly draw on the higher levels of the motivations of followers and, in return, offer increasing opportunities for followers and leaders to grow and develop increasing capacities for effective organizational behavior. Thus, transforming leaders engage the aspirations of followers, tap their motivations, energize their mental and emotional resources, and involve them enthusiastically in the work to be done. This kind of leadership does not merely obtain the compliance of followers; it evokes their personal commitment as they embrace the goals to be achieved as their own, seeing them as an opportunity for a willing investment of their effort. It transforms the roles of both followers and leaders so that they become virtually interdependent,[26] their aspirations, motives, and values merged in mutual commitment to achieve the shared goals. Burns's focus was political leadership, not educational leadership, and he used Gandhi as one well-known exemplar of both transforming and moral leadership. One also thinks of the leadership of Martin Luther King, Jr. But such leadership is not limited to those who appear larger than life on the world stage. Many coaches, in various sports ranging from football to tennis, illustrate effective leadership in their work. Indeed, the metaphor of the coach is popular in speaking of leadership in many kinds of organizations. Many who have followed Burns's scholarly lead have described how readily his concepts of transforming leadership apply to realms other than politics, such as education and business. Increasingly one finds literature that describes the behavior of people in high-performing schools as being consistent with transformational leadership.

We know that members of educational organizations thrive on the experience of being part of an organization that is constantly growing in its capacity to detect and solve its own problems. A school having such characteristics is seen by teachers as a successful and effective place in which to work. For example, a substantial body of research, such as Dan Lortie's classic *Schoolteacher,*[27] tells us that teachers are highly motivated by feeling successful and effective in their teaching. From this, one can conclude that an educational leader in a school might seek to foster a culture that facilitates teaching and enhances the likelihood that one will be successful at it, that energizes and applauds the efforts of teachers, that rewards and supports success in teaching, and that celebrates teaching as a central value in the life of the school. Such a school is likely to have a history that stresses the importance of teaching, heroes who epitomize achievement in teaching, and rituals and ceremonies that celebrate teaching and the successes of teachers. These are likely to be prominent characteristics of the school that are emphasized daily at all levels of the organization. Thus, one can exercise leadership by working with and through teachers to transform the culture of the school and, in the process, transform the very ways in which the leader and the teachers relate to one another. It is widely believed that the vehicle for bringing about such a transformation is a vision of the future that is better, more desirable, more compelling, and more personally fulfilling than the reality of the present time.

Leadership and Vision

The vision that leaders seek to share with followers is a protean thing, continually being revised and annotated by changing values, emerging developments, and events that vindicate or repudiate aspects of the worldview previously held by leaders, followers, or both. Indeed, one of the pivotal activities of leaders is to engage constantly in the dynamic process of stating a vision of things to come; then revising in light of emerging events, ideas, and beliefs; and restating the vision of "where we are and where we are going" that binds the members of the organization in mutual purpose and resolve. But in all its iterations, the vision of a leader is always uplifting, pointing to new directions, calling for progress from where we are to where we want to be, and describing how we will get there. Dramatic examples abound in the realm of politics and social movements: one thinks of Churchill's magnificent rallying cry to the British facing almost certain defeat in World War II, "We shall fight on," the stirring inspiration of Lincoln's low-key Gettysburg Address, and the immortal vision of King's revelation that "I have a dream." Educational leaders rarely have opportunities to exercise such dramatic flair and personal charisma, yet they must always be prepared to articulate their personal vision for the organization as a rallying cry for the daily work to be done.

The purpose of the ongoing process of stating and discussing the vision is to buttress and develop the most critical factors in the development of organizational culture:

the web of shared assumptions, beliefs, and values that unites the group in mutual solidarity. In the ordinary bureaucratic organization these things are rarely examined and discussed, rarely made explicit and public, rarely challenged. Indeed, in ordinary organizations there is little even in the way of vocabulary for talking about such things, and the time-consuming minutiae of professional meetings usually drives such conversation out, so that the norm in the organization's culture is to avoid such discussion altogether.

The goal of forging agreement on the vision or mission of the organization is, ideally, to seek consensus as nearly as it can be practically achieved, but always consensus on a new and better state in the future. In one iteration the statement may not be as clear as it might be, and it must be restated in a hopefully clearer way. Sometimes even the nuance of a word or phrase can produce an unanticipated effect, and the statement must be rephrased more sensitively. Sometimes aspects of the stated vision are unacceptable to some members of the organization and an accommodation must be worked out. But throughout the process, the leader strives always to marshall consensus in support of something better: a higher plane of functioning, an elevated sense of motivation and commitment, an organization that is constantly metamorphosing into something better than it was. The point to remember is that the ongoing discussion of the organizational vision is a crucial dialogue through which the leader and the followers mutually engage in the process of forging the destiny that unites them in common cause. It is, therefore, a powerful engine for the empowerment of teachers. By participating in the never-ending process of creating, maintaining, and evolving a vision of the future of the school, teachers are themselves involved in a process of self-development and growth. Moreover, because the process is open, ongoing, and collaborative, the principal is also engaged in personal self-development and growth: the process engages the leader as much as anyone and in the end helps to forge and refine the leader's own vision.

Engaging in the give-and-take of the ongoing colloquy required to forge and maintain an evolving vision of the organization requires one to rethink assumptions, beliefs, and values that previously guided behavior at work and either reaffirm them or modify them in the light of this reflection as well as in the light of newly emerging realities. The process has a name—reflective practice—and many believe that it is essential if one is to continue to develop and improve one's professional practice over the years rather than to stagnate and become increasingly irrelevant.

Whose Vision Is It, Anyway?

At a time when school reform cries out for leadership rather than bureaucratic command, schools should be evolving from top-down hierarchical management toward a more collaborative, collegial, participative form of leadership. Because the new form of organization facilitates and encourages the active participation of people who are on the lower rungs of the organizational hierarchy, it is sometimes popularly referred to as bottom-up organization. In such an organization the glue that binds the organization's participants together, that motivates them to unite in common purpose, is a vision of a different school, new and better, in the future. But whose vision is it, anyway?

Bureaucrats assume that experts high in the hierarchy are especially qualified to set the goals of the organization and determine how to reach them. The experts may or may not consult those on the lower levels of the organization in so doing. Leaders, on the other hand, assume that those on the lower levels of the organization have valuable knowledge, good ideas, and insights as to what the organization is about that must be an integral part of the mix that we call a vision of the organization.

Leaders assume that the ability to lead is widely distributed throughout the organization and often manifests itself when participants express new ideas, challenge traditional practices, and synthesize and express the ideas of a collegial group. That is why it is important for leaders to empower others to participate fully in the unending processes of creating and refining a vision of the mission of the school. But leadership is not a spectator sport: leaders do not stand passively on the sidelines hoping that others will lead the way and shape the future.

Leaders are not merely catalysts of the ideas of others, much as they encourage and facilitate participation, but have their own clearly thought-out vision of the future, their own sense of direction. Leaders have something important to say in the dialogue about where we are and where we are going, something that engages the aspirations of others and raises their sights as to what can and should be achieved in their work, moves them forward to engage vigorously with others in building a new and better future in the organization. But leadership is not a solo performance, either. The leader's role in the process of developing a vision of the school, in addition to offering ideas and participating in discussion, emphasizes facilitating the involvement of others in an ongoing dialogue about the direction for the future.

One must remember that, by definition, transformational leadership involves mobilizing resources, including human and intellectual resources, *in conflict with others* so as to "arouse, engage, and satisfy the motives of others."[28] Therefore, vision building is not always a placid process but also often requires engagement with different worldviews of people in the group, different temperaments, different personal agendas, different levels of understanding, different hopes and aspirations, and different pedagogical approaches to the future. Therefore, whereas the school principal, for example, must avoid imposing a prepared mission statement on the teachers for ratification by them, he or she must have developed a clearly thought-out position from which to contribute, unhesitatingly and convincingly, to the discussion.

Perhaps the leader can do nothing more important in empowering teachers to create a process for forging and reworking the vision, or mission, of the school than to signal that this process is not only important but also acceptable. Traditionally, schools have not been places where adults can easily share the collegial relationships that are essential to leadership, as distinct from management, and teacher empowerment. The school leader, then, must demonstrate convincingly an interest in promoting collegiality and shared leadership, an interest in shifting the norms of the school's culture from the traditional to more collaborative ways of working together. Making this shift in the cultural norms of the school, translating the intent into daily practices that reduce the sense of isolation that is typical teaching, will more than likely be gradual because teachers have learned, through experience, to be cautious in talking about their work. In traditional schools, teachers rarely see one another practice their craft, rarely discuss pedagogy in a serious way, and almost never deal with such matters in staff meetings, which are ordinarily filled with minor routine matters.

Manipulation and Empowerment

One of the most common criticisms of educational administrators that is emerging in the literature on school reform is the charge that they tend to manipulate followers, often by using a veneer of seemingly participative involvement. By indirection these administrators get followers to pursue ends that the administrators seek while seeming to act on the followers' intentions. Through this manipulation those who are in power maintain their power, whereas followers are induced to believe that the arrangement is appropriate and legitimate, if not inevitable. Teachers, for example, deeply socialized into the traditional ways of schools—having participated in them since they were five years old—generally accept the hierarchical power of principals and superintendents as a reality of life that is both inevitable and legitimate. It is commonplace for teachers who have had their views brushed aside to say to the principal, "Well, just tell me what you want me to do and I'll try my best to do it."

Critical Theory

A group of educational academicians who subscribe to a form of social criticism known as critical theory have been especially sensitive to and vociferous about this perceived shortcoming. Critical theory is a form of social criticism that holds that institutionalized oppression of groups of people in a society—cultural, ethnic, racial, and gender groups—is often supported by the oppressed peoples themselves, who believe the system to actually be in their own best interests. This, critical theorists contend, is achieved by the manipulation of meaning by those in power so as to legitimate the values and beliefs of the power elite. In that view, some critical theorists in the Marxian tradition would say, indeed have said, that workers in capitalist societies are oppressed by the powerful capitalist class but don't perceive it because, through control of the press, education, organized religion, and other social institutions, those in power systematically induce workers to believe that the values and beliefs of the capitalist class are legitimate and in the workers' best interests.

Critical theory is often applied to the analysis of the perceived oppression of non-dominant races, women, the poor, and other social classes in present-day U.S. education.[29] The approach has also been applied to the study of relationships between official school leaders, such as principals, and teachers. Some school leaders mandate that teachers comply with organizational goals or that they embrace particular notions of organizational culture, whereas others induce compliance through more subtle, more manipulative, means. Nevertheless, by the mid-1980s recognition began to grow that bona fide participation by teachers in school affairs is highly desirable yet has traditionally been rare. However, with the recommendation in 1986 by the Carnegie Forum on Education and the Economy that teachers be given "a greater voice in the decisions that affect the school,"[30] the term *teacher empowerment* has been one of the most recurrent buzzwords in school educational circles.

An important aspect of empowerment is that it provides opportunities for teachers to participate actively, openly, and without fear in the endless process of shaping and molding the vision of the school and its culture through iterative discussion. When they do so, at least three things happen that Burns described as essential to transforming leadership:

- Teachers participate actively in the dynamic ongoing processes of leadership by contributing their knowledge, insights, and ideas to the development of the vision for the school.
- They acquire greater personal ownership, and thus a greater sense of personal commitment to, the values for which the school stands and that shape its vision for the future.
- By their active engagement in the process, and by being personally committed to its outcomes, teachers are stimulated to increase their awareness of both the larger mission of the school and the connection of their own daily mundane work to the achievement of that mission.

This process of leadership is very different from the manipulation of followers, guileful or otherwise, by power-wielding leaders that once passed for leadership. It taps the motivations of teachers—their aspirations, beliefs, and values—and enriches the significance of what they do by better connecting their daily work to the larger mission of the enterprise. Thus, transforming leadership inevitably empowers teachers.

Leadership and Management

The rhetoric of reform chic contends that U.S. schools require leadership, not "mere management." This suggests that there is not only a difference between management and leadership but that, moreover, they are mutually exclusive. This view correctly derives from the fact that one manages things, not people, and one leads people, not things. We manage finances, inventories, and programs, for example, but we lead people. Moreover, there is a qualitative difference between managing and leading and, some contend, they are mutually exclusive. Warren Bennis and Burt Nanus, for example, have told us that "managers are people who do things right and leaders are people who do the right thing."[31] Some blame much of our present dearth of educational leadership on the existence of a managerial mystique, long promoted by schools of business as well as schools of education, that taught managers to pay attention to structures, roles, and indirect forms of communications, to ignore the ideas and emotions of people, and to avoid direct involvement of others in leadership. The result has been a professionalization of management that deflected attention from the real business of schools, which is teaching, and conceptualized leadership as emphasis on rules, plans, management controls, and operating procedures.

This often manifests itself in the language of those who confuse schooling and teaching with "the delivery of educational services," and who do so with the cool detachment that a merchant might use to speak of the distribution of goods or the manager of a fast-food restaurant might use to describe the essence of the business. Thus, in schools we too often see

> an emphasis on doing things right, at the expense of doing the right things. In schools, improvement plans become substitutes for improvement outcomes. Scores on teacher-appraisal systems become substitutes for good teaching. Accumulation of credits in courses and inservice workshops become a substitute for changes in practice. Discipline plans become substitutes for student control. Leadership styles become substitutes for purpose and substance. Congeniality becomes a substitute for collegiality. Cooperation becomes a substitute for commitment. Compliance becomes a substitute for results.[32]

There is little question that as the U.S. public school enterprise became markedly more bureaucratized in the decades from 1945 to 1985, emphasis was placed on the bureaucratic concept of leadership, which we now call management. There is also little question that this myopic focus needs to be corrected, that leadership is badly needed in educational institutions at all levels. But we must be cautious about substituting management-bashing for leadership.

Educational leaders must—as must all leaders—be able to manage. John Gardner rightly pointed out that leaders often must allocate resources, deal with budgets, and organize the enterprise in order to enable people to do the work necessary to move the organization toward its vision.[33] He concluded, therefore, that leaders need to be skilled managers well able to deal with the mundane inner workings of organizational life that must be attended to if the vision is to be realized.

It is unarguable that schools have been, and still largely are, organized and administered as bureaucracies or, as the contemporary pejorative expression has it, using the factory as a model. There is little question that most educational administrators conceptualize their work largely in terms of management of operational routines. Clearly this emphasis has tended to thwart the development of leadership in schools while emphasizing management. Therefore, it is unarguable that U.S. schools are generally in need of more and better leadership. But it is false to argue that, therefore, principals should be leaders, not managers, because they need to be both.

Empowerment and Leadership

Recent research and writing on leadership[34] has sharpened the difference between managing and leading. Whereas managers may, and often do, involve other people in various ways in making decisions, leaders go beyond that: leaders are able "to create and communicate a vision that inspires followers."[35] Thus, whereas the main concern of educational administration once was viewed as controlling the behavior of teachers, with planning and decision making closely held in the hands of the hierarchy, the emerging concept is focused on developing a vision that involves followers, inspires them, and motivates their efforts. It is the shared vision of a better school in the future that has the power to transform the relationships between the teachers and the principal, for example, uniting them in mutually sharing the work required to achieve the vision. This is the reason that one hears so much today about the vision of the future as a key element in school leadership.

Creating this mutually shared vision cannot be done without sharing some of the power that was traditionally closely held by those in the administrative hierarchy with the rank and file of the organization: power, for example, in the form of information about the organization, authority to participate freely in making decisions, recognition of the legitimacy of followers as stakeholders in the enterprise, and creating an environment that facilitates the development of trust and open communication that is essential to collaborative group effort. This is the basis for the empowerment of teachers, parents, students, and others who were formerly shut out of the decision making of the organization.

A Moral or Ethical Problem

The notion of empowerment to improve organizational performance is not a new one, having been widely discussed and, to a limited extent, practiced in the 1970s under the banner of organization development, which used the term *power sharing* instead of today's *empowerment.* Indeed, the organization development experience provided us with a wealth of knowledge about techniques that can be used to implement the concept of empowerment by training organization members in such techniques as shared decision making and developing trust and openness so as to create a growth-enhancing culture in the organization. But the failure of the organization development movement was anchored in the entrenched resistance of those who held position power to share their power with others. This resulted in many people holding position power and playing Theory X soft games with their subordinates in which they used various forms of participative methods—holding meetings, calling on people to be open and honest, using the language of participation—while guilefully making sure that no significant power was shared with subordinates.

Today this sort of Machiavellian manipulation is understood as constituting a serious moral or ethical problem, and concern about it is widespread, especially in educational settings. The quality of organizational life in the United States dwindled over the past two or three decades while those in position power steadfastly ducked the issue of empowerment. Many hope that we have now entered a different era in which it is clear that empowerment methods of leadership are all that remain as we attempt to revitalize our schools. Efforts by people with position power to finesse the new imperative for collaboration, to use guile and Machiavellian subterfuge to manipulate appearances without changing realities in power relationships can, in the long run, only impede leadership and threaten our educational organizations even further.

Conclusion

This chapter began with a discussion of the difference between leadership and command, with particular attention to the differences in the role of power in both leadership and command. Clearly, organizational leaders have a range of theories of leadership from which to choose in selecting a leadership style.

- For example, one may choose to use a traditional top-down directive approach, often thought of as bureaucratic. Such an approach assumes that the best information and the best ideas for solving problems are found in the upper echelon of the organization and should be passed down the line to be implemented by those in the lower echelons. This approach predictably creates a transactional relationship with followers in which motivation and effort are circumscribed by the expectations inherent in the agreed-upon transactional relationship.

- An alternative is to choose a more collaborative, or transformative, leadership style in working with others in the belief that useful information and good ideas may well be found anywhere in the organization and should be shared in the leadership process. At its best, collaborative leadership creates a transformational relationship with followers in which they are motivated by uniting with others in a mutual commitment to share in solving problems and creating solutions, as well as by the sense of mutual effort, or team membership, involved.

But the major factor in deciding which approach to use in exercising leadership lies in the belief that one approach will be more effective in producing better outcomes than the other. Educational organizations today are confronted by demands for near-constant change in dealing with problems that are highly complex, often ill-understood, and ambiguous, and with outcomes that are uncertain. Such organizations must be nimble, adaptable, and responsive. The contemporary scientific paradigm of leadership under these conditions is to use a collaborative style that emphasizes teamwork, and it is called "adaptive leadership." The goal of adaptive leadership is to transform the relationship between leader and followers so that participants are energized and motivated by unity of purpose and mutually shared values.

Adult learners, such as teachers, are motivated to learn new ways when they are active participants in their own learning, forging new ideas about the future of their lives at work and participating actively as team members in making the central decisions regarding their work. To move an organization from traditional transactional leadership to transformative leadership requires the development of a new process that is pursued steadfastly over time through which teachers can learn new roles and new skills required for active participation in teamwork and collaboration. This transformative team-building process must include constant attention to the building of greater levels of trust not only between the leader and the followers but among the collaborating followers as well. Thus, transformative leaders understand that leadership is a never-ending process of growth and development—a process of building human capital in the organization.

Reflective Activities

Working on Your Game Plan. It was 11:45 that night late in May when the telephone finally rang. Rising from a comfortable chair before the TV to cross the room to answer it, Marion felt her heart jump a little. It seemed odd, almost childlike, this tingling sense of anticipation and suspense. Marion knew that it would be Sidney Bennigan, the superintendent of schools, who had promised to call with the news after the school board had made its decision at tonight's meeting.

"Hi, this is Sid," Bennigan announced in that characteristically calm, expressionless voice. "Well, congratulations, Marion. The board just voted to name you the new principal of JFK. There was no problem, no hesitation, and the vote was unanimous. They're pretty sure that I found the right person for this job. They like you and that gets you off to a pretty good start." Marion controlled the urge to let out a cheer at such a stroke of good fortune—at last landing what was surely the best principalship in the county!—and said, "I'm delighted, Sid, that's really great! I really appreciate your support in this and I'll do everything I can to justify your confidence in me."

"I know you will, Marion, and I'm sure you have a bright future in the principalship. Otherwise, I never would have nominated you." He quickly added, "Listen, I've got to run. The board's taken a short recess so that I could call you and a couple of other people. And I have

to make those calls. But I want you to call the central registry and get a substitute for yourself tomorrow because I want us to go out to JFK first thing in the morning and I'll introduce you to the teachers and people over there as the new principal-elect. I don't want them to hear about it by the union grapevine, though I imagine that Jack Garvey is on the phone to their association rep right now. So let's meet in my office at 7:30 so that we can be at the school by 8:00."

"Okay," Marion responded. "Sure, I'll be at your office at 7:30."

"Fine," the superintendent said, "and in the meantime you should be thinking about what you plan to do when you officially become the principal starting August 1, how you're going to approach the job. My hunch is that all of these general questions and answers that have been batted around during the past few months will fade into the background now and people will want to know more about how you will actually approach the job in this particular school when the time comes. As we both know, the opening moves are probably important. I don't think that anyone will ask you that tomorrow, but I suspect that they will be wondering. So, you might think about it."

"Okay," Marion said, "I will. And I'll see you in the morning. And thanks again." After hanging up, Marion thought for a moment about the other telephone calls that Sidney Bennigan would be making now, to the other two candidates who had lost out in the end. Turning to Dale with a big grin, Marion said exultantly, "Well, I got it!"

Write two paragraphs that address these questions:

1. What are the three or four most important pieces of advice that you would have for Marion in developing a strategy for approaching

the principalship of JFK? Explain the reasoning behind each of your suggestions.

2. To illustrate how your strategic advice would work, describe at least one specific kind of action or actions that Marion should consider taking in order to implement each of your suggestions. On the other hand, what actions should be avoided, and why?

Suggested Reading

Burns, James MacGregor, *Leadership.* New York: Harper & Row, 1978.

This highly readable Pulitzer Prize–winning volume vividly interprets the contemporary understanding of leadership. The aim of the book is to illuminate the dilemmas of political leadership; hence, it draws many of its examples from great political leaders. However, the lessons for educators are clear and readily understandable. Highly recommended not only for its impeccable scholarship but also for the intellectual quality that is revealed by the open, straightforward writing that makes its ideas easily accessible.

Drath, Wilfred, *The Deep Blue Sea: Rethinking the Source of Leadership.* San Francisco: Jossey-Bass, 2001.

"Too often," Drath observes, "in thinking about leadership we are like persons standing on the shore, captivated by the dancing, sparkling whitecaps on the ocean and entirely missing the deep blue sea. The whitecaps are real enough, but their source lies within the action of the ocean itself." And it is so with organizations as well, he contends: the deep blue sea he refers to is our own educational organization, and understanding it lies well below the surface that is so readily seen. Thus, he introduces us to a new way of thinking afresh about organizations and exercising leadership in them. He emphasizes, as the contemporary leadership paradigm does, facilitating relationships and meaning between and among people and organizations. Strongly recommended.

Heifetz, Ronald A., *Leadership Without Easy Answers.* Cambridge, MA: Belknap Press of Harvard University Press, 1998.

Heifetz brings an extraordinarily broad background to this discussion of the key concepts of adaptive leadership. He clearly illuminates such issues as distinguish-ing between adaptive problems and technical problems and the differences between authority and leadership. His approach is both theoretical and practical and is leavened with his own experiences as a medical doctor, a psychiatrist, and a musician.

Helgesen, Sally, *The Female Advantage: Women's Ways of Leadership.* New York: Doubleday Currency, 1990.

This widely read book argues that men tend to think in linear fashion, lean toward hierarchical organization, emphasize logic, seek power for themselves, are uncomfortable with ambiguity, and are goal oriented, whereas women tend to think in terms of more global connections rather than in straight lines, emphasize human interaction processes rather than hierarchy, have no great interest in personal power, are easily able to tolerate ambiguity, and are process oriented. The result, she believes, is a marked difference in thinking and organizational behavior between men and women—a difference that Helgesen firmly believes gives women a decided advantage as organizational leaders.

Powell, Gary, *Women and Men in Management.* Newbury Park, CA: Sage Publications, 1988.

This entry in the literature on the gender wars in leadership concludes, after closely examining the published research on the subject, that there are few gender differences in the organizational behavior of men and women in similar jobs. Powell believes that faulty research methods account for much of the difference that feminist scholars have been claiming, and that innate differences in the leader behavior of men and women simply do not exist.

Rosener, Judy B., "The Ways Women Lead." *Harvard Business Review,* 68, no. 6 (November-December 1990), 119–25.

Having studied 456 female business executives, Rosener reports that they behave very differently from male leaders in similar positions. She found that men emphasized a command-and-control style (rational decision making, giving orders, appealing to the self-interest of followers), whereas women tended to work more "interactively" (sharing information and power, promoting empowerment, motivating people by appeals to organizational ideals and a shared vision of the future). Many women have found this article appealing, yet it remains highly controversial because the quality of the research design and methods have repeatedly been criticized.

Wheatley, Margaret J., *Leadership and the New Science: Discovering Order in a Chaotic World,* 2nd ed. San Francisco: Berrett-Koehler, 1999.

This is an erudite, witty exploration of new ways of thinking about and exploring science. Not a book focused on education, it draws upon a wide range of sources and people to illustrate the new problems of dealing with uncertainty, emerging new ideas, and rapid change across a broad spectrum of science today. It is highly recommended to educational leaders because it brilliantly shows us that the world of schools is not unique but that leadership problems in the schools are part of a much larger mosaic.

chapter 9

Decision Making

LEARNING OBJECTIVES

After reading this chapter, you should be able to

- Identify the two dominant issues in our society that influence how decisions are made in educational organizations and describe how they are interrelated.

- Identify and describe the organizational characteristics that schools must have in an era dominated by the dynamics of change.

- Identify reasons why this chapter focuses on participative decision making.

- Identify and discuss some key characteristics of important educational problems that limit the usefulness of logico-mathematical decision algorithms.

- Describe how the beliefs and values of those in authority shape the way decisions are made in the school.

- Identify and describe the basic assumption that underlies efforts to improve the decision making of administrators by instructing them in the application of rational, logical models of decision making.

- Identify and describe what Vroom and Yetton called the five leadership styles.

- Briefly describe what it is about the nature of administrative work, its pace and workload, that causes few administrators to use formal decision-making models to guide their behavior.

- Discuss the concept of administration as an art or craft as different from the concept of it as a science.

- Define and describe the concept of participative decision making.

- Explain some important differences between participative and democratic decision making.

- Define the concept of the emergent problem and discuss the implications of such problems for decision making in the school.

ISLLC Standards

STANDARD 1: A school administrator is an educational leader who promotes the success of all students by facilitating the development, articulation, implementation, and steward-ship of a vision of learning that is shared and supported by the school community.

Knowledge

The administrator has knowledge and understanding of:

- information sources, data collection, and data analysis strategies
- effective communication
- effective consensus-building and negotiation skills

Dispositions

The administrator believes in, values, and is committed to:

- the inclusion of all members of the school community
- ensuring that students have the knowledge, skills, and values needed to become successful adults.

Performances

The administrator facilitates processes and engages in activities ensuring that:

- the school community is involved in school improvement efforts
- the vision, mission, and implementation plans are regularly monitored, evaluated, and revised

STANDARD 3: A school administrator is an educational leader who promotes the success of all students by ensuring management of the organization, operations, and resources for a safe, efficient, and effective learning environment.

Knowledge

The administrator has knowledge and understanding of:

- theories and models of organizations and the principles of organizational development
- human resources management and development

Dispositions

The administrator believes in, values, and is committed to:

- making management decisions to enhance learning and teaching
- taking risks to improve schools
- trusting people and their judgments
- accepting responsibility
- involving stakeholders in management processes

Performances

The administrator facilitates processes and engages in activities ensuring that:

- knowledge of learning, teaching, and student development is used to inform management decisions
- emerging trends are recognized, studied, and applied as appropriate
- operational plans and procedures to achieve the vision and goals of the school are in place
- problems are confronted and resolved in a timely manner
- stakeholders are involved in decisions affecting schools
- responsibility is shared to maximize ownership and accountability
- effective problem-framing and problem-solving skills are used
- effective group-process and consensus-building skills are used

STANDARD 5: A school administrator is an educational leader who promotes the success of all students by acting with integrity, fairness, and in an ethical manner.

Dispositions

The administrator believes in, values, and is committed to:

- bringing ethical principles to the decision-making process
- accepting the consequences for upholding one's principles and actions

Performances

The administrator:

- accepts responsibility for school operations
- considers the impact of one's administrative practices on others
- uses the influence of the office to enhance the educational program rather than for personal gain
- treats people fairly, equitably, and with dignity and respect

By definition, as was described in Chapter 8, the exercise of leadership involves working with and through others—individually and in groups—to achieve organizational goals. When the goals of the organization emphasize

- *stability,* refinement, and continued application of existing practices, and
- *maintenance* of existing levels of performance

the contemporary paradigm of organizational studies supports the use of bureaucratic top-down methods as likely to be highly effective ways of working with and through others. However, when the organization is required to effectively confront

- demands for quick, adroit, nimble responses to rapid, pervasive change in the environment while dealing, at the same time, with

- emerging problems arising from the need for change that are ambiguous and ill-understood, and the outcomes of possible alternative solutions are not knowable in advance,

the contemporary paradigm of organizational studies supports the use of collaborative methods as likely to be more effective ways of working with and through others. This is why, though educational leaders have a theoretical choice between using traditional bureaucratic methods to work with and through others or using collaborative methods, under contemporary conditions in educational practice collaborative methods are generally the methods of choice.

These two issues—stability and change—are contrapuntal: they are inseparable parts of virtually every decision in which the educational leader is involved. The effectiveness and quality of decisions that are made in an organization usually reflect the skill with which the leader has orchestrated these two issues.

The fast-paced world of school administration seems, on the one hand, to demand that the leader make decisions quickly, without needless ado, and move on to other pressing business. This creates the temptation to make the decision unilaterally, for the sake of speed and efficiency, and be done with it. On the other hand, it is becoming increasingly clear that healthy organizations characteristically find strength in opening up participation in decision making and empowering relevant people at all levels of the organization to contribute to the quality of the decisions made. There are two reasons for this: first, empowering people to participate in important decisions is highly motivating to them; second, broad participation infuses the decision-making process with the full spectrum of knowledge and good ideas that people throughout the organization have to contribute. This is especially and particularly important in organizations peopled by knowledge workers, such as schools.

As it is for all organizations, the environment of educational organizations today is dominated by the dynamics of change—fast-paced, pervasive, insistent change. To keep pace—or, better yet, to set the pace—it is imperative that schools be nimble, responsive, adaptable, and capable of constantly developing themselves from within (or, as the popular phrase has it, reinventing themselves). It is an increasingly competitive environment. The secure monopoly that school districts once had is no longer secure as attention is increasingly focused on results in the form of student achievement and as competitors promise to produce better results than the established public schools have done. In a real sense the competition is global, not merely local, as clients of educational organizations anxiously compare the results posted by local schools with those in other parts of the world. In this context the educational leader is constantly making judgments as to how to make a decision—more particularly, who should be involved in making it and how these others should be involved in the process.

This chapter, therefore, focuses on participative decision making. It begins, however, with a brief background discussion on decision making in general and a discussion of so-called rational decision making. We then discuss the realities of working in schools, how these influence the behavior of leaders in their decision-making efforts, and the need to develop a theory of decision-making practice. The Vroom-Yetton normative leadership model is presented, which offers guidance in determining how to decide, in terms of involving other people. The Tannenbaum-Schmidt analysis then describes a systematic way of thinking about possible courses of action in confronting issues of participative decision making. This is a very important guide to leadership action and should be studied closely for the implications it has for effective leader behavior. The chapter closes with a simple suggested practical paradigm for shared decision making that can be useful in developing a theory.

The significance of decision making on an organizational and administrative level has a long history. For example, in a landmark book published in 1950, Herbert Simon observed that "a general theory of administration must include principles of organization that will insure correct decision-making."[1] By 1959 Daniel E. Griffiths had proposed a theory that administration *was* decision making.[2] He maintained that, first, the structure of an organization is determined by the nature of its decision-making processes; second, that an individual's rank in an organization is directly related to the control exerted over the decision process; and third, that the effectiveness of an administrator is inversely proportional to the number of decisions that he or she must personally make.

Griffiths's theory, which was highly influential in educational circles for many years, highlights two important concepts: (1) that the administrator's task is to see to it that an adequate decision-making process is in place in the organization and (2) that because such a process is in place, the effective administrator makes relatively few decisions personally, although those few may be particularly potent in their impact on the organization. In this view, the administrator's influence resides more firmly in creating and monitoring the processes through which decisions are made by the organization than in personally making large numbers of the many decisions that are required in any busy complex organization.

However, Simon and Griffiths and their colleagues at that time envisioned that decision making could be rationalized, made logical, systematized, and optimized by applying logico-mathematico methods to the solution of educational problems. Many people believed them then, and many still would like to. With the passage of time, however, it has become apparent that many of our most trenchant educational problems are so ambiguous, multifaceted, and complex that they simply cannot be reduced to algorithms into which various quantitative data can be plugged so as to yield optimum educational decisions. Indeed, since the mid-twentieth century, there has been growing understanding that the human complexities of organizational life in commerce as well as in education sharply limit the usefulness of such decision-making approaches in many kinds of organizations.

Individual versus Organizational Decision Making

An important issue that enters many discussions of decision making is being raised here: the question of individual versus organizational decision making. On the one hand, there is the widely held expectation that persons in administrative positions will personally "be decisive." What that means is far from clear, but it is often taken to mean making decisions swiftly, without delay or temporizing, and clearly, with minimum ambiguity. It often also implies that the individual tends to make decisions that conform to certain accepted qualitative standards: that, for example, decisions are well informed and ethically acceptable. Thus, discussions of administrative decision making often focus on the personal behaviors of individuals who are construed to be "decision makers."

On the other hand, because administration is defined as working with and through other people to achieve organizational goals, it is important to consider the mechanisms by which the organization (and not merely the individual) deals with decision making. In this perspective, the issue begins to turn on the ways in which the *organization* "acts" (or "behaves") in the process of making and implementing *organizational* decisions, rather than on the idiosyncratic behavior of the person in administrative office. For many of the clients of organizations (students and parents, for example), the individual roles of administrators in decision-making processes are obscure and perhaps irrelevant, whereas the "behavior" of the organization is highly proximate and relevant. In this view—although administrators may be seen as implicated—the vital decision-making functions are organizational.

This was illustrated in one university when the heating system was constantly malfunctioning, classrooms were chronically unkempt, and student seating was typically in disrepair. Students were astounded when, in the spring, an ambitious project was undertaken to beautify the campus by planting flowers and shrubs and setting sculptures among the trees. This, of course, prompted outcries from students, such as "What is wrong with this university? It obviously doesn't care what happens in the classrooms. All that matters is what visitors see on the outside!" The implication was, of course, that regardless of the persons who might be involved, somehow the decision-making processes of the university, as an organization, had gone awry.

The discussion of decision making in this chapter recognizes that the personal decision-making style of the administrator is important insofar as it gives rise to the ways in which the organization, as an entity, goes about the unending processes of identifying problems, conceptualizing them, and finding ways of dealing with them. The individual decision making of persons in administrative office takes on significance as organizational behavior chiefly because of its inevitable impact on the behavior of others as it affects the decision-making processes of the organization itself.

This emphasis on the responsibility of the administrator for the nature and quality of the decision-making processes used in an organization is compatible with the contemporary view that the administrator is a key actor in the development of the culture of the organization. That is, decision-making practices are not so much the result of circumstances inherent in a given organization ("the kind of place a school is") as they are the choices of those in authority (namely, administrators) as to how decisions *ought* to be made. These choices are closely tied to assumptions held by administrators on issues that are now familiar to the reader, such as

- what motivates people at work,
- the relative values of collaboration versus directiveness in the exercise of leadership in the workplace,

- the desirability of a full flow of information up, down, and across the organization,
- the best ways of maintaining organizational control and discipline, and
- the value of involving people throughout all levels of the organization in decision making.

Rationality in Decision Making

Even an elementary understanding of contemporary approaches to decision making in organizations requires brief consideration of some of the ways in which we have learned to think about such things. We who live in the Western world tend to use and accept logic, rationality, and science when thinking about concepts such as decision making. This reflects generally held assumptions in our culture about the ways in which we ought to go about making decisions. These assumptions have formed the core of our thinking about such matters.

During the three centuries since the Reformation, the history of Western thought and culture has been dominated by the rise of science, technology, and industry. Scientific thought, with its strong emphasis on logical rationality, has become virtually ingrained in the institutions of our culture. Thus, in seeking explanations of our experiences, we are accustomed to respect the rationality of logical positivism. In short, we have strongly tended to see the solution to all sorts of problems as requiring the application of "engineering" approaches.

This was reflected in Max Weber's analysis of bureaucratic organization. It was epitomized by the work of Frederick Taylor, who, adapting the principles and methods of science to a form of "human engineering" in the workplace, sought to create a science of management which could be applied to everyday problems in the organization. Taylor called it "scientific management" and, as Donald Schön pointed out, "Taylor saw the . . . manager as a designer of work, a controller and monitor of performance . . . [seeking through these roles] to yield optimally efficient production."[3]

The concept of management as a science grew steadily during the first half of the twentieth century, but World War II stimulated its development enormously. This was due to three factors associated with the war:

- The great emphasis on the roles of science and technology in winning the war.
- The development of operations research and systems theory. These involved the application of the rational logic of mathematics modeling to the solution of complex problems ranging from how to reduce the loss of shipping to submarine attack to how to increase the effectiveness of aerial bombing.
- The unprecedentedly vast scale of organizing that was required to manage the global dimensions of the conflict.

The post–World War II era was one of great optimism and energy as industry and business moved rapidly to exploit the ready markets that abounded as a result of the years of wartime shortages everywhere. Confidence in science and technology boomed and the rational, logical methods associated with science soared in acceptance and prestige. It was commonplace to refer to the wartime Manhattan Project as a model for conceptualizing and solving problems: "After all, if we could build an atomic bomb we ought to be able to solve this problem." Government expenditures for research surged to new heights on the "basis of the proposition that the production of new scientific knowledge could be used to create wealth, achieve national goals, improve human life, and solve social problems."[4]

As though to be sure that attention to the importance of the message did not lag, Russia launched *Sputnik I* in the fall of 1957. The United States reacted with another spasm of emphasis on the logic of applying mathematics and science to the solution of problems. Under the leadership of President John F. Kennedy, the United States began a large-scale effort to develop new space technology. Before long, the educational infrastructure of the nation found itself involved in meeting the demands of the space program for scientists and mathematicians, as well as managers trained to apply the concepts of those disciplines to complex organizational challenges. The new rallying cry became, "If we can put a man on the moon, why can't we solve this problem?" The implication was, of course, that the National Aeronautics and Space Administration (NASA) had—since its inception under the presidency of Dwight Eisenhower—developed and demonstrated the effectiveness of a model for complex decision making that was applicable to all sorts of problems, social as well as technological.

During the post–World War II era, another similar model—widely admired and emulated—was proffered by medicine. It emphasized clinical-experimental research as the basis of knowledge:

> The medical research center, with its medical school and its teaching hospital, became the institutional model to which other professions aspired. Here was a solid base of fundamental science, and a profession which had geared itself to implement the ever-changing products of research. Other professions, hoping to achieve some of medicine's effectiveness and prestige, sought to emulate its linkage of research and teaching institutions, its hierarchy of research and clinical roles, and its system for connecting basic and applied research to practice. The prestige and apparent success of the medical and engineering models exerted great attraction for the social sciences. In such fields as education . . . the very language . . . rich in references to measurement, controlled experiment, applied science, laboratories and clinics, was striking in its reverence for those models.[5]

This is precisely the view and the hope so very much in evidence among the supporters of the No Child Left Behind (NCLB) Act as it was created and as it began to unfold in practice.

Rational Decision-Making Models

It is not surprising, therefore, that students of decision making tried to develop, and assist administrators to master, a *science* of making better-quality decisions through the analysis of decision-making processes. An early and major contributor in this effort was Herbert Simon.

Simon's analysis identified three major phases in the process of making decisions. First, there is *intelligence activity*. Not surprisingly, in view of the influence of World War II on postwar thought, Simon used the term *intelligence* much as military people do: the search of the environment that reveals circumstances that call for a decision. The second phase is *design activity*: the processes by which alternative courses of action are envisioned, developed, and analyzed. The third phase in Simon's analysis is *choice activity*—the process of actually selecting a course of action from among the options under consideration.[6]

Simon's great stature as a scholar and his popularity as a consultant to numerous prestigious corporations ensured wide acceptance of his pioneering approach to decision making, which now stands as classic work. Many who were to follow would create a substantial literature devoted to efforts to improve upon his conceptualization, usually by elaborating the number of steps to be found in the process. Thus, one finds numerous models proffered in the extensive literature on decision making. Two basic assumptions incorporated in virtually all of them are based on Simon's work: the assumption that decision making is an orderly, rational process that possesses an inherent logic; and the assumption that the steps in the process follow one another in an orderly, logical, sequential flow (which some refer to as "linear logic"). Such models, and the assumptions on which they are based, became important in the training of administrators and have been widely applied in planned, systematic ways to real-world organizations in the hope of improving their performance.

Peter F. Drucker, a leading organizational scholar whose thinking was very influential in corporate circles from the 1960s to the 1980s, listed the following steps in decision making:

1. Define the problem.
2. Analyze the problem.
3. Develop alternative solutions.
4. Decide on the best solution.
5. Convert decisions into effective actions.[7]

Such a formulation was seen as helping the administrator to organize decision making and make it more systematic, as an alternative to intuitive, perhaps haphazard, "knee-jerk responses" to the flow of events in the busy environment of organizational life. Drucker's model, much elaborated and detailed, was widely applied in corporate and governmental organizations throughout the United States, and it was accepted by many as the essential logic of administrative thought.

Nevertheless, even as the number of models proliferated and efforts to install them in organizations intensified, a widespread disparity between the theoretic notions of the scholars and actual practices of administrators was also apparent. Therefore, further work to improve decision-making models went forward. It was noted, for example, that decision making usually does not terminate with either a decision or the action to implement a decision. In the real world, decision making is usually an iterative, ongoing process whereby the results of one decision provide new information on which to base yet other decisions. Thus, "feedback loops" were added to some process models to ensure that the outcomes of decisions would be considered as future decisions were pondered.

Eventually recognition of this cyclic nature of decision-making processes caused some students of the subject to abandon conventional lists of steps and linear flowcharts in favor of circular depictions. Both the feedback loop concept and the circular concept of decision-making processes illustrate two further assumptions commonly found in the literature on decision making: (1) decision making is an iterative, cyclical process that proceeds over time to provide successive approximations of optimal action, and (2) reaching optimal decisions is the central goal of decision making.

However, it has long been obvious that people in an organization do not tend to search endlessly and relentlessly for the best way of achieving goals. They engage in decision-making procedures to seek alternative ways of doing things only when the organization's performance seems to be falling below some acceptable level. This "acceptable level" of performance is usually not the highest level of performance possible; rather, it is one that is good enough to fit the organization's perception of reality and values.[8] Moreover, once those in the organization sense the need to seek some alternative way of doing things, they tend to seek a course of action that is perceived as sufficient to alleviate the need for action. That is, they tend to make a decision that will relieve the proximate problem but are unlikely to seize the moment as an occasion for moving to some optimal level of performance. This widespread tendency in organizations is called *satisficing*.

Limits on Rationality in Decision Making

As we have explained, much of the scholarly literature on decision making—both organizational and individual—represents the efforts of academicians to uncover and describe the logic assumed by them to be inherent in decision-making processes. Based on these efforts, a number of "models" of decision-making processes have been developed. These models, it has often been assumed, can be useful in facilitating the learning of this logic by administrators so that it may be applied in their work. Many people—including practicing educational administrators, legislators, and school board members trained at a time when these assumptions were essentially unchallenged—persist in the belief that more rigorous application of these efforts to practice is essential to improving organizational performance.

However, ambiguity and uncertainty are dominant characteristics of the real world of the educational administrator. Organizations, their goals, their technologies, and their environments have become so complex that it is difficult to connect causes with effects, actions with outcomes. For example, the volatile nature of the economic, social, and political environments of the educational organization makes it difficult to predict the course of future events with any certitude. This condition is not limited to educational organizations by any means: it is of pressing importance in all forms of organizational life. This has caused researchers to reexamine organizational life more carefully in recent years and, in the process, to question old assumptions concerning the logic and rationality of decision making.

The Gap between Theory and Practice

Scholars commonly seek to improve the performance of administrators by instructing them in the application of rational, logical models of decision making to their work. One of the better examples in the field of education is found in a training manual called *Deciding How to Decide: Decision Making in Schools.*[9] Intended to be the basis for organizing and presenting an in-service workshop to teach administrators when and how to involve others in decision making, the manual is essentially an orderly presentation of Victor Vroom and Philip Yetton's contingency model, which points up with remarkable clarity that the central issue in contemporary leadership is participation in the process of making decisions. The issue is often confused by value-laden arguments over the relative merits of hard-nosed, directive administrative style as contrasted with a more consultative style. Even the eminent Peter Drucker lapses occasionally into contrasting "democratic management," "participatory democracy," and "permissiveness" with the supposed successes of autocratic, tyrannical management that makes decisions by fiat.[10] Clearly, the complexities of modern organizations require decision-making processes carefully selected with an eye to the probability of effectiveness in view of the contingencies in the situation. There may be situations in which an autocratic style is most effective and other situations that call for highly participatory methods for greatest effectiveness. As Vroom and Yetton see it, the problem for the leader is to analyze the contingencies in each situation and then behave in the most effective manner.

Vroom and Yetton tried to specify how leaders ought to behave in order to be effective in view of specific contingencies. The Vroom-Yetton model is not prescriptive, but it can be described as a normative model because it tries to tie appropriate leader behavior to specific contingencies.[11]

Five Leadership Styles

Vroom and Yetton have developed a taxonomy of five leadership styles, as follows:

Autocratic Process

AI. Leader (manager, administrator) makes the decision using whatever information is available.

AII. Leader secures necessary information from members of the group, then makes the decision. In obtaining the information, the leader may or may not tell followers what the problem is.

Consultative Process

CI. Leader shares the problem with relevant members of the group on a one-to-one basis, getting their ideas and suggestions individually without bringing them together as a group; then the leader makes the decision.

CII. Leader shares the problem with members as a group at a meeting, then decides.

Group Process

GI. Leader, acting as chairperson at a meeting of the group, shares the problem with the group and facilitates efforts of the group to reach consensus on a group decision. Leader may give information and express opinion but does not try to "sell" a particular decision or manipulate the group through covert means.

Notice that Vroom and Yetton have described these leadership styles in behavioral terms (for example, "leader decides" or "leader shares the problem with the group") rather than in general terms (for example, "directive style" or "participative style"). They do not imply that one style is more highly valued than others; that issue must be addressed in terms of which behavior works in the specific situation.

Seven Situation Issues

Analysis of the situation begins with *yes* or *no* answers to the following questions:

    A. *Does the problem possess a quality requirement?* One quality might be time: Is this a decision that must be made now, with no time to consult others? Other quality factors might be the desirability of stimulating team development or keeping people informed through participation.

    B. *Does the leader have sufficient information to make a good decision?*

    C. *Is the problem structured?*

    D. *Is it necessary for others to accept the decision in order for it to be implemented?*

    E. *If the leader makes the decision alone, how certain is it that others will accept it?*

    F. *Do others share the organizational goals that will be attained by solving this problem?*

    G. *Are the preferred solutions to the problem likely to create conflict among others in the group?*

Decision-Process Flowchart

The leader can quickly diagnose the situation's contingencies by answering *yes* or *no* to each of these seven questions as they are arrayed on the decision-process flowchart (Figure 9.1). As the flowchart shows, it is possible to identify fourteen types of problems in this way, and the preferred way of dealing with each becomes evident as one follows the chart from left to right.

Given a problem, the first question is, "Does the problem possess a quality requirement?" In effect the question is, "Is one decision preferable to or more rational than another?" If not, then questions B and C are irrelevant, and one follows the flowchart to question D, "Is acceptance of the decision by others important to implementing it?" If not, then it makes little difference as to which of the five leadership styles is utilized: AI,

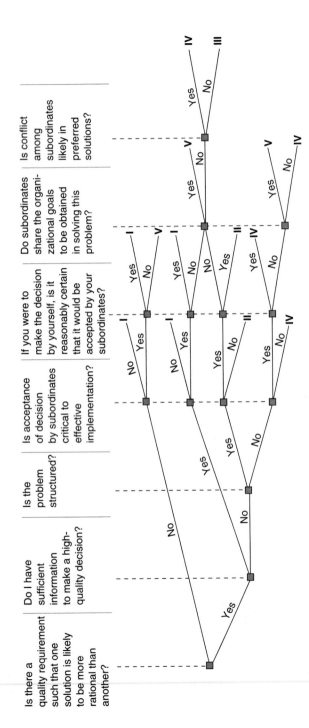

FIGURE 9.1 Vroom-Yetton normative leadership model. From Fred Luthans, *Organizational Behavior*, 2nd ed. (New York: McGraw-Hill Book Company, 1977). p. 458. Reproduced with permission of the McGraw Hill Companies.

I. You solve the problem or make the decision yourself, using information available to you at the time. II. You obtain the necessary information from your subordinate(s), then decide on the solution to the problem yourself. You may or may not tell your subordinates what the problem is in getting the information from them. The role played by your subordinates in making the decision is clearly one of providing the necessary information to you, rather than generating or evaluating alternative solutions. III. You share the problem with relevant subordinates individually, getting their ideas and suggestions without bringing them together as a group. Then *you* make the decision that may or may not reflect your subordinates' influence. IV. You share the problem with your subordinates as a group, collectively obtaining their ideas and suggestions. Then *you* make the decision that may or may not reflect your subordinates' influence. V. You share a problem with your subordinates as a group. Together you generate and evaluate alternatives and attempt to reach agreement (consensus) on a solution. Your role is much like that of a chairperson. You do not try to influence the group to adopt "your" solution and you are willing to accept and implement any solution that has the support of the entire group.

AII, CI, CII, or GII. However, the flowchart clearly suggests that there is a logical basis for utilizing various leadership styles for maximum effectiveness under specific describable circumstances.

However, research conducted in a variety of organizations makes it clear that practicing managers and administrators rarely use such models in their work. Henry Mintzberg, Duru Raisinghani, and Andre Theoret have reported that normative decision-making models have no influence on the behavior of middle- and upper-level corporate managers.[12] James G. March found that decision makers, in fact, tend to make sense of problems not by applying logical models to them but by assessing what kinds of options are actually available to be used in solving them.[13] Paul C. Nutt, after examining seventy-eight different organizations, concluded:

> Nothing remotely resembling the normative methods described in the literature was carried out. Not even hybrid variations were observed.... The sequence of problem definition, alternative generation, refinement, and selection, called for by nearly every theorist seems rooted in rational arguments, not behavior. Executives do not use this process.[14]

A national survey of senior high school principals indicates a similar situation among that group of administrators.[15]

Thus, we have an obvious gap between theory and practice. What does it mean? It could suggest that the administrators and managers whose behavior was studied by the researchers were ill trained and, therefore, unable to use the decision-making models available to them. An equally plausible explanation is that the decision-making models espoused in the scholarly literature arise from assumptions about the nature of administrative work that do not reflect the conditions that the administrator on the job actually encounters. This leads us to consider research that describes the behavior of managers and administrators as it actually occurs on the job.

The Nature of Managerial and Administrative Work

In 1973, Henry Mintzberg reported research that presented detailed descriptions of the activities of the chief executives of five organizations as they were observed in their daily work.[16] The executives whose behaviors were thus recorded were (1) the manager of a consulting firm, (2) the president of an industrial company, (3) the manager of a hospital, (4) a manager of a consumer goods concern, and (5) the superintendent of a suburban school district. This research strikingly reveals, first, that the executive's work is very diverse and requires a broad range of skills, and, second, the pressure that appears to be inherent in the work. More specifically, Mintzberg developed five propositions from his observations:

1. Administrators and managers do a great deal of work, and do it at an unrelenting pace. Each day they attend a number of previously arranged meetings as well as a number of unplanned conferences and interactions, deal with a substantial volume

of mail and paperwork, and handle numerous phone calls. There are seldom any real breaks in the work.

2. In doing their work, administrators characteristically devote a brief period to each of a large number of decisions, and these tend to center on specific, well-defined issues and problems. Important and trivial activities arise in juxtaposition to one another in an unplanned, random way, requiring quick mental shifts from topic to topic. There are many brief contacts with people interspersed with planned meetings of prolonged duration and other activities (such as desk work, telephone calls, unscheduled meetings, and tours) worked into the daily schedule.

3. Administrators prefer to deal with active problems that are well defined and nonroutine. Routine information (such as recurring reports) is given low priority, whereas "fresh" information (even if of uncertain quality) is given high priority.

4. Verbal communication is much preferred. (In Mintzberg's original study, it accounted for over three-fourths of the executives' time and two-thirds of their activities.)

5. Managers maintain working relationships with three principal groups: superiors, subordinates, and outsiders.[17]

This research suggests a great deal about the ways in which administrators go about making decisions, particularly about why few seem to use formal decision-making models in their work. The rhythm of the administrator's workday constitutes a driving force that evokes behavior in ways that are not likely to enter the mind of the contemplative scholar pondering the logic he or she seeks to find in the situation. As Mintzberg noted:

> The work of managing an organization may be described as taxing. The quantity of work to be done, or that the manager chooses to do, during the day is substantial and the pace is unrelenting. After hours, the chief executive (and probably many other managers as well) appears to be able to escape neither from an environment that recognizes the power and status of his position nor from his own mind, which has been well trained to search continually for new information.[18]

Why do managers maintain such a pace and such a workload? Mintzberg thinks it is because the job is inherently open-ended and ambiguous:

> The manager must always keep going, never sure when he has succeeded, never sure when his whole organization may come down around him because of some miscalculation. As a result, the manager is a person with perceptual preoccupation. He can never be free to forget his job, and he never has the pleasure of knowing, even temporarily, that there is nothing else he can do. No matter what kind of managerial job he has, he always carries the nagging suspicion that he might be able to contribute just a little bit more.[19]

In conducting his observations of the administrators he studied, Mintzberg developed a technique that required the frequent recording of code symbols that described behaviors being observed during numerous small time frames during the day. Eventually, these coded entries were reduced and arrayed statistically to produce a detailed, quantified description of the observable behaviors that occurred over the total period of time during which observations were carried out.

A number of studies using the "Mintzberg technique" have examined the on-the-job behavior of such educational administrators as superintendents of schools and school principals.[20] These have substantially confirmed that Mintzberg's propositions apply to the work of school administrators. These administrators work long hours at an unrelenting pace. Their work is characterized by many brief interactions, mostly verbal. Meetings, phone calls, and paperwork account for almost every minute from the moment they enter the office in the morning until they leave in the afternoon or evening.

Mintzberg's use of the term "unrelenting pace" needs a little clarification here. One could conjure up the image of an assembly-line worker being driven at his or her task by the inexorable onrush of work coming down the line, never stopping, never varying. This is not what Mintzberg appeared to mean in describing the work of managers. In the manager's work situation, time becomes an important resource. Unlike the situation of the teacher, however, time for the administrator is a fluid resource rather than a constraining one.

For the teacher, critical time constraints (such as the school year, the school day, the bell schedule, and fixed constraints such as bus schedules and lunch schedules) sharply limit what he or she can do. Administrators, on the other hand, can—and often do—have considerable latitude to vary the pace of their work as it seems appropriate to them. They can take extra time to carefully consider some even unimportant issues at length, if they wish, and seek to save time by making a series of rapid decisions on other matters. Or the administrator who wishes to do so can vary the use of time resources by stretching the workday into the evening, or the workweek into the weekend, and the workyear into the summer and holidays. This is, of course, what many educational administrators commonly do. Thus, the "unrelenting pace" is not necessarily an unvarying pace; it is one in which characteristically the work to be done is never completed, and there is always more to be done. One never knows when the task is finished.

These characteristics of administrative work combine with the ambiguity inherent in the educational system—an ambiguity arising from the unclear goals and priorities of schools and school systems, uncertain methods of evaluating administrative performance, and problematic preferences exercised by various constituency groups—to put considerable pressure on educational administrators. One result, and an additional source of pressure, is that they—like administrators in other fields—seldom stop thinking about their work.[21]

How Administrators Think

Recent research suggests that a source of confusion in the minds of scholars who study organizations and the behavior of administrators in them may be the fact that academic people and administrators tend to think about administrative work in different ways. The models for decision making described in the beginning of this chapter are the products of persons conditioned in the belief that highly logical, linear thinking, sometimes called "scientific thinking," is the single most appropriate way of exploring problems and seeking alternatives in the decision-making process. Largely academics, such observers tend to expect to see administrators behave in much the same ways that they themselves do. They maintain, that is, "that thinking is visible in the form of long reflective episodes during which managers sit alone, away from the action, trying to make logical inferences from facts. Since observers do not see many episodes that look like this, they conclude that managers do not do much thinking."[22] Indeed, much of the in-service training for administrators that emphasizes the so-called models for decision making is little more than an effort to train administrators in formal methods of reflective thought. The assumption underlying such training is that one can improve the decision-making behavior of administrators by improving their skills in logical, reflective thought.

But why is it that researchers report so few occasions in which administrators are observed, as scientists frequently are, thinking reflectively—cogitating, mulling over a problem, considering alternatives in the dispassionate calm of a quiet retreat? Karl Weick proposes three possible explanations. First, they do think but not while they are on the job: "they think at home, on airplanes, in the john, on weekends. . . . Thus, the reason researchers do not see managers think is that managers do not think when the observers are around."[23] The second possibility is that, essentially, managers don't think because they have reduced uncertainty to such an extent and anticipate the future so well that they are confronted by few situations in which they are perplexed or bewildered. The third possibility proposed by Weick (and the one he considers most likely) is that managers think all the time but researchers have missed that fact because, while researchers look for episodes evidencing reflective thinking, managers go at the thinking process quite differently. That is, thinking is inseparably woven into, and occurs simultaneously with, managerial and administrative action.

Thus, when administrators tour, read, talk, supervise, and meet with others, all of those actions contain thought and, indeed, they *are* the ways in which administrators do their thinking. "Connected ideas, which are the essence of thought," Weick explains, "can be formed and managed *outside* the mind, with relatively little assistance from the mind. This is how managers work, and this is why we are misled when we use reflection as an index of how much their work involves thinking."[24] Thus, most of the thinking that administrators do is woven into their actions when their actions are taken with attention, intention, and control; that is, they pay attention to what is happening, impose order on their actions, and correct their performance when it strays from accepted standards.[25]

In considering the ways in which administrators think about their work, it is important to bear in mind that the organizational environment in which the work is done is characterized by ambiguity, uncertainty, and disorder: it is, in a word, messy. Situations that require decisions are often fluid and, therefore, difficult to analyze even after the fact; they are subject to a number of interpretations, often conflicting; and (as will be explained more fully later) they are often not clearly bounded and labeled. In the daily flow of action, administrators typically engage in brief, spontaneous, face-to-face, verbal interaction with others. They are, in other words, constantly "fighting fires." But

fighting fires, which managers do all the time, is not necessarily thick-headed or slow witted. Firefighting has seemed like mindless activity because we have used scientific activity as the ideal case for comparison, because we have thought of thinking as a separate activity that stops when people put out fires, because we have presumed that the only time people think is when they make distinct decisions or solve clearcut problems . . . and because we keep examining things as if they occurred in sequences rather than simultaneously.[26]

A crucial issue is implied in this view: whether administration is, or can be, a science in the traditional sense or whether it is, instead, an art or a craft. Many continue to pursue the notion of administration as the application of management science to organizational problems (much as engineering is the application of physics and mathematics to other sorts of real-world problems), as envisioned earlier in the twentieth century. Those holding this view tend, of course, to emphasize the development of technical rationality in organizational decision making. Others, however—cognizant of the great complexities of human organizations and the uncertainty, instability, and uniqueness that are commonly found in them—recognize the importance of intuitive judgment and skill, the sense of proportion and appropriateness in the context of the traditions and values of the organization's culture. Schön, like Weick, found the thinking of managers closely entwined with the action demanded in their work. He observed:

> Managers do reflect in action. Sometimes, when reflection is triggered by uncertainty, the manager says, in effect, "This is puzzling; how can I understand it?" Sometimes, when a sense of opportunity provokes reflection, the manager asks, "What can I make of this?" And sometimes, when a manager is surprised by the success of his own intuitive knowing, he asks himself, "What have I really been doing?"[27]

Thus, Schön makes clear that the term *art* has a twofold meaning in describing administration: intuitive approaches to understanding situations and also one's reflection, in a context of action, when one encounters events that are incongruent with his or her intuitive understandings.

The reader should note carefully that, in this discussion, we are talking about *trained* intuition.[28] The point is that we can learn—through both formal education and socialization into the organization's culture—to see a complex system as an organic whole as well as being trained (as we commonly are) to see individual parts of the whole. This crucial point is difficult for some observers to accept, perhaps for two main reasons. One is that, in the strong tradition of technical rationality that has long been emphasized in Western culture, the logic of breaking complex phenomena down into relatively simple, quantifiable parts has been thoroughly ingrained in many of us. It seems so sensible, so right, that holistic approaches to complex problems are suspect. It is also probable that recent research on right- and left-hemisphere brain functioning is important to our understanding here. One mode of consciousness, associated with the left hemisphere, is generally described as analytic, rational, sequential, convergent, logical, objective, and linear. The other, associated with the right hemisphere, is characterized as intuitive, holistic, pattern-recognizing, artistic, subjective, and nonlinear. Unquestionably, emphasis has been placed on training left-brain functions in education that stresses logical-positivistic approaches to decision making. If we are to improve the way we apply right-hemisphere functioning to our decision making, it is likely that we will also have to improve our training strategies.[29]

Thus, it is argued that administrators are thinking all the time, that their thinking is closely intertwined with the actions (decisions) they take, and that everyday thinking almost never represents a sequence of steps. This suggests that formal models for decision making have little relevance to everyday administrative thinking and that to try to implement them would run counter to the real world as administrators experience it. In that world, problem situations are experienced holistically and the steps found in the usual decision-making models are considered simultaneously rather than serially. This view suggests that emphasis on holistic thought—which seeks understanding of the complexities, interconnections, ambiguities and uncertainties of educational organizations—might be more fruitful in decision making than the linear and step models proffered in the past.

The Influence of Organizational Culture on Decision Making

Earlier in this book, the concept of organizational culture was discussed as being at the core of understanding organizational behavior such as decision making. Organizational culture involves the norms that develop in a work group, the dominant values advocated by the organization, the philosophy that guides the organization's policies concerning employees and client groups, and the feeling that is evident in the ways in which people interact with one another. Thus, it clearly deals with basic assumptions and beliefs that are shared by members of the organization. Taken together, these define the organization itself in crucial ways: why it exists, how it has survived, what it is about. In the process of developing and becoming part of the way of life in the organization, these values and basic beliefs tend to become solidly—almost unquestioningly—established as "the way we do things here." In this way, they shape the view of the world that members bring to problems and decision making. We speak of "intuition" in the processes of thinking; organizational culture plays a large role in shaping that intuition in that the assumptions and beliefs that compose the essence of organizational culture are largely taken for granted by participants. This is especially so in educational organizations inasmuch as those who work in them are generally highly socialized to the values and central beliefs of the organization through long years of commitment to them.

Consider the educational and work history of professionals in schools and institutions of higher education. Most of these people entered school at the age of five or (at most) six years and have remained in educational organizations, with only brief absences (such as for military service or child rearing), virtually continuously throughout their formative years and the later years in which they established themselves as full adult members of society. As a result, they strongly tend to have "bought into" the values of education and educational organizations and, as professionals in these organizations, are highly committed to their core values, central beliefs, and goals. In the long process of being so thoroughly socialized into the organization—first as pupil, then as student, and, ultimately, as professional—those who work in educational organizations tend strongly to accept the "rules of the game" for getting along and "the ropes" that must be learned in order to become accepted as a member.[30]

In other words, these individuals become members of a set of persons who have a long history of sharing common experiences. These shared experiences have, over time, led to the creation of a shared view of the world and their place in it.[31] This shared view enables people in the organization to make sense of commonplace as well as unusual events, ascribe meaning to symbols and rituals, and share in a common understanding of how to deal with unfolding action in appropriate ways. Such sense making is described by Karl Weick as being central to understanding how people in organizations attribute credibility to interpretations that they have made of their experience.[32] Such a shared view is developed over a period of time during which the participants engage in a great deal of communicating, testing, and refinement of the shared view until it is eventually perceived to have been so effective for so long that it is rarely thought about or talked about anymore: it is taken for granted.[33] This constitutes the development of an *organizational culture.* And it is culture that largely determines how one perceives and understands the world; it is the concept that captures the subtle, elusive, intangible, largely unconscious forces that shape thought in a workplace.[34]

Mintzberg's analysis, which is supported by a number of studies in educational organizations, makes it clear that administrators spend little time in reflective thought. They are active; they spend much of their time communicating, interruptions are frequent, and they have little opportunity to be alone in peace and quiet. But, as Schön and Weick have pointed out, that does not necessarily mean that administrators do not think: it means that their thinking is closely intertwined with their action on the job.

But is their thinking merely random, perhaps geared to the last person they talked with or the latest crisis that has emerged? Probably not. Organizational culture is a powerful environment that reflects past experiences, summarizes them, and distills them into simplifications that help to explain the enormously complex world of the organization. In this sense, the organization—the school, the university—may be understood as a body of thought[35] that has evolved over time and that guides the administrator in understanding what is going on and how to deal with it. This body of thought embodies a highly complex array of subtleties, inconsistencies, and competing truths: it reflects the complexities and delicate balances of the administrator's world. Efforts to reduce this complexity through such simplification processes as imposing decision-making models on it are not likely to be very workable. In this view, therefore, the culture of the organization represents significant thinking prior to action and is implicit in the decision-making behavior of administrators.

The role and power of organizational culture to shape and mold the thinking and, therefore, the decision making of people in organizations is not a new concept by any means. However, only in relatively recent years has it received widespread serious attention from organizational analysts and administrative practitioners alike as an approach to improving the decision making of organizations.

Closing the Gap between Theory and Practice

What guidance does the theoretic and research literature offer for practicing administrators attempting to implement these newer concepts in decision making? One answer is that in selecting an administrative style to use in practice, one needs to examine one's assumptions as to what is the most effective approach to administrative practice. Let us consider briefly how some of the important points of this book come together at this juncture to see where they lead us in administrative decision making.

Administration has been defined as *working with and through people to achieve organizational goals.* It has long been accepted that the functions of administration are planning, organizing, leading, coordinating, and controlling. But the persistent puzzling issue throughout the twentieth century was, what are the most effective ways of performing these functions? As we have described, there are conflicting ways to approach administrative practice: classical approaches and human resources approaches are the leading contenders among the currently competing systems of analysis through which administrative practice is interpreted. Except for those administrators who choose to pursue a mindless eclectic course in their professional work, the administrator must choose between these competing systems of analysis in deciding how to go about his or her professional work. The choice that the administrator chooses to embrace rests largely on the assumptions about the nature of organizations and the people in them.

Theory of Practice

The assumptions that form the foundations of one's professional practice constitute, in the language of Chris Argyris and Donald Schön, a "theory of practice." But we do not always practice what we preach: the actual theory of practice that one uses in deciding what to do is not always explicit, clear, and well reasoned. Indeed, given human frailty, we often espouse one theory and actually act on the basis of another, perhaps conflicting, theory. Therefore, we commonly witness administrators verbalizing their commitment to values that support improving the quality of work life in educational organizations while engaging in actions that are perceived by role referents to be antithetical to such improvement. Thus, as individuals—often enlightened and well intended—we act out the conflict between opposing ideas about organizations and people that has characterized organizational theory for decades.

Human Resources Development

There is a pattern in the history of the competition between the two major conflicting systems of analysis. Over the course of the twentieth century, the classical (or bureaucratic) approach gradually lost credibility in the analysis of *educational* organizations at least, as the organizational problems of schools and universities deepened even as the application of bureaucratic attempts at solution grew and multiplied. Simultaneously, as more sophisticated research was pushed forward, the credibility and usefulness of human resources approaches grew steadily, and that pattern seems likely to continue into the foreseeable future. This pattern is clearly evident in the body of research literature that is being discussed in this book. It is called "human resources development" (HRD). HRD is based on the overlapping theories and concepts of such scholars as Douglas McGregor, Abraham Maslow, Frederick Herzberg, Chris Argyris, Rensis Likert, James March, Karl Weick, and William Ouchi.

McGregor described two sets of conflicting assumptions that administrators tend to hold about people and their attitudes toward work: Theory X, the belief that people are lazy and will avoid work if they can, and Theory Y, the belief that people seek responsibility and want to perform satisfying work. These concepts are now well understood by many administrators.

Maslow's concept of motivation is based on a hierarchy of prepotent needs in which satisfied needs are seen as not motivating people but in which yet unsatisfied needs can be motivators.

Herzberg's work identified "maintenance" factors, such as compensation and working conditions, as not being motivators but as being essential in order for such motivating factors as satisfaction arising from achievement in the work itself and a sense of autonomy on the job to be effective.

Likert conceptualized four management styles (System 1–System 4), each using different styles of leadership, motivation, and conflict management that have predictable outcomes in terms of organizational culture as well as end results in terms of organizational effectiveness. Further, and perhaps more important, Likert pointed out that it is the administrator—who has options from which to choose in deciding what the philosophy of management is to be, how communication is to be carried out, and how decisions shall be made in the organization—who bears major responsibility for the culture that develops in an organization.

Vroom and Yetton lent strong support to Likert's views by demonstrating that administrators are key actors in controlling decision making in the organization, and that this control is exercised by the decision-making style that administrators choose to use.

Argyris's work emphasized the need to develop greater harmony and consistency between the goals of organizations and the human needs of people who work in them, and that this requires replacing directive administrative styles with more participative styles.

James March pointed out that ambiguity and uncertainty characterize the natural state of affairs in organizations, rather than the patterns of predictability and order that administrators have traditionally sought to find in them. Thus, streams of problems, solutions, participants, and opportunities for making choices swirl around, occasionally resulting in decisions, though rarely arrived at in the orderly sequential fashion usually envisioned by formal rational decision-making models.

Karl Weick made it clear that, instead of the close hierarchical cause-and-effect linkages that classical theory assumes to be present in organizations, the instructional activities of schools are characteristically loosely coupled. This loose coupling not only calls traditional assumptions about management methods into question but also creates new visions of how schools can be managed so as to reduce the rigidity and ineffectiveness so frequently observed in them.

William Ouchi and others—including Terrence Deal, Rosabeth Moss Kanter, Edgar Schein, and Marshall W. Meyer—have explained that there are various ways of exercising administrative control in organizations. Although traditional bureaucratic hierarchy is one way, and is often thought to be the only way, in fact, the norms of the culture of an organization evolving throughout its history are an exceedingly powerful means through which administrators exercise influence over others. Furthermore, they explain, the cultures of some organizations are more effective than others in implementing HRD concepts of motivation, leadership, conflict management, decision making, and change.

These HRD perspectives on organization provide a set of assumptions on which to base the practice of administration that are clear alternatives to classical perspectives. Whereas those who choose to use classical bureaucratic perspectives on organization continue to push hard for reducing ambiguity through increasing use of rules and close surveillance, striving for greater logic and predictability through more planning, increased specification of objectives, and tighter hierarchical control, contemporary best thinking in management emphasizes tapping the motivations and abilities of participants while recognizing that disorder and illogic are often ordinary characteristics of effective organizations. Taken together, the assumptions of HRD constitute a theory of decision making, the centerpiece of which is participative methods. Lately, it has been increasingly called the "empowerment" of others.

Participative Decision Making

Much of decision making revolves around issues of participation in solving problems and making decisions. *Participation* is defined as the mental and emotional involvement of a person in a group situation that encourages the individual to contribute to group goals and to share responsibility for them.[36]

Participation in this sense is "mental and emotional involvement"; this is the notion of "ownership" of (or "buying into") decisions. It is genuine ego involvement, not merely being present and "going through the motions." Such involvement is motivating to the participant and, thus, it releases his or her own energy, creativity, and initiative. This is what distinguishes participation from *consent,* which is the major feature of voting on issues or approving proposals.[37] This ego involvement, this sense of ownership, also encourages people to accept greater responsibility for the organization's effectiveness. Having "bought into" the goals and the decisions of the group, the individual sees himself or herself as having a stake in seeing them work out well. This, in turn, stimulates the development of teamwork so characteristic of effective organizations.

The use of participative decision making has two major potential benefits: (1) arriving at better decisions and (2) enhancing the growth and development of the organization's participants (for example, greater sharing of goals, improved motivation, improved communication, better-developed group-process skills). As a practical guide for implementing participative processes in educative organizations, three factors in particular should be borne in mind: (1) the need for an explicit decision-making process, (2) the nature of the problem to be solved or the issue to be decided, and (3) criteria for including people in the process.

Participative Decision Making and Empowerment

Participative decision making requires the interaction of power and influence from two sources: the power and influence of the administrator and the power and influence of others in the organization. In educational organizations these others are generally faculty members, students, and/or community members. When the organization is conceptualized as a traditional bureaucracy, which emphasizes the top-down exercise of hierarchical power, the power of administrators is ordinarily viewed as being in conflict with that of others. Indeed, in such a view the administrator tends to consider it important to husband power, expand it if possible, and limit the power and influence of others. Unionized teachers, on the other hand, consider it important to resist the expansion of the administrator's power and seek to enlarge their own power. These are important elements in establishing and maintaining control of decision making in the organization when the participants are responding to traditional values and beliefs.

Administrators who embrace these traditional views of organization and administration may view the management of participative decision making in the organization as requiring a conflict management approach. In the traditional organization, characterized by boss–worker relationships that we now tend to associate with the stereotypic factory model, the power and influence of the administrator dominates the decision-making process and the followers have little ability to influence the course of events. As Tannenbaum and Schmidt depict in Figure 9.2, this is the situation in which the administrator decides what is to be done and communicates the decision to others to be carried out. But you will notice that this is only the starting point in a dimension of possible behaviors along which the administrator may choose to recognize the power of others to exercise influence on the process. This is the basis for the concept of empowering others in the school.

As Tannenbaum and Schmidt see it, the next step that increases the freedom of followers to influence decision making may occur when the administrator seeks to have followers approve and "buy into" the decision when it is announced to be implemented. This often requires some "selling" of the new idea to the followers. As Figure 9.2 shows, the administrator has a range of other options by which the role of followers in the process may be expanded and their power in decision making increased. For example, referring to the diagram, we can see a possible progression:

- First, permit followers to ask questions after a decision is taken.
- Then offer a tentative decision subject to possible change after discussion with followers, before the administrator finalizes the decision.
- Next, present the problem to followers, and make a decision only after discussion with them to get their opinions.
- And so on until, finally, the organization has the possibility of making many of its most important decisions in a highly collegial and collaborative way.

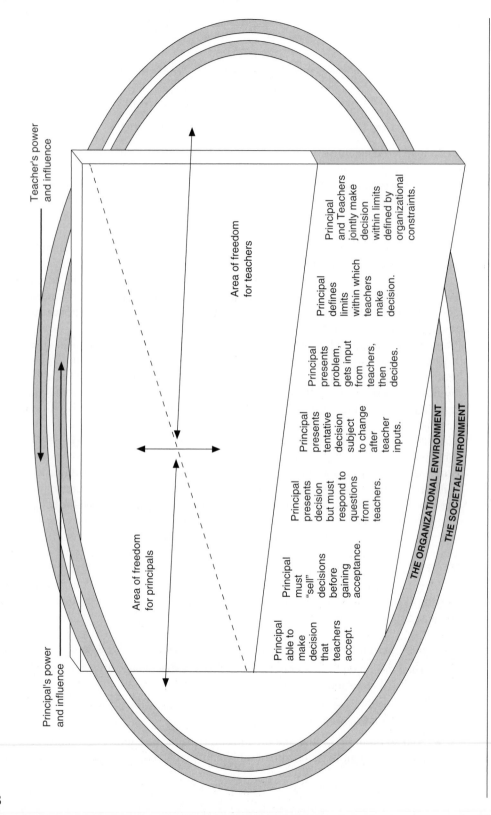

FIGURE 9.2 Leadership style is evident in a range of possible behaviors. Adapted from Robert Tannenbaum and Warren H. Schmidt, "How to Choose a Leadership Pattern," *Harvard Business Review*, 51 (May–June 1973), p. 167. Copyright © 1973 by the President and Fellows of Harvard College; all rights reserved.

The following labels appear within the figure:

Teacher's power and influence

Principal's power and influence

Area of freedom for principals

Area of freedom for teachers

THE ORGANIZATIONAL ENVIRONMENT

THE SOCIETAL ENVIRONMENT

Principal able to make decision that teachers accept.

Principal must "sell" decisions before gaining acceptance.

Principal presents decision but must respond to questions from teachers.

Principal presents tentative decision subject to change after teacher inputs.

Principal presents problem, gets input from teachers, then decides.

Principal defines limits within which teachers make decision.

Principal and Teachers jointly make decision within limits defined by organizational constraints.

In traditional organizations, which are markedly hierarchical, the process of deciding how to make decisions is largely controlled by the administrator, not the followers. In such a case, the progress of the organization from autocratic decision making toward collaborative decision making resides largely in the extent to which the administrator sees power sharing as a win-win proposition, a desirable state of affairs, rather than a threat to administrative hegemony. Many present-day educational organizations, though still hierarchical, have developed collaborative cultures to such an extent that reverting to the more primitive autocratic model would be difficult: the administrator is not so much confronted with the issue of whether others will be involved in decision making but, rather, how and to what extent they will be involved.

Participative or Democratic?

One of the most common, and most serious, errors that leaders can make in organizational decision making is to confuse participative decision making with democratic decision making. In my consulting work with schools it is commonplace to hear a principal exclaim, "Democratic decision making doesn't work! I can't hold a meeting and call for a vote every time we need to make a decision! There just isn't time for that." And that is quite right. Moreover, the teachers do not want to be involved in making every decision; they haven't time for *that,* either. This is where the Tannenbaum-Schmidt model can be very useful both to the administrator and in training the staff about participation. Let's look at some of the issues involved.

In the first place, the concept of democracy is a political one: it refers to government by the people, either directly or through representatives. It generally implies majority rule as determined by voting. It also rests on a specific concept about the relationship between the government and the governed: the governed, the body politic, exercise ultimate power over the government in the voting booth. Though we commonly think of the government as being at the top of a hierarchical organization with the people at the bottom, this is, as you know, a little misleading because in the end the Constitution really has created a government of the people, by the people, and for the people. This concept does not translate to educational organizations.

Educational organizations are inherently hierarchical. The school board is created by the body politic; it simply is not the province of teachers, for example, to control the organization by vote. The board can, and usually does, appoint a superintendent of schools and create an organization through which it manages the schools in the district. Traditionally, school boards have managed the school system directly by creating a central office bureaucracy that reports to the board. A commonplace complaint about school boards is that the boards tend to micromanage to a fault. One of the current hot-button approaches to school reform challenges that time-honored arrangement and proposes that school boards should stop managing schools directly. School boards can do this by using school site management organization, in which individual schools have a much freer hand to make their own decisions but are responsible to the school board for educational results. Alternatively, school boards can enter into contracts with other entities, such as charter school boards or for-profit school management corporations, to operate the schools and be responsible to the school board for educational results. However, the bottom line is that at the school district level the organization is hierarchical, and power is exercised asymmetrically from the top down.

At the school level there surely may be certain issues that, from time to time, the principal might wish to have decided by a ballot of the teachers. But there is scant support in scholarly and research literature for turning the affairs of the school over to the ballot box. School principals and other administrators are educational leaders, and we have discussed the relationship between followers and leaders by which leaders are granted power to act as leaders. The models that have been presented in this chapter (that of Vroom and Yetton and particularly that of Tannenbaum and Schmidt) provide the leader guidance in organizing and managing *participative* decision making, and that should not be confused with *democratic* decision making.

The Tannenbaum-Schmidt model emphasizes the different kinds of behavior exhibited by both the leader and the followers as the participation of the followers becomes more involved and more responsible. Sometimes, on some issues, teachers do want and expect the principal to make decisions and tell them clearly what the decision is. Clearly, this is time efficient for everyone and is a normal way of operating on relatively simple and routine matters. However, at other times and on other issues teachers want to be more involved—and the greater their involvement, the more time is required of them, and teachers are busy people. For that simple and practical reason, therefore, teachers usually participate in making joint decisions with the principal on a relatively limited number of issues that are considered to be very important. The principal can, however, find many kinds of appropriate ways to involve others in decision making so that participation is optimized yet the process is time efficient.

In participative decision making, all organizational members have the right to be heard, to have their views considered, to express feelings, to offer knowledge and information. Thus, they have a right to be part of the process. However, as Tannenbaum and Schmidt have clearly shown, there is a broad range of ways in which the input from participants may be sought and used in the process. As the organization becomes experienced in participative methods, it may very well shift over time from the traditional top-down model across a range of optional ways of working together to the level of true collaboration. However, nowhere in this process is it inherent that the leader is bound by vote of subordinates. In that sense, a school is not a democracy, at its best it is a participative organization.

An Explicit Decision-Making Process

Participation can mean many things. All too often, the process, when not properly attended to, can be seen by participants as vague and ill defined. Under such conditions, people are not sure when to participate or what their proper role is in the process.

The most important decision that a group makes is to *decide how it will make decisions.* This is often one of the most inexplicit facts of organizational life: not uncommonly, people literally do not know who makes decisions or how they are made, let alone know how they individually may participate in the process. It is important, therefore, for the organization to develop an *explicit, publicly known* set of processes for making decisions that is *acceptable to its participants.*

The best time to grapple with this problem is before it is necessary to make a decision. One illustrative way of initiating this process is to convene a meeting of a school faculty (or other work group) for the purpose of reviewing the recent performance of the group. After selecting a few *specific,* recent, decision-making episodes, the group can assess its experience by asking a few questions, such as these: What were the processes by which this decision was reached? Do we all agree that we know how the decision was reached? How do we feel about that way of solving this problem? Should we use similar procedures next time or should we make some changes? What suggestions are there for (1) identifying and defining problems, (2) deciding how to deal with them (and who should be involved), and (3) keeping everyone informed as to what is going on?

Simple steps such as these can begin to focus on the importance attached to the *way* that problems are defined and dealt with—a focus on group process. To be successful, it must be accompanied by an emphasis on developing a climate in the group that supports open communication and stresses the skills required for revealing and working through differences among members of the group.

Readers who seek more specific suggestions and advice on developing explicit decision-making processes in the organization may find it useful to consult the following:

Bradford, Leland P., *Making Meetings Work: A Guide for Leaders and Group Members.* La Jolla, CA: University Associates, 1976.
> The old master shows—among other things—how to turn apathy and indifference into involvement and concern, how to use conflict constructively, and how to arrive at a decision.

Doyle, Michael, and David Straus, *How to Make Meetings Work.* Chicago: Playboy Press, 1976.
> This explicit do-it-yourself manual shows how to make meetings more productive by applying concepts of participative decision making. Excellent for staff development.

Dunsing, Richard J., *You and I Have Simply Got to Stop Meeting This Way.* New York: AMACOM, 1977.
> Emphasizes the need to tailor your approach to meetings based on careful analysis of specific needs in your situation.

Likert, Rensis, and Jane Gibson Likert, "Integrative Goals and Consensus in Problem Solving," in *New Ways of Managing Conflict.* New York: McGraw-Hill Book Company, 1976.
> Excellent short chapter clearly discusses the nature of consensus and its importance to group problem solving.

Schindler-Rainman, Eva, and Ronald Lippitt, with Jack Cole, *Taking Your Meetings out of the Doldrums.* La Jolla, CA: University Associates, 1975.
> A treasure trove of detailed suggestions for making sure that meetings are productive and stimulating.

Schmuck, Richard A., "Developing Collaborative Decision-Making: The Importance of Trusting, Strong and Skillful Leaders," *Educational Technology,* 12, no. 10 (October 1972), 43–47.
> The entire issue of this journal is devoted to organization development in schools.

Schmuck, Richard A., Philip J. Runkel, Janet H. Arends, and Richard I. Arends, *The Second Handbook of Organizational Development in Schools.* Palo Alto, CA: Mayfield Publishing Company, 1977.
> This practical guide to applying organizational development theory and concepts to the improvement of schools is an invaluable resource for the practicing educational leader.

Smith, Carole E., *Better Meetings: A Handbook for Trainers of Policy Councils and Other Decision-Making Groups.* Atlanta: Humanics Press, 1975.

   A must for those meetings that bring school staff members and community people together for joint decision making.

Who Identifies the Problem?

Many would contend that as one contemplates involving others in creating an explicit group decision-making process, an even more fundamental question must be confronted— who decides what problem requires a collaborative solution or decision? For, as has been said many times, the most important step in making a decision is to define the problem. Whoever defines the problem literally controls the decision-making process.

   With this in mind, if you look again at the Schmidt-Tannenbaum model, you will notice that at the lowest levels of group involvement, it is the administrator who decides not only what the problem is but what the solution is. However, as one increases the freedom of others to participate in the decision-making process—that is, as one increases the empowerment of the group—a central factor is, who defines the problem? The trend toward greater empowerment of others is marked by the administrator tending to identify the problem but leaving the options for solving the problem somewhat open to others. At the highest levels of participation, the administrator and the other participants become involved in a more genuine collaborative process of, first, mutually agreeing on the definition of the problem itself and, second, jointly deciding how to deal with it.

Emergent and Discrete Problems

Participative decision making has salience primarily because it tends to produce decisions of better quality than those reached by even highly capable individuals. But some kinds of problems are best solved by expert individuals, whereas other kinds of problems are best solved by groups. To achieve decisions of the highest possible quality, therefore, it is necessary to analyze the situation. Indeed, one of the indicators of a highly skilled group is that its members are able to make such analyses, thereby knowing what problems the group should try to work through and what problems it should refer to appropriate experts.

   Some problems have the following characteristics: (1) the elements of the problem are relatively unambiguous, clear-cut, and often quantifiable; (2) the elements of the problem are readily separable; (3) the solution to the problem requires a logical sequence of acts that may be readily performed by one person; and (4) the boundaries of the whole problem are relatively easy to discern. Problems of this kind may be called *discrete,* and they may well be solved best by an expert individual.

   Some problems are quite different: (1) the elements of the problem are ambiguous, uncertain, and not readily quantifiable; (2) the elements of the problem are so dynamically intertwined that it is difficult to separate them on the basis of objective criteria (in fact, obtaining measurements may be difficult); (3) the solution to the problem requires the continued coordination and interaction of a number of people; and (4) the dimensions and nature of the problem cannot be fully known at the time of decision but will come into better view as iterative processes of dealing with the problem cause it to unfold over time. Such problems may be called *emergent*. The highest-quality solutions to problems of this kind are likely to come from a group of people who (1) are in the best position to possess among them the knowledge necessary to solve the problem and (2) will be involved in implementing the decision after it is made.

A typical discrete problem in a school district is handling school supplies. The myriad problems involved in consolidated purchasing, warehousing, and distributing supplies to schools are relatively clear-cut and can be ordered into a logical sequence by an expert. Indeed, compared with the skilled business manager—with his or her intimate knowledge of the budget, contract law, purchasing procedures, and the vagaries of the school supply market—a group of school district administrators trying to deal with the problem of getting the right supplies at the right price to the right places on time could well be a matter of the blind leading the blind. Similarly, laying out school bus routes for maximum economy and efficiency is normally a discrete problem. The use of mathematical models and computer simulations, now relatively common in larger districts, requires the use of experts who have the requisite technical skills and the techniques for grasping the full dimensions of the problem.

Policy issues in public education, on the other hand, are very often emergent problems. The matter of implementing competency-based education, for example, clearly qualifies as an emergent problem. Often the issue confronts school district administrators on the level of "How shall we implement the decision that has been handed down to us?" rather than in terms of "Should we do it?"

As every educator knows, concepts of competency-based education involve many facets of the school enterprise in dynamic interrelationship, and certainly the specialized knowledge of many individuals in the system must be brought to bear on the problem in highly coordinated fashion even to understand the problem. Therefore a decision to undertake such an endeavor will require commitment to the program by many people, continuous close collaboration and free flow of communication, and recognition that success depends upon an iterative process of decision making as the extent and implications of the problem become apparent.

Many of the problems encountered in the course of day-to-day administrative practice are emergent. Indeed, as education grows more complex, there appears to be less and less certitude that many important issues can be resolved by experts who pass their solutions on to others to implement. Appropriate solutions require free and open communication among a number of individuals who pool and share information. Close collaboration is necessary to weigh and evaluate information in the process of developing an informed judgment as to which of several alternatives might be best. Commitment to the implementation of the solution is essential in order to maintain the collaboration that is the basis of the iterative processes of decision making.

Who Should Participate?

A commonly held erroneous assumption that is often made about participative decision making is that its intent is to involve everyone in every decision. Clearly, this is neither practical nor desirable. Edwin Bridges has suggested two rules for identifying decisions in which it is appropriate for teachers to participate:

1. *The test of relevance.* "[W]hen the teacher's personal stakes in the decision are high," Bridges has stated, "their interest in participation should also be high."[38] Problems that clearly meet this test concern teaching methods and materials, discipline, curriculum, and organizing for instruction.

2. *The test of expertise.* It is not enough for the teacher to have a stake in the decision; if his or her participation is to be significant, the teacher must be competent to contribute effectively. In dealing with the physical education department's program schedule, for example, English teachers may be fitted by training and experience to contribute little or nothing.

I would add that there is a significant third test to use in deciding about which problems the teachers should be consulted:

3. *The test of jurisdiction.* Schools are organized on a hierarchical basis; the individual school and staff have jurisdiction only over those decision-making areas that are assigned to them, either by design or by omission. Problems may be *relevant* to teachers, and the teachers may have the requisite *expertise*, but—right or wrong—they may not have *jurisdiction*. Participation in making decisions that the group cannot implement can lead to frustration at least as great as that caused by simple nonparticipation.

Desire of Individuals to Participate

Another practical consideration is whether individuals themselves wish to be involved in making a decision. The demands of time and personal interest inevitably require each person in the organization to establish (albeit imprecisely, perhaps) some priorities for his or her own time and energies. Chester Barnard pointed out that there are some things in which some individuals simply are not interested: he spoke of such matters as falling within the individual's *zone of indifference.*[39] To seek active involvement of teachers in matters to which they are essentially indifferent is, of course, to court resistance in various forms. It is common, for example, for school principals to seek involvement of teachers, either on a limited basis (for example, limiting participation to expressing views and opinions) or on low-level problems (reserving important decisions for themselves). There is little wonder that teachers are often indifferent to such participation.

There are areas of decision making in which teachers take great personal interest over a sustained period of time; in effect, this area may be described as a *zone of sensitivity.*[40] These matters represent "personal stakes," as it were, and could include such things as teaching assignments and evaluation of professional performance. When dealing with problems that fall within a staff's zone of sensitivity, a high degree of participation in a group-process mode of decision making would, of course, be indicated. The principal would enhance his or her authority with such involvement.

There is a third category of problems in which teachers have something at stake but not enough to make them especially concerned as individuals. These fall in the *zone of ambivalence.*[41] For example, it may be difficult for everyone on the staff to become concerned about preparing the agenda for a professional conference day or scheduling an assembly program. Thus, to avoid needless negative feelings from teachers who feel that they are already overburdened by the unnecessary bureaucratic demands of administrators, involvement of teachers in problems of this sort has to be selective. To be effective, such involvement should be restricted. (For example, have a small representative group deal with the problem or simply be sure to keep everyone informed as the problem is processed to a decision).

Although there are undoubtedly clusters of issues to which teachers may be sensitive, ambivalent, or indifferent, it is not possible simply to assume these generalizations: some assessment should be part of the diagnosis in each situation. When the group is small, it is possible to do this through discussion. In dealing with larger groups, it may be useful to employ a paper-and-pencil inventory as a diagnostic aid. One such technique used by Robert Owens and Edward Lewis in a large senior high school reveals that interest in participating in certain issues may be associated with certain characteristics of teachers. For example, experienced teachers and inexperienced teachers on the same school staff may have dissimilar views toward participation in dealing with specific issues.[42] Thus, Owens and Lewis reported that probationary teachers had much higher interest in learning about such things as the policies and rules of the school, the curriculum that they were to teach, and procedures for supervisory evaluation of their work. Older teachers were more concerned about maintaining traditions of the school and issues pertaining to their involvement in key decisions in the school.

Team Administration

While much attention has recently been given to collaborative behavior within schools, it has also been seen as important in the administration of school districts, where it is usually called team administration. A defining concept of team administration is participative decision making. Robert Duncan stated it succinctly: "Team administration simply refers to genuine involvement—before the fact—of all levels of administration in goal-setting, decision-making, and problem-solving processes."[43] Similarly, a state association of school principals said:

> In place of the unilateral decisions which were made by the superintendent and passed down through the ranks to the level of final implementation, this new format would require a team approach to decision-making, providing an opportunity for all administrative and supervisory personnel to contribute . . . to the process. . . . In return for this participation on the part of . . . principals, the superintendent must be willing to demonstrate his confidence in group processes; he must involve individuals so that they may feel a part of the decisions which are made . . . he must understand that this type of involvement is imperative if the principal is to consider himself a member of an administrative team.[44]

Harold McNally concluded: "The administrative team is a group formally constituted by the board of education and the superintendent, comprising both central office and middle echelon administrative-supervisory personnel, with expressly stated responsibility and authority for participation in school system decision making."[45]

Administrative teams vary considerably in the techniques used for participation in making decisions. Five techniques are commonly found. Ranging from the least participation to the maximum, they are as follows:[46]

1. *Discussion.* Perhaps the simplest level of participation, the discussion of a problem is widely used to ascertain that team members are aware of the problem and that a decision about this problem must be made. When participation is limited to discussion, the administrator makes the decision, but he or she hopes that the others will accept the decision more readily than if he or she were to communicate the decision to them *before* discussion.

2. *Information seeking.* This technique of participation involves more than mere discussion; it also involves the administrator's obtaining information so as to facilitate making a more rational, logical decision.

These types of participation are most useful for decisions that fall within the participants' zone of indifference; presumably, the decisions involved would not be of vital interest to them, and each actual decision would be made by the administrator. The essential purposes of involving others at these levels would be (1) to help the administrator make a better decision and (2) to enhance the likelihood that the decision will be accepted by the group when it is made. To decide matters outside the members' zone of indifference—and to allow them to participate actively—other forms of involvement will be used:

3. *Democratic-centralist.* Undoubtedly the most commonly used procedure, this method consists of the administrator's presenting the problem to the staff and asking for suggestions, reactions, and ideas. The administrator will make the decision, but he or she will try to reflect the staff's participation in the decision.

4. *Parliamentarian.* When the team members themselves must make a decision but it does not appear likely that unanimity or even consensus will prevail, the parliamentarian technique is often used. It offers the great advantage of specifically providing for minority opinions, conflict of ideas and values, and shifting positions in time as issues, facts, and values change. It has the distinct disadvantage of creating winners and losers.

5. *Participant-determining.* The essential characteristic of this procedure is that consensus is required of the group. It would be used when (1) the issues are considered very important to the team members and (2) when it appears that consensus probably can be reached. Because consensus can be looked upon as pressure, the participant-determining method would probably not be used frequently. However, when it is used successfully, it is a powerful decision-making procedure.

Participation Requires High Level of Skills

One of the persistently underrecognized problems in implementing participative decision-making methods is the need to provide participants with training in the group process skills that are needed to make collaboration work well. The intention to collaborate in making decisions is simply not sufficient in itself. Moreover, it is insufficient that only the administrator be skilled in participative methods: it is essential that all participants understand and know how to play their roles effectively.

All too often, it is assumed that every educated adult knows how to take part in a meeting and do it well. That can be a mistake, especially if one seeks to develop collaborative, collegial participation in making decisions in the organization. The mistake becomes more serious as the importance of the decision increases and the consequences of the decision loom larger in the lives of the people involved. At its best, participative decision making in educational organizations uses collaborative group methods, whereas our larger society outside of the school generally emphasizes competitive group methods. For example, whenever we have a meeting, we often unthinkingly assume that the best way to make decisions is by voting, when, in fact, voting is a highly competitive process whereby some people become winners and others become losers. That may be highly appropriate in our democratic political system, but it is generally not appropriate in organizational decision making, wherein the goal is neither victory nor compromise but consensus and empowerment, not win-lose but win-win.

To date, the teaching and practice of collaborative group skills have been virtually absent from university programs of preparation for both teachers and administrators. Therefore, to engage in and develop participative decision making in education, it is important for decision-making groups to have adequate support in the form of access to on-the-job training and technical consultation to help members refine their skills as effective group members. Trust building, conflict management, problem solving, and open communication are among the important skill areas in which members of collaborative groups need ongoing support. Some training and skill development can be done through lectures and workshops, but third-party consultation, in which groups can get impartial feedback on the functioning of their group at work and reflect on their own experiences with the process, is essential.

A Paradigm for Decision Making

Confusion can be a very real hazard in organizational decision making. Unless participants know just what procedures the organization is using to arrive at decisions and what their own role and function will be in the procedures, the advantages ascribed to "democratic" or participatory decision making may well be nullified. It would be difficult to find research support for the possible contention that ambiguity in the decision-making processes in a school is somehow a virtue. In addition to knowing *how* people are to participate in decision making—that is, what their role and functions will be—they must know *when* they will participate.

It is also important that participants understand the orderly steps of the decision-making process as the organization moves toward a decision. These steps can be charted, and in so doing, some of the critical choices to be made can be seen more readily.

A skeleton of a proposed decision-making paradigm might resemble the one in Figure 9.3, which shows the four steps typically involved in reaching a decision: (1) defining the problem, (2) identifying possible alternatives, (3) predicting the consequences of each reasonable alternative, and (4) choosing the alternative to be followed.[47] In Figure 9.3 these four steps are identified by the numbers along the *time* dimension. In practice, individual administrators and their staffs might employ other series of steps, perhaps labeled differently; the suggested paradigm is readily adaptable to any sequence of decision-making behavior. Along the *behavior* dimension, a choice must be made as to who is going to perform each necessary decision-making function. Here, broken lines indicate choices of action that the administrator can elect to make: to involve the staff at any one step, at all of them, or, indeed, not to involve them at all.

In other words, when the administrator receives (or becomes aware of) information indicating the need for a decision, the choice is clear: he or she can either use or ignore the information. If the decision maker elects to act on the information, he or she can logically proceed either (1) by defining the problem or (2) by giving the information to the staff and asking them to define the problem. From then on, the process of decision making can comprise any combination of participation that the decision makers desire. The administrator can handle every phase of the process alone or can utilize any combination of participation by the staff. But we must bear in mind that the administrator has no monopoly on the initiation of participation. The concept of participative decision making requires that all members have access to means of initiating decision-making processes.

Conclusion

The wish to simplify organizational decision making and render it more rational has spawned a large number of decision-making models, each of which seeks to reveal the order and logic of organizational life. A commonplace puzzle, however, is that administrators are infrequently observed—even after training—using such models in their work or spending prolonged periods of time in episodes of reflective thinking. Recent research is giving rise to the understanding that (1) educational organizations and administrative work are far more complex than had formerly been believed and (2) administrators go about the thinking that precedes decision making in ways that differ significantly from that of scholars and researchers. Events in the organizational world rarely occur in a neat sequence; more rarely still does one thing occur at a time. Rather, the administrator is typically confronted with ambiguous circumstances in which a number of events are unfolding simultaneously, various goals and values of the school may be in conflict, and truth may take several forms, yet the need for decisions presses inexorably on at a relentless pace.

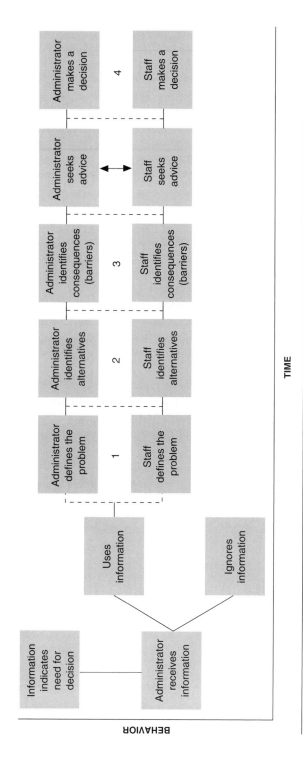

FIGURE 9.3 A paradigm for shared decision making in the school.

329

Furthermore, many organizational problems are ill understood at the time that decisions must be made. They may be described as being emergent problems—that is, they tend to be ambiguous and difficult to define, and the information needed to solve them is scattered among a number of people. Moreover, dealing with emergent problems leads to an iteration of diagnosis and solution by a process of successive approximation over time.

Under these conditions of ambiguity and uncertainty, which are connate characteristics of educational organizations, the trend in organizational decision making in education has been in the direction of empowering teachers and others to participate more fully in making important decisions. This trend is not merely an organizational response intended to placate individuals who have long felt alienated and even oppressed by the traditional top-down decision-making processes of hierarchical organizations. It is primarily intended to improve the quality of decisions by drawing on the knowledge and experience of key people who are closest to the action in the core enterprise of the school: teaching. At the same time, empowerment through participation in decision making tends to more adequately meet intrinsic motivational needs of individuals and to strengthen the growth-enhancing qualities of the organization's culture in ways and to a degree that traditional decision-making methods simply cannot match.

Shifting from traditional methods to participative methods requires administrators to develop a new understanding of power, a new sense of administrative wisdom. Traditionally, it was believed that only limited power was available in the organization and that the wise administrator would garner and husband all that was possible. Thus, empowering teachers and others to participate in decision making would be viewed by the administrator as losing power by giving it away to others. Modern empowering administrators, on the other hand, understand that one gains power by sharing it with others because in collaborative effort the power available to the group multiplies.

The intention to share power with others and increase participation in decision making is, in itself, insufficient to ensure success. Such efforts must be accompanied by the support of ongoing technical training and consultation to help all participants, administrators and others alike, to master the group process skills that are essential to making empowerment succeed. They must also be accompanied by the development of concrete and publicly known processes through which one participates in the collaborative process.

Reflective Activities

1. Make a list of "discrete" problems you believe typically should be handled by principals. Why do you believe the principal should categorize each of these areas as discrete?

2. With what type of "emergent" problems have you been involved when deciding on solutions in the past? Choose one memorable problem and describe the process that was used in the decision-making process. How was the leader involved in organizing the decision-making process? Was the solution acceptable to those in the organization?

3. *Working on Your Game Plan.* The morning after receiving the good news from Superintendent

Sidney Bennigan about being appointed principal to the JFK school, Marion put on a suit that had been bought expressly for the campaign to win the principalship and left home early so as to be sure to be on time at the superintendent's office. Once there—Bennigan, carefully groomed in conservative style as always—the two walked to the school district's Ford Crown Victoria that was one of the perks of the superintendency, and they were soon on their way to the school. Paying careful attention to the road while driving, Sid casually asked, "Well, how do you think you're going to start out at JFK? What do you think you'll do?"

"Well," Marion replied, "I really can't do very much for now, that is until Edith actually retires and I can move into the office in August and take over. I hope in the interim she will fill me in on some background stuff—you know, about the books and supplies that have been ordered, how the files are set up, the schedule, and all of that."

Driving along in silence for a few minutes with lips slightly pursed, Sid said, "Edith Avery is a fine person, and she has served this school district well. She won't push anything on you but I know that, if you ask, she will do all that she can to help you. She's proud of JFK and wants to leave it in good hands." Marion was relieved to have this expectation confirmed, because as sleep had been slow to come last night, it had become clear that there was a great deal that had yet to be learned about the inner workings of JFK.

After driving a few more blocks in silence the superintendent spoke again. "Well, once she's cleared out and you are officially in charge, how do you plan to go about the job? Do you have any sort of strategy in mind?"

"Yes," Marion responded, "I've thought about it. I'm a novice at this job and I don't know this particular school very well. So I think that it's important that I don't go rushing in with a lot of new ideas and get everybody

all shook up and maybe make some blunders in the process. I think that I'll lay low for the first few months, do a lot of looking and listening, get the lay of the land. Then I will know better what I want to change, and by then I'll also know which teachers will be most helpful and which ones are weak, so that I will know how to make my moves more effectively. After all, I'm new to the school and most of the teachers have been there for a while, so I want to make sure that they understand that I respect them and what they have built up at JFK. I want them to respect me, and I want to cultivate their loyalty. So I'm not going in there to turn their world upside down. I'll be low profile."

As Sid drove along silently, Marion continued. "The thing that I'm not sure about is how long the honeymoon period is. I'm sure that there's a period of time when the teachers will be sizing me up, trying to figure me out, during which they'll give me the benefit of the doubt. But that can't last forever. There will come a time when the honeymoon ends and I'll have to make my moves. But I wonder how long that honeymoon lasts. When does it end?" The superintendent turned the car into the long driveway of the school and did not answer until the car had been parked in a reserved space near the main entrance to the school.

Then Sidney Bennigan turned to the new principal and said quietly, "There is no honeymoon period, Marion. If there ever was one, it was during the search and selection process, when no one was committed to you. But from the moment the board voted last night, things are different. From that moment, people will be looking at you through different lenses; you're a principal-elect now, and you soon will be principal of this school. People will be making judgments about you, whether you like it or not, and they'll base those judgments on whatever they see or hear about you, no matter how little they see or hear. From now on every word, every gesture, every act—or lack of an act—on your part will say something about you as the principal of this school. When we go into this school, every encounter will be an opportunity for you to present yourself in the way you want to be understood and accepted. They will not suspend their judgment: they will form opinions about you, one way or another, and you can do a lot to shape those opinions. C'm on," Sid added while opening the car door and getting out. "We've got to get in there."

"Yes," Marion said, "I see. But if I let them know that I intend to listen and observe for a while, to spend some time finding out about the school before I try to make any changes, they'll understand that, won't they?"

Sid looked across the roof of the car and engaged Marion's eyes, saying, "Maybe. But will they accept it? Will that draw their support? I don't know. But maybe first they will want to know who you are and what you stand for, what you believe in."

As the two strode through the glass front doors of the school and entered the spare lobby area of the school, which projected the sterile institutional blandness that is the legacy of architects in schools everywhere, Marion felt uneasiness rising. After all, Edith Avery was nearly a legend around here; it was all well and good to have had the honor of being selected to succeed her but now, Marion realized, was a moment of truth: Marion and Edith were very different people. One could not expect to pick up the reins and go on with the job in the inimitable manner that Edith Avery had honed over the years. On the other hand, one surely must not get in the position of appearing to denigrate, or not appreciate, the accomplishments of the founding principal of the school. After all, Marion had wanted this particular job in no small measure because the school had a reputation of being a good one, with fewer serious problems than some other schools in the district. But these thoughts were quickly brushed aside by the arrival of Edith Avery

as she briskly walked toward them from the school office beaming and, as always, looking the very image of the confident, well-groomed professional who might have been sent out by central casting. "Well, good morning, Sid," she said warmly shaking his hand. Then she turned to Marion and, with a quick handshake, said in her carefully modulated tones, "Welcome, Marion. Congratulations on your appointment. I couldn't be more delighted and I'm very pleased that you were able to come today."

Playing her trademark role of the ebullient hostess to the hilt, she steered the two visitors toward the teachers' room, saying in mock reproach, "Well, Sid, you didn't give us much notice but we've managed. Most of the teachers are already here and are waiting for you. We'll have some coffee and scones and then," turning to Marion, "we'll have a little while to get acquainted with you and hear what you have in store for JFK."

Feeling vaguely rumpled in contrast to Edith's carefully understated classic elegance, Marion really wished that this encounter could somehow be postponed. "Gee," Marion thought, "nobody at the university taught me how to deal with this."

The following questions may be helpful in framing a discussion of this incident with others:

1. If you were coaching Marion, how would you respond to the questions about a honeymoon period in the new job and Sidney Bennigan's views about it? Is it a better theory of practice to go into the school and modestly "lay low" for a while until you feel more secure, or is it better to articulate your own vision of the future in an effort to get others to resonate to it? Give reasons for your theory of practice on this issue.

2. The process of assuming a principalship can take many forms and has many variations. What

kind of planning and preparation could Marion have done in order to be prepared to deal with unexpected opportunities such as the one now faced at JFK?

3. What guidelines or principles—or, if you prefer, what strategies and tactics—do you think are important in planning to assume a school principalship?

Suggested Reading

Bolman, Lee G., and Terrence E. Deal, "Applying the Human Resource Approach," in *Modern Approaches to Understanding and Managing Organizations.* San Francisco: Jossey-Bass, 1984.

> Describes the basis for the human resources management approach to decision making and practical considerations in applying it in practice. Includes discussions of participative methods, organizational democracy, and organization development.

Cunningham, William G., "Decision Making," in *Systematic Planning for Educational Change.* Palo Alto, CA: Mayfield Publishing Company, 1982.

> One of the better discussions of formal decision-making procedures based on conventional logical linear models. Features a description of decision tree analysis that can be very effective in dealing with discrete problems.

Kanter, Rosabeth Moss, "Dilemmas of Participation," in *The Change Masters: Innovation and Entrepreneurship in the American Corporation.* New York: Simon & Schuster, 1983.

> As the title suggests, this chapter explores problems and apparent dilemmas confronting administrators seeking to implement participative decision-making methods and suggests ways of dealing with them.

Wynn, Richard, and Charles W. Guditus, *Team Management: Leadership by Consensus.* Columbus, OH: Charles E. Merrill Publishing Company, 1984.

> An excellent resource for readers who want a detailed, practical guide for implementing participative management in educational organizations.

chapter 10

Conflict in Organizations

LEARNING OBJECTIVES

After reading this chapter, you should be able to

- Define conflict.
- Describe and discuss the concepts of interpersonal conflict, intra-personal conflict, interorganizational conflict, and intraorganizational conflict.
- Describe how bureaucratic theory deals with organizational conflict.
- Differentiate between the concept of conflict and the concept of attack.
- Discuss the view that organizational conflict is endemic, inevitable, and legitimate.
- Describe and discuss how ineffective responses to organizational conflict lead to a decline in organizational health while effective responses lead to improved organizational health.
- Explain how conflict in an organization can lead to desirable outcomes.
- Describe the role of hostility in conflict and why it is important in the management of conflict to reduce hostility.
- Explain why avoidance or denial of conflict is a poor management strategy.
- Compare and contrast the win-lose orientation to conflict with the win-win orientation and explain how these views influence one's strategy of conflict management.
- Describe and discuss *assertiveness* and *cooperativeness* as interrelated dimensions of understanding organizational conflict.
- Describe and show how *avoidance* and *appeasement* are nonmanagement approaches to organizational conflict.

ISLLC Standards

STANDARD 1: A school administrator is an educational leader who promotes the success of all students by facilitating the development, articulation, implementation, and steward-ship of a vision of learning that is shared and supported by the school community.

Knowledge

The administrator has knowledge and understanding of:

- effective communication
- effective consensus-building and negotiation skills

Dispositions

The administrator believes in, values, and is committed to:

- a willingness to continuously examine one's own assumptions, beliefs, and practices

Performances

The administrator facilitates processes and engages in activities ensuring that:

- conflict is managed in the most appropriate manner.

STANDARD 3: A school administrator is an educational leader who promotes the success of all students by ensuring management of the organization, operations, and resources for a safe, efficient, and effective learning environment.

Knowledge

The administrator has knowledge and understanding of:

- theories and models of organizations and the principles of organizational development
- human resources management and development

Dispositions

The administrator believes in, values, and is committed to:

- trusting people and their judgments
- accepting responsibility
- involving stakeholders in management processes

Performances

The administrator facilitates processes and engages in activities ensuring that:

- potential problems and opportunities are identified
- problems are confronted and resolved in a timely manner

- the school acts entrepreneurially to support continuous improvement
- organizational systems are regularly monitored and modified as needed
- stakeholders are involved in decisions affecting schools
- responsibility is shared to maximize ownership and accountability
- effective problem-framing and problem-solving skills are used
- effective conflict resolution skills are used
- effective group-process and consensus-building skills are used
- effective communication skills are used

STANDARD 5: A school administrator is an educational leader who promotes the success of all students by acting with integrity, fairness, and in an ethical manner.

Knowledge

The administrator has knowledge and understanding of:

- various ethical frameworks and perspectives on ethics

Dispositions

The administrator believes in, values, and is committed to:

- bringing ethical principles to the decision-making process
- accepting the consequences for upholding one's principles and actions
- using the influence of one's office constructively and productively in the service of all students and their families

Performances

The administrator:

- examines personal and professional values
- accepts responsibility for school operations
- considers the impact of one's administrative practices on others
- treats people fairly, equitably, and with dignity and respect

Because educational organizations exist only to foster cooperative human endeavor in order to achieve goals that cannot be achieved individually, their organizational ideals normatively emphasize cooperation, harmony, and collaboration. Contemporary literature on schools ordinarily stresses such perceived virtues as empowerment, participation, and collaboration, with little mention of competition and conflict. Yet "the potential for conflict permeates the relations of humankind, and that potential is a force for health and growth as well as destruction. . . . No group can be wholly harmonious . . . for such a group would be empty of process and structure."[1] Thus, because conflict is pervasive in all human experience, it is an important aspect of organizational behavior in education.

Conflict can occur even within a single individual (so-called intrapersonal conflict), typified by approach–avoidance conflict, the common situation in which the person feels torn between the desire to achieve two goals that are incompatible. This leads to feelings of stress and—not infrequently—behavior manifestations (for example, indecisiveness) and even physiological symptoms (for example, hypertension, ulcers). Moreover, conflict runs the gamut of social experience—between individuals, between groups, and between whole societies and cultures.

Conflict can occur *within* persons or social units; it is *intra*personal or *intra*group (or, of course, *intra*national). Conflict can also be experienced *between* two or more people or social units: so-called *inter*personal, *inter*group, or *inter*national conflict. In this chapter, we are not attempting to deal with the broad, general phenomenon of conflict; we will confine the discussion to conflict in organizational life—*organizational conflict* (that is, *intra*organizational conflict). Most commonly, this involves interpersonal conflict and intergroup conflict.

The Nature of Conflict in Organizations

In bureaucratic theory, the existence of conflict is viewed as evidence of breakdown in the organization: failure on the part of management to plan adequately or to exercise sufficient control. In human relations views, conflict is seen in an especially negative light as evidence of failure to develop appropriate norms in the group.

Traditional administrative theory has, therefore, been strongly biased in favor of the ideal of a smooth-running organization characterized by harmony, unity, coordination, efficiency, and order. Human relations adherents might seek to achieve this through happy, congenial work groups, whereas classical adherents would seek to achieve it through control and strong organizational structure. Both, however, tend to agree that conflict is disruptive: something to be avoided.

One of the more dramatic developments in the literature on organizations has been a reexamination of these positions, resulting in some more useful views.

Definition of Conflict

In the vast body of scientific literature, there is no consensus on a specific definition of "conflict."[2] There is general concurrence, however, that two things are essential to any conflict: (1) divergent (or apparently divergent) views and (2) incompatibility of those views.

Thus, Morton Deutsch said simply that "a conflict exists whenever incompatible activities occur."[3] But this incompatibility produces a dilemma—conflict becomes "the pursuit of incompatible, or at least seemingly incompatible, goals, such that gains to one side come out at the expense of the other."[4] We are confronted with the classic, zero-sum, win-lose situation that is potentially so dysfunctional to organizational life; everyone strives to avoid losing and losers seek to become winners. Though a conflict may originate as substantive (that is, "conflict rooted in the substance of the task"[5]), it readily can become affective (that is, "conflict deriving from the emotional, affective aspects of the . . . interpersonal relations").[6] This affective involvement is a central characteristic of conflict in organizations, which may be defined as "the active striving for one's own preferred outcome which, if attained, precludes the attainment by others of their own preferred outcome, *thereby producing hostility.*"[7]

The focus of contemporary application of behavioral science to organizations is precisely this: to manage conflict in the organization so that hostility can be either avoided or minimized. This is *not* the management of hostility; it is the management of conflict so as to reduce or eliminate hostility emanating from it.

Conflict Different from Attacks

There is a distinct difference between organizational conflict and its attendant hostility, on the one hand, and destructive attacks, on the other hand; to treat them alike can be a serious mistake. Kenneth Boulding suggested that we distinguish between malevolent hostility and nonmalevolent hostility.[8] Malevolent hostility is aimed at hurting or worsening the position of another individual or group, with scant regard for anything else, including consequences for the attacker. Nonmalevolent hostility, on the other hand, may well worsen the position of others but is acted out for the purpose of improving the position of the attacker. Malevolent hostility is often characterized by the use of issues as the basis for attack, which are, in reality, not important to the attacker except as a vehicle for damaging the opposition.

Malevolent hostility can, in turn, give rise to "nefarious attacks."[9] These are characterized by (1) the focus on persons rather than on issues, (2) the use of hateful language, (3) the use of dogmatic statements rather than questions, (4) the maintenance of fixed views regardless of new information or argument, and (5) the use of emotional terms.

The key difference between such attacks (whether malevolent, nefarious, or otherwise) and legitimate expressions of conflict lies in the motivation behind them, often not easily discernible. Although considerable (and often vigorous) conflict may erupt over such issues as improving school performance, ways of desegregating a school system, or how to group children for instruction, the parties to the conflict may well be motivated by essentially constructive goals. The key is whether the parties involved want to work with the system or are motivated by a wish to destroy it.

Warren Bennis has described, for example, how—in a period of student disruption at the State University of New York at Buffalo—he labored hard and long to deal with a student takeover of the campus, using his not inconsiderable skills as a third-party facilitator. But it was all to little avail. Looking back, Bennis came to realize that he really had not been in a two-party conflict-management situation at all.[10] The students—to the extent that they were organized—were committed to a set of political goals that had little to do with the educational goals that the university administrators embraced. In this case, the conflict was largely a device being used to achieve carefully masked goals. The student confrontations and rhetoric often were, in fact, malevolent, with little intention of coming to agreement.

Any public education administrator needs to be sensitive to this problem and to be aware of the significant difference between attacks for the sake of destruction[11] and vigorous expression of essentially constructive—though sharply divergent and perhaps unwelcome—views.

Contemporary Views of Conflict

Conflict in organizations is now seen as inevitable, endemic, and often legitimate. This is because the individuals and groups within the human social system are interdependent and constantly engaged in the dynamic processes of defining and redefining the nature and extent of their interdependence. Important to the dynamics of this social process is the fact that the environment in which it occurs is itself constantly changing. Thus, as Chester Barnard pointed out, "inherent in the conception of free will in a changing environment"[12] are social patterns characterized by negotiating, stress, and conflict.

Moreover, there will be conflict in any well-led organization for, as we saw in Chapter 8, leaders marshal and organize resources *in conflict with others.* By definition, leaders marshal resources (people, money, time, facilities, material) so as to achieve new goals. Given the finite resources available in an educational organization, there will invariably be competing ideas of what to do with them: how to use the time, how to involve people, where to spend the money, how to schedule facilities, and so on. Thus, when leadership is present, people in the organization must experience conflict as a normal part of organizational life. The central issue, then, is neither whether organizational conflict is present nor the degree to which it is present. The central issue is how well conflict is managed in the organization.

Effects of Organizational Conflict

This is an important issue because frequent and powerful hostility arising from conflict can have a devastating impact on the behavior of people in organizations. Psychological withdrawal from the hostility—such as alienation, apathy, and indifference—is a common symptom that keenly affects the functioning of the organization. Physical withdrawal—such as absence, tardiness, and turnover—is a widely occurring response to conflict in schools that is often written off as laziness on the part of teachers who have been spoiled by "soft" administrative practices. Outright hostile or aggressive behaviors—including job actions, property damage, and minor theft of property—are far from unknown responses by teachers to conflict situations that appear to be "too hot to handle" or totally frustrating.

Indeed, the behavioral consequences of conflict in educative organizations can be, to put it mildly, undesirable. Ineffective management of conflict (for example, a hard-nosed policy of punishment for "offenses," get-tough practices in the name of administering the negotiated contract, emphasizing the adversarial relationship between teachers and administration) can—and frequently does—create a climate that exacerbates the situation and is likely to develop a downward spiral of mounting frustration, deteriorating organizational climate, and increasing destructiveness, as shown in Figure 10.1.

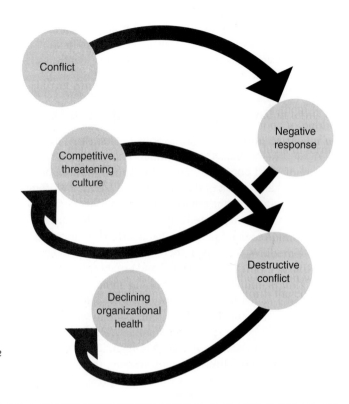

FIGURE 10.1
An ineffective conflict-response-climate syndrome leads to a lower state of organizational health.

Obviously, the health of an organization caught in this syndrome tends to decline. Effective management of conflict, on the other hand (for example, treating it as a problem to be solved, emphasizing the collaborative essence of organizational life), can lead to outcomes that are productive and enhance the health of the organization over time, as shown in Figure 10.2.

The point to be emphasized is that conflict in itself is neither good nor bad; it is (in value terms) neutral. Its impact on the organization and the behavior of people largely depends on the way conflict is treated.

The Criterion: Organizational Performance

To speak of organizational conflict as good or bad, or as functional or dysfunctional, requires one to specify the criteria used in judging. Some people—many with a "humanistic" bias—simply find conflict repugnant and seek to abolish it wherever it may be found. Others are concerned about the internal stress that conflict often imposes on individuals. These, in themselves, are not of central concern in *organizational* terms. One would do well to keep in mind that, after all, there also are people who relish conflict, find it zestful, and seek it out. The issue, then, is the impact of conflict on the performance capability of the organization as a system.

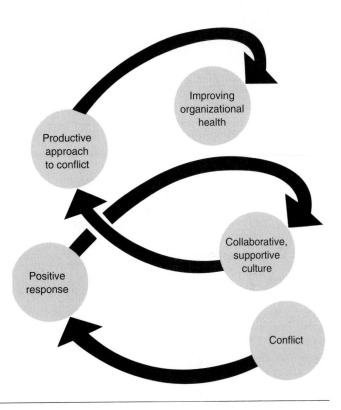

FIGURE 10.2
An effective conflict-response-climate syndrome leads to an improved state of organizational health.

Again, the problems of measuring the productivity of educational organizations and the discussion of the relevance of the school system's or school's internal conditions (that is, organizational culture, interaction–influence system) come to the fore. Thus, the functional or dysfunctional consequences of conflict on educative organizations are understood best in terms of organizational health, adaptability, and stability.

Modern motivation theory makes it clear that challenge, significance, and the need to solve problems are important attributes of work that people find interesting, enjoyable, and, in a word, motivating. Also, as has been seen, concepts of participative leadership rest on the conviction that many people in the organization have good ideas and quality information to contribute to making better decisions in the organization. In this view, Kenneth Thomas observed that

> the confrontation of divergent views often produces ideas of superior quality. Divergent views are apt to be based upon different evidence, different considerations, different insights, different frames of reference. Disagreements may thus confront an individual with factors which he had previously ignored, and help him to arrive at a more comprehensive view which synthesizes elements of his own and other's positions.[13]

Finally, there is growing reason to believe (based on both research and expert opinion) that conflict causes people to seek effective ways of dealing with it, resulting in improved organizational functioning (for example, cohesiveness, clarified relationships, clearer problem-solving procedures).[14] Speaking of society in general, Morton Deutsch observed that

> conflict within a group frequently helps to revitalize existent norms; or it contributes to the emergence of new norms. In this sense, social conflict is a mechanism for adjustment of norms adequate to new conditions. A flexible society benefits from conflict because such behavior, by helping to create and modify norms, assures its continuance under changed conditions.[15]

He went on to caution that rigid systems that suppress conflict smother a useful warning signal, thereby maximizing the danger of catastrophic breakdown.

We all have witnessed repeatedly the wisdom of these observations in national and international events of great and small magnitude. Educators in the United States also have seen it closer to home, where fearful explosions of pent-up hostility have, not infrequently, followed long periods of frustration brought on by organizations that thought they had either crushed or nimbly avoided impending conflict.

Although few who really understand conflict would advocate its deliberate use in organizational life, fewer still would advocate seeking its elimination or avoidance. Rather, by applying concepts of conflict management, the intent is to minimize the destructive potential of conflict, on the one hand, and make conflict as productive, creative, and useful as possible, on the other hand.

The Dynamics of Organizational Conflict

Hostility

Many people say that they do not like conflict, avoid it whenever they can, and may even fear it. This is important to recognize because it leads to one of the least productive and most common approaches to conflict management: denial and avoidance. Therefore, it is not splitting hairs to point out that the aftermath to an episode of conflict is ordinarily more troubling than the conflict itself. Badly managed organizational conflict can generate hostility between the parties, and this can lead to hate, retribution, and antagonism.

A key goal of any approach to the management of conflict is to eliminate or reduce—to manage—the hostility arising from the conflict. But the time to intervene is before conflict arises, rather than afterward. It is important for members of the organization to learn to talk openly about conflict long before the need arises, and to discuss what conflict is and strategies and tactics that may be used to encourage it (yes, encourage it) in ways that will be productive and helpful to everyone.

Although numerous writers have compiled a long list of the causes of organizational conflict, Louis Pondy has classified most of them into three basic types of *latent* conflict:

1. When the organization's resources are insufficient to meet the requirements of the subunits to do their work, there is *competition for scarce resources* (for example, budget allocations, assigned teaching positions, space or facilities).

2. When one party seeks to control the activities "belonging" to another unit (and the second unit seeks to fend off such "interference"), the issue is *autonomy* (for example, protecting one's "turf").

3. When two parties in the organization must work together but cannot agree on how to do so, the source of conflict is *goal divergence* (for example, the school principal and the director of special education have differing views as to how mainstreaming issues are to be settled).[16]

A Contingency View

These latent sources of conflict are unlikely to disappear from organizational life. It is, therefore, important to develop a culture that supports productive approaches to conflict management.[17] Because there are a number of causes of conflict—even when classified or grouped, as above—it is obvious that there is no one best way of managing conflict. As John Thomas and Warren Bennis put it:

> An effective paradigm incorporates what might be termed a "situational" or "contingency" framework, a point of view reflected in much of the current theoretical and empirical work in organizational theory. There is a primary emphasis upon diagnosis and the assumption that it is self-defeating to adopt a "universally" applicable set of principles and guidelines for effecting change or managing conflict.[18]

As a basis for the necessary organizational diagnosis, two concepts concerning conflict are often used: one seeks to understand the internal dynamics of the events that occur in the process of conflict; the other seeks to analyze the external influences that tend to structure the conflict.

A Process View of Conflict

Conflict between two parties appears to unfold in a relatively orderly sequence of events and, unless something intervenes, the sequence tends to be repeated in episodes. Each episode is highly dynamic, with each party's behavior serving as a stimulus to evoke a response from the other. Furthermore, each new episode is shaped in part by previous episodes.

One model of such a process is suggested by Thomas (see Figure 10.3), in which an episode is triggered by the *frustration* of one party by the act of another (for example, denial of a request, diminishment of status, disagreement, or an insult). This causes the participants to *conceptualize* the nature of the conflict—often a highly subjective process that suggests ways of defining and dealing with perceived issues in the conflict. Indeed—as experimental research reported by Robert Blake, Herbert Shepard, and Jane

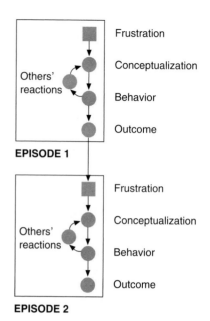

FIGURE 10.3

Process model of conflict episodes between two parties. From Kenneth Thomas, "Conflict and Conflict Management," in *Handbook of Industrial and Organizational Psychology,* ed. Marvin D. Dunnette (Chicago: Rand McNally & Company, 1976), p. 895. Reprinted by permission of Marvin D. Dunnette.

Mouton makes clear—this step of defining the issues and seeking alternative responses is frequently viewed by the parties to the conflict as a simple matter of victory or defeat. Alternatives other than winning or losing are easily overlooked.[19] This is followed by *behavior* intended to deal with the conflict. As Kenneth Thomas explained, understanding the bases for this behavior is a complex matter, but key elements surely include a mix of (1) a participant's desire to satisfy the other's concern (cooperative-uncooperative) and (2) the participant's desire to satisfy his or her own concern (assertive-unassertive).[20] *Interaction* of the parties follows, of course; this is a highly dynamic phase of the process. It can involve escalation or deescalation of the conflict, depending on such factors as the trust level that is established, biases and self-fulfilling prophecies that get in the way, the level of competition between the participants, and the openness and sensitivity each has to the other. The *outcome* of all this—the last stage in an episode of conflict—is not merely some agreement on substantive issues but also includes residual emotions (for example, frustration, hostility, trust—either increased or decreased). These outcomes have potentially long-term effects on the aftermath of a conflict episode, particularly as they set the stage for ensuing episodes.

In commenting on the aftermath as part of a sequence of episodes, Louis Pondy pointed out that

> [i]f the conflict is genuinely resolved to the satisfaction of all participants, the basis for a more cooperative relationship may be laid; or the participants, in their drive for a more ordered relationship may focus on latent conflicts not previously perceived and dealt with.

On the other hand, if conflict is merely suppressed but not resolved, the latent conditions of conflict may be aggravated and explode in more serious form. . . . This legacy of a conflict episode is . . . called "conflict aftermath."[21]

A Structural View of Conflict

Although a process approach to conflict sees it as a *sequence of events,* a structural view tends to see conflict in terms of the *conditions that influence behavior.* For example, every organization has rules and procedures (written and unwritten, formal and informal) that regulate behavior (for example, who talks with whom about what). Rules and procedures often serve to avoid or manage conflict by clarifying such issues as how to proceed, when, and who has what responsibility. Of course, they also can cause or exacerbate conflict by becoming dysfunctional, such as when they lead to rigid, repetitious behavior that does not readily allow for exceptions (the typical bureaucratic "hardening of the categories").

Not infrequently, rules and procedures so complicate the processes of working out a relatively simple conflict through direct negotiation that they in fact create conflict. For example, in one school district an elementary school principal discovered that an order for a certain kind of paper had been cut sharply by an administrative assistant in the office of the assistant superintendent for business. When the principal contacted the administrative assistant to straighten out the matter, she was reminded that her complaint should be routed through the assistant superintendent for elementary education, who could take it up with the assistant superintendent of business, and so on. Needless to say, considerable conflict ensued, much time was lost, and the needed paper finally arrived at the school—in time for *the following* year. The point is that simple rearrangements in the way that even minor decisions are made and differences are negotiated can influence the course of conflict in organizations.

Another structural factor lies in the kinds of people found in the organization, with particular reference to their personality predispositions, such as their attitudes toward authority and the extent and flexibility of their responses to others. In selecting new personnel, for example, many school districts and schools are attracted to candidates who seem to "fit in" over candidates who might add diversity to the staff.

A further structural factor influencing the incidence and nature of conflict in an organization is the social norms of the organization: the social pressures, for example, "to stand up and fight" or "not to rock the boat." The creation of organizational cultures that smooth over friction and frown on open challenge and questioning can make it very difficult to identify and confront conflict at all. Similarly, when secretiveness and restricted communication represent the organizational norm, it is difficult to know if a latent conflict exists, let alone to plan ways of dealing with it. Many administrators of educational organizations instinctively understand this and make it a rule to put as little communication in writing as possible, to assemble people for meetings as infrequently as possible, and—when meetings *must* be held—to be sure to control the proceedings tightly so as to minimize the "risk" of opening up issues that might "cause trouble."

Thus, the structural factors that shape conflict in organizations are strongly influenced by structural factors in the organization itself. In the words of the Likerts:

> The success of [an organization] is influenced greatly by its capacity to achieve cooperative coordination rather than hostile conflict among its functional departments and also to stimulate differences and then to capitalize on them by productive problem-solving leading to creative and acceptable solutions. . . . Institutions based on traditional organizational theory . . . lack the capacity to deal successfully with the conflicts created by the new demands which recently legitimized values are placing on them. . . . Repressive action brings costly backlash.[22]

They, of course, advocate developing a more responsive interaction-influence system through System 4 leadership, developing a supportive climate, deemphasizing hierarchical status, and using consensus for productive (win-win) problem solving.

An Open-Systems View of Conflict

Thus far, we have been discussing organizational conflict entirely in terms of the internal functioning of educative organizations, and this will continue to be the focus of the chapter as a whole. It is, however, vital not to lose sight of the fact that these organizations are open systems; they are interactive with their environments, and much that goes on within them reflects changes in the external environment.

In terms of conflict, a good case in point is P.L. 94-142, which was passed by Congress and signed into law on November 29, 1975. It is a classic example of power-coercive change strategy and probably set the stage for more widespread conflict in U.S. public schooling—at all levels—than anything since the *Brown* school desegregation decision of some two decades earlier. At the highest levels it raised conflicting constitutional issues: the interpretation of the Tenth Amendment that education is a state responsibility and a matter of local control versus the view that P.L. 94-142 is an exercise of federal responsibility to ensure full civil rights to equal opportunity for the unserved (and inadequately served) handicapped.

However, the law also raised conflicts all along the line, from Washington, D.C., to the most remote school classroom in the land. For example, it sought to redefine the prerogatives of teachers to control instruction and related decision making by mandating the inclusion of parents in a participatory role in planning individualized instruction and in a formalized appeal process. The parent—formerly an outsider confined to an advisory role—suddenly became one of the insiders, with new authority in relation to the teacher.

The ability of schools to deal productively with this conflict thrust on them from the larger environment was unclear even as late as 1990 because external initiatives to mandate increasing control of the classroom decisions of teachers were still increasing in number and scope. It is, however, a clear and unambiguous illustration of how conflict—very much involving the internal functioning of schools and school systems—can be imposed on them by rapid change in the external system.

Gerald Griffin and David Rostetter have speculated as to whether Randall Collins's five hypotheses on coercive efforts to deal with coercion and conflict might apply.[23] As they pointed out:

1. Coercion leads to strong efforts to avoid being coerced.
2. If resources for fighting back are available, the greater the coercion applied the more counteraggression is called forth.
3. If resources are not available but opportunities to escape are, the greater the tendency to leave the situation.
4. If resources for fighting back and opportunities to escape are not available, or if there are other strong incentives for staying in the situation (material rewards or potential power), the greater coercion that is applied the greater the tendency to comply with exactly those demands that are necessary to avoid being coerced.
5. If resources for fighting back and opportunities for escape are not available, the . . . tendency to dull compliance and passive resistance [is increased].[24]

In this view, coercion leads to a conflict-hostility-resistance syndrome *within* the organization, very unlike the synergistic, creative, problem-solving culture that characterizes effective organizations. Only time will tell what effect this federal initiative, based on traditional concepts of schools as organizations, will ultimately have.

Approaches to Organizational Conflict

When conflict arises, the almost instinctive response of the parties involved is to adopt a strategy—backed by determination—to *win*. To most people that means, *ipso facto,* that the other party will *lose*.

> Confrontation, non-negotiable demands, and ultimatums have become the order of the day as *the* way of dealing with deep-seated differences. One party marshals all its forces to compel the other party to do what the first has decided it wants. Confrontation is from a fixed position and seeks to mobilize the power to win. Win-lose strategy is used in a variety of situations, such as struggles for civil rights; urban riots; student demonstrations and sit-ins; international conflicts; union-management disagreements; a hearing on next year's budget; a controversy between departments . . . or a controversy between professional staff and the lay board.[25]

The focal point of conflict management is the win-lose orientation and how to deal with it. It is important, first, to understand the dynamics and consequences of win-lose approaches to conflict and, second, to see what alternatives are available.

The Win-Lose Orientation to Conflict

The dynamics of win-lose conflict and their consequences for organizational behavior are well known. Group dynamicists in the 1950s and 1960s conducted extensive research on the phenomena of group conflict—including both experimental work and field observation studies (see the discussion of group dynamics and human relations in Chapter 3).[26]

"A win-lose orientation to conflict is characterized by one basic element," Blake, Shepard, and Mouton observe. "The contesting parties see their interests to be mutually exclusive. No compromise is possible. One must fail at the price of the other's success . . . [and] hope is abandoned of being able to appeal to each other on the basis of reason."[27] The parties to the conflict come to believe that the issues can be settled in one of three ways: (1) a power struggle, (2) intervention by a third party who possesses some sort of power greater than either of them (and this can include public opinion or moral suasion), or (3) fate.

There are two consequences of this approach:

1. *Between the parties to the conflict.* Antagonisms deepen, hostility rises, hope of finding a mutually acceptable solution fades, and as it does the search for such a solution ceases.

2. *Within the groups involved.* Spirits soar as members close ranks in preparation for battle. Differences of opinion, skepticism, and challenge of leadership or the "party line" are frowned on: members are pressured to support the decisions taken, to conform, to "go along," to be loyal to the group or get out. Leadership gravitates rapidly to a very small number of people, who are usually forceful and aggressive. Thus, diversity of opinion, the search for quality ideas, and the broad involvement of members in developing creative responses are snuffed out in the group. This not only hardens the group's position in the conflict itself but also, more importantly, sets the stage for ineffective functioning of the group after the conflict eases.[28]

Experimental studies of conflict[29] make it clear that the perception of individuals and groups is very much involved in conflict—often becoming distorted as the episode unfolds. And, of course, "perception is the key to behavior. The way people see things determines the way they will act. If their perceptions are distorted, the distortions are reflected in their behavior."[30] Thus, judgment is adversely affected by the conflict experience: one tends to become blindly loyal, to become hostile to members of the other group, and to denigrate not only their ideas but their worth as persons. Leaders of the opposition—formerly seen as mature, able people—are now seen as irresponsible and incapable. Indeed, even cognition is affected: in studying proposed solutions to the conflict, it becomes difficult or impossible to see merit in proposals put forth by "the other side," even though they may be in substantial agreement with one's own ideas. Thus, agreement becomes elusive. *Any* sign of questioning the position of one's group or any approval of proposals put forth from the other side is viewed by associates as backing down. Winning becomes everything. The ability to identify alternatives, to be objective, and to suspend judgment while seeking to understand are all badly distorted as one increasingly shares the gung-ho drive of the group for "victory."

In terms of the process model of conflict (described earlier), win-lose is a way of conceptualizing the conflict and gives rise to predictable patterns of behavior in the interaction between parties to the conflict as the episode unfolds. But the consequences, it should be clear, are not limited to the shape and character of the conflict itself. Each of the groups involved in the conflict is powerfully affected in the aftermath. Usually, hostility between the winning group and the losing group is intensified, and subsequent episodes may be expected.

Commonly, the losing group will reject its leaders; very likely it will, in time, begin reappraising what went wrong and start preparing to do better next time. Powerful emotional reactions (resentment—even hatred—and anxiety) are likely to continue to distort the group's functioning, reducing the likelihood that it will develop a climate supportive of self-renewal and creative problem solving. Thus, win-lose solutions to conflict tend to build long-term dysfunctional behaviors that result in a downward spiral of organizational climate, performance, and overall organizational health. A central concern of conflict management, then, is to seek more effective ways of conceptualizing conflict as a basis for more effective behavior.

A Contingency Approach to Conflict

Contingency approaches to management are predicated on the concept that diagnosis of the situation is necessary as a basis for action. In dealing with conflict, the contingency view holds that there is no one best way of managing it under all conditions, but that there are optimal ways of managing conflict under certain conditions. An important aspect of conflict management, then, is to consider (1) alternative ways of managing conflict and (2) the kinds of situations in which each of these various alternatives might be expected to be the most effective, not only in dealing with the critical issues but also in doing so in a way that strengthens the organization.

Diagnosing Conflict

In the first place, it is helpful to ascertain whether conflict *does* exist between the parties or whether a conflict only *appears* (to the parties) to exist. The criterion is whether the two parties seek goals that are actually incompatible.

Frequently, what appears to be a brewing conflict between two parties is, in fact, a misunderstanding. When the problem is recognized as one of distorted perception, as discussed earlier, it is probable that the misunderstanding can be dealt with through explicit goal setting and improved communication. This often requires training individuals and groups in such skills as group goal setting and prioritizing, as well as in communication skills (for example, active listening, seeking feedback to check the receiver's perceptions, using multiple channels).

If a conflict *does* exist, however (that is, the parties do have goals that are mutually incompatible), then it is necessary to select a method of dealing with it as productively as possible from among the many options available. The general principle is that a win-lose approach tends to be the least productive, while a win-win approach—in which both parties win something (though not necessarily equally)—tends to be the most productive.

Collaboration is a process in which the parties work together to define their problems and then engage in mutual problem solving. As a mode of dealing with conflict, this process requires, first, that the parties involved must want to try to use it (will give time and effort to participating). The process also requires that the people involved possess (1) the necessary skills for communicating and working in groups, effectively coupled with (2) attitudes that support a climate of openness, trust, and frankness in which to identify and work through problems.

In situations in which the *will* to do this exists but the skills are not well developed, a facilitator can be brought in to help the groups to learn the necessary skills and engage in the collaborative processes (though the facilitator does not get involved in the substance of decisions, merely the processes for making them). This is the highest level of win-win conflict management because it leaves the groups with new skills and new understandings that they can use in dealing with future problems. It is, of course, a form of organization development (organizational self-renewal). Not the least attribute of collaborative approaches to problem solving is the healthy sense of "ownership" or commitment to the solution arrived at that is unmatched by other approaches. In Likert and Likert's terms it is System 4 management; Blake, Shepard, and Mouton would call it 9, 9 style.

Bargaining, compromise, and other forms of splitting the difference have some elements in common with collaborative problem solving: (1) the parties must be willing to engage in the process (though sometimes they are legally required to do so); (2) there is some move toward collaboration (though usually this is restricted to the negotiators); and (3) the process is basically conciliatory and not in flagrant conflict with the organization's well-being. If the bargaining escalates to mediation or arbitration, the outside third party plays a role quite different from that of the group-process facilitator in a collaborative process: he or she *does* have the power to make judgments and impose decisions on the parties in conflict. Bargaining does seek to develop a long-term relationship between the parties and provides them with a mechanism for dealing with future problems. But bargaining is not a collaborative approach: it recognizes that the two parties are essentially adversaries and may use information as a form of power for strategic purposes.

Neither party wins in the typical bargaining/compromise situation, but then neither party loses. Although the term *bargaining* is readily associated with labor–management relations, negotiation processes are, in fact, widely employed within organizational settings to settle conflicts. For example, when two administrators confer to work out some problems between their divisions, it is not uncommon for them to use negotiating and compromise techniques systematically. If the negotiations do bog down, they may take the problem to their immediate superordinate for mediation (a common feature of the so-called bureaucratic mode of conflict management).

Avoidance (withdrawal, peaceful coexistence, indifference) is often employed when dealing with conflict. Avoidance is useful (1) when it is not likely that the latent conflict really can be resolved ("live with it") or (2) when the issues are not so important to the parties as to require the time and resources to work them out. As Blake and his colleagues pointed out, avoidance can be in the form of a "cease-fire," wherein two groups engaged in a long-term struggle decide to keep in contact, still entrenched in their positions, but not to get locked into combat with each other.[31] An interesting outcome of various avoidance responses to latent conflict is that, although conflict is not inevitable, agreement is impossible. Thus, though a hostile aftermath is avoided, the underlying problems are not dealt with; the latent conflict—with all its hazardous potential—remains, ready to become manifest at any time.

Power struggle is, of course, the effort by each party to win, regardless of the consequences for the other party. Although conflict, in itself, may be seen as having some beneficial potential for organizations (or, at least, as being nondestructive), this mode of dealing with it is viewed almost universally as being destructive. It is the classic win-lose situation.

A Contingency Approach to Diagnosis of Conflict

An important aspect of diagnosis for the conflict manager is to ascertain the way each party to the conflict has conceptualized the situation.

Kenneth Thomas contended that it is common, in a conflict situation, to emphasize the extent to which a party is willing to cooperate with another party but to overlook a second critical factor: the party's desire to satisfy his or her own concerns.[32] Thus, in his view, two critical behavioral dimensions shape the way one conceptualizes conflict:

1. *Cooperativeness,* which is the extent to which one wishes to satisfy the concerns of the other.
2. *Assertiveness,* which is the extent to which one wishes to satisfy her or his own concerns.

These are seen as independent dimensions, as shown in Figure 10.4. Thus, in diagnosing conflict as conceptualized by the parties involved, the issue becomes more than merely a matter of cooperating or "acting professionally": cooperation can be viewed as literally a sacrifice of one's own needs.

From this analysis, Thomas identified five principal perspectives that may be used in conceptualizing conflict and behaviors commonly associated with those perspectives:

1. *Competitive* behavior is the search to satisfy one's own concerns at the expense of others if need be. As shown in Figure 10.5, it is a high competitive–high uncooperative orientation. The effect is domination of the situation (as, for example, in hard-nosed contract negotiations in which nothing is yielded and every advantage is exploited). It is the classic win-lose view of conflict.

2. *Avoidant* (unassertive–uncooperative) behavior is usually expressed by apathy, withdrawal, and indifference. This does *not* mean that there is an absence of conflict but that it has been conceptualized as something not to deal with. Hence, the latent conflict remains and may be viewed differently at another time.

3. *Accommodation* (high cooperativeness–low assertiveness) is typified by appeasement: one attends to the other's concerns while neglecting his or her own. This

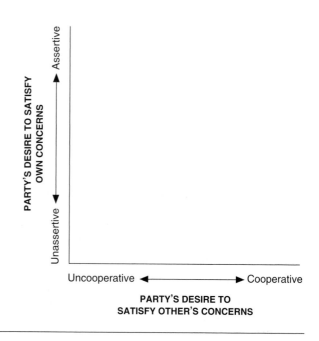

FIGURE 10.4

Assertiveness and cooperativeness are independent dimensions in conflict. Based on Kenneth Thomas, "Conflict and Conflict Management," in *Handbook of Industrial and Organizational Psychology*, ed. Marvin D. Dunnette (Chicago: Rand McNally & Company, 1976), p. 900. Reprinted by permission of Marvin D. Dunnette.

FIGURE 10.5

Five orientations to conflict related to assertiveness and cooperativeness. From Kenneth Thomas, "Conflict and Conflict Management," in *Handbook of Industrial and Organizational Psychology*, ed. Marvin D. Dunnette (Chicago: Rand McNally & Company, 1976), p. 900. Reprinted by permission of Marvin D. Dunnette.

orientation may be associated with a desire to maintain a working relationship even at some sacrifice of one's own interests.

4. *Sharing* orientation (moderate assertiveness–moderate cooperativeness) often leads to compromise (trade-offs, splitting the difference, horse-trading).

5. *Collaborative* orientation to conflict (high assertive–high cooperative) leads to efforts to satisfy fully the concerns of both parties through mutual problem solving. The solution to the conflict is a genuine integration of the desires of both sides. The concept is win-win.

This approach to the analysis of conflict helps to assess the kinds of strategies that might be most usefully employed in managing it (for example, bargaining, power, or collaboration). The goal, of course, is to manage the conflict in such a way that it will be as productive as possible for the organization while minimizing destructive consequences. It is important, therefore, to consider the potential long-run consequences resulting from the aftermath of conflict.

For example, avoidance or appeasement can be appealing responses because—in the short run—they are likely to head off the difficulties of seeking genuine solutions and have the added advantage of requiring the least in terms of organizational energy, time, and resources. But they do not solve the problem that triggered the conflict, nor do they develop the organization's capacity to deal productively with conflict.

Bargaining does help to develop the internal capacity of the organization to deal with conflict. But bargaining is not designed to produce optimal solutions: in the process of horse-trading, neither side emerges completely satisfied, and quite likely the more skilled, hard-nosed negotiator will walk away with more than his or her opponent does. Bargaining is essentially an adversarial procedure—if not downright underhanded—using "dirty tricks" and wily ploys to gain advantage. These often engender resentment and mistrust, both dysfunctional attitudes in organizational life.

Competitive win-lose power plays and collaborative problem solving require the most energy, time, and resources. The essentially different consequences of each mode have already been described. Because the aftermath and long-term consequences of win-lose power struggles are well known to be dysfunctional and those of collaboration functional, few who are concerned about enhancing the organization's performance would fail to choose collaboration—whenever practical—as the most desirable conceptualization of conflict, and competition as least desirable.

Because avoidance and appeasement are really *non*management of conflict, we are left with three basic general strategies for dealing with it: collaboration, bargaining, or power. Figure 10.6, which summarizes the essential characteristics of each of these strategies, also shows how bargaining incorporates certain features of both collaboration and power strategies. In this sense, bargaining serves as a bridge between power strategies and collaboration, making it possible—though far from inevitable—to move, over time, organizational processes from win-lose power struggles to win-win collaborative problem solving.

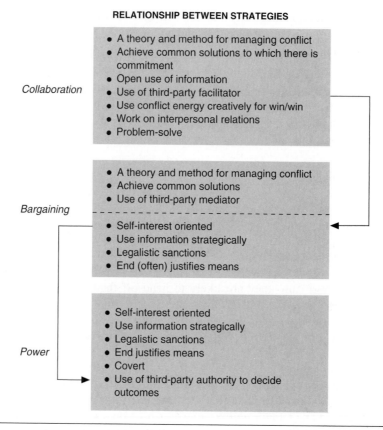

RELATIONSHIP BETWEEN STRATEGIES

Collaboration
- A theory and method for managing conflict
- Achieve common solutions to which there is commitment
- Open use of information
- Use of third-party facilitator
- Use conflict energy creatively for win/win
- Work on interpersonal relations
- Problem-solve

Bargaining
- A theory and method for managing conflict
- Achieve common solutions
- Use of third-party mediator
- -
- Self-interest oriented
- Use information strategically
- Legalistic sanctions
- End (often) justifies means

Power
- Self-interest oriented
- Use information strategically
- Legalistic sanctions
- End justifies means
- Covert
- Use of third-party authority to decide outcomes

FIGURE 10.6   Relationship between conflict management strategies. From C. Brooklyn Derr, *Managing Organizational Conflict: When to Use Collaboration, Bargaining and Power Approaches* (Monterey, CA: Naval Postgraduate School, 1975), p. 12. Reprinted by permission.

Conclusion

Organizational conflict has been discussed in this chapter chiefly in terms of two-party clashes within the organization. Whereas conflict was once thought to signal a failure of the organization, it is being increasingly recognized as a normal and legitimate aspect of human social systems. Thus, conflict is not only inevitable but, contrary to earlier views, it can serve a useful function by stimulating creative solutions to problems.

Whether organizational conflict is destructive or constructive depends to a large extent on how it is managed. The day is over for the wily school administrator who could head off or terminate conflict with deft tricks or a swift exercise of power. Healthy organizations—characterized by well-developed problem-solving mechanisms and a collaborative climate—are able to identify conflict and deal with it in a collaborative way that leaves the organization stronger and more well developed rather than weakened and wracked with hostility.

Ways of handling conflict in school districts and schools have been heavily influenced by the people who have been consulted for advice or by third-party intervention. Especially with the spread of collective bargaining, school districts have turned increasingly for advice to people trained and conditioned to view conflict in adversarial, combative terms (lawyers and, not infrequently, professional negotiators and mediators), rather than to people trained and conditioned to view it as a phenomenon of organizational behavior (applied social scientists, organizational psychologists). Too often this has produced essentially destructive, win-lose strategies and tactics. Frequently it has been associated with the denigration of proposals to seek more productive approaches as being "unrealistic."

This chapter has proposed a way of diagnosing conflict in a given situation as a basis for choosing an appropriate management strategy. Clearly, there is no one best way of managing conflict in organizations. There are a number of ways, each suited to circumstances in a particular situation. The basic principle in choosing a way of managing conflict, however, is to use the approach most likely to minimize the destructive aspects (for example, hostility) and to maximize the opportunities for organizational growth and development (for example, to develop greater trust, to improve problem solving).

Finally, no phase of conflict management is more critical than diagnosing the situation. Frequently the processes of conceptualizing, or analyzing, conflict confuses effects with causes. For example, a superintendent of schools asked a consultant, "What are some of the ways that I can deal with conflict in this school district?" When asked what kind of conflict he was talking about, the superintendent replied, "Well, you know, we had that teachers' strike and it was pretty bad here. Now the teachers are back at work, but we have a lot of bad feeling everywhere. You know—hostility. We have to do something about it. What can we do?" Although, as I have explained, hostility is an important aspect of conflict, it is important to bear in mind that hostility does not describe a conflict, itself. Hostility is an emotional reaction that is all too often part of the outcome or aftermath of an episode of conflict. But trying to ameliorate hostile feelings is, perhaps, dealing with a symptom rather than a cause. If we fail to diagnose the conflict correctly and deal with the causes, the conflict will continue in latent form, ready to manifest itself at a later time.

Reflective Activities

1. **Handling Conflict:** Complete the following conflict management activity by Author Allan Dornseif.* *Please place a 5 (most likely),*

*Allan Dornseif, *Pocket Guide to School-Based Decision Making #5* (Arlington, VA: Association for Supervision and Curriculum Development, 1996).

a 4 (next most likely), to 1 (least likely) next to the courses of action you would take under each of the four cases that follow. Answer from what you would most likely do if you were the person described in the situation.

CASE ONE

Pete is the lead teacher of a five-teacher middle school teaching team. Recently he has noticed that Sarah, a teacher from across the hall, has been dropping in on Linda, the reading teacher in Pete's team, almost every fifth period to borrow something and chat a few minutes. It's only for a short time but class noise and attention appear to be worsening. Others on the team seem to have some resentment of the minor intrusion. If you were Pete, you would:

_____ a. Talk to Linda and tell her to limit conversations to break periods.

_____ b. Ask the principal to tell the other team members to keep their teachers in their own classrooms.

_____ c. Confront both teachers the next time you see them together, find out what they are up to, and inform them of the problem as you see it.

_____ d. Say nothing now; it would be silly to make a big deal out of a few minutes.

_____ e. Try to keep the rest of the team at ease; it is important that they all work well together.

CASE TWO

Ralph is head of the new computerized management system. His department consists of a state-of-the-art computer system and a staff of five. The work is exacting. Inattention or improper procedures could create costly damage to the system, bad output, or a serious breach of confidential information. Ralph suspects that Jim is drinking too much, maybe even on the job, but at the least he appears to be a bit "high." Ralph feels that he has some strong indications, but he knows he does not have a "case." If you were Ralph, you would:

_____ a. Confront Jim outright, tell him what you suspect and why, and that you are concerned for him and for the operation of the department.

_____ b. Ask Jim to keep his habit off the job; what he does *on* the job is part of your business.

_____ c. Not confront Jim right now; it might either turn him off the job or drive his drinking further underground.

_____ d. Tell Jim that drinking on the job is illegal and that if he gets caught you will do everything you can to see that he is fired.

_____ e. Keep a close eye on Jim to see that he is not causing serious mistakes.

CASE THREE

Sally is the district curriculum specialist and has been appointed by the superintendent to gather data for teaching improvement. On separate occasions, two teachers on the committee have come to her with different suggestions for reporting test results. Since the superintendent will see the progress the teams are making, Paul wants to send the test results directly to the superintendent and then to the teaching teams. Jim thinks the results should go directly to the teaching teams so they can take corrective action right away. Both ideas seem good; the superintendent has been extremely busy completing this project, and there is no specific procedure for routing the reports. If you were Sally, you would:

_____ a. Decide who is right and ask the other person to go along with the decision.

_____ b. Wait and see; the best solution will become apparent.

_____ c. Tell both Paul and Jim not to get uptight about their disagreement. It is not that important.

_____ d. Get Paul and Jim together and examine both of their ideas closely for the best approach.

_____ e. Send the data to the superintendent with a copy to the lead teachers (although it's a lot more work for staff and will be more expensive).

CASE FOUR

Jean is president of the PTA. From time to time in the past, the school council and the staff have "tapped" the PTA for volunteers to augment several projects. This has not been a problem since parents have been very willing to cooperate. Lately, however, there is an almost constant demand for volunteers to help on various new projects. Many parents are no longer available and the rest of the "real workers" must now make up for the shortage. Parents are beginning to complain that they are being used. If you were Jean, you would:

_____ a. Let it go for now; the extra projects will be over soon.

_____ b. Try to smooth things over with the volunteers and with the council and principal. Everyone is doing this for the kids, after all. We cannot afford a conflict.

_____ c. Tell the council and the staff they can each have only two volunteers.

_____ d. Go to the principal and council chair and talk about how these demands for additional help could best be met without overloading the volunteers.

_____ e. Go to the council chair and get him to call off or postpone the council's projects.

STYLES OF DEALING WITH CONFLICT

When faced with a controversy, we often rely on an "instinctive" approach that reflects our attitudes and behavior. From our background and experiences, most of us have developed an approach that we prefer and with which we are most comfortable as we face potential conflict situations. Two issues are at stake, however, in group conflict situations.

The values we assign to these two issues determine our preferred strategy of dealing with conflict. We can approach a potential conflict situation with five possible methods.

Muscle

When using this method, the need for confrontation is high to accomplish goals and establish or maintain one's status but low in its need to maintain harmonious feelings and smooth working relationships. This style is assertive, aggressive, and competitive. This is a win-lose situation. People using this approach often feel they have moral certitude in their position. "I am the boss. Just do it!"

Most people view this as an approach that other people use, not them. Since more people rely on a muscle approach, however, it may be an unknowing personal choice.

Reconciliation

Harmonizing is the opposite of using muscle. Here the concern for people, feelings, and smooth working relationships is high, while the need to accomplish goals and maintain status is low. This style is one of accommodating, giving in, and acquiescing to preserve relationships while resolving the conflict, at least temporarily. Sometimes we say "agreeing to disagree" or "peaceful coexistence." Usually it means that we quietly sweep the issue under the rug and hope it stays there. (It rarely does.)

Harmony

Bargaining or negotiation is about equal in its need to maintain harmony in relationships and to accomplish goals. It is a "middle ground," aimed at achieving compromise in order to resolve conflict. This is used when pressure to win is not too great, and the parties find it possible to work out an equitable bargain or "split the difference." In this situation there is no loser but no winner either.

Retreat

Avoiding or withdrawal is the other end of the muscle approach. It is low on both the need to maintain relationships and the need to accomplish goals. This approach is aimed at not becoming involved with conflict and the strong feelings it may generate. Retreat is usually a temporary solution.

Collaboration

Solving problems through the collaboration of people and groups attempting to reach consensus on issues is high both on the need to maintain relationships and the need to accomplish goals. It is aimed at finding a new set of goals incorporating ideas and concerns of both parties, which leads to growth in the working relationship. This style stresses working together for a mutual solution to conflicts.

Facing the issues together, all parties need a strong commitment to finding a solution to which all can agree. This approach requires a high investment of energy with no guarantee that the problem can be solved effectively. It is the most positive approach, however, which engenders trust. Its success makes a greater potential for using this approach in future conflict situations.

Each of these approaches has its own advantages and disadvantages, its strengths and weaknesses. In itself, no one style is "better" than another. However, each approach has a different thrust and different consequences. Constructive conflict management calls for the ability to read the situation and apply the best strategy.

Different stages of conflict may call for different approaches. In the initial stages of bargaining, for example, both parties are likely to use muscle to establish the issues in which they are most interested. Later, as bargaining continues, each party must assume a negotiating style if a compromise is to be reached. If the parties can develop a mutual trust, the problem-solving approach of collaboration is best for the long term.

Activity Score Sheet Directions: For each case write the number you placed next to each letter.

The column with the highest number shows your preferred method of resolving conflict in these type of situations. Reflect on your scores. Are your scores what you would expect?

Insert Ranking for Each Letter

Case

	Retreat	Reconciliation	Harmony	Muscle	Collaboration
One	d.	e.	a.	b.	c.
Two	c.	e.	b.	d.	a.
Three	b.	c.	e.	a.	d.
Four	a.	b.	c.	e.	d.
Totals					
Style					

2. Review Louis Pondy's three basic types of latent conflict. For each type of conflict (competition for scarce resources, autonomy, and goal divergence) provide an example from your experience. Using Kenneth Thomas's model of conceptualizing conflict, identify the type of orientations that were involved in each scenario. Who were the players in the conflict, and what strategies did they and the organizational leaders use to respond to the conflict? Did the outcomes have positive or negative effects on organizational health?

3. *Working on Your Game Plan.* Meetings with staff members present prime opportunities for educational leaders to engage in conflict management. However, in school meetings conflict is often latent: unrecognized, "papered over," ignored and thus denied, or simply not acknowledged. Latent conflict is virtually impossible to manage productively. Therefore, a first step in managing conflict is to make the conflict manifest: acknowledge it; get it on the table so that it can be described, discussed, and managed. A common problem in school staff meetings, however, is that people behave in tacitly agreed-on ways to prevent conflict from being acknowledged and managed. As described in this chapter, this is ordinarily attributable to the fear of hostility.

As you reflect on your own experience with staff meetings at school after you've read this chapter, prepare three key coaching tips that you might offer a school principal to improve the planning and conducting of staff meetings so as to incorporate conflict management strategies and tactics. Start each of your coaching tips with a specific recommended action or procedure. Then describe your rationale for recommending the action.

For example, one might recommend that the principal form an advisory group made up of staff members who will work collaboratively to develop the agendas for staff meetings. The model for doing this might very well be the

Tannenbaum-Schmidt model. The rationale for this recommendation is twofold: first, empowering teachers to exercise greater influence over the meetings that they must attend will have a salutary effect in improving the climate of the meetings so as to increase consensus; second, this will, in turn, make it easier, and more likely, that issues of conflict can be acknowledged and discussed.

Suggested Reading

Beckhard, Richard, "The Confrontation Meeting," *Harvard Business Review,* 45 (March-April 1967), 149–155.

Description of "an activity that allows a total management group, drawn from all levels of the organization, to take a quick reading on its own health, and—*within a matter of hours*—to set action plans for improving it" (p. 149). Provides a specific design for a one-day meeting that can be used to deal with the stress of a crisis that helps the group (1) diagnose the situation, (2) set goals and priorities collaboratively, (3) develop a plan of action, and (4) implement the plan on both a short-range and a long-range basis.

Derr, C. Brooklyn, *Managing Organizational Conflict: When to Use Collaboration, Bargaining and Power Approaches.* Monterey, CA: Naval Postgraduate School, 1975.

Proposes a contingency approach. Pointing out that collaboration, bargaining, and power approaches all are appropriate in the management of organizational conflict under certain conditions, the author explains how to diagnose the contingencies in different situations. Benefits and drawbacks for each strategy, under varying conditions, are discussed.

Likert, Rensis, and Jane Gibson Likert, *New Ways of Managing Conflict.* New York: McGraw-Hill, 1976.

After analyzing the causes of increasing organizational conflict, this book describes procedures for substituting System 4 (win-win) problem-solving strategies for the win-lose approach that usually leaves one party to a conflict frustrated and embittered. A highly specific, practical, how-to book with some explicit applications to schools that should be helpful to practitioners.

Wynn, Richard, *Administrative Response to Conflict.* Pittsburgh: Tri-State Area School Study Council, School of Education, University of Pittsburgh, 1972.

In this twenty-three-page monograph the author attempts to distill contemporary concepts of organizational conflict into practical advice for school superintendents, school board members, and other public school practitioners. It emphasizes that the organizational climate appears to predispose an organization toward either productive conflict or destructive conflict and that the administrator influences this climate by his or her administrative style and values.

Yankelovich, Daniel, *The Magic of Dialogue: Transforming Conflict into Cooperation.* New York: Simon & Schuster, 1999.

Leaders in the ongoing struggle to forge a broad consensus on the goals, purposes, and methods of schooling must continually strive to improve communication between the parties to the debate. In this book, a social scientist and scholar in communication offers methods to help leaders master communication skills that they need to be more effective in resolving problems and achieving shared goals. The term *dialogue,* as Yankelovich uses it, has a specific meaning and is not merely a synonym for "conversation." He shows how to use dialogue to strengthen relationships, dissolve stereotypes, overcome mistrust, achieve mutual understanding, and shape visions grounded in shared purposes. Some have objected that this book is merely a systematic presentation of common sense. The problem is, however, that common sense is often one of the first things out the window when opposing forces contend over schooling. This valuable book takes the leader back to fundamentals—always, as any athlete will testify, a good idea when things are not going well.

chapter **11**

Motivation

LEARNING OBJECTIVES

After reading this chapter, you should be able to

- Identify and describe the three patterns of human behavior that indicate motivation.

- Identify, compare, and contrast intrinsic views of motivation with behaviorist views.

- Summarize and discuss the central findings about motivation of the Western Electric Studies.

- Describe Howard Gardner's approach to multiple intelligences and how it relates to motivation in the organization.

- Describe and discuss Carl Jung's understanding that individuals are motivated by inner forces, that these vary widely from person to person, but that there are patterns of these inner motivational forces that we call personality types.

- Summarize and describe the Myers-Briggs Type Indicator as an aid to understanding personality types.

- Describe the ideas about motivation that arise from John Atkinson's contention that everyone is driven by two learned characteristics: the desire to achieve success and the desire to avoid failure.

- Describe and discuss David McClelland's belief that there is a link between high achievement motivation as a sociocultural norm and the economic productivity of a people.

- Summarize and describe Maslow's theory of motivation as a hierarchy of needs.

- Explain the dynamic interplay that Herzberg described between motivating factors and maintenance factors in the workplace.

- Explain how $B = f(p \cdot e)$ expresses motivation as a result of the interaction between the person and the environment.

ISLLC Standards

STANDARD 2: A school administrator is an educational leader who promotes the success of all students by advocating, nurturing, and sustaining a school culture and instructional program conducive to student learning and staff professional growth.

Knowledge

The administrator has knowledge and understanding of:

- applied motivational theories
- diversity and its meaning for educational programs
- adult learning and professional development models
- school cultures

Dispositions

The administrator believes in, values, and is committed to:

- lifelong learning for self and others
- the benefits that diversity brings to the school community

Performances

The administrator facilitates processes and engages in activities ensuring that:

- all individuals are treated with fairness, dignity, and respect
- students and staff feel valued and important
- the responsibilities and contributions of each individual are acknowledged
- lifelong learning is encouraged and modeled
- there is a culture of high expectations for self, student, and staff performance
- student and staff accomplishments are recognized and celebrated

STANDARD 3: A school administrator is an educational leader who promotes the success of all students by ensuring management of the organization, operations, and resources for a safe, efficient, and effective learning environment.

Knowledge

The administrator has knowledge and understanding of:

- theories and models of organizations and the principles of organizational development
- human resources management and development

Dispositions

The administrator believes in, values, and is committed to:

- trusting people and their judgments
- accepting responsibility

- high-quality standards, expectations, and performances
- involving stakeholders in management processes

Performances

The administrator facilitates processes and engages in activities ensuring that:

- stakeholders are involved in decisions affecting schools
- responsibility is shared to maximize ownership and accountability
- human resource functions support the attainment of school goals

STANDARD 5: A school administrator is an educational leader who promotes the success of all students by acting with integrity, fairness, and in an ethical manner.

Knowledge

The administrator has knowledge and understanding of:

- various ethical frameworks and perspectives on ethics

Dispositions

The administrator believes in, values, and is committed to:

- bringing ethical principles to the decision-making process
- subordinating one's own interest to the good of the school community

Performances

The administrator:

- examines personal and professional values
- considers the impact of one's administrative practices on others
- treats people fairly, equitably, and with dignity and respect

Now that organizational behavior has been described as arising from interactions between the person in the organization and characteristics of the organizational environment, or $B = f(p \cdot e)$, this chapter focuses on the person—the individual—in that equation. The previous chapters of the book focused on characteristics of the organizational environment in the equation.

The Meaning and Patterns of Motivation

Motivation deals with explanations of why people do the things they do. Why, for example, do some teachers regularly come to work and do as little as necessary, whereas others are full of energy and ideas and throw themselves zealously into the job? Why do some principals seem to focus only on the day-to-day operations in the school with no apparent vision of where the school should be headed, whereas others seem to embrace a clear, coherent vision of the school as it ought to be and pursue it consistently over the course of years? Why are some professors boring, monotonous lecturers whose classes students avoid, whereas other professors are so enthusiastic, vibrant, and creative that their classes are interesting, always fresh, and so popular with students that they are closed out early during registration?

For millennia, the mysteries of why people behave as they do have fascinated dramatists, artists, writers, composers, philosophers, theologians, and other observers of the human condition, as the libraries and museums of the world attest. For a century now, scholars have added their efforts to probing the enigma of human motivation and have produced a body of literature that is staggering in scope and size and illuminating as well. From all this we have learned a great deal about the links between motivation and human behavior, and we still have more to learn. This chapter discusses some of what we know and the pragmatic implications of that knowledge for the practice of leadership in educational organizations.

Although many theories of motivation exist, with new ones appearing every year, and much disagreement about them among scholars, there is also substantial agreement on what we are talking about when discussing motivation. Scholars generally agree, for example, that when we observe the variation in human behavior in organizations, at least three motivational patterns are evident.

First Pattern: Direction in Making Choices

One of the first indicators of motivation is the apparent pattern of choices that individuals make when confronted with an array of possible alternatives. When a person attends to one thing rather than others, the observer may make some motivational inference from the behavior of choosing but, of course, cannot know what actually caused the choice to be made. For example, one teacher might habitually arrive at school early in the morning, pick up the mail promptly, and proceed briskly to the classroom to prepare for the day's work so as to be ready and relaxed before the students arrive. Another teacher might wander in much later, chat and socialize in the office until the last moment, then dash to the classroom to begin work by fumbling with papers as the students sit at their desks waiting. A similar example is the professor who, seeing the academic job as demanding only three days a week on campus, regularly spends two days on the golf course or at the tennis club, whereas a colleague spends every spare moment studying and preparing articles for publication in academic journals that not only do not pay for them but also reject three times more manuscripts than they publish.

Second Pattern: Persistence

A second critical indicator of motivation is the persistence with which one pursues the chosen course of action. One dimension of persistence is the amount of time a person devotes to the chosen activity. Whether it is refinishing antiques or creating plans for a new teaching project, some people will work intensely for long hours seeking to produce meticulous, high-quality results, whereas others may give the task a "lick and a promise," consider the result good enough to get by, and let it go at that. Indeed, an individual may show great persistence in pursuing one activity meticulously and show remarkably little persistence in pursuing another. Another dimension of persistence is observed when an individual returns to a task time and again to achieve the desired results. Some teachers, for example, never seem to have the job done and frequently take work home to spend more hours on it, whereas others usually close up shop as soon as the buses have left and won't think about their work again until tomorrow. Some professors pull old yellowed lecture notes from the file year after year, whereas others spend many hours every year not merely editing, revising, and polishing their lectures but creating new methods of instruction in the hope of making classes not only more informative but more interesting as well.

Third Pattern: Intensity

The intensity with which a person attends to doing something is a third behavioral indicator that seems to be linked to motivation. One person can work with apparent high energy, seemingly concentrating intensely, engrossed in the work, whereas another might be observed to be much less intensely involved when attending to a task. Observations of intensity have to be interpreted more carefully than observations of either direction or persistence, because factors beyond the control of the individual may be involved, such as the environment and the skill of the individual. For example, observing work behavior in environments where there are many uncontrolled interruptions, as is common in some schools, makes it difficult to determine whether the level of intensity is a matter of individual choice or the result of environmental disturbance. Similarly, an individual may be observed as being little involved as a participant in meetings, apparently merely waiting quietly for the time to pass that will bring the meeting to a close. The problem here could easily be environmental, such as a social climate in the meeting not being conducive to participation; or it may be that the individual has never developed the behavioral attitudes and skills that one needs to participate confidently in the give-and-take of effective meetings; or it may simply be that the topic under consideration is neither interesting nor relevant to the individual.

The Extrinsic-Intrinsic Debate

Two major approaches dominated thinking about motivation in organizational behavior during the twentieth century. One has been described as *The Great Jackass Fallacy*.[1] That is the age-old metaphor of the carrot and the stick, which prescribes that a combination of proffering some mix of rewards and punishments is a way to motivate people in organizational life. It is associated with behaviorist psychology in which external control of the individual is emphasized.

The other approach, associated with both cognitive psychology and humanist psychology, emphasizes the psychic energy of internal thoughts and feelings as the primary source of motivation.

Extrinsic, or Behaviorist, Views

Managers have traditionally sought to motivate people with a carrot and a stick. They long ago found that people who are hurt tend to move in order to avoid pain and that people who are rewarded tend to repeat the behavior that brought the reward. This is a behaviorist concept of motivation, and it has long been highly influential in management thought. Managers using such techniques would say, "We're motivating the employees!"

The behaviorist view of motivation, that people can be motivated through manipulation of positive reinforcers (the carrot) and negative reinforcers (the stick), has been widely embraced and used in educational organizations. Merit pay plans, demands for accountability, emphasis on formal supervision, annual performance reviews tied to reappointment to position, and "teacher recognition days" are but a few of the many ways that this motivational concept is routinely used in public school praxis. In the same vein, universities often practice an "up-or-out" policy to motivate newly appointed junior faculty members. They are commonly given a stipulated number of years to demonstrate growing research production through publication of their works; at the end of the time period, they know that they may be either rewarded for their behavior by being promoted and granted tenure or punished by dismissal.

Intrinsic Views of Motivation

Some contend that the behaviorist approach has nothing to do with motivation. As Frederick Herzberg said of the carrot-and-the-stick approach, "Hell, you're not motivating them. You're moving them."[2] Herzberg's observation points to a major criticism of the behaviorist approach to motivation: it in fact does not deal with motivation at all.

The view is that although people can be *controlled* by external forces such as rewards and punishments, a crucial factor in the *motivation* of people lies within the individuals themselves. The cognitive and humanistic views of motivation spring from an understanding of people as unfolding and developing both physiologically and psychologically from biological givens. The internal capacities of individuals, primarily emotional and cognitive, give rise to feelings, aspirations, perceptions, attitudes, and thoughts, and it is these that can be motivating or demotivating. In this view, motivation is thought of as creating conditions in the organization that facilitate and enhance the likelihood that the internal capacities of members will mature both intellectually and emotionally, thus increasing their motivation. In sum, the behaviorist tends to view motivation as something that one does *to* people, whereas the cognitive or humanist tends to view motivation as tapping the inner drives of people by creating growth-enhancing environments.

Individual and Group Motivation

Let's now focus on the motivation of people in organizations, as distinguished from the more general, broader concept of motivation of individuals qua individuals. A crucial point to remember in understanding organizational behavior is that, as a member of an organization, the person does not act alone and independently: the organization member always acts as a member of a group, and that concept is probably central to understanding organizational behavior. Groups are dynamic social systems that establish interdependent relationships between and among people.

Thus, if you find yourself hurrying along a crowded city street, you would hardly think of the throng as a group of which you are a member. On the other hand, if you step to the curb and take your place in a queue to wait for a bus, you have joined a group, albeit a primitive one. The members of that group, the bus queue, share certain purposes, values, and expectations for behavior that bond them in common purpose and modify not only your own behavior but your attitudes and beliefs as well. Thus, if someone had the temerity to cut in line near the head of the queue, you would probably become concerned and join with fellow group members in remonstrating with the individual in an effort to get him to abide by the behavioral norms tacitly shared by the group.

The character and quality of the group's internal dynamics are often described in terms of group cohesion and morale. These dynamics of the group give rise, in turn, to basic assumptions and values that are shared between and among the members of the group as "truth" and "reality." The latter point, which is the essence of group climate and culture, was discussed in greater depth in Chapter 6.

The power of group norms in motivating people at work, having been first clearly identified in the Western Electric Studies almost eighty years ago, is well established in the literature of organizational behavior and is widely understood and accepted. Let's take a moment to consider once again and more exactly what was learned in those studies.

The Western Electric Studies Revisited

Most students of education have heard something about the Hawthorne Studies or the Western Electric Studies, if in no other way than to have learned about the so-called Hawthorne effect, about which I shall say more in a moment. This classic research has had such profound impact on the understanding of motivation at work, and has been so widely misunderstood in educational circles, that we should take a moment to review it here. This discussion draws on only two of the many studies that composed this very sizable research project.

The Illumination Studies

The Hawthorne Works of the Western Electric Company, located in Cicero near Chicago, was chosen as the site for an experimental study that was started in 1924 and ended ten years later. This particular site was selected for the experiment largely because the management of Western Electric was considered enlightened and likely to be cooperative with the investigators. The purpose of the study was to find out how much illumination was required to achieve the maximum output from workers.

Two groups of employees doing similar work under similar conditions were chosen, and records of output were kept for each group. The intensity of the light under which one group worked was varied, while that under which the other group worked was held constant. By this method, the investigators hoped to isolate from the effect of other variables, the effect of changes in the intensity of illumination on the rate of output.[3]

But in the early stages of the research the investigators were disappointed; it soon became obvious that no simple relationship existed between the intensity of illumination and the workers' rate of output. "The employees [reacted] to changes in light intensity in the way they assumed they were expected to react," George Homans reported, "that is, when light intensity was increased, they were expected to produce more; when it was decreased, they were expected to produce less. A further experiment was designed to demonstrate this point."[4] The lightbulbs were changed so that the workers were allowed to assume that there would be more light when, in fact, other bulbs of the same power had been installed. Of course, as we now know, each change of bulbs resulted in some increase in output by the workers regardless of the level of illumination that they provided. Clearly, the workers in the experimental group were responding to *their perceptions* of the expectations of the experimenters and not to the changes in the physical environment. Thus, the workers were responding to *psychological* factors that motivated their behavior at work and, at the time of the experiments, the nature of these psychological factors was unknown to the investigators.

The significance of this study was not lost on the researchers. Whereas traditional management theory would have posited that changes in the physical environment would have an impact on worker productivity, this experiment showed a direct relationship between productivity and *psychological* phenomena, such as the expectations of others and being the focus of attention. This is sometimes called the "Hawthorne effect," which has often been misinterpreted by many educators as suggesting that merely paying attention to people, changing some things in their environment, and expecting higher achievement from them will increase their motivation. As we shall see, there is much more to it than that.

The Relay Inspection Group Studies

After the study on the relationship between illumination and productivity was concluded, leaving more questions than answers, a new experimental study was organized in the Hawthorne Works involving workers who assembled telephone relays. The researchers used a control group, which worked in the regular shop, and an experimental group, which was given a separate work area. To initiate the experiment,

the operators who had been chosen to take part were called in for an interview in the office of the Superintendent of the Inspection Branch [remember, this was in 1927, and the workers all were women]. . . . The nature of the test was carefully explained to these girls and they readily consented to take part in it. . . . They were assured that the object of the test was to determine the effect of certain changes in working conditions, such as rest periods, midmorning lunches, and shorter working hours. They were especially cautioned to work at a comfortable pace, and under no circumstances to try to make a race of the test. This conference was only the first of many that were to be held during the course of the experiment. Whenever any experimental change was planned, the girls were called in, the purpose of the change was explained to them, and their comments were requested. Certain suggested changes which did not meet with their approval were abandoned.[5]

Working methodically for over a year, the researchers kept careful production records while trying different experimental interventions: rest pauses, special lunch periods, a shorter working day, and a shorter working week. Throughout the period of the experimental work, output rose slowly and steadily. In each period of the experiment, output was higher than in the preceding period. Finally, the work conditions of the group were, with the consent of the workers, returned to the same as they had been prior to the start of the research (no rest periods, no special lunch periods, a regular-length workday and workweek). The result: productivity *continued to rise*. In fact, "the output of the group continued to rise until it established itself on a high plateau from which there was no descent until the time of discouragement and deepening economic depression which preceded the end of the test" in 1933.[6] In sum, the group had (1) become more productive and (2) had maintained that high productivity even after the experimental interventions were taken away. If rest periods and shorter working hours, plus the "special attention" of being in an experimental group, could not account for the change, what could?

Central Findings of the Studies

It took a number of people some years to analyze all the data and gradually put together a picture of what had happened. The salient facts are these:

1. The workers liked the experimental situation and considered it fun.
2. The new form of supervision (encouraging them to work at a normal pace and not to try to hurry) made it possible for them to work freely and without anxiety.[7]
3. The workers knew that what they did was important and that results were expected.
4. The workers were consulted about planned changes, often by the superintendent himself, and during that process were encouraged to express their views and were, in fact, permitted to veto some ideas before they were ever implemented.
5. As a result, the group itself had changed and developed during the course of the experiment. Though the last step of the experiment was an attempt to return the group to the original conditions of work by taking away the experimental rest periods, new hours, and the like, it was in fact impossible to return the group to its original state because the group itself had been transformed. It had become more cohesive, it had developed a distinctive esprit, and it was functioning at a significantly more mature level than it had been in the beginning.

In sum,

> the women were made to feel that they were an important part of the company. . . . They had become participating members of a congenial, cohesive work group . . . that elicited feelings of affiliation, competence, and achievement. These needs, which had long gone unsatisfied at work, were now being fulfilled. The women worked harder and more effectively than they had previously.[8]

Or, in the vernacular of today's educational reform, the women had been empowered, had participated in making decisions that were important to them and their work, had been treated in ways that fostered personal feelings of dignity and respect, and had gained "ownership" of their work and how it was performed. However it is expressed, clearly this experience had transformed the group into a much more effective team than it had been before, as the sustained increase in productivity over time showed.

Impact of the Studies

One very interesting aspect of this research is that at the time, when it was not unknown for companies routinely to send goons to beat up dissident workers, it was so unusual for a company to relate to workers in these ways that many years passed before it dawned on anyone (except a very few advanced scholars) what had happened in the Hawthorne plant during those experiments. For decades, many students of organization and management chose to believe that the Hawthorne Studies showed that if you pay a little attention to people by changing some of their working conditions, their motivation will take an upward tick and productivity will increase. This misreading of the research is often called the Hawthorne effect.

However, it is now clear that the Western Electric Studies set the stage for the evolution of widespread research seeking to better understand the nature and needs of human beings at work and to apply this knowledge to the development of more effective organizations. Drawing on that large and still growing body of research, plus extensive practical experience in applying the emerging new knowledge to a variety of organizations, we now understand that the higher productivity achieved during the Western Electric research resulted from the fact that under participative leadership the groups of workers themselves developed greater cohesiveness, higher morale, and values that were highly motivating. Once collaborative group processes had been established, the individual participants were no longer merely working side by side, but became interrelated in ways that were unique to that specific group. Today, of course, that is commonly called teamwork and it is at the heart of motivational concepts in work groups. Moreover, as the Western Electric Studies showed, once established, teamwork can become not only a powerful motivator but one that tends to endure. Though school boards, school administrators, and managers who like to view themselves as being tough failed for decades to understand the power and significance of this simple, crucial discovery even as it was being reconfirmed in study after study over the years, it eventually emerged in the 1980s as the central idea in the transformation of organizational life and leadership in U.S. business and industry and, eventually, education.

Contemporary Views of the Western Electric Studies

The Western Electric Studies are arguably the most seminal research of the twentieth century on organizational behavior in the workplace. They illumined a whole new approach to understanding the subject and paved the way for such modern notions as participative management, democracy in the workplace, empowerment, and more. The foundations of organization and management as we know it today, including the field of organizational behavior, were built on the Western Electric Studies and they have stood the test of time and trial for seven decades. Contemporary scholarship developed on those foundations has added a great deal to our knowledge, but little of it has dimmed the luster of that early seminal research.

Individual Differences

Thus far, the discussion has dwelt on some notable *environmental* factors in the basic organizational behavior equation, $B = f(p \cdot e)$. We turn now to a discussion of useful ways of thinking about the differences in the intrinsic characteristics of the *person* in that dynamic concept. One question about motivation that commonly arises is, what gets people "turned on" or "turned off"? Why is it, for example, that one person will select a particular thing to do, stick with it, and work intensively on it, whereas another person might show no interest whatever? Psychologists call this "turning on" to something, this energizing of human behavior, "arousal": it is clearly an internal aspect of self, seemingly involving emotional processes as well as cognitive processes, a characteristic that lies close to the personality of the individual. Clearly, then, the individual brings unique personal characteristics to the dynamic social interaction processes of the group. The characteristics of these internal capacities literally determine how one perceives the environment and makes judgments about it.

In Praise of Diversity

In today's world, when all people of good will seek to avoid the bigotry of stereotyping and labeling of others, any effort to type or categorize people tends to be met with suspicion. Yet the fact is

> that people are different from each other, and no amount of getting after them is going to change them. Nor is there any reason to change them, because the differences are probably good, not bad. People are different in fundamental ways. They *want* different things; they have different motives, purposes, aims, values, needs, drives, impulses, urges. Nothing is more fundamental than that. They *believe* differently: they think, cognize, conceptualize, perceive, understand, comprehend, and cogitate differently.[9]

Because such inner attributes—cognitions, urges, values, perceptions, and so on—are crucial in prompting us to say what we say and do what we do, the individual differences between and among us can and do evoke a vast range of behaviors. From those behaviors we can deduce a great deal about the motivations of individuals and create useful descriptive categories. But one must be extremely cautious not to slip into the error of labeling one behavioral style good and another bad.

Because what is being discussed here is the inner characteristics of the person, their temperament or personality, we are unsure of the extent to which they are either learned or innate. We are therefore unsure of the extent to which they can be intentionally modified. Some take a fairly absolutist view of this, comparing psychological type to other fixed characteristics. For example, just as short persons cannot make themselves tall and one cannot change the pattern of fingerprints or the color of the eyes, one cannot change inner drives and attributes. Others believe that some modification of inner characteristics may be possible but always at the risk of distorting, destroying, or scarring the original instead of transforming it into something new.

However, a problem in this debate is the all too common tendency to confuse various ways of perceiving, thinking, feeling, and behaving as shortcomings or flaws that need to be corrected. Keirsey and Bates reminded us of the Pygmalion story from Greek mythology and cautioned that efforts to sculpt others so that they conform to our own standard of perfection are doomed to failure at the outset.[10] Educators deal with this all the time: for example, we may understand, and perhaps accept, the idea of multiple intelligences, yet in our schools there is powerful social and cultural pressure to put a premium on certain kinds of intelligences, especially the linguistic and logical-mathematical, and value the others less in varying degrees. Thus, the logic of American cultural traditions prods schools to emphasize and extol in the official curriculum languages, math, and sciences for all students and tends to marginalize music, the arts, and bodily kinesthetic opportunities for development. In the minds of many Americans, for example, a "good" kindergarten curriculum stresses formal instruction in reading, language, and arithmetic and "wastes" little time on activities in which children move about, engage others in play, and participate in physical activities.

So we proceed from the assumption that people are fundamentally different in many ways, that we can understand important patterns of those differences, and that we can learn to make that understanding work productively for us. The converse assumption would be that people are, or should be, fundamentally all alike and our goal is to get them to behave alike. That, however, appears to be a twentieth-century confusion that arises from the growth of democracy in the Western world: the idea that if we are equals, then we must be alike.[11] Today, in the twenty-first century, we celebrate a different idea: as we are equals, we may be different from one another.

Understanding and accepting diversity between and among people in a nonjudgmental way is important to understanding and working with organizational behavior in education. In praxis, this means that educational administration and leadership emphasizes creating environments in organizations that simultaneously

- foster and enhance the growth and development of participants in terms of their own perceptions, needs, aspirations, and self-fulfillment and
- accept the fact that not only do individuals differ from one another but that this diversity can be a source of great strength to the organization.

Archetypes

We commonly make the great diversity between and among people manageable by thinking of individuals as archetypes: "Oh," we say, "he's that kind of guy!" or "Did you hear what she asked? That's vintage Harriet Smith!" Psychologists do the same thing.

- Howard Gardner described the differences between and among people in terms of seven kinds of intelligence.
- Based on the work of Carl Jung, many psychologists describe individuals in terms of their temperaments, or personality types.
- Not a few psychologists, such as Carol Gilligan, have used gender as a lens to examine and understand individual differences in organizational life.

Human Intelligence

Earlier in this book we discussed intelligence as a critical variable in the ways in which people differ. In his landmark book on human intelligences—which set forth the concept of multiple intelligences—Howard Gardner drew attention to the shift during the twentieth century of philosophers and psychologists from focusing on the external objects of the physical world in explaining human behavior to focusing on the mind, and especially cognitive thought, which depends so heavily on symbols such as from language, mathematics, the visual arts, body language, and other human symbols.[12] As we described in Chapter 2, Gardner explained that there are several kinds of intelligence and that they are independent of one another; each kind enables a person to engage in intellectual activity in different ways.

In describing the historical underpinnings of his theory of multiple intelligences, Gardner recounted the noted meeting between William James, the first world-renowned psychology scholar from the United States, and Sigmund Freud, which took place in Worcester in 1909. The occasion was Freud's only trip to the United States, which was at the invitation of G. Stanley Hall, the psychologist who was then president of Clark University. The meeting between Freud, who had already achieved celebrity in Europe, and the aging James is acclaimed in the history of the development of psychology because it set the stage for the eventual emergence of modern psychology that was to transcend the radical behaviorism that was so dominant in the United States at that time.

"What united Freud and James," Gardner explains, "and what set them apart from the mainstream of psychology both on the Continent and in the United States, was a belief in the importance, the centrality, of the individual self—a conviction that psychology must be built around the concept of the person, his personality, his growth, his fate. Moreover, both scholars deemed the capacity for self-growth to be an important one, upon which depended the possibility of coping with one's surroundings."[13] Curiously, Gardner did not mention the presence of another person on that historic occasion who was to play a pivotal role in explaining human personality and its capacity for self-growth and adaptation to the environment. Carl Jung, then thirty-four and a close collaborator of Freud's, would soon thereafter break away from his older colleague and create new ways of understanding the differences between and among individuals that have proven to be invaluable in understanding organizational behavior.

Temperament and Organizational Behavior

Early psychology was dominated by the notion that people are motivated from within by a single instinct. The scholar's challenge was to identify that instinct. To Freud it was eros, which manifested itself in different guises at different times. Adler thought that the motivating instinct was to acquire power. Others thought that the desire for social belonging was the central motivational instinct. To the existentialists it was the search for self that informed and drove our behavior. "Each appealed to instinct as purpose, and each made one instinct primary for everybody."[14]

Carl Jung's masterwork on motivation revealed that this was not so, that individuals are motivated by different inner forces and there is wide variation in these motivational forces from person to person. But Jung identified a pattern in these individual differences. Understanding the pattern of individual differences enables one to better understand the behavior of others and to predict their likely behaviors under different circumstances. This was the basis for understanding the concept of "personality types."

Like Freud, his senior and sometime mentor, Carl Jung was a clinical psychologist. Having observed many people in his clinical practice, he began to think that the personalities of various individuals could be sorted into categories according to types. He compared his observations with studies of literature, mythology, and religions and found that the idea was often used by writers and other observers of human behavior. He published a treatise on the subject in 1920, and a student of his translated it into English in 1923;[15] both publications were largely ignored. Why? Because "in 1923, other approaches to psychology were dominant in Europe and North America. Freudian psychology was in vogue in Europe and on both American coasts, while grass-roots America was under the overwhelming influence of behaviorism. Scientific circles of the time regarded Jung as mystical and his approach antithetical to their own penchant for logic and facts."[16]

The Four Psychological Types

Cutting through the confusion that abounds in trying to understand the essential personality differences between and among people, Jung's observations led him to a simple analysis: there are three basic dimensions of human personality, and the "mix" of these dimensions varies from person to person although they cluster into patterns that are called "psychological types." In the 1950s, as we shall describe, Isabel Myers and her mother, Katheryn Briggs, added a fourth dimension to the analysis, laying the basis for identifying four psychological types—or four temperaments—of people, an analysis that is widely accepted today.

When we speak of four psychological types, we are speaking of the ways in which people perceive the world around them, how they interpret what they perceive, and how they form judgments about their perceptions—that is, the extent to which people are

(1) introverted or extraverted,* (2) sensing or intuitive, (3) thinking or feeling, and (4) perceiving or judging. From the perspective of psychological types, therefore, there is no objective independent reality that we call the environment: the "real" environment depends largely on how one perceives and interprets it. This is an important point in understanding organizational behavior and a central tenet of postmodern thought: the reality of organizational life lies largely in the eye of the beholder. An understanding of one's own temperament not only puts one in a better position to understand how one sees and deals with the organizational world but also gives one greater ability to understand the behavior of others in the organization.

Four Basic Dimensions of Human Personality

The Myers-Briggs Type Indicator (MBTI) is a paper-and-pencil instrument that seeks to identify sixteen different patterns of action that people are likely to follow in responding to certain situations. The sixteen patterns of action are combinations of four dimensions that describe the preferences that one might have in dealing with the situations. Three of the dimensions were described by Jung in the 1920s:

- introversion-extraversion
- sensation-intuition
- thinking-feeling

Myers and Briggs used these three dimensions as scales to create the MBTI. As one would in creating such a personality inventory, they devised questions to represent these scales to which people taking the test would respond. During their work, Myers and Briggs created a fourth dimension that they believed was needed:

- perceiving-judging

The MBTI became popular in U.S. corporate organizations as a self-assessment instrument for those who wanted to learn more about themselves as managers as well as about their colleagues. It has also been used in corporate training programs to help work groups gain a better understanding of ways to become more effective in dealing with various types of colleagues in the organization. Aside from its uses as a self-assessment instrument, the dimensions on which the MBTI is built provide an interesting way to analyze and understand organizational behavior.

Introversion-Extraversion

Jung "used the term *attitude* to refer to the ways that individuals direct their psychic energy. He described two attitudes: the extraverted and the introverted."[17] Some people character-

---

*The atypical spelling of the word *extraversion* became the accepted spelling in the subject index of *Psychological Abstracts* in 1974 and has been the accepted spelling in the literature on individual differences since that time.

istically receive great psychic energy from external sources: people, events, and things in the environment. Typically these are very sociable individuals who like to talk to people and play and work with them; they find that meeting and interacting with others is not only fun, but also that it invigorates them and recharges their psychic batteries. They are the extraverts, and whether at work, at play, or on vacation, they gravitate to other people and want to be involved where the action is. Working alone in quiet places is wearisome to the extravert, who tends to find such activities as research in the library or puzzling alone over a complex problem tiring and draining.

Introverts, on the other hand, though they usually like people and often enjoy being around them, tend to find socializing taxing, tiring, draining of their energies rather than energizing. The introvert prefers quiet, even being alone at times, and in this environment is recharged and invigorated.

These dimensions—introversion and extraversion—are useful in thinking about motivation because they reveal deep-seated orientations as to how one literally perceives the world, where one gets information about the world, and how one makes judgments about what is real in the world. Two individuals, one an extravert and the other an introvert, tend to experience identical events differently, understand them differently, and respond to them differently. This said, it is important to remind ourselves that one is not *either* an introvert *or* an extravert. This is a dimension that describes the intensity of a personality characteristic; although each of us may tend to emphasize either extravert attitudes or introvert attitudes, most of us find that both attitudes coexist in each of us.

Sensation-Intuition and Thinking-Feeling

In describing the ways in which different types of people related to their environments, Jung saw that there were two rational functions, thinking and feeling, and two nonrational functions, sensing and intuition. These allude to how one experiences, judges, and reacts to events in the environment. Normally one, or perhaps two, tend to dominate in an individual. These four functions are summarized as follows:

> The rational functions, thinking and feeling, evaluate and judge information. *Thinking* uses principled reasoning, logic, and impersonal analysis to evaluate information and situations. To make a judgment, criteria are sufficiency of data, validity, and reasonableness. *Feeling*, by contrast, uses empathy or personal values to make a judgment. Of prime importance in feeling is the impact a judgment will have upon another person. The feeling person calculates subjectively whether a judgment is important or unimportant, valuable or useless.
>
> The [nonrational] functions, sensing and intuition, simply receive and process information without evaluating or judging it. *Sensation* is sense perception, or perception mediated by the bodily senses. Its focus is on concrete, tangible realities in the present. Sensing types of people distrust ideas that cannot be supported by the facts. *Intuition* is perception through the unconscious. The intuitive individual can arrive at a perception without being aware of the concrete basis for that perception. Intuitive types of people can make leaps from the past or the present to future possibilities, and they can perceive complex connections among various phenomena.[18]

Perceiving-Judging

As Myers and Briggs developed an instrument for identifying personality types (about which more will be said in a moment), they added a fourth dimension of behavior that people use in dealing with the world around them: perceiving and judging. A *perceiving* person is one who tends to use either sensing or intuition in making sense of the environment. On the other hand, one who tends to use either thinking or feeling in interactions with the environment is described as a *judging* type of individual.

The Myers-Briggs Type Indicator (MBTI)

After World War II, when the field of psychology underwent extraordinary ferment in which many alternatives to traditional academic behaviorism emerged, Jung's idea that these "psychological types" existed and could be identified was revisited. Myers and Briggs triggered widespread interest in the possibilities and uses of this idea when they created a simple questionnaire that was said to be reliable and valid in determining the psychological type of individuals. The MBTI[19] makes it easy to use the four behavioral dimensions that have just been described to sort people out according to the preferences that they tend to use in dealing with the world around them. The MBTI and its offshoots have also been widely advocated in popular literature for individuals to use as a way of assessing their own personality type.[20] To anyone who would be an educational leader, having a clear understanding of how one functions in the world—how one "reads" the environment, the kinds of information one attends to, how one interprets what is perceived—is, of course, a great advantage in dealing effectively with many kinds of people.

The idea of different personality types as a set of lenses through which one may view and understand the behavior of men and women in the organization is an interesting—and, many find, useful—alternative to the lenses demanded by, for example, radical feminist psychology, which generally describes men and women as perceiving and functioning differently and explains the differences in terms of the cultural norms associated with gender. There is little doubt that, as Carol Gilligan made clear, "psychology has persistently and systematically misunderstood women," including their motives, and when men view the world differently than women do, "the conclusion is that something may be wrong with women."[21] There is also little doubt that psychology has little understood the whole concept of personality types.

Introversion-Extraversion

For example, about 75 percent of the population are thought to have extraverted attitudes and about 25 percent are thought to be introverted.[22] But as Gilligan pointed out in discussing sex differences in psychological attitudes, "it is difficult to say 'different' without saying 'better' or 'worse' since there is a tendency to construct a single scale of measurement [in one's mind]," and the same is true in dealing with introversion-extraversion. Just as some people tend to think there is something wrong with women who do not conform to male-dominated norms of motivation,[23] so in Western cultures it is common to think that there is something wrong with those individuals who prefer a little peace and quiet, perhaps some solitude, and a little territorial breathing room. "Indeed," noted Keirsey and Bates, "Western culture seems to sanction the outgoing, sociable and gregarious temperament. The notion of anyone wanting or needing much solitude is viewed rather often as reflecting an unfriendly attitude."[24] When one considers that the attitudes of people in non-Western cultures often tend to be more supportive and approving of those who prefer to direct their psychological energy inward than those whose energy is primarily directed outward, it becomes clearer that Jung was at least close to being right in believing that introversion-extraversion reveals some combination of innate, inherited attitudes, skills that reflect learning to conform to cultural norms. For example, the introverted individual may very well learn the social skills and attitudes to deal effectively with the expectation that one occasionally attends large, noisy cocktail parties as part of professional life. The extravert, on the other hand, may learn to "work the room" expertly. The difference is that the introvert will find the experience demanding, perhaps tiring, while the extravert will find it exhilarating and just plain fun.

A Dimension Rather Than Either-Or

In thinking about introversion-extraversion attitudes, however, it must be underscored that we are dealing with a dimension with two poles: introversion at one end and extraversion at the other. One's attitude will lean toward one pole or the other, but it would be rare indeed to find a "pure" type. Thus, an introvert is not totally without the ability to enjoy other people, to socialize, or to share with them, nor is an extravert unable to enjoy concentrating on lonely tasks or a break away from the "pressure cooker" of the organization. It is the balance, chiefly between sociability and territory, that identifies types in this dimension.

Intuition-Sensation

Intuition and sensation are ways of thinking about the world around us. Although differences in introversion-extraversion are important differences between and among people, intuition-sensation differences may be, more than any of the other factors in personality typing, "the sources of the most miscommunication, misunderstanding, vilification, defamation, and denigration. *This difference places the widest gulf between people.*"[25] This is probably due in large part to the fact that these two ways of receiving information about our environment are opposites, polarities—not a continuum. One who relies on sense perception to get information probably cannot also use intuition simultaneously. These two lenses on the world are opposites, and when one individual operates on the basis of sensation and the other on the basis of intuition, the groundwork is laid for misunderstanding.

Sensation is sense perception—that is, perception as it is received and processed by the body, such as sight, sound, touch, taste, and feel. Sensation is real, seemingly tangible, in the immediate here and now. The person who prefers to be informed by sensation tends to be one who relies on facts and observation, who trusts the lessons drawn from practical experience, emphasizes the demonstrable, and tends to ask, "How do you know?"

The polar opposite of sensation, intuition, is a very different way of gathering information with which to make sense of the world around us. Rather than sense perception received and mediated through the body, intuition is perception through the unconscious.[26] Individuals who depend on intuition for information about the environment often develop an insight without knowing exactly the bases for it. They are often quick to spot patterns and connections between and among elements of complex situations, though they are not sure how they saw them. Intuitive people tend to be able to project from the present to future possibilities. They like ingenuity and often express themselves through metaphor, fantasy, and fiction. Many times, of course, they are impatient with the attention to detail of sensation-oriented colleagues and view them as plodding and unimaginative. For their part, sensation-oriented people—who emphasize being sensible, practical, and no-nonsense—often find intuitive colleages impractical and unaware of realities.

The intuition-oriented person can be impatient with insistence on facts and hard evidence, tends to use metaphor and imagery, and often fails to notice details in observation that the sensation-oriented person notes at once. The intuitive individual, not infrequently to the despair of the sensation-oriented individual, often speaks about future possibilities for making things better; tends to bounce from one vision to another, often leaving a project before it is completed to take up another; and talks a lot about the future, about what may be possible, creative, and imaginative. As we have seen, using the examples of intelligences, personality types, and gender, many psychologists focus on the role that various personal characteristics play in motivation. These personal characteristics are thought to be basic to motivation: in large measure they literally construct the environment of the individual by defining and describing what is perceived and understood; they cause a person to attend to one thing rather than another; they explain why the individual is persistent in some tasks and desultory in others. Sense making, viewed through the lenses of individual differences, is informed by the way one thinks, feels, and experiences as one interacts with the organizational environment.

To what extent are these personal characteristics innate or learned? In pragmatic terms, we don't know: for scholars, the debate continues. However, many theories of motivation have been constructed on the assumption that humans universally respond to certain innate needs, and new theories of this sort appear every year.

Intrinsic Motivation

Other than behaviorist theories of motivation, which emphasize motivational factors external to the individual (e.g., the carrot and the stick), two main streams of motivational thought exist: the cognitive perspective and the humanistic perspective. Both view motivation as intrinsic, or arising from within the individual.

Cognitive Views of Motivation

One cognitive perspective on motivation is based on the belief that human beings have an innate inner drive to understand the world, to make sense of it, to gain control over their lives, and to become increasingly self-directed. This is thought to give rise to certain innate characteristics that arouse and energize individuals to work toward these ends. Following Piaget, the cognitive perspective assumes that people are motivated by a need for order, predictability, sensibleness, and logic in dealing with the world. This is equilibrium, an idea central to Piaget's theory.[27] Piaget used the term *equilibration* to describe the processes of seeking equilibrium. In applying the notion of equilibrium to organizational life, one would tend to emphasize organizational routines to develop regularity, predictability, and dependability as desirable motivating processes.

Achievement Motivation

John Atkinson thought that every individual was driven by two learned characteristics: the desire to achieve success (n Achievement or n Ach) and/or the desire to avoid failure.[28] Some people are high in their n Ach and low in the need to avoid failure (low avoidance), whereas others are low in their n Ach and high in avoidance of failure (high avoidance). The behaviors of people with these two different motivational traits obviously tend to be different. Atkinson's work, which was carried on and extended by his close colleague and longtime collaborator, David McClelland, has had enormous impact on thinking about the behavior of managers in corporate America and in conceptualizing entrepreneurship in free market capitalism. Woven into achievement motivation theory is a very strong element of competition.

It would appear that high n Ach people thrive on competition and find it zestful and energizing, whereas high avoidance people tend to shun competition and find it stressful. But it should be made clear that the approach-avoidance concept is about *potential in human characteristics*: one may exhibit high avoidance behavior in some situations, yet in other circumstances one's n Ach motives may be aroused and one may engage in highly competitive behavior. A shy, self-effacing young woman, for example, may shun public appearances and large, glittering celebrity parties, yet step onstage before a world-class orchestra and an audience of thousands and deliver a brilliant violin solo knowing that the critics as well as her older colleagues listen perceptively, looking for the slightest flaw.

In the literature on achievement, success-oriented people (high approach to success—low in avoidance of failure) are extolled as achieving beyond and above the standards, beating the competition, being winners. High approach people are epitomized in the stereotype of the American entrepreneur as mythologized during the Reagan/Bush presidencies: hard-driving, risk taking, tough, relentless, narrowly focused on achieving a limited goal, driven by the clock, often with little consideration for others. Failure avoiders (low approach–high avoidance), on the other hand, act more defensively, are more careful to avoid losses, and often restructure the situation so that failure may be redefined as success.

Although people high in n Ach anticipate and savor success and victory in competition, their counterparts seek to avoid humiliation and failure. Just as achievers work hard and relentlessly to assure success, failure avoiders may tend toward inaction or may lower their aspirations to more closely match their perception of the likelihood of success. One has to be very careful, however, not to overgeneralize too glibly. Failure avoiders can, and often do, strive very hard, and are often highly successful in the process. Covington described it as "a frontal assault on failure—avoiding failure by succeeding! . . . These fear-driven successes can be extraordinary," he explained. "Many failure-threatened students are merit scholar finalists, class valedictorians, and National Science Fair winners. Despite such outward signs of success, however, being driven to succeed out of fear may be the ultimate academic ordeal. The individual's sense of worth comes to depend to an increasingly perilous degree on always succeeding, relentlessly, and against lengthening odds."[29] Yet the central point should not be missed: those who seek to avoid failure can be, and often are, highly motivated people.

Ferdinand Hoppe did landmark research on the roles of self-confidence, expectations, and aspirations in the motivation of people when he was Kurt Lewin's laboratory assistant in 1930–1931. Martin Covington described Hoppe's experimental work, which both Atkinson and McClelland surely knew well, in this way:

> Professor Lewin's laboratory [in Berlin] was crowded with the research paraphernalia of his time, including an odd conveyor-belt contraption that allowed a series of pegs to move on circular rollers at a uniform rate of speed, much like a row of ducks in a shooting gallery. This unlikely apparatus would provide the key to the question of how, psychologically, humans define success and failure. There are few consistent yardsticks when it comes to judging whether or not a particular achievement is successful—certainly not in the same sense that we can objectively measure height, weight, or temperature. Success and failure mean different things to different people. The same accomplishment can elicit pride in one person and self-rebuke in another, giving rise to the truism that 'one [person's] success is another [person's] failure.' However, for all the subjectivity involved, these judgments do proceed in lawful ways, as Hoppe was to discover.
>
> Hoppe invited an assortment of local tradespeople and university students to practice tossing rings on the moving pegs at various distances from the target. He found that some subjects felt satisfied after placing, say, 8 rings, whereas others expressed extreme frustration at only 12 correct tosses. Additionally, Hoppe found that the performance level needed to arouse feelings of success changed over time for each individual. A score that was initially judged a success might well be considered unacceptable on a later practice trial.
>
> Hoppe's revelation prompted a cascade of crucial insights. For instance it was now possible to give meaning to the concept of *self-confidence,* another psychological state of mind like success and failure. There is no accounting for self-confidence in objective terms. Some individuals may discern a gleam of hope in a situation that seems hopeless to everyone but themselves. At the same time, others may express a vote of no confidence despite the fact that they have everything going for them. Basically, self-confidence reflects the extent to which the individual believes himself or herself able to win the prize, to turn back the foe, or in Hoppe's experiment to toss enough rings correctly.[30]

McClelland and the "Spirit of Capitalism"

Having identified the need to achieve and the avoidance of failure as personality traits that are relatively stable and had some value in predicting behavior in various circumstances, McClelland proceeded to extend his thinking to the larger society and to the economic growth of nations around the world. His hypothesis was that, first, highly motivated people can change society itself, and therefore, second, a society experiences economic growth when it promotes the advancement and use of achievement motivation by its people. This could be done, McClelland believed—and many still believe strongly—by placing high value on the orientation to achievement and teaching this value in the home and in the schools, as well as teaching the attitudes, skills, and habits that might develop high n Ach.

Thus, McClelland elevated discourse on motivation to the realms of social, political, and economic policy. For example, in order to transform a society into a highly motivated society with a "spirit of capitalism," which he called *The Achieving Society,*[31] McClelland advocated child-rearing practices and schooling as primary points of intervention.

The belief that there is a link between high achievement motivation as a socio-cultural norm and the economic productivity of a people is remarkably similar to Max Weber's observations during the Belle Epoch that led to his work *The Protestant Ethic and the Spirit of Capitalism.*[32] Weber lived at a time when both Roman Catholicism and Protestantism were vigorous social forces omnipresent in the daily lives of people in European nations, having a powerful impact on their ethical beliefs as well as child-rearing practices and schooling. Thus, it was significant when Weber observed that the productivity and economic development of European Protestant countries and European Roman Catholic countries differed from one another. Weber believed that the "Protestant ethic"—with its emphasis on individual faith and independence, rejection of personal pleasure, and the belief that hard work is inherently good—accounted for much of the observed difference. As one can imagine, this view aroused a good deal of controversy over the years; however, it also has had a powerful impact on Western thought about the inner versus outer issues in motivation. Moreover, the extensive research carried out by McClelland and his followers lends strong support to the notion that the society that emphasizes the need for personal achievement, hard work, and personal responsibility may be inculcating the characteristics that will ultimately lead to the society's high productivity and economic development. Indeed, in our time, with the humiliating demise of communism, we have witnessed an unfolding of this line of thought as the Eastern European countries of the old Soviet empire struggle to transform their societies and their economies by trying to cast off the demotivating hand of Soviet-style bureaucracy and adopt the outlook, values, and work behavior of free market capitalist cultures.

In studying the need for achievement as a motivational force, McClelland discovered that individuals varied in their need for achievement, or to be successful, with some having a high need to achieve and some having less of such a need. He also discovered that other people actually have a fear of success. Matina Horner raised the possibility that fear of success is a gender-related issue.

Fear of Success

How do we find out the strength of a person's need for achievement and the strength of a person's need to avoid failure? A basic research technique that McClelland used was to have the person take the Thematic Apperception Test (TAT). The person taking the TAT is shown a picture or given a brief story line and is asked to write a story, or complete an already started story, which, in effect, tells his or her version of what the picture or story line portrays. This is what psychologists call a "projective" technique, somewhat akin in concept to the familiar Rorschach "ink-blot" test. The idea is, of course, that different people see different things in the events depicted and, therefore, tell different stories, just as Jung would have predicted.

Fear of Success as a Gender Issue

Because the TAT has been administered by many psychologists over the years, an extensive database of results was generated, which was analyzed for trends. One trend that emerged was that "sex role turns out to be one of the most important determinants of human behavior; psychologists have found sex differences in their studies from the moment they started doing empirical research."[33] One difference that caught the attention of Matina Horner was that women tend to experience more anxiety than men when confronted with situations of competitive achievement. As you have seen, McClelland's studies of men had identified two general characteristics that influenced their perception of what they saw in the TAT pictures and story lines: one was the hope or expectation of success and the other was fear of failure. Do women perceive the same options or do they perceive something different?

In doing research for her Ph.D. at the University of Michigan in 1968, Horner demonstrated that women tend to see something different, and she identified it as a third motivation: fear of success.[34] Why would a woman fear success in a competitive situation? One answer is the woman's perception of a dilemma that men do not experience: that success will bring a loss of culturally defined femininity.

One of the test items that Horner used began, "After first term finals, Anne finds herself at the top of her medical school class." In analyzing the stories that women wrote to complete this introduction, Horner commented, "when success is likely or possible, threatened by the negative consequences they expect to follow success, young women become anxious and their positive achievement strivings become thwarted."[35] She concluded that this fear of success "exists because for most women, the anticipation of success in competitive achievement activity, especially against men, produces anticipation of certain negative consequences, for example, the threat of social rejection and loss of femininity."[36]

A Women's Issue?

Since the publication of Horner's work, there has been much discussion of fear of success in direct competition as a significant factor in the motivation of women. In the first place, however, it is not limited to women. In the second place, it is but a part of the complex human dynamics involved in dealing with issues of competition.

For example, it is commonplace for bright students to conceal their academic prowess, often using elaborate performances to avoid being thought a "brain" by their peers, one who is highly successful in the supposedly competitive environment of the school. Dissembling is a common strategy for these students. They may conceal the fact that they have actually studied and may consistently perform below par to avoid being singled out by their peers as a winner. Indeed, it appears that one way students avoid appearing too bright in the eyes of others, yet preserve their inner sense of being bright, is to exert little effort. If one is to fail, it is a better excuse that one didn't try than that one was not able.[37]

The Humanistic Perspective

Although the cognitive perspective on motivation is that we are motivated from within to make sense of the world as we perceive it, to exercise control of our lives, and to be inner directed, the humanistic perspective is that personal needs to constantly grow and develop, to cultivate personal self-esteem, and to have satisfying human relationships are highly motivating drives. This perspective is a "searching to understand what goes on inside us—our needs, wants, desires, feelings, values, and unique ways of perceiving and understanding what causes us to behave the way we do . . . it is what teachers practice as they help students to see the personal relevancy of what they are learning."[38]

Accordingly, motivation is internal—not something that is done *to* us—and emphasizes nurturing an inherent ongoing human proclivity to continue growing, developing and maturing, and being enriched by new experiences. Hence, one is always in the process of becoming. In this view there is no such thing as an unmotivated person. As Arthur Combs put it, "People are always motivated; in fact, they are never unmotivated. They may not be motivated to do what we would prefer they do, but it can never be truly said that they are unmotivated."[39] The experienced teacher who shows little enthusiasm for the latest twist in curriculum and instruction being advocated by the superintendent, the kind of teacher who is commonly described by such clichés as "deadwood" and "burned out," and who is often targeted for "weeding out," is not unmotivated: that teacher may not be motivated to do what the superintendent would prefer, but probably sees little connection between what is being demanded and her or his own internal sense of fulfillment.

Abraham Maslow: Motivation as a Hierarchy of Needs

One of the most powerful and enduring ways of understanding human motivation was developed by Abraham Maslow, who, unlike the experimental psychologists of his day, decided to study the motivation patterns shown by people as they lived. He believed that people are driven from within to realize their full growth potential. This ultimate goal is sometimes called *self-fulfillment,* sometimes *self-realization,* but Maslow called it *self-actualization.* Some people—such as Eleanor Roosevelt, Thomas Jefferson, and Albert Einstein, all of whose lives Maslow studied—achieve self-actualization in the course of their lives, and many people do not, but all strive in that direction.

The genius of Maslow's work lies in the hierarchy of needs that he constructed: that human needs start with survival, then unfold in an orderly, sequential, hierarchical pattern that takes us toward continued growth and development.[40] The hierarchy is shown in Figure 11.1. *Prepotency* is the term that Maslow used to describe the fact that one cannot be motivated by a higher need until the lower needs are first met. For example, we all start out with the need to survive, and the basics for that are food, water, clothing, and shelter. The

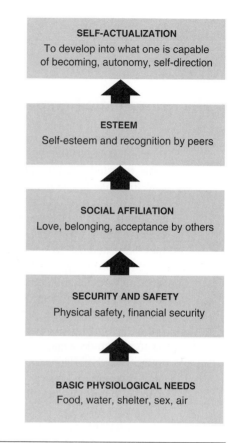

FIGURE 11.1
Hierarchy of needs as used in Maslow's theory of motivation.

next higher need is safety: to be without fear of physical or psychological harm. The need for survival is prepotent, however: one cannot attend to the need for safety unless the needs for survival are first met. As the need for safety is met, one seeks affiliation: belonging, acceptance by others, love. Once one's prepotent needs for affiliation are adequately met, one is motivated by the next higher need in the hierarchy, the need for self-esteem: this comes from recognition and respect from others.

Deficiency Needs and Growth Needs

The lower four needs in Maslow's hierarchy are called *deficiency needs* because (1) their deficiency motivates people to meet them and (2) until the deficiencies are met, people find it difficult to respond to a higher-order need. Thus, the teacher who feels unsafe at school is unlikely to be highly motivated to seek acceptance by other members of the faculty or by the need for recognition or approval. In such a case, in Maslow's view, trying to create a more supportive, accepting climate in the school or to use participative methods of decision making are likely to be more problematic than if the prepotent need—the need for safety—had first been met.

The higher-order needs are called *growth needs,* and they are different. The growth needs are never fully met: for example, as one learns more and develops aesthetic appreciation, the need for growth is not met; rather, it expands. The music aficionado never wearies of fine music but studies more, collects recordings, and continues attending concerts, always striving to achieve greater depth and scope of understanding and new levels of appreciation. Civil War buffs may not satisfy their curiosity by reading a book and visiting a battlefield or two: they may soon be involved to the extent of using their weekends and vacation time to attend seminars, travel to historic sites, and otherwise pursue their quest for knowing and understanding with increasing energy.

As the need for growth and self-development expands, we can understand why many people motivated by growth needs seem insatiable in their search for knowledge and understanding. Many develop an enormous scope of interests, and others probe ever more deeply into their understanding of fewer interests. Thus, responding to growth needs leads to increased growth; the cycle of personal growth is seemingly endless.

This is a very different perspective on motivation than behaviorist views, which primarily emphasize carefully regulated rewards and punishments: the prospect of modest annual increases in compensation and ultimately an unpretentious retirement income as the reward for being a "good" teacher; the threat of being demoted or sacked for being a "poor" teacher. The hierarchy-of-needs view of motivation envisions the realistic possibility of generating enormous psychic energy within and among teachers and principals, and seeing that energy expand and increase over time: first, by meeting their deficiency needs and, second, by encouraging their growth and development needs. This is the essence of creating growth-enhancing environments in schools as an organizational approach to motivating participants.

Application to Work Motivation

Lyman Porter adapted Maslow's concept of hierarchy of needs to creating growth-enhancing environments in work organizations.[41] An interpretation of his work is shown in Figure 11.2. In Porter's view, Maslow's hierarchy fits the organizational environment better by adding a new level in the hierarchy: *autonomy.*[42] This refers to the individual's need to participate in making decisions that affect him or her, to exert influence in controlling the work situation, to have a voice in setting job-related goals, and to have authority to make decisions and latitude to work independently. Using Porter's concept of the needs hierarchy, it is relatively easy to see the ways in which work organizations, such as school districts, schools, and institutions of higher education, can be sources for fulfilling these motivating needs.

Porter went on to conduct research that is interesting because it is representative of a whole line of inquiry that followed. Among the characteristics he attempted to measure concerning the managers he studied were the following:

1. To what extent the need characteristic (of any level of the hierarchy) was being met by the manager's job.

2. To what extent the manager thought the job should meet the need characteristic.

SELF-ACTUALIZATION
Working at full potential
Feeling successful at work
Achieving goals viewed as significant

AUTONOMY
Control of work situation, influence in
the organization, participation in
important decisions, authority to
utilize organizational resources

SELF-ESTEEM
Titles, feeling self-respect, evidence of
respect by others, status symbols,
recognition, promotions, awards, being
part of "insiders" group

AFFILIATION
Belonging to formal and informal work
groups, friendships, professional
associations and unions, acceptance by
peers beyond the immediate organization

SECURITY
Pay, union, seniority, retirement plan,
tenure, such legal concepts as "due process"
and "fairness," statutory and policy
protections establishing orderly evaluation
and "RIF" procedures, the negotiated contract,
insurance plans

FIGURE 11.2
A hierarchy of work motivation based
on Porter's model.

The differences between the first question (to what extent need was being met) and the second question (to what extent the job should meet the need) provide a measure of either (1) the amount of *need satisfaction* the person is experiencing or (2) the perceived *need deficiency* that the person is experiencing. Research such as this has been conducted widely in an effort to understand the relationship between need satisfaction and/or need deficiency and the performance of people on the job.[43]

Because such studies "contend that human behavior is goal-directed toward fulfilling unsatisfied needs, an individual's need satisfaction should be related to his job performance. And, as Maslow's theory would predict, higher-order needs should be more closely linked to job performance than lower-order needs that can be readily satisfied."[44] One generalization that seems to arise from the substantial body of research of this kind is that it is situation-bound. That is, when or where times are good and jobs plentiful, such research tends to pick up little concern for the lower-order needs (for example, security and physiological needs) because they are not a significant part of reality. But when or where there is employment instability, there appears to be a closer connection between the lower-order needs and job satisfaction. This admittedly general observation may be disconcerting to those who seek a broad, generally applicable explanation of human motivation.

It is probably unrealistic to assume that teachers are, as a group, motivated by any particular needs inducement that is applicable only to that group; the variables among teachers are too great to expect that. There are personal variables, such as life and career goals, and differing family and financial obligations. There also are differing situational contingencies; teachers who work in schools where they may have their coats stolen, or be robbed, or be in danger of being raped may very well reveal needs dispositions that are different from those of teachers in a more secure environment. Again, the point being emphasized here is the critical importance of the function of situational contingencies in attempting to describe, explain, and predict the needs inducements that lie behind the behavior of people in educational organizations.

With this caveat in mind, we should consider the studies reported by Thomas Sergiovanni and his associates, which sought to find out "at what level teachers are with respect to the hierarchy [of prepotent needs]. We need to know their level of prepotency"[45] for the simple reason that we cannot (according to the hierarchy-of-needs theory) motivate insecure teachers by offering them greater autonomy or, on the other hand, motivate teachers seeking autonomy by offering them security. Perhaps worse is the likelihood that "freshly trained school executives who overestimate the operating need level of teachers and scare them off with ultraparticipatory self-actualizing administration are as ineffective as others who deny teachers meaningful satisfaction by underestimating operating need levels."[46] To shed light on what he calls the "operating need levels" of teachers, Sergiovanni and his colleagues conducted two studies: one of the teachers and administrators of an upstate New York suburban school district and the other of the teachers in thirty-six Illinois high schools.

These studies are of interest on two levels: (1) the data-gathering instruments and techniques for analyzing the data that were used demonstrate one way to study systematically important situational contingencies in the motivation of people in educative organizations, and (2) the results drawn from the populations they studied provide some useful insights.[47] In general, "esteem seems to be the level of need operation showing greatest need deficiency for these professionals. Large deficiencies are also reported for autonomy and self-actualization, and these gaps will continue to rise as teachers make gains in the esteem area."[48] In other words, these studies suggest that (in the populations studied and at the time of the study) the teachers—overall, as a group—(1) had satisfied the lower-order needs and (2) were generally ready to respond to higher-order needs. They felt reasonably secure and reasonably affiliated with their colleagues, and, therefore, more of these kinds of inducements were unlikely to be very motivating. But were these teachers to be given opportunities to feel better about themselves and opportunities to have greater influence in the processes of making decisions, these would likely be highly motivating opportunities. But the groups of people studied were not monolithic: the researchers report (not surprisingly, to be sure) some differences related to age (in this case, age probably was an indicator of where individuals were in the development of their careers). They found, for example, that the younger teachers (that is, those aged twenty to twenty-four) seemed to be the most concerned with esteem. Slightly older teachers (aged twenty-five to thirty-four), on the other hand, showed the most unmet motivational needs across the board. One could speculate that this is the period in a teacher's career when he or she hits a dead end: for most, there will be little opportunity for professional growth, advancement, and significant achievement in the years ahead. Perhaps even more disturbing, however, are some insights concerning older teachers (forty-five years or over). At first glance, the data seemed to indicate that older teachers had the smallest need deficiencies of all; this tends to suggest that, in the later years of their careers, teachers were finding their work rather highly motivating at all levels. When the researchers examined this phenomenon, however, there appeared to be quite a different explanation: older teachers "are not getting more in terms of need fulfillment as the years go by but, rather, are expecting less. Levels of aspiration seem to drop considerably with age. Teachers become more 'realistic' or resigned to things as they are."[49]

The significance of findings such as these looms very large, indeed, to those who are concerned with improving the effectiveness of public schools. There is strong support for believing that job security, salaries, and benefits—though far from being irrelevant to teachers—have little likelihood of motivating them. A greater motivational need, it seems clear, is for teachers to achieve feelings of professional self-worth, competence, and respect; to be seen increasingly as people of achievement, professionals who are influential in their workplaces, growing persons with opportunities ahead to develop even greater competence and a sense of accomplishment. But in an era in which public schools (and, increasingly, institutions of higher education) have been pervaded by a powerful sense of adversarial relationships between teachers and management, there appears to be little support from the organizational hierarchy of many schools to meet these needs. Indeed, the negotiating posture of most school districts has been highly defensive on this point, viewing every gain by teachers in opportunities to develop their autonomy and participation and to increase their scope of influence as a loss of jealously guarded management authority and prerogatives.

Similarly, the widespread loss of confidence in the effectiveness of schools has led to a rash of actions that have had a direct impact on the motivating environment of educative organizations. Reductions in force (RIF), slashed budgets, mandated competency programs, legislated school reforms, and massive federal interventions at the local school level all—of course—have laudable intent in terms of overall social policy. But in terms of Maslow's needs hierarchy theory of motivation, as applied to the organizational behavior of people at work in schools, they tend to produce disastrous results in combination.

Herzberg's Two-Factor Theory of Motivation

The two-factor theory of motivation posits that motivation is not a single dimension describable as a hierarchy of needs but rather is composed of two separate, independent factors:

1. *Motivational factors,* which can lead to job satisfaction.
2. *Maintenance factors,* which must be sufficiently present in order for motivational factors to come into play and when not sufficiently present can block motivation and can lead to job dissatisfaction.

The work of Frederick Herzberg began to appear some twelve years after Maslow's and has become widely influential in management thought around the world, particularly in profit-making organizations. He started with systematic studies of people at work, thereby producing an empirically grounded theory rather than using an "armchair" approach. In his research Herzberg asked people to recall the circumstances in which (1) they had, at specific times in the past, felt satisfaction with their jobs and in which (2) they similarly had been dissatisfied with their jobs.[50] Analysis of the responses indicates that there is one specific, describable cluster or group of factors that is associated with motivation and satisfaction at work and another, equally specific, group of factors that is associated with dissatisfaction and apathy. Perhaps no other theory of motivation at work has been more extensively researched and argued about than this, and in all likelihood none has been as widely applied to complex organizations.

Traditionally, it had been believed that the opposite of job satisfaction is job dissatisfaction; thus, by eliminating the sources of dissatisfaction from work, the job would become motivating and satisfying. But Herzberg suggested that this is not so, that the opposite of satisfaction is no satisfaction (see Figure 11.3). Thus, by eliminating sources of dissatisfaction, one may placate, pacify, or reduce the dissatisfaction of a worker, but this does not mean that such reduction either motivates the worker or leads to job

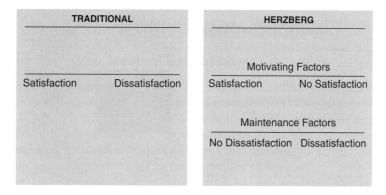

FIGURE 11.3 Traditional concept of job satisfaction-dissatisfaction contrasted with Herzberg's concept.

satisfaction. For example, salary, fringe benefits, type of supervision, working conditions, climate of the work group, and attitudes and policies of the administration can be sources of dissatisfaction. However, if one improves the salary-benefit "package" and working conditions and develops a more humane, concerned administration, one can expect to reduce dissatisfaction, but one cannot expect to motivate the workers by such means. Such conditions as these, taken together, originally were called "hygiene" factors. That term was chosen because—to Herzberg, at least—they have a preventive quality. They are being called increasingly "maintenance" factors, however, and that is the appellation that is used in this book.

Motivation appears to arise from a separate cluster of conditions, different from and distinct from those related to the sources of dissatisfaction. For example, achievement, recognition, the challenge of the work itself, responsibility, advancement and promotion, and personal or professional growth appear to motivate people and are, therefore, associated with job satisfaction. They are called "motivating factors" or "motivators."

The theory, which is shown schematically in Figure 11.4, suggests that it is not possible to motivate people at work through maintenance factors. Reducing class size, developing a more amiable atmosphere, and improving the fringe benefits may well do two things: (1) reduce or eliminate the dissatisfaction of teachers and (2) create conditions wherein they may be motivated. But these kinds of efforts in themselves are not motivat-

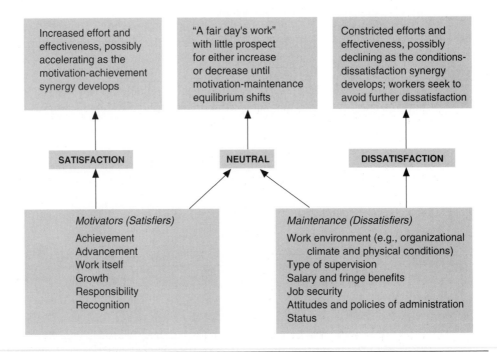

FIGURE 11.4   Model of Herzberg's motivation-maintenance theory.

ing. It does not follow, however, that the maintenance factors are unimportant: minimum levels must be maintained if we are to avoid so much dissatisfaction that motivators will not have their expected effect. For example, failure to keep the salary schedule at a level that teachers think is reasonable or threats to job security can generate such dissatisfaction that teachers cannot respond to opportunities for professional growth, achievement, or recognition. Thus, although maintenance factors are not in themselves motivating (or do not lead to job satisfaction), they are prerequisite to motivation.

An important concept in the two-factor theory is that people tend to see job satisfaction as being related to such intrinsic factors as success, the challenge of the work, achievement, and recognition, whereas they tend to see dissatisfaction as being related to such extrinsic factors as salary, supervision, and working conditions. In other words, they attribute motivational characteristics to themselves and attribute dissatisfaction to characteristics of the organization. In this context, Herzberg has suggested three main ideas for those who would practice his theory:

1. *Enrich the job,* which involves redesigning the work that people do in ways that will tap the motivation potential in each individual. This would include making the job more interesting, more challenging, and more rewarding.

2. *Increase autonomy* on the job. The reader is specifically cautioned to note here that it was not suggested that complete autonomy be somehow granted to workers but that autonomy be increased. This suggests more participation in making decisions as to how the work should be done.

3. *Expand personnel administration* beyond its traditional emphasis on maintenance factors. The focus of personnel administration should be on increasing the motivational factors present in the work. In this view, school districts in which personnel administration focuses almost exclusively on such things as contract administration, the routines of selection-assignment-evaluation-dismissal, and the details of teacher certification and pension plans are attending to important things but not to motivating things. Because 80 percent or more of the current operating budget of many school districts is allocated directly to salaries, wages, and related items, it would seem that the personnel function should be deeply involved in creating or redesigning jobs that motivate the incumbents and thus increase the effectiveness or productivity of the district's employees. This is the view that, for many, underlies the concept of "human resources administration" in contrast to more traditional views of personnel administration.

Herzberg's motivation-maintenance theory has been widely accepted and applied to the management of organizations, especially to U.S. business and industrial corporations. It has, at the same time, provided the basis for considerable academic debate. The four principal criticisms that crop up in that debate are often expressed as follows:

1. Herzberg's basic research methods tended to foreshadow the responses he got. When things went well and people felt satisfied, they tended to take the credit for it; but when things went badly on the job and the respondents were not satisfied, they tended to project the fault onto other people or onto management.

2. The reliability of his research methods is also open to question. The research design required a number of trained individuals to score and interpret the responses from the respondents. Obviously, there may be some differences in the way individuals do the rating, with one rater scoring a response in one way and another rater scoring a similar response in another way (so-called interrater reliability).

3. No provision in the research covers the likely possibility that a person may get satisfaction from one part of his or her job and not from another part.

4. The theory assumes that there is a direct relationship between effectiveness and job satisfaction; yet the research studies only satisfaction and dissatisfaction and does not relate either of them to the effectiveness (or productivity) of the respondents.

The first three of these criticisms are easily dealt with as merely representing typical problems of designing research that requires us to infer causes of behavior from observations of the behavior itself. They make the basis for nice arguments, but in fact, Herzberg's research—after exhaustive review in the literature over a period of two decades—must be accepted as representing the state of the art. The fourth criticism, however, is not so simple.

There is a chicken-or-the-egg aspect to the research literature on job satisfaction and its presumed link to effectiveness on the job. Roughly, investigators with a human relations orientation tend to think that satisfied workers are likely to be productive. Herzberg, however, is among those scholars who tend to think that satisfaction at work arises from the work itself or, more precisely, that job satisfaction comes from achievement. There is a massive body of research literature in this area; because of methodological problems as well as ideological conflicts, the overall results are inconclusive. Conversely, scant support exists for the notion that dissatisfied workers are likely to be more effective than those who report a higher level of satisfaction; the question, then, revolves around the sources of satisfaction (that is, maintenance factors or motivating factors). The Herzberg theory has been tested numerous times in school situations and—in this organizational setting, at least—appears to be well supported.

Ralph Savage, using interviews to obtain data from Georgia teachers, reported that Herzberg's theory was generally supported,[51] as did Rodney Wickstrom in reporting a study of teachers in the Province of Saskatchewan, Canada.[52] Gene Schmidt studied 132 high school principals in districts in the Chicago suburbs and found that, again, the two-factor theory appeared to be strongly supported by these school administrators, indicating that "recognition, achievement, and advancement are major forces in motivating them to lift their performance to approach their maximum potential."[53] In operational terms, this investigator concluded that "encouragement and support for administrators who desire to be creative, to experiment with new educational programs, and to delve into different educational endeavors are needed to allow more opportunities for achievement."[54]

Thomas Sergiovanni, in the late 1960s, after replicating Herzberg's work among teachers, reported that the theory appeared to be supported.[55] His findings were that achievement and recognition were very important motivators for teachers, along with the work itself, responsibility, and the possibility of growth. Among the dissatisfiers reported were (not surprisingly) routine housekeeping, taking attendance, paperwork, lunch duty, insensitive or inappropriate supervision, irritating administrative policies, and poor relationships with colleagues and/or parents. Sergiovanni made the point that advancement, frequently an important motivator in studies conducted in private-sector corporations, was missing in the study of teachers. On this significant point, he observed that "advancement was simply not mentioned by teachers because teaching as an occupation offers so little opportunity for advancement. If one wishes to advance in teaching, he must leave teaching for a related education profession such as administration, supervision, and counseling."[56]

Comments on Herzberg's Two-Factor Theory

Herzberg's two-factor theory of motivation was developed through research in which people were asked to describe critical incidents in their work lives that involved motivation and job satisfaction. Subsequently, it has been strongly supported by additional research carried out by a number of investigators using similar techniques. Together, these provide strong support for the concept. However, some investigators find it troubling that studies that use other research techniques generally fail to support the theory.

Herzberg's theory has been widely influential, however, and commonly appears in the literature of business and industry as well as that of education. Although some advocate abandoning it in favor of the newer and more complex expectancy theory, the two-factor theory remains a powerful explanation of motivation in the workplace.

Integration of Herzberg's and Maslow's Theories

Some of the essential differences between Maslow's hierarchy-of-needs theory and Herzberg's motivation-maintenance theory have already been pointed out. The central difference is that Maslow thought of every need as a potential motivator, with the range of human needs in a prepotent hierarchical order, whereas Herzberg argued that only the higher-order needs are truly motivating (the lower-order needs being conceptualized as maintenance factors). Another difference—not quickly apparent, perhaps—is that Maslow's was a general theory of human motivation, concerned, as Stephen Robbins puts it, "with the person's needs 24 hours a day,"[57] whereas Herzberg tried specifically to illuminate motivational issues in the workplace.

Nevertheless, a comparison of the two theories, as shown in Figure 11.5, reveals that they are basically highly compatible and, in fact, support one another. We feel (as Figure 11.5 shows) that the Porter version of the hierarchy-of-needs model lends itself to such a comparison, for the simple reason that such basic physiological drives as the need for food, water, and air have little relevance for motivating behavior at work in U.S. educational organizations. Even so, we agree with Robbins:

> The lower-order needs on Maslow's hierarchy tend to closely approximate the maintenance factors as outlined by Herzberg. Salary, working conditions, job security, [school district] policy and administration, and supervision are generally physiological and safety-oriented needs. In contrast, the intrinsic motivational factors of recognition, advancement, responsibility, growth, achievement, and the work itself tend to be closely related to the desire for esteem and self-actualization. The integrated model would also suggest that organizations have traditionally emphasized lower-order needs. If workers are to become motivated on their

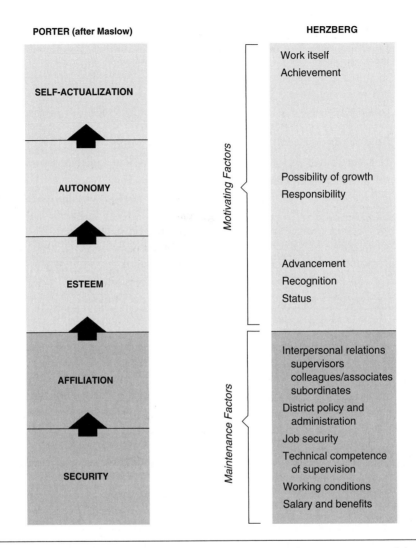

FIGURE 11.5 Need-priority model compared with motivation-maintenance model.

jobs, it will be necessary for administrators to make the alterations necessary to stimulate the motivational factors in the [jobs themselves].[58]

Conclusion: General Principles

Motivating people who work in schools is not a simple matter and it cannot be reduced to a simple, certainly not a mechanical, procedure or set of procedures. Each of the two factors in the motivational process, the idiosyncratic personality of the individual and the idiosyncrasies of the organization's environment, is complex, and the precise nature of their interactions is not fully known. The school practitioner therefore must proceed, not with aphorisms or simple reductionism, but with an intelligent holistic approach that takes these complex variables into account. Here are some pragmatic principles that will help to support such an approach:

1. Individuals are not motivated only by their own internal perceptions, needs, and characteristics or only by external demands, expectations, and environmental conditions, but by an interaction of the two: the generalization is $B = f(p \cdot e)$.

2. The educational leader or administrator is an important part of the organizational environment with which the organization's members interact and therefore, by definition, is important in determining the nature and quality of their motivation.

3. Short-term behavioral changes can often be achieved by highly controlling strategies such as threats of serious punishments, promises of meaningful rewards, and forced competition, but these should not be confused with motivation. Such direct, coercive attempts to motivate may be useful in bringing about changes in behavior when immediate action is required in crisis situations, for example, when the performance of a teacher is so unacceptable that the school cannot wait for corrective action. Indeed, in a case such as this, the controlling strategy might have a beneficial effect by permitting the teacher to achieve enough success at work so as to become responsive to motivational needs of a higher order than survival. However, even if well intended, when highly controlling strategies are used consistently enough to lead people to feel coerced, intimidated, and manipulated, members tend to lose interest and, indeed, to develop motivational goals and strategies of their own that resist those of the organization.[59]

4. To induce and sustain long-term evolution of motivation of organizational members requires a facilitative approach, one that encourages and supports members in their efforts to grow and develop their ways of perceiving the environment they work in, their personal goals, feelings, and beliefs. A facilitative approach might, for example, seek to encourage members of the organization always to be moving up Maslow's hierarchy of needs over time, always in the direction of self-actualization, with the goal of encouraging all members to become all that they can be.

5. One strategy for developing a facilitative approach to motivation in educational organizations is to change the environment factor in $B = f(p \cdot e)$, that is, to create growth-enhancing environments. This involves working with the organizational culture and organizational climate. It is in this realm that the educational leader emerges as a key actor in the environment of the organization.

Reflective Activities

1. Using the information in our text concerning the "Four Psychological Types" and the Myers-Briggs Type Indicator, write a self-assessment concerning these concepts. Describe the predominant types that you believe you possess. Give examples of behaviors that illustrate your self-assessment.

2. Using John Atkinson's characterizations of achievement motivation, complete a self-assessment and give specific examples of why you think you meet your self-assessed achievement-motivation criteria.

3. Assuming that all lower-order needs have been met (in Maslow's theory), and using Herzberg's "motivating factors," complete the following: Develop a plan to meet the higher-order needs of school personnel. You may choose to focus on a specific school level (for example, elementary) or develop a generic plan that would be good for any school level. Within your plan be sure to briefly outline at least two major programs, projects, or activities that will help meet higher-order needs in the faculty or staff.

4. *Working on Your Game Plan.* Over time you have observed a lot of school principals and other people working in schools. Think about those observations and relate them now to what you have read in this book. Then create two lists. First, list five things that principals do that are highly motivating to teachers. Then list five things that principals do that kill motivation in teachers. After creating the two lists, describe what generalizations for educational leadership you draw from your observations.

Suggested Reading

Benfari, Robert, with Jean Knox, *Understanding Your Management Style: Beyond the Myers-Briggs Type Indicators.* Lexington, MA: D.C. Heath and Company, 1991.

   This book applies four theoretical orientations to the understanding of one's own personality structure: (1) the Myers-Briggs Type Indicators, which are drawn directly from Jung's theory of personality; (2) the needs that motivate you; (3) the conflict management style that you use; and (4) the kinds of power that you use. It stresses the importance of assessing your own personality characteristics so that you can work from your own strengths. It's a do-it-yourself book, in a way, complete with a self-assessment test that you can take. It is also scholarly, sound, and readable.

Covington, Martin V., *Making the Grade: A Self-Worth Perspective on Motivation and School Reform.* New York: Cambridge University Press, 1992.

   While this book is focused on the motivation of students in the classroom, rather than on the motivation of adults who work in the educational organization, it is an informative and provocative discussion that has much to say to those who are interested in organizational behavior in education. Drawing heavily on the work of Atkinson and McClelland, Covington starts with the thesis that "every achievement situation implies the promise of success as well as the threat of failure. This means that all achievement situations involve approach-avoidance conflict to one degree or another" (p. 32). Entwined with this approach-avoidance, in which many students wind up struggling to avoid failure in school, is the sense of self-worth of the individual. A scholarly yet highly practical resource for educational leaders.

Gilligan, Carol, *In a Different Voice: Psychological Theory and Women's Development.* Cambridge, MA: Harvard University Press, 1982.

   In describing this book on the dust jacket, Lawrence Kohlberg said, "Carol Gilligan believes that psychology has persistently and systematically misunderstood women—their motives, their moral commitments, the course of their psychological growth." Gilligan describes her research into these areas and what her findings mean. This has become one of the most frequently cited works in the field of women's psychology.

Keirsey, David, and Marilyn Bates, *Please Understand Me: Character and Temperament Types.* Del Mar, CA: Prometheus Nemesis Book Company, 1984.

   This book explains the psychological types of Carl Jung and provides a useful vocabulary and phraseology for applying the Jung-Myers concepts of different types to one's work in organizations. As the title suggests, it focuses on the communication distortions and blockages that commonly arise between and among different kinds of people who perceive and respond to the world in different ways. Readers can get feedback on their own psychological type by taking *The Keirsey Temperament Sorter* found on pp. 5–13.

c h a p t e r

12

School Reform

LEARNING OBJECTIVES

After reading this chapter, you should be able to

- Describe and explain the theory that underlies free market approaches to school reform.

- Describe the views of market theorists of school reform and organizational behavior.

- Describe school reform as an investment opportunity.

- Explain what investors mean when they speak of education as "the next health care."

- Differentiate between the concepts of contracting and privatization in education.

- Describe the theory and practice of standards-based school reform.

- Describe the school district as a political-legal concept.

- Explain the relationship between the concept of standards-based school reform and the concept of the school district.

- Explain what is meant when standards-based school reform is described as an example of command-and-control management.

- Describe the theory and practice of whole school reform.

- Explain the role of autonomy of the school in school reform.

- Define and describe school site management.

- Describe and discuss the new roles for school boards proposed by the Education Commission of the States.

- Describe the Coalition of Essential Schools, or Accelerated Schools, or the Comer School Development Program as approaches to whole school reform.

- Describe and discuss the proposals on teacher education put forward by the American Council on Education in 1999.

ISLLC Standards

STANDARD 3: A school administrator is an educational leader who promotes the success of all students by ensuring management of the organization, operations, and resources for a safe, efficient, and effective learning environment.

Knowledge

The administrator has knowledge and understanding of:

- theories and models of organizations and the principles of organizational development
- operational procedures at the school and district levels
- legal issues impacting school operations

Dispositions

The administrator believes in, values, and is committed to:

- taking risks to improve schools
- trusting people and their judgments
- high-quality standards, expectations, and performances

Performances

The administrator facilitates processes and engages in activities ensuring that:

- emerging trends are recognized, studied, and applied as appropriate
- the school acts entrepreneurially to support continuous improvement
- organizational systems are regularly monitored and modified as needed
- stakeholders are involved in decisions affecting schools

STANDARD 5: A school administrator is an educational leader who promotes the success of all students by acting with integrity, fairness, and in an ethical manner.

Knowledge

The administrator has knowledge and understanding of:

- the philosophy and history of education

Dispositions

The administrator believes in, values, and is committed to:

- the ideal of the common good
- the right of every student to a free, quality education

STANDARD 6: A school administrator is an educational leader who promotes the success of all students by understanding, responding to, and influencing the larger political, social, economic, legal, and cultural context.

Knowledge

The administrator has knowledge and understanding of:

- principles of representative governance that undergird the system of American schools
- the role of public education in developing and renewing a democratic society and an economically productive nation
- the law as related to education and schooling
- the political, social, cultural, and economic systems and processes that impact schools
- models and strategies of change and conflict resolution as applied to the larger political, social, cultural, and economic contexts of schooling
- global issues and forces affecting teaching and learning
- the dynamics of policy development and advocacy under our democratic political system

Dispositions

The administrator believes in, values, and is committed to:

- education as a key to opportunity and social mobility
- recognizing a variety of ideas, values, and cultures
- the importance of a continuing dialogue with other decision makers affecting education

Performances

The administrator facilitates processes and engages in activities ensuring that:

- the environment in which schools operate is influenced on behalf of students and their families
- communication occurs within the school community concerning trends, issues, and potential changes in the school environment
- there is ongoing dialogue with representatives of diverse community groups
- the school community works within the framework of policies, laws, and regulations enacted by local, state, and federal authorities
- public policy is shaped to provide quality education for students
- lines of communication are developed with decision makers outside the school community

The last two decades of the twentieth century witnessed a remarkable quickening and expansion of efforts to reform U.S. schools. It is a virtual certainty that these efforts will continue and that they will dominate the environment of leadership in schools well into the twenty-first century. As explained briefly in Chapter 4, the term *school reform* often means very different things to different people because they use various theories in trying to understand and explain such things as education, schools as organizations, and human behavior.

As discussed earlier, the term *school reform* generally connotes planned efforts by those external to the school to cause changes, or restructuring, to occur within the school. Chapter 7 described in some detail three major theoretical strategies that dominate the field:

- Empirical-rational strategies depend largely upon the invention or discovery of new ways of doing things and persuading schools to adopt them. Such approaches include the development of new curriculum packages, new teaching techniques (such as scripted teaching), or more demanding education, training, and licensing of teachers.

- Power-coercive strategies are distinguished by the willingness to use sanctions (especially political and financial sanctions) to force schools to adopt change. These are characteristically expressed as legislation, judicial decisions, government regulations, and executive orders accompanied by financial sanctions to heighten their coercive power. An excellent example was the enactment of the No Child Left Behind Act of 2001. The scope and coercive power of this massive legislative effort were unmatched by any previous effort undertaken to force changes in the schools.

- Organizational self-renewal strategies focus on helping those in the school to strengthen the climate and culture of the school, improve its organizational health, and develop its ability to detect and solve its own problems. This usually involves helping those in the school to improve their own ability to detect and solve problems so that they make better decisions, deal with conflict more productively, and improve motivation and morale. The goal is the development of an organization that is continually renewing itself over time in response to changes in its environment.

To be effective, power-coercive strategies require the exercise of power so overwhelming that the organization is compelled to change in response. Adherents of power-coercive strategies for school reform normally start out with little concern for or interest in organizational behavior issues in the schools. The third category of school reform seeks to change schools from the inside-out through processes of organizational self-renewal. As described in Chapter 7, when the leader's theory of practice is based on the strategy of organizational self-renewal, organizational behavior issues are central in the leader's practice.

Market-Based School Reform

Some who would reform public schooling in the United States believe that the notion of public schools that are democratically controlled by the body politic should be abandoned. Instead, they propose that a new system should replace democratic, direct control of schools—as one normally finds in U.S. school districts—with the indirect control of the marketplace. This view of school reform tends to be shared by two main groups: market-oriented theorists, who tend to see government organizations as phenotypically inferior to market-oriented organizations, and business investors, who see private control of education as a potential source of vast profits.

One of the early and widely popular expositions of this iconoclasm was the book *Politics, Markets, and America's Schools,* by John Chubb and Terry Moe, which was published in 1990 by the Brookings Institution. In this scholarly polemic, all educational reforms that had ever been tried were totally dismissed and the authors' own theoretical concept—sometimes called the "voucher system"—was argued as being flawless, though, at that time, it had never been tried. Markets, the authors insisted, by their very nature, foster the autonomy that is required for schools to be effective. In the marketplace, they theorized, the ineffective schools simply disappear for want of customers to purchase their products. Democratic control, they argued on the other hand, inherently fosters bureaucracy that simply smothers the autonomy necessary for effective schools. Under bureaucracy, according to this view, ineffective schools continue to stay in business regardless of their ineffectiveness.

The shift from democratic direct control to indirect marketplace control would be accomplished by providing the parents of every child with a voucher. Payable by the public treasury, the voucher could be used to pay for tuition in any school—public or private, sectarian or nonsectarian—that met minimal state standards and that would accept the student. Admission criteria would be established by each school—subject, of course, to such minimal state regulation as nondiscrimination requirements. With this simple, strongly argued proposal, Chubb and Moe stirred a national debate on parent–student choice in the marketplace as an alternative to direct democratic control of public schooling that had prevailed in the United States for well over a century.

In order to work, free market school reform requires the existence of schools to make up a market in which parents and students can actually shop for the school of their choice that will accept their vouchers. By 1998 pilot state-approved voucher programs were functioning in Milwaukee and Cleveland, cities that permit vouchers to be used in either religious or nonreligious private schools. Across the United States at the dawn of the twenty-first century there was a great deal of controversy and not a little confusion about school choice and vouchers.

- In some school districts, for example, simply permitting children to transfer to another public school within the district was hailed as being school choice akin to a voucher system. This is often called "districtwide choice" or "intradistrict choice."

- At least fourteen states permit students to choose to attend public schools within the state but outside their home school districts. Though this is also sometimes hailed as evidence that vouchers have a long history in U.S. education, that interpretation is a bit of a stretch. There has, in fact, been a practice of long standing in states where isolated rural school districts may be so sparsely populated that the district chooses not to operate its own schools. These are called "nonoperating" school districts. They have customarily been legally required by the state to pay tuition to other school districts, and sometimes to private schools, on behalf of the pupils and students who reside in the nonoperating district. It remains a fairly common practice today at the secondary school level in rural communities. In today's lexicon, this practice does not constitute a voucher plan.

- A voucher plan permits students and parents to obtain tuition vouchers on demand, which they may use to attend any public or private schools wherever they may be, regardless of whether or not the district in which they reside operates schools.

Despite what may seem to educators to be a great deal of news coverage and public discussion, the public is widely confused about or unaware of what school vouchers are. In November 1999, nine years after the appearance of the Chubb and Moe book, Public Agenda conducted a study that revealed that 63 percent of people interviewed across the country reported knowing "very little" or "nothing" about vouchers. In the two school districts that were then experimenting with vouchers, the figure was a surprising 60 percent. "It isn't that people are undecided," Public Agenda reported, "as much as that they are unaware. The vast majority of the public knows very little about school vouchers, charter schools, or for-profit schools. This lack of familiarity extends to both parents and nonparents, ordinary citizens and local civic leaders, and cuts across all lines of geography and demographics."[1] Public Agenda pointed out that this finding does not mean that people do not care, nor does it mean that they are satisfied with schools as they are: it simply means that they do not know about the alternatives being discussed. Public Agenda went on to point out that the public *must* know what options may be under consideration in the education arena. As Public Agenda put it, the public has a big stake in this educational debate and has a right to exercise informed consent in participating in it.

Economic Theory and School Reform

The origin of the concept of school vouchers is generally credited to Milton Friedman, a staunchly conservative economist. Friedman developed economic views that were strongly opposed to those of John Maynard Keynes, which dominated economic and political thought for most of the twentieth century. Keynes advocated public works programs and other government spending programs in free markets to stimulate employment and the economy, and to provide such social programs as health care and education. After World War I until well after World War II, Keynesian economics underlay the economic and political policies of many Western nations, including the New Deal of the United States.

Friedman, however, was a pioneer of the now-fashionable idea of open markets free of government interference or control. In that context, Friedman developed the notion that schooling should not be a service provided by the government but should be a part of the free market system. Although Friedman did very little to put the idea into practice, many of his followers have done so. Thus, the theory that drives market-based school reform, including voucher plans, arises from economic thought. We will not try to delve deeply into economic theory here, but some points are highly relevant to the idea of tuition vouchers and market-based school reform and should be considered by school leaders.

Economics is the science of how a society chooses to allocate scarce resources to best meet competing needs.[2] Education Professor Herbert J. Walberg has been a leader in trying to adapt market theory to the organization and control of public schooling in the United States. Walberg and Bast explain that economic activity takes place in four sectors: governments, households, civic or nonprofit institutions, and the marketplace. Each sector has its own rules and ends. Activity in government and civic institutions, for example, generally takes the form of voting or giving or receiving commands. Within households, rules commonly resemble a kind of primitive communism. In the marketplace, the primary activities are purchase, sale, savings, and investment.[3]

In this context, one can look on schooling as an economic issue because the necessary resources—money for such requirements as buildings, facilities, equipment and materials, teachers, and administrators—are scarce and must be bid for in competition with other demands. Whereas people in the United States have traditionally chosen to make decisions about schooling within the framework of democratic political control, it is plausible to the free market advocate that we can choose to shift from that public policy value to the marketplace if we wish. Naturally, in a booming economic era that characteristically celebrates free market entrepreneurship and denigrates government, the free market protagonists tend to view this as highly desirable.

A large problem looms before the free market advocate and everyone else who entertains this seemingly simple idea: it is the enormous size and complexity of the public schooling enterprise in the United States, which are rendered incalculably greater when one considers the scope of the human variables involved in this enormous human social system. Nationally in the United States we are talking about 14,772 school districts with 111,486 K–12 public and private schools that enroll 52,217,000 pupils and students and employ 3,071,000 teachers. Since the notion of rational choice lies close to the heart of economic theory, how can one be confident that—in an enterprise of this enormous human and social scale and obvious diversity—rational choice can and will prevail in the arena of the free marketplace? Fortunately, Walberg believes, there is a disarmingly simple answer. It should be well understood by school leaders because it has immense implications for leadership and organizational behavior in an era of market competition and school vouchers.

Whereas education leaders are intensely interested in the complexities of such human issues as motivation, collaboration, and conflict management, we are told that the economist chooses to ignore such things:

> The economist solves the problem of complexity by assuming *as little as possible* about the motivation of the actors he is studying . . . [and] asserts only that human agents will tend to choose rationally among the choices they face. . . . Rational choice theory is silent on whether or not the agents' ends are rational or desirable in any way except that they are voluntarily chosen by the agent over other ends.[4]

In other words, it is the incentives and the rules of the marketplace that give rise to behavior, and the economist is not particularly involved in the values or attitudes that may or may not contribute to the decision-making processes of either individuals or societies. This is why economists so often emphasize the notion of *rational* choice—that is, making decisions in the marketplace that are perceived to be in one's economic self-interest. This is, of course, very troublesome from the organizational behavior perspective—which assumes that nothing is more important in understanding organizations than the psychosocial factors in the human dimension of the organization.

Much of the work of those who favor free market strategies in educational reform is financially supported by conservative think tanks and often cited by conservative news columnists such as William Raspberry, whose column appears in the *Washington Post* and is widely syndicated. Both the think tanks and those who elect to represent them tend to advocate, as a transcendent truism, the ideology that free market solutions to public policy issues are intrinsically superior to all other solutions. This applies in particular to those solutions that they like to call "government" solutions (as in *government schools,* a term that appears frequently in discussions of market-driven school reform). Walberg, for example, has written numerous tracts—closely reasoned and carefully documented—to forcefully argue this thesis. But the sources on which Walberg depends for evidence to support his strident advocacy of abandoning public schooling and embracing for-profit corporate schools in the marketplace are very thin on research and long on opinions that express ideological chutzpah from the economic realm of academe. In Walberg's copious and finely detailed ad hominem arguments, one is hard pressed to find a scintilla of support for even the possibility that government schools and their administrators have a shred of value. Economist Thomas Sowell, whose work was described in Chapter 2, similarly assails public education as a partisan advocate instead of revealing the balanced temperament and perspective that one normally associates with in scholarly analyses. For example, Sowell is so anxious to destroy the roots of professional preparation for teaching—that is, the preparation programs in teacher education in U.S. colleges and universities—that he argues that the contracts of all the professors of education should be bought out and the faculty members dismissed so that the programs in which they teach may be eradicated. In his view, the cost would be readily justified by the benefit of being rid of professors of education. As you will see a little later in this chapter, the American Association for Higher Education would vigorously beg to differ with that suggestion.

In addition to a survey of present-day evidence of the superiority of private enterprise and free competition in education to all other approaches, Andrew Coulson has sought to develop a historical rationale to advance the claims of marketplace approaches to schooling. His discourse in *Market Education: The Unknown History*[5] ranges from the ancient civilizations of Athens and Rome, through the Islamic world and the Middle Ages, to nineteenth-century Great Britain and the United States. His intent is to demonstrate that what he calls "market education" has consistently been shown to be superior to all other approaches since the time of Aristotle. Coulson sums up the findings of his study this way:

> [A] recurrent theme emerged from the hum of the centuries: Competitive educational markets have consistently done a better job of serving the public than state-run educational systems. The reason lies in the fact that state school systems lack four key factors that history tells us are essential to educational excellence: choice and financial responsibility for parents, and freedom and market incentives for educators. School systems that have enjoyed these characteristics have consistently done the best job of meeting both our private educational demands and our shared educational goals.[6]

Perhaps. Some readers, however, see in this scholarly discourse merely evidence that the dynamic tension inherent in the controversy of marketplace versus democratic control of schooling has waxed and waned for millennia, that it has often been as contentious as it is today, and that its long run on the stage of history testifies to the fact that it has, despite Coulson's claim, never been resolved.

However, those who have turned their attention to economic theory in the organization and control of public schooling have stirred up intense debate on important issues and elevated those issues to the realm of public discourse. If you recall the discussion in Chapter 6 about the role of fundamental assumptions and values that underlie the formation of culture, the marketplace advocates have raised questions about fundamental assumptions that are rarely thought about, much less discussed. In view of the widespread concern about the state of public schooling in the United States, it is altogether appropriate for us to reconsider our long-unexamined assumptions and either keep them, revise them, or replace them. Advocates of marketplace concepts of schooling have proffered some powerful criticisms and some genuine new alternatives to traditional ways of providing public schooling, such as the idea of school choice and vouchers, that merit thoughtful consideration—and many people are considering these ideas at this time. They have raised serious doubt as to the viability of public schooling as it has been known in the United States for well over a century. It seems highly probable that their proposals will have a deep effect on the organization and administration of public schooling in the United States for years to come. One group that has listened attentively to the widespread discontent of U.S. citizens about the state of public schooling, as well as the proposals from the free market advocates, is that small but growing group of investors who see public schooling as a rare opportunity for potentially high—possibly huge—profits on their business investments in education at all levels.

School Reform as Investment Opportunity

Perhaps you remember Michael Milken, the former junk bond king. Well, he's an education entrepreneur now. He heads up a corporate conglomerate known as the Knowledge Universe that owns a number of companies that span preschool education to corporate training.[7] In 1998 he met with Arthur Levine, president of Teachers College, Columbia University, to discuss issues of corporate involvement in public education reform. "The message was," President Levine later recalled, "you guys are in trouble and we're going to eat your lunch." This was understood by Levine not as a direct challenge but as a predatory threat.[8]

Many investors, not a few with very deep pockets, have heard the hue and cry of unhappiness over public schooling in the United States—especially the notion of searching for marketplace alternatives to the existing system—and have been attracted to it as a potential high-profit investment. For example, Paul Allen, who cofounded Microsoft with Bill Gates, has heavily invested in education businesses. Some of them, as we shall describe in a moment, are directly involved in teaching and schooling, but always with a view to electronic networking and what educators tend to call "distance learning." For example, one of his businesses is Charter Communications, the fourth largest cable company in the

United States. It went public with an initial public offering of its stock in 1999 that garnered $3.23 billion from investors who apparently think that the company has profitable prospects.[9] Allen envisions this company as part of a "wired world" that he is trying to create, which very likely will include the dissemination of educational products such as courses of instruction.

Many investors plunged into the business beginning in the late 1990s, often riding the stock market boom of the time by raising hundreds of millions of dollars in venture capital to finance yet-to-be-developed enterprises. These efforts were commonly represented by well-known individuals from public life who would be readily recognized and trusted by investors. Former Governor of Tennessee Lamar Alexander, once hailed as an "education governor" and a presidential hopeful, provided leadership for such an investment group. William F. Weld, a former governor of Massachusetts, who had faced stiff political resistance to his advocacy of for-profit schooling, sought to help Leeds Equity Partners III raise a huge venture capital fund investment in for-profit schooling beginning with $150 million in start-up money. By 2003 William F. Bennett, well-known perennial critic of public education, was heading a business called K12, which relied heavily on the Internet to provide curriculum and instruction to partner schools in California, Colorado, Idaho, Ohio, and Pennsylvania, as well to individuals throughout the nation who desired support and guidance in providing home schooling for their children. A number of relatively small companies have tested the waters in for-profit educational management, with varying degrees of success. Among them are

- Advantage Schools, Incorporated, which opened two schools in 1997 and added six more a year later and eight more in 1999. By 2002 they had enrolled about 9,000 students in nine states.
- Beacon Education Management, Incorporated, which contracts with a few school districts to run districts schools and charter schools.
- SABIS Educational Systems, Incorporated, which manages four charter schools in Massachusetts and Michigan.

Clearly, by 2003, the largest and best known of the for-profit education-management corporations continued to be Edison Schools, Incorporated. It was founded as The Edison Project in 1992, after obtaining an initial contract to manage four schools with about 2,000 pupils. The corporation grew during the next decade, with a number of reverses and recoveries along the way. In the 2002–2003 school year Edison claimed that it managed 150 public schools with some 84,000 pupils enrolled in twenty-three states and the District of Columbia.* Based on this, Edison liked to advertise that it was the third largest school system in the United States. This is a bit of a stretch, of course, because few would describe its schools as comprising a school system. Nevertheless, Edison Schools had clearly established itself as the pacesetter in the business of managing public schools for profit. Edison is a publicly traded equity corporation that has consistently lost money

---

*Edison's school enrollment numbers are a little suspect because they count pupils in some grades twice: once for middle school and again for elementary school.

throughout its history, even as its number of clients has grown. Consequently, the price of its stock has declined markedly as this process unfolded.

On December 21, 2001, a few hours after the classrooms of the Philadelphia public schools had been emptied for the annual holidays, Governor Mark Schweiker of Pennsylvania and the mayor of Philadelphia, John Street, announced a takeover by the state of the city's floundering school system. This was to have been a major coup for Edison Schools, which had arranged as part of the deal to take over the management of forty-five of the city's failing schools and thus hoped to make a major breakthrough in the development of its business. Philadelphia was the seventh largest school district in the United States, and the takeover was the largest in history, involving some 210,000 students and 27,000 employees. However, when the secretly negotiated deal became public, a firestorm of controversy resulted. An advertising blitz costing over $400,000 may have boomeranged on Edison in a community that was deeply concerned about the future of its educational enterprise. In the end Edison was awarded twenty schools to manage, while six other community agencies, including universities and charter school operators, were awarded the rest. The challenges confronting everyone running schools in Philadelphia are daunting, and the outcome of this intervention remains in doubt and so, for that reason, does the future of Edison Schools.

Edison's chairman is Benno C. Schmidt, Jr., formerly president of Yale University.[10] Its chief executive officer is Christopher C. Whittle, who created and formerly headed Whittle Communications, the firm that offers the highly controversial Channel One to the nation's junior and senior high schools.[11] Edison's chief operating officer is Christopher Cerf, a noted Washington litigator who practices before the Supreme Court and was formerly associate counsel to President Bill Clinton. Edison Schools' home office is in New York City.

Edison contracts to manage schools chiefly for school districts and for the boards of charter schools. Its preferred organizational pattern is K–12. In a new-school start-up Edison prefers to begin with a K–5 school and expand by adding additional grades each year. However, Edison has also contracted to manage a number of existing schools. The Edison Schools are organized so that teams of teachers can work with the same students for several years. Edison also emphasizes the use of electronic technology (with a computer on every teacher's desk and in the home of every student), an extended school day and school year, and a broad, rigorous curriculum.

The majority of Edison Schools qualify for Title I; 60 percent of its students are eligible for free or reduced lunch, 15 percent receive English as a second language (ESL) services, and 9 percent receive special education services. In the fall of 1999, Edison gave the overall demographics of the schools under its management as follows:

- 45 percent African American
- 32 percent Caucasian
- 18 percent Hispanic
- 2 percent Asian
- 2 percent other

Edison Schools, it should be noted, remain public schools, open to all students, and the company is accountable for the performance of the schools to local authority with whom it has a contract—usually the school board of the district or the charter school board.

TesseracT (formerly Educational Alternatives, Incorporated, EAI), based in Eagan, Minnesota, made quite a splash in 1993 when it moved boldly and was awarded a contract to run the entire school district in Hartford and another contract to run ten schools in Baltimore. However, controversy erupted in both places and EAI, squeezed for money and unable to demonstrate that it was reaching promised goals, saw both contracts canceled. The firm still runs its flagship school in Eagan. TesseracT's approach is child centered and warmly humanistic, with a supportive learning climate undergirding a broad curriculum adapted to the interests and the abilities of the students. The name TesseracT, by the way, comes from Madeleine L'Engle's fanciful science fiction story in which two children travel through space in search of their father, who had been working on a wrinkle in time.[12]

Nobel Learning Communities, based in Media, Pennsylvania, claims to operate the largest chain of private schools in the country: 140 preschools, elementary schools, and middle schools, as well as three schools for learning-challenged children with special needs. Some of these are charter schools, and others are sponsored by corporations. The organization specifically seeks to offer parents an alternative to public school systems, and it places great emphasis on the claim that its students achieve above national norms on standardized tests.

Advantage Schools, based in Boston, has contracted to manage eight charter schools in seven states. These are rather formal schools that emphasize a "Code of Civility," zero tolerance for disruptive behavior, safe school environments, and school uniforms. Similarly, instruction tends to be formal. Teachers typically deliver well-crafted whole-class lessons to which students are often expected to respond in chorus. Instruction tends to be highly structured, with, for example, phonics emphasized in reading in classes of fifteen students or fewer. Advantage Schools are also attractive, well-equipped places often using renovated facilities—ranging from older schools to a former mill to a remodeled department store—that are spacious, architecturally striking, colorful, and altogether attractive places in which to be.

Higher education has also attracted serious attention from investors. Leeds Equity Partners III, mentioned earlier, is focusing on providing professional training and certification in such fields as business, law, psychology, and medicine. The organization believes that training in these fields can be offered profitably if it can harness the Internet as a vehicle for instruction. Many students, it reasons, would be attracted to programs that permit them to pursue studies without taking much time off from work to commute to even local campuses. Productivity Point International, one of Michael Milken's groups, offers an extensive array of online courses geared to the needs of businesspeople for software technical training. The University of Phoenix, the largest private university in the nation, has established at least twenty-two campuses around the country and offers an extensive array of degree-granting programs that range from undergraduate through doctoral degrees in specialties that have great appeal to working professionals. With heavy reliance on online instruction and other distance learning techniques plus campuses placed so as to be handy to a large population of prospective students, the University of Phoenix does not try to emulate traditional universities but instead offers programs that are a clear alternative for busy working people. Many established universities have already felt this competition and are themselves plunging into the development of distance learning, which will make it more convenient for students to attend campuses in their own communities with less need for commuting.

All of these corporate excursions into K–12 schooling for profit are of recent vintage, few if any predating 1990, so that their track record is thin at best. Naturally, those who are invested in them and who work in them are busily trying to put the best foot forward and are making claims that are often more hopes than evidence of success. Nevertheless, it is clear that there is at least a market niche for their products, and they are working hard to reach their ambitious goals. Entrepreneurs work in ways that are very different from those of the bureaucrats in the world of public schools. One great difference lies in the fact that entrepreneurs bring startup money to the project, sometimes substantial amounts of it. They are thus able to undertake a project with strong resources and a long-term perspective, depending on substantial financing from their investment capital to let them ride out the inevitable surprises and difficulties that are bound to arise in a startup project. Unlike the restrictive mind-set of public school bureaucracies, in which new programs must demonstrate their effectiveness almost at once, entrepreneurs are willing to spend money in order to make money and are determined to have the time that is necessary to develop the project and make it work. For those reasons, while there is at this point little evidence that the students attending for-profit schooling achieve at higher levels than those attending government schools, it appears certain that their growing financial backing will make them increasingly serious competitors as time goes on. But their strength comes from more than money: they have ideas that seriously challenge the traditional orthodoxy of both the pedagogical and the organizational ideas of public schooling.

Contracting versus Privatization

There is often some confusion between the concept of contracting and the concept of privatization, and it is important to be clear about the difference. School districts have, for many years, contracted for many kinds of services. Corporate people generally call it "outsourcing." It is commonplace, for example, for school districts to contract with vendors for food services, transportation services, or janitorial services. Increasing numbers of school districts are contracting with temporary personnel companies to provide substitute teachers when they are needed. In a similar vein, school districts or the school boards of charter schools may contract with vendors to operate schools for them. This is the business that firms such as Edison Schools are in. They contract to operate public schools for the school district.

Privatization is something quite different: it envisions eliminating or bypassing public schools, what some like to call "government" or "state" schools, in favor of privately owned and controlled schools. Such schools may be sectarian or nonsectarian, for-profit or not-for-profit, but they are neither run by the school district nor under contract to the school district. They are owned by some entity and governed by a board representing that entity. They are not under direct democratic control of the body politic. Privatization of schooling is favored by those who advocate market-driven choice. It is also favored by those who want to wrest the control of schooling from the mechanisms of direct democratic control.

Investors risking money in the $700 billion U.S. educational sector not only see it as a huge market involving enormous sums of money, but also they tend to think of education as being a potential source of profits in the future, as health care was for investors in the 1980s and 1990s. Once again, as was the case in health care, they believe that corporate management can transform large portions of a fragmented cottage industry of independent nonprofit institutions into a consolidated, professionally managed, money-making set of businesses that include all levels of education. As in health care, the profits that the investors hope for must be squeezed out of the enterprise by reducing costs, increasing efficiency, and rationalizing the use of resources. These are hard-nosed businesspeople intent on realizing a high return on investment in ventures that pose what they regard as acceptable levels of risk. Neither ideologues nor theoreticians, their theories-in-use nonetheless are the marketplace theories posited by economists. But they are pragmatists: these ways of investing and making money have worked for them before, and they are confident that they will do so again.

Standards-Based School Reform

Chapter 2 described and discussed standards-based school reform, which has been growing steadily and gathering strength since the first educational summit meeting was convened by President George Bush in 1989. Educational leaders should recognize that this is very different from market-driven strategies: it operates from different assumptions and different theories of action. At the core, standards-based school reform is a political strategy: it accepts and seeks to work within the direct democratic political system under which public schooling has been controlled in the United States for some two centuries. At the operational level, it is an organizational strategy: more exactly, it seeks to greatly strengthen the hierarchical command-and-control power of the states over public schooling. Let us explain.

After being ratified by New Hampshire in 1788, the Constitution went into effect. Within a year, elections were held, and on April 30, 1789, George Washington was inaugurated as president, John Adams as vice president, the elected members of the two houses of Congress took office, and the federal government was organized and started operating from its headquarters on Wall Street in New York City. It was a busy year in New York: courts had to be organized, judges appointed, emissaries commissioned to foreign nations, a financial crisis arising from the debts incurred by the states during the American Revolution had to be straightened out, and national defense had to be provided for—but no one in New York had to think about education. It wasn't in the federal Constitution.

However, at the same time that so much was going on in New York, each of the thirteen states was engaged in writing and adopting its own constitution. The framers of the constitutions in each of the states quickly noted that nothing had been said about education in the federal Constitution. Therefore, each state included in its constitution a commitment to provide for schooling.

In time, after the adoption of the state constitution, the legislature of each state—as representatives of the body politic—wrote and adopted statutes that spelled out how the mandate for public schooling in the state constitution would be carried out. There were differences in the constitutional language from state to state and differences in the statutory arrangements as well. But there was, from the beginning, also a remarkable consistency among the states as to how public schooling would be organized and governed under state authority. From this process of representative democracy a pattern and structure developed—ultimately in all fifty states—that was original and unique in the world. It was, and still is, a source of admiration and bafflement for people around the world: like jazz, it is distinctly American.

To implement the responsibility of the state to provide public schooling, the legislators had many options for arrangements from which to choose. They could easily have elected to create a centralized bureaucratic organization, like the department of motor vehicles, or the state police, or the state court system. Interestingly enough, they all chose not to do this, and all adopted one pattern with variations: to decentralize the organization and administration of public education.

The pattern was to create school districts within the state. In some states (notably those in New England), the boundaries of the school district usually are identical to the boundaries of the town.[13] In many states, the boundaries of the school district are coterminous with the boundaries of the county or parish. Some state legislatures created school districts whose boundaries coincided with the boundaries of neither the town, the city, nor the county, which makes it possible to have several school districts in a single county or even within a single city.[14]

Despite these political and organizational variations, school districts have in common a unique characteristic: they are created by the state for the purpose of conducting *state* business at the local level, in this case education. Sometimes lawyers call such an entity a *quasi-corporation.* This is very different from a *municipal corporation,* which is created by the state to conduct *local* business such as police and sanitation services and zoning for land use.

Thus, in school districts we have a local school board, usually elected but sometimes appointed, to carry out the state responsibility to provide for education in the district. In carrying out their mandate, school boards are under the general supervision of the state education department and, through them, the state legislature. Thus, while education is a responsibility of the state and there is a state education bureaucracy that oversees the local school districts, we in the United States speak often about the importance of local control. This bespeaks the encouragement, by the body politic of the state, of direct democratic participation by citizens residing in the school district not only in electing their local representatives but also in having a voice in local educational policy issues.

Perhaps the clearest and simplest example of this political concept in practice was seen in New England. For nearly 200 years it was common practice in New England towns to have an annual school meeting, separate from the annual town meeting, to discuss educational matters, adopt the school budget, and elect members to the school board or school committee. This is still the practice in some small New England towns today.[15]

This arrangement for the organization and administration of public schooling emerged at the beginning of the second millennium as a critical issue in education reform. We shall come back to this issue when we examine the significant new proposals that were put forward by the Education Commission of the States in 1999 to reform public schooling through changes in school governance. But for the moment, let us return to the strategy of reform through education standards and the relationship that it has with the basic concepts that underlie the traditional governance arrangement just described.

Instead of seeking to bypass or extirpate the public control of schooling through democratic political processes, as advocates of market-driven approaches would, the advocates of standards-based school reform have sought to work within and strengthen the existing system. Beginning with the first summit meeting on education in 1989, forces were set in motion to reenergize the existing political arrangements and make them work powerfully for school reform. The president of the United States convened and participated in that first summit meeting, and principal invitees included the governors of the states—many of whom came—which not only lent weight to the proceedings but also attracted the press and their cameras: it became an important and widely publicized media event. Other important actors were invited and attended, including state legislators, movers and shakers from the corporate world, and key state-level bureaucrats, whose participation and support were critical to making high-level decisions become reality "back home" in the states. Instead of being marginalized or bypassed, these key actors were involved as important participants in action plans for school reform. In a sense, they were owners of the ideas and thus were committed to seeing that they worked.

For good or ill, the standards-based school reform movement is a classic example of command-and-control organization and management. The concept is that educational standards are determined at the state level and turned into mandates that are passed down the hierarchy to the school district to be implemented. Compliance is monitored by the state by administering mandatory statewide standardized tests. It is a strategy that follows the long-established political-legal arrangements that the states themselves created when they wrote their constitutions—except for one point: it marginalizes participation at the level of the local school district. Whereas the tradition for organizing and administering schooling in the states has tended to give considerable weight, if not primacy, to local control, the current standards-based movement of school reform strongly reasserts the authority of the state. Conceptually, the standards-based school reform movement reasserts the primacy and authority of the state in educational policy and practice and redefines the authority relationship between the school district and the state that had developed over a period of many years.

As described in Chapter 2, the standards-based school reform movement has been vigorous and powerful. Two summit meetings followed the original historic summit meeting, which were attended by politically powerful people: the president, many governors, legislators, and corporate executives. Predictably, these initiatives have produced dramatic widespread changes in schooling. This became evident early on when standardized tests mandated by the states increased in frequency. It was soon underscored when the test results began to be used by states to develop "report cards" to grade individual schools, with sometimes dire consequences for the schools that were deemed to be failing. Soon, school districts began to use the tests in deciding who was qualified to be promoted from grade to grade and who was qualified to graduate from high school. This has become known as "high-stakes testing." All of these initiatives were proposed and advocated at the three educational summit meetings held between 1989 and 1999.

The history of this top-down movement is striking in how little attention has been paid to critical issues at the school level and at the level of individual pupils and students that result from the energetic top-down exercise of coercive power, such as the following:

- The impact that new standards and high-stakes testing have on the daily experience of pupils and students in school.
- The curricular, instructional, and organizational transformations that they demand of schools.
- The long-term effects of this new concept of school experience on the pupils and students themselves—for example, on their educational and career planning.

The presidents of the National Education Association and the American Federation of Teachers were invited to attend the 1999 summit meeting as a first step in reaching out to the teaching profession as the reformers planned steps to tie test results to the compensation of teachers as well as to the promotion of students through the grades and, ultimately, graduation from high school. At the same time, there was a rising tide of alarm being expressed by parents who were dismayed as they began to understand the possible consequences to their children of high-stakes testing in the new era of tougher educational standards. Perhaps reacting to that alarm, Secretary of Education Richard W. Riley issued a call in his seventh annual State of American Education speech in 2000 for a "midcourse review" of the standards movement. This was not a call to halt the movement but to "make sure everybody understands what the standards movement is all about." State leaders and educators, he said, "need to listen hard to legitimate concerns." He went on to point out that standards should be challenging but realistic, adding that "Setting high expectations does not mean setting them so high that they are unreachable except for a very few."

Whole School Reform

The third strategy of school reform, whole school reform, is predicated on two basic elements that have been learned about school reform since the mid-1980s and that are now widely incorporated into the theory of practice of many education leaders:

- First, we have not been very successful at learning how to improve the effectiveness of schools by using top-down command-and-control methods from the federal level, the state level, or even the school district level.

- Second, there has been a great deal of demonstrated success in improving the effectiveness of schools by working to renew individual schools from the inside out. This approach means that every school is expected to meet the same standards, but every school writes its own script.

Efforts to improve school performance by seeking to implement and orchestrate change from the school district central office, or from the state education department, or even from a federal agency have historically failed notoriously to improve the achievement of students at the individual school level, even when compliance is closely monitored and audited. Such efforts commonly take the form of issuing—from the top policy level down the hierarchy to the operating level, the schools—directives, uniform policies, detailed curricula for the schools to follow, requirements to follow selected textbooks, and so on. Efforts such as these are called "systemic reform" because they are based on the understanding that the public school enterprise is an orderly, rational system, just as an army in the eighteenth century was supposed to be, and the belief that the proper "marching orders" from the top to the schools coupled with adequate control measures will get the desired results. It is an attractive idea to many who have little experience with the quotidian realities of schools and teaching and impatiently seek simple solutions to complex problems. However, repeated Sisyphean experiences with this way of working with schools, which those in the schools often castigate as micromanaging, has left systemic reform with few adherents except some bureaucrats in some state education departments or in the central offices of a few large school systems.

Increasing School Autonomy

One solution has been site-based management, which is an effort to decentralize decision making in the system by shifting some important decisions from the central office of the state or the district to the school. In some cases in which the concept was enthusiastically embraced by the central office, important instructional, personnel, and financial decisions have been delegated to the schools. These decisions have then been made by principals and teachers. In management jargon, this creates a flatter organization. Layers of bureaucracy are stripped away, decisions are made close to where the work is done, less time is devoted to bureaucratic paperwork and delays, and the happy result should be that the school is more responsive, more nimble, more quickly adaptable, and more effective. This management strategy has become virtually standard procedure in revitalizing for-profit organizations in the corporate world, while it remains highly unusual in the world of public schools.

Sadly, however, experience with site-based management in public schooling has been mixed. Some school districts, mostly moderate-sized suburban districts, have implemented on-site management to good effect. In many instances, however—especially in city school districts, where schooling problems often seem intractable—school boards and their central office bureaucracies are reluctant to cede their power to schools. Too frequently school site-based management results in limited authority being transferred to the schools, and decision making at the school level ranges from marginal to illusory.

Yet the question remains: what undermines the effectiveness of principals and teachers? The answer of a long-time student of New York City education strikes a chord with those who are experienced at working in schools:

> A school system that seeks to restrict initiative by imposing an elaborate command-and-control mechanism, that attempts to manage all of its employees through uniform and burdensome mandates and regulation, that stamps out efforts to find a different (perhaps better) way of educating children, and that lacks meaningful standards for what children should learn but has elaborate standards for the delivery of mediocre services.[16]

Thus, school reform is recognized as an issue in organization and behavior: the crux is recreating the school organization—the operational level of the school district—so as to energize teachers and principals, motivate them, encourage them to collaborate in mutual problem solving, and engage their personal commitment to achieving their own deeply held goals and aspirations. It involves organizing to encourage the development in the school of a culture of leadership, energized motivation, shared decision making, and—above all—creating a growth-enhancing climate of success for both children and adults.

By the dawn of the twenty-first century, there was growing agreement among those seeking school reform that ways had to be found to change the relationship between schools and the bureaucracies of states and school districts that have traditionally controlled them. Perhaps this was part of the new amalgam that Giamatti had described, a new fusion of ideas about the political control of public schooling in the United States with a fresh understanding that school reform is nurtured not in governmental bureaucracies but in individual schools. This new, growing agreement was given a powerful lift by a significant report from the Education Commission of the States[17] on the governance of U.S. schools that was unveiled in November 1999.

The report, titled "Governing America's Schools: Changing the Rules," was the product of a long and careful study by a distinguished eighteen-member commission. In it, educational leaders from the states came to grips with the reality that twenty years of school reform have wrought significant changes:

> Nearly two decades of intensive reform and innovation have dramatically altered the landscape of American public education. Standards are in place in most states and districts, providing the basis for new ways of measuring and attaching consequences to the performance of students, teachers and schools. A variety of promising new national and state initiatives focused on improving teacher quality are under way. Charter schools, classroom technology, comprehensive school reform models and other innovations have changed the look and feel of public education, providing parents and students with a greater range of options and opportunities. . . . At the same time, there is unprecedented interest in the lessons to be learned from the experiences and accomplishments of districts and schools that are doing a good job of preparing students for the world that awaits them.[18]

The report strongly supports the political structure of public schooling that has endured in the Republic for over two centuries and suggests ways in which it should be adapted to contemporary circumstances. The commission report detailed two approaches within this framework from which the embattled school districts of the United States can choose:

- One choice would be for a school district to be "a system of publicly authorized, publicly funded and *publicly operated schools,* based on some of the more promising trends within the prevailing system of public education governance."[19] School districts opting for this form of governance would continue to hire superintendents and principals, bargain with unions, and operate schools, which they hold accountable for results. A significant departure from the past, however, would be that schools would prepare their own budgets based on standard funding from the district, allocate resources as they felt necessary, and hire and fire teachers. In short, this option would institutionalize decentralization of school districts (site-based management) and lead to a reduction of bureaucratized governance of the schools.

- A second option would be "a system of publicly authorized, publicly funded, and *independently operated schools,* based on some of the more promising alternatives to the prevailing system of public education governance."[20] This model envisions the school district as principally a contractor in which schools are run by independent organizations under charters that may be granted to them by the school district. The organizations that may bid to run schools could run the gamut from for-profit corporations to teacher collaboratives, but all would be largely free from governmental regulations yet accountable for results to the school district.

The publication of this set of proposals initiated a nationwide dialogue about the choices for the future of local school boards. However, it is significant that the tenor of both suggestions is twofold:

- Either of the two models would increase the autonomy of individual schools as they seek to develop more flexible and adaptive responses to pressures for change.

- Each model would, instead of giving schools the right to choose students, empower parents to choose the best schools for their children.

Neither of the alternative proposals suggested an increase in the power and authority of the bureaucracies of school districts. At the same time, each of the proposals would result in an increase in the power and authority of school boards to govern because they could quickly alter their relationship with a school if it failed to meet the standards for performance that two parties—the school and the school board—had established. In the case of charter schools, for example, the district school board could terminate contracts with contractors that were not performing up to the specifications in their contracts. Either of the approaches suggested by the Education Commission of the States, however, calls for the following:

- Strengthening, not discarding, the public school system.
- Allowing money to follow the child to the school that he or she attends.
- Providing information on student, teacher, and school performance to parents and community members.

- Giving parents more choice about where their children attend school.
- Granting individual schools greater control over their personnel and budgets.
- Focusing accountability systems on improved student achievement.
- Redefining the role of teachers' unions.
- Strengthening the role of school boards.[21]

Support for School Leaders

The concept is one of shifting authority and responsibility from the central office bureaucracy of the school district to the individual school so that the school can become more nimble, sure-footed, quickly adaptable, and increasingly effective. Autonomy brings greater opportunity for the school leader to be more effective in making a difference. It also greatly increases responsibility for results. As the central office bureaucracy is diminished, the school leader can look there less and less for guidance or to pass the buck up the line. Whole school educational reform is transforming the school principalship into a very different, very demanding opportunity for those who want to be leaders.

Under these changed circumstances, school leaders must not allow themselves to be isolated and left to go it alone. More than ever, school leaders need support, need to reach out and connect with people who have something pertinent and useful to offer: ideas, collegiality, support, feedback, helpful experience, people skills, or knowledge needed for this new era. One can no longer assume that senior people in the bureaucracy know the answers to contemporary leadership problems: very often the most effective help must come from peers who are facing similar problems. To fill this need, a number of resource organizations have arisen since the mid-1980s. We will examine three examples.

Coalition of Essential Schools

The Coalition of Essential Schools (CES)[22] operates nationwide, with about twenty-four CES centers working directly with more than 1,000 schools. Its chairman is Ted Sizer, who was a coprincipal of the Francis W. Parker Charter Essential School, a grade 7–10 school in Devens, Massachusetts, in its first year.[23] CES supports a very well organized, active, and highly diverse program that encourages whole school reform—and that includes the parents—through methods that are personal, encourage members to be part of a learning community through networking and sharing information, and model the ideals of democracy and equity. A top priority is collaboration and critical friendship: colleagues who coach one another, prod, encourage, share, and reflect as they learn together how to meet the challenge to make schools more effective. This is done through local networks, direct services to schools from CES centers, and national and regional seminars and conferences.

One CES program deals with school design and leadership. It focuses on practical problems confronting school leaders, such as staffing patterns and school schedules that facilitate building teams and collaborative work in support of teaching and learning in the school. It does this, however, in ways that are consonant with a clear theoretical framework that the coalition believes is essential to effective long-term school improvement.

Among the practical and often difficult topics addressed by the CES school design and leadership program are the following:

- Strategic planning.
- Managing organizational change.
- Restructuring school time, budgets, and staffing.
- Accountability systems.
- Team building.

Many practitioners like the CES approach. It is eminently practical for them yet operates at a strong intellectual level. For example, one of the principles that CES advocates and supports is as follows:

> Ultimate administrative and budget targets should include substantial time for collective planning by teachers, competitive salaries for staff and an ultimate per pupil cost not to exceed that at traditional schools by more than 10 percent. To accomplish this, administrative plans may have to show the phased reduction or elimination of some services now provided students in many traditional schools.[24]

Working with others to develop practical ways of implementing such a clear-cut, no-nonsense goal is found by many participants to be not only a valuable learning experience but exhilarating as well.

Accelerated Schools

The National Center for the Accelerated Schools Project,[25] based at Stanford University, has eleven regional centers and coordinates a nationwide program that seeks to facilitate the transformation of more than 1,000 elementary and middle schools in some forty states. The goal of this project is to bring all students into the educational mainstream by the end of elementary school so that they can perform at the level appropriate to their age group. The organization uses the term *accelerated*

> because at-risk students must learn at a faster rate than more privileged students—not at a slower rate that drags them farther and farther behind. Only an enrichment strategy, not a remedial one, can offer hope for reversing the present educational crisis of at-risk students. . . . It may seem strange to talk of acceleration for at-risk students. This is a strategy usually reserved for "gifted and talented" students [while, ordinarily] we slow down the learning of children who lack educational advantages.[26]

Therefore:

- Instead of labeling certain children as slow learners, Accelerated Schools have high expectations for all students.
- Instead of slowing down the pace of instruction for at-risk students, Accelerated Schools combine relevant curriculum, powerful and diverse instructional techniques, and creative school organization to accelerate the progress of all students.

- Instead of simply complying with "downtown" decisions made without teacher input, Accelerated Schools' staff systematically identify their own unique challenges and search out solutions to those challenges.[27]

Comer School Development Program

Under the leadership of psychiatrist James Comer, the Child Study Center of Yale University sponsors the School Development Program, which provides coaching, networking, training, and other support services to schools that are seeking to improve their effectiveness. The School Development Program started in 1968 in the two lowest-achieving schools, which were virtually in Yale's backyard, in New Haven. By 1999 it had grown to a network of 721 schools, mostly K–6 but also some middle schools and high schools, and research and evaluations indicate that the program is effective in increasing academic achievement, improving behavior, increasing attendance, and bolstering the self-concept of students.

Three teams give the School Development Plan its unique approach in each individual school:

- A school planning and management team develops a comprehensive school plan that gives direction to the school improvement processes in such areas as school climate, staff development, and public relations.
- A student and staff support team—which includes counselors, social workers, special education teachers, and others—focuses on teacher training related to the School Development Plan.
- A parent team promotes the involvement of parents in all areas of school life.

The program emphasizes the development of an organizational culture in the school that is characterized by no-fault problem solving, consensus decision making, and collaborative working relationships.[28]

The Catalog of School Reform Models

Information about twenty-nine reputable schoolwide models of school reform are found in *The Catalog of School Reform Models,* published by the prestigious Northwest Regional Educational Laboratory (NWREL) since 1998. It is available in paper form and may also be downloaded from the NWREL website (www.nwrel.org/scpd/catalog). This catalog, with the authoratative imprimatur of NWREL, is constantly reviewed and updated. For a model of school reform to be included and maintained in the catalog its sponsors must reapply at regular intervals, providing NWREL with detailed information such as a description of the model, where it is in use, its history and record of evaluations, types of assistance that are available to schools that are interested in adopting the model, contact information, and costs involved in adopted the model. The catalog provides a mine of valuable information on research-based whole-school reform for the school leader looking for ideas and help in developing a school improvement program. The school-reform models included in the catalog are sponsored by reputable organizations that have programs that are and have been functioning in schools all over the United States for some years.

Teacher Education and School Reform

Inevitably as school reform unfolded, increased attention was focused on the education of teachers. Not only was there rising dissatisfaction with the achievement of students in schools, and therefore with the quality of instruction that they received, but also there was a rising teacher shortage by 1999. The shortage loomed ominously in the future as enrollments in schools were on the rise while, at the same time, school reform efforts were pushing class sizes down. The problem was compounded by the fact that with increased employment and educational opportunities available to women, the once seemingly endless supply of bright young women filling the need for teachers in school classrooms had dwindled sharply.

At the same time, many colleges and universities took the position that teacher education was unworthy to be included in the august ranks of academe. Yale University's example was not atypical: it simply abolished the small department of education that it once had. In many institutions of higher education, schools of education struggled with little support and often were isolated from either the leadership of the university or the faculty in the other schools. By the year 2000, however, universities were being called both to account and to action in taking responsibility for meeting the need to educate and train the 2.5 million new teachers who would be needed in the United States in the first decade of the twenty-first century.

National Network for Educational Renewal (NNER)

John Goodlad has, for many years, worked "on the assumption that we will not have better schools without better teachers, but we will not have better teachers without better schools in which teachers can learn, practice, and develop."[29] This assumption underlies the NNER, which involves 33 colleges and universities, more than 100 school districts, and some 500 partner schools. For example, members of the NNER range from the Connecticut School–University Partnership to the University of Wyoming, from the Hawaii Institute for Educational Partnerships to Texas A&M University, and from Miami University to the South Carolina Network for Educational Renewal.

NNER seeks the simultaneous renewal of schools and the education of teachers. In working toward this goal, it is guided by nineteen postulates. The first three of these postulates convey the direction that the NNER is taking:

- Programs for the education of the nation's educators must be viewed by institutions offering them as a major responsibility to society, and must be adequately supported and promoted and vigorously advanced by the institution's top leadership.

- Programs for the education of educators must enjoy parity with other professional education programs, full legitimacy and institutional commitment, and rewards for faculty geared to the nature of the field.

- Programs for the education of educators must be autonomous and secure in their borders, with clear organizational identity, constancy of budget and personnel, and decision-making authority similar to that enjoyed by the major professional schools.[30]

The American Council on Education Initiative

In October 1999 the prestigious American Council on Education (ACE) sounded a clarion call urging every U.S. college and university president to action. The call was titled *To Touch the Future: Transforming the Way Teachers Are Taught*. The line "to touch the future," the ACE explained, came from Christa McAuliffe, the teacher who died in the 1986 *Challenger* explosion. When McAuliffe was asked why she wanted to be the first teacher to fly into space, she replied, "Don't you understand? I am a teacher. Every day, through my students, I touch the future." Belatedly, the ACE had come to understand that the teachers now being prepared in U.S. universities and colleges "will be responsible for teaching the very children who, before the middle of the 21st century, will be the country's movers and shakers, its workers and savers, its leaders and caretakers, its engines of social and economic well-being."[31]

The proposal was to first conduct an external audit of all 1,300 teacher-education programs in the country—much as has become routine in medical and law schools. Fewer than half of the teacher education programs in the United States are independently accredited in this way. But, furthermore, the ACE urged college and university presidents to put the education of teachers at the top of their agendas, calling teacher education the responsibility of the entire university. The view—novel in academe—was that schools of education alone cannot make all of the improvements that are needed in teacher education. They must have the support and participation across the entire campus to do what has to be done. Finally, and importantly, the ACE report called for great increases in research on teacher education to improve the programs. It noted that federal spending for educational research is about $300 million per year and proposed that it be increased to $3 billion per year.

The Flexner Report on Medical Education as Precedent

These sweeping proposals for improving teacher education, both Goodlad's and the ACE's, bring to mind what may be a historic parallel in medical education that occurred nearly a century ago. While medical education stands today in U.S. universities as a bright and shining model for professional education in the university—with its emphasis on rigor, a strong research base, and guided clinical practice—it was not so a century ago. In 1910 a commission headed by Abraham Flexner studied the 155 medical schools in the country and found three-quarters of them substandard. Indeed, it found only one—at Johns Hopkins in Baltimore—to match the standards of the best medical training in Europe.[32] Following Flexner's sweeping proposals for reform in medical education, many of the existing substandard medical schools were closed and the concept of medical schools that we know today began to emerge. The process not only transformed medical education in the university but also, as a direct result, the entire practice of medicine mutated into the much-admired model of professional practice that we take for granted today. That is why some believe and hope that Goodlad's and the ACE's proposals may ultimately turn out to be far more potent in the reform of education in the United States than we may suspect.

Conclusion

On the threshold of the twenty-first century, school reform was the single overarching concern that drove, with great energy, the direction that public education was taking in the United States. Three major strategies for school reform—each based on a different theory of action—jousted with one another for dominance in the highly competitive arena. The advocates of two of these strategies—market-based reform and standards-based reform—started out professing little interest in issues of organizational behavior in schools. One group reasoned that the power of market competition would somehow coerce schools to do whatever they had to do in order to become more effective or they would simply not survive in the marketplace. Another group reasoned that the exercise of overwhelming down-the-line political and bureaucratic coercion would produce a similar result. In the end, however, all reforms were transmuted into designs and strategies for organizational self-renewal in individual schools, and their understanding and working effectively with organizational behavior is the primary determinant of success.

Belatedly, higher education was beginning to show a heightened awareness of the connections between the university, teacher education, and the effectiveness of public schooling. There was some hope that reforming teacher education and educational research at the university level might trigger a powerful and far-reaching transformation in the practice of education, much as the reform of medical education had transformed the practice of medicine early in the twentieth century. Clearly, the strategists in academe believed that a normative-reeducative strategy—one that would populate the schools with more highly educated people—would bring about the changes within the schools that would, in the end, stimulate and facilitate organizational renewal, and thus reform.

Reflective Activities

1. Select one of the reform initiatives identified in this chapter. Go to the research literature and find a study that evaluates the school reform you chose. Locate at least one article that is a true research study, either quantitative or qualitative. Read it and then summarize its findings in one or two paragraphs. Don't choose an article that simply talks about the program components or one that is a "war story" that touts the program's effectiveness by stating how well the authors "think" it worked in a school or district. Find an article that describes the pro-

gram's effectiveness based on such dependent variables as test scores, school climate studies, and qualitative interviews and observations by researchers. Share your summary with others in your class. Discuss the pros and cons of each of the reform initiatives. Which of these reforms has great promise in helping schools improve?

2. *Working on Your Game Plan.* At this point you have, it is hoped, parts of the game plan that you have been working on, along with some further ideas about educational organization and leadership. Now the challenge is to review these thoughts, written and not yet written, and pull them together to develop a more complete draft statement about your understanding of organizational behavior in education—a first draft of your personal game plan for educational leadership. A way to get started would be to identify ten to twenty "this I believe" kinds of state-

ments about educational leadership and educational organizations. After each statement, write a sentence or two that explain briefly why you hold that belief.

For example, we might start out with this statement: *If highly motivated teachers are important to educational excellence, then a school must have a climate that is open and growth enhancing.* We think this in large part because the literature on motivation, notably Maslow's and Herzberg's theories, suggests that people are highly motivated by opportunities in which they can grow and mature as individuals. The research literature on organizational climate also supports the view that a growth-enhancing climate is highly motivating.

How would you, at this point, define your game plan as a work in progress?

Suggested Reading

Chubb, John E., and Terry M. Moe, *Politics, Markets and America's Schools.* Washington, DC: Brookings Institution, 1990.

Historically this is an important book because it was so instrumental in popularizing the idea of school vouchers. It is scholarly, carefully written, and analytic. But it is suspect for many readers because it totally dismisses all forms of education reforms except what the publisher, the Brookings Institution, has advocated for years. Their central argument is that the two alternatives discussed— democratic control and market control—have very different consequences for the organization and performance of schools. Markets, the authors contend, foster the autonomy that schools need to make themselves more effective, and democratic control, they contend, fosters bureaucracy that smothers autonomy and hence effectiveness. Every school leader should read—no, carefully study—these challenging ideas.

Goodlad, John I., *Educational Renewal: Better Teachers, Better Schools.* San Francisco: Jossey-Bass, 1998.

Goodlad masterfully interweaves the culture of the schools and the processes by which the teachers in those schools are educated to work in them. The question is,

what comes first—good schools or good teacher education programs? The answer, according to Goodlad, is that both must come together.

Kohn, Alfie, *The Schools Our Children Deserve: Moving Beyond Traditional Classrooms and "Tougher Standards."* New York: Houghton Mifflin Company, 1999.

This is a book about tougher standards versus better education: the costs of overemphasizing achievement, the arrogance of top-down coercion, the case against standardized testing, and confusing harder with better. It's a good book, insightful, fact-filled, and provocative, and it deserves a place in every discussion about school reform.

Ravitch, Diane, and Joseph P. Viteritti, eds., *New Schools for a New Century: The Redesign of Urban Education.* New Haven, CT: Yale University Press, 1997.

This sophisticated, wide-ranging discussion focuses on schooling in U.S. cities, where our problems are the most intractable. A tour de force for educators who want to understand schooling problems in the contemporary United States, not as slogans or catch phrases but as they are in the real world. Though marred by the authors' predisposition to accept charters, contracting, and *anything* but what we have had in the past, it is nonetheless a tough-minded assessment of where we are and where we are going in urban schooling.

Sarason, Seymour B., *Charter Schools: Another Flawed Educational Reform?* New York: Teachers College Press, 1998.

Sarason has long been one of the most sensitive and supportive observers of the problems of public schooling. In this discussion he draws on his impressive understanding of the creation of organizational settings to raise tough questions about—not challenges to—the idea of charter schools. It may seem strange to some that he draws on a variety of examples, including the history of the Manhattan Project, to examine the problems of charter schools, but he does, and with a remarkably helpful effect.

Vance, Mike, and Diane Deacon, *Think Out of the Box.* Franklin Lakes, NJ: Career Press, 1995.

We think that we've done well to have gotten this far without mentioning the notion that one should "think out of the box." However, the idea may have started with this book. If you like your management thought light and easy, this is the book for you. It has been phenomenally successful in corporate management circles.

Notes

THE ISLLC STANDARDS FOR SCHOOL LEADERS

1. Joseph Murphy, "Reculturing Educational Leadership: The ISLLC Standards Ten Years Out," paper prepared for the National Policy Board for Educational Administration, September 2003, www.npbea.org/Resources/catalog.html, 30.
2. Joseph Schneider, "Issues Related to the Revamping of the ISSLC and ELCC Standards" (working draft), paper prepared for the National Policy Board for Educational Administration, 2005.
3. Ibid.

CHAPTER 1: IN SEARCH OF A PARADIGM

1. We are indebted to Edgar Schein's analysis of the relationships between basic assumptions, values and beliefs, and behavior; his views are described more fully later in this book. See Edgar H. Schein, *Organizational Culture and Leadership* (San Francisco: Jossey-Bass, 1985).
2. We now have extensive documentation and literature on this. See, for example, Theodore R. Sizer, *Horace's School: Redesigning the American High School* (New York: Houghton Mifflin, 1992).
3. Benjamin S. Bloom, Edward J. Furst, Walker H. Hill, and David R. Krathwohl, *Taxonomy of Educational Objectives: Cognitive Domain* (New York: David McKay, 1956).
4. Cleo H. Cherryholmes, *Power and Criticism: Poststructural Investigations in Education* (New York: Teachers College Press, 1988), p. 29.
5. Ibid., p. 30.
6. See, for example, Michel Foucault, *Power/Knowledge* (New York: Pantheon Books, 1980). For a broader overview of Foucault's ideas, see Hubert Dreyfus and Paul Rabinow, eds., *Michel Foucault: Beyond Structuralism and Hermeneutics,* 2nd ed. (Chicago: University of Chicago Press, 1983).
7. Cherryholmes, *Power and Criticism,* p. 35.
8. Sharon Welch, "An Ethic of Solidarity and Difference," in *Postmodernism, Feminism, and Cultural Politics: Redrawing Educational Boundaries,* ed. Henry A. Giroux (Albany: State University of New York Press, 1991), pp. 83–84.
9. Ibid., p. 84.
10. Thomas S. Kuhn, *The Structure of Scientific Revolutions* (Chicago: University of Chicago Press, 1962).
11. Lawrence Van Gelder, "Thomas Kuhn, 73; Devised Science Paradigm" [obituary], *The New York Times,* June 19, 1996, p. B7.
12. Though he did not invent the term *paradigm,* his use of the term was instrumental in popularizing it in American English in the late twentieth century.
13. Jason Epstein, "A Dieter's Dilemma," *The New York Times Magazine,* August 25, 2002, Section 6, p. 58.
14. Walter C. Willett, *Eat, Drink, and Be Healthy: The Harvard Medical School Guide to Healthy Eating* (New York: Simon and Schuster, 2001).
15. Richard Klee, "Humanistic Perspective," in *Humanistic Psychology: A Source Book,* ed. I. David Welch, George A. Tate, and Fred Richards (Buffalo, NY: Prometheus Books, 1978), p. 4.
16. Richard A. Schmuck and Patricia A. Schmuck, *A Humanistic Psychology of Education: Making the School Everybody's House* (Palo Alto, CA: National Press Books, 1974), p. 45.
17. Ibid., p. 49.
18. B. F. Skinner, *The Technology of Teaching* (New York: Appleton-Century-Crofts, 1968), p. 26. Emphasis added.
19. Perhaps his opus magnum was *Love Is Not Enough* (New York: The Free Press, 1949).
20. The following discussion on the differences between the approaches used by psychologists and sociologists to making schools better follows Amy Stuart Wells, "Backers of School Change Turn to Sociologists," *The New York Times,* Education Supplement, Wednesday, January 4, 1989, p. 17.
21. Ibid.
22. Henry A. Murray and others, *Explorations in Personality* (New York: Oxford University Press, 1938).
23. Lewin originally stated it as $B = f(P, E)$. See Kurt Lewin, *A Dynamic Theory of Personality* (New York: McGraw-Hill Book Company, 1935).
24. Carl R. Rogers, *On Becoming a Person* (Boston: Houghton Mifflin, 1961).
25. Kathy Kiely and Tamara Henry, "Will No Child Be Left Behind?" *USA Today,* December 17, 2001, p. 4D.
26. Kenneth A. Dodge, Martha Putallaz, and David Malone, "Coming of Age: The Department of Education," *Phi Delta Kappan* (May 2002), p. 674.
27. Douglas B. Reeves, "Galileo's Dilemma: The Illusion of Scientific Certainty in Educational Research," *Education Week,* May 8, 2002, p. 44.
28. U.S. Department of Education, *Class Size and Students at Risk: What Is Known? . . . What Is Next?,* April 1998, accessed November 25, 2005, www.ed.gov/pubs/ClassSize/academic.html.
29. Tennessee State Department of Education, *The State of Tennessee's Student/Teacher Achievement Ratio (STAR) Project: Final Summary Report 1985–1990* (Tennessee

State Department of Education, 1990); Jeremy Finn and Charles M. Achilles, "Tennessee's Class Size Study: Findings Implications, Misconceptions," *Educational Evaluation and Policy Analysis,* 21 (1999), 97–109.

30. National Education Association, "Stand Up for Children: *Pontiac v. Spellings,*" accessed November 25, 2005, www.nea.org/lawsuit/index.html.

31. No Child Left Behind. Section 9527(a).

32. Interstate School Leaders Licensure Consortium, *Standards for School Leaders* (Washington, DC: Council of Chief State School Officers, 1996).

33. Mortimer Adler, *The Paedeia Proposal: An Educational Manifesto* (New York: Macmillan, 1982).

34. David Perkins, *Smart Schools: Better Thinking and Learning for Every Child.* New York: The Free Press, 1982, p. 55.

35. Ibid.

CHAPTER 2: TOWARD A THEORY OF PRACTICE

1. Diane Ravitch, *Troubled Crusade: American Education, 1945–1980* (New York: Basic Books, 1983).

2. Lynn Olson, "Tugging at Tradition," *Education Week,* XVIII (April 21, 1999), 25.

3. Ibid.

4. *Education Week,* XVIII, no. 32 (April 21, 1999), 26.

5. Ibid., p. 25.

6. Ibid.

7. National Education Association of the United States, Commission on the Reorganization of Secondary Education, *Cardinal Principles of Secondary Education* (Washington, DC: Government Printing Office, 1918).

8. *Education Week,* XVIII, no. 32 (April 21, 1999), 28.

9. Hyman G. Rickover, *Education and Freedom,* with a foreword by Edward R. Murrow and a preface by Charles Van Doren (New York: Charles E. Dutton, 1959).

10. John Holt, *How Children Fail* (Boston: Little, Brown and Company, 1953).

11. Albert Lynd, *Quackery in the Public Schools* (New York: Greenwood Press, 1969).

12. Jonathan Kozol, *Death at an Early Age: The Destruction of the Hearts and Minds of Negro Children in the Boston Public Schools* (Boston: Houghton Mifflin, 1967).

13. Herbert Kohl, *36 Children* (New York: New American Library, 1967).

14. David C. Berliner and Bruce J. Biddle, *The Manufactured Crisis: Myths, Fraud, and the Attack on America's Public Schools* (Reading, MA: Addison-Wesley Publishing Company, 1995), p. 3.

15. *A Nation at Risk* (Washington, DC: The National Commission on Excellence in Education, 1983).

16. Evans Clinchy, "Magnet Schools Matter," *Education Week* (December 8, 1993), 28.

17. Clark Kerr, "Is Education Really All That Guilty?" *Education Week* (February 27, 1991), 30.

18. Thomas Sowell, *Inside American Education: The Decline, the Deception, the Dogmas* (New York: The Free Press, 1993), from the book jacket.

19. Ibid., pp. 296ff.

20. Ibid., p. 296.

21. Ibid., pp. 296–97.

22. David C. Berliner and Bruce J. Biddle, *The Manufactured Crisis: Myths, Fraud, and the Attack on America's Public Schools* (Reading, MA: Addison-Wesley Publishing Company, 1995).

23. Ibid., p. 9.

24. The series is available in book form: Gerald R. Bracey, *The Truth about America's Schools: The Bracey Reports, 1991–1997* (Bloomington, IN: Phi Delta Kappa, 1997).

25. Richard Rothstein, *The Way We Were? The Myths and Realities of America's Student Achievement.* (New York: The Century Foundation [formerly The Twentieth Century Fund], 1998).

26. Ibid., Chapter 2.

27. Ibid.

28. Ibid. Emphasis added.

29. Vance Packard, "Are We Becoming a Nation of Illiterates?" *Reader's Digest,* April 1974, 81–85.

30. Charles C. Walcutt, *Tomorrow's Illiterates: The State of Reading Instruction Today* (Boston: Atlantic Monthly Press, 1961), xiii–xvi, 7.

31. Ibid.

32. Jeanne Chall, *Learning to Read: The Great Debate.* (New York: McGraw-Hill Book Company, 1967).

33. Edward L. Butterworth, "You Have to Fight for Good Schools," *Education Digest* (December, 1958), 83.

34. Pauline Maier, *American Scripture: Making the Declaration of Independence* (New York: Alfred A. Knopf, 1997).

35. From a statement signed by fifty-two internationally known scholars published in *The Wall Street Journal,* Tuesday, December 13, 1994.

36. Richard J. Herrnstein and Charles Murray, *The Bell Curve: Intelligence and Class Structure in American Life* (New York: The Free Press, 1994).

37. Thomas J. Bouchard, Jr., "Breaking the Last Taboo," *Contemporary Psychology* May 1995 (Vol. 40, No. 5), www.apa.org/journals/ ell.html.

38. Quoted in Stephen J. Gould, *The Mismeasure of Man* (New York: W. W. Norton, 1981), pp. 159–60.

39. Howard Gardner, *Frames of Mind: The Theory of Multiple Intelligence* (New York: Basic Books, 1983), p. 25.

40. Howard Gardner, *Multiple Intelligences: The Theory in Practice* (New York: Basic Books, 1993), p. xxiii.

41. Ibid., p. 239.

42. Norman Mailer quoted in Benjamin Lowe, *The Beauty of Sport: A Cross-Disciplinary Inquiry* (Englewood Cliffs, NJ: Prentice-Hall, 1977), p. 255.

43. Gardner, *Frames of Mind,* p. 239.

44. Op. cit.

45. Ibid., pp. 324–25.

46. David Perkins, *Outsmarting IQ: The Emerging Science of Learnable Intelligence* (New York: The Free Press, 1995), p. 16.
47. Ibid., p. 14.
48. Ibid.
49. Ibid., pp. 14–15.
50. Ibid., p. 15.
51. Ibid., p. 7.
52. Ray Marshall and Marc Tucker, *Thinking for a Living: Education and the Wealth of Nations* (New York: Basic Books, 1992), p. 67.
53. David Perkins, *Smart Schools: Better Thinking and Better Learning for Every Child* (New York: The Free Press, 1992).
54. Ibid., p. 3.
55. Ibid. Emphasis added.
56. Ibid. Emphasis added.
57. Ibid. Emphasis added.
58. Steven J. Stein and Howard E. Book, *The EQ Edge: Emotional Intelligence and Your Success* (Toronto: Stoddart, 2000), p. 14.
59. Ibid.
60. E. D. Hirsch, Jr., *Cultural Literacy* (Boston: Houghton Mifflin, 1987). See also E. D. Hirsch, Jr., William G. Rowland, Jr., and Michael Stanford, eds., *A First Dictionary of Cultural Literacy: What Our Children Need to Know* (Boston: Houghton Mifflin, 1996).
61. Kathy A. Zahler and Diane Zahler, *Test Your Countercultural Literacy* (New York: Arco, 1989).
62. Robert J. Marzano, John S. Kendall, and Barbara B. Gaddy, "Deciding on Essential Knowledge," *Education Week,* XVIII, no. 32 (April 21, 1999), 49.
63. Howard Gardner, "Toward Good Thinking on Essential Questions," *The New York Times,* September 11, 1999, p. A15.
64. Ibid., p. A17.
65. E. D. Hirsch, Jr., "Finding Answers in Drill and Rigor," *The New York Times,* September 11, 1999, p. A15.
66. Alfred J. Marrow, *The Practical Theorist: The Life and Work of Kurt Lewin* (New York: Teachers College Press, 1977), pp. 94–95.

CHAPTER 3: MAINSTREAMS OF ORGANIZATIONAL THOUGHT

1. Paul R. Mort and Donald H. Ross, *Principles of School Administration* (New York: McGraw-Hill Book Company, 1957), p. 4.
2. Woodrow Wilson, "The Study of Administration," *Political Science Quarterly,* 2, no. 2 (June 1887), 197–222.
3. Frederick Taylor, *The Principles of Scientific Management* (New York: Harper & Row, Publishers, 1911), p. 8.
4. For a vivid description of this period and the power of business and industrial leaders to force their values on school administrators, see Raymond E. Callahan, *Educa-*

tion and the Cult of Efficiency (Chicago: University of Chicago Press, 1962).
5. Amitai Etzioni, *Modern Organizations* (Englewood Cliffs, NJ: Prentice-Hall, 1964), p. 21.
6. Henri Fayol, *General and Industrial Management,* trans. Constance Storrs (London: Sir Isaac Pitman & Sons, 1949), p. 14.
7. Ibid., p. 15.
8. Fayol's work was published in French in 1916 (when he was chief executive of a mining firm) and immediately received wide acclaim in Europe. His views became dominant and remained so well into the 1940s following their appearance in English translation, in *Papers on the Science of Administration,* eds. Luther Gulick and L. Urwick (New York: Columbia University, Institute of Public Administration, 1937).
9. Richard H. Hall, "The Concept of Bureaucracy: An Empirical Assessment," *The American Journal of Sociology,* 69, no. 1 (July 1963), 33.
10. J. P. Mayer, *Max Weber and German Politics* (London: Faber & Faber, 1943), p. 128.
11. Raymond E. Callahan, *Education and the Cult of Efficiency* (Chicago: University of Chicago Press, 1962).
12. Ellwood P. Cubberly, *Public School Administration: A Statement of the Fundamental Principles Underlying the Organization and Administration of Public Education* (Boston: Houghton Mifflin, 1916), pp. 337–38.
13. David B. Tyack and Robert Cummings, "Leadership in American Public Schools before 1954: Historical Configurations and Conjectures," in *Educational Administration: The Developing Decades,* eds. Luvern L. Cunningham, Walter G. Hack, and Raphael O. Nystrand (Berkeley, CA: McCutchan, 1977), 61.
14. Luther Gulick and L. Urwick, eds., *Papers on the Science of Administration* (New York: Institute of Public Administration, Columbia University, 1937).
15. Luther Gulick, *Administrative Reflection on World War II* (University, AL: University of Alabama Press, 1948).
16. These studies, often called the Western Electric Studies, may be known to the reader for another reason: they also led to identification of the so-called Hawthorne effect, which became important in improving techniques of behavioral research. These studies are summarized in Fritz J. Roethlisberger and William J. Dickson, *Management and the Worker* (Cambridge, MA: Harvard University Press, 1939).
17. Jacob L. Moreno, "Contributions of Sociometry to Research Methodology in Sociology," *American Sociological Review,* 12 (June 1947), 287–92.
18. Robert F. Bales, *Interaction-Process Analysis: A Method for the Study of Small Groups* (Reading, MA: Addison-Wesley Publishing Company, 1950).
19. Benjamin Wolman, "Leadership and Group Dynamics," *Journal of Social Psychology,* 43 (February 1956), 11–25.
20. Robert F. Bales, "The Equilibrium Problem in Small Groups," in *Working Papers in the Theory of Action,* eds.

Talcott Parsons, Robert F. Bales, and Edward A. Shils (Glencoe, IL: The Free Press, 1953).

21. Helen H. Jennings, *Leadership and Isolation,* 2nd ed. (New York: Longman, 1950).

22. Lewin, who defined *field theory* in social psychology, is often thought of as the father of social psychology. See his "Field Theory and Experiment in Social Psychology: Concepts and Methods," *American Journal of Sociology,* 44 (1939), 868–96, and "Group Decision and Social Change," in *Readings in Social Psychology,* eds. Theodore M. Newcomb and Eugene L. Hartley (New York: Holt, Rinehart & Winston, 1947), pp. 330–44.

23. Muzafer Sherif, *An Outline of Social Psychology* (New York: Harper & Row, 1948).

24. Dorwin Cartwright, "Influence, Leadership, Control," in *Handbook of Organizations,* ed. James G. March (Chicago: Rand McNally, 1965), p. 2.

25. Van Miller, *The Public Administration of American School Systems* (New York: Macmillan, 1965), pp. 544–45.

26. As distinguished from a collection of individuals.

27. This discussion follows that of Max G. Abbott, "Intervening Variables in Organizational Behavior," *Educational Administration Quarterly,* 1, no. 1 (Winter 1966), 1–14.

28. See, for example, John K. Hemphill and Alvin E. Coons, *Leader Behavior Description* (Columbus: Ohio State University Press, 1950). For later research using their concept, see Andrew W. Halpin and B. J. Winer, *The Leadership Behavior of the Airplane Commander* (Columbus: Ohio State University Press, 1952); and Andrew W. Halpin, "The Behavior of Leaders," *Educational Leadership,* 14 (1956), 172–76.

29. Daniel Griffiths, "Administrative Theory," *Encyclopedia of Educational Research,* ed. R. L. Ebel (Toronto: Macmillan, 1969), p. 18.

30. Neal Gross, *Who Runs Our Schools?* (New York: John Wiley & Sons, 1958).

31. Daniel E. Griffiths, *Administrative Theory* (New York: Appleton-Century-Crofts, 1959).

CHAPTER 4: ORGANIZATIONAL THEORY IN THE MODERN PERIOD

1. Luvern L. Cunningham, "Leaders and Leadership: 1985 and Beyond," *Phi Delta Kappan,* 67 (September 1985), 20.

2. Education Commission of the States, "Tracking the Reforms," *Education Week* (September 18, 1985), 18.

3. Denis P. Doyle and Terry W. Hartle, "Leadership in Education: Governors, Legislators, and Teachers," *Phi Delta Kappan,* 67 (September 1985), 24.

4. Douglas M. McGregor, *The Human Side of Enterprise* (New York: McGraw-Hill Book Company, 1960), pp. 37–57.

5. Chris Argyris, *Management and Organizational Development* (New York: McGraw-Hill Book Company, 1971), pp. 1–26.

6. Thomas J. Sergiovanni, "Beyond Human Relations," in *Professional Supervision for Professional Teachers,* ed. Thomas J. Sergiovanni (Washington, DC: Association for Supervision and Curriculum Development, 1975), p. 11.

7. Ibid.

8. Albert F. Siepert and Rensis Likert, "The Likert School Profile Measurements of the Human Organization" (paper presented at the American Educational Research Association National Convention, February 27, 1973), p. 3.

9. Ibid., p. 4.

10. Robert R. Blake and Jane Srygley Mouton, *Building a Dynamic Corporation through Grid Organization Development* (Reading, MA: Addison-Wesley, 1969).

11. Gordon L. Lippitt, *Organizational Renewal: Achieving Viability in a Changing World* (New York: Appleton-Century-Crofts, 1969).

12. Paul Berman and Milbrey Wallen McLaughlin, *Federal Programs Supporting Educational Change, Volume VIII: Implementing and Sustaining Innovations* (Santa Monica, CA: Rand Corporation, 1978).

13. Charles B. Perrow, *Organizational Analysis: A Sociological View* (Monterey, CA: Brooks/Cole Publishing Co., 1970), pp. 3–4.

14. Ludwig von Bertalanffy, "An Outline of General Systems Theory," *British Journal of Philosophical Science,* 1 (1950), 134–65. A more complete work, by the same author, is *General Systems Theory* (New York: George Braziller, 1968).

15. Andre Lwoff, "Interaction among Virus, Cell and Organization," *Science,* 152 (1966), 1216.

16. F. Kenneth Berrien, "A General Systems Approach to Organizations," in *Handbook of Industrial and Organizational Psychology,* ed. Marvin D. Dunnette (Chicago: Rand McNally & Company, 1976), p. 43.

17. Ronald G. Corwin, "Models of Educational Organizations," in *Review of Research in Education,* ed. Fred N. Kerlinger and J. B. Carroll (Itasca, IL: F. E. Peacock, Publishers, 1974), p. 263.

18. Andrew W. Halpin and Don B. Croft, *The Organizational Climate of Schools* (Washington, DC: Cooperative Research Report, U.S. Office of Education, 1962).

19. Some examples are James G. Anderson, *Bureaucracy in Education* (Baltimore: The Johns Hopkins University Press, 1968); Neal Gross and Robert E. Herriott, *Staff Leadership in Public Schools: A Sociological Inquiry* (New York: John Wiley & Sons, 1965). These may be compared with later studies, such as the Rand investigations of educational change conducted by Berman and McLaughlin. See, for example, Paul Berman and Milbrey Wallin McLaughlin, *Federal Programs Supporting Educational Change, Volume VII: Factors Affecting*

Implementation and Continuation (Santa Monica, CA: Rand Corporation, 1977), especially pp. 16–20.

20. Erving Goffman, *The Presentation of Self in Everyday Life* (New York: Doubleday & Co., Anchor Books, 1959): A later study in a similar vein by the same author is *Encounters* (Indianapolis: The Bobbs-Merrill Company, 1961).

21. The term *role* is a highly useful metaphor that is widely used in human relations research and practice. Because there is such extensive literature on role theory in psychiatry, psychology, sociology, and education, not surprisingly there is some imprecision attached to the use of this metaphor. It should be clear, however, that what is under discussion here is a psychological concept and not merely job titles or job descriptions. For discussion of the problem of definition, see Theodore R. Sarbin and Vernon L. Allen, "Role Theory," in *The Handbook of Social Psychology,* vol. 1, 2nd ed., eds. Gardner Lindzey and Elliot Aronson (Reading, MA: Addison-Wesley Publishing Company, 1968).

22. Robert Boguslaw, *The New Utopians: A Study of System Design and Social Change* (Englewood Cliffs, NJ: Prentice-Hall, 1965), pp. 170–77.

23. The material presented here on role set is based on Warren G. Bennis, *Changing Organizations* (New York: McGraw-Hill Book Company, 1966), pp. 193–96.

24. Robert L. Kahn, Donald M. Wolfe, Robert R. Quinn, and J. Diedrick Snoek, *Organizational Stress: Studies in Role Conflict and Ambiguity* (New York: John Wiley & Sons, 1964).

25. The following discussion of role allocation is based on Kenneth D. Benne and Paul Sheats, "Functional Roles of Group Members," *Journal of Social Issues,* 4, no. 2 (Spring 1948), 41–49.

26. Ibid., pp. 43–44.

27. Ibid., pp. 44–45.

28. Jacob W. Getzels and Egon G. Guba, "Social Behavior and the Administrative Process," *The School Review,* 65 (Winter 1957), 423–41. This version of the organization as a sociopsychological system is based upon the earlier work of Talcott Parsons and was first suggested by Getzels in 1952 in his "A Psycho-Sociological Framework for the Study of Educational Administration," *Harvard Educational Review,* 22, no. 4 (1952), 235–46. Later, in collaboration with Egon Guba, the model was developed to include *psychological* concepts (such as personality), *sociological* notions (for example, role expectation), *anthropological* concepts of culture, and *social-psychological* concepts (for example, group norms and organizational climate). This more elaborate model—the so-called Getzels-Guba model—is discussed later in this chapter (see Figure 4.14).

29. Jacob W. Getzels, "Administration as a Social Process," in *Administrative Theory in Education,* ed. Andrew W. Halpin (Chicago: Midwest Administration Center, University of Chicago, 1958), p. 157.

30. There is extensive literature on the authoritarian personality. Classic works are Theodore W. Adorno, Else Frenkel-Brunswik, Daniel J. Levinson, and R. N. Sanford, *The Authoritarian Personality* (New York: Harper & Row, Publishers, 1950); and Milton Rokeach, *The Open and Closed Mind* (New York: Basic Books, Publishers, 1960).

31. Mary Lynn Crow and Merl E. Bonney, "Recognizing the Authoritarian Personality Syndrome in Educators," *Phi Delta Kappan,* 57, no. 1 (September 1975), 40.

32. Frederick W. Taylor, *The Principles of Scientific Management* (New York: Harper & Row, Publishers, 1911), pp. 42–43.

33. Chester I. Barnard, *The Functions of the Executive* (Cambridge, MA: Harvard University Press, 1938), p. 57.

34. Ibid., p. 55.

35. Ibid., p. 57.

36. John M. Pfiffner and Frank P. Sherwood, *Administrative Organization* (Englewood Cliffs, NJ: Prentice-Hall, 1960), p. 299.

37. The following discussion is adapted from Robert G. Owens and Carl R. Steinhoff, *Administering Change in Schools* (Englewood Cliffs, NJ: Prentice-Hall, 1976), pp. 60–63 and 143 and is based on the concepts developed by Harold J. Leavitt cited below.

38. This view is based on the concepts developed by Harold J. Leavitt, *Managerial Psychology,* 2nd ed. (Chicago: University of Chicago Press, 1964). See also by the same author "Applied Organizational Change in Industry: Structural, Technological, and Humanistic Approaches," in *Handbook of Organizations,* ed. James G. March (Chicago: Rand McNally & Company, 1965), pp. 1144–70.

39. See, for example, Wendell L. French and Cecil H. Bell, Jr., *Organizational Development* (Englewood Cliffs, NJ: Prentice-Hall, 1973), pp. 183–85, whose description is reflected in this discussion.

40. John I. Goodlad, "Educational Leadership: Toward the Third Era," *Educational Leadership,* 35, no. 4 (January 1978), 330.

41. Fremont E. Kast and James E. Rosenzweig, *Contingency Views of Organization and Management* (Chicago: Science Research Associates, 1973), p. ix.

42. Dennis Moberg and James L. Koch, "A Critical Appraisal of Integrated Treatments of Contingency Findings," *Academy of Management Journal,* 18, no. 1 (March-June 1975), 109–24.

43. Donald Hellriegel and John W. Slocum, Jr., *Organizational Behavior: Contingency Views* (St. Paul: West Publishing Co., 1976), p. 6.

44. Paul R. Lawrence and Jay W. Lorsch, *Organization and Environment* (Homewood, IL: Richard D. Irwin, 1967).

45. Stephen P. Robbins, *The Administrative Process: Integrating Theory and Practice* (Englewood Cliffs, NJ: Prentice-Hall, 1976), pp. 272–73.

CHAPTER 5: THE HUMAN DIMENSION OF ORGANIZATION

1. Donald A. Schön, *Educating the Reflective Practitioner* (San Francisco: Jossey-Bass, 1987), p. 3.
2. Ibid., pp. 4–5.
3. Wayne K. Hoy and Cecil G. Miskel, *Educational Administration,* 2nd ed. (New York: Random House, 1982), p. 82.
4. T. Barr Greenfield, "Theory About Organization: A New Perspective and Its Implication for Schools," in *Administering Education: International Challenge,* ed. M. G. Hughes (London: Athlone, 1975), p. 71.
5. Ibid., p. 81.
6. Robert W. Heller, James A. Conway, and S. L. Jacobson, "Here's Your Blunt Critique of Administrative Preparation," *The Executive Educator* (September 1988), 18–30.
7. Roland S. Barth and Terrence E. Deal, *The Effective Principal: A Research Summary* (Reston, VA: Association of Secondary School Principals, 1982).
8. James Bryant Conant, *Two Modes of Thought: My Encounters with Science and Education* (New York: A Trident Press Book, 1964).
9. Carl R. Rogers, "Toward a Science of the Person," *Journal of Humanistic Psychology* (Fall 1963), 17–31.
10. Arthur Blumberg, *School Administration as a Craft: Foundations of Practice* (Boston: Allyn and Bacon, 1988).
11. Charles E. Bidwell, "The School as a Formal Organization," in *Handbook of Organizations,* ed. James G. March (Chicago: Rand McNally & Company, 1965).
12. Karl E. Weick, "Educational Organizations as Loosely Coupled Systems," *Administrative Science Quarterly,* 21 (March 1976), 1.
13. John W. Meyer and Brian Rowan, "The Structure of Educational Organizations," in *Organizational Environments: Ritual and Rationality,* eds. John W. Meyer and W. Richard Scott (Beverly Hills, CA: Sage Publications, 1983), p. 74.
14. For examples see Van Cleve Morris, Robert L. Crowson, Emanuel Hurwitz, Jr., and Cynthia Porter-Gehrie, *The Urban Principal: Discretionary Decision Making in a Large Educational Organization* (Chicago: College of Education, University of Illinois at Chicago Circle, 1981); and N. A. Newberg and A. G. Glatthom, *Instructional Leadership: Four Ethnographic Studies of Junior High School Principals* (final report of Grant Number NIE G-81-0088, 1983) (Washington, DC: National Institute of Education).
15. Meyer and Rowan, "The Structure of Educational Organizations," p. 75.
16. Economists have long recognized the value of human resources. See, for example, Gary S. Becker, "Investment in Human Capital: A Theoretical Analysis, *The Journal of Political Economy* (Supplement), 70 (October 1962); and Theodore W. Schultz, "Capital Formation by Education,"

The Journal of Political Economy, 68 (December 1960), 3–72.
17. Chris Argyris, "Human Problems with Budgets," *Harvard Business Review,* 31 (January-February 1953), 97–110.
18. Rensis Likert, *The Human Organization: Its Management and Value* (New York: McGraw-Hill Book Company, 1967), p. 148.
19. Ray A. Killian, *Human Resource Management* (New York: AMACOM, 1976), p. 140.
20. William A. Firestone and Bruce L. Wilson, *Using Bureaucratic and Cultural Linkages to Improve Instruction: The High School Principal's Contribution* (Eugene: Center for Educational Policy and Management, College of Education, University of Oregon, 1983), pp. 14–15.
21. Terrence E. Deal and A. Kennedy, *Corporate Cultures: The Rites and Rituals of Corporate Life* (Reading, MA: Addison-Wesley Publishing Company, 1982); and Lee G. Bolman and Terrence E. Deal, *Modern Approaches to Understanding and Managing Organizations* (San Francisco: Jossey-Bass, 1984).
22. Thomas J. Peters and Robert H. Waterman, Jr., *In Search of Excellence: Lessons from America's Best-Run Companies* (New York: Harper & Row, Publishers, 1982).
23. Rosabeth Moss Kanter, *The Change Masters: Innovation and Entrepreneurship in the American Corporation* (New York: Simon & Schuster, 1983).
24. Edgar H. Schein, *Organizational Culture and Leadership* (San Francisco: Jossey-Bass, 1985).
25. S. C. Purkey and M. S. Smith, "School Reform: The District Policy Implications of the Effective Schools Literature," *The Elementary School Journal,* 85 (December 1985), 353–89.
26. Ibid., p. 355.
27. Ibid.
28. Ibid., p. 357.
29. Ibid.
30. This discussion follows the analysis of Purkey and Smith, "School Reform," pp. 358–59.

CHAPTER 6: ORGANIZATIONAL CULTURE AND ORGANIZATIONAL CLIMATE

1. Alfred J. Marrow, David G. Bowers, and Stanley E. Seashore, *Management by Participation* (New York: Harper & Row, Publishers, 1967).
2. Terrence E. Deal, "Cultural Change: Opportunity, Silent Killer or Metamorphosis?" (unpublished paper, no date).
3. Chester I. Barnard, *Functions of the Executive* (Boston: Harvard University Press, 1938).
4. Philip Selznick, *TVA and the Grass Roots* (Berkeley: University of California Press, 1949).
5. Marshall W. Meyer and associates, eds., *Environments and Organizations* (San Francisco: Jossey-Bass, 1978).

6. Andrew W. Halpin and Don B. Croft, *The Organizational Climate of Schools* (Chicago: Midwest Administration Center, The University of Chicago, 1962).

7. Bernard Clark, "The Organizational Saga in Higher Education," in *Managing Change in Educational Organizations,* J. Victor Baldridge and Terrence E. Deal, eds. (Berkeley, CA: McCutchan, 1975).

8. Michael Rutter, Barbara Maughan, Peter Mortimore, and Jane Ouston, with Alan Smith, *Fifteen Thousand Hours: Secondary Schools and Their Effects on Children* (Cambridge, MA: Harvard University Press, 1979).

9. Deal, "Cultural Change," p. 6.

10. Renato Tagiuri, "The Concept of Organizational Climate," in *Organizational Climate: Exploration of a Concept,* Renato Tagiuri and George H. Litwin, eds., (Boston: Harvard University, Division of Research, Graduate School of Business Administration, 1968). See also Carolyn S. Anderson, "The Search for School Climate: A Review of the Research." *Review of Educational Research,* 52 (Fall 1982), 368–420, and Cecil Miskel and Rodney Ogawa, "Work Motivation, Job Satisfaction, and Climate," in *Handbook of Research on Educational Administration,* ed. Norman J. Boyan. (New York: Longman, 1988).

11. William Ouchi, *Theory Z: How American Business Can Meet the Japanese Challenge* (Reading, MA: Addison-Wesley Publishing Company, 1981).

12. Ibid., p. 165.

13. Thomas J. Peters and Robert H. Waterman, Jr., *In Search of Excellence: Lessons from America's Best-Run Companies* (New York: Harper & Row, Publishers, 1982).

14. Ibid., p. 282.

15. Peters and Waterman, *In Search of Excellence,* p. 319.

16. Edgar H. Schein, "How Culture Forms, Develops, and Changes," in *Gaining Control of the Corporate Culture,* Ralph H. Kilmann, Mary J. Saxton, Roy Serpa, and Associates, eds. (San Francisco: Jossey-Bass, 1985), pp. 19–20.

17. Ibid., p. 20.

18. Ralph H. Kilmann, Mary J. Saxton, and Roy Serpa, "Five Key Issues in Understanding and Changing Culture," in Kilmann and others, *Gaining Control of the Corporate Culture,* p. 5.

19. Ibid.

20. Terrence E. Deal, "Cultural Change: Opportunity, Silent Killer, or Metamorphosis?" in *Gaining Control of the Corporate Culture* (revision of previously unpublished paper), p. 301.

21. Ibid.

22. Ralph H. Kilmann, "Five Steps for Closing Culture-Gaps," in Kilmann and others, *Gaining Control of the Corporate Culture,* p. 352.

23. Alan L. Wilkins and Kerry J. Patterson, "You Can't Get There from Here: What Will Make Culture Projects Fail," in Kilmann and others, *Gaining Control of the Corporate Culture,* p. 267.

24. George C. Homans, *The Human Group* (New York: Harcourt, Brace, & World, 1950), p. 123.

25. A. Paul Haire, *Handbook of Small Group Research* (New York: The Free Press, 1962), p. 24.

26. A. R. Cohen and others, *Effective Behavior in Organizations,* 3rd ed. (Homewood, IL: Richard D. Irwin, 1984), p. 62.

27. Schein, "How Culture Forms, Develops, and Changes," in Kilmann and others, *Gaining Control of the Corporate Culture,* p. 21.

28. Ibid., pp. 19–20.

29. Ralph H. Kilmann, Mary J. Saxton, and Roy Serpa, "Five Key Issues in Understanding and Changing Culture," in Kilmann and others, *Gaining Control of the Corporate Culture,* p. 5.

30. Ibid.

31. Terrence E. Deal, "Cultural Change: Opportunity, Silent Killer, or Metamorphosis?" in Kilmann and others, *Gaining Control of the Corporate Culture,* p. 301.

32. Halpin and Croft, *The Organizational Climate of Schools.*

33. Rosabeth Moss Kanter, *The Change Masters: Innovation and Entrepreneurship in the American Corporation* (New York: Simon & Schuster, 1983), p. 149.

34. George C. Homans, *The Human Group* (New York: Harcourt, Brace, & World, 1950), p. 123.

35. Haire, *Handbook of Small Group Research,* p. 24.

36. Kurt Lewin, *Principles of Topological Psychology* (New York: McGraw-Hill Book Company, 1936).

37. Garlie A. Forehand and B. Von Haller Gilmer, "Environmental Variations in Studies of Organizational Behavior," *Psychological Bulletin,* 62, no. 6 (December 1964), 361–82.

38. James G. March and Herbert A. Simon, *Organizations* (New York: John Wiley & Sons, 1959).

39. Renato Tagiuri, ed., *Research Needs in Executive Selection* (Boston: Harvard University, Graduate School of Business Administration, 1961).

40. The contemporary concept of block scheduling should not be confused with what was called "block scheduling" from 1940 through the 1980s. The former version normally divided the high school day into one-hour blocks of "recitation periods" (typically forty-two minutes long), which made scheduling with file cards and cup hooks fairly simple. One had either single periods (as for English, math, or foreign languages) or double periods (which provided time for lab sessions, as in science, for example). Contemporary block scheduling is much more complex and requires computer assistance to make it work.

41. Roger G. Barker describes the theory of behavior settings and ways of studying them in *Ecological Psychology: Concepts and Methods for Studying the Environment of Human Behavior* (Stanford, CA: Stanford University Press, 1968).

42. Roger G. Barker and Paul V. Gump, eds., *Big School, Small School* (Stanford, CA: Stanford University Press, 1964).

43. Leonard L. Baird, "Big School, Small School: A Critical Examination of the Hypothesis," *Journal of Educational Psychology,* 60 (1969), 253–60.

44. Leonard L. Baird, "The Relation of Vocational Interests to Life Goals, Self-Ratings of Ability and Personality Traits, and Potential for Achievement," *Journal of Educational Measurement,* 7 (1970), 233–39.

45. Susan Chira, "Is Smaller Better? Educators Now Say Yes for High School," *New York Times,* Wednesday, July 14, 1993, p. A1.

46. Seymour B. Sarason, *The Culture of the School and the Problem of Change* (Boston: Allyn and Bacon, 1971).

47. Seymour B. Sarason, *The Creation of Settings and Future Societies* (San Francisco: Jossey-Bass, 1972).

48. This field is well surveyed in Marvin D. Dunnette, ed., *Handbook of Industrial and Organizational Psychology* (Chicago: Rand McNally & Company, 1976).

49. Theodore R. Sizer, *Horace's Compromise: The Dilemma of the American High School* (Boston: Houghton Mifflin Company, 1984).

50. Ernest L. Boyer, *High School: A Report on Secondary Education in America* (New York: Harper & Row, Publishers, 1983).

51. John I. Goodlad, *A Place Called School: Prospects for the Future* (St. Louis: McGraw-Hill Book Company, 1983).

52. Wilbur B. Brookover and others, "Elementary School Social Climate and School Achievement," *American Educational Research Journal,* 15, no. 2 (Spring 1978), 302.

53. James S. Coleman and others, *Equality of Educational Opportunity* (Washington, DC: Government Printing Office, 1966).

54. Christopher Jencks and others, *Inequality* (New York: Basic Books, 1972).

55. Brookover and others, "Elementary School Social Climate and School Achievement," p. 316.

56. Ibid., p. 317.

57. Rutter and others, *Fifteen Thousand Hours.*

58. Ibid., p. 178.

59. Joyce L. Epstein, ed., *The Quality of School Life* (Lexington, MA: D.C. Heath and Company, 1984).

60. Rudolf H. Moos, *Evaluating Educational Environments* (Palo Alto, CA: Consulting Psychologists Press, 1979).

61. Andrew W. Halpin and Don B. Croft, *The Organizational Climate of Schools* (U.S.O.E. Research Project, Contract No. SAE 543-8639, August 1962).

62. Henry A. Murray and others, *Explorations in Personality* (New York: Oxford University Press, 1938), p. 124.

63. For a full description of Stern's extensive research in this field, see George G. Stern, *People in Context: Measuring Person-Environment Congruence in Education and Industry* (New York: John Wiley & Sons, 1970).

64. George G. Stern, "Characteristics of Intellectual Climate in College Environments," *Harvard Educational Review,* 31 (Winter 1963), 5–41.

65. Carl R. Steinhoff, *Organizational Climate in a Public School System* (U.S.O.E. Cooperative Research Program, Contract No. OE-4–255, Project No. S-083, Syracuse University, New York, 1965).

66. See, for example, Carl R. Steinhoff and Lloyd Bishop, "Factors Differentiating Preparation Programs in Educational Administration: U.C.E.A. Study of Student Organizational Environment," *Educational Administration Quarterly,* 10 (1974), 35–50; and Lloyd Bishop and Carl R. Steinhoff, "Organizational Characteristics of Administrative Training Programs: Professors and Their Work Environments," *Journal of Educational Administration,* 13 (1975), 54–61.

67. Rensis Likert and Jane Gibson Likert, *New Ways of Managing Conflict* (New York: McGraw-Hill Book Company, 1976), pp. 218–19.

68. David G. Bowers, *Systems of Organization: Management of the Human Resource* (Ann Arbor: University of Michigan Press, 1976), pp. 2–3.

69. Rensis Likert, *New Patterns of Management* (New York: McGraw-Hill Book Company, 1961), p. 144.

70. Likert and Likert, *New Ways of Managing Conflict,* Chapter 12.

71. Likert, *New Patterns of Management,* p. 181.

CHAPTER 7: ORGANIZATIONAL CHANGE

1. Matthew B. Miles, "Some Properties of Schools as Social Institutions," in *Change in School Systems,* ed. Goodwin Watson (Washington, DC: National Training Laboratories, NEA, 1967), p. 20.

2. National Commission on Excellence in Education, *A Nation at Risk* (Washington, DC: Government Printing Office, 1983).

3. Evans Clinchy, "Magnet Schools Matter," *Education Week,* December 8, 1993, p. 28.

4. Seymour B. Sarason, *The Predictable Failure of Educational Reform: Can We Change Before It's Too Late?* (San Francisco: Jossey-Bass, 1990).

5. Ibid., p. 73.

6. Ibid., p. 72.

7. Ibid.

8. Paul R. Mort and Donald H. Ross, *Principles of School Administration* (New York: McGraw-Hill Book Company, 1957), p. 181.

9. Paul R. Mort, "Educational Adaptability," in *Administration for Adaptability,* ed. Donald H. Ross (New York: Metropolitan School Study Council, 1958), pp. 32–33.

10. "Kindergarten Education, 1967–68." *NEA Research Bulletin,* 47, no. 1 (March 1969), 10.

11. Paul R. Mort and Francis G. Cornell, *American Schools in Transition* (New York: Teachers College, Columbia University, 1941).

12. A. G. Grace and G. A. Moe, *State Aid and School Costs* (New York: McGraw-Hill Book Company, 1938), p. 324.

13. Austin D. Swanson, "The Cost-Quality Relationship," in *The Challenge of Change in School Finance,* Proceedings of the Tenth Annual Conference on School Finance (Washington, DC: Committee on Educational Finance, National Education Association, 1967), pp. 151–65.

14. Richard O. Carlson, *Adoption of Educational Innovations* (Eugene: Center for the Advanced Study of Educational Administration, University of Oregon, 1965).

15. For a full description of PSSC, see Paul E. March, "The Physical Science Study Committee: A Case History of Nationwide Curriculum Development" (unpublished doctoral dissertation, Graduate School of Education, Harvard University, 1963).

16. Two other taxonomies that are widely used are those developed by (1) Daniel Katz and Robert L. Kahn, and (2) Ronald G. Havelock. There is substantial agreement among the three taxonomies. For a discussion, see Robert G. Owens and Carl R. Steinhoff, *Administering Change in Schools* (Englewood Cliffs, NJ: Prentice-Hall, 1976), Chapter 4.

17. David L. Clark and Egon G. Guba, "An Examination of Potential Change Roles in Education," in *Rational Planning in Curriculum and Instruction,* ed. Ole Sand (Washington, DC: National Education Association, 1967).

18. Such as the Biological Sciences Curriculum Study (BSCS), the Physical Sciences Study Committee (PSSC), the Chemical Bond Approach Project (Chem Bond or CBA), and the School Mathematics Study Group (SMSG).

19. Gerald Zaltman, David Florio, and Linda Sikorski, *Dynamic Educational Change: Models, Strategies, Tactics, and Management* (New York: The Free Press, 1977), p. 77.

20. Robert Chin, "Basic Strategies and Procedures in Effecting Change," in *Educational Organization and Administration Concepts, Practice and Issues,* ed. Edgar L. Morphet and others (Englewood Cliffs, NJ: Prentice-Hall, 1967).

21. Homer Garner Barnett, *Innovation: The Basis of Cultural Change* (New York: McGraw-Hill Book Company, 1953).

22. Matthew B. Miles, *Innovation in Education* (New York: Columbia University Press, 1964), p. 14.

23. Robert Chin and Kenneth D. Benne, "General Strategies for Effecting Changes in Human Systems," in *The Planning of Change,* 2nd. ed., ed. Warren G. Bennis, Kenneth D. Benne, and Robert Chin (New York: Holt, Rinehart & Winston, 1969).

24. Group on School Capacity for Problem Solving, *Program Plan* (Washington, DC: National Institute of Education, June 1975), p. 1.

25. Paul Berman and Milbrey Wallin McLaughlin, *Federal Programs Supporting Educational Change, Volume VIII: Implementing and Sustaining Innovations* (Santa Monica, CA: Rand Corporation, May 1978), p. iii.

26. This study is fully reported in eight volumes under the general title, *Federal Programs Supporting Educational Change* (Santa Monica, CA: Rand Corporation).
   Volume I: *A Model of Educational Change* by Paul Berman and Milbrey Wallin McLaughlin (1975).
   Volume II: *Factors Affecting Change Agent Projects* by Paul Berman and Edward Pauley (1975).
   Volume III: *The Process of Change* by Peter W. Greenwood, Dale Mann, and Milbrey Wallin McLaughlin (1975).
   Volume IV: *The Findings in Review* by Paul Berman and Milbrey Wallin McLaughlin (1975).
   Volume V: *Executive Summary* by Paul Berman, Peter W. Greenwood, Milbrey Wallin McLaughlin, and John Pincus (1975).
   Volume VI: *Implementing and Sustaining Title VII Bilingual Projects* by Gerald Sumner and Gail Zellman (1977).
   Volume VII: *Factors Affecting Implementation and Continuation* by Paul Berman and others (1977).
   Volume VIII: *Implementing and Sustaining Innovations* by Paul Berman and Milbrey Wallin McLaughlin (1978).

27. Group on School Capacity for Problem-Solving, p. 1.

28. Ibid., p. 4.

29. Ibid., p. 5.

30. T. Barr Greenfield, "Organizations as Social Inventions: Rethinking Assumptions about Change," *Journal of Applied Behavioral Science,* 9, no. 5 (1973), 551–74.

31. Chris Argyris, *Integrating the Individual and the Organization* (New York: John Wiley & Sons, 1964), p. 123.

32. Matthew B. Miles, "Planned Change and Organizational Health: Figure and Ground," in *Change Processes in the Public Schools,* ed. Richard O. Carlson and others (Eugene: Center for the Advanced Study of Educational Administration, University of Oregon, 1965), p. 17.

33. Adapted from Miles, "Planned Change," pp. 18–21.

34. Rensis Likert, *New Patterns of Management* (New York: McGraw-Hill Book Company, 1961).

35. Gordon L. Lippitt, *Organizational Renewal: Achieving Viability in a Changing World* (New York: Appleton-Century-Crofts, 1969).

36. Matthew B. Miles and Dale G. Lake, "Self-Renewal in School Systems: A Strategy for Planned Change," in *Concepts for Social Change,* ed. Goodwin Watson (Washington, DC: National Training Laboratories, NEA, 1967).

37. Far West Laboratory, "A Statement of Organizational Qualification for Documentation and Analysis of Organizational Strategies for Sustained Improvement of Urban Schools" (paper submitted to Program on Local Problem-Solving, National Institute of Education, San Francisco, 1974).

38. John I. Goodlad, *The Dynamics of Educational Change: Toward Responsive Schools* (New York: McGraw-Hill Book Company, 1975), p. 175.

39. Gerald Zaltman, David H. Florio, and Linda A. Sikorski, *Dynamic Educational Change: Models, Strategies, Tactics, and Management* (New York: The Free Press, 1977), p. 89.

40. Michael Fullan, Matthew B. Miles, and Gib Taylor, *OD in Schools: The State of the Art, Volume I: Introduction and Executive Summary.* Final report to the National Institute of Education, Contract Nos. 400-77-0051-0052 (Toronto: Ontario Institute for Studies in Education, August 1978), p. 14.

41. The following discussion of OD concepts and force-field analysis is from Robert G. Owens and Carl R. Steinhoff, *Administering Change in Schools* (Englewood Cliffs, NJ: Prentice-Hall, 1976), pp. 142–48.

42. See, for example, Spencer Wyant, *Organizational Development from the Inside: A Progress Report on the First Cadre of Organizational Specialists* (Eugene: Center for the Advanced Study of Educational Administration, University of Oregon, 1972).

43. Jack R. Gibb, "TORI Theory: Consultantless Team-building," *Journal of Contemporary Business,* 1 (Summer 1972), 33–34.

44. The concepts of force-field analysis and the three-step cycle of organizational change are generally credited to Kurt Lewin, "Frontiers in Group Dynamics," *Human Relations,* 1 (1947), 5–41. The definitive work in this field by Lewin is *Field Theory in Social Science* (New York: Harper & Row, Publishers, 1951).

45. Lewin, "Frontiers in Group Dynamics," p. 35.

46. Paul Hersey and Kenneth H. Blanchard, *Management of Organizational Behavior: Utilizing Human Resources,* 3rd ed. (Englewood Cliffs, NJ: Prentice-Hall, 1977), p. 2.

47. Michael Fullan, Matthew B. Miles, and Gib Taylor, *OD in Schools: The State of the Art* (Toronto, Ontario: Ontario Institute for Educational Studies, 1978), 4 volumes.

48. Philip J. Runkel and Richard A. Schmuck, *Findings from the Research and Development Program on Strategies of Organizational Change at CEPM-CASEA* (Eugene: Center for the Advanced Study of Educational Administration, Center for Educational Policy and Management, University of Oregon, 1974), p. 34.

49. John I. Goodlad, *The Dynamics of Educational Change: Toward Responsive Schools* (New York: McGraw-Hill Book Company, 1975), p. xi.

50. Ibid., p. 113.

51. Ibid.

52. Ibid., p. 115.

53. Ibid., p. 135.

54. Ibid., pp. 139–40.

55. Fullan, Miles, and Taylor, *OD in Schools,* p. 2.

56. Ibid.

CHAPTER 8: ADAPTIVE LEADERSHIP

1. Margaret J. Wheatley, *Leadership and the New Science: Discovering Order in a Chaotic World* (San Francisco: Berrett-Koehler, Publishers, 1999).

2. Ronald A. Heifetz, *Leadership Without Easy Answers* (Cambridge, MA: Belknap Press of Harvard University Press, 1994).

3. Paul Thurston, Renee Clift, and Marshall Schacht, "Preparing Leaders for Change-Oriented Schools," *Phi Delta Kappan,* 75, no. 3 (November 1993), 262.

4. Warren Bennis and Burt Nanus, *Leaders: The Strategy for Taking Charge* (New York: Harper & Row, Publishers, 1985), p. 15.

5. Jacob W. Getzels, "Theory and Research on Leadership: Some Comments and Some Alternatives," in *Leadership: The Science and the Art Today,* eds. Luvern L. Cunningham and William J. Gephart (Itasca, IL: F.E. Peacock, Publishers, 1973), pp. 40–41. Emphasis in the original.

6. Meryl Reis Louis, "Putting Executive Action in Context: An Alternative View of Power," in *Executive Power,* eds. Suresh Srivastva and others (San Francisco: Jossey-Bass, 1986), p. 111.

7. This section is adapted from John R. P. French and Bertram Raven, "The Bases of Social Power," in *Studies in Social Power,* ed. Dorwin Cartwright (Ann Arbor: Institute for Social Research, University of Michigan, 1959). Many later writers have sought to extend the list for their own purposes, but the French and Raven work is still definitive.

8. W. Warner Burke, "Leadership as Empowering Others," in *Executive Power,* ed. Suresh Srivastva and others, pp. 56–57.

9. David C. McClelland, *Power: The Inner Experience* (New York: Irvington, 1975), p. 18.

10. James MacGregor Burns, *Leadership* (New York: Harper & Row, Publishers, 1978), p. 18.

11. Andrew W. Halpin, *Theory and Research in Administration* (New York: Macmillan, 1966), p. 86.

12. Bernard M. Bass, ed., *Stogdill's Handbook of Leadership: A Survey of Theory and Research,* rev. & exp. ed. (New York: The Free Press, 1981).

13. David Keirsey and Marilyn Bates, *Please Understand Me: Character and Temperament Types* (Del Mar, CA: Prometheus Nemesis Book Company, 1984), p. 129. Emphasis in the original.

14. General H. Norman Schwartzkopf quoted in *U.S. News and World Report,* Vol. 110, May 27, 1991 (20), p. 36.

15. The English word *bureaucracy* is taken from the French *bureaucratie.* In French, *bureau* means "office." The ending comes from the Greek, *kratie,* meaning "rule." Literally, then, bureaucracy is the rule of offices.

16. David Bradford and Allan Cohen, *Managing for Excellence: Developing High Performance in Contemporary Organizations* (New York: John Wiley & Sons, 1984), p. 26.

17. Burns's original term, *transforming,* has been transmogrified by followers in the literature to include such variations as *transformational* and *transformative.*
18. Burns, *Leadership.*
19. Bernard Bass, *Leadership and Performance Beyond Expectations* (New York: The Free Press, 1985).
20. Bennis and Nanus, *Leaders: The Strategies for Taking Charge.*
21. Rosabeth Moss Kanter, *The Change Masters: Innovation and Entrepreneurship in the American Corporation* (New York: Simon & Schuster, 1983).
22. Judy B. Rosener, "Ways Women Lead," *Harvard Business Review* (November–December 1990), 119–25.
23. Thomas J. Sergiovanni, *Moral Leadership: Getting to the Heart of School Reform* (San Francisco: Jossey-Bass, 1992).
24. Burns, *Leadership,* p. 4.
25. Ibid.
26. Ibid., p. 21.
27. Dan C. Lortie, *Schoolteacher: A Sociological Study* (Chicago: University of Chicago Press, 1975).
28. Burns, *Leadership,* p. 18.
29. The literature on critical theory in education is large, and growing. See, for example, Gary L. Anderson, "Toward a Critical Constructivist Approach to School Administration: Invisibility, Legitimation, and the Study of Non-Events," *Educational Administration Quarterly,* 26 (1990), 1, 38–59; William Foster, *Paradigms and Promises: New Approaches to Educational Administration* (Buffalo, NY: Prometheus Books, 1986); Peter Watkins, "Leadership, Power, and Symbols in Educational Administration," in *Critical Perspectives on Educational Leadership,* ed. John Smyth (Philadelphia: The Falmer Press, 1989), pp. 9–37.
30. Carnegie Forum on Education and the Economy, *A Nation Prepared: Teachers for the 21st Century* (New York: The Forum, 1986), p. 24.
31. Bennis and Nanus, *Leaders: The Strategies for Taking Charge.*
32. Sergiovanni, *Moral Leadership: Getting to the Heart of School Improvement,* p. 4.
33. John W. Gardner, *On Leadership* (New York: The Free Press, 1989).
34. Notably the work of James MacGregor Burns, *Leadership* (New York: Harper & Row, Publishers, 1978) and Warren Bennis and Burt Nanus, *Leaders* (New York: Harper & Row, Publishers, 1985).
35. Warren H. Schmidt and Jerome P. Finnegan, *The Race Without a Finish Line: America's Quest for Total Quality* (San Francisco: Jossey-Bass, 1992), p. 22.

CHAPTER 9: DECISION MAKING

1. Herbert A. Simon, *Administrative Behavior* (New York: Macmillan, 1950), p. 1.
2. Daniel E. Griffiths, *Administrative Theory* (New York: Appleton-Century-Crofts, 1959), p. 89.
3. Donald A. Schön, *The Reflective Practitioner: How Professionals Think in Action* (New York: Basic Books, 1983), p. 237.
4. Ibid., p. 39.
5. Ibid.
6. Herbert A. Simon, *The New Science of Management Decision* (New York: Harper & Row, Publishers, 1960), p. 2.
7. Peter F. Drucker, *Management: Tasks, Responsibilities, and Practices* (New York: Harper & Row, Publishers, 1974), pp. 19–20.
8. James G. March and Herbert A. Simon, *Organizations* (New York: John Wiley & Sons, 1958).
9. *Deciding How to Decide: Decision Making in Schools.* Project Leadership Presenter's Guide prepared by the Research-Based Training for School Administrators Project (Eugene: Center for Educational Policy and Management, College of Education, University of Oregon, 1983).
10. Drucker, *Management,* pp. 264–65.
11. Victor H. Vroom and Philip W. Yetton, *Leadership and Decisionmaking* (Pittsburgh: University of Pittsburgh Press, 1973).
12. Henry Mintzberg, Duru Raisinghani, and Andre Theoret, "The Structure of 'Unstructured' Decision Processes," *Administrative Science Quarterly,* 21 (June 1976), 246–75.
13. James G. March, "Footnotes to Organizational Change," *Administrative Science Quarterly,* 26 (December 1981), 563–77.
14. Paul C. Nutt, "Types of Organizational Decision Processes," *Administrative Science Quarterly,* 29 (September 1984), 446.
15. National Association of Secondary School Principals, *The Senior High School Principalship* (Reston, VA: National Association of Secondary School Principals, 1978).
16. Henry Mintzberg, *The Nature of Managerial Work* (New York: Harper & Row, Publishers, 1973).
17. These five points are summarized from Mintzberg, *The Nature of Managerial Work,* pp. 28–48.
18. Ibid., p. 30.
19. Ibid.
20. For examples see Van Cleve Morris, Robert L. Crowson, Emanuel Hurwitz, Jr., and Cynthia Porter-Gehrie, *The Urban Principal: Discretionary Decision-Making in a Large Educational Organization* (unpublished manuscript, University of Illinois at Chicago, 1981). This study was elaborated into a book by the same authors entitled *Principals in Action: The Reality of Managing Schools* (Columbus, OH: Charles E. Merrill Publishing Company, 1984). Also see Nancy J. Pitner, "Descriptive Study of the Everyday Activities of Suburban School Superintendents: The Management of Information" (unpublished doctoral dissertation, The Ohio State University, 1978).

21. Mintzberg, *The Nature of Managerial Work;* Sune Carlson, *Executive Behavior: A Study of the Work Load and the Working Methods of Managing Directors* (Stockholm: Strombergs, 1951); Pitner, "Descriptive Study of the Everyday Activities of Suburban School Superintendents"; William H. Whyte, Jr., "How Hard Do Executives Work?" *Fortune* (January 1948), 108–11.

22. Karl E. Weick, "Managerial Thought in the Context of Action," in *The Executive Mind,* ed. Suresh Srivastva (San Francisco: Jossey-Bass, 1983), p. 222.

23. Ibid., pp. 222–23.

24. Ibid., p. 222. Emphasis in the original.

25. Ibid., pp. 226–27.

26. Ibid., p. 236.

27. Schön, *The Reflective Practitioner,* pp. 240–41.

28. T. R. Blackburn, "Sensuous-Intellectual Complementarity in Science," *Science,* 172 (1971), 1003–07.

29. Louis R. Pondy, "Union of Rationality and Intuition in Management Action," in *The Executive Mind,* ed. Suresh Srivasta (San Francisco: Jossey-Bass, 1983).

30. Edgar H. Schein, "Organizational Socialization and the Profession of Management," *Industrial Management Review,* 9 (1968), 115; John Van Manaan, "Breaking In: Socialization to Work," in *Handbook of Work, Organization and Society,* ed. Robert Dubin (Chicago: Rand McNally & Company, 1976); R. R. Ritti and G. R. Funkhouser, *The Ropes to Skip and the Ropes to Know* (Columbus, OH: Grid, 1982).

31. Edgar H. Schein, *Organizational Culture and Leadership* (San Francisco: Jossey-Bass, 1985), p. 6.

32. Weick, "Managerial Thought."

33. Schein, *Organizational Culture,* p. 7.

34. Terrence E. Deal, "Cultural Change: Opportunity, Silent Killer, or Metamorphosis?" in *Gaining Control of the Corporate Culture,* ed. Ralph H. Kilmann, Mary J. Saxton, Roy Serpa, and associates (San Francisco: Jossey-Bass, 1985).

35. Karl E. Weick, "Cognitive Processes in Organizations," in *Research in Organizational Behavior,* Vol. 1, ed. Barry M. Staw (Greenwich, CT: JAI Press, 1979), pp. 41–74.

36. Kenneth Davis, *Human Behavior at Work: Human Relations and Organizational Behavior,* 4th ed. (New York: McGraw-Hill Book Company, 1972), p. 136.

37. Mary Parker Follett, "The Psychology of Consent and Participation," in *Dynamic Administration: The Collected Papers of Mary Parker Follett,* ed. Henry C. Metcalf and Lyndall Urwick (New York: Harper & Row, Publishers, 1941), pp. 210–12.

38. Edwin M. Bridges, "A Model for Shared Decision Making in the School Principalship," *Educational Administration Quarterly,* 3, no. 1 (Winter 1967), 52.

39. Chester I. Barnard, *The Functions of the Executive* (Cambridge, MA: Harvard University Press, 1938).

40. Robert G. Owens and Edward Lewis, "Managing Participation in Organizational Decisions," *Group and Organization Studies,* 1 (1976), 56–66.

41. Ibid.

42. Ibid.

43. Robert Duncan, "Public Law 217 and the Administrative Team," *Indiana School Boards Association Journal,* 20 (1974), 10.

44. Ohio Department of Elementary School Principals, *The Administrative Team,* (1971), 2–3.

45. Harold J. McNally, "A Matter of Trust," *National Elementary Principal,* 53, no. 1 (November-December 1973), 23.

46. The five types of participation discussed here are from Edwin M. Bridges, "A Model for Shared Decision Making in the School Principalship," *Educational Administration Quarterly,* 3, no. 1 (Winter 1967), 52–59.

47. Ibid., p. 53.

CHAPTER 10: CONFLICT IN ORGANIZATIONS

1. James MacGregor Burns, *Leadership* (New York: Harper & Row, Publishers, 1978), p. 37.

2. Kenneth Thomas, "Conflict and Conflict Management," in *Handbook of Industrial and Organizational Psychology,* ed. Marvin D. Dunnette (Chicago: Rand McNally & Company, 1976), p. 890.

3. Morton Deutsch, *The Resolution of Conflict: Constructive and Destructive Processes* (New Haven, CT: Yale University Press, 1973), p. 10.

4. Bernard Berelson and Gary A. Steiner, *Human Behavior: An Inventory of Scientific Findings* (New York: Harcourt Brace Jovanovich, 1964), p. 588.

5. H. Guetzkow and J. Cyr, "An Analysis of Conflict in Decision-making Groups," *Human Relations,* 7 (1954), 369.

6. Ibid.

7. Rensis Likert and Jane Gibson Likert, *New Ways of Managing Conflict* (New York: McGraw-Hill Book Company, 1976), p. 7. Emphasis added.

8. Kenneth E. Boulding, *Conflict and Defense: A General Theory* (New York: Harper & Brothers, Publishers, 1962), pp. 152–53.

9. Richard Wynn, *Administrative Response to Conflict* (Pittsburgh: Tri-State Area School Study Council, 1972), pp. 7–8.

10. Warren G. Bennis, *The Leaning Ivory Tower* (San Francisco: Jossey-Bass, 1973).

11. For advice on how to deal with "nefarious attacks," see Wynn, *Administrative Response to Conflict.*

12. Chester I. Barnard, *The Functions of the Executive* (Cambridge, MA: Harvard University Press, 1938), p. 36.

13. Thomas, "Conflict and Conflict Management," p. 891.

14. The research (none of it in schools) has been summarized by Thomas, "Conflict and Conflict Management."

15. Deutsch, *The Resolution of Conflict,* p. 9.

16. Louis R. Pondy, "Organizational Conflict: Concepts and Models," *Administrative Science Quarterly,* 12 (September 1967), 296–320.

17. Most writers in this field today use the term *conflict management,* connoting an ongoing organizational process that is heuristic and supportive of organization development over time. To many, the term *conflict resolution* carries the connotation of seeking final, conclusive solutions that will terminate even latent conflict—an unlikely event.
18. John M. Thomas and Warren G. Bennis, *Management of Change and Conflict* (Baltimore: Penguin Books, 1972), p. 20.
19. Robert R. Blake, Herbert A. Shepard, and Jane S. Mouton, *Managing Intergroup Conflict in Industry* (Houston, TX: Gulf Publishing Company, 1964).
20. Thomas, "Conflict and Conflict Management," p. 900.
21. Pondy, "Organizational Conflict."
22. Likert and Likert, *New Ways of Managing Conflict,* p. 7.
23. Randall Collins, *Conflict Sociology: Toward an Explanatory Science* (New York: Academic Press, 1975).
24. Gerald Griffin and David Rostetter, "A Conflict Theory Perspective for Viewing Certain Problems Associated with Public Law 94–142" (paper presented at the American Educational Research Association, Atlanta, GA, March 1978), p. 4.
25. Likert and Likert, *New Ways of Managing Conflict,* p. 59.
26. The research literature is rich and fascinating. See, for example, Muzafir Sherif and Carolyn W. Sherif, *Groups in Harmony and Tension* (New York: Harper & Brothers, Publishers, 1953); Muzafir Sherif and others, *Intergroup Conflict and Cooperation: The Robbers Cave Experiment* (Norman: Institute of Group Relations, University of Oklahoma Book Exchange, 1961); Morton Deutsch, "The Effects of Cooperation and Competition upon Group Process: An Experimental Study," *American Psychologist,* 4 (1949), 263–64; and—also by Deutsch—*The Resolution of Conflict.*
27. Blake, Shepard, and Mouton, *Managing Intergroup Conflict,* p. 18.
28. Likert and Likert, *New Ways of Managing Conflict,* p. 61.
29. Such as the works of Deutsch, Blake, and Sherif mentioned above.
30. Likert and Likert, *New Ways of Managing Conflict.*
31. Blake, Shepard, and Mouton, *Managing Intergroup Conflict,* p. 63.
32. Thomas, "Conflict and Conflict Management."

CHAPTER 11: MOTIVATION

1. Harry Levinson, *The Great Jackass Fallacy* (Boston: Harvard University Press, 1973).
2. Quoted in William Dowling, ed., *Effective Management and the Behavioral Sciences* (New York: AMACOM, 1978), p. 44.

3. George C. Homans, "The Western Electric Researches," in *Human Factors in Management,* ed. Schuyler Dean Hoslett (New York: Harper and Brothers, 1951), p. 211.
4. Ibid., p. 211.
5. Ibid., pp. 214–15.
6. Ibid., p. 217.
7. Ibid.
8. Paul Hersey and Kenneth H. Blanchard, *Management of Organizational Behavior: Utilizing Human Resources,* 3rd ed. (Englewood Cliffs, NJ: Prentice-Hall, 1977), p. 46.
9. David Keirsey and Marilyn Bates, *Please Understand Me: Character and Temperament Types* (Del Mar, CA: Prometheus Nemesis Book Company, 1984), p. 2.
10. Ibid., p. 2.
11. Ibid.
12. Howard Gardner, *Frames of Mind: The Theory of Multiple Intelligences* (New York: Basic Books, 1983), p. 25.
13. Ibid., p. 238. Obviously, as late as 1983, neither Gardner nor his publisher took seriously the notion of gender-free writing that prevails today.
14. Keirsey and Bates, *Please Understand Me,* pp. 2–3.
15. Carl Jung, *Psychological Types* (Princeton, NJ: Bollingen Series, 1971).
16. Robert Benfari with Jean Knox, *Understanding Your Management Style: Beyond the Myers-Briggs Type Indicators* (Lexington, MA: Lexington Books, D.C. Heath and Company, 1991), pp. 4–5.
17. Ibid., p. 6.
18. Ibid., p. 8. Emphasis in the original.
19. Published by the Center for Applications of Psychological Type, P.O. Box 13807, Gainesville, FL 32604.
20. Two such books have already been mentioned: Benfari, *Understanding Your Management Style* and Keirsey and Bates, *Please Understand Me.*
21. Lawrence Kohlberg, on the dust jacket of Carol Gilligan, *In a Different Voice: Psychological Theory and Women's Development* (Cambridge, MA: Harvard University Press, 1982).
22. Keirsey and Bates, *Please Understand Me,* p. 16.
23. Gilligan, *In a Different Voice,* p. 14.
24. Keirsey and Bates, *Please Understand Me,* p. 16.
25. Ibid., p. 17.
26. Benfari, *Understanding Your Management Style,* p. 8.
27. Jean Piaget, "Problems in Equilibration," in *Topics in Cognitive Development: Vol. 1. Equilibration: Theory, Research and Application,* eds. Marilyn H. Appel and Lois S. Goldberg (New York: Plenum Press, 1977), pp. 3–13.
28. John W. Atkinson and George H. Litwin, "Achievement Motivation and Test Anxiety Conceived as Motive to Approach Success and Motive to Avoid Failure," *Journal of Abnormal and Social Psychology,* 60 (1960), 52–63.
29. Martin V. Covington, *Making the Grade: A Self-Worth Perspective on Motivation and School Reform* (Cambridge: Cambridge University Press, 1992), p. 89.

30. Ibid., p. 26.

31. David C. McClelland, *The Achieving Society* (New York: The Free Press, 1961).

32. Max Weber, *The Protestant Ethic and the Spirit of Capitalism,* trans. Talcott Parsons (New York: Scribner, 1930). The original was published in German in 1904.

33. David C. McClelland, *Power: The Inner Experience* (New York: Irvington, 1975).

34. Matina S. Horner, "Sex Differences in Achievement Motivation and Performance in Competitive and Non-competitive Situations" (Ph.D. Dissertation, University of Michigan, 1968). University Microfilms #6912135.

35. Ibid., p. 171.

36. Ibid., p. 125.

37. Jonathan Brown and Bernard Weiner, "Affective Consequences of Ability versus Effort Ascriptions: Controversies, Resolutions, Quandries," *Journal of Educational Psychology,* 76 (1984), 146–58.

38. Don E. Hamachek, "Humanistic Psychology: Theory, Postulates and Implications for Educational Processes," in *Historical Foundations of Educational Psychology,* eds. John A. Glover and Royce R. Ronning (New York: Plenum Press, 1987).

39. Arthur Combs, "Motivation and the Growth of Self," in *Perceiving, Behaving, and Becoming: Association for Supervision and Curriculum Development Yearbook* (Washington, DC: National Education Association, 1962), pp. 83–98.

40. Abraham Maslow, *Motivation and Personality,* 2nd. ed. (New York: Harper & Row, Publishers, 1970).

41. Lyman W. Porter, "A Study of Perceived Need Satisfaction in Bottom and Middle-Management Jobs," *Journal of Applied Psychology,* 45 (1961), 1–10.

42. Ibid.

43. For example, Edward E. Lawler III and Lyman W. Porter, "The Effect of Job Performance and Job Satisfaction," *Industrial Relations* 6 (1967), 20–28; and David G. Kuhn, John W. Slocum, and Richard B. Chase, "Does Job Performance Affect Employee Satisfaction?" *Personnel Journal,* 50 (1971), 455–60.

44. Don Hellriegel and John W. Slocum, Jr., *Management: A Contingency Approach* (Reading, MA: Addison-Wesley Publishing Company, 1974), p. 308.

45. Thomas J. Sergiovanni and Fred D. Carver, *The New School Executive: A Theory of Administration* (New York: Dodd, Mead & Company, 1973), pp. 58–59.

46. Ibid., p. 59.

47. This research is summarized and documented in ibid., pp. 56–63.

48. Ibid.

49. Ibid., p. 61.

50. Frederick Herzberg, *Work and the Nature of Man* (Cleveland: World Publishing Company, 1966), p. 56.

51. Ralph M. Savage, "A Study of Teacher Satisfaction and Attitudes: Causes and Effects" (unpublished doctoral dissertation, Auburn University, 1967).

52. Rodney A. Wickstrom, "An Investigation into Job Satisfaction among Teachers" (unpublished doctoral dissertation, University of Oregon, 1971).

53. Gene L. Schmidt, "Job Satisfaction among Secondary School Administrators," *Educational Administration Quarterly,* 12 (1976), 81.

54. Ibid., p. 81.

55. Sergiovanni and Carver, *The New School Executive,* pp. 75–78.

56. Ibid., p. 77.

57. Stephen P. Robbins, *The Administrative Process: Integrating Theory and Practice* (Englewood Cliffs, NJ: Prentice-Hall, 1976), p. 312.

58. Ibid., p. 312.

59. Richard M. Ryan and Jerome Stiller, "The Social Contexts of Internalization: Parent and Teacher Influences on Autonomy, Motivation, and Learning," in *Advances in Motivation and Achievement, Vol. 7: Goals and Self-Regulatory Processes,* eds., Martin L. Maehr and Paul R. R. Pintrich (Greenwich, CT: JAI Press, 1991), pp. 115–49.

CHAPTER 12: SCHOOL REFORM

1. Public Agenda, *On Thin Ice: How Advocates and Opponents Could Misread the Public's Views on Vouchers and Charter Schools* (New York: Public Agenda, 1999), p. 1.

2. Milton Friedman, *Price Theory* (Chicago: Aldine Publishing, 1976), p. 1.

3. Herbert J. Walberg and Joseph L. Bast, "Understanding Market-Based School Reform," *Heartland Report* (October 21, 1998), 4.

4. Ibid., p. 5. Emphasis in the original.

5. Andrew J. Coulson, *Market Education: The Unknown History* (Brunswick, NJ: Transaction Publishers, 1999).

6. Andrew J. Coulson, "Are Public Schools Hazardous to Public Education?" *Education Week* (April 7, 1999).

7. Leapfrog Toys makes products for reading and language; Knowledge Learning operates a chain of day care centers; Teacher Universe assists in using classroom technology; MindQ Publishing sells multimedia learning systems; Productivity Point International sells technology training to corporations.

8. Edward Wyatt, "Investors See Room for Profit in the Demand for Education," *The New York Times,* November 4, 1999, 1.

9. One indicator of investor enthusiasm: in the initial public offering of Charter Communications the stock was quickly bid up from $3.75 per share to $22.75 per share in the first day.

10. Whose father was highly successful in finding and backing profitable start-up ventures and thought to have invented the term *venture capital.* One of his many successes was Minute Maid orange juice.

11. Channel One broadcasts a ten-minute daily newscast accompanied by two minutes of sponsored commercials into classrooms of about 12,000 participating schools,

thus reaching about 8 million students between the ages of thirteen and eighteen. Participating schools receive a satellite dish, two VCRs, and a nineteen-inch television monitor for each participating classroom.

12. Madeleine L'Engle, *A Wrinkle in Time* (New York: Bantam Doubleday, 1981).

13. In the New England states even cities are also considered to be towns. So, for example, the geographic boundaries of the city of West Haven are the same as for the West Haven School District.

14. In the state of New York, for example, the mammoth City School District of the City of New York (with 1,100 schools) covers five counties (Manhattan, the Bronx, Staten Island, Queens, and Brooklyn) and has a single school board, while upstate Erie County, which includes the city of Buffalo, has twenty-nine school districts (including the Buffalo City School District), some of which have as few as four schools and each district having its own independent school board.

15. In the early years of my career as a teacher and school administrator in rural New England, the generally accepted practice was to hold the annual town meeting on the morning of a designated day. Then, following a community lunch, the school meeting would be convened that same afternoon.

16. Diane Ravitch and Joseph P. Viteritti, eds., *New Schools for a New Century: The Redesign of Urban Education* (New Haven, CT: Yale University Press, 1997), p. 4.

17. The Education Commission of the States was created by the National Governors' Conference in 1966 under the leadership of North Carolina's Governor Terry Sanford, following a proposal by James Bryant Conant. Currently, forty-nine states are members along with Puerto Rico, the District of Columbia, American Samoa, and the Virgin Islands. Each member state is represented in ECS by seven commissioners, including the governor, legislative leaders, the chief state school officer, school board members, school administrators, and other educational professionals.

18. Education Commission of the States, *Governing America's Schools: Changing the Rules*. Report of the National Commission on Governing America's Schools, Execu-tive Summary (Denver, CO: Education Commission of the States, 1999), p. 1.

19. Ibid.

20. Ibid., p. 2. Emphasis in the original.

21. *Education Week* (November 10, 1999), 17.

22. Coalition of Essential Schools, 1814 Franklin Street, Suite 700, Oakland, CA 94612.

23. Sizer is also the author of a trio of distinguished books about the American high school: *Horace's Compromise: The Dilemma of the American High School* (New York: Houghton Mifflin, 1984); *Horace's Hope: What Works for the American High School* (New York: Houghton Mifflin, 1995); and *Horace's School: Redesigning the American High School* (New York: Houghton Mifflin, 1996).

24. Coalition of Essential Schools, *Ten Common Principles* (Oakland, CA: The Coalition, 1999), p. 2.

25. Stanford University, CERAS 109, Stanford, CA 94305-3084.

26. *Accelerated Schools,* 1, no. 1 (Winter 1991), 1.

27. Ibid.

28. School Development Program, *Overview of the School Development Program* (New Haven, CT: Yale Child Study Center, 1999), pp. 1–2.

29. Center for Educational Renewal, *National Network for Educational Renewal* (Seattle: Institute for the Study of Educational Policy, University of Washington, 1999), p. 2.

30. Center for Educational Renewal, *Nineteen Postulates Necessary for the Simultaneous Renewal of Schools and the Education of Educators* (Seattle: Institute for the Study of Educational Policy, University of Washington, 1999), p. 1.

31. Center for Policy Analysis, *To Touch the Future: Transforming the Way Teachers Are Taught. Executive Summary* (Washington, DC: American Council on Education, 1999), p. 1.

32. Abraham Flexner, *Medical Education in the United States and Canada: A Report to the Carnegie Foundation for the Advancement of Teaching* (New York: Arno Press, 1910).

Glossary

Administration   Working with and through other people to achieve organizational goals.

Bargaining   The process of negotiating the terms of an agreement that involves give-and-take and, often, compromise.

Behaviorist psychology (behaviorism)   The branch of human psychology that deals with the study of directly observable objective evidence of behavior, such as measurable and quantifiable responses to stimuli, and specifically eschews introspective evidence, such as emotions, perceptions, motives, thoughts, and attitudes. (*See also* cognitive psychology; social psychology; and humanistic psychology.)

Bureaucracy   Literally, from the French (after Max Weber), rule or authority of offices. Thus an organization characterized by a pyramidal hierarchy of authority in the form of official offices, top-down centralized decision making, emphasis on rules and regulations, and impersonality in human interactions. Contrast with human resources development.

Change process   The life-cycle theory of organizational change, which views change as an endless process in the life of an organization, is the most widely acclaimed theoretical model. It is a three-stage model that starts with (1) unfreezing existing practices and behaviors, followed by (2) the development of new practices and behaviors, then (3) institutionalizing and standardizing the newly developed practices and behaviors.

Charter schools   Public schools that operate under special charter from the state, or under contract from a school board, that frees them from certain restraints and requirements so that they can pursue innovative teaching methods that are expected to improve the achievement of students.

Classical organizational theory   A theory of organization that embodies basic ideas from bureaucracy and scientific management such as the scalar principle, unity of command, and span of control.

Cognitive psychology   The branch of human psychology that studies the mental processes that mediate between stimulus and response, especially such processes as creativity, perception, thinking, and problem solving. (*See also* behaviorist psychology; social psychology; and humanistic psychology.)

Collaborate   To work jointly with others, especially in intellectual efforts such as solving problems and setting goals.

Conflict, organizational   A situation in which two or more parties hold divergent, or apparently divergent, views that are incompatible.

Contingency theory   The concept that no single approach to organization and administration is superior to all others in all cases; that the best approach is contingent upon variable factors in the context of the situation.

Espoused theory   Theory to which one publicly subscribes. Superintendents of schools, for example, often espouse a culture of collegiality, trust, and teamwork as essential to the school district's plan for achieving educational excellence.

Exception principle   The classical principle of organization that recurring decisions should be codified in standardized written form such as rules, standard operating procedures, regulations, and operations manuals, thus freeing administrators to deal only with exceptions to the rules.

Feedback   The flow of information that an organization or an individual receives that provides information about the impact that the behavior of the organization or the individual is having on others.

Homeostasis   The tendency of an open social system to regulate itself so as to stay constantly in balance with its environment, which permits it to adapt to changes in the environment.

Hostility   Behavior intended to hurt or worsen the position of another individual or group.

Human capital   The concept that the knowledge that people have—their skills, attitudes, and social skills—are valuable assets to the organization and, because they are assets, can increase or decrease in value over time, depending on how they are managed.

Human relations   Broadly refers to the interactions among people in all kinds of social situations in which they seek through mutual action to achieve some purpose. Applicable to two people seeking to develop a happy and productive life together, organizations such as a business firm or school, or entire societies.

Human resources development   A set of assumptions about organization that emphasizes the primacy of the conscious thinking of persons in the organization, their abilities, and their socialization to the values and purposes of the-organization as a basis for coordination and motivation. Contrast with bureaucracy.

Humanistic psychology   An approach to the study of human psychology that focuses on human interests, values, dignity, and worth and recognizes the capacity of human beings to increase self-realization through reason. (*See also* social psychology.)

Leadership   After James MacGregor Burns, the processes of mobilizing, in conflict or in competition with others, institutional, political, psychological, and other resources so as to arouse and satisfy the motives of followers. Thus, a dynamic interactive relationship between members of a group and an individual collectively acknowledged by the group as a leader.

Motivation   The forces that cause people to behave as they do. Thought by behaviorists to be extrinsic (the carrot and the stick) and by others to be intrinsic (cognitive and emotional, e.g., feelings, aspirations, attitudes, thoughts, perceptions).

Naturalistic research   Research conducted in the natural setting using observational methods that are designed to avoid distorting or disturbing the natural setting.

Neoclassical organization theory   Classical organizational concepts that are manifested in contemporary form. For example, the educational standards movement, high-stakes testing, and accountability programs are based on classical concepts of organization and hence are neoclassical ideas.

Organization   An orderly, functional social structure (such as a business, political party, or school) characterized by identifiable people who are members of the organization and an administrative system.

Organization development   Any of a variety of processes by which an organization improves its ability to make better-quality decisions about its affairs.

Organization self-renewal   The concept that effective change cannot be successfully imposed on an organization from the outside but is a process of developing an increasing internal capacity for continuous problem solving and goal setting.

Organizational behavior   Both a field of scientific inquiry that seeks to understand the behavior of people in organizational contexts and a field of professional practice that seeks to apply that knowledge from the social sciences to practical problems of organizational leadership and administration.

Organizational climate   After Renato Tagiuri, the characteristics of the total environment in a school building. Often called the "atmosphere," the "tone," the "personality," or the "ethos" of the school.

Organizational culture   Those enduring traditions, values, and basic assumptions shared by people in an organization over time that give meaning to the work of the organization and establish the behavioral norms for people in the organization.

Organizational health   The extent to which the organization, over time, achieves its goals, maintains itself internally, and adapts to changes in its environment. The healthy organization shows a pattern of increasing its ability to do these things over the course of time.

Performance-based assessment   An alternative to machine-scored multiple-choice tests in assessing student achievement. Normally requires the student to perform tasks such as writing an essay, demonstrating the method of solving a problem, or conducting a science demonstration.

Power   The ability to exercise control, authority, or influence over others either as an official right of office or by mutual agreement with the others.

Qualitative research   Research that seeks to understand human behavior and human experience from the point of view of those being studied rather than the point of view of the researcher.

Rationalistic research   The concept that controlled experimental research is the epitome of research methods but that nonexperimental methods are acceptable if they are quantitative and observe certain procedural safeguards.

Reflective practice   A process in which one reflects on and thinks through the dissonances that inevitably arise between theory and practice and seeks to bring about greater harmony between espoused theory and theory of action.

Reify   To think of an abstraction, such as organization, as though it were material and concrete. People often reify organizational structure, although it is intangible.

Scalar principle   Commonly, the concept of line and staff, which holds that authority in the organization should flow in as unbroken a line as possible from the top policy-making level down through the organization to the lowest member.

School choice   The concept that parents may choose the schools their children may attend at public expense rather than the schools that the school district may designate. Ordinarily, public, private, or religious schools may be chosen.

School reform   A generic term that includes all kinds of efforts to improve the apparent effectiveness of schools. The three principal competing approaches to school reform are (1) market-based strategies, (2) setting and enforcing content standards, and (3) school improvement and development.

Scientific management   The view of management that formalizes differentiated roles between management and workers; the asymmetrical exercise of power and discipline from the top down, in which management plans and sets goals and workers execute the required tasks. Originated with the work of Frederick W. Taylor.

Self-actualization   To achieve or attain one's maximum potential as a human being.

Self-esteem   To have a sense of confidence, pride in oneself, and self-respect.

Site-based management   Attempts to shift decision making from the central administrative offices of the school district to the school.

Social psychology   The branch of human psychology that studies group behavior and the influence of social factors (such as group norms) on the personalities, attitudes, motivations, and behaviors of individuals. (*See also* behaviorist psychology; cognitive psychology; and humanistic psychology.)

Social sciences   Collectively, the scholarly and scientific disciplines devoted to the study of human society and the relationships between individuals in and to society. Usually includes sociology, psychology, anthropology, economics, political science, and history.

Social system   A collectivity of individuals who are bound together by common bonds or purposes. Herds of cattle and flocks of birds are social systems in the animal world. Among humans, street gangs and lunch groups are examples of informal social systems. Church congregations, schools, and business firms—being more clearly structured—are examples of more formal social systems.

Social systems theory   The concept that organizations are best understood as dynamically interactive social systems.

Sociometry   The study of interpersonal relationships using quantitative methods that reveal the strength and direction of preferences between and among individuals in a social system.

Sociotechnical systems theory   The concept that an organization is best understood as the dynamic interaction of four subsystems: technology, structure, task, and people.

Span of control   The principle of classical organizational theory that the number of people reporting to a supervisor should be limited to a number thought to be manageable.

Standards, academic content   Specification of those things that every student should know and be able to do in the so-called core subjects (usually, but not necessarily limited to, mathematics, the sciences, geography, and the English language). Advocates of academic content standards normally believe that they should apply equally to all students, regardless of linguistic or cultural heritage, special learning needs, race, or socioeconomic status.

Standards, discipline-based   Performance standards established for student learning in various academic disciplines, such as mathematics, music, the English language, economics, reading, sciences, history, geography, foreign languages, and physical education.

Standards, performance   Define and specify what minimal information and insights or skills students must acquire in order to meet the specifications framed by academic content standards. Students are usually expected to demonstrate their levels of achievement in the academic content standards either on some form of standardized paper-and-pencil tests or by performing tasks, such as writing an essay.

Systems theory   The concept, generally accepted in both the physical and social sciences, that all observations of nature are embedded in complex, dynamically interactive systems.

Theory   Systematically organized knowledge that is thought to explain things and events that are observed in nature.

Theory in use   Also called *theory of action* is the actual theory that is manifest in the behavior of an individual or group. One's theory in use, or theory of action, may differ from the espoused theory (see above). It is inferred from the behaviors of individuals rather than from their words. Dissonance between espoused theory and theory in use is commonplace in organizational leadership.

Theory of practice   The broad theoretical amalgam that guides and gives direction to one's professional practice, as distinguished from a practice in which one responds in *ad hoc* fashion as events unfold.

Total quality management   An approach to management, adopted from business and industrial management, that focuses on satisfying the client and, to achieve that end, emphasizes involving workers in continual decision-making processes that seek unending improvement in the way the organization functions.

Unity of command   The classical principle of organization that no one in an organization should receive orders from more than one superordinate.

Voucher   A chit or written authorization drawn upon the public treasury, usually issued by a state, that can be used by parents to pay tuition for the schooling of their children at a private school, a religious school, or an out-of-district public school.

Name Index

Subject Index